Exchanging Terrorism Oxygen for Media Airwaves:

The Age of Terroredia

Mahmoud Eid
University of Ottawa, Canada

A volume in the Advances in Human and
Social Aspects of Technology (AHSAT)
Book Series

Managing Director:	Lindsay Johnston
Production Editor:	Jennifer Yoder
Development Editor:	Allison McGinniss
Acquisitions Editor:	Kayla Wolfe
Typesetter:	Deanna Jo Zombro
Cover Design:	Jason Mull

Published in the United States of America by
Information Science Reference (an imprint of IGI Global)
701 E. Chocolate Avenue
Hershey PA 17033
Tel: 717-533-8845
Fax: 717-533-8661
E-mail: cust@igi-global.com
Web site: http://www.igi-global.com

Library of Congress Cataloging-in-Publication Data

Exchanging terrorism oxygen for media airwaves : the age of terroredia / Mahmoud Eid, editor.
     pages cm
  Includes bibliographical references and index.
  Summary: "This book presents a timely and thorough discussion on the integration of terrorism and the media, exploring the influence of traditional and new media on global terrorism"-- Provided by publisher.
   ISBN 978-1-4666-5776-2 (hardcover) -- ISBN 978-1-4666-5777-9 (ebook) -- ISBN 978-1-4666-5779-3 (print & perpetual access) 1. Terrorism and mass media. 2. Terrorism in mass media. 3. Terrorism--Press coverage. 4. Terrorism. I. Eid, Mahmoud, 1970-
  P96.T47E93 2014
  303.6'25--dc23
                                        2013050676

This book is published in the IGI Global book series Advances in Human and Social Aspects of Technology (AHSAT) (ISSN: 2328-1316; eISSN: 2328-1324)

British Cataloguing in Publication Data
A Cataloguing in Publication record for this book is available from the British Library.

All work contributed to this book is new, previously-unpublished material. The views expressed in this book are those of the authors, but not necessarily of the publisher.

For electronic access to this publication, please contact: eresources@igi-global.com.

Advances in Human and Social Aspects of Technology (AHSAT) Book Series

Ashish Dwivedi
The University of Hull, UK

ISSN: 2328-1316
EISSN: 2328-1324

MISSION

In recent years, the societal impact of technology has been noted as we become increasingly more connected and are presented with more digital tools and devices. With the popularity of digital devices such as cell phones and tablets, it is crucial to consider the implications of our digital dependence and the presence of technology in our everyday lives.

The **Advances in Human and Social Aspects of Technology (AHSAT) Book Series** seeks to explore the ways in which society and human beings have been affected by technology and how the technological revolution has changed the way we conduct our lives as well as our behavior. The AHSAT book series aims to publish the most cutting-edge research on human behavior and interaction with technology and the ways in which the digital age is changing society.

COVERAGE

- Activism & ICTs
- Computer-Mediated Communication
- Cultural Influence of ICTs
- Cyber Behavior
- End-User Computing
- Gender & Technology
- Human-Computer Interaction
- Information Ethics
- Public Access to ICTs
- Technoself

IGI Global is currently accepting manuscripts for publication within this series. To submit a proposal for a volume in this series, please contact our Acquisition Editors at Acquisitions@igi-global.com or visit: http://www.igi-global.com/publish/.

Titles in this Series

For a list of additional titles in this series, please visit: www.igi-global.com

Women in IT in the New Social Era A Critical Evidence-Based Review of Gender Inequality and the Potential for Change
Sonja Bernhardt (ThoughtWare, Australia)
Business Science Reference • copyright 2014 • 274pp • H/C (ISBN: 9781466658608) • US $195.00 (our price)

Gamification for Human Factors Integration Social, Education, and Psychological Issues
Jonathan Bishop (Centre for Research into Online Communities and E-Learning Systems, Belgium)
Information Science Reference • copyright 2014 • 362pp • H/C (ISBN: 9781466650718) • US $175.00 (our price)

Emerging Research and Trends in Interactivity and the Human-Computer Interface
Katherine Blashki (Noroff University College, Norway) and Pedro Isaias (Portuguese Open University, Portugal)
Information Science Reference • copyright 2014 • 580pp • H/C (ISBN: 9781466646230) • US $175.00 (our price)

Creating Personal, Social, and Urban Awareness through Pervasive Computing
Bin Guo (Northwestern Polytechnical University, China) Daniele Riboni (University of Milano, Italy) and Peizhao Hu (NICTA, Australia)
Information Science Reference • copyright 2014 • 440pp • H/C (ISBN: 9781466646957) • US $175.00 (our price)

Gender Divide and the Computer Game Industry
Julie Prescott (University of Bolton, UK) and Jan Bogg (The University of Liverpool, UK)
Information Science Reference • copyright 2014 • 321pp • H/C (ISBN: 9781466645349) • US $175.00 (our price)

User Behavior in Ubiquitous Online Environments
Jean-Eric Pelet (KMCMS, IDRAC International School of Management, University of Nantes, France) and Panagiota Papadopoulou (University of Athens, Greece)
Information Science Reference • copyright 2014 • 325pp • H/C (ISBN: 9781466645660) • US $175.00 (our price)

Uberveillance and the Social Implications of Microchip Implants Emerging Technologies
M.G. Michael (University of Wollongong, Australia) and Katina Michael (University of Wollongong, Australia)
Information Science Reference • copyright 2014 • 509pp • H/C (ISBN: 9781466645820) • US $265.00 (our price)

Innovative Methods and Technologies for Electronic Discourse Analysis
Hwee Ling Lim (The Petroleum Institute-Abu Dhabi, UAE) and Fay Sudweeks (Murdoch University, Australia)
Information Science Reference • copyright 2014 • 546pp • H/C (ISBN: 9781466644267) • US $175.00 (our price)

www.igi-global.com

701 E. Chocolate Ave., Hershey, PA 17033
Order online at www.igi-global.com or call 717-533-8845 x100
To place a standing order for titles released in this series, contact: cust@igi-global.com
Mon-Fri 8:00 am - 5:00 pm (est) or fax 24 hours a day 717-533-8661

To everyone who suffered from a terrorist act or a media stereotype

Editorial Advisory Board

Table of Contents

Section 7
Terrorism & Media over a Decade

Section 8
Rationality & Responsibility

Detailed Table of Contents

Chapter 1

Offering a conceptualization of the relationship between terrorism and the media in this introductory chapter, Mahmoud Eid introduces and defines a new term. Terroredia is the interactive, codependent, and inseparable relationship between terrorism and the media, in which acts of terrorism and their media coverage are essentially exchanged to achieve the ultimate aims of both parties—exchanging terrorism's wide-ranging publicity and public attention (i.e., oxygen) for media's wide-ranging reach and influence (e.g., airwaves).

Section 1
Terrorism & Media

Chapter 2

This chapter critically analyzes discussions and definitions of terrorism in an attempt to contribute to an objective understanding of terrorism. Mahmoud Eid discusses subjectivity in defining terrorism, the distinctive nature of the contentious concept of terrorism in comparison to other forms of violence, and how communication and media are fundamental in achieving terrorism's ultimate aim of obtaining public attention. The chapter concludes with eliminating controversial definitional items and features and introducing a definition of terrorism.

Chapter 3

This chapter explores the relationship shared between terrorism and the media. Robert Hackett describes how the media cover terrorism and state violence to deconstruct the relationship between violence and communication tools in modern day. This chapter seeks to investigate whether media and terror are two entirely separate categories or two sides of the same hideous coin—mediated terror, terrorizing media, or simply media terror.

Section 2
Terrorism Manifestations & Media Representations

Chapter 4

Jonathan R. White, Grand Valley State University, USA

This chapter examines the tactical aspects of terrorism, beginning with a focus on the nature of war and conflict in the 21st century. Jonathan R. White suggests that technology, economic structures, and communication have changed the way war is waged. Next, the chapter focuses on the specific actions that constitute the tactics of terrorism, examining tactical innovations within various campaigns. It concludes with an analysis of tactical force multipliers, and highlights the role of the media within this context.

Chapter 5

John Downing, Southern Illinois University, USA

This chapter begins with a comparative overview of violence against civilians in war, terrorist actions, and in torture. This is followed by related comparisons between the United States post-9/11, Britain during the civil war in Northern Ireland 1969-2000, and France during and since the Algerian armed liberation struggle of 1954-1962. John Downing then proceeds to a critical-discourse analysis of the U.S. Fox Television channel's highly successful dramatic series, *24*. This analysis explores how several of this series' themes (e.g., political violence, counter-terrorism, racism, and torture) interact with the post-9/11 social and political environment.

Section 3
Terrorism Types & Media Stereotypes

Chapter 6

Gus Martin, California State University, USA

This chapter identifies and discusses terrorist typologies, which refer to descriptive classifications explaining the quality of political violence from distinct political and social environments in the modern era. While definitional debate exists surrounding the lines of categorization, Gus Martin provides a detailed description of eight terrorist typologies: New Terrorism, state terrorism, dissident terrorism, religious terrorism, ideological terrorism, international terrorism, criminal dissident terrorism, and gender-selective terrorism. In addition to the exploration of these typologies, Martin also discusses the emerging recognition of newly defined typologies.

Chapter 7

Georgios Terzis, Vrije Universiteit Brussel, Belgium & Global Governance Institute, Belgium

This chapter analyzes different stereotypes used by the media in the coverage of terrorist events, discussing topics such as media stereotypes of different terrorist groups, how media responses differ according to the type of terrorism, and the characteristics of the communication medium. Georgios Terzis also analyzes how these stereotypes are formulated by the use of simple and complex rhetorical techniques related to the invention, arrangement, style, memory, and delivery applied. These analyses are further investigated against the backdrop of the basic social determinants of journalism.

Section 4
Terrorism Tactics & Media Strategies

Chapter 8

Brigitte L. Nacos, Columbia University, USA

This chapter reconsiders arguments surrounding contagion theories, contending that old and new media are important carriers of the virus of hate and instrumental in tactical and ideological contagion. Given the advances in communication and information technology and changes in the global media landscape during the last decade or so, contagion theories have become further developed. Brigitte L. Nacos explores the various dimensions of this evolution and the current status of contemporary contagion theories.

Chapter 9

Randal Marlin, Carleton University, Canada

This chapter looks at aspects of how different English and French Canadian newspapers, as examples, covered the push for war on Iraq. It includes reflections on the use of language in reporting on the war itself. Randal Marlin identifies some comparisons regarding media coverage of the current apparent resolve by the United States, Israel, and allies to apply force to Iran to prevent getting a nuclear-weapon capability. The central concern is with the media role in fear mongering and propaganda for war.

Section 5
Terrorism Functioning & Media Employing

Chapter 10

Dana Janbek, Lasell College, USA

This chapter explores the ways in which terrorist groups operate in today's world, focusing on the operation of terrorism and the different elements that play a role in this operation. Dana Janbek presents a solid overview of relevant topics while borrowing examples from a range of organizations to illustrate the different elements of the terrorist operations. This chapter highlights specific examples of historically significant events from various parts of the world that mark changes in the overall terrorist operations. Finally, the chapter looks at how terrorist groups have operated historically and examines current developments and trends that will influence the future of terrorist operations.

Chapter 11

Muhammad Ayish, American University of Sharjah, UAE

This chapter draws on research findings and practical experiences around the world to identify prime actors associated with the challenges embedded in employing the media during terrorism to describe their objectives, tactics, and channels of communication. Muhammad Ayish identifies four categories of media users: media institutions, terrorist organizations, governments, and citizen groups. The chapter discusses enduring issues associated with each actor's use of media and calls for evolving new conceptual frameworks for understanding media use during terrorism. The chapter concludes by arguing that while we seem to have a huge pool of research findings and practical experiences related to employing the media during terrorism, we seem to have a critical shortage in how we conceptually account for the different variables that define the use of media in terrorism situations.

Section 6
New Terrorism & New Media

Chapter 12

Mahmoud Eid, University of Ottawa, Canada

This chapter reviews discussions surrounding new terrorism, explains its key characteristics and features, and demonstrates the dual role of the media and information technologies. Mahmoud Eid compares the new and conventional terrorism in terms of all aspects of functioning to conclude that regardless of the label—new or old—attention should be focused on the act and the actors, whether the ways they function utilize the conventional or adapt with the most recent technologies, media, and weapons, and most crucially, recognizing how fast and efficient terrorists are in utilizing the most advanced media and information technologies.

Chapter 13

Pauline Hope Cheong, Arizona State University, USA

This chapter discusses the role of new(er) media in facilitating the transmediated spread of extremist narratives, rumors, and political parody. Drawing from recent case studies based upon multi-modal analyses of digital texts on social media networks including blogs, vlogs, Twitter, and Jihadist sites associated with acts of terror in Asia, Middle East, and North America, Pauline Hope Cheong illustrates how digital transmediation significantly works to construct counter narratives to government counter insurgency operations and mainstream media presentations. In discussing these examples, the chapter demonstrates how the new media points to varied narratives and reifies notions of national security, global politics, terrorism, and the media's role in framing the "War on Terrorism."

Section 7
Terrorism & Media over a Decade

Chapter 14

Maura Conway, Dublin City University, Ireland

This chapter explores the changes that have taken place in the role and functioning of the Internet in terrorism and counter-terrorism in the past decade. Maura Conway traces the shift in focus from a preoccupation with the threat of so-called "cyberterrorism" in the period pre- and immediately post-9/11 to the contemporary emphasis on the role of the Internet in processes of violent radicalization. The cyberterrorism threat is explained as over-hyped herein and the contemporary focus, by researchers and policymakers, on the potential of the Internet as a vehicle for violent radicalization viewed as more appropriate, albeit not without its difficulties.

Chapter 15

Samuel P. Winch, Penn State – Harrisburg, USA

This chapter examines the photographic reportage of the Associated Press wire service photojournalists during the Arab Spring and the decade that preceded it to determine if a measurable shift in coverage did occur. In this, Samuel P. Winch investigates media depictions of the visible elements of Middle East unrest–from Libya to Pakistan–in the ten-year period from 2002 through the revolutions in Egypt, Tunisia, and Libya in 2011. An examination of news photographs during the period shows subtle shifts in the imagery.

Section 8
Rationality & Responsibility

Chapter 16

Joseba Zulaika, University of Nevada, USA
William A. Douglass, University of Nevada, USA

This chapter focuses on advocating the deconstruction of terrorism upon the discourse itself: its premises, beliefs, fears, definitions, rhetorical devices, imaginary constructions of the enemy, the inability to distinguish ritual bluff from actual combat, the logic of taboo, the injunction not to humanize the terrorist other, and moral self-righteousness. Joseba Zulaika and William A. Douglass argue that by undermining its claims to apocalyptic powers and fears, terrorism would lose credibility as an effective rhetorical ploy and bellicose weapon for insurgents and governments alike.

Chapter 17

Mahmoud Eid, University of Ottawa, Canada

This chapter questions the effectiveness of media performance during times of terrorism through the examination of their decision-making processes in terms of rationality and responsibility. Mahmoud Eid explains that the numerous media decisions that are usually made under severe stress during times of terrorism require the interweavement of ethics and rational thinking in strategic and goal-directed media decision-making processes to achieve more desired outcomes.

Preface

Modern terrorism is codependent on the media. Terrorists of our era are much more aware of their relationship with the media and understand how they can benefit the most from using them. Moreover, they are even more aware of how to avoid being "used" by the media. On one hand, there are many incidents in history when the media were used by terrorists and their sympathizers. On the other, terrorists themselves have been used by the media that broadcast their actions without necessarily transmitting their messages. Inevitably interacting together throughout the long history of terrorism, today terrorists and media personnel are increasingly becoming more able to maximize their mutual benefits.

Media coverage provides terrorists with their ultimate aim—gaining public attention—without which their acts are seemingly invisible; hence, the popular saying of former British Prime Minister Margaret Thatcher, "publicity is the oxygen of terrorism." Acts of terrorism provide the media with top-stories through which they can broadcast more airwaves, print more texts, and upload more digital data bytes, achieving their ultimate aim of reaching wider audiences. This exceptional relationship between terrorism and the media feeds mainly from the mutual aim of influencing the public.

Exchanging Terrorism Oxygen for Media Airwaves: The Age of Terroredia provides comprehensive understandings of a wide range of issues surrounding terrorism in relation to both the traditional and the new media. I introduce the new term *Terroredia* to explain the phenomenal relationship between terrorists and media personnel for achieving goals of both parties. Terrorists' awareness of how to use the media and how to avoid being used by them is in conflict with the media's efforts to benefit from covering acts of terrorism while carefully avoiding to be used by terrorists—creating a relationship whose adversaries are competing and increasingly becoming able to maximize their payoffs from one another.

This monumental book is the first attempt to look into some fundamental aspects of *Terroredia*, mirroring terrorism and the media within specific contexts of interrelated relationships. Leading, well known, and widely published international scholars who are engaged in the most relevant, cutting-edge practices and theorization have contributed chapters in this book in their respective specializations in terrorism and media studies. The book's structure follows a unique strategy that divides the arrays of interrelated chapters into two perspectives—"terrorism-focused" and "media-focused"—mirroring each other throughout all eight sections of the book. This "mirror" format demonstrates to readers various elements inherited in the relationship between terrorism and the media. Each section includes two chapters—the first is terrorism-focused and the second is media-focused—which both cover the theme of the section about a major context within which both terrorism and the media are interrelated.

In Chapter 1, titled "Terroredia: Exchanging Terrorism Oxygen for Media Airwaves," I discuss the unique relationship between terrorism and the media that has been long evident in history and academia, which has grown strong and widely influential due to modern advancements in communication and information technologies. Mutual interaction, dependency, and inseparability have characterized the co-existence of terrorists and media personnel. Looking into the various dynamics, discussions, and descriptions of this relationship, I offer a conceptualization of this relationship by introducing and defining a new term—*Terroredia*.

The first section of the book (Terrorism and Media) discusses the aspects of both understanding terrorism and understanding the media during times of terrorism. The terrorism-focused Chapter 2, titled "Understanding Terrorism," critically analyzes discussions and definitions of terrorism in an attempt to contribute to an objective understanding of terrorism. I discuss subjectivity in defining terrorism, the distinctive nature of the contentious concept of terrorism in comparison to other forms of violence, and how communication and media are fundamental in achieving terrorism's ultimate aim of obtaining public attention. The chapter concludes with eliminating controversial definitional items and features and introducing a definition of terrorism. The media-focused Chapter 3, titled "Understanding Media during Times of Terrorism," explores the relationship shared between terrorism and the media. Robert Hackett describes how the media cover terrorism and state violence to deconstruct the relationship between violence and communication tools in modern day. This chapter seeks to investigate whether media and terror are two entirely separate categories or two sides of the same hideous coin—mediated terror, terrorizing media, or simply media terror.

The second section of the book (Terrorism Manifestations and Media Representations) discusses the aspects of both terrorism manifestations and media representations. The terrorism-focused Chapter 4, titled "Terrorism Manifestations," examines the tactical aspects of terrorism, beginning with a focus on the nature of war and conflict in the 21st century. Jonathan R. White suggests that technology, economic structures, and communication have changed the way war is waged. Next, the chapter focuses on the specific actions that constitute the tactics of terrorism, examining tactical innovations within various campaigns. It concludes with an analysis of tactical force multipliers, and highlights the role of the media within this context. The media-focused Chapter 5, titled "Media Representations of Terrorism," begins with a comparative overview of violence against civilians in war, terrorist actions, and in torture. This is followed by related comparisons between the United States post-9/11, Britain during the civil war in Northern Ireland 1969-2000, and France during and since the Algerian armed liberation struggle of 1954-1962. John Downing then proceeds to a critical-discourse analysis of the U.S. Fox Television channel's highly successful dramatic series, *24*. This analysis explores how several of this series' themes (e.g., political violence, counter-terrorism, racism, and torture) interact with the post-9/11 social and political environment.

The third section of the book (Terrorism Types and Media Stereotypes) discusses the aspects of both terrorism types and media stereotypes. The terrorism-focused Chapter 6, titled "Types of Terrorism," identifies and discusses terrorist typologies, which refer to descriptive classifications explaining the quality of political violence from distinct political and social environments in the modern era. While definitional debate exists surrounding the lines of categorization, Gus Martin provides a detailed description of eight terrorist typologies: New Terrorism, state terrorism, dissident terrorism, religious terrorism, ideological terrorism, international terrorism, criminal dissident terrorism, and gender-selective terrorism. In addition to the exploration of these typologies, Martin also discusses the emerging recognition of newly defined typologies. The media-focused Chapter 7, titled "Media Stereotypes of Terrorism," analyzes different stereotypes used by the media in the coverage of terrorist events, discussing topics such as media stereotypes of different terrorist groups, how media responses differ according to the type of terrorism, and the characteristics of the communication medium. Georgios Terzis also analyzes how these stereotypes are formulated by the use of simple and complex rhetorical techniques related to the invention, arrangement, style, memory, and delivery applied. These analyses are further investigated against the backdrop of the basic social determinants of journalism.

The fourth section of the book (Terrorism Tactics and Media Strategies) discusses the aspects of both terrorism tactics and media strategies. The terrorism-focused Chapter 8, titled "Tactics of Terrorism," reconsiders arguments surrounding contagion theories, contending that old and new media are important carriers of the virus of hate and instrumental in tactical and ideological contagion. Given the advances in communication and information technology and changes in the global media landscape during the last decade or so, contagion theories have become further developed. Brigitte L. Nacos explores the various dimensions of this evolution and the current status of contemporary contagion theories. The media-focused Chapter 9, titled "Media-Related Strategies and 'War on Terrorism,'" looks at aspects of how different English and French Canadian newspapers, as examples, covered the push for war on Iraq. It includes reflections on the use of language in reporting on the war itself. Randal Marlin identifies some comparisons regarding media coverage of the current apparent resolve by the United States, Israel, and allies to apply force to Iran to prevent getting a nuclear-weapon capability. The central concern is with the media role in fear mongering and propaganda for war.

The fifth section of the book (Terrorism Functioning and Media Employing) discusses the aspects of both terrorism functioning and media employing. The terrorism-focused Chapter 10, titled "Functioning of Terrorism," explores the ways in which terrorist groups operate in today's world, focusing on the operation of terrorism and the different elements that play a role in this operation. Dana Janbek presents a solid overview of relevant topics while borrowing examples from a range of organizations to illustrate the different elements of the terrorist operations. This chapter highlights specific examples of historically significant events from various parts of the world that mark changes in the overall terrorist operations. Finally, the chapter looks at how terrorist groups have operated historically and examines current developments and trends that will influence the future of terrorist operations. The media-focused Chapter 11, titled "Employing of Media during Terrorism," draws on research findings and practical experiences around the world to identify prime actors associated with the challenges embedded in employing the media during terrorism to describe their objectives, tactics, and channels of communication. Muhammad Ayish identifies four categories of media users: media institutions, terrorist organizations, governments, and citizen groups. The chapter discusses enduring issues associated with each actor's use of media and calls for evolving new conceptual frameworks for understanding media use during terrorism. The chapter concludes by arguing that while we seem to have a huge pool of research findings and practical experiences related to employing the media during terrorism, we seem to have a critical shortage in how we conceptually account for the different variables that define the use of media in terrorism situations.

The sixth section of the book (New Terrorism and New Media) discusses the aspects of both new terrorism and new media. The terrorism-focused Chapter 12, titled "New Terrorism and Media," reviews discussions surrounding new terrorism, explains its key characteristics and features, and demonstrates the dual role of the media and information technologies. I compare the new and conventional terrorism in terms of all aspects of functioning to conclude that regardless of the label—new or old—attention should be focused on the act and the actors, whether the ways they function utilize the conventional or adapt with the most recent technologies, media, and weapons, and most crucially, recognizing how fast and efficient terrorists are in utilizing the most advanced media and information technologies. The media-focused Chapter 13, titled "New Media and Terrorism," discusses the role of new(er) media in facilitating the transmediated spread of extremist narratives, rumors, and political parody. Drawing from recent case studies based upon multi-modal analyses of digital texts on social media networks including blogs, vlogs, Twitter, and Jihadist sites associated with acts of terror in Asia, Middle East, and North America, Pauline Hope Cheong illustrates how digital transmediation significantly works to construct counter narratives to government counter insurgency operations and mainstream media presentations. In discussing these examples, the chapter demonstrates how the new media point to varied narratives and reify notions of national security, global politics, terrorism, and the media's role in framing the "War on Terrorism."

The seventh section of the book (Terrorism and Media over a Decade) discusses the most recent developments on terrorism and the media. The terrorism-focused Chapter 14, titled "From 'Cyberterrorism' to 'Online Radicalism,'" explores the changes that have taken place in the role and functioning of the Internet in terrorism and counter-terrorism in the past decade. Maura Conway traces the shift in focus from a preoccupation with the threat of so-called "cyberterrorism" in the period pre- and immediately post-9/11 to the contemporary emphasis on the role of the Internet in processes of violent radicalization. The cyberterrorism threat is explained as over-hyped herein and the contemporary focus, by researchers and policymakers, on the potential of the Internet as a vehicle for violent radicalization viewed as more appropriate, albeit not without its difficulties. The media-focused Chapter 15, titled "From 'Angry Arab' to 'Arab Spring,'" examines the photographic reportage of the Associated Press wire service photojournalists during the Arab Spring and the decade that preceded it to determine if a measurable shift in coverage did occur. In this, Samuel P. Winch investigates media depictions of the visible elements of Middle East unrest—from Libya to Pakistan—in the ten-year period from 2002 through the revolutions in Egypt, Tunisia, and Libya in 2011. An examination of news photographs during the period shows subtle shifts in the imagery.

The last section of the book (Rationality and Responsibility) questions both terrorism/counterterrorism rationality and media responsibility during terrorism. The terrorism-focused Chapter 16, titled "Questioning Terrorism/Counterterrorism Rationality," focuses on advocating the deconstruction of terrorism upon the discourse itself: its premises, beliefs, fears, definitions, rhetorical devices, imaginary constructions of the enemy, the inability to distinguish ritual bluff from actual combat, the logic of taboo, the injunction not to humanize the terrorist other, and moral self-righteousness. Joseba Zulaika and William A. Douglass argue that by undermining its claims to apocalyptic powers and fears, terrorism would lose credibility as an effective rhetorical ploy and bellicose weapon for insurgents and governments alike. The media-focused Chapter 17, titled "Questioning Media Responsibility during Terrorism," questions the effectiveness of media performance during times of terrorism through the examination of their decision-making processes in terms of rationality and responsibility. I explain that the numerous media decisions that are usually made under severe stress during times of terrorism require the interweavement of ethics and rational thinking in strategic and goal-directed media decision-making processes to achieve more desired outcomes.

It is hoped that this book will be of interest to students, researchers, scholars, media personnel, policymakers, and the general public. The multifaceted contents of this book can serve readers across various disciplines, such as communication, conflict resolution, criminology, crisis management, cultural studies, information and communication technologies, international relations, media, national security, political science, psychology, sociology, and terrorism. Readers are well served with intensive chapters that include great details and specific topics, which are grouped under major themes, such as definitions and understandings of terrorism and the role of the media during times of terrorism, terrorism manifestations and media representations of terrorism, types of terrorism and media stereotypes of terrorism, tactics of terrorism and media-related strategies, functioning of terrorism and employing of media during terrorism, new terrorism and the media and the new media and terrorism, contemporary cases of terrorist-media interactions, and the rationality of terrorism/counterterrorism and the corresponding media responsibility.

Mahmoud Eid
University of Ottawa, Canada

Chapter 1
Terroredia:
Exchanging Terrorism Oxygen for Media Airwaves

Mahmoud Eid
University of Ottawa, Canada

ABSTRACT

Terrorism and the media have a unique relationship that has been long evident in history and academia. Due to modern advancements in communication and information technologies, the relationship has grown strong and widely influential. Mutual interaction, dependency, and inseparability have characterized the co-existence of terrorists and media personnel. Looking into the various dynamics, discussions, and descriptions of this relationship, this chapter offers a conceptualization of this relationship by introducing and defining a new term. Terroredia *is the interactive, codependent, and inseparable relationship between terrorism and the media, in which acts of terrorism and their media coverage are essentially exchanged to achieve the ultimate aims of both parties—exchanging terrorism's wide-ranging publicity and public attention (i.e., oxygen) for media's wide-ranging reach and influence (e.g., airwaves).*

It is highly unlikely for people to believe that terrorists and media personnel could be best friends forever. One's initial thoughts may be that friendship is considered a positive phenomenon while terrorism is a pejorative term. However, on second thought—after a thorough reconnaissance—many might agree to this metaphoric statement. Strong friendships can exist among the same and different kind of criminals. This is not to say that media personnel are criminals; moreover, terrorists have not been even considered normal criminals, if at all, by many individuals, groups, organizations, and states, depending on which adversary in a

terrorist event they side with. Instead, it goes without much argument that friends usually help, if not necessarily benefit from, each other. The unique relationship between terrorists and media personnel can be extremely helpful for each party, not only to achieve their ultimate goals, but also to survive. This had been the case all over the long history of terrorism, persists in our present time, and will certainly continue to evolve in the future.

Modern terrorism "can be understood as an attempt to communicate messages through the use of orchestrated violence" (Tsfati & Weimann, 2002, p. 317). Terrorists use the media as a key

DOI: 10.4018/978-1-4666-5776-2.ch001

mechanism to communicate a message to "members of the public that are not directly harmed by the violence" that "could be harmed by future attacks" (Braithwaite, 2013, p. 96). Brigitte L. Nacos (2007) asserts that understanding terrorism should focus on the centrality of communication via the media in terrorists' calculations of the actions' consequences, the likelihood of gaining media attention, and the likelihood of gaining entrance into the triangle of political communication (between civil society, government decision-makers, and the media).

Since the introduction of the printing press, there has been always a relationship between terrorism and the media that has been growing stronger over time due to modern development of media and communication technologies (Eid, 2013). Numerous studies have discussed this relationship (e.g., Alexander & Latter, 1990; Alger, 1989; Biernatzki, 2002; Cho et al., 2003; Crelinsten, 1989; Elmquist, 1990; Finn, 1990; Freedman & Thussu, 2012; Grinyaev, 2003; Kelly, 1989; Nacos, 2000, 2003a, 2003b, 2005, 2006, 2007, 2012; Picard, 1990; Protheroe, 1990; Robinson, 2000; Steuter, 1990; Wittebols, 1992). This relationship "has existed for centuries," since the time when the means pre-mass media relied on "after the event word-of-mouth dissemination;" its roots are "traceable to nineteenth century anarchists and their concept of 'propaganda of the deed'" (Surette, Hansen, & Noble, 2009, p. 360).

Terrorists have become increasingly aware of their relationship with the media; they are clever in achieving utmost benefits through both using the media in the best way of obtaining public attention and also avoiding to be used by the media. The media are terrorism's "'two-edged weapons' used both by and against it" (Combs, 2013, p. 166). They are "instruments of terrorism," "agents in the spread of terroristic acts," and "tools for manipulation by both terrorists and their adversaries" (Schmid & Jongman, 2008, p. 111). The media "are not simply external actors passively bringing the news of terrorist incidents to global audiences but are increasingly seen as active agents in the actual conceptualization of terrorist events" (Freedman & Thussu, 2012, p. 10). They possess great abilities to enhance or diminish terrorism stories and ideas (Eid, 2013). The media are "the primary vehicle that the public has come to know and thus fear terrorism" (Chermak, 2003, p. 6). Meanwhile, terrorists sometimes "feel 'used' by the media which pick up their action, but offer no guarantee of transmitting their message" (Schmid, 1989, p. 559). To avoid manipulations of their messages by the media, terrorists have found new media and the Internet to be good alternatives through which they can produce and publicize their messages.

Terrorism has become "mediaized" as demonstrated in the direct links between terrorists, political processes, and the success of media outlets (Louw, 2003). As Former British Prime Minister Margaret Thatcher once said "publicity is the oxygen of terrorism" and that terrorists "understood this and acted accordingly" (Nacos, 2006, p. 208). Terrorists choreograph events to leverage media coverage during and after their attacks (Surette, Hansen, & Noble, 2009). The media that play a fundamental role in relation to terrorism are not only limited to press, radio, television, or Internet news, they involve "the whole of the contemporary mediascape" (Conway & McInerney, 2012, pp. 4-5), including films, television entertainment, television drama, graphic novels, computer games, and so on. These "multiple media . . . transmit powerful images" and "help to trigger highly emotional responses to the terrorist event;" through television, the Internet, and other networked information technologies, "we see terrorism everywhere in real time, all the time" (Der Derian, 2005, p. 26). Particularly, television has become the leading news medium through which terrorist events are framed for audiences (Biernatzki, 2002). Media organizations and professionals have a powerful influence on audiences and have the ability to impact public opinion; the framing of their messages is particularly important, as they "provide us [with] information about different events [that have] happened in the world, often within hours of any occurrence" (Ali et al., 2012, p. 1464). The media are also culprits of spinning information to frame the interests of their organizations or countries in a positive light (Boggs, 2002).

There has been a long debate around the media's role during terrorism; while there is "a strong need of independent and free media to disseminate information to the general public," there is a concern "that freedom of press may also become source of promoting terrorism" (Nasir, Khan, & Jalil, 2013, p. 715). Publicity is argued to be more effective and beneficial for terrorists when their acts are committed in societies where the media are either free or irresponsible because the media may report news in ways that make their governments unable to apprehend terrorists; on the contrary, it is almost pointless for terrorists to commit their acts in countries where the media are fully controlled and censored because the media are never allowed to present officials unfavorably (Devine & Rafalko, 1982). Also, many blame the media "for rewarding terrorist acts with disproportionate coverage that plays into the hands of terrorists" (Nacos, 2000, p. 175). Thus, the role of the media in relation to terrorism has been viewed within different models. For instance, the "culpable-media" model and the "vulnerable media" model have explained the media's role in that the former implies that media coverage of terrorism ultimately incites more terrorism, producing more media coverage, while the latter sympathizes with the media denying them to be causes of terrorism but obliged to cover terrorism (Barnhurst, cited in Biernatzki, 2002).

The relationship between terrorism and the media has been described in various terms, such as: "theater of terror" (Weimann & Winn, 1994); "marriage of convenience" (Sadaba, 2002); "media-oriented terrorism" (Martin, 2006); and "mass-mediated terrorism" (Nacos, 2007). Overall, there is a general agreement that this relationship is "symbiotic" (e.g., Anderson, 2003; Lockyer, 2003; Pfeiffer, 2012; Surette, Hansen, & Noble, 2009; Wilkinson, 1997).

However, I argue that the relationship between terrorism and the media requires inquiry that goes beyond the simple process of "symbiosis," which implies both "interaction" and "mutual dependence." This is because the term symbiosis refers to an interactive relationship of mutual benefit or dependence. Instead, inquiry into the relationship between terrorism and the media must combine the notion of interaction with issues pertaining to symmetrical and asymmetrical "codependency." The idea of codependency may involve some sort of control or manipulation if the relationship is imbalanced. However, it is challenging, while possible in rare instances, to find a perfect process of codependency; instead, an imbalance is most common. Hence, codependency can be symmetrical or asymmetrical. While symmetrical relationships indicate equality, as both parties are equally dependent on each other to function, asymmetrical relationships indicate that one party is more or less dependent than the other. Being more common, it is important to note that asymmetrical codependency can sometimes demonstrate a parasitic relationship in which one entity is the parasite and the other is the host. Moreover, the two entities can manipulate, leverage, or abuse each other for their own betterment. This is true of the relationship between terrorism and the media as the media coverage of some terrorist events can be more, (sometimes) equally, or less beneficial to terrorists than the media personnel, depending on the nature of the tactic of terrorism, the terrorist's obtained volume of public attention and other achieved goals, and the direct profits and benefits gained by the media.

While the interaction, the symmetrical codependency, and the asymmetrical parasitic codependency between terrorism and the media warrant the term "relationship," they also imply a process of exchange (or exchanging). Each party has methods of strength or power; albeit in the meantime, requires basic needs to survive. Terrorism has tactics of violence, force, and coercion while the media have the power of reaching and influencing the opinions, attitudes, and behaviors of wide-ranging audiences. Meanwhile, in order for both to survive, terrorists seek to garner public attention and the media seek to find top-stories to sell. In a sense, both parties target wide-ranging audiences (although for different purposes); hence, they interact in a highly toxic relationship that involves a process of exchange necessary for their survival. The exchanging process contributes to the survival of each party; acts of terrorism provide media stories that result in more broadcasting airwaves, press texts, and digital data bytes, while the media coverage brings public attention to terrorists—the oxygen necessary for their existence. The more the audiences are widespread the more both parties benefit and achieve their goals—i.e., the more they survive and grow. This point is fundamental in emphasizing the inevitable and inseparable benefits both terrorists and media personnel share. Therefore, this multifaceted relationship that is rooted in interaction, codependency, and inseparability necessitates a representative term. Thus, I introduce the term *Terroredia* and its following definition to reflect on this relationship.

Terroredia is the interactive, codependent, and inseparable relationship between terrorism and the media, in which acts of terrorism and their media coverage are essentially exchanged to achieve the ultimate aims of both parties—exchanging terrorism's wide-ranging publicity and public attention (i.e., oxygen) for media's wide-ranging reach and influence (e.g., airwaves).

The equation in this relationship is simple; the more terrorist attacks accumulate, the higher the multiplication of media broadcasting airwaves, press texts, and digital data bytes. The reverse is also true; the higher the level of exacerbation, sensationalization, and manipulation by the media, the more terrorist attacks are committed.

Terroredia can be understood in conjunction with the emergence of the idea of "new terrorism" (e.g., Martin, 2006; Rich, 2013), in that new terrorism is partly characterized by causing extraordinary massive damages and the use of new tactics. Terroredia in our present era can result in newly born tactics of terrorism, such as cyber-terrorism. Cyber-terrorism is one example of the modern tactics of terrorism that can cause huge harm in numerous industries and fields. Cyberspace, which is a new medium of communication and information technologies, is a unique battlefield for terror (e.g., Anderson, 2003; Conway & McInerney, 2012; Conway, 2006; Tsfati & Weimann, 2002) and hate (Nacos, 2012), giving birth to cyber-terrorism (e.g., Berner, 2003; Breen, 2008; Denning, 2000; Ducol, 2012; Eid, 2010; Gearson, 2002; Hensgen et al., 2003; Laqueur, 2000; Matusitz & Minei, 2009; Matusitz, 2009, 2005; Mitliaga, 2001; Poland, 2005; Simons, 2010; Weimann, 2005), which has become effective in achieving terrorist goals.

With the advancement of modern information technologies and the Internet, terrorists gain public attention through not only the mainstream media but also the new media, including those of their own. In fact, terrorists use the Internet as a tool both to gain and to disseminate information; as a medium through which they "engage in publicity, propaganda and, ultimately, psychological warfare" (Conway, 2006, p. 283). The advent and growing use and popularity of the Internet has allowed for a transformation in the ways in which terrorists communicate with their adversaries, making the dissemination of their ideas to their target audiences much easier, faster, and exactly as intended without any alteration (Soriano, 2012; Weimann, 2005). The Internet provides terrorists with "unprecedented level of direct control over the content of their message(s)" allowing them the great ability "to manipulate not only their own image, but also the image of their enemies" (Conway, 2006, p. 284). Also, with the advancement of information technologies, "one should expect a rise in international terrorist activity" (Grinyaev, 2003, p. 87). Publicity of terrorism "encourages imitation—the 'copycat phenomenon'" (Clutterbuck, 1982, p. 165).

Terroredia is two-directional. Terrorism and the media "can appear to become locked in a relationship of considerable mutual benefit" (Wilkinson, 1997, p. 52). Terrorists need the media coverage "to influence others" and "to propagate a strong message of intimidation"; meanwhile, they "give the media a huge drama that involves a gripping story" (Bergin & Khosa, 2007, p. 1). The relationship can be viewed as a public relations strategy through which the media provide terrorists with access to the public and the acts of terrorism are the symbols of terrorist message and cause (Somerville & Wood, 2007). Terrorists use the media "as a conduit for their political message to be heard by the target audience, whilst supplying 'exciting news' for the media" (Lockyer, 2003, p. 1). In the relationship, "the terrorist demand for recognition via publicity is intimately linked to the media's appetite for increasing sales with sensational stories" (Sadaba, 2002, p. 219). The media play "a crucial role in facilitating the psychological processes that intensify the public's fears and apprehension" (Breckenridge & Zimbardo, 2007, p. 116). Indeed, "the media play an increasing role not only in the recording and reporting of terrorist events, but also in the process of target selection and actions taken by terrorist groups;" hence, contemporary terrorist tactics and targets are selected with the ultimate goal of delivering messages to wide-ranging audiences (Surette, Hansen, & Noble, 2009, p. 360). While the media explain how terrorists choose their target and commit the acts, terrorists tailor both in ways that attract the media to disseminate their message creating a terror-inspiring effect (Bassiouni, 1981).

In order for terrorists to achieve their goals, they "need the attention of the mass media to manipulate, threaten, intimidate, or co-opt the general public, specific groups and individuals,

and government officials," and the more their acts are brutal the more media coverage is substantial (Nacos, 2000, p. 176). On the media side, they strive to attract viewers—in this, they are awarded financial gains. When the media cover events such as hostage-takings or hijackings, they are awarded a bountiful source of highly attractive and compelling stories for audiences (Wilkinson, 1997). Suicide bombings also represent a recently growing tactic of terrorism perpetrated by terrorists worldwide. The attention generated by suicide attacks demonstrates the strong hold that terrorist activity can have on the media (e.g., Atran, 2003; 2006; Schweitzer & Ferber, 2005). Suicide attacks instigate mass terror among audiences. In this tactic of terrorism, the media are fixated and mesmerized by the severity of such attacks; meanwhile, terrorists are able to disseminate their messages through media platforms. Thus, "[t]he primary target is not those actually killed or injured in the attack, but those made to witness it" (Atran, 2003, p. 1534).

Terroredia is fueled by a vicious cycle of violence, media attention, and public fear. The media commonly obsess over terrorist events, as the dramatic spectacle of death, violence, and war is known to attract audiences out of fear. The media frequently impose the word "terrorism," loosely and meaninglessly, referring to events and actors only to "persuade people to read newspapers and watch television news" (Bruce, 2013, p. 29). Events such as 9/11 illustrate "the struggle, and failure, of media discourse to contain unique events within dominant modes of understanding" (Wark, cited in McMillian, 2004, p. 394). Moreover, media coverage of terrorist events can transform a specific incident into a global drama, inducing audience involvement similar to that of melodramas (e.g., Altheide, 1987; Brown, 1990).

The ways in which the media frame terrorist events can spark strong emotional reactions among audiences (Boyle et al., 2004). Unfortunately, these reactions and the promotion of fear are precisely what make terrorists survive, making them able to disrupt communities and disseminate their messages. The events of 9/11 sparked a boom of discussion surrounding how the media and terrorists interact (e.g., Abrahamian, 2003; Albright, Abrams, & Panofsky, 2009; Alsultany, 2013; Boyle et al., 2004; De Goede, 2008; Hammond, 2003; Hoffman, 2002; Ismail & Berkowitz, 2009; Louw, 2003; Mazumdar, 2004; Merola, 2013). For instance, some argued that the perpetrators of 9/11 were able to leverage media coverage to amply the fear produced by their acts (Mythen & Walklate, 2006). The event "set the bar for future terrorist attacks as terrorists escalate carnage to capture and maintain media and public attention" (Blum, Asal, & Wilkenfeld, 2005, p. 166). Simultaneously, the media seem to thrive on this coverage; through dramatic news reporting and chaotic images, they are able to captivate audiences and fuel the media machine. However, inquiry into the relationship between terrorism and the media emerged prior to 9/11 (e.g., Altheide, 1987; Brown, 1990; Delli Carpini & Williams, 1987; Held, 1997; Sandler, Tschirhart, & Cauley, 1983; Weimann & Winn, 1994; Wilkinson, 1997; Wittebols, 1991). The events of 9/11 simply solidified the ways in which terrorists (state and non-state) are dependent on the media to communicate symbols and ideas that are necessary to their cause. They "conformed to a long-standing tradition of terrorism as 'propaganda of the deed'—namely executing highly visible, violent acts designed for maximal symbolic impact" (Louw, 2003, p. 211).

In Terroredia, each party "gives the other what it wants", as for terrorism the "biggest single motivation" is "to gain publicity by attracting the attention of the mass media," while the media "are motivated by the need to attract an audience" because they "stand or fall by selling advertising" and "purely professional motivations" (Clutterbuck,

1982, p. 166). Media coverage can be perceived as "the lifeblood" of terrorism, without which "the terrorist act would resemble the proverbial tree falling in the forest: if no one learned of an incident, it would be as if it had not occurred" (Nacos, 2000, p. 175). Therefore, publicity is strategic in the terrorism decision-making calculations of increasing the return of carrying out attacks, as it enhances the ability to propagandize terrorist ideology and to recruit new members, supplies terrorists with critical real-time tactical information (e.g., particular political pressures that can be exploited during negotiations), and increases the negotiating power of terrorists during some tactics of terrorism such as hostage-takings by increasing the political value of those taken captive (Drakos & Gofas, 2006). On the other hand, news media are competitive and lucrative businesses that thrive on action and controversy; hence, they sensationalize terrorism stories to boost ratings and grab the attention of audiences (Eid, 2013).

Intensive research into Terroredia is required. This book is the first attempt to look into some individual aspects of Terroredia, mirroring terrorism and the media within specific contexts of interrelated relationships. The first section of the book discusses the aspect of both understanding terrorism and understanding the media during times of terrorism. Similarly, the following sections of the book discuss other various aspects: terrorism manifestations and media representations; terrorism types and media stereotypes; terrorism tactics and media strategies; terrorism functioning and media employing; and new terrorism and new media. Finally, the most recent developments on terrorism and the media are discussed, and both terrorism/counterterrorism rationality and media responsibility during terrorism are questioned.

REFERENCES

Abrahamian, E. (2003). The US media, Huntington and September 11. *Third World Quarterly*, *24*(3), 529–544. doi:10.1080/0143659032000084456

Albright, K., Abrams, C. B., & Panofsky, A. L. (2009). After the fall: The changing experiential conditions of post-9/11 New York and their political implications. *The American Behavioral Scientist*, *53*(1), 80–98. doi:10.1177/0002764209338787

Alexander, Y., & Latter, R. (Eds.). (1990). *Terrorism and the media: Dilemmas for government, journalists and the public*. Washington, DC: Brassey's.

Alger, D. E. (1989). *The media and politics*. Upper Saddle River, NJ: Prentice Hall.

Ali, Z., Iqbal, A., Jan, M., & Ahmad, A. (2012). Coverage of Pak-U.S. relations on issue of counter terrorism by U.S. leading news magazines. *Middle-East Journal of Scientific Research*, *15*(10), 1464–1471.

Alsultany, E. (2013). Arabs and Muslims in the media after 9/11: Representational strategies for a postrace era. *American Quarterly*, *65*(1), 161–169. doi:10.1353/aq.2013.0008

Altheide, D. L. (1987). Format and symbols in TV coverage of terrorism in the United States and Great Britain. *International Studies Quarterly*, *31*(2), 161–176. doi:10.2307/2600451

Anderson, A. (2003). Risk, terrorism, and the internet. *Knowledge, Technology & Policy*, *16*(2), 24–33. doi:10.1007/s12130-003-1023-7

Atran, S. (2003). Genesis of suicide terrorism. *Review Social Science*, *299*, 1534–1539. PMID:12624256

Atran, S. (2006). The moral logic and growth of suicide terrorism. *The Washington Quarterly*, *29*(2), 127–147. doi:10.1162/wash.2006.29.2.127

Bassiouni, M. C. (1981). Terrorism, law enforcement, and the mass media: Perspectives, problems, proposals. *The Journal of Criminal Law & Criminology*, *72*(1), 1–51. doi:10.2307/1142904

Bergin, A., & Khosa, R. (2007). The Australian media and terrorism. *ASPI: Australian Strategic Policy Institute*, *11*, 1–8.

Berner, S. (2003). Cyber-terrorism: Reality or paranoia? *South African Journal of Information Management*, *5*(1), 1–4.

Biernatzki, W. E. (2002). Terrorism and mass media. *Communication Research Trends*, *21*(1), 3–27.

Blum, A., Asal, V., & Wilkenfeld, J. (2005). Nonstate actors, terrorism, and weapons of mass destruction. *International Studies Review*, *7*, 133–170. doi:10.1111/j.1521-9488.2005.479_1.x

Boggs, C. (2002). Militarism and terrorism: The deadly cycle. *Democracy and Nature*, *8*(2), 241–259. doi:10.1080/10855660220148598

Boyle, M. P., Schmierbach, M., Armstrong, C. L., McLeod, D. M., Shah, D. V., & Pan, Z. (2004). Information seeking and emotional reaction to the September 11 terrorist attacks. *Journalism & Mass Communication Quarterly*, *81*(1), 155–167. doi:10.1177/107769900408100111

Braithwaite, A. (2013). The logic of public fear in terrorism and counter-terrorism. *Journal of Police and Criminal Psychology*, *28*, 95–101. doi:10.1007/s11896-013-9126-x

Breckenridge, J. N., & Zimbardo, P. G. (2007). The strategy of terrorism and the psychology of mass-mediated fear. In B. Bongar, L. M. Brown, L. E. Beutler, J. N. Breckenridge, & P. G. Zimbardo (Eds.), *Psychology of terrorism* (pp. 116–133). New York: Oxford University Press.

Breen, G.-M. (2008). Examining existing counter-terrorism tactics and applying social network theory to fight cyberterrorism: An interpersonal communication perspective. *Journal of Applied Security Research*, *3*(2), 191–204. doi:10.1080/19361610802135888

Brown, W. J. (1990). The persuasive appeal of mediated terrorism: The case of the TWA flight 847 hijacking. *Western Journal of Speech Communication*, *54*, 219–236. doi:10.1080/10570319009374337

Bruce, G. (2013). Definition of terrorism: Social and political effects. *Journal of Military and Veteran's Health*, *21*(2), 26–30.

Chermak, S. (2003). Marketing fear: Representing terrorism after September 11. *Journal for Crime. Conflict and the Media*, *1*(1), 5–22.

Cho, J., Boyle, M. P., Keum, H., Shevy, M. D., McLeod, D. M., Shah, D. V., & Pan, Z. (2003). Media, terrorism, and emotionality: Emotional differences in media content and public reactions to the September 11th terrorist attacks. *Journal of Broadcasting & Electronic Media*, *47*(3), 309–327. doi:10.1207/s15506878jobem4703_1

Clutterbuck, R. (1982). Terrorism and urban violence. *Proceedings of the Academy of Political Science*, *34*(4), 165–175. doi:10.2307/3700978

Combs, C. C. (2013). *Terrorism in the twenty-first century*. Boston: Pearson.

Conway, M. (2006). Terrorism and the internet: New media – new threat? *Parliamentary Affairs*, *59*(2), 283–298. doi:10.1093/pa/gsl009

Conway, M., & McInerney, L. (2012). Terrorism in old and new media. *Media. War & Conflict*, *5*(1), 3–5. doi:10.1177/1750635211434349

Crelinsten, R. D. (1989). Terrorism and the media: Problems, solutions, and counterproblems. *Political Communication and Persuasion*, *6*(4), 311–339. doi:10.1080/10584609.1989.9962881

De Goede, M. (2008). Beyond risk: Premediation and post-9/11 security imagination. *Security Dialogue*, *39*(2-3), 155–176. doi:10.1177/0967010608088773

Delli Carpini, M. X., & Williams, B. A. (1987). Television and terrorism: Patterns of presentation and occurrences, 1969 to 1980. *The Western Political Quarterly*, *40*(1), 45–64. doi:10.1177/106591298704000105

Denning, D. E. (2000). Activism, hacktivism, and cyberterrorism: The internet as a tool for influencing foreign policy. *Computer Security Journal*, *16*(3), 15–35.

Der Derian, J. (2005). Imaging terror: Logos, pathos and ethos. *Third World Quarterly*, *26*(1), 23–37. doi:10.1080/0143659042000322883

Devine, P. E., & Rafalko, R. J. (1982). On terror. *The Annals of the American Academy of Political and Social Science*, *463*, 39–53. doi:10.1177/0002716282463001004

Drakos, K., & Gofas, A. (2006). The devil you know but are afraid to face: Underreporting bias and its distorting effects on the study of terrorism. *The Journal of Conflict Resolution*, *50*(5), 714–735. doi:10.1177/0022002706291051

Ducol, B. (2012). Uncovering the French-speaking jihadisphere: An exploratory analysis. *Media. War & Conflict*, *5*(1), 51–70. doi:10.1177/1750635211434366

Eid, M. (2010). Cyber-terrorism and ethical journalism: A need for rationalism. *International Journal of Technoethics, 1*(4), 1–19. doi:10.4018/jte.2010100101

Eid, M. (2013). The new era of media and terrorism. [Review of the three books *Terrorism in the twenty-first century, Mass-mediated terrorism: The central role of the media in terrorism and counterterrorism*, and *Fueling our fears: Stereotyping, media coverage, and public opinion of Muslim Americans*]. *Studies in Conflict and Terrorism, 36*(7), 609–615. doi:10.1080/1057610X.2013.793638

Elmquist, S. (1990). The scope and limits of co-operation between the media and the authorities. In Y. Alexander & R. Latter (Eds.), Terrorism and the media: Dilemmas for government, journalists and the public (pp. 74-80). Washington, DC: Brassey's (US), Inc.

Finn, J. E. (1990). Media coverage of political terrorism and the first amendment: Reconciling the public's right to know with public order. In Y. Alexander & R. Latter (Eds.), Terrorism and the media: Dilemmas for government, journalists and the public (pp. 47-56). Washington, DC: Brassey's (US), Inc.

Freedman, D., & Thussu, D. K. (2012). Introduction: Dynamics of media and terrorism. In D. Freedman, & D. K. Thussu (Eds.), *Media & terrorism: Global perspectives* (pp. 1–20). London: Sage. doi:10.4135/9781446288429.n1

Gearson, J. (2002). The nature of modern terrorism. *The Political Quarterly, 73*(1), 7–24. doi:10.1111/1467-923X.73.s1.3

Grinyaev, S. (2003). The mass media and terrorism: A Russian view. *European Security, 12*(2), 85–88. doi:10.1080/09662830412331308086

Hammond, P. (2003). The media war on terrorism. *Journal for Crime. Conflict and the Media, 1*(1), 23–36.

Held, V. (1997). The media and political violence. *The Journal of Ethics, 1*(2), 187–202. doi:10.1023/A:1009797007570

Hensgen, T., Desouza, K. C., Evaristo, J. R., & Kraft, G. D. (2003). Playing the cyber terrorism game towards a semiotic definition. *Human Systems Management, 22*(2), 51–61.

Hoffman, B. (2002). Rethinking terrorism and counterterrorism since 9/11. *Studies in Conflict and Terrorism, 25*(1), 303–316. doi:10.1080/105761002901223

Ismail, A., & Berkowitz, D. (2009). Terrorism meets press system: The *New York Times* and *China Daily* before and after 9/11. *Global Media Journal, 4*(1), 15-28.

Kelly, M. J. (1989). The seizure of the Turkish embassy in Ottawa: Managing terrorism and the media. In U. Rosenthal, M. T. Charles, & P. T. Hart (Eds.), *Coping with crises: The management of disasters, riots and terrorism* (pp. 117–138). Charles C. Thomas Publisher.

Laqueur, W. (2000). *The new terrorism: Fanaticism and the arms of mass destruction.* New York: Oxford University Press.

Lockyer, A. (2003). *The relationship between the media and terrorism.* The Australian National University: Strategic and Defence Studies Centre.

Louw, P. E. (2003). The war against terrorism. *Gazette: The International Journal for Communication Studies, 65*(3), 211–230. doi:10.1177/0016549203065003001

Martin, G. (2006). *Understanding terrorism: Challenges, perspectives, and issues.* Thousand Oaks, CA: Sage Publications, Inc.

Matusitz, J. (2005). Cyberterrorism: How can American foreign policy be strengthened in the information age? *American Foreign Policy Interests, 27*(2), 137–147.

Matusitz, J. (2009). A postmodern theory of cyberterrorism: Game theory. *Information Security Journal: A Global Perspective, 18*(6), 273-281.

Matusitz, J., & Minei, E. (2009). Cyberterrorism: Its effects on health-related infrastructures. *Journal of Digital Forensic Practice, 2*(4), 161–171. doi:10.1080/15567280802678657

Mazumdar, R. (2004). Cracks in the urban frame: The visual politics of 9/11. In Sarai reader 04: Crisis/media (pp. 209-216). Delhi, India: Sarai, the Centre for the Study of Developing Societies.

McMillian, N. (2004). Beyond representation: Cultural understandings of the September 11 attacks. *Australian and New Zealand Journal of Criminology, 37*(3), 380–400. doi:10.1375/acri.37.3.380

Merola, L. M. (2013). Transmitting the threat: Media coverage and the discussion of terrorism and civil liberties since 9/11. *Behavioral Sciences of Terrorism and Political Aggression, 5*(1), 1–19. doi:10.1080/19434472.2011.571531

Mitliaga, V. (2001). Cyber-terrorism: A call for governmental action? In *Proceedings of 16ᵗʰ BILETA Annual Conference*. Retrieved October 9, 2009, from http://www.bileta.ac.uk/01papers/mitliaga.html

Mythen, G., & Walklate, S. (2006). Communicating the terrorist risk: Harnessing a culture of fear? *Crime, Media, Culture, 2*(2), 123–142. doi:10.1177/1741659006065399

Nacos, B. L. (2000). Accomplice or witness? The media's role in terrorism. *Current History (New York, N.Y.), 99*(636), 174–178.

Nacos, B. L. (2003a). Terrorism as breaking news: Attack on America. *Political Science Quarterly, 118*(1), 23–52. doi:10.1002/j.1538-165X.2003.tb00385.x

Nacos, B. L. (2003b). The terrorist calculus behind 9-11: A model for future terrorism? *Studies in Conflict and Terrorism, 26*(1), 1–16. doi:10.1080/10576100390145134

Nacos, B. L. (2005). The portrayal of female terrorists in the media: Similar framing patters in the news coverage of women in politics and in terrorism. *Studies in Conflict and Terrorism, 28*(5), 435–451. doi:10.1080/10576100500180352

Nacos, B. L. (2006). *Terrorism and counterterrorism: Understanding threats and responses in the post-9/11 world*. New York: Longman.

Nacos, B. L. (2007). *Mass-mediated terrorism: The central role of the media in terrorism and counterterrorism*. Lanham, MD: Rowman & Littlefield Publishers.

Nacos, B. L. (2012). *Terrorism and counterterrorism*. Boston: Longman.

Nasir, M., Khan, A. A., & Jalil, H. H. (2013). Exploring the relationship between media and terrorism: A panel study of south Asian countries. *Economic Bulletin, 33*(1), 714–720.

Pfeiffer, C. P. (2012). Terrorism and its oxygen: A game-theoretic perspective on terrorism and the media. *Behavioral Sciences of Terrorism and Political Aggression, 4*(3), 212–228. doi:10.1080/19434472.2011.594629

Picard, R. (1990). News coverage as the contagion of terrorism: Dangerous charges backed by dubious science. In Y. Alexander & R. Latter (Eds.), Terrorism and the media: Dilemmas for government, journalists and the public (pp. 100-110). Washington, DC: Brassey's (US), Inc.

Poland, J. M. (2005). *Understanding terrorism: Groups, strategies, and responses*. Upper Saddle River, NJ: Pearson Education, Inc.

Protheroe, A. H. (1990). Terrorism, journalism, and democracy. In Y. Alexander & R. Latter (Eds.), Terrorism and the media: Dilemmas for government, journalists and the public (pp. 64-69). Washington, DC: Brassey's (US), Inc.

Rich, P. B. (2013). Understanding terror, terrorism and their representations in media and culture. *Studies in Conflict and Terrorism, 36*(3), 255–277. doi:10.1080/1057610X.2013.755915

Robinson, P. (2000). The policy-media interaction model: Measuring media power during humanitarian crisis. *Journal of Peace Research, 37*(5), 613–633. doi:10.1177/0022343300037005006

Sadaba, T. (2002). Each to his own… September 11 in Basque media. *Television & New Media, 3*(2), 219–222. doi:10.1177/152747640200300214

Sandler, T., Tschirhart, J. T., & Cauley, J. (1983). A theoretical analysis of transnational terrorism. *The American Political Science Review, 77*(1), 36–54. doi:10.2307/1956010

Schmid, A. P. (1989). Terrorism and the media: The ethics of publicity. *Terrorism and Political Violence, 1*(4), 539–565. doi:10.1080/09546558908427042

Schmid, A. P., & Jongman, A. J. (2008). *Political terrorism: A new guide to actors, authors, concepts, data bases, theories, & literature.* London: Transaction Publishers.

Schweitzer, Y., & Ferber, S. G. (2005). *Al-Qaeda and the internationalization of suicide terrorism.* Jerusalem, Israel: Jaffe Center for Strategic Studies.

Simons, G. (2010). *Mass media and modern warfare: Reporting on the Russian war on terrorism.* Bulington, VT: Ashgate.

Somerville, I., & Wood, E. (2007). Public relations, politics and the media. In A. Theaker (Ed.), *The public relations handbook* (pp. 32–51). New York: Routledge.

Soriano, M. R. T. (2012). The vulnerabilities of online terrorism. *Studies in Conflict and Terrorism, 35*(4), 263–277. doi:10.1080/105761 0X.2012.656345

Steuter, E. (1990). Understanding the media/terrorism relationship: An analysis of ideology and the news in Time magazine. *Political Communication and Persuasion, 7*(4), 257–278. doi:10.1080/10584609.1990.9962902

Surette, R., Hansen, K., & Noble, G. (2009). Measuring media oriented terrorism. *Journal of Criminal Justice, 37,* 360–370. doi:10.1016/j.jcrimjus.2009.06.011

Tsfati, Y., & Weimann, G. (2002). Terror on the internet. *Studies in Conflict and Terrorism, 25*(5), 317–332. www.terrorism.com doi:10.1080/10576100290101214

Weimann, G. (2005). Cyberterrorism: The sum of all fears? *Studies in Conflict and Terrorism, 28*(2), 129–149. doi:10.1080/10576100590905110

Weimann, G., & Winn, C. (1994). *The theater of terror: Mass media and international terrorism.* New York: Longman.

Wilkinson, P. (1997). The media and terrorism: A reassessment. *Terrorism and Political Violence, 9*(2), 51–64. doi:10.1080/09546559708427402

Wittebols, J. H. (1991). The politics and coverage of terrorism: From media images to public consciousness. *Communication Theory, 1*(3), 253–266. doi:10.1111/j.1468-2885.1991.tb00018.x

Wittebols, J. H. (1992). Media and the institutional perspective: U.S. & Canadian coverage of terrorism. *Political Communication, 9*(4), 267–278. doi:10.1080/10584609.1992.9962950

KEY TERMS AND DEFINITIONS

Asymmetrical: Having parts that fail to correspond; to lack in symmetry.

Codependency: Two entities are mutually dependent on each other, while the level of dependence can vary.

Cyber-Terrorism: The use of cyberspace to plan and implement acts of terrorism.

Public Attention: Fascination or concentration from the people constituting a community, state, nation, or society.

Publicity: The gaining of public notice.

Symmetrical: Equality and correspondence of two or more parts.

Terroredia: Terroredia is the interactive, codependent, and inseparable relationship between terrorism and the media, in which acts of terrorism and their media coverage are essentially exchanged to achieve the ultimate aims of both parties—exchanging terrorism's wide-ranging publicity and public attention (i.e., oxygen) for media's wide-ranging reach and influence (e.g., airwaves).

Section 1
Terrorism & Media

Chapter 2
Understanding Terrorism

Mahmoud Eid
University of Ottawa, Canada

ABSTRACT

People all over the globe have become very familiar with the term terrorism due to its common and worldwide occurrence. Terrorism has been committed by states, governments, organizations, groups, and individuals throughout its long history. Despite the large number of definitions by governments, global institutions, academics, politicians, security experts, and journalists, there has been no single universally agreed-upon definition of terrorism so far for a variety of reasons. This chapter critically analyzes discussions and definitions of terrorism in an attempt to contribute to a fair and balanced understanding of terrorism. It discusses how subjectivity has been an obstacle in understanding terrorism due to the pejorative nature of the term. Debates around the highly contentious concept of terrorism in terms of its distinctive nature, motivations, goals, and means in comparison to other forms of violence are discussed, and several definitions of terrorism are analyzed. It is evident that obtaining public attention is the ultimate aim of terrorism in relation to communicating specific messages and both the use of and by the media. While definitions of terrorism struggle to demonstrate exhaustive lists of descriptions, traits, components, conditions, and elements of terrorism, disagreements on these definitional items and features create ambiguities in understanding terrorism. The chapter, then, concludes with discussions on eliminating controversial and subjective definitional items and features to introduce a definition that can help provide an objective understanding of terrorism.

RECOGNIZING THE DILEMMA

Nearly everyone across the globe has become familiar with the word "terrorism" (Bankoff, 2003), given the fact that almost every day a terrorist incident occurs somewhere in the world (Kupperman, van Opstal, & Williamson, 1982). In a broad, yet vague, understanding, the word "terrorism" can be applied to numerous social relations and interactions. For example, "men terrorize women; adults terrorize children; humans terrorize animals; and so on" (Bergesen & Lizardo, 2004, p. 38). However, this understanding is far separate from tactics of terrorism used by states, organizations, groups, and individuals that are motivated by specific predetermined agendas.

State terrorism (against a state's own people) and state-sponsored terrorism (against the people

DOI: 10.4018/978-1-4666-5776-2.ch002

of another state) have occurred throughout the long history of terrorism. Governments "may use their legal apparatus and even their military forces to terrorize segments of their own populations" (Jaggar, 2003, p. 176). While nations (e.g., Iraq, Syria, and Iran) have been repeatedly accused of involvement in state-sponsored terrorism, some wars (e.g., the U.S. 2003 war on Iraq) have also been seen as acts of state terror (e.g., Combs, 2013; Eid, 2008). Terrorist organizations require the support of networks able to fund activities in regions outside conflicts; hence, there exist an international network of groups that cooperate informally and formally with each other in many ways, such as ideological and theological alliances; organizational assistance; propaganda and psychological warfare; financial help; recruitment support; intelligence sharing; supply of weapons; operational activities; and availability of sanctuaries (Alexander, 2006). Terrorist groups and individuals carry out activities that range from playing support roles (e.g., fundraising; lobbying through front institutions; coercing, intimidating, and manipulating communities; and propagating hate) to planning and preparing terrorist attacks (e.g., procuring weapons and materials and abusing regulations).

Terrorism is international; so has to be counterterrorism. A helpful step towards a universal cooperation among nations of the globe in the prevention of terrorism is an agreement on a common definition; however, the United Nations has been struggling to provide a definition that is accepted by all nations (Bruce, 2013). The United Nations produced an interim draft definition in 2001, which down-plays political justification and lists acts of violence as terrorism if they are "resulting or likely to result in major economic loss, when the purpose of the conduct, by its nature or context, is to intimidate a population, or to compel a Government or an international organisation to do or abstain from doing any act" (cited in Bruce, 2013, pp. 26-27). In 2010, the Head of the UN Counter-Terrorism Committee Execu-

tive Directorate said that "the fact that there was not a universal definition of terrorism presented a challenge . . . nations are hampered by an inability to define and criminalise terrorism" and this remains a problem in achieving transnational counterterrorism (Bruce, 2013, p. 27).

The fight against terrorism seems to be as hard as the attempt to define it. International institutions and scholars have acknowledged the struggle to define the highly contentious concept of terrorism (e.g., Chakravorti, 1994; Coady, 2004; Devine & Rafalko, 1982; Ganor, 2002; Gibbs, 1989; Hoffman, 2006; Poland, 2005; Ruby, 2002; Schmid & Jongman, 2008; Teichman, 1989). Despite the comprehensive discussions in the literature of defining terrorism, a consensus on an appropriate definition is still far from reach. Well-established global institutions, academics, politicians, security experts, and journalists have defined terrorism, focusing on various angles; however, there has been no single fully or universally agreed-upon definition of terrorism. Many explain that the concept of terrorism is difficult to define (e.g., Atran, 2003; Davis et al., 2013; Fletcher, 2006; Ganor, 2002; Oberschall, 2004; Schmid & Jongman, 2008; Symeonidou-Kastanidou, 2004; Waldron, 2004).

The attempt to define the term terrorism is faced with various difficulties, including its: long history; various and different forms or tactics; pejorative nature; polemical and rhetorical use; and rapidly changing nature. Walter Laqueur explains that it is "so difficult to find a generally accepted definition" of terrorism because: 1) "only things which have no history can be defined" but terrorism "has had a very long history"; and 2) "there has not been a single form of terrorism, but many, often with few traits in common" (2000, p. 6). Terrorism also holds negative connotations to which nobody would desire to be attributed (Copeland, 2001). The use of the term "is often polemical and rhetorical;" it "can be a pejorative label, meant to condemn an opponent's cause as illegitimate rather than describe behavior" (Crenshaw, 2000, p. 406). The nature of terrorism is rapidly changing, rendering "many traditional definitions misleading" (Lesser, 1999, p. 85).

This chapter critically analyzes discussions and definitions of terrorism in an attempt to contribute to an objective understanding of terrorism. In doing so, it discusses how subjectivity causes an obstacle in understanding terrorism when used in a large number of definitions to describe the Other due to the pejorative nature of this term. Actors of terrorism are identified to include states, governments, organizations, groups, and individuals. Terrorism is a contentious concept that attracts extensive debates around its distinctive nature in comparison to other forms of violence in terms of motivations, goals, and means. Obtaining public attention is the ultimate aim of terrorism in relation to communicating specific messages and both the use of and by the media. The present analysis of a wide range of definitions and discussions of terrorism employs an ascending approach in demonstrating how descriptions and characteristics of terrorism have been adding-up, moving from simple to comprehensive definitions. While definitions of terrorism struggle to demonstrate exhaustive lists of descriptions, traits, components, conditions, and elements of terrorism, debates around these definitional items and features create ambiguities in understanding terrorism. Hence, the chapter concludes with discussions on eliminating controversial and subjective definitional items and features and introducing a definition of terrorism that can help provide a fair and balanced understanding of this term.

LABELING THE OTHER

The Self-Other dichotomy is evident in the dilemma of defining terrorism. Most discussions around defining terrorism try to come up with definitions that generally describe "what they do is terrorism and is unjustified, whereas what we and our friends do is not terrorism but a justified response to it, or is justified self-defense" (Held,

2004, p. 65). Terrorism is a pejorative socially constructed label, which if given to an action, "it becomes difficult to treat it in a value-neutral manner" (Biernatzki, 2002, p. 3). The label "terrorism" is used to describe the use of violence opposed by the person or government using the label; hence, it can be seen more as a discursive practice than as valid categorization of violence (Beiber, 2003). It is a word "with intrinsically negative connotations that is generally applied to one's enemies and opponents, or to those with whom one disagrees and would otherwise prefer to ignore" (Hoffman, 2006, p. 23).

The fundamental differences between terrorism and the legitimate uses of violence are ignored. This is reflected in the popular canard: someone's terrorist is another's freedom fighter. If one identifies with the victim or the target of an act of violence, then the act is considered terrorism; whereas if one identifies with the actor, the act is not terrorism (e.g., Copeland, 2001; Hoffman, 2006). Hence, terrorism is, unsurprisingly, more prolific in the rhetoric of politicians than of scholars: it is "a convenient label to attach to someone you dislike" (Beiber, 2003, p. 46). Benjamin Netanyahu of Israel defines terrorism as "the deliberate and systematic murder, maiming, and menacing of the innocent to inspire fear for political ends" (cited in Beinin, 2003, p. 12). Interestingly, this same definition can be applied to both parties in the Israeli-Palestinian conflict, depending on the party with which one can take side. Being that the term terrorism carries "tremendous (negative) evaluative or emotive weight, people have an incentive to ensure that, if possible, it is applied to their dangerous political adversaries or to persons or programs that they disagree with strenuously on other grounds" (Waldron, 2004, p. 33).

Terrorism is "differently valued depending on one's perspective" (Goody, 2002, p. 140). Many collectives and individuals have defined terrorism in "the form that suits their bias or perspective," including alliances of nations, academics and researchers, legal professionals, health professionals, counterterrorism and law enforcement agencies, "governments that wish to protect their citizens, governments that wish to repress their citizens, terrorist groups and the media"; all have a "different agenda, even within their groups" (Bruce, 2013, p. 29). In fact, "the decision to call someone or label some organization 'terrorist' becomes almost unavoidably subjective, depending largely on whether one sympathizes with or opposes the person/group/cause concerned" (Hoffman, 2006, p. 23). For example, governments "characteristically define 'terrorism' as something only their opponents can commit, as something only those who seek to change policies, or to attack a given political system or status quo can engage in" (Held, 2004, p. 62). Terrorism is a "deeply contested concept," its use "tends to be politicized" (Crenshaw, 2000, p. 406), and therefore defining it is "a highly subjective, even ethno-centric exercise" (Lesser, 1999, p. 85). Definitions of terrorism are controversial because labeling actions as "terrorism" promotes "condemnation of the actors;" hence, "a definition may reflect ideological or political bias" (Gibbs, 1989, p. 329).

It is claimed that more than two hundred definitions of terrorism are used worldwide; nearly half of them by governments and well-established organizations (Copeland, 2001). What are sometimes called "official" definitions include those of: The United Nations;[1] The United Nations General Assembly;[2] The U.S. Congress;[3] The U.S. Department of Defense;[4] The U.S. Federal Bureau of Investigation (FBI);[5] The U.S. Department of Homeland Security;[6] and The U.S. Department of State.[7] These definitions are criticized for adopting somewhat narrow approaches in defining terrorism, reflecting only on the priorities and particular interests of the defining institution, and giving sole power to the institution to determine the acts of terrorism. An analysis of the various definitions of terrorism by U.S. departments reveals common elements (when assigned to individual suspects, they may be labeled and detained as terrorists),

constructing "a composite American definitional model"[8]; these elements "indicate that the United States has adopted a fairly narrow and legalistic approach to defining terrorism" (Martin, 2006, p. 48). Each of these definitions "reflects the priorities and particular interests of the specific agency involved" (2006, p. 31). As well, definitions such as those by the UN General Assembly and the FBI have the limitation of terror to "criminal" or "unlawful" acts, giving only authorities the power to determine whether or not an act is criminal/unlawful (Biernatzki, 2002).

COMMITTING THE ACTION

Terrorism can be committed by non-state, state, and state-sponsored actors. Most definitions of terrorism limit applications of the term to non-state actors (individuals, groups, and organizations). They usually put these actors in opposition or confrontation against governments and states, whether directly or through violence against their public. For example, despite his acknowledgment that terrorism "is a weapon or method which has been used throughout history by both states and sub-state organizations" (Beiber, 2003, p. 47), Paul Wilkinson still defines terrorism as the "resort to violence for political ends by unauthorised, non-governmental actors in breach of accepted codes of behaviour regarding the expression of dissatisfaction with, or dissent from or opposition to, the pursuit of political goals by the legitimate authorities of the State whom they regard as unresponsive to the needs of certain groups of people" (Wilkinson, 1974, p. 79).

However, other definitions acknowledge that terrorism is also perpetrated by states (e.g., Falk, 2003; Goody, 2002; Laqueur, 2000; O'Kane, 2012). States "can terrorize and can use soldiers, airplanes, and tanks to do so" (Held, 2004, p. 63). They "may engage in terrorism covertly as well as overtly, using unofficial militias" (Jaggar, 2003, p. 176). The non-state terrorist attacks are even sometimes direct responses or retaliation due to the terrorism initiated by the state; an action justified as "terror begets terror" (Berezovsky, 2005, p. 59).[9] Terrorism has been used by governments to suppress revolution as well as by revolutionaries who have sought to achieve power over a government; it has been used by individuals and by organizations (Garrison, 2004). While a terrorist action "normally characterizes activities against an overpowerful state, . . . [it] can also be said to mark the reaction of states to such attempts at opposition" (Goody, 2002, p. 140).

State terrorism is used against a state's own people, while state-sponsored terrorism is directed against the people of another state (Biernatzki, 2002). State terrorism is "the earliest and most dangerous form of terrorism" (Symeonidou-Kastanidou, 2004, p. 18). It "causes far more harm than nonstate terrorism, because states typically have access to resources far more powerful and destructive than those available to individuals or to nonstate groups" (Jaggar, 2003, p. 176). State-sponsored terrorism has been "espoused, in an unbridled fashion, by democratically elected governments" (Symeonidou-Kastanidou, 2004, p. 19). It is exercised "when the government of one state funds and supports terrorism carried out by members of groups or states not under its control" (Held, 2004, p. 63). Also, it is sometimes committed by "individuals acting on behalf of states in time of war and peace" (Bassiouni, 1981, p. 1).

DISTINGUISHING THE CONCEPT

The term "terrorism" is derived from the Latin word "terror," which originally meant "physical trembling" and later included "the emotional state of extreme fear" (Crenshaw Hutchinson, 1972, p. 383). Etymologically, "to terrorize" means "to prevail, by inducing terror" (Symeonidou-Kastanidou, 2004, p. 18). Therefore, terrorism is linked to "terror" which is "a state of mind, created by a level of fear that so agitates body

and mind that those struck by it are not capable of making an objective assessment of risks anymore" (Schmid, 2005, p. 137). The word "terror" had entered "the West's political vocabulary as a name for French revolutionaries' actions against their domestic enemies in 1793 and 1794. It referred to governmental repression, most directly in the form of executions" (Tilly, 2004, p. 8).

Delving deeper into the concept may aid in reaching a proper understanding of terrorism that distinguishes its nature from other forms of violence. In doing so, it is important to look into the characteristics of terrorism, the variables that have been most recurring in the discussions about it, its distinction from other types (mainly political violence) and forms (e.g., crime and warfare) of violence, and its justifications (if any). The analysis of discussions and definitions of terrorism is presented here in an ascending approach; demonstrating how descriptions and characteristics of terrorism have been adding-up, moving from simple to comprehensive definitions. On the foundational level, definitions and discussions of terrorism include mainly the actors (non-state, state, and state-sponsored) and highlight its reliance on violence. Then, they move on to accumulate a few or many of its descriptions and characteristics such as: crime, warfare, illegitimate, unlawful, political, deliberate, covert, systematic, psychological harm, fear, intimidation, victims, goals and motivations, targeting wide public attention, and using the media.

Donald Black (2004) argues that, what he calls, "pure terrorism" is social control. Black explains that it belongs to the same family as law, gossip, ostracism, ridicule, and other processes that define and respond to deviant behavior. In comparison to homicide, assault, riot, lynching, vigilantism, feud, guerrilla, and war, Black distinguishes pure terrorism as: 1) self-help, the handling of a grievance with aggression; 2) collective violence; 3) entails logic of collective liability: vulnerability attaches to a social location (e.g., a particular nationality, religion, or ethnicity) rather than to wrongful conduct by those attacked; 4) recurrent, a series of episodes over time; 5) mass violence that kills or maims a large number; 6) unilateral-one-sided, rather than reciprocal; 7) covertly well-organized; and 8) a form of quasi-warfare.

As an alternative to a definition of terrorism, George P. Fletcher suggests "an account of terrorism as the concept is actually used," proposing to "reflect on eight variables that seem to recur" in discussions about terrorism (2006, p. 901). These variables are: violence; intentions; victims; wrongdoers; just cause; organization; theatre; and no guilt, no regrets (Fletcher, 2006). Terrorism is premised on the violent attack on life and security of human beings; however, its official definitions seem to focus very heavily on the element of intention or purpose. Most definitions of terrorism stress that the victims must be either civilians or innocent people and juxtapose the wrongdoers as private actors against the state. The slogan that someone's terrorist is another's freedom fighter accurately highlights the problem: can a good cause justify the use of horrendous means? Assumptions exist in definitions that actors are part of cells, groups, or organizations. Terrorism always has a theatrical aspect, as effective terrorism is always a dramatic event that captures headlines for long periods; otherwise, it cannot communicate the threat of terror to the public at large. Finally, terrorists are perceived to act without feelings of guilt or remorse.

The use of violence is at the heart of any act of terrorism. Particularly, terrorism "is political violence" (Held, 2004, p. 63); hence, many definitions of terrorism "share one common element" that is terrorism is a "politically motivated behavior" (Perl, 2001, p. 5).[10] For example, terrorism is defined "as violence directed, as a matter of political strategy, against innocent persons" (Devine & Rafalko, 1982, p. 40). Acts of terrorism are considered political violence because they are carried out for a particular agenda; for instance, an assassination would not be considered a tactic of terrorism without a political motive. If the motive is criminal, it would be considered a crime (Beiber, 2003). This understanding is debated due to the legitimacy that is sometimes attributed to political violence. Political violence is generally considered "a legitimate, justifiable means to wage a long-term ideological battle against a hostile government;" it has been "ubiquitous throughout human history" as "many governments have met with their demise through the means of coup d'etat, by which the rulers of the government are overthrown by violent means" (Cohan, 2006, p. 910). The distinction between political violence and terrorism lies in that the former is often perceived to be morally justified, while the latter is not; albeit in both there are atrocities and violations of human rights (Cohan, 2006, p. 915). However, making a coherent distinction between them is still difficult as freedom fighters and terrorists "are not mutually exclusive categories. Terrorists can also fight for national liberation, and freedom fighters can also carry out inhumane atrocities" (Ibid, p. 916).

Thus, the question is whether or not terrorism can be defended under any circumstances. The overwhelming discussions among scholars on the legitimacy of terrorism confirm that nothing can justify acts of terrorism. However, some argue that terrorism can only be justified in very specific situations. For example, it can be justified as the absolute last weapon of the oppressed if: 1) it is used against a form of power that uses illegitimate violence; 2) the circumstance excludes all other possibilities for action; 3) it is only directed against those who are responsible for the practice of illegitimate violence; 4) its sole aim is to neutralize those people as practitioners of violence and not to harm them further; and 5) one has taken precautions against unwanted side-effects or has seen to it that these are at any rate kept within restricted limits (Thomassen, 1992).

Although terrorism is about violence, "not every form of violence is terrorism" (Laqueur, 2000, p. 8). Therefore, the concept of terrorism has to be placed in a relational context with other forms of violence (Beiber, 2003). One less severe way of defining terrorism considers it as something in itself unethical, as a crime, or as a form of justifiable warfare. In this way, terrorists are to be treated as prisoners of war and not as criminals. However, George P. Fletcher suggests a "better way to think of terrorism," which "is not as a crime but as a different dimension of crime, a higher, more dangerous version of crime, a kind of super-crime incorporating some of the characteristics of warfare" (2006, p. 900).

The distinction between "a criminal terrorist act of violence" and "a merely criminal act of violence" is "that the direct victim is generally not the ultimate target of the violence" as "victimization serves . . . as an amplifier to convey a message" (Schmid, 2005, pp. 138-139). To distinguish terrorism from both ordinary crimes and acts of war, Alison M. Jaggar characterizes terrorism "to refer to intentional attacks on private citizens carried out with the objective of promoting some political goal by creating terror in the population attacked" (2003, p. 176). As well, Jonathan R. White, suggesting simplicity in defining terrorism, offers this definition: "Terrorism occurs outside the 'rules' of warfare and criminal activity. Terrorism uses violence or threatened violence against innocent people to achieve a social or political goal. Terrorism is a method of fighting somewhat greater than civil disorders and somewhat less than guerilla warfare" (2006, p. 7).

Linked to the comparison of terrorism with other forms of violence is the issue of illegitimacy. Walter Laqueur defines terrorism as "the illegitimate use of force to achieve a political objective by targeting innocent people" (cited in Bruce, 2013, p. 27). Terrorism can be the use of, or the threat of using violence. The targeting is carried out deliberately. Brigitte L. Nacos defines terrorism as "political violence or the threat of violence by groups or individuals who deliberately target civilians or noncombatants in order to influence the behavior and actions of targeted publics and governments" (Nacos, 2012, p. 32).

Most theories of terrorism rest upon and revolve around the assumption that the primary purpose of terrorism is to inflict psychological harm upon a public audience (Braithwaite, 2013). Fear is among the psychological emotions "such as panic, chaos, unrest, fear, paranoia, anxiety, anger, grief, and a sense of tragedy" (Loza, 2007, p. 142) created by terrorist events. Terrorist violence "aims to create a climate of extreme fear" (Wilkinson, cited in Bennett, 1999, p. 50). In this view, Walter Laqueur defines terrorism as "a form of political or criminal violence using tactics designed to change behaviour through fear" (1987, p. 74). Similarly, terrorism is defined as "a type of political violence, which uses the threat or act of violence to create an atmosphere of fear for the advancement of a political agenda" (Beiber, 2003, pp. 46-47). Additional psychological effects such as intimidation and demoralization are also added-up in definitions taking this view. For example, Roger W. Fontaine defines terrorism as a "political action employing extraordinary violent means to achieve the largely psychological effect of intimidation and demoralization on the part of a nation's regime and its populace" (1988, p. 4).[11]

Discussions and definitions of terrorism exchangeably refer to motivations (or reasons, demands, etc.) and goals (or ends, objectives, purposes, etc.). The unclear distinction sometimes happens as a result of the similarity of the descriptions of motivations and goals. For example, terrorist acts can be described as motivated by "religious" beliefs and/or aiming at "religious" ends. Overall, motivations and goals are described in relation to: racial, ethnic, or religious conviction (Ignatieff, 2004); political victory (Thomassen, 1992)[12]; coercion (Biernatzki, 2002)[13]; religious[14] or ideological[15] aim (Bergesen & Lizardo, 2004; Ganor, 2002); and general,[16] political,[17] or social change[18] (Coady, 2004; Garrison, 2004; Kushner, 1998).

COMMUNICATING THE MESSAGE

Terrorist events are meant to communicate messages to much wider audiences than those directly involved. Terrorism is meant "to intimidate a watching popular audience by harming only a few, . . . to hurt, not to destroy" (Crenshaw, 2000, p. 406). Destruction, killing, or injuries are not necessarily the ultimate goals of terrorists; instead, their most important goal is "public information as a communication strategy" (Hirschmann, 2000, p. 299). A fundamental aim of terrorism is "to create public attention or even sympathy" (Hirschmann, 2000, p. 299). The media play a crucial role in achieving this goal; hence, terrorists rely heavily on media coverage (Hirschmann, 2000). Acts of terrorism "are purposely brutal to create an atmosphere of fear while publicizing the terrorists' cause. As the public becomes numb to their acts of violence, terrorists ratchet up the carnage to maintain media interest" (Enders & Sandler, 2005, pp. 467-468). Meanwhile, the media sometimes use terrorists and their attacks to communicate specific ideological or political messages that were not necessarily intended by the acts or their perpetrators, in order to fulfill or achieve personal or institutional agendas or gain some benefits.

Definitions of terrorism reflect on this ultimate goal of wide-ranging public attention, targeting audiences far beyond the immediately troubled. This goal is rationalized within definitions of terrorism in relation to: 1) coercing to comply with the demands; 2) infusing a psychological effect of fear; and 3) affecting policy change. Terrorism is defined as the "use and/or threat of repeated violence in support of or in opposition to some authority, where violence is employed to induce fear of similar attack in as many non-immediate victims as possible so that those so threatened accept and comply with the demands of the terrorist" (Rosie, 1987, p. 7).[19] It is "a set of methods of combat rather than an identifiable ideology or movement, and involves premeditated use of

violence against (primarily) non-combatants in order to achieve a psychological effect of fear on others than the immediate targets" (Bjorgo, cited in Bruce, 2013, p. 27). As well, terrorism is "a form of psychological warfare in which the terrorist is attempting to affect policy change by influencing individual fears and attitudes—notably amongst a population much wider than the immediate targets" (Friedland & Merari, cited in Braithwaite, 2013, p. 96).

With communication as the focal point, Ronald D. Crelinsten understands terrorism as "a form of coercive, violent communication, taking a behavioural approach rather than a motive-based or perpetrator-based approach" (2002, p. 83). Using this behavioral approach, terrorism is defined as the "combined use and threat of violence, planned in secret and usually executed without warning, that is directed against one set of targets (the direct victims) in order to coerce compliance or to compel allegiance from a second set of targets (targets of demands) and to intimidate or to impress a wider audience (target of terror or target of attention)" (Crelinsten, 2002, pp. 83-84). Similarly, and in line with communicating a specific message, terrorism is defined as "systematic threat or use of violence, whether for or in opposition to established authority, with the intention of communicating a political message to a group larger than the victim group by generating fear and so altering the behavior of the larger group" (Claridge, cited in Garrison, 2004, p. 276).

EXHAUSTING THE TOPIC

Definitions and discussions of terrorism have not been limited to what has been demonstrated in this chapter so far. In fact, other descriptions, traits, components, conditions, and elements of terrorism are used to define and explain terrorism. The more the definitions of terrorism move from being simple to comprehensive, the more descriptions, traits, components, conditions, and elements of terrorism are used.

Definitions and discussions include descriptions of the acts of terrorism such as: covert, secretive, furtive, or clandestine; premeditated, deliberate, or calculated; shocking or unexpected; and persistent or systematic. Walter Laqueur defines terrorism as "the use of covert violence by a group for political ends" (1987, p. 72).[20] Rex A. Hudson defines a terrorist action as "the calculated use of unexpected, shocking, and unlawful violence against noncombatants (including, in addition to civilians, off-duty military and security personnel in peaceful situations) and other symbolic targets perpetrated by a clandestine member(s) of a subnational group or a clandestine agent(s) for the psychological purpose of publicizing a political or religious cause and/or intimidating or coercing a government(s) or civilian population into accepting demands on behalf of the cause" (Hudson, 1999, p. 12). Terrorism is also defined as "systematic and persistent strategy of violence practiced by a state or political group against another state or political group through a campaign of acts of violence . . . with the intent of creating a state of terror and public intimidation to achieve political ends" (Ezeldin, 1987, p. 40). As well, terrorism is defined as "the premeditated, deliberate, systematic murder, mayhem, and threatening of the innocent to create fear and intimidation in order to gain a political or tactical advantage, usually to influence an audience" (Poland, cited in Coady, 2004, p. 38).

Fernando Reinares distinguishes three traits that define terrorism: "Firstly, it is an act of violence that produces widespread disproportionate emotional reactions such as fear and anxiety which are likely to influence attitudes and behaviour. Secondly, the violence is systemic and rather unpredictable and is usually directed against symbolic targets. Thirdly, the violence conveys messages and threats in order to communicate and gain social control" (cited in Bruce, 2013, p. 27).

Comprehensive definitions of terrorism tend to include exhaustive lists of basic components. For example, in summarizing the basic components of a definition of terrorism, Martha Crenshaw Hutchinson suggests that:

1. Terrorism is part of a revolutionary strategy—a method used by insurgents to seize political power from an existing government.
2. Terrorism is manifested in acts of socially and politically unacceptable violence.
3. There is a consistent pattern of symbolic or representative selection of the victims or objects of acts of terrorism.
4. The revolutionary movement deliberately intends these actions to create a psychological effect on specific groups and thereby to change their political behavior and attitudes. (Crenshaw Hutchinson, 1972, p. 385)

In providing also a comprehensive definition of terrorism, Jack P. Gibbs (1989) has discussed specific conditions of terrorism; "Terrorism is illegal violence or threatened violence directed against human or nonhuman objects, provided that it: (1) Was undertaken or ordered with a view to altering or maintaining at least one putative norm in at least one particular territorial unit or population; (2) Had secretive, furtive, and/or clandestine features that were expected by the participants to conceal their personal identity and/or their future location; (3) Was not undertaken or ordered to further the permanent defense of some area; (4) Was not conventional warfare and because of their concealed personal identity, concealment of their future location, their threats, and/or their spatial mobility, the participants perceived themselves as less vulnerable to conventional military action; *and* (5) Was perceived by the participants as contributing to the normative goal previously described (*supra*) by inculcating fear of violence in persons (perhaps an indefinite category of them) other than the immediate target of the actual or threatened violence and/or by publicizing some cause" (Gibbs, 1989, p. 330).

Distinguishing terrorists from other criminals and irregular fighters and terrorism from other forms of crime and irregular warfare, Bruce Hoffman (2006) concludes that terrorism is

- Ineluctably political in aims and motives;
- Violent—or, equally important, threatens violence;
- Designed to have far-reaching psychological repercussions beyond the immediate victim or target;
- Conducted *either* by an organization with an identifiable chain of command or conspiratorial cell structure (whose members wear no uniform or identifying insignia) or by individuals or a small collection of individuals directly influenced, motivated, or inspired by the ideological aims or example of some existent terrorist movement and/or its leaders; and
- Perpetrated by a subnational group or non-state entity. (Hoffman, 2006, p. 40, *emphasis in original*)

Accordingly, Hoffman defines terrorism as "the deliberate creation and exploitation of fear through violence or the threat of violence in the pursuit of political change. All terrorist acts involve violence or the threat of violence. Terrorism is specifically designed to have far-reaching psychological effects beyond the immediate victim(s) or object of the terrorist attack. It is meant to instill fear within, and thereby intimidate, a wider "target audience" that might include a rival ethnic or religious group, an entire country, a national government or political party, or public opinion in general. Terrorism is designed to create power where there is none or to consolidate power where there is very little. Through the publicity generated by their violence, terrorists seek to obtain the leverage, influence, and power they otherwise lack

to effect political change on either a local or an international scale" (Hoffman, 2006, pp. 40-41).

Alex P. Schmid led a study in 1984 that is considered a very useful guide to academic thought by many researchers in the field of terrorism. It examined 109 definitions of terrorism, obtained in a survey of leading academics in the field, and found out 22 frequently used "definitional elements" (Schmid & Jongman, 2008, pp. 5-6). These elements are: violence, force (83.5%); political (65%); fear, terror emphasized (51%); threat (47%); (psychological) effects and (anticipated) reactions (41.5%); victim-target differentiation (37.5%); purposive, planned, systematic, organized action (32%); method of combat, strategy, tactic (30.5%); extranormality, in breach of accepted rules, without humanitarian constraints (30%); coercion, extortion, induction of compliance (28%); publicity aspect (21.5%); arbitrariness; impersonal, random character; indiscrimination (21%); civilians, noncombatants, neutrals, outsiders as victims (17.5%); intimidation (17%); innocence of victims emphasized (15.5%); group, movement, organization as perpetrator (14%); symbolic aspect, demonstration to others (13.5%); incalculability, unpredictability, unexpectedness of occurrence of violence (9%); clandestine, covert nature (9%); repetitiveness; serial or campaign character of violence (7%); criminal (6%); and demands made on third parties (4%).

At the end of this exercise, Schmid "volunteered" the following definition: "Terrorism is a method of combat in which random or symbolic victims serve as an instrumental *target of violence*. These instrumental victims share group or class characteristics which form the basis for their selection for victimization. Through previous use of violence or the credible threat of violence other members of that group or class are put in a *state of chronic fear (terror)*. This group or class, whose members' sense of security is purposefully undermined, is the *target of terror*. The victimization of the target of violence is considered extranormal by most observers from the witnessing audience on the basis of its atrocity, the time (e.g., peace-time) or place (not a battlefield) of victimization, or the disregard for rules of combat accepted in conventional warfare. The norm violation creates an attentive audience beyond the target of terror; sectors of this audience might in turn form the main object of manipulation. The purpose of this indirect method of combat is either to immobilize the target of terror in order to produce disorientation and/or compliance, or to mobilize secondary *targets of demands* (e.g., a government) or *targets of attention* (e.g., public opinion) to changes of attitude or behaviour favouring the short or long-term interests of the users of this method of combat" (Schmid & Jongman, 2008, pp. 1-2, *emphasis in original*).

CLEARING THE NOISE

As discussions and definitions of terrorism grow from simple to comprehensive, and as debates amplify around what can be agreed-upon and what cannot for various reasons, it becomes essential to go through a process of filtration. I prefer to call this "clearing the noise" in order to focus only on the most reasonable definitional items and features to be included in a fair and balanced understanding or definition of terrorism.

Defining terrorism should be clean from any attribution to specific ethnicity, culture, religion, geography, affiliation, demographic, or ideology, simply because it happens in relation to any of each. In addition, despite the fact that definitions of terrorism "range from the very short to the ver-bose, the use of politically sensitive and subjective adjectives like 'innocent,' 'civilian,' 'unarmed,' 'illegal,' 'merciless killing' or 'unjustified,' fail to provide a clear understanding of terrorism" (Garrison, 2004, p. 276). For example, Virginia Held declines "to make targeting civilians a defin-ing feature of terrorism" (2004, p. 68). Terrorism does not only target civilians or noncombatants; otherwise some attacks on military groups, ships,

and camps should not have been then labeled as acts of terrorism.

Focusing on the nature of the act of terrorism rather than on the identity of the perpetrators and victims or the nature of the cause allows for a more objective analysis of terrorism (Garrison, 2004). It is important to understand that a "terrorist is a terrorist, no matter whether or not you like the goal s/he is trying to achieve, no matter whether or not you like the government s/he is trying to change" (Richardson, cited in Bruce, 2013, p. 26). For example, motivations behind terrorism can be a misleading factor to understand terror-ism. Defining terrorism should "focus more on defining terrorist acts, giving less emphasis to the motivation behind the acts" (Perl, 2001, p. 6). Similarly, goals are less distinctive of terrorist acts than the means. Political ends sought such as social justice, national independence, and equal treatment for a minority are "viewed widely as legitimate political goals and often have much popular support;" hence, what is "distinctive about terrorism is not its ends but the means: violence" (Oberschall, 2004, p. 26). In achieving their main goals (e.g., attracting attention, getting their demands recognized, and winning respect or gaining legitimacy), terrorists appear to have seven main tactics; ranked from the most to least frequently used: bombings, assassinations, suicide missions, hijackings, kidnapping, missile attacks, and mass disruption/mass destruction (Nacos, 2006). Cyber-terrorism can be also added to the list as a modern tactic of terrorism (Eid, 2010).

UNDERSTANDING THE TERM

Understanding terrorism is vital to creating effec-tive ways for counterterrorism. However, although understanding terrorism is more important than defining it (Waldron, 2004), the majority of dis-cussions about terrorism tend to emphasize the necessity of the latter to achieve the former.

Over the past few decades, the nature of terrorism has changed; its activities are more lethal. While prior to 1990s most terrorist attacks were based on political objectives that were best achieved through agendas that balanced inflicting bloodshed to gain international media attention but not such as to completely alienate public support, recent terrorist attacks seem carefully planned to cause the maximum possible injury (Bankoff, 2003). Recently "there are more varieties" of terrorism, compared to what existed many years ago; many of which "are so different from those of the past and from each other" to the extent that the term terrorism "no longer fits some of them" (Laqueur, 2000, p. 6). Nacos agrees with Laqueur's suggestion that "new and multiple definitions are needed to get a better handle on the distinctive features of different kinds of political violence committed by different types of actors" (Nacos, 2012, p. 32). It is also argued that without a definition of terrorism, "it is impossible to formulate or enforce international agreements against terrorism" (Ganor, 2002, p. 300). Defining terrorism is important for "the law, inasmuch as legislators often seek to distinguish terrorist crimes from other crimes" (Waldron, 2004, p. 6). It is useful to distinguish terrorism "from other types of violence and identify the characteristics that make terrorism the distinct phenomenon of political violence that it is" (Hoffman, 2006, p. 34).

In an attempt, then, to provide an objective understanding of terrorism that benefits from the present analysis of definitions and discussions about terrorism and focuses on the most reasonable definitional items and features, it is inevitable to introduce the following definition of terrorism.

Terrorism is the persistent, shocking, premeditated, covert and/or overt, individual and/or collective, and direct and/or indirect threat and/or use of conventional and/or modern and military and/or nonmilitary tactics of violence, force, and/or coercion that is/are initiated and/or retaliated by and against individuals, groups, organizations, governments, and/or states, on national, transnational, and/or international levels, resulting in complete or partial severe loss/injury of lives, destruction/damage in properties, and/or other physical atrocities and inducing terror and/or other psychological effects, in order to gain wide-ranging public attention beyond that of the immediate targets, through the use of and/or by traditional and/or new media, communicating messages that may (or not) be rooted in specific motivations, aiming to help achieve specific predetermined agenda and/or desired ends.

REFERENCES

Alexander, Y. (2006). Introduction. In Y. Alexander (Ed.), *Counterterrorism strategies: Success and failures of six nations* (pp. 1–8). Washington, DC: Potomac Books.

Arce, D. G., & Sandler, T. (2007). Terrorist signaling and the value of intelligence. *British Journal of Political Science*, *37*, 573–586. doi:10.1017/S0007123407000324

Atran, S. (2003). Genesis of suicide terrorism. *Review Social Science*, *299*, 1534–1539. PMID:12624256

Bankoff, G. (2003). Region of risk: Western discourses on terrorism and the significance of Islam. *Studies in Conflict and Terrorism*, *26*(6), 413–428. doi:10.1080/10576100390242929

Bassiouni, M. C. (1981). Terrorism, law enforcement, and the mass media: Perspectives, problems, proposals. *The Journal of Criminal Law & Criminology*, *72*(1), 1–51. doi:10.2307/1142904

Beiber, F. (2003). Approaches to political violence and terrorism in former Yugoslavia. *Journal of Southern Europe and the Balkans*, *5*(1), 39–51.

Bennett, S. (1999). Commercial aircraft bomb-proofing technologies: A social science critique. *Risk Management*, *1*(3), 49–61. doi:10.1057/palgrave.rm.8240004

Berezovsky, B. (2005). Putin is terrorist number one. *New Perspectives Quarterly*, *22*(1), 59–61. doi:10.1111/j.1540-5842.2005.00730.x

Bergesen, A. J., & Lizardo, O. (2004). International terrorism and the world-system. *Sociological Theory*, *22*(1), 38–52. doi:10.1111/j.1467-9558.2004.00203.x

Biernatzki, W. E. (2002). Terrorism and mass media. *Communication Research Trends*, *21*(1), 1–42.

Black, D. (2004). The geometry of terrorism. *Sociological Theory*, *22*(1), 14–25. doi:10.1111/j.1467-9558.2004.00201.x

Braithwaite, A. (2013). The logic of public fear in terrorism and counter-terrorism. *Journal of Police and Criminal Psychology*, *28*, 95–101. doi:10.1007/s11896-013-9126-x

Bruce, G. (2013). Definition of terrorism: Social and political effects. *Journal of Military and Veteran's Health*, *21*(2), 26–30.

Chakravorti, R. (1994). Terrorism: Past, present and future. *Economic and Political Weekly*, *29*(36), 2340–2343.

Coady, C. A. J. (2004). Terrorism and innocence. *The Journal of Ethics*, *8*(1), 37–58. doi:10.1023/B:JOET.0000012251.24102.a5

Cohan, J. A. (2006). Necessity, political violence and terrorism. *Stetson Law Review*, *35*(3), 903–981.

Collins, S. D. (2004). Dissuading state support of terrorism: Strikes or sanctions? An analysis of dissuasion measures employed against Libya. *Studies in Conflict and Terrorism*, *27*(1), 1–18. doi:10.1080/10576100490262115

Combs, C. C. (2013). *Terrorism in the twenty-first century*. Boston, MA: Pearson.

Copeland, T. (2001). Is the new terrorism really new? An analysis of the new paradigm for terrorism. *The Journal of Conflict Studies*, *21*(2), 91–105.

Crelinsten, R. D. (2002). Analysing terrorism and counter-terrorism: A communication model. *Terrorism and Political Violence*, *14*(2), 77–122. doi:10.1080/714005618

Crenshaw, M. (2000). The psychology of terrorism: An agenda for the 21st century. *Political Psychology*, *21*(2), 405–420. doi:10.1111/0162-895X.00195

Crenshaw Hutchinson, M. (1972). The concept of revolutionary terrorism. *The Journal of Conflict Resolution*, *16*(3), 383–396.

Davis, J. M., Planje, E., Davis, C. J., Page, J., Whitely, M., O'Neil, S., & West, D. (2013). Definitions of war, torture, and terrorism in Great Britain, Northern Ireland, Australia, Canada, and the United States. In K. Malley-Morrison, S. McCarthy, & D. Hines (Eds.), *International handbook of war, torture, and terrorism* (pp. 27–48). New York: Springer.

Devine, P. E., & Rafalko, R. J. (1982). On terror. *The Annals of the American Academy of Political and Social Science*, *463*, 39–53. doi:10.1177/0002716282463001004

Eid, M. (2008). *Interweavement: International media ethics and rational decision-making*. Boston, MA: Pearson.

Eid, M. (2010). Cyber-terrorism and ethical journalism: A need for rationalism. *International Journal of Technoethics*, *1*(4), 1–19. doi:10.4018/jte.2010100101

Enders, W., & Sandler, T. (2005). Transnational terrorism 1968-2000: Thresholds, persistence, and forecasts. *Southern Economic Journal*, *71*(3), 467–482. doi:10.2307/20062054

Ezeldin, A. (1987). *Terrorism & political violence: An Egyptian perspective*. Chicago, IL: Office of International Criminal Justice, University of Illinois at Chicago.

Falk, R. A. (2003). A dual reality: Terrorism against the state and terrorism by the state. In C. W. Kegley (Ed.), *The new global terrorism: Characteristics, causes, controls* (pp. 53–59). Upper Saddle River, NJ: Prentice Hall.

Fletcher, G. P. (2006). The indefinable concept of terrorism. *Journal of International Criminal Justice*, *4*(5), 894–911. doi:10.1093/jicj/mql060

Fontaine, R. W. (1988). *Terrorism: The Cuban connection*. New York: Crane Russak.

Ganor, B. (2002). Defining terrorism: Is one man's terrorist another man's freedom fighter? *Police Practice and Research*, *3*(4), 287–304. doi:10.1080/1561426022000032060

Garrison, A. H. (2004). Defining terrorism: Philosophy of the bomb, propaganda by deed and change through fear and violence. *Criminal Justice Studies*, *17*(3), 259–279. doi:10.1080/1478601042000281105

Gibbs, J. P. (1989). Conceptualization of terrorism. *American Sociological Review*, *54*(3), 329–340. doi:10.2307/2095609

Goody, J. (2002). What is a terrorist? *History and Anthropology*, *13*(2), 139–143. doi:10.1080/0275720022000001219

Held, V. (2004). Terrorism and war. *The Journal of Ethics*, *8*(1), 59–75. doi:10.1023/B:JOET.0000012252.68332.ff

Hirschmann, K. (2000). The changing face of terrorism. *Internationale Politik und Gesellschaft*, *3*, 299–310.

Hoffman, B. (2006). *Inside terrorism*. New York: Columbia University Press.

Hudson, R. A. (1999). *The sociology and psychology of terrorism: Who becomes a terrorist and why?* Washington, DC: Federal Research Division: Library of Congress. doi:10.1037/e622272007-001

Ignatieff, M. (2004). *The lesser evil: Political ethics in an age of terror*. Toronto: Penguin Canada. doi:10.3366/edinburgh/9780748618729.001.0001

Jaggar, A. M. (2003). Responding to the evil of terrorism. *Hypatia*, *18*(1), 175–182. doi:10.1111/j.1527-2001.2003.tb00787.x

Kupperman, R. H., van Opstal, D., & Williamson, D. (1982). Terror, the strategic tool: Response and control. *The Annals of the American Academy of Political and Social Science, 463*, 24–38. doi:10.1177/0002716282463001003

Kushner, H. (1998). *Terrorism in America: A structured approach to understanding the terrorist threat*. Springfield, IL: Charles C Thomas.

Laqueur, W. (1987). *The age of terrorism*. Boston: Little Brown.

Laqueur, W. (2000). *The new terrorism: Fanaticism and the arms of mass destruction*. New York: Oxford University Press.

Lesser, I. O. (1999). Countering the new terrorism: Implications for strategy. In I. O. Lesser (Ed.), *Countering the new terrorism* (pp. 85–144). Santa Monica, CA: Rand Corporation.

Loza, W. (2007). The psychology of extremism and terrorism: A middle-eastern perspective. *Aggression and Violent Behavior, 12*(2), 141–155. doi:10.1016/j.avb.2006.09.001

Martin, G. (2006). *Understanding terrorism: Challenges, perspectives, and issues*. Thousand Oaks, CA: Sage Publications, Inc.

Nacos, B. L. (2006). *Terrorism and counterterrorism: Understanding threats and responses in the post-9/11 world*. New York: Longman.

Nacos, B. L. (2012). *Terrorism and counterterrorism*. Boston: Longman.

O'Kane, R. H. T. (2012). *Terrorism*. Harlow, UK: Pearson.

Oberschall, A. (2004). Explaining terrorism: The contribution of collective action theory. *Sociological Theory, 22*(1), 26–37. doi:10.1111/j.1467-9558.2004.00202.x

Perl, R. F. (2001). *Terrorism, the future, and U.S. foreign policy*. Washington, DC: Congressional Research Service, The Library of Congress.

Poland, J. M. (2005). *Understanding terrorism: Groups, strategies, and responses*. Englewood Cliffs, NJ: Pearson Education, Inc.

Rosie, G. (1987). *The dictionary of international terrorism*. New York: Paragon House.

Ruby, C. L. (2002). The definition of terrorism. *Analyses of Social Issues and Public Policy (ASAP), 2*(1), 9–14. doi:10.1111/j.1530-2415.2002.00021.x

Schmid, A. P. (2005). Terrorism as psychological warfare. *Democracy and Security, 1*, 137–146. doi:10.1080/17419160500322467

Schmid, A. P., & Jongman, A. J. (2008). *Political terrorism: A new guide to actors, authors, concepts, data bases, theories, & literature*. London: Transaction Publishers.

Symeonidou-Kastanidou, E. (2004). Defining terrorism. *European Journal of Crime Criminal Law and Criminal Justice, 12*(1), 14–35. doi:10.1163/1571817041268883

Teichman, J. (1989). How to define terrorism. *Philosophy (London, England), 64*(250), 505–517. doi:10.1017/S0031819100044260

Thomassen, N. (1992). *Communicative ethics in theory and practice* (J. Irons, Trans.). New York: St. Martin's Press.

Tilly, C. (2004). Terror, terrorism, terrorists. *Sociological Theory, 22*(1), 5–13. doi:10.1111/j.1467-9558.2004.00200.x

United Nations. (1999). *International convention for the suppression of the financing of terrorism*. Article 2(b) Adopted by the General Assembly of the United Nations in resolution 54/109 on 9 December 1999. Retrieved January 20, 2014, from http://www.un.org/law/cod/finterr.htm

Waldron, J. (2004). Terrorism and the uses of terror. *The Journal of Ethics, 8*(1), 5–35. doi:10.1023/B:JOET.0000012250.78840.80

White, J. R. (2006). *Terrorism and homeland security*. Mason, OH: Thomson Wadsworth.

Wilkinson, P. (1974). *Political terrorism*. London: Macmillan.

KEY TERMS AND DEFINITIONS

Desired End: The expected or wanted outcome.

Fear: A psychological effect of distress sparked by impeding pain, danger, or evil.

Media: The means of mass communication through platforms such as television, newspapers, magazines, and the Internet that reach and influence people widely.

Political Violence: Force instigated in the name of political ideologies.

State Terrorism: Acts of terrorism perpetrated by a state or government against its own people.

State-Sponsored Terrorism: Acts of terrorism funded, planned, or perpetrated by a nation state against another nation.

Terror: An emotional state of immense and intense fear.

Terrorism: There are numerous definitions of terrorism suggested by organizations and scholars. The suggested definition in this chapter is as follows: Terrorism is the persistent, shocking, premeditated, covert and/or overt, individual and/or collective, and direct and/or indirect threat and/or use of conventional and/or modern and military and/or nonmilitary tactics of violence, force, and/or coercion that is/are initiated and/or retaliated by and against individuals, groups, organizations, governments, and/or states, on national, transnational, and/or international levels, resulting in complete or partial severe loss/injury of lives, destruction/damage in properties, and/or other physical atrocities and inducing terror and/or other psychological effects, in order to gain wide-ranging public attention beyond that of the immediate targets, through the use of and/or by traditional and/or new media, communicating messages that may (or not) be rooted in specific motivations, aiming to help achieve specific predetermined agenda and/or desired ends.

ENDNOTES

1. The United Nations defines terrorism as an "act intended to cause death or serious bodily injury to a civilian, or to any other person not taking an active part in the hostilities in a situation of armed conflict, when the purpose of such act, by its nature or context, is to intimidate a population, or to compel a government or an international organization to do or to abstain from doing any act" (United Nations, 1999).

2. The UN General Assembly defines terrorism as "criminal acts intended or calculated to provoke a state of terror in the general public, a group of persons or particular persons for political purposes . . . whatever the considerations of a political, philosophical, ideological, racial, ethnic, religious or other nature that may be invoked to justify them" (cited in Biernatzki, 2002, p. 3).

3. The U.S. Congress defines an act of terrorism as "an activity that—(A) involves a violent act or an act dangerous to human life that is a violation of the criminal laws of the United States or any State, or that would be a criminal violation if committed within the jurisdiction of the United States or of any State; and (B) appears to be intended (i) to intimidate or coerce a civilian population; (ii) to influence the policy of a government by intimidation or coercion; or (iii) to affect the conduct of a government by assassination or kidnapping" (cited in Atran, 2003, p. 1534).

4. The U.S. Department of Defense defines terrorism as "the calculated use of unlawful violence or threat of unlawful violence

to inculcate fear; intended to coerce or to intimidate governments or societies in the pursuit of goals that are generally political, religious, or ideological objectives" (cited in Hoffman, 2006, p. 31).

5. The FBI defines terrorism as "the unlawful use of force or violence against persons or property to intimidate or coerce a Government, the civilian population, or any segment thereof, in furtherance of political or social objectives" (cited in Biernatzki, 2002, p. 3; Bruce, 2013, p. 28; Coady, 2004, p. 38; Hoffman, 2006, p. 31).

6. The U.S. Department of Homeland Security defines terrorism as "any activity that involves an act that: is dangerous to human life or potentially destructive of critical infrastructure or key resources; and . . . must also appear to be intended (i) to intimidate or coerce a civilian population; (ii) to influence the policy of a government by intimidation or coercion; or (iii) to affect the conduct of a government by mass destruction, assassination, or kidnapping" (cited in Hoffman, 2006, p. 31).

7. The U.S. Department of State, using the definition of terrorism contained in Title 22 of the United States Code, Section 2656f(d), defines terrorism as "premeditated, politically motivated violence perpetrated against noncombatant targets by subnational groups or clandestine agents, usually intended to influence an audience" (cited in Atran, 2003, p. 1534; Bruce, 2013, pp. 27-28; Hoffman, 2006, p. 31; Hudson, 1999, p. 12; Ruby, 2002, p. 10).

8. Terrorism is "a premeditated and unlawful act in which groups or agents of some principal engage in a threatened or actual use of force or violence against human or property targets. These groups or agents engage in this behavior intending the purposeful intimidation of governments or people to

affect policy or behavior with an underlying political objective" (Martin, 2006, p. 48).

9. While acknowledging that taking 1,000 children and parents hostage at a school in Beslan, ending in the death of hundreds, is terrorism, Boris Berezovsky calls Vladmir Putin as "terrorist No. 1" because "terror begets terror" and that Putin initiated the terror in Chechnya when Russian troops under his command committed genocide, killing and wounding 10,000 children (2005, p. 59).

10. Other definitions added-up a few more elements. For example, Cindy C. Combs explains that terrorism is "an act composed of at least four crucial elements: (1) It is an act of violence, (2) it has a political motive or goal, (3) it is perpetrated against civilian noncombatants, and (4) it is staged to be played before an audience whose reaction of fear and terror is the desired result" (2013, p. 15).

11. Similarly, Daniel G. Arce and Todd Sandler define terrorism as "the premeditated use, or threat of use, of violence by individuals or subnational groups to obtain a political or social objective through intimidation of a target audience, beyond that of the immediate victims" (2007, p. 573).

12. The major objective of terrorism "is not the winning of a military victory, nor the fulfilling of private motives such as revenge or enrichment. It is a political manifestation and normally aims at winning a political victory" (Thomassen, 1992, p. 219).

13. William E. Biernatzki defines terrorism as "the exercise of violence or the threat of violence against an unarmed and/or unsuspecting population to coerce it to meet the demands of the aggressor" (2002, p. 5, *emphasis in original*).

14. Albert J. Bergesen and Omar Lizardo define terrorism as "the premeditated use of violence by a nonstate group to obtain a political,

religious, or social objective through fear or intimidation directed at a large audience" (2004, p. 38).

15. Boaz Ganor defines terrorism as "the deliberate use or the threat to use violence against civilians in order to attain political, ideological and religious aims" (2002, p. 288).

16. Arthur H. Garrison defines terrorism as "the use of force or violence or the threat of force or violence to change the behavior of society as a whole through the causation of fear and the targeting of specific parts of society in order to affect the entire society" (2004, p. 273, *emphasis in original*).

17. Brian Jenkins defines terrorism as "the use or threatened use of force designed to bring about political change" (cited in Coady, 2004, p. 38).

18. Harvey Kushner defines terrorism as "the use of force (or violence) committed by individuals or groups against governments or civilian populations to create fear in order to bring about political (or social) change" (1998, p. 10).

19. Similarly, terrorism is defined as the "use, or threat of use, of violence by an individual or a group, whether acting for or in opposition to established authority, when such action is designed to create extreme anxiety and/or fear inducing effects in a target group larger than the immediate victims with the purpose of coercing that group into acceding to political demands of the perpetrators" (Wardlaw, cited in Garrison, 2004, p. 276).

20. Also focused on the covert description, terrorism is defined as "covert violence against non-combatants for the purpose of creating an atmosphere of fear and of intimidating a wide audience, so as to advance a social or political agenda" (Collins, 2004, p. 2, *emphasis in original*).

Chapter 3
Understanding Media during Times of Terrorism

Robert Hackett
Simon Fraser University, Canada

ABSTRACT

Political violence, including terrorism, can be regarded as a form of (distorted) communication, in which media spectacles play an integral role. Conversely, mass-mediated communication can be regarded as a form of violence, and even terror, in several respects. Media are often propagandistic facilitators to state terror. More broadly, they may help to cultivate a political climate of fear and authoritarianism, contributing to conflict-escalating feedback loops. Even more broadly, beyond media representations, dominant media institutions are arguably embedded in relations of global economic, social, and cultural inequality—constituting a form of structural violence. Notwithstanding its democratic potential, the Internet does not comprise a clear alternative in practice, and neither censorship of terrorist spectacles nor the intensified pursuit of dominant forms of journalistic "objectivity" offer viable ways to reduce the media's imbrication with violence. Three potentially more productive strategies explored in this chapter include reforming the media field from within through the paradigm of Peace Journalism, supporting the development of alternative and community media, and building movements for media reform and democratization.

INTRODUCTION

The deformed human mind is the ultimate dooms-day weapon (Thompson, 1980, p. 52).

I was reminded of that stark warning by the late British historian E.P. Thompson while listening to Canadian Broadcasting Corporation radio host Rex Murphy in November 2011. On his program *Cross-Country Checkup*, Murphy was interviewing Terry Glavin, a journalist and writer, about

DOI: 10.4018/978-1-4666-5776-2.ch003

Glavin's (2011) latest book (titled *Come from the Shadows*), on Canada's so-called "mission" in Afghanistan. That is, following 9/11, Canadian troops participated in the subsequent invasion of Afghanistan, on the basis of a shifting rationale that arguably had never been adequately debated. Was it about preventing further attacks, overthrowing the Taliban regime, protecting women's rights, rebuilding a failed nation, or other unstated geo-political objectives?

Murphy's telephone caller was a military man from Winnipeg. Asked whether he thought the "mission" was "worth it," the caller indicated it was good for the Canadian armed forces, because it gave them a chance to put their training and tools to "practical" use. On the face of it, that is an extraordinary statement from the perspective of human morality. It appears to justify invasion, bombing and war, and the massive organized spending of blood and treasure, on the grounds that they give the military a chance to try out its weapons. Would anybody argue for burning villages as a means of testing new fire engines? Interestingly, Rex Murphy did not challenge the caller's answer, but instead simply thanked him for his service to Canada.

That brief radio exchange, I suggest, is part of a broader pattern. Since the 9/11 terrorist attacks, and particularly the advent of the Conservative government of Stephen Harper, there has been a well-funded effort to militarize Canada's culture (Richler, 2012). That campaign helps to explain why recent official Canada Day celebrations are festooned with tanks and military equipment on which youngsters are invited to play; why the Harper government is rescuing from its erstwhile historical obscurity the War of 1812 against the U.S. as a symbol of Canadian identity, to take its place alongside the battle of Vimy Ridge during the inter-imperialist slaughter of World War I; and why professional hockey teams have special games honoring the military (Shipley, 2013). Canada's hegemonic media have often followed suit, providing prominent, respectful, and often emotive treatment of the 158 Canadian men and women who have died in the Afghan "mission" since 2002, while paying far less attention, for example, to the approximately *10,000* Canadian workers who have died on the job in the same time period.

Emerging debates around such shifts towards militarization are linked to Canada's involvement in war and armed conflict. However, as the internationally respected Norwegian peace scholar Johan Galtung (1990) has tirelessly argued, the trajectory of war begins long before the first shot is fired. War is typically preceded by euphemisms, lies, the glorification of combat and military, desensitization to violence, and a process of "othering" vis-à-vis a designated enemy. Cultural violence helps to lay the groundwork for the physical violence of war. The form of public storytelling known as journalism, along with other genres of mediated communication, are central to contemporary cultural processes.

Therefore, it is not absurd to ask whether media and terror are two entirely separate categories. Or might they be two sides of the same hideous coin—mediated terror, terrorizing media, or simply, media terror?

VIOLENCE AS COMMUNICATION

Violence can sometimes be acknowledged as a form of communication. Distorted, limited, destructive, immoral, counterproductive perhaps, certainly monologic rather than dialogic, but a kind of communication nevertheless. Long before 9/11, two European peace researchers argued that a defining characteristic of insurgent terrorism was the use of politically motivated violence against victims who were not the primary targets of the action (Schmid & de Graaf, 1982). Rather, the targets are other groups—typically, enemy governments or publics or rival groups and potential supporters. Schmid and de Graaf (1982) saw it as no coincidence that the mass media and modern insurgent terrorism (the Russian social-revolutionaries' use of "propaganda of the deed") emerged at the same historical moment—towards the end of the 19th century.

The televised spectacle is integral to contemporary insurgent terrorism. The fanatics who planned 9/11 clearly calculated that the first aircraft crashing into the twin towers would generate a nation-wide, real-time audience for the second plane's stunning and traumatizing arrival. Political communication scholar Eric Louw (2005) identified a variety of goals that al-Qaeda achieved through its choreographed violence. Specifically, it created fear, anger, and thirst for revenge throughout the United States; it demonstrated American vulnerability; it boosted recruitment and morale for al-Qaeda and other Islamicist groups; it propagandized al-Qaeda's cause; and it generated political polarization throughout the world—dangerous for humanity, but politically useful to elements on both (discursively constructed) "sides" in the subsequent "war on terror."

However, modern terrorism was originally an instrument *of* rather than *against* state power—that is, Robespierre's Reign of Terror during the French Revolution (Schmid & de Graaf, 1982). "State violence, particularly state terrorism that operates in violation of accepted human rights or international law, often prefers to hide in the shadows—but not always" (Hackett, 2007b, p. 3). Counter-insurgency campaigns often include both direct violence and efforts to "win hearts and minds" through public relations and media manipulation (Louw, 2005, p. 248). States may also use violence itself as a form of one-sided communication. The show trials of authoritarian states, intended to intimidate potential dissidents, are one example. During the Vietnam War, the U.S. government spoke of the bombing of Hanoi as a way to "send a message" to the North Vietnamese government. In this context, one might contemplate the brand-name of the 2003 U.S. invasion of Iraq: "Shock and Awe" (Hackett, 2007b). Was it demonstrative violence intended in part to dramatize the potential consequences of defying the imperial world order?

MEDIA AS VIOLENCE

If terrorism is a distorted form of communication, can mass-mediated communication also be a form of terror?

One common view sees news media as at least unwitting accomplices of insurgent terrorists, by not only spreading their messages and psychological impact, but also by enhancing their legitimacy and recruitment efforts. Liebes and Kampf (2004) argue that in the changed media ecology (including the emergence of al-Jazeera) since 9/11, global journalism has turned terrorists into regular sources, and even cultural "superstars."

That is a contestable view, at least in the North American context, where mainstream media are far more likely to focus on the destructive actions and future threat of insurgent terrorism, rather than on its grievances or even the social conditions that breed it. A more plausible case can be made that media are more typically handmaidens of state terror. With honorable exceptions, the American media largely uncritically amplified the Bush government's now discredited claims about Saddam Hussein's weapons of mass destruction and links to 9/11, or at the very least, failed to question the accuracy, logic, and evidentiary basis for the Bush narrative. That media role is now widely regarded as a key to unleashing the enormously costly invasion and occupation that followed (Schechter, 2003).

Beyond such overtly political/propagandistic functions, hegemonic media have in some respects helped to nurture a culture of terror. Why did so many New Yorkers express a sense of "surrealism" at the 9/11 destruction of the twin towers? Perhaps because the attack was the materialization of a catastrophe already embedded cinematically in the public imagination, one that has been primed by a profit-driven, commercially oriented film and television industry to expect a dystopic future—or none at all. Social theorist Klaus Theweleit has provocatively suggested that the "producers of catastrophe films are of course terrorists, simply in a milder form" (Theweleit, cited in Herz, 2006, p. 53).

Add to the mix a local commercial television journalism that emphasizes mayhem—fires, crime, collisions, and murder—and the American mediascape has the makings of what the late communication scholar George Gerbner considered a degrading, inhumane, and even toxic cultural environment. In his lifelong research on how media "cultivate" particular perceptions of and orientations to the world, Gerbner showed that heavy TV viewers were disproportionately likely to distrust other people, to see the world as a threatening place, and to support authoritarian approaches to social problems—a phenomenon he labeled the Mean World Syndrome (Gerber et al., 1986; Morgan, 2002).

With the presence of a stronger public service broadcaster, Canadian television (still the primary source of news for most Canadians) has not gone so far down the "mayhem" path, compared to commercial American television. Yet impressionistically, and as implied at the start of this chapter, Canadian media have not been immune to the tendency to emphasize insurgent terrorism and to celebrate military power.

If hegemonic media help to cultivate a culture and a politics of fear, such a cultural environment creates incentives for politicians and governments to appeal to "security," resulting in military strength and crime crackdowns as a fast track to popularity. Conversely, it presents opportunities for politicians to avoid climate crisis, poverty, inequality, corporate corruption, and other pressing issues that might disrupt business as usual—the kinds of issues raised globally by the 2011 Occupy Wall Street protest movement. It is a political culture that fuels the military-industrial complex, the private security industry, the small arms trade, a gated community/Fortress America mentality, and a foreign policy that arguably practices state terrorism, economic exploitation, and cultural domination. Could one concoct a better recipe to foster fear amongst dominant groups, hatred amongst subordinate populations, and a cycle of terror and counter-terror?

What is at the root of media-as-terror? Some see a link forged by technology (Hackett, 2007a), one that arguably continues to strengthen along with

dramatic changes in communication and media technologies (Karmasin et al., 2013). Terrorism and communication interact with one another, as "from an anthropological viewpoint, violence can be seen as a specific form of communication" (Ibid, p. xi). A generation ago, Jerry Mander (1978) analyzed a host of what he considered to be inherent technological biases in television, a medium that, two decades into the Internet era, is still the primary source of news for most Canadians and Americans. He asserts that television favors death, commodities, artificially highlighted events, compressed time, charismatic leaders, fast-paced and fixation-inducing techniques, and war rather than peace:

War is better television than peace. It is filled with highlighted moments, contains action and resolution, and delivers a powerful emotion: fear. Peace is amorphous and broad. The emotions connected with it are subtle, personal and internal. These are far more difficult to televise (Mander, 1978, p. 323).

That is a plausible argument, so long as we do not essentialize television as a medium. Any comprehensive international survey would show that TV is quite capable of offering diverse and thoughtful programming. It is not inherently a violence-promoting medium. What is important is the governing logic—the political economy—within which the medium is institutionalized. Gerbner argued that the prevalence of violent programming in American commercial TV and films was shaped not mainly by audience preferences, but by profit-making strategies, such as the relative ease with which "action films" could be translated and exported to overseas markets (Morgan, 2002). After all, the onscreen dialogue of actors such as Sylvester Stallone and Bruce Lee is not replete with culturally specific nuances.

During the 1990s, one of America's leading environmentalist writers taped one day's worth of programming available on the 100 cable channels in one Virginia community. Asking himself, "What would the world look like if this was your source of information"?, Bill McKibben (1999) spent a mind-numbing year viewing the tapes and found the essential message to be one of narcissistic consumerism: "You, the person watching the television, you are the most important thing on Earth. Everything revolves around you." He concluded that:

The thing to fear from [commercial] television is less the sight of [people] mowing each other down with machine guns than the sight of people having to have every desire that enters their mind gratified immediately . . . that kind of culture is going to be a violent one, no matter what images one shows. Television hasn't done this by itself, of course, but it's the anchor and central idol of this system of values that dominates us (McKibben, 1999, pp. 45-46).

More broadly, Majid Tehranian (2002) argues that the world's media are dominated by state and commercial/corporate organizations, tied respectively to the logics of identity and commodity fetishism. Such media generate political or commercial propaganda that too often constructs hostile and demonizing images of the Other—fertile cultural soil for the weeds of terrorism. Global media also generate a "fishbowl effect," in which the exaggerated opulence portrayed in American television programs (the "lifestyles of the rich and famous") is on display to the rest of the world, an excellent mechanism for breeding resentment. Thus, he says, the "envy and hatred generated by global communication seems to have outpaced mutual understanding, respect and tolerance" (Tehranian, 2002, p. 59).

Lynch and McGoldrick (2005) hypothesize one way that media representations may contribute, even if unwittingly, to the escalation of conflict. They posit a "feedback loop" between journalism and political realities, as governments and other powerful sources create "facts" (e.g., policy statements, statistics, initiatives, etc.), intending to have them "reported in such a way as to pass on a preferred or dominant reading" (Lynch & McGoldrick, 2005, p. 218). In that process, sources rely on their own previous observations of media to anticipate the nature of news coverage, which will favor some courses of action over alternative options. For instance, if incidents of political violence are reported without context, a "crackdown" may be incentivized.

Further, media terror is not only about media representations of violence or media's presumably unwitting role in its escalation. Media themselves are a *form* of structural violence, which Lynch and McGoldrick define as a structure, often understood as a system of political, social, or economic relations, that creates "barriers that people cannot remove . . . an *invisible form* of violence, *built into* ways of doing and ways of thinking," a form that "includes economic exploitation, political repression and cultural alienation" (2005, pp. 59-60, *emphasis in original*). Through the dominant global media, perhaps the world is wired in such a way as to reproduce the social and economic inequalities and cultural hierarchies that fuel the resentment, ignorance, and desperation underlying political extremism and insurgent terrorism. Writing in the wake of the 1980s New World Information and Communication Order movement, which called *inter alia* for more equal information flows between the global North and South, Jorg Becker (1982) attacked the liberal notion that the extension of transnational information flows necessarily promotes peace. Deriding the typical research focus on the effects of media (representations of) violence on their audiences, Becker reframed the issue: media are embedded in, and help to reproduce, relations of inequality within and between nations. In his words:

If mass-media reception as well as production are at once expression and motor of structural violence; if communications technology can be understood, historically, only as an integral part of the emerging military industrial complex; if the access to and the power over the mass media are unequal and unbalanced . . . then the mass media can fulfill their original hoped for function as "peace-bringers" [only] under rare and exceptional circumstances. The representation of violence in the mass media, then, is part and parcel of the universal violence of the media themselves (Becker, 1982, p. 227).

Since the 1980s, media globalization (i.e., the emergence of global media and advertising markets, the rise of transnational media conglomerates, etc.) has arguably (sometimes) moderated state authoritarianism or promoted notions of human rights. However, its relationship to democratization is at best contradictory (Zhao & Hackett, 2005). Its dark side reveals an equally repressive role. First, global media frequently facilitate and legitimize relations of inequality, hostility, and hierarchy, whether through the nationalist biases and blind spots of news organizations with a basis in a particular state, or through promoting the consumerist lifestyles available only to a minority of the world's people and at huge environmental costs. Second, the very structure of hegemonic media excludes the global majority from participation in public discourse, whether through overt censorship or through market mechanisms that embody a logic of one dollar-one vote, rather than one person-one vote.

Thus, what about the Internet? Debates about the Internet's impact on public communication, particularly journalism, are well rehearsed. Technophiles emphasize its perceived contributions to democracy, including its potential for interactivity and many-to-many communication, its capacity to evade or bypass censorship, to hold journalists and propagandists accountable to a more diverse marketplace of ideas, to facilitate transnational mobilization by democratization movements, and to vastly broaden the range of voices and information in the public domain.

However, do digital networks promote the kind of dialogic and inclusive communication that can drain the swamps of hatred? Do they reduce the cultural and structural violence (such as severe economic inequality) that can breed physical violence, including the resort to insurgent terrorism? Simply to state the question that bluntly is to invite a realistic skepticism. Most obviously, the Internet provides new tools and conduits for propaganda and recruitment by organized hate and terror groups—from the Websites of white supremacist organizations, to the video recorded beheadings notoriously posted by al-Qaeda. More subtly, the "digital divide" in access and effective use of the Internet parallels and reinforces rather than challenges the distribution of cultural, political, and economic power globally—the kind of mediated structural violence that Becker (1982) warned about three decades ago. Responding to the question of whether the Internet promotes global understanding, British media scholar James Curran (2012) summarizes the research this way:

[T]he idea that cyberspace is a free, open space where people from different backgrounds and nations can commune with each other and build a more deliberative, tolerant world overlooks a number of things. The world is unequal and mutually uncomprehending (in a literal sense); it is torn asunder by conflicting values and interests; it is subdivided by deeply embedded national and local cultures (and other nodes of identity such as religion and ethnicity); and some countries are ruled by authoritarian regimes. These different aspects of the real world penetrate cyberspace, producing a ruined tower of Babel with multiple languages, hate Websites, nationalist discourses, censored speech and over-representation of the advantaged (Curran, 2012, p. 11).

Thus, the extent to which the Internet exacerbates or ameliorates the preconditions of terrorism, or even constitutes an extension of a culture of terror, is not predetermined by its technological potentialities. Rather, it is shaped by the way that it is inserted in political, economic, and social relations.

BEYOND MEDIA TERROR?

In advancing the concept of media terror, I would never suggest that the everyday work of reporters—professionals trying their best to deliver honest accounts of the day's events—is the moral equivalent of suicide bombing. Their respective intentions and immediate impact differ, it goes without saying, and that matters. Additionally, the category "media" is far too general, conflating organizations of different size, orientation, governing logic, and quality.

Still, in a world where politics and conflict are increasingly mediatized, one need not accept all the arguments in this chapter to acknowledge that dominant national and global media, generically speaking, are too often implicated in relations and acts of violence, and the politics of fear. Is there a way to dismantle the media/terror nexus?

The censorship of terrorist spectacles, in a misguided effort to deprive insurgent terrorists of the publicity they need, is hardly an option. Censorship would undermine a core putative function of media—to assist audiences in surveying the social and political environment, obviously including violent assaults on social order. Moreover, a censored press would deepen the shadows around the problem of state terrorism and sharpen the hierarchies of access that comprise a form of structural violence. In any event, outside of very closed regimes, censorship of terrorist spectacles is not likely to be effective in the era of the Internet and eyewitness accounts from online citizen journalists (Allan, 2004).

Nor does the pursuit of "objectivity," as it is normally understood and practiced within western journalism, offer a way out. To the contrary, as numerous authors have shown, the "regime of objectivity" in hegemonic North American media too often ties journalism to narrow official optics and to war propaganda (Hackett & Zhao, 1998). What specific mechanisms may have that effect? They include the heavy dependence on "authoritative" sources, such as government and corporate spokespeople; the conventions of "balance" that lead to the representation of conflict as two-sided zero-sum affairs in which one side's gain is the other's loss; and the focus on timely events (e.g., today's suicide bombing) rather than context, structures, and processes, such as poverty, political dysfunction, foreign meddling, or military occupation—or more positively, grassroots peace-building (Lynch & McGoldrick, 2005). Such contexts may help audiences understand the complexities of conflicts and alternative options for conflict resolution, but news media often avoid them, partly because they are more difficult to narrate than a single event, and partly for fear of opening the door to accusations of "bias."

Rather than doing more of what does not work, the challenge is to find ways that media can contribute to a more humane culture, to genuinely representative and transnational public spheres, and to the prevention or transformation of conflicts into non-violent conflict management and/or resolution. Briefly, three strategies can be suggested.

One approach is to reform the journalism field from within. It is unreasonable to expect journalists or media organizations to reduce levels of violence and terror on their own. However, there are signs that practicing journalists and journalism educators are aware that they may be unwitting contributors to conflict escalation, and they are thinking through alternative ways to report conflict. Since the 1990s, a reform movement known as Peace Journalism (PJ) has emerged. It has found particularly fruitful soil in societies—such as Indonesia and the Philippines—that have been riven by internal conflict in which media were perceived to play a role, and where media institutions have opportunities and incentives to seek new roles and professional norms at a time of political transition from brutal dictatorships (Hackett, 2006). Simply put, its public philosophy is "when journalists make choices—of what stories to report and about how to report them—that create opportunities for society at large to consider and value non-violent responses to conflict" (Lynch & McGoldrick, 2005, p. 5).

Originally proposed by Galtung (1990), PJ draws upon the insights of the emergent discipline of conflict analysis. It comprises a mode of analysis and evaluation, a toolkit of alternative practices for reporting particular conflicts, and a campaign for change by journalists and activists. Looking beyond the overt violence that is the stuff of conventional journalism, which is regarded as tantamount to War Journalism (WJ), PJ calls attention to the context of attitudes, behavior, and contradictions, and the need to identify a range of stakeholders broader than the "two sides" engaged in violent confrontation. If WJ presents conflict as a zero-sum tug-of-war, PJ invites journalists to reframe conflict as a cat's cradle of relationships between various stakeholders. It calls on journalists to identify the needs and objectives that underlie conflicts, and to include a broader range of sources, particularly victims and peace-builders, working for creative and non-violent solutions. It keeps eyes open for ways of transforming and transcending the hardened lines of conflict, and pays heed to aggression and casualties on all sides, avoiding the conflict-escalating trap of emphasizing "our" victims and "their" atrocities. By contrast with much conventional reporting of war and terrorism, PJ looks beyond direct physical violence, to explore the structural and cultural violence (e.g., racism, militarism, etc.) that may underlie conflict situations (Hackett, 2010).

While its prescription for media change may be appealing to many, PJ in many ways runs against the grain of governing logics in dominant news media. These include the attractiveness of war as a televisual spectacle; the difficulties of constructing "peace" as a saleable narrative; the symbiosis between economic, political, and media elites at national and global levels; the organizationally convenient dependence on official and military sources; the relatively high cost of contextual and localized reporting at a time when major media conglomerates (at least in North America) are slashing investment in journalism; and the national basis of much of the world's news media and their audiences (notwithstanding the recently hypothesized emergence of the global newsroom).

Thus, a second approach to media change suggests itself: support alternative and community journalism as a field of practices, projects, networks, and practitioners rooted in civil society, parallel to, but also challenging and influencing hegemonic journalism, and with far greater independence from corporate, state, and military power.

While there are debates in the burgeoning literature about how to define alternative journalism, an ideal type might include these characteristics: participatory models of production; challenges to established media power (including the professionalization and highly capitalized economy of commercial journalism and the division between media producers and audiences); more bottom-up ways of scanning and reporting the world, challenging conventional elite-oriented and ideologically conservative news values; and a positive orientation to social movements, social change, and/or marginalized communities (Atton, 2009; Atton & Hamilton, 2008; Hackett & Zhao, 1998; Hackett, 2010).

To be sure, some alternative media may be linked to movements that advocate violence or that lack a commitment to universal human rights and/or other-oriented ethics. Within the broad spectrum of ethnic diaspora media, for instance, some amplify the most militant or uncompromising views. However, at their best, alternative media share with PJ a commitment to social justice, to the critical analysis of social structure beyond the everyday spectacles of conventional news, and to the exposure and removal of the cultural and structural violence that can breed terrorism.

Speculatively, the media most likely to meet these criteria are those linked to communities seeking to protect themselves from direct violence, or linked to oppositional social movements seeking democratization in the face of structural violence.

Even at its best, however, as the very term "alternative" journalism implies, it typically speaks to and for politically or culturally marginalized communities, and lacks the resources to transform public communication in the culture as a whole. Thus, a third avenue for enhancing the media's potential to reduce cultural and structural violence is suggested—media reform. It entails intervening in institutional fields adjacent to the media—notably politics and social movements—to change the environment of journalism, the gravitational pulls to which it is subject. One key aspect of journalism's institutional environment is state policy regarding culture and communication. Here, there are very encouraging signs. Citizen movements have emerged in a number of countries, demanding democratic reform of state communication policies to help bring forth more accountable, diverse, humane, and representative media (Hackett & Carroll, 2006; McChesney, 2004). In recent years, similar efforts by civil society organizations have been directed towards democratizing global media governance, such as the Campaign for Communication Rights in the Information Society (O Siochru, 2005). More broadly, social justice movements struggling to project their voice in the public arena could help shift the environment of journalism, particularly by lending a portion of their resources to support media reform organizations like the Campaign for Press and Broadcasting Freedom in the U.K.,

freepress.net in the U.S., openmedia.ca in Canada, or their counterparts in South Korea, Taiwan, and elsewhere. Mobilized audiences, demanding "real news" as a condition of their own empowerment, could also make a difference.

It would be extremely naïve, of course, to believe either that media transformation can occur in the absence of determined movements for broader social change, or that media change alone can prevent insurgent terrorism, state terrorism, or cultural and structural violence. However, media are clearly part of the nexus of forces at play. We should take comfort in the fact that people can still be outraged by overt acts of terror. While Dobkin (cited in Lee, 2007) cautions that we are en route to normalizing state counter-terror and repression, we have not yet reached the point portrayed in Terry Gilliam's satirical film *Brazil*, when a terrorist bomb exploding in a restaurant attracts no attention from those diners not immediately eviscerated. Can those of us in the globe's gated communities extend our sense of outrage to forms of structural violence that do not immediately threaten us? Ultimately, a terror-free world requires an "enabling environment" for entrenching popular communication rights, empathizing with those we have been taught to see as the Other, and transcending a politics of fear and hate.

ACKNOWLEDGMENT

The author thanks Mahmoud Eid for editorial assistance. Portions of this chapter are drawn from Hackett (2012, 2010, and especially 2007b).

REFERENCES

Allan, S. (2004). The culture of distance: Online reporting of the Iraq war. In S. Allan, & B. Zelizer (Eds.), *Reporting war: Journalism in wartime* (pp. 347–364). London: Routledge.

Atton, C. (2009). Alternative and citizen journalism. In K. Wahl-Jorgensen, & T. Hanitzsch (Eds.), *The handbook of journalism studies* (pp. 265–278). New York: Routledge.

Atton, C., & Hamilton, J. F. (2008). *Alternative journalism.* Los Angeles, CA: Sage.

Becker, J. (1982). Communication and peace: The empirical and theoretical relation between two categories in social sciences. *Journal of Peace Research, 19*(3), 227–240. doi:10.1177/002234338201900302

Curran, J. (2012). Reinterpreting the Internet. In J. Curran, N. Fenton, & D. Freedman (Eds.), *Misunderstanding the internet* (pp. 3–33). London: Routledge.

Galtung, J. (1990). Cultural violence. *Journal of Peace Research, 27*(3), 291–305. doi:10.1177/0022343390027003005

Gerbner, G., Gross, L., Morgan, M., & Signorielli, N. (1986). Living with television: The dynamics of the cultivation process. In J. Bryant, & D. Zillman (Eds.), *Perspectives on media effects* (pp. 17–40). Hillsdale, NJ: Lawrence Erlbaum Associates.

Glavin, T. (2011). *Come from the shadows: The long and lonely struggle for peace in Afghanistan.* Vancouver, BC: Douglas & McIntyre.

Hackett, R. A. (2006). Is peace journalism possible? Three frameworks for assessing structure and agency in news media. *Conflict and Communication Online, 5*(2), 1–13.

Hackett, R. A. (2007a). Journalism versus peace? Notes on a problematic relationship. *Global Media Journal, 2*(1), 47–53.

Hackett, R. A. (2007b). Media terror? *Media Development, 46*(3), 3–6.

Hackett, R. A. (2010). Journalism for peace and justice: Towards a comparative analysis of media paradigms. *Studies in Social Justice, 4*(2), 145–164.

Hackett, R. A. (2012). Militarizing Canadian culture: Our government and media not just excusing war, but glorifying it. *The CCPA Monitor, 18*(8), 39.

Hackett, R. A., & Carroll, W. K. (2006). *Remaking media: The struggle to democratize public communication.* London: Routledge.

Hackett, R. A., & Zhao, Y. (1998). *Sustaining democracy? Journalism and the politics of objectivity.* Toronto: Garamond.

Herz, M. (2006). Prime time terror: The case of La Jetee and 12 Monkeys. In A. P. Kavoori, & T. Fraley (Eds.), *Media, terrorism, and theory: A reader* (pp. 53–68). Lanham, MD: Rowman & Littlefield.

Karmasin, M., Melischek, G., Seethaler, J., & Wöhlert, R. (2013). Perspectives on the changing role of the mass media in hostile conflicts. In J. Seethaler, M. Karmasin, G. Melischek, & R. Wöhlert (Eds.), *The role of the mass media in hostile conflicts from World War I to the war on terror* (p. ix-1). Chicago: University of Chicago Press.

Lee, P. (2007). Editorial. *Media Development, 56*(3), 2.

Liebes, T., & Kampf, Z. (2004). The PR of terror: How new-style wars give voice to terrorists. In S. Allan, & B. Zelizer (Eds.), *Reporting war: Journalism in wartime* (pp. 77–95). London: Routledge.

Louw, E. (2005). *The media and political process.* London: Sage.

Lynch, J., & McGoldrick, A. (2005). *Peace journalism*. Stroud, UK: Hawthorn Press.

Mander, J. (1978). *Four arguments for the elimination of television*. New York: William Morrow.

McChesney, R. W. (2004). *The problem of the media: U.S. communication politics in the twenty-first century*. New York: Monthly Review Press.

McKibben, B. (1999). Living second hand: An environmental view of the mass media. In K. Duncan (Ed.), *Liberating alternatives: The founding convention of the cultural environment movement* (pp. 43–47). Cresskill, NJ: Hampton Press.

Morgan, M. (Ed.). (2002). *Against the mainstream: The selected words of George Gerbner*. New York: Peter Lang.

Richler, N. (2012). What we talk about when we talk about war. Fredericton: Goose Lane Ed.s.

Schechter, D. (2003). *Embedded: Weapons of mass deception*. Amherst, NY: Prometheus Books.

Schmid, A. P., & de Graaf, J. (1982). *Violence as communication: Insurgent terrorism and the Western news media*. London: Sage.

Shipley, T. (2013). The NHL and the new Canadian militarism. *Canadian Dimension, 47*(2), 32–34.

Siochru, O. S. (2005). Finding a frame: Towards a transnational advocacy campaign to democratize communication. In R. A. Hackett & Y. Zhao (Eds.), Democratizing global media: One world, many struggles (pp. 289-311). Lanham, MD: Rowman & Littlefield.

Tehranian, M. (2002). Peace journalism: Negotiating global media ethics. *Harvard Journal of Press/Politics, 7*(2), 58-83.

Thompson, E. P. (1980). Protest and survive. In E. P. Thompson, & D. Smith (Eds.), *Protest and survive* (pp. 9–61). Harmondsworth, UK: Penguin.

Zhao, Y., & Hackett, R. A. (2005). Media globalization, media democratization: Challenges, issues and paradoxes. In R. Hackett, & Y. Zhao (Eds.), *Democratizing global media: One world, many struggles* (pp. 1–36). Lanham, MD: Rowman & Littlefield.

KEY TERMS AND DEFINITIONS

Communication Technologies: Interactive digital tools used to share information.

Media Reform: Proposed attempts to reform mass media towards an agenda that is in alignment with public needs and away from corporate interests.

Military Conflict: A clash, battle, or struggle between armed forces.

Peace Journalism (PJ): A public philosophy in which journalists make choices about what and how to report, to create opportunities for considering and valuing non-violent responses to conflict.

Political Identity: An individual's or a community's political affiliation.

Propaganda: Information, ideas, or rumors deliberately disseminated to help or harm a person, group, nation, movement, institution, etc.

War Journalism (WJ): A type of journalistic conduct that instigates the audience and society to support war and conflict.

Section 2
Terrorism Manifestations & Media Representations

Chapter 4
Terrorism Manifestations

Jonathan R. White
Grand Valley State University, USA

ABSTRACT

This chapter examines the tactical aspects of terrorism. It begins by focusing on the nature of war and conflict in the 21st century, suggesting that technology, economic structures, and communication have changed the way war is waged. It argues that small groups of aggrieved people may conduct campaigns of unconventional warfare against individual nations or international alliances. Although such violence is manifested in many ways, it is typically labeled as "terrorism." The chapter also demonstrates how large groups and nation states may participate in terrorist activities by either using terrorist tactics or supporting terrorist groups. The next part of the chapter focuses on the specific actions that constitute the tactics of terrorism, examining tactical innovations within various campaigns. The chapter concludes with an analysis of tactical force multipliers, and it introduces the role of the media within this context.

INTRODUCTION

Terrorism is a method of fighting. It involves asymmetrical attacks; that is, small outgunned and outmanned subnational units that launch assaults on a larger foe outside the rules of conventional warfare (Jenkins, 2006). Terrorism involves crime because terrorists violate criminal laws while engaging in violence against innocent people for political purposes (Cooper, 2001; Crenshaw, 1983). Terrorism is also a means of communicating a political, religious, or ideological message (Schmid & Jongman, 2005). As a result, it requires modernity with access to technology and the contemporary media. With no stage or mass mediated violence, terrorism has limited impact (Black, 2004).

DOI: 10.4018/978-1-4666-5776-2.ch004

This chapter will focus on the tactics, ideological meanings, and applications of terrorism. Terrorist tactics are simple and straightforward, but the social processes surrounding them make the tactical aspects of terrorism quite complex. Accordingly, this chapter will identify the basic tactics of terrorism, discuss the manner in which power is amplified, provide a framework for understanding terrorism within the changing nature of modern conflict, and explain the importance of communication. While terrorism has a range of meanings, the unit of analysis in this chapter is considered small to large subnational groups. Such groups may act with state support, but they do not act as official agents of the state. Accordingly, an ideological death squad operating outside the legal norms of a state fits the definition.

States acting with unconventional military force and those repressing a population with police or military power are not included. The focus will also be on political, ideological, and religious groups operating outside the law.

TACTICS AND IDEOLOGIES

Terrorism is ever changing. Terrorist organizations change tactics and strategies frequently, which can strain the capabilities of authorities to respond effectively (Thackrah, 2013). If security forces can chart the organizational structure of terrorist groups, they can be tracked and destroyed. As a result, terrorists seek to form complex organizations and networks (Latora & Marchioni, 2004). They change structures over time and operate with extended secrecy (White, 2012). Such changes allow groups to maintain complex social networks (Sageman, 2004). Thus, flexibly means survival. When a network is penetrated, security and flexibility are compromised giving security forces an opportunity to destroy key links inside the organization (Arquilla & Ronfeldt, 1996; Arquilla, Ronfeldt, & Zanini, 1999).

It is important to note that terrorism is not new. Distinguished scholars such as Walter Laqueur (1999) trace terrorism back for hundreds of years. However, massive death and destruction require modernity and technology. Modern terrorists wage a war in the shadows, blurring the distinction between war and peace. Access to instruments that can kill hundreds of people at a time and the ability to deliver death from great distances is a product of the modern world (Burleigh, 2009). Terrorism is a form of communication, and operations vary in terms of the message. In other words, terrorists operate within an informational aura while targeting a specific audience; operations change with the meaning of the message and its receiving audience. Today, small numbers of like-minded people can gather on an international level and wreak havoc that was unimaginable in the past.

Their message and violence are communicated immediately throughout the world (Hoffman, 2006).

Various scholars and analysts believe that the tactics of terrorism are simple (Brackett, 1996; Jenkins, 1987; O'Connor, 2006; Parachini, 2003; White, 2012). Although they can be described and grouped in a variety of ways, terrorist tactics involve shootings (e.g., assassinations, drive-bys, random assaults, etc.), physical assault, bombing, arson, and other forms of control mediated by violence (e.g., kidnappings, hostage incidents, hijackings, etc.).

Brian Jenkins (1984, November; 2004a, 2004b) summarizes these activities by categorizing six basic tactics of terrorism: bombing, hijacking, arson, assault, kidnapping, and hostage taking. Attacks can range from a simple shooting spree to a massive attack with a technological weapon. These actions become terrorism when they are conducted for political purposes guided by an ideological framework. Thomas R. O'Connor (2006) posits a slightly different typology, citing five basic tactics delivered in four modes. The tactics include:

1. Rolling where terrorists use a moving vehicle;
2. Ambush attacks;
3. Standoffs where terrorists are barricaded;
4. Boutiques involving multiple simultaneous attacks (also known as swarm attacks); and
5. Revenge attacks against symbolic targets.

The modes used to deliver such attacks are derived from conventional traditional weapons, advanced technological weapons, cyber-attacks, and the utilization of narcotics as an instrument of terrorism. A close examination reveals few differences between Jenkins and O'Connor; specifically, delivery may be complicated, but the tactics are simple.

If tactics are simple, terrorism is not. Complexity arises from the organizational structures and networks supporting terrorism and the criminal conspiracies inherent to terrorist plots. Complex operations such as multiple bombings or assaults require a great deal of planning and logistical support. While simple attacks—such as shooting sprees—are much easier to plan and coordinate, they can be complex. Even simple attacks involve planning and psychological preparation in secrecy. For instance, a plan must provide for coverage of the event, as it does no good to kill or destroy without a public audience. The immediate victims of any attack are not the intended victims. The target of a terrorist attack is the audience that will experience events through some type of medium. Therefore, communication becomes essential because the message is the purpose of any attack (Ross, 2007).

It is understood that intricate attacks become extremely complex. For example, consider the series of coordinated subway bombings in London in 2005. The attack involved four suicide bombers with backpacks. Three of the attackers were able to board London subways and explode their bombs within subway cars, and a fourth bomber detonated explosives on a city bus. The tactic was fairly simple; it involved building four bombs and setting them off. However, the logistics supporting the operation were another matter. The attack involved long-term planning, international travel, training, and a support structure, which was controlled by a highly sophisticated network in Pakistan (Storm & Eyerman, 2008). In this case, this was far from "leaderless resistance."

When the London bombings are compared to the relatively simple case of Jerry and Joe Kane, the level of complexity is reduced. Joe Kane and his father Jerry were part of the sovereign citizen movement in the United States. The teenaged Kane was a believer in the ideology due to long-term socialization within his family. In 2010 Kane and his father were driving outside of West Memphis, Arkansas in a vehicle that had a "constitutional" license plate. After two police officers stopped the car, the elder Kane confronted them with multiple bogus documents. The officers tried to make sense of the documents, and as they did so Joe Kane exited the vehicle with an assault rifle. Both officers were killed in the ensuing shootout, and the Kanes were killed in a confrontation with law enforcement the next day (Harris, 2010). This was a spontaneous action with virtually no planning, demonstrating the essence of "leaderless resistance."

These two examples are important when discussing the tactical nature of terrorism, because ideas about the complexity of terrorism have generated debate. This is symbolized by a recent exchange between Bruce Hoffman (2008a, 2008b) and Marc Sageman (2008). Hoffman reviewed Sageman's book, *Leaderless Jihad,* in *Foreign Affairs.* He argued that Sageman failed to grasp the nature of modern terrorism because he did not understand the complex organizational structures required to launch sophisticated terrorist attacks. Sageman responded to this critique by citing cases. Essentially, the main point in the debate focused on organizational structure. Did terrorists get their power from a network with a leaderless internal dynamic, or did intricate hierarchies control terrorist operations? Cases such as the London bombings and the murders in West Memphis, Arkansas, suggest that there is a range of methods and there is merit to both positions (Hoffman, 2008c).

Organizations and tactical operations are conducted by groups of individuals who assign meanings to events that happen around them. Interpreting social reality forms meanings, and people take actions based on their understandings. Thus, the decision to take any action is based on the subjective interpretation of reality. Terrorists select their methods and targets based on such meanings. Tactics cannot be separated from motivation, decision-making, and ideology (Arena & Ariggo, 2004). Groups of people operating within an organizational structure move within social space; this movement direction is dependent on the interpretation of reality. However, a descriptive analysis of ideology and tactics does very little to solve a security problem. A better tactical understanding can be gained by looking at the interpretations that cause a group to move. Groups moving toward violence may practice terrorism. Opening opportunities to express and mollify social grievances may open opportunities for alternative decision-making (Black, 2004).

Whether a lone individual engages in a spontaneous attack or a complex organization supports a group of people in multiple assaults, there are three key decision points that have tactical implications, according to John Horgan (2005, 2009). The first involves the decision to join a terrorist group; that is, it is one thing to support a cause, but it is another to take direct action. Joining a group represents the first direct action taken by a potential terrorist. The decision to engage in actual violence is the second crucial decision point. Finally, after engaging in violence, many people want to leave. Escaping could be possible, if opportunities were available, such as the provision of escape routes fostered by government policies. Horgan (2005) believes that terrorism cannot be countered by challenging radical ideologies or religious beliefs. Instead, he suggests that a more effective policy would involve counter-tactics aimed at individuals during these three critical decision points.

Ideology is important when deciding whether or not to join a group, but belief systems are less important at the other two decision points. An ideology based on political or religious doctrine provides the basis for making a decision. It can come in several forms, such as long-term socialization, identifying with a victimized community, accepting a sacred story, a sudden conversion experience, or a psychological crisis (Juergensmeyer, 2009; Stern, 2003). After joining a group, however, other mechanisms affect decisions (Helfstein, 2012). The traditional social bonds that form within communities are more important in influencing the direction of the group's movement and individual decisions made within the circle of people.

Tactics are also affected by the message a group is trying to convey, as communication is the lifeblood of terrorism. The ultimate tactical goal of any terrorist attack is to communicate some type of point; it may be to promote an ideology, force political change, or simply to create fear. This implies that any form of communication—whether reports created internally or coverage by mainstream media—has a tactical purpose. However, communication is not objective. Both terrorist organizations and security forces utilize communication as a weapon, and it influences the way attacks and counterattacks take place.

Selective targeting is essential for both terrorists and security forces. While terrorists seem to employ unlimited indiscriminate murder, only the most nihilistic terrorists could carry this out in practice. Terrorists need people to support their cause, as terrorists claim to represent a victimized population. If casualties include supporters, potential supporters, or innocents related to supporters, the victims may turn against their supposed representatives. A backlash of this nature was experienced by al-Qaeda in 2005. Ayman al Zawahiri, then the number two leader in al-Qaeda, wrote a scathing letter to the leader, Abu Musab al Zarqawi, chastising him for the number of innocent Iraqis being killed in such attacks (al-Zawahiri, 2005). Although random killing appears to be a terrorist tactic, even terrorists must select targets with some care. Innocent people have symbolic power, but terrorists cannot kill the people they claim to represent for long periods of time, as poor targeting leads to a backlash.

The same principle is applicable to security forces, and it can be illustrated by looking at the drone campaign against various branches of al-Qaeda. Both Presidents George W. Bush and Barack Obama assumed they had the power to strike and kill suspected terrorists in foreign lands. One of the primary instruments employed for this purpose was an unmanned drone armed with precision missiles. The purpose was to locate a suspect in impenetrable regions in Pakistan, Yemen, Somalia, and other venues through drone reconnaissance or other means of intelligence. An armed drone, flown remotely from the United States, would be dispatched to the site, the target would be located, and the missile would be fired. A number of al-Qaeda leaders and suspected terrorists were killed in this manner. The problem is that exploding warheads cause other casualties; when bombs explode, flying ordinance does not discriminate its victims. Combatants and non-combatants are killed and maimed resulting in resentment and may drive neutrals or even allies to the terrorist cause (Mothana, 2012).

FORCE MULTIPLIERS AND THE ILLUSION OF POWER

Terrorism exists in an aura. Its power comes from the ability to disrupt the normal routines of life with violence and to make people believe that such disruption can happen at any time. This impact of terrorism is similar to that of violent crime. People want to feel socially secure in familiar areas; they accept that some areas, high crime districts, for example, are dangerous, but they want to believe that their neighborhood is peaceful and relatively free of crime. When violent crime occurs in a person's own neighborhood, the residents are impacted. They begin to believe that there is no safe haven in daily routines and that life is in a constant state of violent fluctuation. Terrorists seek to create the same feeling by forcing a mass audience to participate as vicarious victims of an attack.

Horrific mass mediated violence creates the illusion of power. The attacks of 9/11 were terrible and had a tremendous impact on U.S. policies and the structure of operation of governmental functions. To be sure, the ability to disrupt social activities on such a large scale represents power, but it is nowhere near the amount of power needed to defeat the United States. It would be farcical to

think of an al-Qaeda force massing off the shores of New York City and moving in to destroy military forces and occupy territory—terrorists know this, and this is not their goal. In fact, their goals are to project power and cause governments to react. As a result of 9/11, the United States launched two wars, created a new cabinet level department, launched a domestic security industry, deployed troops in undeclared wars, and created a new massive system of domestic criminal intelligence. All of this happened because 19 men in airplanes carried out four suicide attacks.

Terrorists mediate fear through symbolic actions. The example of 9/11 is illustrative of the process, but it applies to almost all terror attacks. For example, a Ku Klux Klan cross burning ignites more than flames; the symbolism in this activity creates fear. Tortured bodies left in a large garbage dump during El Salvador's civil war were messages from death squads to a variety of audiences ranging from would-be revolutionaries to humanitarian workers and the Catholic Church. Suicide bombing is a powerful method of communication; it not only symbolizes power to break the norm, it demonstrates a willingness to sacrifice life for the cause. Such events happen outside the normal flow of everyday life, and the resulting aura suggests that terrorists are powerful enough to do it again—anytime, anywhere.

Force multipliers are crucial because they help to sustain the aura; that is, they magnify symbolic power. A force multiplier refers to the ability to increase striking power. Most scholars and analysts acknowledge three force multipliers used in terrorism: media coverage, technology, and transnational support (White, 2012). The media give terrorists power; it is drama—made for television drama. As attacks are aired repeatedly, the symbolic power of a single attack is increased. Most news organizations have come to realize that their reports can easily become part of the event, and they have taken steps to control this. In response, terrorist organizations have responded by creating their own media outlets—for instance,

Webpages become a means to transmit messages. Further, for example, al-Qaeda Central, located in Pakistan, runs a television station called "The Cloud." It broadcasts its own reports, sends taped footage to news outlets, and also uses the Internet to post videos and propaganda messages. Additionally, al-Qaeda in the Arabian Peninsula publishes an online instructional magazine called *Inspire*, which contains articles on tactics, weapons, and recruitment.

Technology multiplies force in two manners. Obviously, it can be used in an attack to increase the number of casualties and victims. While modern weapons give terrorists an important force multiplier, modern implements can also be turned into weapons. Joe Stack flew a small airplane into a federal building in Austin, Texas to strike the Internal Revenue Service in 2010 (Heining, 2010). Car bombs, bureaucratically called "vehicle born improvised explosive devices," have been a staple of terrorism for decades. Terrorists can also strike technological targets. For example, natural gas travels through a network of pipelines controlled by computer systems. If a cyber-attack were to gain temporary control of the system, hackers could disable pressure controls and cause explosions throughout the system. Power grids, train lines, aircraft ground controls, and many other systems could be attacked in the same manner.

Transnational support is a crucial force multiplier. Organizations that span international borders increase their striking power. Foreign supports may send financial aid or contraband from afar. The greatest transnational force multiplier involves the ability to create a protected base in one country while conducting terrorism in another. The Haqqani network in Pakistan and Afghanistan exemplifies this situation. The Haqqanis and their allies have planned multiple simultaneous attacks in secure areas of Kabul. They have conducted difficult suicide bombings against targets that were thought to be protected, and they have successfully launched attacks in the West from remote areas of Pakistan.

Some scholars believe that religion is a potential fourth force multiplier (Juergensmeyer, 2003, 2009; Laqueur, 1999; Stern, 2003; White, 2001). Their contention is that religion increases the ideological fanaticism. Other scholars disagree, saying that religious terrorists are no more violent than politically motivated terrorists, and the importance of religion is reduced once a person joins a group (Berman, 2009; Helfstein, 2012; Rapoport, 1988). Despite the difference of opinion about the amount of violence, the orientations of political and religious terrorists differ. Political terrorists fight for a better world and they want to improve circumstances in this life, requiring political support to accomplish these goals. Religious terrorists fight to change the cosmos to the image of their chosen deity, and they often fail to see the need for political support (Aslan, 2010). Religious terrorists are free to engage in massive violence because they fight for a deity, in theory. In practice, even religious terrorists must limit violence and select targets. However, religion can motivate an entire network, such as the Haqqanis, and it is a powerful tool for recruiting operators and supporters. Therefore, religion has the power to multiply force.

THE TRANSFORMATION OF CONFLICT

If terrorism is ever changing, so is the practice of war. Principles like massing troops, surprising enemies, ensuring adequate supplies, and maintaining maneuverability and momentum are constant. These principles are as applicable to Alexander the Great's conquest of Persia as they are to coalition forces operating in Afghanistan. Tactics and practices, however, change continually. Technology and ideology are two of the main forces that impact the tactical aspects of war, and this has changed the scope of conflict in the modern world.

David Bell (2007) posits a controversial yet well-supported argument about the transformation of conflict in the era of the French Revolution. Orthodox historiography maintains that warfare changed because of nationalism and revolutionary spirit. Unlike the limited territorial wars that dominated Europe and much of the world from 1648 until 1789, massed conscripted armies of the Napoleonic period fought wars seeking the total destruction of their enemies. The French prompted this change by fighting for the ideology of the revolution. Bell argues against this tradition. He states that the meaning of war changed with the revolution. Prior to 1789 war was considered to be normal, ongoing, and part of social life. It was to be waged by courtly gentlemen, and most importantly, it was to be limited. War's purpose was to obtain a political advantage in a stable international system. The advent of total war came when armies of the revolution developed a new ethos. The new purpose of war was to destroy the enemy, or to utterly impose the victor's will on the enemy. This, Bell maintains, caused the nature of war to be transformed.

This style of thinking dominates contemporary military doctrine (Barnett, 2005a, 2005b). The American concept of conflict has been deeply influenced by the Prussian general and military philosopher Carl von Clausewitz (1780-1831), who began studying conflict during the nationalistic wars against Napoleon (1795-1815). Joining the Prussian Army as a 12 year-old drummer boy to fight against France, he came to believe that the French Revolution created a new type of war, and he began to study war as a philosophical problem (Clausewitz, 1984).

The strength of the French, Clausewitz reasoned, came from their ability to place the nation in arms; that is, to rally the people to the belief that all citizens of a nation are potential soldiers or supporters of the military. To defeat the French, Germany had to become a nation in arms, unite under a democracy, and employ its own citizen soldiers. The proof of victory would come when Germany's political will could be imposed on France. Clausewitz joined a group of reformers and tried to modernize the Prussian Army. He understood that war had been transformed, and his philosophical treatise *On War* (1984) summarizes the concept of total war. Most members of Western armed forces read Clausewitz in staff schools before being promoted to command ranks. They are taught to think in the terms that Bell (2007) describes—total war (Cebrowsky, 2004; Cebrowsky & Barnett, 2003).

Bell (2007) argues warfare transformed during the Napoleonic period and that the world is in a similar transformation today. The problem is that many people—including political and military leaders—do not seem to realize it. Speaking in front of a TED (Technology, Entertainment, Design) meeting in California, Thomas P. M. Barnett (2005b) illustrates this dilemma. The United States has the world's largest and best military forces, he states. In fact, it is so powerful that no country wants to challenge the U.S. in a standard conventional manner—the manner of fighting since the total wars of the French Revolution. The U.S. Air Force can be used as an illustration. Despite many military ventures since the Vietnam War, Barnett says that the last U.S. fighter pilot to actually shoot down an enemy plane had reached the rank of brigadier general in 2005. The thousands of flight-qualified officers in the Air Force and Navy have no aerial combat experience because no single nation can challenge American air power. Yet, the United States will be challenged with violence, and if enemies cannot fight by the rules of total war, they will invent a new set of rules to level the playing field.

Barnett (2005b) says the economic structure of the world has reassembled political geography, supporting the transformation away from total war. The modern world is dominated by three economic zones: nations that dominate the global economy, less wealthy nations that have special products allowing them to participate in parts of the economy, and nations who have nothing.

Wealthy nations cannot afford to engage in conventional war with each other; it would be massively destructive, and destroying the interlocked nature of the global economy would financially ruin the victor. In short, the rich nations cannot afford to fight one another. However, poorer nations have the incentive to fight when they feel victimized. When they fight, Barnett concludes, they do not fight by the rules of the dominant powers. Why fly against the U.S. Air Force if you cannot win? Why not send a suicide bomber into a place the Air Force cannot defend?

If Barnett (2005b) is correct, the post-Cold War era has ushered in a new type of conflict similar to the argument Bell (2007) introduces in the transformation from limited to total war. The world is shifting (or has shifted) into a new age of limited war. Subnational forces or surrogates of nations in the second or third economic tier will attack the economically dominated system when they feel victimized. Terrorists, however, are not attacking state power; they are attacking the idea of Western culture—the culture of the dominant economic system. Their war is with a global system that they fear and loathe, and they resent the economic structure of the world. This is applicable from radical Islamic militancy to violence within the sovereign citizen movement in the United States. Modern conflict is aimed at the infrastructure of everyday life and the symbols that define that structure (Homer-Dixon, 2002; Stevenson, 2003). One of the forms of modern conflict is terrorism.

The major tactical problem is that Western policies have not recognized the transformation of war (Cebrowsky, 2004). Tactical changes in modern terrorism signal a return to limited war. Terrorists only strike front line combat-ready forces by stealth. They favor attacks on military forces at rest or those assigned to policing functions. Targeting has also shifted from military forces to societal structures. Civilians, symbols, and physical infrastructures become the targets of attack in a war beyond traditional definitions.

In Bell's (2007) historical analysis and Barnett's (2005b) political theory, warfare is in the process of transformation.

BEATING THE WRONG WAR DRUM

If Barnett's (2005b) thesis is correct, terrorism is a product of the transformation of war. It operates with simple tactics inside complex networks and social structures. It blurs the distinction between war and peace. The rules of conflict have been changing since World War II, and homeland security is taking place within a changing tactical environment. Brian Jenkins (2006) speaks of the types of wars America will face on a spectrum of conflict ranging from small, short counterterrorist operations to major military conflicts. These findings are reinforced by many military analysts. However, the structure of conventional war has changed since World War II; there is a need to recast our mode of thinking about conflict in new images that differ from conventional war (Clark, 2001; Gordon & Trainor, 2006; Ricks, 2006). The United States and most of the world's leading economic powers have failed to do so.

The problem inside this transformation, at least for the militarily dominant United States, is that terrorism has been approached within the metaphor of conventional war—total war inherited from the age of Napoleon. Shortly after 9/11, President George W. Bush addressed the nation, stating that America and its allies were at war with terrorism. Despite the Constitution having no provision for declaring war on a concept, federal and local bureaucracies embraced the metaphor of war for combating terrorism, and the American military even used an acronym for it: GWOT, the Global War on Terrorism. More recently, President Barack Obama has redefined America's approach to terrorism as a criminal justice problem where military force is used to augment legal power (Kimery, 2009).

Louise Richardson (2007), a dean at Harvard University, says that the United States made four primary mistakes after 9/11. First, the government allowed a small group of people to force it into declaring war on terrorism. This was a declaration against a concept with no clear means of victory. Second, it confused the relationship between al-Qaeda and Iraq, partially causing an unnecessary war. Third, authorities failed to transmit factual information about terrorism. Instead of focusing on the low probabilities and risks of terrorism, officials changed the course of government. Finally, the government allowed the incident to be defined by public hysteria. She concludes that the United States played into the hands of the terrorists.

Retired CIA terrorism specialist Paul Pillar (2005), now teaching at Georgetown University, says that America has had sufficient historical experience to deal with terrorism. Violence in the 20th century ranged from a 1919 bombing campaign to the waves of ideological left- and right-wing terrorism during the century's last decades. These events were handled within the context of American law, and the country did not reorganize government or declare war on terrorism to do so. Given the events of the 1990s, the country should have been preparing sound policies to control the threat of terrorism by preventing it where possible and competently responding to events that could not be stopped. This did not occur, Pillar concludes, because the U.S. approach to terrorism is based on incorrect public perceptions instead of objective examinations of security problems. American policy makers tend to react to terrorism with populism and emotion rather than to plan for it within the context of a national security policy.

Failure to understand the nature of modern terrorism comes with a cost. Historian John W. Dower (2010) believes the war metaphor failed the country after 9/11 because it militarized the problem of terrorism. In fact, the United States has been militarizing foreign policy issues since World War II. Dower argues that enemies are demonized when political situations are militarized. This led to targeting civilians, mass fire bombings, and nuclear weapons during the Second World War. After the war, Americans assumed they could control foreign relations and diplomatic problems with military force, and this spilled into the country's response to 21st century terrorism. The American response was based on a faulty theory of militarized solutions to social problems. The attacks of 9/11 were interpreted within a culture of war.

Most terrorism experts have argued that counterterrorism is primarily an affair for law enforcement, not the military (Cooper, 1978; Jenkins, 1984; Sageman, 2004; Scheuer, 2002; Wardlaw, 1982; Wilkinson, 1974). When a problem goes beyond the capabilities of the criminal justice system, limited military force should be used to augment legal power. When antiterrorist operations are viewed mainly as a military matter, however, problems arise. The purpose of police power is to restore normalcy through the legal system. Military forces seek victory. After 9/11 basic human rights were ignored. Torture, cruel treatment, limitless detention, and continuous monitoring were justified under the umbrella of controlling enemy combatants (Martinez, 2008; Suskind, 2008). The intelligence services were diverted from their role of information gathering and clandestine operations, and they were assigned to paramilitary functions, clandestine prison services, and criminal interrogation. Proven interview techniques within acceptable Western legal norms are crucial to controlling terrorism, but they were frequently ignored—often at the direction of the executive branch of government. Operating outside legal norms established within the rule of law is not only ineffective; it increases sympathy for the very terrorists causing the security problem (McCoy, 2006).

As the Iraqi war entered its insurgency phase, the United States Army War College and the law school of the University of Virginia co-sponsored a conference on terrorism. They drew participants from several different professional areas, including the military and intelligence communities. The presenters argued that the social interpretative framework surrounding the meaning of terrorism has important diplomatic, legal, and military consequences, and the participants unequivocally emphasized the importance of differentiating between war and terrorism. Essentially, they concluded, war and terrorism are two different entities. The former is framed in the context of destroying an enemy through force. Terrorism, however, is a complicated conspiratorial activity requiring the nuances of criminological analysis and responses within the criminal justice system (Owens, 2005).

The conference summary concluded that the United States defined the events of 9/11 within the context of war rather than approaching it with the flexibility of the American legal system. This limited the options the United States could apply to counterterrorist operations. It also caused the U.S. to respond to terrorism as if it were merely a tactical problem rather than grasping the complexity of the situation. Not only did this reinforce the dangers of defining terrorism solely within the context of military affairs, it caused policymakers to ignore the other dimensions of terrorism (Owens, 2005). There are a variety of effective responses to terrorism far beyond the realm of military force. If terrorism is simply viewed as an extension of war, these options seem to disappear.

THE INFORMATION ENVIRONMENT

Terrorism may cause a nation or a coalition of nation states to enter into conflict with a non-state entity. This may become extremely complex requiring coordinated responses from diplomats, the intelligence community, military leaders, and representatives of the legal system. This is a problem for criminal law and the agencies charged with enforcing it. Police departments should not become military or secret intelligence organizations. Law enforcement has three primary responsibilities—duties that existed long before 9/11. These responsibilities include:

- Maintaining public safety;
- Collecting criminal intelligence; and
- Sharing information in a legal manner.

None of these activities requires extra-constitutional authority, nor do they imply that police tactics should be militarized. Most importantly, there is no need for special paramilitary law enforcement units beyond those needed for high-risk response. In fact, closer relations with local communities enhance the national defense role of policing. Militarization, which inevitably builds barriers between the police and the public, actually detracts from law enforcement's ability to protect a community and serve the nation (Carter, 2009; Murray, 2005).

It is important to note that terrorism is taking place within a new set of rules or "rule set," in the words of Thomas Barnett (2005a). When Barnett discusses rules sets, he is talking about the unwritten norms or even formal agreements that govern military confrontations during particular periods of history. Although nations can pose a security threat, the threat from terrorism comes from sub-national terrorist networks, militant ideologies, and lone groups or actors. Modern military forces, especially those of the world's major powers, are preparing to fight the next big war, and this dominates the military thought of the world's major power, the United States of America. Yet, terrorism is conducted far outside the realm of "the next big one" and the rule set in which it would be governed. Anti-terrorism policies are aimed at protecting lives and property, securing the infrastructure, maintaining order at special events, protecting officials, maintaining the rule of law, and, most importantly, preserving democratic values and the rights of citizenship. Such functions are conducted within a rule set defined by criminal law, and not the rules of war.

The primary job of law enforcement in preventing terrorism is to stop criminal activity within networks. Terror networks require technology, tactical doctrine, organizational structure, social support, and narrative. Technology, a traditional force multiplier for terrorist groups, is crucial. It allows a small group to operate on more sophisticated levels. Organizations have abandoned the old hierarchy that defined terrorist groups in the post-World War II era. Today, groups range from simple chains to, small hubs, to all-channel networks. Some are controlled by command structures; others operate autonomously under the power of a network. Tactical doctrine is formed by the control mechanism for the network (Arquilla & Ronfeldt, 2001).

The last two factors, social support and narrative, involve communication and control of information. Groups must effectively maintain internal and external social relations. This builds trust and identity. Narrative is myth—it provides a story, the *raison d'etre*. The group must accept the story, but outsiders may embrace the narrative if they feel victimized and they sympathize with the goals of a terrorist group. Good communication generates sympathy and support. When popular groups operate with a strong narrative, terrorist groups are strong and long lasting. Therefore, terrorism brings a struggle for control of the information environment.

Terrorists exist within an appearance of projected power. They manipulate information internally with a myth that casts actions and causes in heroic terms. They attempt to export a mythic aura to the community of victims that they claim to represent. They attack symbols to manipulate messages to various publics, including their enemies, potential recruits, their own membership, and sympathizers. Simple tactics are camouflaged by social complexity and control of information. Fear is the key to effective terrorism, and it can

be developed and maintained when terrorists create the illusion that they can disrupt the norms of everyday life at any time and any point they desire. Terrorists want to control the stories they narrate, and they do so by creating fear.

Yet, despite any aura of fear, terrorism is merely a method of fighting. Attacks are composed of simple tactics and delivered in a variety of complex ways. The impact of attacks is multiplied by transnational support, technology, religion, and the media. All media are critical because they help communicate all types of messages, including the message of fear. Terrorism is one of the manifestations of changes in the nature of warfare, and at times it blurs the distinction between war and peace. Law enforcement agencies should have the primary role in controlling and preventing terrorism, but they can be supplemented by military power when necessary. Failure to recognize the nature of terrorism can lead to misguided policies, military metaphors, and security failures.

The centrality of the message and the medium is crucial to both terrorist organizations and security forces. Both sides vie to have favorable images in broadcast, print, or their own internal media. Violence at the scene of an attack is horrific, but the strategic struggle takes place afterward on YouTube, al-Jazeera, CNN, and *Inspire* magazine—for, each side wants media control. The late Richard Clutterbuck (1975) explains the reason that competition to control the information environment never stops. All media, he maintained, is a loaded neutral weapon laying in the center of a street fight. The first side that picks it up gets to shoot.

CONCLUSION

This chapter's focus on tactical aspects of terrorism reveals the multifaceted nature of terrorism today. Through an exploratory analysis of a variety of terrorist methods and techniques, it becomes clear that conflict in the 21st century has changed due to new aspects of our society. Technology, communication, and economic structures are three main elements that are considered to have a great amount of impact on how war is waged. That is, terrorism—campaigns of unconventional warfare against individual nations or international alliances by small groups of aggrieved people—has taken on many new characteristics. It has taken on a persona that, while retaining primary resemblances to traditional methods, incorporates the many new strands of contemporary global interactions. These tactics, although often associated with traditional terrorist ideologies (i.e., extremists, religious fanatics, etc.), are also employed by nation states.

While vast changes in terrorist tactics have been demonstrated in this chapter, it is important to acknowledge that they remain simple. This is not to say that the true nature of terrorism is uncomplicated—as it is considered a highly complex notion—however, the basics of the tactics are understood to be simple. This understanding of how terrorism functions and the tactics that fuel terrorism is necessary for developing comprehensive and effective strategies for countering these tactics. Through analysis and accurate categorization, it becomes possible to understand the mechanics of recruitment, strategy, execution, and response to the tactics of terrorism in modern day. This competence can allow for the development of increasingly proficient counter-terrorism tactics, which are needed in today's global climate of conflict uncertainty.

As expressed by Barnett (2005a), terrorism today has taken up a new set of rules. As changes in communication and technology spawn constant innovation and the global economy continue to grow increasingly close, our world and the methods of exchange interact with how clashes and combat unfold. Thus, awareness of the ways in which terrorist adapt to these changes—with specific regard to their tactics—unveils a realm of knowledge fundamental to comprehending and reducing the incidence of terrorist conflict. Although a wide body of knowledge exists surrounding these tactics today, further inquiry into the changes and developments in terrorism tactics will aid in the creation of the awareness and dexterity needed to reduce and understand terrorism.

REFERENCES

al-Zawahiri, A. (2005). *Letter from Ayman al-Zawahiri to Abu Musab al-Zarqawi*. Council on Foreign Relations. Retrieved May 16, 2012, from http://www.cfr.org/iraq/letter-ayman-al-zawahiri-abu-musab-al-zarqawi/p9862

Arena, M., & Arrigo, B. (2004). Identity and the terrorist threat: An interpretive and explanatory model. *International Criminal Justice Review, 14*, 124–163.

Arquilla, J., & Ronfeldt, D. (1996). *The advent of netwar*. Santa Monica, CA: RAND Corporation.

Arquilla, J., & Ronfeldt, D. (2001). *Networks and netwars: The future of terror, crime, and militancy*. Santa Monica, CA: RAND Corporation.

Arquilla, J., Ronfeldt, D., & Zanini, M. (1999). Networks, netwar, and information-age terrorism. In I. O. Lesser, B. Hoffman, J. Arquilla, D. Ronfeldt, & M. Zanini (Eds.), *Countering the new terrorism* (pp. 39–41). Santa Monica, CA: RAND Corporation.

Aslan, R. (2010). *Beyond fundamentalism: Confronting religious extremism in the age of globalization*. New York: Random House.

Barnett, T. P. M. (2005a). *The Pentagon's new map: War and peace in the twenty-first Century*. New York: Putnam's.

Barnett, T. P. M. (2005b, February). *Thomas Barnett draws a new map for peace*. [podcast radio program]. Monterey, CA: TED Talks. Retrieved May 5, 2012, from http://www.ted.com/talks/thomas_barnett_draws_a_new_map_for_peace.html

Bell, D. A. (2007). *The first total war: Napoleon's Europe and the birth of war as we know it*. New York: Houghton Mifflin Company.

Berman, E. (2009). *Radical, religious, and violent: The new economics of terrorism*. Boston: MIT Press.

Black, D. (2004). The geometry of terrorism. *Sociological Theory, 22*(1), 14–25. doi:10.1111/j.1467-9558.2004.00201.x

Brackett, D. W. (1996). *Holy terror: Armageddon in Tokyo*. New York: Weatherhill.

Burleigh, M. (2009). *Blood and rage: A cultural history of terrorism*. New York: Harper.

Carter, D. L. (2009). *Law enforcement intelligence: A guide for state, local and tribal agencies*. United States Department of Justice. Retrieved July 30, 2010 from, http://www.cops.usdoj.gov/pdf/e09042536.pdf

Cebrowsky, A. K. (2004). *Netwar*. Paper presented at the Assistant Secretary of Defense Conference on Special Operations. Alexandria, VA.

Cebrowsky, A. K., & Barnett, T. P. M. (2003). The American way of war. In *Proceedings of U.S. Naval Institute*, (pp. 42-43). Retrieved July 30, 2013, from http://thomaspmbarnett.com/globlogization/2010/8/12/blast-from-my-past-the-american-way-of-war-2003.html

Clark, W. (2001). *Waging modern war*. New York: Public Affairs.

Clausewitz, C. (1984). *On war* (M. Howard, & P. Paret, Trans.). Princeton, NJ: Princeton University Press.

Cluterbuck, R. C. (1975). *Living with terrorism*. London: Faber & Faber.

Cooper, H. H. A. (1978). Terrorism: The problem of the problem of definition. *Chitty's Law Journal, 26*(3), 105–108.

Cooper, H. H. A. (2001). Terrorism: The problem of definition revisited. *The American Behavioral Scientist, 44*(6), 881–893. doi:10.1177/00027640121956575

Crenshaw, M. (1983). The concept of revolutionary terrorism. *The Journal of Conflict Resolution, 16*(3), 383–396.

Dower, J. W. (2010). *Cultures of war.* New York: W. W. Norton.

Gordon, M. R., & Trainor, B. E. (2006). *Cobra II: The inside story of the invasion and occupation of Iraq.* New York: Pantheon Books.

Harris, D. (2010, July 1). Deadly Arkansas shootings by Jerry and Joe Kane who shun U.S. law. *ABC News.* Retrieved 3 July, 2013, from http://abcnews.go.com/WN/deadly-arkansas-shooting-sovereign-citizens-jerry-kane-joseph/story?id=11065285

Heining, A. (2010, February 18). Who is Joe Stack? *The Christian Science Monitor.* Retrieved June 12, 2012, from http://www.csmonitor.com/USA/2010/0218/Who-is-Joe-Stack

Helfstein, S. (2012). Edges of radicalization: Ideas, individuals and networks in violent extremism. *Combating Terrorism Center at West Point: United State Military Academy.* Retrieved February 17, 2012, from http://www.ctc.usma.edu/posts/edges-of-radicalization-ideas-individuals-and-networks-in-violent-extremism

Hoffman, B. (2006). *Inside terrorism.* New York: Columbia University Press.

Hoffman, B. (2008a). The myth of grass roots terrorism. *Foreign Affairs, 87*(3), 133–138.

Hoffman, B. (2008b). Hoffman replies. *Foreign Affairs, 87*(4), 165–166.

Hoffman, F. G. (2008c). Al Qaeda's demise or evolution? *United States Naval Institute Proceedings, 134*(9), 18–22.

Homer-Dixon, T. (2002). The rise of complex terrorism. *Foreign Affairs, 81*(1), 52–62.

Horgan, J. (2005). *The psychology of terrorism.* New York: Routledge. doi:10.4324/9780203496961

Horgan, J. (2009). *Walking away from terrorism.* New York: Routledge.

Jenkins, B. (1984, November). The who, what, when, where, how, and why of terrorism. In *Proceedings of the Detroit Police Department Conference on Urban Terrorism: Planning or Chaos?* Detroit, MI: Detroit Police Department.

Jenkins, B. (1987). Will terrorists go nuclear? In W. Laqueur, & Y. Alexander (Eds.), *The terrorism reader.* New York: Meridian.

Jenkins, B. (2004a). The operational code of the jihadists: A briefing prepared for the Army science board. *RAND Corporation.* Retrieved July 30, 2013, from http://www.au.af.mil/au/awc/awcgate/army/asb_op_code_jihadists.pdf

Jenkins, B. (2004b). Where I draw the line. *The Christian Science Monitor.* Retrieved July 3, 2013, from http://www.csmonitor.com/specials/terrorism/%20lite/expert.html

Jenkins, B. (2006). *Unconquerable nation: Knowing our enemy, strengthening ourselves.* Santa Monica, CA: RAND Corporation.

Juergensmeyer, M. (2003). *Terror in the mind of God: The global rise of religious violence.* Berkley, CA: University of California Press.

Juergensmeyer, M. (2009). *Global rebellion: Religious challenges to the secular state from Christian militias to Al Qaeda.* Berkeley, CA: University of California Press.

Kimery, A. L. (2009, August 13). Rejection of Jihadist, war on terrorism terms draws fire, debate. *Homeland Security Today.* Retrieved July 3, 2013, from http://www.hstoday.us/blogs/the-kimery-report/blog/rejection-of-jihadist-war-on-terrorism-terms-draws-fire-debate/7a2ac6715e2f3671f040bfca2cb55f57.html

Laqueur, W. (1999). *The new terrorism: Fanaticism and the arms of mass destruction.* New York: Oxford University Press.

Latora, V., & Marchioni, M. (2004). How the science of complex networks can help developing strategies against terrorism. *Chaos, Solitons, and Fractals*, *20*(1), 69–75. doi:10.1016/S0960-0779(03)00429-6

Martinez, J. S. (2008). Process and substance in the war on terror. *Columbia Law Review*, *108*(5), 1013–1092.

McCoy, A. W. (2006). *A question of torture: CIA interrogation from the Cold War to the War on Terror*. New York: Henry Holt Company.

Mothana, I. (2012, June 13). How drone strikes help al Qaeda. *The New York Times*. Retrieved June 13, 2012, from http://www.nytimes.com/2012/06/14/opinion/how-drones-help-al-qaeda.html

Murray, J. (2005). Policing terrorism: A threat to community policing or just a shift in priorities? *Police Practice and Research*, *6*(4), 347–361. doi:10.1080/15614260500293986

O'Connor, T. R. (2006). The criminology of terrorism: History, law, definitions, typologies. *Cults and Terror*. Retrieved June 14, 2012, from http://www.cultsandterror.org/sub-file/TOConnor%20Lecture.htm

Owens, D. D. (2005). Law versus war: Competing approaches to fighting terrorism. *Strategic Studies Institute, US Army War College*. Retrieved November 10, 2011, from http://www.au.af.mil/au/awc/awcgate/ssi/boyne_law_terr.pdf

Parachini, J. (2003). Putting WMD terrorism into perspective. *The Washington Quarterly*, *26*(4), 37–50. doi:10.1162/016366003322387091

Pillar, P. (2005). Perceptions of terrorism: Continuity and change. *Strategic Studies Institute, US Army War College*. Retrieved June 25, 2012, from http://www.au.af.mil/au/awc/awcgate/ssi/boyne_law_terr.pdfhttp://www.strategicstudies-institute.army.mil/pubs/display.cfm?pubID=613

Rapoport, D. (1988). *Inside terrorist organizations*. New York: Columbia University Press.

Richardson, L. (2007). *What terrorists want: Understanding the enemy, containing the threat*. New York: Random House.

Ricks, T. E. (2006). *Fiasco: The American military adventure in Iraq*. New York: Penguin.

Ross, J. I. (2007). Deconstructing the terrorism-news media relationship. *Crime, Media, Culture*, *3*(2), 215–225. doi:10.1177/1741659007078555

Sageman, M. (2004). *Understanding terror networks*. Philadelphia, PA: University of Pennsylvania.

Sageman, M. (2008). *Leaderless Jihad: Terror networks in the twenty-first century*. Philadelphia, PA: University of Pennsylvania Press.

Scheuer, M. (2002). *Through our enemies' eyes: Osama bin Laden, radical Islam, and the future of America*. Washington, DC: Potomac Books.

Schmid, A. P., & Jongman, A. J. (2005). *Political terrorism: A new guide to actors, authors, concepts, data bases, theories, and literature*. Summerset, NJ: Transaction Books.

Stern, J. (2003). *Terror in the name of God: Why religious militants kill*. New York: Harper Collins.

Stevenson, J. (2003). How Europe and America defend themselves. *Foreign Affairs*, *82*(2), 75–90. doi:10.2307/20033505

Storm, K. J., & Eyerman, J. (2008). *Interagency cooperation: Lessons learned from the London subway bombings*. Office of Justice Programs, United States Department of Justice. Retrieved May 15, 2012, from http://www.ojp.usdoj.gov/nij/journals/261/coordination.htm

Suskind, R. (2008). *The way of the world: A story of truth and hope in the age of terrorism*. New York: Harper Collins.

Thackrah, J. R. (2013). *Dictionary of terrorism.* New York: Routledge.

Wardlaw, G. (1982). *Political terrorism: Theory, tactics, and counter-measures.* London: Cambridge University Press.

White, J. R. (2001). Political eschatology: A theology of antigovernment extremism. *The American Behavioral Scientist, 44*(6), 937–956. doi:10.1177/00027640121956601

White, J. R. (2012). *Terrorism and homeland security.* Belmont, CA: Cengage.

Wilkinson, P. (1974). *Political terrorism.* New York: Wiley.

KEY TERMS AND DEFINITIONS

Communication Tools: Apparatuses used to connect people and share information.

Counter-Terrorism Tactics: Methods used to oppose, stop, and prevent terrorism.

Developments in Terrorism: Changes and/or growth in different aspects of terrorism.

Modern Warfare: Contemporary forms of conflict.

Power Structures: Modes of building and organizing ascendency.

Technology: A branch of knowledge that deals with the creation and use of technical means and their interrelation with life and society.

Terrorist Tactics: Modes, procedures, or weapons employed by terrorists to achieve specific desired outcomes.

Chapter 5
Media Representations of Terrorism

John Downing
Southern Illinois University, USA

ABSTRACT

This chapter begins with a comparative overview of violence against civilians in war, terrorist events, and torture. The comparisons are between the United States since the 9/11 attacks, Britain during the civil war in Northern Ireland 1969-2000, and France during and since the Algerian armed liberation struggle of 1954-1962. The discussion covers the general issues involved, and then summarizes existing research on British and French media representations of political violence. This chapter then proceeds to a critical-discourse analysis of the U.S. Fox Television channel's highly successful dramatic series, 24. The series is currently considered one of the most extended televisual reflections on the implications of 9/11. Political violence, counter-terrorism, racism, and torture are central themes demonstrated in this television series. It is argued that the show constructs a strangely binary imaginary of extremist and moderate "Middle Easterners" while simultaneously projecting a weirdly post-racist America. In particular, the series articulates very forcefully an ongoing scenario of instantaneous decision-making, under dire impending menace to public safety, which serves to insulate the U.S. counter-terrorist philosophy and practice from an urgently needed rigorous public critique.

INTRODUCTION: VIOLENCE AGAINST CIVILIANS, PAST AND PRESENT

[O]ne of the immanent possibilities of the state's monopoly of violence is the transgression of those very legal frameworks which in theory act to limit its arbitrariness. It is at this point that we talk of states becoming terroristic, or of employing unacceptable techniques (such as torture) whose use they themselves would wish to deny, dissimulate or euphemize (Schlesinger, 1991, p. 9).

DOI: 10.4018/978-1-4666-5776-2.ch005

The main empirical focus of this chapter is the political discourse of the Fox TV series *24* (2001-2010).[1] To understand its influence on U.S. culture, however, we need to set it in a much larger comparative and indeed historical, political, and cultural context (Downing, 2007). To do so, this chapter first provides a comparative overview of violence against civilians in war, terrorist events, and torture. Comparisons are drawn between the United States since the terrorist events of September 11, 2001, Britain during the civil war in Northern Ireland 1969-2000, and France during and since the Algerian armed liberation struggle of 1954-1962. This exploration covers the general issues involved and includes a summary of existing research on British and French media representations of political violence. These specific analyses are explored to demonstrate the prevalence of violence against civilians in a historical context.

However, while terrorism has become an emerging concern among governments and civilians alike, the deliberate infliction of death and mutilation on *non*-combatants—as war policy—is hardly new to human history. For instance, think: World War II and its precursors—the British onslaught on Kurdish and Arab villages in Iraq in 1920 (Glancey, 2003, April 19), the 1931 Japanese military invasion of China (You-Li, 1993), the Italian assault on Ethiopia, Gernika of 1935 (Baratieri, 2010; Steer, 2012)—put an end to the intra-European code in practice, although the old public rhetoric persists to this very day in terminology such as "smart bombs" and "minimum collateral damage." That rhetoric's continued use pays tribute in some measure to the persistent reluctance of most humans to contemplate the savagery of war, for if that were not so, these soothingly hypocritical obfuscations would not need to be deployed. In particular, the old soldier-to-soldier battles evaporated with the saturation ("carpet") bombing of Hamburg in July 1943, of Dresden in August 1944, and of some 60 other German cities, amounting to 20% of the total residential area of the country and killing 300,000 civilians (Beck, 1986). This was followed by the saturation bombing of Tokyo and other Japanese cities in March 1945 (resulting in some 170,000 deaths), which only then culminated in the nuclear attacks on Hiroshima and Nagasaki (Grayling, 2006).

The predominance of the Air Force and of bombing from a safe distance in U.S. military strategy dates from that period (Sherry, 1987), a strategy which the South East Asian War (1965-1975), the Iraq and Afghanistan Wars, and the Bush Administration's threats against Iran, demonstrated to be still paramount. A frequently cited study by Sivard (1991) suggests that over the 20th century the civilian percentage of wartime deaths rose from 5% in World War I to over 50% in World War II, to around 90% by 1990. Thus, the gigantic 15,000-pound "daisy-cutter" bombs deployed in Afghanistan—the total heartlessness of this mocking military term is truly evocative of the hypocrisy of America's democratic global mission—had a pristine pedigree. The cluster bombs so beloved of the U.S. military high command both multiply immediate civilian casualties and scatter the equivalent of landmines and booby-traps that will be set off by casual contact later (Wiseman, 2003, December 16), especially when projected from remote ground-based missile-launchers. Depleted uranium bomb casings have their own long-term civilian impact, yet to be fully assessed by independent scientists.

Yet, if one reduces direct U.S. army casualties by bombing at a distance, you reduce domestic opposition to war, especially since the Vietnam disaster. The high proportion of Black and Latino soldiers in the U.S. Army also muffles public reaction to their deaths and mutilation, not in the abstract, but in the sense of their having close social connections to the White majority. The more that war opposition gets tamped down, the freer across the planet is the hand left to the transnational military-industrial complex, with the United States as its principal policeman.

The rhetoric for public consumption on casualties also sharply varies, depending on whether it refers to the home team or the away team. Many Americans likely know that approximately 2,400 were killed in the Pearl Harbor attack, that 58,000 U.S. troops were killed in the South East Asian war, and that approximately 3,000 were killed in the 9/11 attacks. Yet far fewer have an idea even to the nearest million of the numbers of Japanese or Vietnamese civilians killed in World War II or in the U.S. war in South East Asia, and as a matter of Bush Administration policy, no numbers are offered, except in individual news stories, of Iraqis (Ramadani, 2004) or Afghanis killed by U.S. forces since 9/11. If the figures of Iraqi, Vietnamese, Korean, or Japanese civilian deaths had been as consistently rehearsed in U.S. news media as the losses suffered by Americans, this ignorance would arguably have been a great deal less. When, in a 1995 Smithsonian Institute exhibit on the nuclear attacks on Japan this silence looked like being ruptured, even that momentary breach was ferociously sutured over—a full 50 years afterwards (Bird & Lifschultz, 1998).

On occasions when silence does break, when it is impossible any longer to deny the scale of annihilation achieved or torture practiced, then the default—and passionate—response has generally been to claim that what was done was the lesser of two evils. Bombed Vietnamese hamlets were better than Communist ones, a flattened Hiroshima and Nagasaki were better than pursuing a long-drawn-out war, and unless the United States wished to be seen as a permanent soft target, a vast crowd of Arabs and assorted Muslims definitely had to be seen to have helped to pay for 9/11 with their own lives—predominantly their children's lives, in practice.

This defense would be much more ethically credible if it did not usually have to wait to be dragged out in answer to the evidence of huge slaughter, if it were for example routinely accompanied by a forthright acknowledgment of the monumental levels of suffering entailed on the other side. "Shock and awe" in Baghdad was not a firework display, as U.S. media exultantly portrayed it. It communicated what the U.S. military is prepared to do to civilians.

CIVILIAN WAR CASUALTIES VS. TERRORISM CASUALTIES

Yet after 9/11, "terrorism"—meaning *non*-state violence against civilians—has become The Pre-Eminent Evil (this capitalization is not meant to imply endorsing it). It has also become the default rationale around the world among regimes glad to find a U.S.-supported justification for their own repression of civilians (e.g., Russian forces in Chechnya). "Terrorism's" conspicuous utility lies in its open-endedness. No state can be negotiated with to end this war, no one can finally assert with total confidence that there are no terrorists left. Consequently, it is marvelously pliable, an infinite resource from which to rationalize not only war, but extensive political surveillance, the abrogation of citizens' legal protections, secret trials, and politicized violence: torture, subhuman jail conditions, assassination squads, and renditions. Piece by piece, perhaps, not all at once on U.S. soil.

However, in the longer term, as Danner (2004) has forthrightly argued, neither Abu Ghraib, nor Guantánamo, nor the Pakistani or Egyptian jails to which the U.S. government transported terrorism suspects to be tortured in its "extraordinary rendition" programs, *need* be external to the United States even though in this transitional period their location was precisely selected so as to be beyond the jurisdiction of U.S. courts and protections (Golden, 2004; Golden & Van Natta, 2004). If this logic of "anti-terrorism" becomes hegemonic and is cumulatively endorsed by U.S. courts and major media, there will be seen to be no long-term reason to "keep the gloves on" or defend the general public's civil liberties inside the United States.

Thus, *non*-state terrorist attacks on civilians have become quite successfully defined as the ultimate public horror, which automatically justifies new forms of *state* repression and violence (against civilians). The fascistoid military government of Argentina in the period 1976-1983, covertly supported by the U.S. administration in 1976, similarly justified its systematic arbitrary arrests, torture, and physical disappearance of some 30,000 citizens, mostly labor union leaders, teachers and psychiatrists, in the name of a war against terrorism. In reality, the statistics clearly demonstrate that deaths and injuries from leftist guerrilla attacks in the years immediately preceding the junta's 1976 coup d'état were comparatively puny in number (García, 1995). Argentina's policy was influenced by French government policy on the Algerian revolution and by the Nazis' and Spanish dictator Franco's disappearance policies. It was more or less on the same scale as the CIA's Phoenix Program implemented in southern Vietnam a little earlier, in 1967 (Valentine, 2000), which targeted the civilian infrastructure of the National Liberation Front. In the process it eliminated perhaps 40,000 Vietnamese, systematically using torture as well as assassination (McCoy, 2006).

In the United States in the aftermath of 9/11 and during the very muted public debate about interrogation tactics in Afghanistan and Guantánamo, voices were raised arguing that in times of crisis civil protections might indeed have to be put on hold. Prominent among these was Allan Dershowitz, the energetically self-publicizing Harvard University, and trial, lawyer. His argument was, in line with the publication of the Aussaresses memoir, that the Eighth Amendment to the U.S. Constitution, outlawing "cruel and unusual punishment," might be protected if specific warrants to torture were issued in cases of extreme threat to national security. Mr. Dershowitz's thirst for the public spotlight was one thing, but his injection of this logic into public debate certainly did nothing to protect the prisoners in Guantánamo, Abu Ghraib, and elsewhere, who overwhelmingly had only their own blood on their hands, put there by their captors. In a public, many of whose members were complacent with any revenge for 9/11, his intervention gave extra fuel to the Bush Administration's claim that it was resolutely attacking the roots of terrorism.

In a moment we will revisit the logic of this anti-terrorism strategy through a discussion of Chomsky and Herman's construct of "wholesale" and "retail" terrorism, but first let us review how the U.S. government's "anti-terrorist" repression strategy has had companions-in-arms over the years, both Britain and France (notwithstanding the frenzied fraternal-imperialist brouhaha about the Iraq War between the U.S. and French administrations). Subsequently, we will compare media coverage of terrorism between these three nations.

NORTHERN IRELAND AND ALGERIA: THE UNITED STATES IS NOT AN ISOLATE

The story is definitely not just an American one (not that any cause for celebration or relief are to be inferred). We need to recognize how the British regime in Northern Ireland since 1969 and the French regime in Algeria in the period 1954-1962—and since—mirror many of the trends just summarized.

In 2001, retired French general Paul Aussaresses (2001) published a book not only acknowledging that he and the French army had organized the systematic torture of Algerians during the 1954-1962 insurgency, but also vigorously defending the practice. He further insisted that top government ministers at the time, such as Socialist Party leaders Guy Mollet and Interior Minister François Mitterrand (subsequently two-term president), had been fully *au fait* with this; a claim of which we need not feel compelled to be skeptical.

This was hardly news for those Algerians whose family members had been subjected to torture or murdered, or among relatives of the million or more Algerian villagers forcibly herded en masse into concentration camps.[2] Or to the politically informed, left or right, in France. Nonetheless, the defiant acknowledgment of torture by a general himself involved in it, and the subsequent letter of support signed by some 500 past and present French generals, was a classic case of insistent justification of merciless brutality the French establishment had long and systematically denied, despite attempts by French and Algerian individuals and organizations, from the first years of the independence war, to get it acknowledged and stopped. That story is not only a 50-year-old one;

the violent repression that plagued Algeria since 1992 represented, very plausibly, a continuation in new circumstances of the Franco-Algerian political economy of terror.[3] Furthermore, Jean-Marie Le Pen (then leader of the neo-fascist *Front National*), who had been a paratrooper in Algeria, publicly defended his activities as a torturer during that war. The Franco-Algerian past and present are thus intimately conjoined.

The Northern Ireland scenario from 1969 onwards held both parallels and contrasts with the foregoing (Schlesinger, 1991). The numbers killed were far fewer than in Iraq or Algeria, and the patterns of repression and terrorization of populations, whilst evident, were seemingly more restrained. McGuffin (1974) produced the first account of the British army's interrogation methods (e.g., hooding, standing for very long periods of time spread-eagled, subjection to continuous white noise or loud noise, sleep deprivation, beatings, kickings, etc.). In a 1978 ruling, the European Court of Human Rights officially declared these practices not to be torture, but nonetheless to be inhumane, degrading, and contrary to European Union human rights standards.

There was in addition to these practices, however, a sinister program of targeted assassinations, often organized via the British government's Force Research Unit, or the heavily Loyalist northern Ireland police hierarchy, passing the names of alleged Republican terrorists to Loyalist paramilitaries, who would be the ones to do the actual killing. Some 150 individuals may have been disposed of in this way (Murray, 2003). The most notorious case of direct British government executions was the 1988 street liquidation in Gibraltar of three unarmed terrorist *suspects* by a British government counter-terrorist unit (Ruddock, 1996). The overall "shoot-to-kill" policy was long vigorously denied by the government, with one senior police chief investigating the case forced into early retirement and with another having his office torched to destroy his documentation (Ibid). Finally in 2003 the Force Research Unit was officially declared to have been a "rogue" unit (Bamber & Palmer, 2003).

Neither in Algeria, Northern Ireland, or the "Middle East" did the French, British, nor American states simply stomp in. There was an armed insurrection against French colonial rule, designed to bring it to an end, there was a similar insurgency designed to close out British rule in northern Ireland (a majority of deaths were caused by that insurgency) (Sutton, 1994), and the murderous 9/11 attacks did happen. In every case, therefore, the insurgents too generated civilian casualties and routinely defined them as the necessary costs of war. However, in both Algeria, and much later in Afghanistan and Iraq, the devastation within the camp of the poor and dispossessed was out of all proportion to the death-toll for the French and the Americans: ten times higher (one million) for Algerians, and in Iraq approximately 200 times higher than 9/11 (Cole, 2006).

Not that the Iraqis had created 9/11, nor that the U.S. military were the direct agents of this huge carnage in its entirety. However, even within the fake rationales of the Bush Administration for its inroads into Afghanistan and Iraq, the sustained savagery of the reprisals was out of all proportion to the devastations of 9/11, and the architects of the invasion itself *were* direct agents of the ensuing civil war, which accounted for a majority of the fatalities.

Thus emerges a comparable pattern of state behavior across these three nations, involving both torture as a matter of policy, and savagely disproportionate state retaliation for *non*-state political violence.

"DEMOCRATIC" STATE VIOLENCE

This question inevitably leads us to evaluate the argument by Chomsky and Herman (1979) that terrorism comes in two forms, state or "wholesale" violence, and insurgent or "retail" violence.

Their position is unequivocal, that during the Cold War era major Western states, the United States in the lead, perpetrated far more numerous and wholesale acts of terroristic violence than did insurrectionary guerrillas and terrorists. Yet in those states' official and media discourse the designation "terrorist" was entirely reserved for the retail merchants of destruction. The states, in this rhetoric, were acting only, and legitimately, to protect or extend national security, order, and democracy. Chomsky and Herman point by way of refutation to the Indonesian bloodbath of 1966, the Indochina War through 1975, and (in their later writings) Latin America and the Middle East, for proof positive that these rationales were and are a grotesque fiction, an up-ending of the truth.

Schlesinger (1991), despite sharp differences at a series of points with Chomsky and Herman's analyses, sets out to establish fundamentals in his essay quoted from at the beginning of this chapter, and cites Max Weber, in turn citing Leon Trotsky, that a defining characteristic of the modern state is its claim to a *legitimate monopoly* on the means of violence. This is not the only facet of the modern state, but arguably it is its bedrock dimension. Thus, in the discussion of terrorism, the question shifts from its social-ethical to its political-ethical dimension. The argument becomes a pragmatic one about who is politically enabled to be violent, not the absolutist Gandhian or Tolstoian question of whether *anyone* is so entitled.

The Chomsky and Herman argument is hard to dismiss in the face of historically grounded statistics of death and destruction. The Israeli-Palestinian statistics since 2000, with a ratio of six Palestinians killed for every one Israeli (If Americans knew, 2013, May 15) are actually less asymmetrical than a number of other such "wholesale-retail" scenarios. The point is *not* to blot out those horrors for Palestinians and Israelis or soften them, but to mark the even more terrifying savagery that has marked the state's supposedly legitimate use of violence against those within the realm it has defined as its own domain (which, for the U.S. regime *since Jefferson*, has repeatedly meant anywhere it chose on the planet). Unless we are to subscribe to a Hobbesian statolatry, or a kneejerk "America-the-beautiful," we cannot avert our gaze from this.

Schlesinger's argument does not move into this terrain, but simply seeks to complicate the nature of political violence, avoiding the heavily freighted associations of the term "terrorism." But does his, or Chomsky and Herman's position, imply we should regard "retail" political violence—non-state terrorism—as somehow acceptable? In my judgment, only those predisposed to smear any or all of these writers could reasonably answer in the affirmative. On the other hand, as with Herman and Chomsky's rhetorical "jiu-jitsu" with the term "propaganda" (Herman & Chomsky, 1988), their redefinition of non-state terrorism as "retail" risks downplaying it, not just ethically but also politically. Its capacity to be harnessed as a justification for intensifying the state's repressive armory and expanding its targets is a very dangerous dimension to neglect.

There is therefore a triangular issue:

1. The state's privileged and self-legitimated access to the means of violence, at home and abroad, and how it uses them against civilians—particularly how the U.S. regime does so at this point in history;

2. The political violence of *non*-state agents; and

3. The uses of terror and torture by the state against presumed or real agents in the second category.

We now turn to studies of media coverage of these processes, first in Britain and France.

BRITISH AND FRENCH MEDIA COVERAGE OF POLITICAL VIOLENCE

It is impossible to do more than indicate the main lines of research to date, without any pretense that the research literature itself is comprehensive in scope. An important study is by Schlesinger, Murdock, and Elliott (1983), one of the few that seeks to compare, contrast, and relate television news and entertainment formats' representations of terrorism. They note that in the British case there was a time-lag quite often between news coverage and fictional coverage, but that fictional coverage frequently drew upon stories of some months beforehand to lend itself a sense of immediacy, and in so doing often translated the news frame into a dramatic genre. The television show *24* represents an extended illustration of precisely this process.

Most other studies focus just on terrorism and news. Fleury-Villatte (2000) and De Bussière, Méadel, and Ulmann-Mauriat (1999) register, for different periods, passing instances of fictional entertainment, but their emphasis is fundamentally on news, news magazines, and documentaries. Elsewhere, Schlesinger (1987) investigates in some detail the often tense relationship between the TV news channels and the British government over coverage of Northern Ireland in the period up to 1986, concentrating on the mostly successful tactics used by successive administrations to intimidate untrammeled reporting of the crisis.

Taken together, the studies by De Bussière, Méadel, and Ulmann-Mauriat (1999) and Fleury-Villatte (2000), covering respectively 1954-1962 and 1962-1992, come closest to a connected narrative evaluating a variety of media, but always with a predominant concentration on news and journalism. This tends to lead to a restricted focus not just on "what was missed out," including torture, but also the political violence experienced by the *pieds-noirs*[4], the *harkis*[5] and anti-war demonstrators.[6]

The very significant power of dramatic representation is not addressed in these studies. However, Hennebelle, Berrah, and Stora (1997) focus on cinematic portrayals. Six of these were banned by the French government. Stora (2007) engages with the history of the powerful Italian/Algerian feature film *Battle of Algiers* (1966), shot in graphic documentary style. This film was kept from French cinemas for a number of years, not by the government, but due to threats against movie theatres from anti-independence and veterans' groups. It was first shown on a French TV channel in 2004. Thus, part of the French story of media coverage of state terrorism and torture during and since the Algerian independence war, is movie censorship from below as well as from above.

At the same time, the Fleury-Villatte (2000) study uncovers the fascinating extent to which masses of film footage rejected out of hand at the time by news editors had nonetheless been shot *and* subsequently archived. This clearly reflected the division of labor and very often of viewpoints between journalists in the field and their safely ensconced superiors. Fleury-Villatte includes as an appendix a lengthy interview with Pierre Abramovici, producer of a documentary on the fascistic Secret Armed Organization (Organisation Armée Secrète, OAS), which set off a terrifying series of anti-civilian bombs and assassinations in 1961-1962, in the hope of compelling the French government to hang on to Algeria. His account of the material he uncovered in the process, that gave the lie to continuing regime propaganda, is illuminating.

British media coverage of Northern Ireland is summarized much more briefly (Downing & Husband, 1995). For some 45 years following the initial foundation of the Protestant-dominated state-ling/"province" in 1920, British media pursued a policy of news neglect, malign, or otherwise. For most intents and purposes, the Six Counties separated from the rest of Ireland were not on the British media radar. With the rise of the U.S. civil rights movement, and a corresponding student-led movement in Northern Ireland in 1967-1969, British media briefly swung into focus and even a strong measure of support for the students. However, with the resurgence of an armed separatist nationalist movement from 1969 onwards, British broadcast media increasingly operated within the general parameters of government policy.

When they did not, all hell broke loose at government level. It was short of direct soviet-type controls, but nonetheless sufficient to dissuade all but the most trenchant of journalists and editors from addressing Northern Ireland issues in depth and with honesty (e.g., Curtis, 1984; Schlesinger, 1987).

Even so there was a period early in the Troubles during which contradictory tendencies expressed themselves. Bloody Sunday 1971, when British troops opened fire on a peaceful and unarmed Catholic demonstration in Derry, the second city of Northern Ireland, killing approximately 13 and wounding others, was telecast that Sunday in considerable detail, as had been the violent attack on an unarmed march some 18 months before. The British state immediately whitewashed the murderous attack, only recanting its subterfuges approximately 30 years later. Yet the visual image of the dead and wounded at the rally was not one that would smoothly dissipate.

To summarize: there is no single continuing study of all facets of media representation of political violence in either nation. Nonetheless, the state's attempts to shape and censor terrorism news coverage are self-evident. Equally evident are sustained attempts by some media professionals to function independently of the state's dictates and pressures. The case of *24*, however, represented a very sustained fictional echo of news coverage of Bush Administration policies to combat terrorism, and a dramatic endorsement of them. It offered only the rarest signs of dissent, portraying resistance in the Cabinet to a declaration of martial law (Series Five), or to setting up Arab-American internment camps (Series Six).

It illustrated well what Andersen (2006) refers to as "militainment"—the interpenetration of the military and entertainment establishments, which in an era of mostly sagging journalistic standards may come to figure as the U.S. public's chief form of access to current events.

24 AS A CASE-STUDY IN MEDIA REPRESENTATION OF "TERRORISM"

Originally put into development in 2000, and first heralded in the trade press in spring 2001, *24* was evidently not sparked by 9/11, although those events and their aftermath clearly influenced the script's formation at points thereafter—and, inevitably, the U.S. and global television audiences' appropriations of the series. Launched in November 2001, it was in due course successfully nominated for numerous Emmy's and Golden Globes, and sold very widely around the world (Littleton, 2002; Schneider, 2002; The Hollywood Reporter, 2002). At the height of its popularity in early 200s, *24* regularly attracted 10-15 million viewers and subsequently released DVD versions of each series on the market (Stetler, 2013).

The show aired its much-anticipated finale after eight seasons in 2010, however, the Fox network announced in the spring of 2013 that it would be launched a 12-episode series in May 2014. While the show's original format—a story that plays out in real time over a 24-hour period—will remain, the producers chose to skip and condense some hours to reduce the show to a 12-hour format. The new version will also entail a subtitle, *24: Live Another Day*, and is said to be picking up the plot from where the series left off (Ibid). Fans of *24* spanned beyond American borders, attracting global audiences due to its gripping plotlines related to counterterrorism drama in the United States. However, it is suggested that the depiction of these themes are, in many ways, an illustration of Andersen's (2006) thesis of "militainment."

Aside from the first episode of the second series, which was run without commercials as a loss-leader, it lent itself to easy gibes from the Left, in that the real running time minus ads was closer to 42 minutes than 60. Even nuclear crises, it seemed, would respectfully wait for commercials to air before daring to proceed further. In addition to this, the series writers and producers were committed to the "surprise twist," which meant that each episode worked very hard to generate a mass of unexpected cliffhangers.

The fact that there were always at least three simultaneous plots running kept this momentum busy for the most part:

1. Terrorist attacks on a presidential candidate, then president (Series One-Three), then assassinated by order of his successor (beginning of Series Five);
2. Terrorist attacks on the intimate associates of the chief counter-terrorism operative, the series hero; and
3. Convoluted machinations inside the various presidents' own teams and the counter-terrorism organization, both of them penetrated to various degrees by "the bad guys" (though neither we nor "the good guys" know initially whom to trust).

The few individuals in whom, pretty well, the audience was invited to place its unquestioning trust were David Palmer the presidential candidate/president/ex-president, his brother Wayne (president in Series Six), the chief counter-terrorism operative Jack Bauer, his girlfriend in Series Four-Six, and a very small scatter of lesser government and counter-terrorism officials. Even these latter, though never suborned, were wont to be distracted from counter-terrorism by purely personal and emotional dramas.

Series 1 mostly revolved around the frantic attempts of Jack Bauer (Kiefer Sutherland) to protect from terrorist attacks and kidnappers David Palmer, the presidential candidate (Dennis

Haysbert), and his own wife and teenage daughter. The terrorists seized Bauer's wife and daughter as hostages to neutralize Bauer's consummate protection skills for the president. Series Two revolved around a threat to detonate a nuclear device in Los Angeles, and a plot to unseat David Palmer, now president, from office. Bauer's daughter found herself once more simultaneously in a series of calamities which constantly threatened to distract Bauer from his prime task, but he manfully continued to juggle both responsibilities successfully, a model to us all of how to combine serious parenting with counter-terrorist dedication. Parallel with Bauer's family trials went the vivid tensions in the president's own family, centered principally around his ruthless and power-obsessed wife, Sherry Palmer, a Lady MacBeth/Hillary Clinton character played to the hilt by Penny Johnson Jerald.

Series Three had Jack Bauer struggling to defeat a conspiracy to unleash a weaponized virus, which initially appeared to involve Mexican drug cartel barons, but was actually led by a disillusioned British ex-operative, Stephen Saunders. In Series Four, Bauer combatted terrorists led by a certain Marwan Habib, who was trying to cause nuclear power plant meltdowns all over the United States, and succeeded in one case. They shot down Air Force One, very seriously wounding the U.S. president on board, and finally launched a nuclear missile at Los Angeles. In the course of these events, Bauer was involved in a firefight inside the Chinese Embassy in Washington, DC in which a senior Chinese official accidentally got shot dead by his own embassy guards. They blamed Bauer.

Series Five saw Bauer once again trying to stop terrorist nerve gas attacks (two actually take place, one in a shopping mall, the other in a hospital). It eventually emerges that the plot originated with the new U.S. president, and that Bauer's own brother, not previously seen in the series, was master-minding the operation, intent on protecting U.S. oil interests in Central Asia.

At the series end, the plot defeated, a Chinese commando squad seized Jack in retaliation for his role in the embassy attack (Series Four) and to extract information from him.

In Series Six, bearded, exhausted and virtually speechless after 20 months of unsuccessful Chinese interrogation, he had just been released in order to deal with terrorists led by a certain Abu Fayed, but manipulated by an ultra-nationalist Russian general. As the series commenced, these charmers had been setting off bombs in U.S. cities for 11 weeks, with 900 fatalities. They also had possession of five "suitcase" nuclear bombs, one of which they detonated 20 miles north of Los Angeles. They eventually were disposed of, but the Chinese and Russian governments were far from being out of the picture, since Chinese operatives had accessed a crucial circuit board from one of the "suitcase" bombs, which could give them access to Russian defense codes, and the Russian government threatened a military attack unless it was restored to them.

The series' links, like the overall links of News Corp.'s Fox television channel, were very close indeed to the Bush White House, and to the Bush Administration's vitriolically Rightist media spokespeople, such as radio and television commentator Rush Limbaugh. On June 23, 2006, a Heritage Foundation press conference celebrated the series, with lead speakers being Michael Chertoff, Secretary of Homeland Security, and Limbaugh, who took pains to announce that Vice-President Cheney and then-Defense Secretary Donald Rumsfeld were "huge" fans. Both speakers lavishly praised the show. One of its two producers, Robert Cochran was present to adorn the occasion. Its executive producer, Joel Surnow, was profiled in *The New Yorker* (Mayer, 2007). A close friend of Limbaugh's, Surnow is an energetic and very well-placed media activist for the political Right, who "would like to counter the prevailing image of Senator Joseph McCarthy as a demagogue and a liar" (Mayer, 2007, p. 80).

The three related facets of *24* that I shall examine are its representations of ethnicity; of the "soul" of terrorism; and of torture.

Ethnicity

Ethnicity's relevance in the series' narrative to broader social narratives—quite often leaching into religion when the series features characters from the "Middle East"—lies in the political categorization of citizens in periods of real or declared national security crises. In one way or another, this crisis-categorization process has exceptionally deep roots in U.S. historical culture (Downing, 2007). "Racial" profiling since 9/11 officially focused on people of a supposedly "Middle Eastern" appearance (Akram & Karmely, 2005), although in practice in the United States, Britain, and France the prime targets for special searches and stop and search procedures were people of color in general.

Thus, the situation proved ambivalent, with traditionally salient racist categories, defining African Americans, Latinos, and Pacific Asians as both inferior and threatening, jostling for position within the United States with newer ones marking out Arabs, "Middle Easterners," and Muslims as the new prime enemy. These Orientalist frames had been injected with new life during the 1980-1981 U.S. Embassy hostage episode in Teheran, and kept on the simmer through 9/11 and since by routinely anti-Palestinian coverage of the Israeli occupation. In the United States the ideological premise was that in the face of terrorism, and with the claimed total success of the Black civil rights movement, the nation stood united and cohesive, immune to its traditional divisions. *24* articulated this premise incessantly.

In *24* Arabs, "Middle Easterners" and Muslims—the contemporary U.S. prime Other—were systematically binarized into the virtuous and the hideous (Alsultany, 2012). Not unlike the "good Indian"/"vicious Indian" binary in the Hollywood Western.

For example, an imam of one U.S. mosque was shown to be fully cooperative and to find terrorism totally repugnant (Series Two). In the same series another Arab, initially entirely distrusted by Bauer and his associates, ends up seriously injured by terrorists and then killed by street thugs precisely because he is a "Middle Easterner." However, despite the fact that if only they were not so stupid, thuggish, and blinded by their prejudices, he is the one person at that point who has the necessary information to stop the nuclear device being detonated which will inexorably also affect them. In Series Six, the second in command at the counter-terrorism office is an Arab American woman; and a Muslim rights organization leader is ready to be wrongly incarcerated in order to glean information from suspected terrorists in the same detention center, telling his civil rights lawyer girlfriend "Stop being a lawyer for one damned *minute*!"

Another Series Two character, not defined explicitly as Iranian, but with the first name Reza, is scripted initially to appear suspicious, and the potentially sinister fiancé of a naïve White American girl, who does not appear to have a clue what she is getting into. The ultimate plot twist, however, is that she herself is the trained and merciless terrorist who hesitates only a brief second before shooting dead, on her wedding day, both her fiancé and a Black FBI agent. We shall come back to her, but her fiancé turns out to be a tragic and good-hearted victim, not in the least sinister after all. The script here deliberately played with, and against, common expectations in the U.S. public. Yet in Series Six, a well-meaning but tragically naïve White family rushes to protect their neighbor's teen son Ahmed from another neighbor's retaliation for the bomb outrages, only shortly afterwards to find him threatening to kill them if they do not help him deliver a nuclear switch to the terrorists.

Thus in many cases the villains are indeed Arabs (lead villains include Syed Ali in Series Two, Habib Marwan in Series Four, Abu Fayed in Series Six), or Iranians (Navi Araz in Series Four), though never explicitly distinguished from Arabs except for those who know Persian names. Thus, the TV series reproduces a conventional news media bifurcation of "extremist" vs. "moderate" Muslim/Arab, a splendidly flattening rhetorical exercise pretending to diversity (does not the very adjective "moderate" imply that it would really be preferable, cleaner, not to be a Muslim at all?).

In Series One, the primary terrorists are Serbs, not Arabs, obviously echoing the systematic demonization of all Serbs that took place during the monumental civil strife in former Yugoslavia in the years leading up to the development of this drama. They are seeking revenge on the presidential candidate and on Jack Bauer, because Bauer had been the lead hitman in an undercover targeted assassination of a Serb terrorist, green lighted by presidential candidate Palmer when he had been Senate Intelligence Committee chair. The hit, it emerged, had liquidated several of the terrorist's family members, but not him or his younger brother. However, as the saga continues, it also emerges that—as with some other terrorist activist groups we see in action during the series—they are in turn being manipulated behind the scenes by individuals who will use them to achieve their evil ends, but will equally discard them without a backward glance. Thus, all the Serb terrorists are eventually killed at the close of Series One, but it is made explicit that there are still more deadly—and domestic American—forces at work, whose agenda to dispose of President Palmer remains to be activated. In Series Five, a leading terrorist is heavily implied to be a Chechen, Vladimir Bierko (unaccountably sporting a British accent).

The series sometimes suggests that Arabs and Muslims are liable to be used as a smokescreen by people with genuinely terroristic designs. In Series Six, the Arab terrorists are manipulated by an ultra-nationalist Russian general who despises them and "the West" equally and hopes to get both "sides" to destroy each other. Indeed, some of the most dangerous and ruthless people in the series are not only White (Saunders in Series Three, Henderson in Series Five), but also include ranking members of the Los Angeles counter-terrorism unit, and of successive presidents' cabinets, including the president himself in Series Five (who looks and sounds remarkably like Richard Nixon).

There is no reference at any point to White racism: even at moments of the highest tension, people disagree with each other, scream at each other, plan to dispose of each other, but with never the whisker of a racist slur or attitude. The urban street-scum in the earlier phase of the series who intermittently erupted into the action to complicate it further, were all White. There are two Black U.S. presidents, yet not even their direst foes trouble to allude to their blackness. The Black Chief of Staff of the counter-terrorism unit, prominent in Series Four and Five, is a paragon of dedication, so much so that when Bauer is forced to shoot him in Series Six, the impregnable Jack permits himself the rare emotional self-indulgence of vomiting. The only dangerous and ruthless Black character is the first President Palmer's wife, but no one makes derogatory reference to her Blackness. This clearly posits a "post-racist" scenario, where White racism has vanished.

Overall, the series draws upon current national stereotypes aplenty, especially those enshrined in ongoing news media stories—Mexican drug barons, Serb terrorists, Chechen and Russian terrorists, Chinese secret agents, as well as Arab and Iranian terrorists. It produces an absurdly binarized definition of U.S. inhabitants of "Middle Eastern" origin. Further, it projects a fantastic, denialist remove from the ongoing realities of contemporary U.S. racism. There is plenty in *24* to help inculcate and intensify fear in the U.S. public. There is zero to acknowledge the reality of "racial" profiling on the multiple levels it is practiced, or to block the de-humanization of "Middle Easterners" into stick figures labeled okay or vicious.

The "Soul" of Terrorism

There are terrorists aplenty in these series, and they include some of "us," not least the character of Nina, with whom at the beginning of Series One, Jack Bauer has just concluded an affair, but who is still his chief assistant. Apparently 120% loyal to him and to his desperate attempts to protect his estranged wife and daughter, she then turns out at the close of Series One to have been scheming throughout to have the presidential candidate assassinated—but not for the Serbian terrorists. Sherry Palmer, the President's wife, is in cahoots with a high-level group threatening to detonate the nuclear device in Los Angeles. In Series Five, even the U.S. president is organizing a terroristic conspiracy, albeit with the goal of securing Central Asian oil reserves to sustain the U.S. economy. Terrorists-Я-Us! This complicates *24* a little as regards stock tropes of Muslims, Arabs, and "Middle Easterners," and that is in its favor. Women, too, have equal opportunity to be terrorists with men, though in terms of some patriarchal tropes, that makes the situation more than doubly dangerous and especially evil.

At the same time, the representation of one terrorist in Series Two has a particular fascination. She is Marie Warner, younger sister of Kate Warner and fiancée of the initially suspicious-looking Reza. Both sisters' father does contract research work for the CIA. Both sisters speak Arabic, Marie seemingly well, and Kate more haltingly. Whereas the Serb terrorists in Series One had an explicit and comprehensible agenda, to avenge the accidental slaughter of their family by Bauer's assassination squad on then-Senator Palmer's orders, Marie Warner was different. She had seemingly imbibed a Jihadist netherworld perfectly clear to her, but utterly opaque to reasoning or feeling humans. Prepared virtually without emotion to kill her fiancé on their wedding day, to see her father jailed and interrogated on suspicion of bankrolling terrorists, and even to threaten to shoot her own sister (whom we have seen standing by her through thick and thin), her character becomes entirely enigmatic. All the more so because of her entirely credible spoiled and narcissistic character-acting in the earlier part of Series Two, where political logic plays no apparent role whatsoever in her demeanor.

Marie Warner is, not least, prepared to see the nuclear device detonated in Los Angeles because ultimately the devastation will serve many more people than those killed, maimed and bereaved, as she explains to her incredulous sister at a climactic moment. The conversation is the closest *24* takes us to understanding what makes the traitor-terrorist tick. She tells her sister their father works for the CIA. "So what?" replies her sister. "So *what*? Do you have any idea of what suffering they cause around the world?," retorts Marie. "[But] . . . you don't want all those innocent people to die?," Kate says to her disbelievingly, and as Marie responds by threatening to shoot her, Kate tells her she does not believe she will shoot her. Marie: "I will. Because this is more important than your life. Or my life." And when herself shot a moment later in the shoulder by Bauer, and subsequently interrogated by him, she snarls "Nobody is innocent in this country!"

In the final episode of Series Two we see her chained in a perspex holding cage, with her father desperately trying to communicate with her through the perspex, to hear from her some explanation that can comfort him. She is entirely silent, almost autistic-seeming, bathed in bright light that makes her bleached hair wispy and renders her eyes in shadow and hence entirely opaque. Her whitened face is expression-less, a frozen mask, sharply contrasting with the grieved, shocked and horrified faces of her father and sister. The background music is quiet but eerie, a kind of aural representation of a strange and deeply terrifying alienation psychosis. Marie calls Kate back for a moment as she and her father are leaving, a brief little smile of vicious triumph crosses

her face, and she says to Kate: "You think you'll be safe out there? You won't be."

This scene is visually and aurally definitive. The domestically reared terrorist is framed in ways quite similar to the depiction of American communists in McCarthy era Hollywood movies: completely devoid of human emotion, family warmth, or estimable values, and prepared to sacrifice many millions for their horrific cause. These scenes and their accompanying dialogue pinpoint Marie as the ultimate alien, resonating with Osama bin Laden's ideology of collective guilt, yet as "white-bread" as they come. This scenario connects to Bauer and President Palmer's terroristic torture actions, justified in the interests of saving multiple lives, but in *24*'s narrative *these servants of the State* are the retail terrorists, and *Marie* is the wholesale terrorist.

Terrorists and thugs who capture Bauer and members of his family are shown to be totally devoid of human feelings, killer-coyotes at best, sadistic monsters at worst. Bauer himself is injected with a heart-stopping substance to get him to talk (Series Two); terrorist Navi Araz shoots his brother without emotion, and is only by chance stopped from shooting his own teenage son (Series Four). Those trying to activate weapons of mass destruction only think in terms of vast casualties, some of them gloatingly. We know they are guilty up front, so their moral entitlement not to be tortured is narratively zero.

The foreign wholesale terrorists in many cases are acting out of absolute rage at the United States, and cannot be reasoned with. Their ambition is to see American streets "flowing with blood" (Series Six), to strike at "financial centers, transportation hubs, population centers" (Series Five). In the case of the "insider" terrorists, their motivations vary, from fury at having been mistreated as former counter-intelligence operatives (i.e., Saunders, Henderson), to politically highly-placed individuals (patriots-gone-bad) trying to sway the course of American policy rather than—as they see it—watch the United States be destroyed by wrong-headed policies. Thus, in Series Six Deputy Chief of Staff Reed Pollock tries to assassinate his President and a repentant terrorist leader, in order to stop both the ex-terrorist from broadcasting officially to the U.S. public, and to pin the President's murder on him.

Torture

This plays a very major role throughout the series, clearly pivoting upon the "Dershowitz dilemma." It also offers sadistic pleasures to viewers, with Bauer multiply tortured, smoke rising from his skin as he screams in pain (Series Two); with Bauer's shoulder opened up and assaulted at its neural ganglion by a terrorist, and with another counter-terrorism operative assaulted repeatedly with an electric drill (Series Six). We watch several times a terrorist's body arc in agony under officially sponsored torture (Series Five). We also watch in unhappy or happy ghoulish fascination as staff of the counter-terrorism unit choke, their bodies thrash helplessly, and they die, through exposure to nerve gas (Series 4). As Sontag observed, "It seems that the appetite for pictures showing bodies in pain is as keen, almost, as the desire for ones that show bodies naked" (2003, p. 41).

Two of the series' unequivocal heroes themselves engage in torture for noble ends (Andersen, 2006). Bauer is shown denying pain-medication and any medical assistance to a terrorist he has just shot in the shoulder, to try to compel her quickly to talk (Series Two), and in Series Five shooting a terrorist's wife in the leg and threatening to put a second bullet in her kneecap to force her husband to talk. President Palmer is shown ordering electro-shock to get a member of his own Cabinet to yield information about his co-plotters in planning the threatened detonation of a nuclear device in Los Angeles.

Central to the narrative of *24* are a series of highly time-sensitive situations, almost every one being of supreme urgency, leaving hardly any time to consider alternatives, and requiring drastic defensive action. "There's no *time* for that!" is a frequently repeated line. Perhaps the limit was reached in Series Three when Bauer amputates someone's arm in order to block the spread of a deadly virus to the population at large. Each segment of each program starts and closes with a ticking clock, showing seconds as well as hours and minutes. The use of two, three, and four split screens at the beginning and at commercial breaks through each episode, showing characters in each of the sub-plots, intensifies the sense of pace and urgency. Cell phones are everywhere and enable extreme rapidity of action—the series is an ongoing commercial for the merits of extensive National Security Agency surveillance. Ford SUVs reliably and swiftly—product placement in full gear—switch the players from one site to another. In the midst of all the mayhem, however, the worst expletive ever heard in the series is "Dammit!," a remarkable acknowledgment of U.S. TV audiences' sensitivity to cursing as contrasted with the series producers' insensitivity to torture.

Prime virtues implicitly extolled in these situations are decisiveness, the readiness to opt for the least bad outcome, *and the moral courage to swallow one's own moral scruples*. Both Jack Bauer and David Palmer exhibit these qualities, including the last, whereas by contrast many of those around them have no moral scruples to swallow. We are pitchforked into situation after situation in which we have to trust Bauer and Palmer's essential goodness and moral probity, and indeed must hope that their application of torture *will do the trick in time*. We end up invited to trust authority to deploy pain, though not in the abstract, only via the characters we have come to screen-know rather well and in whom we therefore have confidence. The targeted assassinations of Serb terrorists, which are the prior backdrop for much of Series One, are presented passingly, a bread-and-butter daily matter, without any hint that state power was being illegitimately deployed for overseas murder (the charge laid against Serbian president Milošević during the Bosnian civil war).

As a logical-ethical proposition, viewers may even find themselves corralled into subscribing to the narrative's ethical priorities. But as always, it is essential to stand back and ask ourselves in how many cases, were we permitted to issue an opinion in the first place, would the shadowy figures in the world's counter-terrorist units be likely to pursue this hierarchy of values rather than others? And without seizing upon the innocent, as in Guantánamo, to prove they are hard at work solving the case? Particularly with the evidence of what we do know of their history around the world, why would we ever trust their values or judgment once they have virtually untrammeled power?

To fully understand *24*'s narrative, however, requires more than a post-9/11 perspective. Profoundly enshrined in U.S. historical culture and nationalist imagery is the visual trope of encirclement by barbaric enemies, of being lethally imperiled (Downing, 2007). This frame has been sedimented but also watered for at least four centuries, and in that sense 9/11 and the Bush Administration's responses constitute only the latest chapter in an ongoing imperialist nationalism born of fear, born of the manipulation of fear, and born of the experience of suffering retaliation for prior violence. There is still more involved at present in terms of the political economy of oil and other mineral deposits, in terms of Islamicist millenarianism, and still other factors, but this nationalist lens is crucial within the force field we inhabit.

CONCLUSION

The three nations discussed here have many more nuances and contradictions than it have been possible to engage with in this short space. So too in certain respects do their discourses and practices of politically motivated violence. So also have been their media representations over time, whether in news or fiction.

Nonetheless, there are certain key resonances. There is the arrogation of the term "terrorist" to cover only *non*-state political violence, plus its framing as unacceptable and therefore as justifying state repressive violence against non-combatants. There is the almost universal readiness to use civilian targets as legitimate while simultaneously lamenting that accidents are inevitable. There was in Britain and France for long the denial of the state's torture practices, while in the United States they have in recent years been justified by the White House (while jesuitically denying they can be described as torture), and legitimated, perhaps for many, via *24*. Perhaps "legitimated" may put it too strongly, and it would be more accurate to conceptualize the process as both the expansion of the U.S. and global public's threshold of tolerance and our fascination with watching succulent violence.

Media, which challenge these positions, or at least challenge their application to the given case, are rather rare. In the United States, *The New York Review of Books*, in France *Le Monde Diplomatique*, and in Britain *The Independent* and *The Guardian*, have been the most significant established media organs to operate as if they were actually independent of government on these issues. Otherwise, only radical small-scale media and Internet networks have tried to introduce some light into a darkening public sphere. Much was hoped for with the installation of the Obama administration, but its celebration of ongoing drone attacks in Pakistan and Afghanistan largely mirrored the dominance of the U.S. Air Force and its never-ending trumpeting of bombing as the heart of U.S. foreign policy. So much for "soft power"…

…police and the OAS needs no further comment. This episode has been the subject of numerous publications and demonstrations in recent years, but once again has not benefited from any official investigation to the time of writing.

REFERENCES

Akram, S. M., & Karmely, M. (2005). Immigration and constitutional consequences of post-9/11 policies involving Arabs and Muslims in the United States: Is alienage a distinction without a difference? *University of California Davis Law Review*, *38*(3), 609–700.

Alsultany, E. (2012). *Arabs and Muslims in the media: Race and representation after 9/11*. New York: New York University Press.

Andersen, R. (2006). *A century of media, a century of war*. New York: Peter Lang Publishers.

Aussaresses, P. (2001). *Services spéciaux Algérie 1955-1957*. Paris: Perrin.

Bamber, D., & Palmer, A. (2003, March 31). UK forces aided Ulster loyalists. *The Age*. Retrieved March 31, 2003, from http://www.theage.com.au/articles/2003/03/30/1048962644995.html?oneclick=true

Baratieri, D. (2010). *Memories and silences haunted by fascism: Italian colonialism, MCMXXX-MCMLX*. Bern, Switzerland: Peter Lang.

Beck, E. R. (1986). *Under the bombs: The German home front, 1942-1945*. Lexington, KY: The University Press of Kentucky.

Benramdane, D. (2004, March). Les rouages d'une guerre secrete. *Le Monde Diplomatique*. Retrieved July 3, 2013, from http://www.monde-diplomatique.fr/2004/03/BENRAMDANE/11094

Bird, K., & Lifschultz, L. (Eds.). (1998). *Hiroshima's shadow*. Branford, CT: The Pamphleteers Press Inc.

Chomsky, N., & Herman, E. (1979). *The Washington connection and third world fascism: The political economy of human rights* (Vol. 1). Boston: South End Press.

Cole, J. (2006, November 10). 655000 dead in Iraq since Bush. *Informed Comment*. Retrieved July 17, 2013, from http://www.juancole.com/2006/10/655000-dead-in-iraq-since-bush.html

Curtis, L. (1984). *Ireland: The propaganda war*. London: Pluto Press.

Danner, M. (2004). *Torture and truth: America, Abu Ghraib and the war on terror*. New York: NYRB Books.

De Bussière, M., Méadel, C., & Ulmann-Mauriat, C. (Eds.). (1999). Radios et télévision au temps des evènements d'Algérie. Paris: L'Harmattan.

Downing, J. D. H. (2007). The imperiled American: Visual culture, nationality, and U.S. foreign policy. *International Journal of Communication*, *1*(1), 318–341.

Downing, J. D. H., & Husband, C. H. (1995). Media flows, ethnicity, racism and xenophobia. *The Electronic Journal of Communication*, *5*(2), 91–95.

Fleury-Villatte, B. (2000). *La mémoire télévisuelle de la guerre d'Algérie*. Paris: Institut National de l'Audiovisuel/L'Harmattan.

García, P. (1995). *El drama de la autonomía militar*. Madrid: Alianza Editorial.

Glancey, J. (2003, April 19). Our last occupation: Gas, chemicals, bombs: Britain has used them all before in Iraq. *The Guardian*. Retrieved July 3, 2013, from http://www.guardian.co.uk/comment/story/0,3604,939608,00.html

Golden, T. (2004, October 24). After terror: A secret reviewing of military law. *The New York Times*. Retrieved July 17, 2013, from http://www.nytimes.com/2004/10/24/international/worldspecial2/24gitmo.html?_r=0

Golden, T., & Van Natta, D. (2004, October 25). Threats and responses: Tough justice, administration officials split over stalled military tribunals. *The New York Times*. Retrieved July 17, 2013, from http://query.nytimes.com/gst/fullpage.html?res=9D05E4D7163DF936A15753C1A9629C8B63

Grayling, A. C. (2006). *Among the dead cities: Is the targeting of civilians in war ever justified?* London: Bloomsbury Publishing.

Hennebelle, G., Berrah, M., & Stora, B. (Eds.). (1997). *La guerre d'Algérie à l'écran*. Paris: Éditions Corlet-Télérama.

Herman, E. S., & Chomsky, N. (1988). *Manufacturing consent: The political economy of the mass media*. New York: Pantheon.

Hollywood Reporter. (2002, April 16). *24 seeing ratings action*. Author.

If Americans Knew. (2013, May 15). Retrieved July 17, 2013, from http://www.ifamericansknew.org

Littleton, C. (2002, October 31). 24 return kick-starts Fox just in time for Nov. sweep. *The Hollywood Reporter*. Retrieved July 22, 2013, from http://www.imdb.com/news/ni0187566/

Mayer, J. (2007, February 19). Whatever it takes: The politics of the man behind 24. *The New Yorker*. Retrieved July 3, 2013, from http://www.newyorker.com/reporting/2007/02/19/070219fa_fact_mayer

McCoy, A. W. (2006). *A question of torture: CIA interrogation from the Cold War to the war on terror*. New York: Metropolitan/Owl Books, Henry Holt & Company.

McGuffin, J. (1974). *The guinea-pigs*. Harmondsworth, UK: Penguin Books.

Murray, R. (2003). *State violence: Northern Ireland 1969-1997*. Cork, Ireland: Mercier Press.

Ramadani, S. (2004, April 9). Iraqis told them to go from day one. *The Guardian*. Retrieved July 3, 2013, from http://www.guardian.co.uk/comment/story/0,1188857,00.html

Rivoire, J.-B., & Aggoun, L. (2004). *Françalgérie: Crimes et mensonges d'État*. Paris: La Découverte.

Ruddock, A. (1996). Unarmed and dangerous: The Gibraltar killings meet the press. In M. Morgan, & S. Leggett (Eds.), *Mainstream(s) and margins: Cultural politics in the 90s* (pp. 143–158). Westport, CT: Greenwood Publishing Group.

Schlesinger, P. (1987). *Putting reality together: BBC news*. London: Routledge.

Schlesinger, P. (1991). *Media, state and nation: Political violence and collective identities*. London: Sage Publications.

Schlesinger, P., Murdock, G., & Elliott, P. (1983). *Televising terrorism: Political violence in popular culture*. London: Comedia.

Schneider, M. (2002, August 15). FX to clock 24 Labor Day marathon. *Daily Variety*. Retrieved July 22, 2013, from http://variety.com/2002/scene/news/fx-net-to-clock-24-marathon-on-sept-1-1117871260/

Sherry, M. (1987). *The rise of American air power*. New Haven, CT: Yale University Press.

Sivard, R. L. (1991). *World military and social expenditures 1991*. Washington, DC: World Priorities Inc.

Sontag, S. (2003). *Regarding the pain of others*. New York: Farrar, Straus & Giroux.

Steer, G. L. (2012). *The tree of Gernika: A field study of modern war*. London: Faber & Faber.

Stetler, B. (2013, May 13). Revival of 24 is more like 12. *The New York Times*. Retrieved August 30, 2013, from http://www.nytimes.com/2013/05/14/business/media/fox-to-bring-back-24-and-jack-bauer.html?_r=0

Stora, B. (2007). Still fighting: The battle of Algiers, censorship and the memory wars. *Interventions, 9*(3), 65–70. doi:10.1080/13698010701618596

Sutton, M. (1994). *Bear in mind these dead: An index of deaths from the conflict in Ireland (1969-1993)*. Belfast, Ireland: Beyond the Pale Publications.

Tassadit, Y. (2004, February). Révélations sur les camps de la guerre d'Algérie. *Le Monde Diplomatique*. Retrieved July 3, 2013, from http://www.monde-diplomatique.fr/2004/02/TASSA-DIT/11020

Valentine, D. (2000). The phoenix program. New York: Authors Guild Backinprint.com.

Wiseman, P. (2003, December 16). Cluster bombs kill, even after shooting ends. *USA Today*. Retrieved July 3, 2013, from http://www.usatoday.com/news/world/iraq/2003-12-10-cluster-bomb-cover_x.htm

You-Li, S. (1993). *China and the origins of the Pacific War, 1931-1941*. New York: St. Martin's Press.

KEY TERMS AND DEFINITIONS

24: An American television series produced by the Fox network that outlines the trials and tribulations of a Counter Terrorism Unit Agent in the United States.

Censorship: A process to censor; i.e., to inhibit or distort activity.

Ethnocentrism: A belief in the inherent superiority of one's own ethnic group or culture.

Militainment: Entertainment with military themes.

Post-9/11 Media Coverage: Media coverage that occurred following the attacks on the United States on September 11, 2001.

Racial Profiling: The use of an individual or community's race or ethnicity by law enforcement as a key factor in deciding whether to engage in enforcement.

Terrorism in History: The role, characteristics, and acts of terrorism in the past.

ENDNOTES

1. An earlier version of this chapter was published in *The Democratic Communiqué, 21*(2), (2007). I am grateful to the editors for permission to reproduce much of it here.

2. Estimates vary from one to two million Algerians forcibly herded into new settlements, mostly women and children, who by the close of the war were dying of malnutrition at the rate of 500 a day (Tassadit, 2004, February). The resonance with the U.S. "pacified hamlets" strategy in the Vietnam War is quite striking.

3. The extreme violence unleashed in Algeria in the decade following the abrogated 1992 national elections, costing between 100,000 and 200,000 lives, while still too shrouded in official shadows to be able to characterize with complete confidence, is a further part of the story connected with France, given the very close continuing relations between the Algerian and French governments (Benramdane, 2004, March). See Rivoire and Aggoun (2004) for an analysis that pinpoints close collaboration between the French and Algerian secret services in the slaughter and in the interests of French access to Algerian energy reserves.

4. Literally, the "Black Feet," a term of derision aimed at the descendants of dirt-poor farmers from France and Spain who had been settled in Algeria in the 19th century.

5. Arab Algerians who had served in considerable numbers in the French army, and thus were defined as the ultimate traitors, worse still than the *pieds-noirs*, by the post-revolution regime.

6. Notably, the largely Algerian-resident Paris demonstration in favor of Algerian independence of October 17th, 1961, in which the police (under the direction of the then city police chief, ex-Nazi collaborator Maurice Papon, who would eventually be put on trial for his crimes during the Nazi era) executed out of hand several hundred Algerian demonstrators and threw their corpses into the Seine. The evident solidarity of feeling between the Paris.

Section 3
Terrorism Types & Media Stereotypes

Chapter 6
Types of Terrorism

Gus Martin
California State University, USA

ABSTRACT

Terrorist typologies are descriptive classifications explaining the quality of political violence arising from distinct political and social environments. Although many terrorist typologies are accepted without controversy by analysts, some are the subject of definitional debate. Accepted typologies include the following: the new terrorism, state terrorism, dissident terrorism, religious terrorism, ideological terrorism, and international terrorism. Sub-classifications of accepted typologies include nationalist terrorism, ethno-national terrorism, and racial terrorism. In contradistinction to accepted typologies, other classifications are conceptually "cutting-edge" and the subject of definitional debate. These include gender-selective terrorism and criminal terrorism (often referred to as "narco-terrorism"). Nevertheless, there is growing recognition that gender-selective and criminal terrorism are features of the modern global terrorist environment. This chapter identifies and discusses terrorist typologies in the modern era, including the emerging recognition of newly defined typologies.

INTRODUCTION

Security experts and scholars in the modern era have defined and described terrorism within the context of systematic typological classifications (Barkan & Snowden, 2001; Eherenfeld, 1990; Hoffman, 2006; Lacqueur, 1999; Marsden & Schmid, 2011; Purpura, 2007; Rubenstein, 1974; Tucker, 2000; White, 2009; Zafirovski & Rodeheaver, 2013). Typological classifications or typologies have been used across disciplines as a means of organizations apparently related phenomena (Marsden & Schmid, 2011). The identification of patterns and organization of things and ideas is beneficial in many regards, a primary

utility of typology "is the greater conceptual clarity they allow" (Ibid, p. 159).

Prior to departing into this discussion on the categorization of terrorism typologies, it is important to emphasize the multifaceted nature of terrorism and its typologies. That is, not only does the term "terrorism" vary depending on geographical, political, or cultural factors (to name a few), the ways in which typologies within this definition are organized are also versatile. Thus, despite the definitional debate that exists surrounding the lines of categorization, this chapter explores eight terrorist typologies, which will be explained within the following contexts:

DOI: 10.4018/978-1-4666-5776-2.ch006

- **The New Terrorism:** The modern terrorist environment that arose during the end of the 20th century, culminating in the September 11, 2001 terrorist attacks in New York City. The New Terrorism is characterized by the threat of mass casualty attacks from dissident terrorist organizations, new and creative organizational configurations, transnational religious solidarity, and redefined moral justifications for political violence.
- **State Terrorism:** Terrorism "committed by governments against perceived enemies. State terrorism can be directed externally against adversaries in the international domain or internally against domestic enemies" (Martin, 2013, p. 4).
- **Dissident Terrorism:** Terrorism "committed by nonstate movements and groups against governments, ethno-national groups, religious groups, and other perceived enemies" (Martin, 2013, p. 4).
- **Religious Terrorism:** "Terrorism motivated by an absolute belief that an otherworldly power has sanctioned—and commanded—the application of terrorist violence for the greater glory of the faith. Religious terrorism is usually conducted in defense of what believers consider to be the one true faith" (Martin, 2013, p. 4).
- **Ideological Terrorism:** Terrorism motivated by political systems of belief (ideologies), which champion the self-perceived inherent rights of a particular group or interest in opposition to another group or interest. The system of belief incorporates theoretical and philosophical justifications for violently asserting the rights of the championed group or interest.
- **International Terrorism:** "Terrorism that spills over onto the world's stage. Targets are selected because of their value as symbols of international interests, either within

the home country or across state boundaries" (Martin, 2013, p. 5).
- **Criminal Dissident Terrorism:** This type of terrorism is solely profit-driven, and can be some combination of profit and politics. For instance, traditional organized criminals accrue profits to fund their criminal activity and for personal interests, while criminal-political enterprises acquire profits to sustain their movement (Martin, 2013).
- **Gender-Selective Terrorism:** Terrorism directed against an enemy population's men or women because of their gender. Systematic violence is directed against men because of the perceived threat posed by males as potential soldiers or sources of opposition. Systematic violence is directed against women to destroy an enemy group's cultural identity or terrorize the group into submission.

While these eight typologies strives to provide a comprehensive and contemporary dicussion of typologies, it is important to note that this list is not exhaustive or conclusive. That is, terrorism is ever-changing—thus, patterns and the task of cateogorization is constantly in motion.

THE NEW TERRORISM

A New Terrorism has come to typify the terrorist environment in the modern era (Lesser et al., 1999; Mockaitis, 2008; Neumann, 2009). It is distinguishable from previous environments because the New Terrorism promotes abstract goals and objectives, engages in mass casualty attacks, seeks to impose extensive social and psychological disorder, and threatens to obtain and wield weapons of mass destruction. The New Terrorism has also adopted creative organizational systems, including independent, non-hierarchical, cell-based networks. Using these core features, modern terrorists regularly engage in asymmetrical attacks, embed cell-based networks in countries far afield from the region of conflict, purposely select and attack "soft" civilian and government targets, and utilize modern communication and networking technologies.

Fault Lines of Conflict

Religion is a principal motivation underpinning the New Terrorism (Mockaitis, 2008). It is important to acknowledge that the al-Qaeda network and other Islamist networks were instrumental in embedding the strategy and tactics of the New Terrorism in the modern terrorist environment (Fallows et al., 2005). Their successes and failures have been keenly observed and replicated by other extremist individuals and groups. Religious extremists believe that the employment of these tactics will boost the success of their agendas, allow them to obtain extensive publicity, and will ultimately deter challenges from their adversaries (Martin, 2013).

New political fault lines have been opened as international terrorist movements and domestic insurgencies seek to supplant established social and governmental norms with a redefined global order. These fault lines have resulted in confrontations involving antagonists who define their causes as defensive in nature—that is, established societies and governments who claim to wage a defensive war on terrorism, versus religious insurgents who claim to wage a defensive holy war to protect and purify their religion. This confrontation epitomizes an active terrorist environment, and the incidence of major terrorist events frequently rises to noteworthy degrees of intensity. In recent years, the frequency of terrorist attacks consistently rises and falls; 11,023 in 2005, to 14,443 in 2006, 14,435 in 2007, 11,725 in 2008, and 10,999 in 2009 (United States Department of State Publication Office of the Coordinator of Counterterrorism, 2009).

The Morality of Asymmetrical Warfare

Terrorist violence has historically been directed against targets possessing maximum symbolic value (Nia, 2010). Until recently (and with occasional high-profile exceptions), terrorist target-acquisition and methodologies were reasonably selective, and frequently modified to correspond to the terrorists' estimation of who should be designated as a championed group or as an adversary. In the modern era, the New Terrorism's moral compass allows for the selection of tactics and targets, which may include the use of high-yield weapons against indiscriminate targets and considerable concentrations of non-combatants.

Unprecedented destruction and damage can now be inflicted against broadly symbolic targets; terrorists must simply design a justification for doing so, and convince fellow believers in the righteousness of the justification. The New Terrorism and the new morality permit terrorists to rationalize maximum fatalities as an objective in itself. Modern terrorists do not necessarily seek to overthrow specific governments or force governments to reconsider standing policies. Instead, goals and objectives are arguably more basic and simple—to render maximum damage and casualties with the sole purpose of terrorizing large segments of a target population and thereby disrupt their societal stability.

Thus, the violence in the modern terrorist environment exemplifies the application of the concept of asymmetrical warfare by international and domestic terrorists (Cordesman, 2002). They regularly engage in irregular, unanticipated, and virtually unpredictable tactics and target selection. Terrorists intentionally strike at unanticipated targets and apply unique and idiosyncratic tactics. Terrorist movements have been largely successful in maintaining the initiative and disrupting new and traditional security measures through the creative application of asymmetrical warfare.

The international security establishment has had some success in adapting to this style of conflict, but terrorists continue to circumvent new and traditional security measures.

STATE TERRORISM

Government-initiated political violence is potentially the most destructive manifestation of terrorist violence. Being that extensive resources are readily available to the state, an great level of violence is quite plausible. Dissident terrorists simply do not possess the same resources, manpower, organizational ability, or immediacy of repression as available to governments. The state's ability to engage in repression, proxy warfare, and other acts of violence greatly outstrips in scale most potential acts of violence by virtually all dissident terrorist groups, with the exception of environments wherein communal groups wage civil war against each other.[1] Governments have used terrorism as an instrument of foreign policy, as well as directed terrorist violence domestically (Westra, 2012). When pursuing such policies, states select from a range of overt and covert alternatives in the domestic and international systems.

State Terrorism as Foreign Policy

Internationally, governments define their national interest within the contexts of economic, ideological, or political priorities, and advocate or protect these priorities either in cooperation or competition with the international community. In extreme circumstances, some regimes have aggressively promoted their priorities through policies of coercion or violence. Many examples are found of governments that have engaged in terrorism as foreign policy. As a practical matter, this is arguably a logical policy option because states cannot always deploy their armed forces internationally with a reasonable likelihood of successfully achieving their strategic goals and objectives. For states pursuing aggressive international goals and objectives, state-sponsored terrorism is more efficient and carries a lower risk of serious and lasting consequences.

Most state sponsorship of terrorism as foreign policy is conducted covertly in order to increase deniability. When adopted as policy, it is relatively inexpensive, less risky than open warfare, and can be beneficial. Governments sponsoring terrorist movements as proxies can thereby disrupt enemy interests while at the same time bring pressure for favorable policy outcomes. In essence, such proxy warfare can coerce rivals with minimum risk to the proxy's sponsor.

State Terrorism as Domestic Policy

All governments, ranging in legitimacy from democracies to dictatorships, apply domestic authority to preserve order and uphold internal security. All governments also respond when domestic authority is threatened by attempting to restore order. When this occurs, some regimes adopt repressive options, sometimes with extreme violence and coercion. Thus, domestic terrorism by governments represents the official application of policies of authoritarian suppression and terrorization. Intimidation and compulsion are applied to counter activism by defined enemies of the state who have been officially declared to be threatening to the preferred order.

Government agents carrying out domestic terrorist campaigns are often members of state security institutions such as the police and military. However, some regimes frequently arm and unleash unofficial personnel who obey directives and orders from government officials. Such unofficial personnel include paramilitary civilians, covert death squads, and mercenary soldiers for hire.

The Quality of State Terrorism

The state has the ability to engage in many varieties and degrees of terrorist violence. The scale of state-sponsored violence can range in intensity from targeted displays of repression to long-term suppression campaigns either domestically or internationally. Iadicola and Shupe summarize the scale of state-sponsored violence as including the following:

- In warfare, the conventional military forces of a state are marshaled against an enemy. The enemy is either a conventional or guerrilla combatant and may be an internal or external adversary. This is a highly organized and complicated application of state violence.

- In genocide, the state applies its resources toward the elimination of a scapegoat group. The basic characteristic of state-sponsored genocidal violence is that it does not differentiate between enemy combatants and enemy civilians; all members of the scapegoat group are considered to be enemies. Like warfare, this is often a highly organized and complicated application of state violence.

- Assassinations are selective applications of homicidal state violence, whereby a single person or a specified group of people is designated for elimination. This is a lower scale application of state violence.

- Torture is used by some states as an instrument of intimidation, interrogation, and humiliation. Like assassinations, it is a selective application of state violence directed against a single person or a specified group of people. Although it is often a lower scale application of state violence, many regimes will make widespread use of torture during states of emergency. (Iadicola & Shupe, 1998, pp. 276-289)

Many experts and scholars who regard the scale and intensity of violence as essential to understanding state terrorism have engaged in detailed analysis of the quality of state violence. Thus, "some analysts distinguish between oppression and repression. Oppression is essentially a condition of exploitation and deprivation . . . and repression is action against those who are seen to be threats to the established order" (Sederberg, 1989, p. 59).

The Future of State Terrorism

Future terrorist environments will continue to include organized terrorism by the state. Government-sponsored terrorism will remain as a potent typology and challenge for international stability and domestic liberty. Repressive states will continue to adopt terrorism as a domestic policy option, and internationally antagonistic states will support proxies and use other measures as foreign policy. Authoritarian regimes will continue to promote and protect state authority when their regimes are threatened, or when they deem such measures to be in their best interest.

Established policies of domestic suppression will remain as viable options for authoritarian regimes. Repressive systems will continue to deploy the police, military, and paramilitary forces internally to suppress dissent and terrorize others into complying with the established order. It is quite plausible that the immediate future will witness enhanced surveillance and communication capabilities because of improvements in these technologies. Recent past examples of massive repression, genocide, and the deployment of illicit weapons of mass destruction against perceived enemy ethno-national populations suggest that some regimes will continue to adopt such policies.

Aggressive governments will continue to arm and support sympathetic proxies internationally when deemed to be prudent and efficient. Recent history has demonstrated that such support can be a relatively prudent and inexpensive substitute to conventional confrontation.

DISSIDENT TERRORISM

Nonstate actors and those sympathetic to their cause have historically justified political violence as a necessary step toward ultimately achieving justice or liberation. Revolutionaries, insurgents, assassins, and other violent dissidents have rationalized their actions as necessary measures to defend and achieve the goals of a justifiable cause (Lutz, & Lutz, 2013). Dissidents have historically adopted tactics that range in scale from high-intensity and long term "wars of national liberation" in 20th century insurgencies to individual suicide bombers and assassins who attack perceived enemies, often sacrificing themselves in the process.

Reasons for dissident terrorism are relatively uncomplicated. Dissidents often foment rebellion against governments and socio-political systems because perceived grievances have been ignored by or caused by these governments and systems (Blake et al., 2012; Lutz & Lutz, 2013). The decision to engage in terrorism is itself rationalized because tactical and weapons selection must be adapted by the weak when at war with the strong. In this regard, the truism that the end justifies the means is commonly adhered to. Thus, dissident terrorists justify their behavior as legitimate resistance to chronic state repression or socio-economic exploitation. Absent violent resistance, the reasoning goes, the state or social system will not act to address the problems of repression and exploitation.

The following analysis is derived and adapted from a model first explicated by Peter C. Sederberg (1989). Although the broad categories are defined and discussed specifically for the purposes of this discussion, the same or similar terms have been adapted and defined by other experts. They are nevertheless very useful for critical analysis of dissident terrorism. The definitional categories are revolutionary, nihilist, and nationalist dissident terrorism.

Revolutionary Dissident Terrorism

Revolutionary dissidents possess a fairly clear vision of the reasons for their insurgency. Their immediate objective is to overthrow an existing government or overturn a repressive socio-economic order. Their eventual goal is to replace the old order—thought to be oppressive and corrupt—with a well-designed new order, which is envisioned as fair, progressive, and honest (Martin, 2013). In this, revolutionary dissident terrorists may not be seeking to create a separate national identity, but instead a new society or way of life (Ibid).

For example, some Islamist dissidents envision a new society—often a reestablished Caliphate—in which the application of God's law (*shari'a*) will build a spiritually pure new order. Likewise, Marxist revolutionaries have historically advocated the creation of a classless society built under the wise central planning of a Communist Party. Being that revolutionary dissidents usually have fewer armed followers than the governments and societies they oppose, their only pragmatic path to victory is to destabilize society or the government, thus demonstrating the vulnerability of their adversaries.

Nihilist Dissident Terrorism

Nihilism is grounded in a 19th century philosophical movement of young dissenters in Russia who held that nationalism, religion, and traditional values (especially family values) are the reason for ignorance in society (Likar, 2011). Only scientific truth can overcome these ignorant belief systems. Nihilism has no clear vision for what to replace existing society with, only that its institutions and belief systems are intolerable (Nonneman, 2010). Nihilism was historically a totally pessimistic and unconstructive philosophy, but interestingly the original anarchists adapted nihilist philosophy to anarchist revolutionary agitation.

Many modern dissidents have adopted nihilistic tendencies and interpretations of the existing order. There exists among many dissidents a fundamental rejection of the existing order with little vision for what a new order will bring. Destruction is itself a goal with little consideration given to building a new society; victory is defined as overthrowing the old society. Nihilists also consider the existing order to be regressive, corrupt, and oppressive. However, they hold that the present government or society is so intolerable, that the overthrow of itself must be the final objective. Modern nihilists often argue that their cause will bring justice to society, but this is a vaguely articulated assertion with no explanation about how to build a new order other than destroying an older one. With no practical political blueprint to build upon, nihilist dissidents have consistently been consigned to the political margins of society. Thus, they have yet to successfully orchestrate broad-based revolutionary uprisings or mount sustained guerrilla campaigns against conventional security forces (Martin, 2013). The only armed alternative has been terrorism.

Nationalist Dissident Terrorism

Nationalism champions the political and national desires of people distinguished by their identities. Such identities are defined by their ethnic, religious, racial, or national heritages. A historically typical pattern of subordination because of these identities has led to resistance against the suppressive group or interest. The championed group live in an environment perceived to be intolerable and oppressive, and nationalists with the group seek to assert the rights of the group. Being that the core motivation is one's ethno-national or other identity, the ultimate goals of nationalist dissidence range from egalitarian political integration, to partial autonomy, to regional autonomy, to outright national independence.

Nationalism is a historically ubiquitous reaction to perceived political or economic exploitation. It has arisen when a minority lives among a majority group, or when a majority group is dominated by a repressive government. In such circumstances, when national identity is defined by regional, ethnic, or cultural distinctions, political solidarity and resistance can occur. As a practical matter, terrorism has been adopted by nationalist dissidents seeking to assert their rights. This occurs in environments wherein warfare or guerrilla insurgencies would not be successful.

The Future of Dissident Terrorism

The late 20th century experienced a decline in ideological insurgency and terrorism, and a concomitant increase in nationalist and otherwise cultural political violence. Nationalist and cultural conflicts occasionally erupted on a massive scale, with large numbers of casualties. Ethno-nationalist and religious terrorism became predominant patterns of conflict, as did stateless terrorist movements. Communal conflicts and violent religious extremism have supplanted the East-West ideological conflicts of the Cold War. Such patterns of conflict reflect the "clash of civilizations" scenario theorized by Professor Samuel Huntington, and debated by experts (Huntington, 1996).

RELIGIOUS TERRORISM

Religious terrorism has come to the fore as a predominant typology in the modern terrorist environment (Jones, 2008; Juergensmeyer, 2003). In the new millennium, terrorism motivated by faith has challenged nations and the international community by virtue of its increased frequency, potential scale of violence, and worldwide scope (Stern, 2003). With the exception of ethno-nationalist conflict, the international community has experienced a relative decrease in the incidence of secular terrorism. Formerly predominant terrorist environments dominated by ideologies of class conflict and anticolonial liberation have been supplanted by aggressive new sectarian movements and ideologies. Although widespread optimism for reform grew during the 2011 Arab Spring uprisings, support for sectarian movements remain strong and entrenched among many populations. Consideration of this fact leads to the following conclusion:

[I]t is perhaps not surprising that religion should become a far more popular motivation for terrorism in the post–Cold War era as old ideologies lie discredited by the collapse of the Soviet Union and communist ideology, while the promise of munificent benefits from the liberal-democratic, capitalist state . . . fails to materialize in many countries throughout the world (Hoffman, 2006, p. 86).

The central features of religious terrorism explain why many religious adherents justify faith-motivated violence. This type of terrorism is a form of political violence that is motivated by an absolute belief that an otherworldly power has sanctioned and commanded the use of violence for the greater glory of religious faith (Martin, 2013). The otherworldly power (one's deity) is believed to favor those who commit faith-motivated violence, and therefore will reward the perpetrators in a paradise-like afterlife.

Religious terrorism is distinctive, and arguably unique, in that it can arise within multivariate historic, ethno-national, and social contexts. Its fundamental features are that it arises from the present circumstances of ethno-national groups, contemporary tendencies within religions, and socio-political environments. Unlike ideological and nationalist activism, religious activism is believed by adherents to be the fulfillment of faith in one's religion's purpose.

Primary and Secondary Motives for Religious Terrorism

The application of religious faith as a justification for terrorist violence has occurred in several ways, and is dependent on the political, social, and cultural environments of religious dissident movements. For example, in some environments religion can be a central and primary motive for terrorist violence. In other environments, it can be a secondary motive in that it is a feature in a people's social and cultural identity, which serves as an intersecting and ubiquitous connection to rally to.

When religion serves as a primary motive for rebellion, it is adopted as the center of an insurgency's political, social, and revolutionary agenda. Thus, religion is the principal motivating factor for their conduct. When religion serves as a secondary motive for rebellion, it is one of several aspects defining the insurgency's identity and political program. Thus, in many ethno-nationalist and revolutionary movements, religion may be a feature of their identity and thereby a factor in building solidarity, but their primary motivation is rooted in their secular (rather than sectarian) identity. This forms the primary motivation for their behavior, and religion the secondary motivation.

The Future of Religious Terrorism

Terrorism motivated by religion is likely to continue to be a predominant feature of the modern terrorist environment. Faith-motivated terrorism existed during the previous environment dominated by ideological and anti-colonial terrorism, it expanded in scale and scope to challenge domestic and international stability, and the death of Osama bin Laden has not heralded an endgame to the threat from religious terrorism. Religious terrorists continue to be able to recruit fresh adherents to their cause, and have been adept at positioning semiautonomous cells in countries far afield from their theaters of operation. Trends suggest that religious terrorists will continue to operate internationally against symbolic targets and domestically against enemy regimes.

IDEOLOGICAL TERRORISM

Ideological extremists justify their behavior by promoting systems of belief that explain collective socio-economic circumstances, and offer interpretations of how to configure an ideal society (Pellicani, 2003). Paul Wilkinson (2001), for example, categorized terrorist groups by political motivation or ideological orientation, listing them under headings such as nationalism, racism, separatism, and vigilantism, to name a few. Although there have existed many manifestations of ideological extremism, most if not all claim to defend or promote a greater good (Katz, 2004). A few have risen to the level of intricate philosophical traditions, such as Marxism and anarchism. Others simply promote nationalist exclusivity, as found in some regions of Europe, Africa, and the Middle East. Others reflect rather paranoid trends existing in some societies, such as the New World Order conspiracy theories found in the Patriot movement in the United States. Any of these trends can also overlay religious, ethnic, or racial extremist tendencies; in such cases the ideological mix can be quite intolerant and combustible.

Core Ideological Beliefs

Several ideologies—anarchism, Marxism, and fascism—epitomize core belief systems that have at time served as an ideological underpinning for political violence.

Anarchism

Anarchism was historically an ideology championing exploited peasant and working classes (Meltzer, 1996; Sheehan, 2003). It is a leftist philosophy, which arose as an ideological manifestation of the social conflicts of the mid-19th century in Europe, which culminated as revolutions in several countries in 1848 (Fosl, 2013). Anarchist philosophers in Russia, Italy, and elsewhere were among the first leftists to champion the downtrodden, resist monarchy and central government control, and oppose the ownership of private property. Anarchists developed a reputation as bombers and "king killers" because of their many successful attacks and assassinations. For example, they assassinated Russian Czar Alexander II in 1881, French President Sadi Carnot in 1894, Austro-Hungarian Empress Elizabeth in 1898, Italian King Umberto I in 1900, and American President William McKinley in 1901. Traditional anarchism reached its high tide during the Spanish Civil War, but declined after the defeat of the Republican government. Modern anarchists tend to not follow the historical pattern of terrorism, although there have been a few terrorist conspiracies.

Marxism

Karl Marx is the founder of a longstanding philosophical and political ideological tradition adopted by proponents ranging from relatively moderate social democrats to extreme Maoist and Stalinist revolutionaries. Marx and his compatriot Friedrich Engels claimed that their brand of socialism was a scientific process in which human advancement and social progress is the outcome of many eras of socio-economic upheavals and revolutions. This scientific process occurs during successive eras when certain inherent "contradictions" based on the working group's unequal relationship to the means of production results in conflict between laboring groups and the ruling status quo group. Revolution and other processes inevitably overthrow the ruling status quo group, thereby resulting in a new society, a new labor relationship, new contradictions, and a new rearrangement of society. Marx and Engels argued that the final era of social evolution will be a Communist era, which will result from the overthrow of the capitalist system by the industrial working class. Marx, Engels, and orthodox Marxists believed that workers would build a dictatorship of the proletariat, create a new Communist society, and design a newly egalitarian social system.

Marxist revolutions, insurgencies, and terrorist campaigns occurred in dozens of societies throughout the 20th century. Many insurgents engaged in terrorism as a kind of "poor man's warfare" against better armed and trained opponents. Some Marxist movements and groups in Europe, Latin America, and the United States, waged urban terrorist campaigns to destabilize their governments. They were sometimes successful, such as in Argentina and Uruguay, but the outcomes were that harsh dictatorships were established that violently suppressed the insurgencies. Marxist governments were established in Russia, China, Cambodia, Vietnam, and elsewhere; these regimes often engaged in ideological state terrorism when attempting to build their new Communist orders.

Fascism

Fascism is a rightist ideological movement that was formed as a counterpoint to anarchism and Marxism, and which peaked during World War II. Since the fascist high tide, a few regimes have been established with fascist tendencies. Fascism initially began as a grass-roots movement growing out of the social turmoil of Europe following the World War I and the Great Depression. In reaction to the Communist revolution in Russia, and the threat of Communist agitation elsewhere, right-wing movements organized themselves as popular movements in Europe.

The elements of fascism include extreme nationalism, championing the superiority of a favored nationality or system, and possibly upholding the superiority of a racial group. Fascism is anti-Communist, suspicious of democracy, distrusts

monarchs, and usually anti-intellectual. Fascist regimes have forcefully required unquestioned obedience to law, order, and the regime. Cultural conservatism is often at the center of fascist ideology, frequently creating nationalistic interpretations of fundamental values such as service to the state, the Christian church as an institution, and traditional roles for women. Authoritarian control is centralized in the state, sometimes centered on a charismatic leader, and other times in a ruling elite such as a military junta.

Following the defeat of the Nazi and Italian Fascist regimes during World War II, occasional regimes took power such as in Greece, Argentina, and the longstanding Falangist regime in Spain. Such regimes engaged in internal campaigns of terror. Dissident right-wing terrorism has rarely been sustained as long-term terrorist campaigns. However, paramilitary activity in Latin America is an exception to this general profile. Paramilitaries in Colombia, El Salvador, and elsewhere were armed and trained to wage counter-insurgencies against leftist insurgents. These campaigns were often quite repressive.

The Future of Ideological Terrorism

Most leftist conflicts were resolved during the late 20th century, and few continued into the new millennium. Anti-colonial wars of national liberation were fought and either won or lost, and domestic leftist terrorist campaigns were defeated. However, several Marxist insurgencies continued into the new millennium, albeit many fewer than during the height of the Cold War. Fascist and other rightist regimes likewise transitioned into more moderate regimes during the late 20th century. Some neo-fascist and neo-Nazi movements persist well into the new millennium, and can be expected to engage in lower-intensity violence, as can occasional outbreaks of paramilitary activity.

INTERNATIONAL TERRORISM

International terrorism is conceptually uncomplicated, and its selection as a tactic by violent extremists is logical. Conceptually, it is terrorism that occurs far afield from the immediate theater of conflict (Trapp, 2011). The conflict "spills over" into the international arena as a way to attract the attention of the international community to give heed to the grievances of parties to a domestic conflict. Symbolic interests are targeted because they represent selected international interests that will be noticed by the global community. Modern international terrorism began to occur frequently beginning in the late 1960s because of the immediate publicity given to the perpetrators' grievances. Such attacks were relatively low-cost in comparison to the propaganda benefits reaped on the international stage, as opposed to limiting attacks to domestic arenas. When successful, domestic causes can become central items on the international agenda.

Selection of international terrorism as a tactic is a deliberate attempt to attract immediate media attention, thereby allowing comparatively weak movements to receive maximum exposure. Attacking symbolic targets with international profiles may result in global media exposure that would otherwise be impossible. Small insurgent movements understand that symbolic extortion, bombings, hijackings, assassinations, and kidnappings are very successful in the international arena. Thus, successful incidents often manipulate global media, political, and political opinion. It has become quite common for domestic insurgents and groups to deliberately seek out targets representing their domestic agenda in another country. Violent extremists have learned from experience that linkages can be readily established for their domestic agenda via international terrorism.

CRIMINAL DISSIDENT TERRORISM

The modern era has witnessed cooperation between transnational organized crime groups and terrorist movements. This cooperation represents a serious problem for the international community. This is considered a common cause between organized crime groups and terrorist movements in that their interests converge as classic market supply and demand. Essentially, a global demand for specified goods by extremists, and supplying this demand by criminal organizations. Some insurgencies have become self-sustaining by involving themselves in transnational criminal enterprises such as trafficking in drugs. In some locales, criminal gangs, and cartels directly confront governments in drug-producing countries, thus giving rise to modern narco-terrorist environments.

Modern transnational organized crime specializes in trafficking people, arms, and drugs. This system of international illicit enterprise is extensive. Some enterprises have become large illicit businesses, often deploying paramilitary units of enforcers. Both production of drugs and transnational trafficking have generated enormous profits for participants, and because of this criminal organizations have participated in documented examples of terrorist violence. This has usually occurred within two environments: first, violence undertaken by profit-motivated traditional criminal enterprises; and second, violence undertaken by politically motivated criminal-political enterprises.

Traditional Criminal Enterprises

Traditional criminal enterprises are motivated by sheer profit, and seek to maximize revenues from their illicit activities. Such enterprises seek a stable environment for their activities, and are by nature apolitical. However, when their illicit activities are threatened by governmental anti-criminal activity, they can resist in an extreme manner—often violently. The motivation behind such violent resistance is not to destroy the social system or overthrow the government, but rather to stabilize a supportive environment for their activities. Active political participation is secondary to the viability of their illicit enterprise. For example, some anti-crime campaigns have been vigorously opposed by cartels in Colombia and Mexico. Such resistance is not ubiquitous, but it has nevertheless occurred frequently.

Criminal-Political Enterprises

Political dissidents became increasingly involved in transnational organized crime. This tactic is a matter of practical deliberation because enormous profits that may be reaped from the arms and drug trades, and because governmental suppliers can be fickle mentors. In Asia and Latin America, some insurgent movements have made the strategic choice to occupy drug-producing regions in order to increase their own independent viability. Thus, an insurgent group can theoretically secure its political and financial autonomy from state interference and sponsorship by carving a niche in an illicit enterprise. The modern terrorist environment has witnessed a pragmatic convergence of transnational organized crime, political extremism, and illegal trafficking. Smuggling in arms and drugs is mutually beneficial to insurgents and illicit criminal organizations; such cooperation is a manifestation of classic *laissez faire* market participation. It is logical for cooperative associations to be established between politically-motivated dissidents and illicit enterprises.

The Future of Criminal Dissident Terrorism

The demand for drugs, arms, and people virtually guarantee that traditional criminal enterprises will aggressively supply these goods in a very active international market. As a result, such enterprises will continue to be viable and versatile, and willing to direct terrorist violence against governments and law enforcement agencies when challenged by these institutions. Political dissident insurgencies will likely continue to participate in the illicit marked because of the erratic nature of support from sympathetic regimes. Self-sustaining insurgencies will rely on illicit trade, as has occurred in Latin America and Asia. Linkages between transnational crime and political extremism will logically continue into the foreseeable.

GENDER-SELECTIVE TERRORISM

Political violence directed against an enemy population based on gender is a controversial concept. Although such violence can be subsumed under any of the other terrorist typologies propounded by experts, evidence exists that women and men have been specifically selected for violent treatment because of their gender. For instance, males have been massacred en masse, females have been the victims of mass rape, and both genders have faced the threat of gender-associated violence during times of war and conflict (Martin, 2013). Such violence should be considered as a specific classification of terrorism.

Gender-selective terrorism is the methodical use of political violence specifically directed against women and men because of their gender. Such gender-directed violence usually occurs as a consequence of political conflict. For example, enemy males may be declared to be potential fighters and selected for execution. Or, enemy women may be selectively abused and terrorized as a way to destroy an enemy group's cultural identity. Thus, gender-selective terrorism is an intentional application of political violence specifically targeting men or women of an enemy group. It frequently occurs during group-level communal conflict and can rise to a scale of intensity that is genocidal in nature. The scale of intensity thus ranges from communal violence caused by roving guerrilla bands, to armies in the field, to well-organized abuse as an application of deliberate policy.

Terrorism against Women

State Terrorism against Women

State-initiated terrorism against women involves violence by armies or proxies and paramilitaries. Because this type of violence is an outcome of intentional policies, it is specifically intended to terrorize an enemy into accepting political dominance, or to destroy a culture through genocidal violence. Such violence occurs during wars of conquest, or when a potential insurgency or other rebellion is perceived by an indigenous group. Such violence can be extensive and extreme in scale.

Dissident Terrorism against Women

Armed insurgents and paramilitary units are usually responsible for dissident terrorism against women. Modern ethnic cleansing sweeps, designed to remove enemy groups from desired swaths of land, often involve violence directed against the women of an enemy population. Women and girls are perceived to represent the cultural identity of enemy groups, and as such they are singled out for violent treatment. Such campaigns occur in environments where conflict may be ethno-national, religious, or ideological in nature. Because of the overarching nature of these environments, the reporting of violence directed against women in such circumstances is often overshadowed by other political considerations.

CONCLUSION

Scholarly research on the typological classifications of terrorism is useful for understanding terrorist environments and specific terrorists. It also allows for an exploration of the motivations that guide terrorists, which can aid in developing counter-terrorism methods tailored specifically to the type of attack or threat. However, it should be mentioned that while this chapter provides a detailed overview of what are known to be some of the most prominent typologies, some scholars and analysts suggest that others exist. Further, trends that develop in the world in which terrorism exists are constantly in motion; innovation in communication technologies, global interconnectedness, and the mechanisms of weaponry and violence all contribute to shifts in these categories.

Despite these changes, it is important to continue research in the realm of terrorist typologies, as it forges new understandings of how terrorists behave and plan their destruction. That is, being aware of and in-tune with what drives those committing acts of violence and deviance motivates an aptitude for success in countering these issues. However, while terrorism is commonly associated with violent fanatics and raging individuals, this chapter also provides an in-depth exploration of state terrorism. This type of terrorism is potentially the most destructive manifestation of terrorist violence, as those who hold positions of great power and are often trusted by citizens carry it out. Despite the variations in danger and threat, all terrorism typologies are spectacles of fear and destruction; therefore, they must be monitored and categorized for continued sophistication of counter strategies.

REFERENCES

Barkan, S. E., & Snowden, L. L. (2001). *Collective violence*. Boston: Allyn & Bacon.

Blake, C., Sheldon, B., Strzelecki, R., & Williams, P. (2012). *Policing terrorism*. London: Learning Matters.

Cordesman, A. H. (2002). *Terrorism, asymmetric warfare, and weapons of mass destruction: Defending the U.S. homeland*. Westport, CT: Praeger.

Ehrenfeld, R. (1990). *Narco terrorism*. New York: Basic Books.

Fallows, J., Bergen, P., Hoffman, B., & Simon, S. (2005). Al Qaeda then and now. In K. J. Greenberg (Ed.), *Al Qaeda now: Understanding today's terrorists* (pp. 3–26). Cambridge, UK: Cambridge University Press. doi:10.1017/CBO9780511510489.004

Fosl, P. S. (2013). Anarchism and authenticity, or why SAMCRO shouldn't fight history. In G. A. Dunn, & J. T. Eberl (Eds.), *Sons of anarchy and philosophy: Brains before bullets* (pp. 201–214). West Sussex, UK: John Wiley & Sons. doi:10.1002/9781118641712.ch18

Hoffman, B. (2006). *Inside terrorism*. New York: Columbia University Press.

Huntington, S. P. (1996). *The clash of civilizations and the remaking of world order*. New York: Touchstone.

Iadicola, P., & Shupe, A. (1998). *Violence, inequality, and human freedom*. Dix Hills, NY: General Hall.

Jones, J. (2008). *Blood that cries out from the Earth: The psychology of religious terrorism*. New York: Oxford University Press. doi:10.1093/acprof:oso/9780195335972.001.0001

Juergensmeyer, M. (2003). *Terror in the mind of God: The global rise of religious violence*. Berkley, CA: University of California Press.

Katz, S. M. (2004). *Raging within: Ideological terrorism*. Minneapolis, MN: Lerner Publications Company.

Laqueur, W. (1999). *The new terrorism: Fanaticism and the arms of mass destruction*. New York: Oxford University Press.

Lesser, I., Arquilla, J., Hoffman, B., Ronfeldt, D. F., & Zanini, M. (1999). *Countering the new terrorism*. Santa Monica, CA: RAND.

Likar, L. E. (2011). *Eco-warriors, nihilistic terrorists, and the environment*. Santa Barbara, CA: Praeger.

Lutz, J., & Lutz, B. (2013). *Global terrorism*. New York: Routledge.

Marsden, S. V., & Schmid, A. P. (2011). Typologies of terrorism and political violence. In A. P. Schmid (Ed.), *The Routledge handbook of terrorism research* (pp. 158–200). New York: Routledge.

Martin, G. (2013). *Understanding terrorism: Challenges, perspectives, and issues*. Thousand Oaks, CA: Sage Publications.

Meltzer, A. (1996). *Anarchism: Arguments for and against*. Edinburgh, UK: AK Press.

Mockaitis, T. R. (2008). *The new terrorism: Myths and reality*. Stanford, CA: Stanford University Press.

Neumann, P. (2009). *Old and new terrorism*. Malden, MA: Polity Press.

Nia, M. M. (2010). From old to new terrorism: The changing nature of international security. *Global Studies Journal, 18*, 1–20.

Nonneman, G. (2010). Terrorism and political violence in the Middle East and North Africa. In A. Siniver (Ed.), *International terrorism post-9/11: Comparative dynamics and responses* (pp. 12–36). New York: Routledge.

Pellicani, L. (2003). *Revolutionary apocalypse: Ideological roots of terrorism.* Westport, CT: Praeger.

Purpura, P. P. (2007). *Terrorism and homeland security: An introduction with applications.* Burlington, MA: Elsevier.

Rubenstein, R. E. (1974). *Alchemists of revolution: Terrorism in the modern world.* New York: Basic Books.

Sederberg, P. C. (1989). *Terrorist myths: Illusion, rhetoric, and reality.* Englewood Cliffs, NJ: Prentice Hall.

Sheehan, S. (2003). *Anarchism.* London: Reaktion Books.

Stern, J. (2003). *Why religious militants kill: Terror in the name of God.* New York: HarperCollins.

Trapp, K. N. (2011). *State responsibility for international terrorism.* Oxford, UK: Oxford University Press. doi:10.1093/acprof:oso/9780199592999.001.0001

Tucker, J. B. (Ed.). (2000). *Toxic terror: Assessing terrorist use of chemical and biological weapons.* Cambridge, MA: MIT Press.

United States Department of State Publication Office of the Coordinator of Counterterrorism. (2009). *Country reports on terrorism.* Retrieved July 30, 2013, from http://www.state.gov/documents/organization/141114.pdf

Westra, L. (2012). *Faces of state terrorism.* Leiden, The Netherlands: Brill. doi:10.1163/9789004225695

White, J. R. (2009). *Terrorism and homeland security.* Belmont, CA: Wadsworth Cengage Learning.

Wilkinson, P. (2001). Current and future trends in domestic and international terrorism: Implications for democratic government and the international community. *Strategic Review for Southern Africa, 23*(2), 106–123.

Zafirovski, M., & Rodeheaver, D. G. (2013). *Modernity and terrorism: From anti-modernity to global terror.* Leiden, The Netherlands: Brill. doi:10.1163/9789004242883

KEY TERMS AND DEFINITIONS

Criminal-Dissident Terrorism: A type of terrorism that is solely profit-driven and can be some combination of profit and politics.

Gender-Selective Terrorism: Terrorism directed against an adversary population's men or women because of their gender.

Ideological Terrorism: Terrorism motivated by political systems of belief (ideologies), which champion the self-perceived inherent rights of a particular group or interest in opposition to another group or interest.

International Terrorism: Terrorism that occurs globally. Targets are selected because of their value as symbols of international interests, either within the home country or across state boundaries.

New Terrorism: The modern terrorist environment in which the functioning state of terrorism is characterized by utilization of new structure of networking, acquisition of high-intensity weapons, use of asymmetrical methods for massive casualties, and clever use of new media and information technologies.

Religious Terrorism: Terrorism motivated by an absolute belief that an otherworldly power has sanctioned the application of terrorist violence for the greater glory of the faith. Religious terrorism is usually conducted in defense of what believers consider to be the one true faith.

State Terrorism: Acts of terrorism that are committed by governments against perceived opponents.

Chapter 7
Media Stereotypes of Terrorism

Georgios Terzis
Vrije Universiteit Brussel, Belgium & Global Governance Institute, Belgium

ABSTRACT

This chapter analyzes different stereotypes used by media when covering terrorism events. It discusses topics such as: media stereotypes of different terrorist groups, how media responses differ according to the type of terrorism, type of medium (e.g., print, broadcast, and on-line), location of the headquarters of the medium (regional subjectivity), the audience of the medium (national, transnational, or international), and the political affiliation and market orientation of the medium. This chapter attempts to provide an additional analysis of the way that these stereotypes are formulated by the use of basic and not so basic rhetorical techniques of the invention, arrangement, style, memory, and delivery applied. All the above are analyzed against the background of the basic social determinants of journalism: political pressures and censorship, technological possibilities, news management and public relations strategies of the army, economic pressures and professional culture, and the basic news values or news selection criteria (e.g., timing of the event, negativity, meaningfulness, and reference to elite nations and persons).

INTRODUCTION

Some scholars believe that acts of terrorism are nothing without the publicity from media, and terrorism results from freedom of the press (Biernatzki, 2002; Jenkins, 1983; Laqueur, 1976). However, they ignore that terrorism groups exist for thousands of years preceding the establishment of the press and when press was heavily censored.

Many justify these ideas with evidence that television (now combined with the Internet) is the leading news medium, and television and the Internet allow for strong visual impact and can play with the audiences' emotions. Ramonet says

that "events which produce strong pictures [and emotional shock] . . . consequently go to the top of the news hierarchy" (cited in Biernatzki, 2002, p. 5). Therefore, all terrorists need to do is create visual situations in which they can gain attention and spread fear.

Yet others, such as Wardlaw, argue that "there is no clear evidence that publicity (by the media) is responsible for significantly affecting the occurrence of terrorism" (cited in Biernatzki, 2002, p. 6). Two models developed by Barnhurst (1991) further analyze the situation. In the "culpable-media model" media are seen as part of the cycle: media coverage of terrorism causes more acts

DOI: 10.4018/978-1-4666-5776-2.ch007

of terrorism, which stimulate increased media coverage. It was found, however, that if coverage of terrorist attacks is censored from the media, even larger acts of violence might be resorted to (Biernatzki, 2002). The "vulnerable media model" depicts the media as victims of terrorism because, "any control on coverage, even a natural one, will be ineffective because terrorists can shift to other forms of communication by striking vulnerable points in the infrastructure of liberal societies" (Ibid, p. 7).

Despite the above, the reality is that terrorists might be given the floor to speak to the media, but they never actually have real "access" to the media; they are not given an opportunity to define the agenda, the platform, or the issues to be discussed. It is always the case that the final spin on the story is given to journalists relying on official sources, making them responsible for the "framing" of the story (Gitlin, 1984).

It is this "framing," which is defined by official sources, that usually defines the stereotyping of terrorist groups. For example, media publicity is received by al-Qaeda, however, they never gain real access to the media in the sense of defining the agenda and receiving positive framing from mainstream media. As Schmid and de Graaf point out, while terrorists may still have considerable influence on the way the media report on their actions, their opponents, "the government and its security forces, are in fact the main sources for the media" (1982, p. 98) and they always have the "last word," (i.e., the opportunity to comment, or "the last reply" and determine the "spin" of the story).

Further, as Brian McNair (2003) explains, the audience observes limited elements of attacks—such as the bomb exploding or the suspect waving his weapon. However, they are rarely provided with the justification, historical background, or political context of the event taking place. Kelly and Mitchell describe the basic model of terrorism stereotyping "by sapping terrorism of its political content, the media turn the crusader into a psychopath" (1981, p. 288).

TERRORISM AND MEDIA COVERAGE

Terrorists know that their activity is 10% violence and 90% publicity, whereas the US response in Afghanistan and Iraq is 90% violence and 10% strategic communications (Taylor, 2009, p. 14).

It should be noted that it is not the purpose of this chapter to discuss extensively the term "terrorism." Instead, this chapter focuses on the part of the definition that sees terrorism as a media management strategy with which terrorists try to reach different audiences, and the "reaction" of the media to this strategy, targeting mainly but not exclusively on the stereotypes they use.

Regional Subjectivity

There are several ways to categorize terrorist groups, such as separatist, revolutionary, religious, and social—with their communication strategies varying accordingly. One of the ways is based on the geography of their operations, as national, transnational, international, or global. The majority of the terrorist organizations operate within national borders for the majority of their actions (e.g., Euskadi Ta Askatasuna (ETA) in Spain, Chechens in Russia, the Shining Path in Peru, or the Partiya Karkerên Kurdistan (PKK) in Turkey). Moreover, there are terrorist organizations that have national goals but also perform terrorist acts transnationally (e.g., the Tamil Tigers). Additionally, there are terrorist organizations that both operate transnationally and also have transnational goals (e.g., the Irish Republican Army) and finally, there are also terrorist organizations that have global goals and actions (e.g., al-Qaeda).

Further, several ways to classify the media exist; for instance, the geographical base of the headquarters and the audience of the media also influence the stereotyping of the terrorists. There are geographical- and audience-based definitions of media, which classify them as:

- National media produced for a national audience (e.g., *ABC* Network, *The Washington Post*);
- National media with transnational mission (e.g., *Deutsche Welle*, BBC World Service);
- International media, which are characterized by a form of cooperation between two or three countries (e.g., Arte);
- Pan-regional media (e.g., *Euronews*, *al-Jazeera*); and
- Global media (e.g., *Financial Times*, *CNN International*) (Bruggemann & Schulz-Forberg, 2009).

These geographical bases of terrorist groups and media primarily define stereotyping characteristics of media coverage. This includes the way that media report specific terrorist acts and which facts they incorporate in that specific report—depending on the definition of the terrorist organization.

For the media that share a geographical base with the terrorist group, for example, if the terrorist organization is considered a separatist-domestic one (e.g., the IRA for the UK media, ETA for Spain, PKK for Turkey), the usual trend of the national media is to follow the government line. If it is a revolutionary-domestic organization then the media will tend to follow the ideology of their news organization (i.e., left wing media will tend to be more sympathetic though never supportive). While if it is a social terrorist group, the local news coverage will almost always be given negative reporting.

In the case of international media the coverage and stereotyping tends to be different. Fewer people in the western world pay attention to international news on a regular basis than in the past. Often, a major event will take place, increasing the media coverage and audience awareness, until interest wanes and a new event occurs. The Pew Research Center released a study in 2008, which demonstrated that 53% of Americans track international news as it develops, but only 42% consistently follow international news coverage (Willnat & Martin, 2012).

A vicious circle with a negative spiral has been created by the decline of the actual coverage of international news events by most major news agencies. Between 1988 and 2010 a decline of 56% occurred: "NBC, ABC and CBS featured more than 4,800 foreign news stories [during broadcasts] in 1989 . . . such coverage dropped to about 2,700 stories in 2010," (Willnat & Martin, 2012, p. 497). A similar trend is true for print media, in which front page foreign "newshole" stories dropped from 27% in 1987 to 11% in 2010, with an all-time low of 6% during the 2008 Presidential race (Ibid, p. 497).

The decline in foreign coverage can be blamed on the lack of interest from audiences and the closing of foreign bureaus abroad. Pamela Constable, a foreign correspondent, explained in 2007:

In the 1980s, American TV networks each maintained about 15 foreign bureaus; today they have six or fewer. . . . Aside from a one-person ABC bureau in Nairobi, there are no network bureaus left at all in Africa, India or South America (cited in Willnat & Martin, 2012, p. 496).

National Public Radio (NPR) in the U.S. is the only exception to this rule, having increased its foreign bureaus from 6 to 17 in the past ten years and has part-time correspondents in two more countries. Lacking first-hand knowledge, many reporters have turned to news sources that are closer to conflict areas, such as *al-Jazeera* (located in Qatar) and *DEBKAfile* (based in Jerusalem), in order to obtain a variety of information (Biernatzki, 2002).

Parachuting foreign correspondents for short periods of time with the purpose of covering "hot topic" incidents can lead to an increase in stereotyping in several ways. First, the reporter most likely lacks substantial "local knowledge." That is, he or she will most likely not have the advantage of having lived in the country for a period of time and therefore will not be fully aware of cultural aspects—such as the history between warring groups—and will not know many local contacts to whom questions can be addressed. Secondly, in the rush to break a story, official sources' facts may not be checked thoroughly. Finally, once the event is over, or loses the attention of the audience/media agency, the journalist leaves the locale, rarely with any follow up.

When a reporter is unfamiliar with the history of why certain events occur or the general culture of the country in which the event occurred *and* is pressed for time, it is easier (for both the reporter and the short news format) to fall back on pre-existing stereotypes. In 2002, a panel discussion held at American University in Washington, DC concerning U.S. and European media coverage of the "war on terror" confirmed that "The U.S. tendency to want to portray everything in 'black and white' hinders presentation of an accurate understanding of terrorism" (Biernatzki, 2002, p. 11).

In general, three factors influence the international coverage of a national terrorist group: the historical relations between the two countries; the political relations of the current governments; and the existence of similar groups in both countries. Here, all kinds of double standards are revealed, as some actions for similar goals receive completely different coverage. For example, if there is no proximity or historical connection (e.g., colony) with the country that the domestic terrorists operate in, then the coverage is usually very short and often works as a warning for possible travelers to this county. In such cases, coverage is commonly completely striped of any ideology. For instance, ETA coverage of bombings in Majorca in Greek media may be neutral, but the same media might be much more sympathetic to similar attacks of PKK in Turkey due to the animosity between the two countries.

Medium Type and New Media

Furthermore, the type of medium widely influences the type of reporting and stereotyping you apply to the reporting, for two main reasons: *speed and space*. Speed is paramount for broadcast and on-line media and, due to the 24-hour news circle of the media, it is much more difficult for media practitioners to double check facts. Moreover, broadcasting formats that are dictated by strict time limits of 60 or 90 second formats for radio or perhaps two to three minutes for television. This requires a huge amount of language compression in order to fit the essentials of a story in the limited number of words in these formats.

Furthermore, it is perhaps an indirect result of the reduction of number of foreign correspondents that more and more people (and terrorists) need to rely on new media. The age of new media technologies does allow terrorists to have some access to an audience. New media technologies not only offer terrorists countless ways to interact with one another, but also to create and disseminate videos of their own. They do not need to rely solely on traditional media in order to promote their messages (Seib, 2012).

Ownership

Additionally, there are also three more divisions that influence media stereotypes of terrorism, such as the divisions between *elite vs. popular media, public vs. private, left vs. right wing*. For example, political divisions often times supersede regional divisions, and thus we see left wing media from different regions providing similar reporting of the same terrorist event (especially of revolutionary terrorist groups) compared with right vs. left wing media from the same region. The coverage of right-wing newspapers from Latin America and Europe of groups such as the Zapatistas or the Shining Path is much more similar and "unfavorable" to their causes than left and right wing newspapers from the same region.

STEREOTYPES AND RHETORICAL TECHNIQUES IN REPORTING TERRORISM

Stereotypes are simplified images people create, most often when confronted with a person or situation that is judged as being different. Within seconds, the observation of, interpretation of and value judgment of the difference is unconsciously registered in one's mind. What should be a three-step process more often occurs in one step, leading people to generalize and determine whether or not the observed difference is superior or inferior to the sense of self of the individual making the judgment(s) (van Ginneken, 1998).

Stereotypes made by observation do not even require that people talk with one another, and the fewer interactions one has with people perceived as being different, the stronger a prejudice will form. On the other hand, when a person has frequent interaction with people of a different group (i.e., age, gender, race, nationality, etc.) stereotypes are less likely to be concretely held on to. Collective judgments are even easier to create, simply by observing the external signs (e.g., physical features, type of dress, etc.) of people (van Ginneken, 1998).

The media often perpetuate collective judgments when the subjects of conflict or terrorism are covered. Creating a sense of nationalism and love of one's own country and hatred of the country's enemies including and especially those perceived as terrorists is the most fundamental way to create a collective identity, which is then used to make the value judgments against observed differences. One way this action occurs in the media is through the process of ethnocentrism, William Grahm Sumner's term used to describe a view of the world in which one's own group (or ethnicity) is at the center of everything, with all others scaled and rated in reference to this ideology (cited in van Ginneken, 1998).

Ethnocentrism can be an unintentional process, practiced by individual journalists or media agencies as a whole. It can be linked to media

subjectivity and stereotyping, usually presented in opposition to media objectivity. Media objectivity does not exist; most big media organizations today even refrain from using the term, preferring instead terms such as "balanced reporting." Journalists make a number of decisions when they practice reporting in seeking, evaluating, selecting, writing and presenting "facts," which are all subjective relative to the person who is writing the story and the medium in which the story is reported. These decisions also need to be made by journalists when they report terrorism acts.

The classic question of course is who is a terrorist? Is victory the only difference between a terrorist and a national hero? In other words, is everyone in a violent conflict usually involved in "terrorism," but only the loser is held accountable for those actions, while the winner who becomes a "government" enjoys the monopoly on violence and gets away with the actions and, more importantly for our analysis, receives favorable media coverage?

This is a widely held belief among national reporters, foreign correspondents, as well as communication and international affairs academics who never fail to remind us that several of the governments of some of the most established democracies today in the world were once labeled as terrorists or performed acts of state terrorism, including the U.S., Israel, France, and the South African governments, as well as some more recent examples such as the Irish Republican Army (IRA) and the Kosovo Liberation Army (McNair, 2003).

In such cases, journalists may be under pressure to apply the first part of rhetoric described by Leith (2011): invention. Invention is the initial process used to develop arguments for and against a statement or idea that the audience can easily identify with, the purpose being to convince the audience to agree with (or, even better, to believe in) the idea presented by the journalist.

Ethos on the other hand, is a rhetorical tactic used by the journalist to appear as a trustworthy source and works best when the common assumptions of the audience are mirrored by the speaker/ writer, or in our case, the media. Ethos is the most commonly used technique by official sources, which they appeal to their "elected" authority, the army (objectivity away from politics, e.g., presentation by Colin Powel of the Iraq WMD dossier in the UN) or by the "objective" secret services (MI5 "dodgy" dossier by the British Government).

The other part of rhetoric—logos—involves reasoning through the available evidence. The reporter tries to connect the points of his/her argument to reach a conclusion that the audience can also easily reach, often through the use of "commonplaces" (i.e., the set of premises that reasoned logic starts from) (Leith, 2011). Commonplaces are culturally specific assumptions that are deeply rooted in society—so much so that "they can pass for universal truths" (Ibid, p. 65). Interestingly, the same evidence, from the exact same event, can be used to argue for and against any statement or idea. This is how media from different backgrounds (e.g., political affiliations, different regions, etc.) can portray the same or similar events in different lights.

A striking example of the media's portrayal of a terrorist is that of Anders Behring Breivik, the Norwegian man who killed 77 people in July 2011. Despite his manifesto and his instance that he is sane, the media is trying to portray him not as a terrorist, but as a mentally unstable person who needs psychiatric help. The idea that a white man, from a western country, would consciously commit acts of terrorism is not an argument the media—nor many of the prosecutors of the case— want to portray. It is not logical and it does not fit any commonplaces in our societies.

For instance, when the initial reports of the massacre in Norway broke, many large news agencies immediately pointed to al-Qaeda as either the perpetrators or the source of inspiration for the attacks. Even after Breivik was caught, *The New York Times* was still trying to link Breivik to al-Qaeda. In his article "Terrorism by other name," Pranaya SJB Rana quotes Richard Silverstein, who points out the fallacy of *The New York Times*, p.

Are the only terrorists in the world Muslim? If so, what do we call a right-wing nationalist capable of planting major bombs and mowing down scores of people for the sake of the greater glory of his cause? If even a liberal newspaper like the Times can't call this guy a terrorist, what does that say about the mindset of the western world? (Silverstein, cited in Rana, 2011, July 29, p. 1)

On the other hand, Richard Reid, also known as "the Shoe Bomber" who tried to blow up a U.S.-bound flight in December 2001, was always portrayed as a terrorist by the media, and never once was there mention of performing psychological tests on him. Though born in the UK, Reid converted to Islam and looks physically different from Breivik. In 2002, he was sentenced to three life sentences.

When reporting terrorism the media can also use appeals to the pathos, another rhetorical technique. Any attempt to stir the emotions of an audience (ranging from sadness to excitement) is an appeal to pathos. Instead of calling on the logic of your audience, the appeal to pathos secretly urges them to become emotionally involved in the subject, often through strong visuals and terrifying facts (Leith, 2011).

Another part of rhetoric, according to Leith (2011), is "arrangement." When giving a speech, or writing a story, one is advised to have six parts (which Leith adopted from *Ad Herennium*):

1. **Exordium:** Establish yourself, get the attention of the audience, employ ethos.
2. **Narration:** Set out basic facts as understood by most people.
3. **Division:** Explanation of what you and your opponents agree/disagree on.

4. **Proof:** Provide arguments for your case, employ logos.
5. **Refutation:** Attack your opponents' claims.
6. **Peroration:** Summary of main points and conclusion.

To further expand, in the exordium, the journalist wants to lay out for the audience the tone and direction of the message. This can be achieved through "discussing our own person, the person of our adversaries, that of our hearers, and the facts themselves" (*Ad Herennium* handbook, cited in Leith, 2011, p. 84). To have a strong narration, it must be brief, clear and plausible. This is one of the most important parts of the speech in which one is able to frame (or spin) the elements of the debate in order to show one's side. Not much further explanation can be added to "division," simply that one should not dwell too long on what is agreed upon—the objective of most speeches/articles is to prove one's point, not someone else's—nor for the section of proof, in which one simply sets out to make a case for or against something or someone.

It is possible to reverse the order of proof and refutation, and often wise to do so when your own case is weak. This way, you can attack your opponent so strongly that few people will notice your weak argument(s) that follow (the most typical technique used by official sources again terrorists). Another trick is to discredit the witnesses (or supporters) of the view you oppose (British Government's approach to the one million anti-war demonstrators). Finally, in the peroration, one really hammers home the point—it can be a place to motivate people to action, to bring them to tears. This final section is where the overall tone of your message is delivered—the way you leave the audience greatly influences what they will (or will not) do next.

Another part of rhetoric is style. Style is often divided into three types—high/grand, low/plain, and middle. Leith describes high/grand style as "rhetorical," "elaborate" and "stuffed with ex-

tended metaphors" (2011, p. 117). He attributes "grander or address, but with a flinty, plain-spoken grip" to middle style, and "clarity, brevity and the effect of sincerity" to low/plain style (Ibid, p. 118). Jokes, especially self-depreciating ones about the speaker, and sounds effects are very important stylistic tools.

In addition, the importance of memory is stronger than one might think. Being spoken to, as opposed to being read to, is a much better way to make the audience feel connected to you and have them pay attention. It takes a good command of the material—the ability to think it though freely and out loud—and practice in order to sound spontaneous and confident when speaking in public.

Finally, the last part of rhetoric is delivery. Delivery can be considered the most important part of speech giving. Words can be beautiful, terrifying or moving on paper, but the way in which the message is delivered will make or break the speaker and his/her argument. Delivery is also important in written works, but for this approach the author must anticipate the reader's reactions. During a speech, the audience is visible and audible; therefore the speaker must react accordingly in order to do a good job.

JOURNALISM CULTURES

The question that arises from all the above of course is why the media and journalists in particular follow these patterns of stereotyping. Among journalists worldwide, there is a general ideological consensus that journalism is:

- A professional service to the public;
- Carried out in organizational contexts;
- Mainly oriented towards facts;
- Provides timely and relevant information; and
- Requires at least some intellectual autonomy and independence (Hanitzsch et al., 2012).

Yet there are emerging debates on the "institutional roles" (the function of journalism in society), "epistemologies" (the nature and reality of accepted evidence) and "ethical ideologies" (the way in which journalists respond to ethical dilemmas while reporting) of journalism (Hanitzch et al., 2012, p. 474). As a result a number of influences on the work of journalists around the world have been classified, not least by one of the biggest research programs—the Worlds of Journalism Study (2013). This research explores and explains these three factors in great deal, providing guidance and detailed information on the ways in which these elements of journalism interact with this profession.

The positions that journalists take in relation to these three factors while reporting terrorism is the one that determines their use of stereotypes for the different groups or individuals that they report and the news values and selection criteria that they apply.

News Values and Selection Criteria

In today's world of a trillion Web pages and massive increase of news exchange through social networking, news selection is more paramount than ever. Even the famous WikiLeaks case proved that no one was able to read and comprehend 250,000 emails unless traditional media would go through them, analyze them, and report about them.

It is well known that journalists and editors must select some news stories from the vast cosmos to make available to the public, but it is less known how the selection is made. Often, the selection of news can be considered as a reflection of the power structures of society and of the news medium.

Scholars have identified groups of taxonomies in order to determine what constitutes a "good" international news story, with six factors intrinsic to the story and six factors external to the story (Galtung & Ruge, 1965; Golding & Elliott, 1979; Harcup & O'Neill, 2001; Schultz, 1982). The first of the six factors, which are often evaluated by journalists and editors as essential to news worthy story is *clarity* of implication on audience. This refers to the cultural and/or geographic relevance of the subject matter to the audience. That is, the closer an event is to the audience, the more likely the audience will want to be informed. Secondly, the elements of *entertainment/amusement/surprise* for the audience are very important and closely considered by news editors. Examples of such stories include "human interest" stories, "feel-good" stories, and unexpected or rare events. A third factor relates to *power*. Stories on elite nations, people, or institutions are more universally covered than stories of less-known people and institutions. For instance, two billion people reportedly watched the Royal Wedding of Prince William and Catherine Middleton. There are an estimated 7 billion people on Earth, only 2.35 billion of which have access to TV. All satellite channels provided the live broadcast to TV viewers, with many also providing it to online viewers. The fourth and fifth types of stories of particular importance are closely related: *life* (stories with good news, such as rescue or cures to diseases) and *death* (stories with bad news, such as conflict, violence, and negative events; the magnitude of death is also important). The sixth and final intrinsic factor of a "good" news story is the concept of a "*balanced diet*." Editors try to find a good balance of news *composition*—between foreign and domestic stories and *co-optation*—which means some stories that are normally not very newsworthy, will be covered if they relate to a major story.

Second are the six factors that are external to a news story but still impact whether or not the story is chosen as news. The first group of factors is *timing and frequency*. Events that are sudden (e.g., terrorist attacks) as opposed to gradual or long-term (e.g., systematic rape of women and girls leading to disease and other social issues in Africa) often have precedence in the nightly news or on the front pages of newspapers. Similarly, stories that are *predictable* or a *continuation* of subjects that are already in the news are favored due to the perception that the audience will already be familiar with the subject and will want to know more about it, as opposed to learning about a new subject. Second, competition between journalists and news agencies, called *intermedia agenda setting*, will lead different news agencies to cover similar stories, especially since one agency has already determined the information as newsworthy and no one wants to lose their audience due to a lack of coverage on a "'hot' topic." A third factor external to the news story but still very much considered is the *political spin and corporate news/public relations* surrounding the story. A story that is prefabricated (i.e., already researched and written) is easier to select for the news than one that could be more important but not researched or written. This directly links to the modern-day problems of time constraints and 24-hour news coverage that audiences expect today. A fourth factor is logistics (i.e., financial and technical). News agencies must decide which stories to spend extra money and equipment on (e.g., travel costs). Though the fifth factor, *where selection takes place*, may appear closely related to the intrinsic factor of "clarity of implication," a distinction can be made between the two. Regional differences in where news selection is made (e.g., *CNN* shows the missiles taking off, while *al-Jazeera* shows them landing); the type of medium used (e.g., print, broadcast, online, etc.); and institutional differences (e.g., private versus state, left versus right, etc.) can all impact which news is provided to the audience. Finally, *who* selects the news can also impact coverage. The different identities of media practitioners (refer to the discussion on social determinants above) must always be kept in mind.

The series of subjective decisions and the valuation of the news selection criteria mentioned above are mainly based on the social determinants of journalism defined by McNair (1998). In detail, media research (Frohardt & Temin, 2003; Hartmann & Husband, 1974; Jager & Link, 1993;

Luostarinen, 1999; Terzis, 2001; van Dijk, 1991; 1997) clearly demonstrates the *conditions* under which these "social determinants of journalism" operate, affect and are affected in the reporting of terrorism. That is, one should reflect on the following possible journalism culture characteristics of the elements of the basic social determinants:

- **Professional Culture:** Such as the absence of a journalism code of ethics; professional ideology that regards journalism as a necessary tool to defend the national interests; poor training of media personnel and the absence (or lack of enforcement) of media laws, absence of strong national journalists unions, isolation of journalists from international associations, political, ethnic, religious, and regional homogenous composition of the journalism corps.
- **Organizational Constraints:** Such as deadline pressures often not allowing in-depth/balanced reporting, 60 or 90 seconds reporting formats; limited and/or biased newsgathering techniques.
- **Technical Constraints and Possibilities:** Such as lack of media reach and accessibility, outdated equipment.
- **Political Pressures:** Such as censorship; traitor labeling; intimidation by the sources or the political establishment; lobbying; regulation; the interlocking interests of the media; the politicians and the business sector.
- **Economic Pressures:** Such as destroyed market conditions; fierce unregulated commercialization; lack of pluralism, market forces that promote sensational journalism.
- **Source Tactics and Strategies:** Such as intimidation of the journalist by the government sources; public relations/conflict spin doctors; manipulation of Preparatory Defence Information (PDI)/abuse of information campaigns for the psychological national defense by the army.

Furthermore, one needs to take into consideration that peer pressure is also experienced by journalists in various forms in different regions in the world, for example:

1. By reading a number of additional newspapers and following various news broadcasts on a daily basis in order to keep up with the news agenda of their competitors and peers, journalists perceive and translate the accentuated perception of the mainstream opinion expressed in the media as the dominant discourse and in some regions that puts great pressure on journalists.

2. Since journalists tend to predominantly socialize with other journalists, peer pressure is constant. Consequently, when journalists perceive their opinion as a dissident one, they are very much reluctant to express it and risk becoming labeled by their colleagues as unpatriotic or even traitors.

The media managerial elites tend to socialize with their own kind, as well as with the social, political and economic elites of the country and as a result become peers and part of the status quo of the country. The political and economic elites exert great pressure on the media managerial elite, especially in relation to reports about terrorism, when they are or feel that they might be threatened.

The increasing levels of the six categories of "basic social determinants of journalism," of professional culture, organizational and technical constraints, political and economic pressures, and source tactics and strategies create different media cultures, which with the increasing levels of peer pressure when reporting terrorism acts contribute towards the increased production of media content that in itself contributes to stereotyping when reporting terrorism.

The result of all these "basic social determinants of journalism" is the simultaneous development of a "spiral of silence" (Noelle-Neumann,

1973, p. 108) by "dissident" journalists who experience their opinions as marginalized and deviant and a "spiral of stereotyping speech" by journalists who realize that their opinions have become mainstream, and thus feel the need to exaggerate.

In the current climate of huge unemployment, insecurity and the prevalence of the new types of media employments such as part time or freelance, no reporter is willing to look in any way favorable in his/her coverage of the terrorists in fear of been labeled as a traitor, and knows that no employer or trade union (if s/he is one of the lucky few that stills belongs to one) will be supportive of him/her and take the risk to annoy audiences and advertisers as well as the political establishment (official sources). In general, media has become much more "risk avert" due to the insecurities created by harsh economic conditions.

CONCLUSION

We hope this paper has exposed some ways in which the media is influenced (sometimes even pressured) to report acts of terrorism in different ways, depending on the situation and audience. In addition, we hope to have opened a debate on the relationship between media and terrorism: do they (both the media and acts of terrorism) thrive because of or in spite of one another? One must not forget that we defined terrorism as a 'media management strategy' but due to information and time constraints, we often find the political motives of terrorists being cut from media coverage of acts of terrorism. This leads to creating stereotypes and providing the audience with very little substance.

By exposing how the basic social determinants of journalism cultures work in the process of terrorism reporting, we hope to have made readers more aware of the ways that media stereotyping of terrorism groups works. Finally, it is important to note that despite the changing nature of journalism, due to—for instance—the introduction of new communication technologies, reliance remains on official sources for media reporting. Usually, journalists adhere to the opinions and stereotypes of the government, leaving terrorist groups with media coverage, but not the access they would like to spin the story in their favor.

Thus, media stereotyping of the news reporting of terrorism first reflects the stereotyping of the official sources providing information about terrorists and second the condition of journalists today who tend to exhibit and increasing "proactive obedience" to follow those official sources almost verbatim due to the current situation in the media sector.

At a media conference in May 2007, Dr. John Horgan's opening address challenged both government officials and journalists to understand that there is a difference between the media's coverage of terrorism and incitement of terrorism. Horgan proposes to change the "tendency for governments to think of media purely in terms of their utility to the opposing forces" (2007, p. 4). He says that the view of "if terrorists can use the media to challenge the state, the state can use the media to defeat terrorism" is an over-simplification (Ibid, p. 5). He argues that this is particularly the case because the media are not simply a tool; they are also part of society. For him, when reporting acts and the effects of terrorism, the media should also inquire, explain, and provide contextual information about the events. Thus, with further research an inquiry into this field, it is hoped that the media and policies related to this entity will take the initiative to initiate better practices that demonstrate greater social responsibility.

ACKNOWLEDGMENT

The author wishes to thank Marina Lynch who worked as a research assistant for this chapter.

REFERENCES

Barnhurst, K. G. (1991). Contemporary terrorism in Peru: Sendero luminous and the media. *The Journal of Communication, 41*(4), 75–89. doi:10.1111/j.1460-2466.1991.tb02332.x

Biernatzki, W. E. (2002). Terrorism and mass media. *Communication Research Trends, 21*(1), 1–27.

Bruggemann, M., & Schulz-Forberg, H. (2009). Becoming pan-European? Transnational media and the European public sphere. *The International Communication Gazette, 71*(8), 693–712. doi:10.1177/1748048509345064

Frohardt, M., & Temin, J. (2003). Use and abuse of media in vulnerable societies. *United States Institute of Peace*. Retrieved July 30, 2013, from http://www.usip.org/sites/default/files/sr110.pdf

Galtung, J., & Ruge, M. (1965). The structure of foreign news: The presentation of the Congo, Cuba and Cyprus crises in four Norwegian newspapers. *Journal of Peace Research, 2*(1), 64–90. doi:10.1177/002234336500200104

Gitlin, T. (1984). *The whole world is watching: Mass media in the making and unmaking of the new left*. Berkley, CA: University of California Press.

Golding, P., & Elliott, P. (1979). *Making the news*. London: Longman.

Hanitzsch, T. et al. (2012). Worlds of journalism: Journalistic cultures, professional autonomy, and perceived influences across 18 nations. In D. H. Weaver, & L. Willnat (Eds.), *The global journalist: In the 21st century* (pp. 473–494). New York: Routledge.

Harcup, T., & O'Neill, D. (2001). What is news? Galtung and Ruge revisited. *Journalism Studies, 2*(2), 261–280. doi:10.1080/14616700118449

Hartmann, P., & Husband, C. (1974). *Racism and the mass media: A study of the role of the mass media in the formation of white beliefs and attitudes in Britain*. London: Davis-Poynter.

Horgan, J. (2007). *Preventing incitement to terrorism and radicalisation: What role for the media?* Paper presented at the EuroMed Conference. Dublin, Ireland.

Jager, S., & Link, J. (1993). *Die vierte gewalt: Rassismus und die medien*. Duisburg: DISS.

Jenkins, B. M. (1983). Research in terrorism: Areas of consensus, areas of ignorance. In B. Eichelman, D. A. Soskis, & W. H. Reid (Eds.), *Terrorism: Interdisciplinary perspectives* (pp. 153–177). Washington, DC: American Psychiatric Association.

Kelly, M. J., & Mitchell, T. H. (1981). Transnational terrorism and the Western elite press. *Political Communication, 1*(3), 269–296. doi:10.1080/10584609.1981.9962729

Laqueur, W. (1976). The futility of terrorism. *Harper's Magazine, 252*(1510), 99-105.

Leith, S. (2011). *You talkin' to me? Rhetoric from Aristotle to Obama*. London: Profile Books Ltd.

Luostarinen, H. (1999). *Media and collective identities*. Unpublished Manuscript.

McNair, B. (1998). *The sociology of journalism*. London: Oxford University Press.

McNair, B. (2003). *An introduction to political communication*. London: Routledge.

Noelle-Neumann, E. (1973). Return to the concept of the powerful mass media. *Studies in Broadcasting, 9*, 67–112.

Rana, P. S. J. B. (2011, July 29). Terrorism by other name. *The Kathmandu Post*. Retrieved July 30, 2013, from http://www.ekantipur.com/the-kathmandu-post/2011/07/28/related_articles/terrorism-by-other-name/224547.html

Schmid, A. P., & de Graaf, J. (1982). *Violence and communication: Insurgent terrorism and the western news media*. London: Sage.

Schulz, W. F. (1982). News structure and people's awareness of political events. *International Communication Gazette, 30*(3), 139–153. doi:10.1177/001654928203000301

Seib, P. (2012). *Real-time diplomacy: Politics and power in the social media era*. New York: Palgrave MacMillan. doi:10.1057/9781137010902

Taylor, P. M. (2009). Public diplomacy and strategic communications. In N. Snow, & P. M. Taylor (Eds.), *Routledge handbook of public diplomacy* (pp. 12–16). London: Routledge.

Terzis, G. (2001). Think local, teach global: National identity and media education. *Media Development, 48*(3), 62–66.

van Dijk, T. A. (1991). *Racism and the press*. London: Routledge.

van Dijk, T. A. (Ed.). (1997). *Discourse as structure and process*. London: Sage.

van Ginneken, J. (1998). *Understanding global news: A critical introduction*. London: Sage Publications.

Willnat, L., & Martin, J. (2012). Foreign correspondents—An endangered species? In D. H. Weaver, & L. Willnat (Eds.), *The global journalist: In the 21ˢᵗ century* (pp. 495–510). New York: Routledge.

Worlds of Journalism Study. (2013). Retrieved July 30, 2013, from http://www.worldsofjournalism.org/pilot.htm

KEY TERMS AND DEFINITIONS

Journalism: The occupation of news reporting.

Journalism Ethics: Principles of ethics and good practice specific to the challenges faced by journalists.

Media Framing: The ways in which the media frame events.

News Management: The organization and control of news reporting in media outlets.

Public Relations: The practice of managing the spread of information among individuals, organizations, and the public.

Terrorism in the Media: Media depictions and/or representations of terrorism.

Terrorism Stereotypes: A thought adopted about terrorism; thoughts or beliefs may or may not accurately reflect reality.

Section 4
Terrorism Tactics & Media Strategies

Chapter 8
Tactics of Terrorism

Brigitte L. Nacos
Columbia University, USA

ABSTRACT

In the late 1960s and early 1970s, Palestinian terrorists staged a number of spectacular hijackings of commercial airliners, exploited the often prolonged hostage situations to win massive news coverage of their political grievances, and seemed to inspire other groups to use the same tactics to highlight their grievances and demands. While the bombing of facilities was in the past and remains today the preferred mode of terrorist attacks, terrorists have also carried out assassinations, suicide missions, and kidnappings with various tactics fashionable at certain times and less so during other periods. For that reason, terrorism scholars, government officials, and journalists have pondered the question of mass-mediated contagion for decades without agreeing whether news about terrorist attacks inspires copycat strikes. Given the advances in communication and information technology and changes in the global media landscape during the last decade or so, this chapter reconsiders arguments surrounding contagion theories and contends that old and new media are important carriers of the virus of hate and instrumental in tactical and ideological contagion.

INTRODUCTION

On July 22, 2011, Anders Behring Breivik, a 32-year old Norwegian, detonated a car bomb near government buildings in Oslo killing eight people. He then made his way to the nearby island of Utoya, where he shot to death 69 people, most of them teenagers, in a camp of the Norwegian Labor Party's Youth League. From his arrest through his trial in the spring of 2012, Breivik justified his deeds as defensive actions of a Christian crusader against the onslaught of Muslim immigrants and Norway's "Islamic colonization." The particular

targets were liberal multiculturalist because they support immigration. Breivik revealed in court that he had consulted various media accounts, especially the Internet, to study the tactics of terrorist groups and lone wolves in order to determine how to carry out his own attacks. He was well informed about the ingredients of the truck bombs used in the first World Trade Center Bombing in 1993 and the Oklahoma City Bombing two years later. But most of all he studied the tactics of al-Qaeda Central and like-minded groups calling them "the most successful revolutionary movement in the world." In spite of their opposing views and goals,

DOI: 10.4018/978-1-4666-5776-2.ch008

Breivik expressed his admiration for al-Qaeda's tactics and suggested that they should inspire his fellow nationalists as they inspired him and his actions. "I have studied each one of their actions, what they have done wrong, what they have done right," he told the court. "We want to create a European version of Al Qaeda."

Breivik had hoped to copycat another and particular gruesome al-Qaeda tactic, the beheading of captured enemies. Obviously informed that former Norwegian Prime Minister Gro Harlem Brundtland had scheduled a visit at the youth camp on the day of his attack, he planned to take her hostage, decapitate her and post the video of her execution on the Internet. To his regret, when he arrived on the island, Brundtland had already returned to the mainland.[1]

In this case, a terrorist used his trial as global propaganda stage and an opportunity to describe in considerable detail that he was *directly* influenced by the reported tactics of other groups and individuals, when he planned his own terror attacks. Media conduced contagion, however, comes in different forms and is not always as obvious as in the case of Anders Breivik as the following example demonstrates.

On April 19th, 1995 Timothy McVeigh ignited a homemade truck bomb that destroyed the Alfred P. Murrah Federal Building in downtown Oklahoma City, killed 168 persons, injured close to 700 others, and triggered massive news coverage in the United States and abroad. Five days later the director of the California Forest Association, Gilbert Murray, was killed instantly when he opened a small package that had been mailed to his office. The enclosed message revealed that the sender was the mysterious person, dubbed "Unabomber" by the FBI, who had killed already two other people and injured 23 via mail bombs since 1978. That same day, *The New York Times* received a letter from the Unabomber threatening another deadly mailing unless the newspaper published a 35,000-word manifesto he had written to explain his motives. It is difficult to imagine

that there was not any link between the non-stop coverage of the terrorist spectacle in Oklahoma City on the one hand and the timing of the simultaneous mailings to Murray's office and the *Times* on the other. My guess was then and is now that the Unabomber, Theodore Kaczynski, was miffed because of the relatively modest news his mail bombs had received over the years compared to the tremendous attention the mass media paid to the Oklahoma City bombing. More importantly, whereas McVeigh's grievances and motives were prominently covered since he had intentionally posited clues in his car (i.e., references to the lethal clashes between federal agents and anti-government groups and individuals at Waco and Ruby Ridge), there had been no definitive news about the Unabomber's causes in the wake of his long mail bombing trail.

Thus, he wasted no time to finally get his share of media attention and recognition of his causes by sending off another mail bomb and a threatening letter to the country's leading newspaper. By September 1995, when *The Washington Post* published his full-length manifesto "Industrial Society and Its Future"—sharing the printing costs with *The New York Times*—the Unabomber had already overtaken McVeigh as terrorist newsmaker-in-chief and seen his causes widely publicized and discussed in the mass media.

If the deadly mail bomb, the letter to the *Times*, a follow-up threat to bomb the Los Angeles airport contained in a letter to the *San Francisco Chronicle*, and a host of demands and threats communicated to several newspapers and magazines were indeed inspired by the high volume and nature of news about Oklahoma City in order to get comparable coverage—and I believe that they were—it is impossible to prove media-related contagion here unless the imprisoned Kaczynski were to confirm such an effect with respect to the timing of a terrorist bombing and a threat some time in the future.

While this case speaks to the difficulty of finding conclusive evidence for *direct* media-induced contagion with respect to terrorism, it encourages the exploration of media content about terrorist incidents, methods, and, most importantly, ideologies as an agent of terrorist infection. In the following, I revisit the media contagion hypothesis as it relates to terrorism and, to a lesser extent for comparative purposes, to violence-as-crime.

Contagion theories have been forwarded and rejected with respect to terrorism for several decades—often in the context of media effects. While some scholars deny such relationships (Picard, 1986; Schlesinger, Murdock, & Elliot, 1984), the notion of mass-mediated contagion seems commonsensical and is supported by anecdotal accounts and systematic research (Schmid & de Graaf, 1982; Weimann & Winn, 1994).

More than 20 years ago, Robert G. Picard attacked the news-as-contagion theory as "backed by dubious science," arguing that "literature implicating the media as responsible for the contagion of terrorist violence has grown rapidly, but, under scrutiny, it appears to contain no credible supporting evidence and fails to establish a cause-effect relationship" (Picard, 1986, p. 1). He cited the minimal press effect findings of social scientists in the 1940s and 1950s in support of his rejection of the media contagion theory (Picard, 1991). What he failed to mention was that ample and far from "dubious" research, starting in the 1960s, found far stronger media effects on audiences (most notably with respect to agenda setting, framing, and priming) than the minimal effect school.

Writing with Northern Ireland and domestic terrorism in mind, Schlesinger, Murdock, and Elliott (1984) also rejected the idea that the media are spreading the virus of political violence as ignoring the intelligence and good judgment of news consumers and especially television audiences.

However, based on their quantitative analysis of media reporting (or non-reporting) of terrorist incidents and subsequent terrorist strikes of the same type (i.e., hijackings, kidnappings) Gabriel Weimann and Conrad Winn concluded that their data "yielded considerable evidence of a contagion effect wrought by coverage." More specifically, these scholars found that "television coverage was associated with a shortened lag time to emulation in the case of kidnapping, attacks on installations, hijackings, bombings, and assassinations" (1994, p. 277).

Alex P. Schmid and Janny de Graaf (1982) concluded that:

The media can provide the potential terrorist with all the ingredients that are necessary to engage in this type of violence. They can reduce inhibitions against the use of violence, they can offer models and know-how to potential terrorists and they can motivate them in various ways (Schmid & de Graaf, 1982, p. 142).

Similarly, Brian Jenkins asserts that:

Initial research tentatively suggests that heavy media coverage of hijackings, kidnappings and other hostile seizures carried out by terrorists increases the likelihood that similar incidents will occur in the period immediately following. A recent Rand analysis of embassy seizures during the last decade shows them occurring in clusters, clearly suggesting a contagion effect (Jenkins, 1981, p. 6).

Assumptions or inferences about contagion in the area of violent crimes are often based on observations and statistical data in the context of particularly horrific incidents. For example, Berkowitz and Macaulay (1971) studied crime statistics in the aftermath of the assassination of President John F. Kennedy in 1963 and two mass killings in 1966, when Richard Speck killed eight nurses in Chicago and Charles Whitman shot 45 persons from a tower at the University of Texas. It was found that "[s]tatistical and graphic data from 40 U.S. cities indicate" that those incidents "were followed by unusual increases in the number of violent crimes" (Berkowitz & Macaulay, 1971, p. 238). While the scholars characterized theses cases as "widely published crimes" (Ibid, p. 241) and implied a relationship between heavy news coverage of the three incidents and subsequent jumps in the number of violent crimes, they did not argue that most such crimes are instigated by media reports.

More recently, Loren Coleman (2004) explored the links between the Columbine school shooting in 1999, when high school students Eric Harris and Dylan Klebold killed 12 and injured 23 fellow students, some 400 similar incidents in the following years, and the Virginia Tech campus shooting in 2007, when student Seung-Hui Cho killed 32 people and wounded many others. In many of these cases the killers revealed the copycat nature of their violence by referring directly or indirectly to the Columbine massacre. In Coleman's words, the copycat effect occurs "when the media makes [sic] an event into a 'hot death story' and then via behavior contagion, more deaths, suicides, murders, and more occur in a regularly predictive cycle" (2007p. 1).

However, just as the media-terrorism connection is embraced and contested by communication, media, and terrorism scholars, there is also disagreement about the impact of media reporting on violent crimes. In a comprehensive, recent review of the relevant literature, one expert in the field cautioned:

Despite the vast volume of published literature that has concluded that the causal link between media violence and antisocial behavior is established, there have been more cautious and even dissenting voices that have challenged the strong effects position. Some writers have accepted that media violence can influence viewers, but not all the time and not always to the same degree in respect of different members of the audience (Gunter, 2008, p. 1063).

As for mass-mediated diffusion of terrorism, the strongest arguments against connections between media content and terrorist incidents are made by those who fear that the notion of the media as agent of terrorist contagion will strengthen the hands of governments in efforts to curb or alter terrorism-related content and thereby interfere with freedom of the press and expression. I share those concerns and oppose censorship categorically. But these concerns must not prevent us from considering possible connections between media content and terrorism contagion and find mitigating factors without media restrictions from government or other outside forces.

OBSERVATIONS AND REVELATIONS

The probably most cited example for media related contagion of violence or the threat thereof is that of D. B. Cooper, who in November 1971 hijacked a commercial airliner on the flight from Portland to Seattle under the threat of detonating a bomb in his briefcase. After receiving a $200,000 ransom and two parachutes at the Seattle-Tacoma Airport and ordering the crew to fly at the lowest possible altitude to Las Vegas, he jumped out of the plane and was never seen again. In the wake of heavy media coverage and the release of songs and a motion picture devoted to his daredevil heist, Cooper became a cult hero. More importantly, he inspired a series of copycat hijackings by other criminals during which the hijackers asked for ransom money and parachutes along the lines of Cooper's example.

As for terrorism, the perhaps best evidence of contagious media content comes from captured terrorists or ex-terrorists. According to Weimann and Winn, "Several biographical studies of terrorists show that many were motivated by a desire to emulate the publicity achievements of precursors" (1994, p. 218). This is exemplified in the case of

South Moluccan nationalists who hijacked trains in the Netherlands on two occasions in the 1970s to dramatize their plight and admitted reportedly after their arrest that their deeds were inspired by a similar attack plotted by Arab terrorists (Schmid & de Graaf, 1980, November).

COPYCATTING TERRORIST METHODS/TACTICS OF ATTACK

In the case of the South Moluccan train hijackers, media reports affected simply what method of attack the group selected as most likely to succeed from what one would assume were several options the extremists considered. This seems to be a quite common media-related contagion effect that explains why particular *modes* of terrorist attacks tend to come in clusters or waves. Thus, beginning with the hijacking of commercial airliners by Palestinian terrorists in the late 1960s, other Palestinian and non-Palestinian groups followed suit so that there was a cluster of hijackings with passengers held hostage. This method remained attractive in the 1980s and beyond. But as airlines and governments improved their security systems, the takeover of planes became more risky. While terrorists continued to hijack planes and in the case of the "Achille Lauro" a cruise ship, it was no longer the preferred method of attack. Instead, terrorist groups embraced other means of attacking different targets and victims, for example, embassy takeovers. Based on incident data collected by the Rand Corporation, Brian Jenkins found that the 43 successful embassy takeovers and five unsuccessful attempts between 1971 and 1980 occurred in 27 countries and targeted the embassies of many countries—albeit most of all those of the United States and Egypt. "Like many other tactics of terrorism, hostage-taking [in embassies] appears to be contagious," Jenkins concluded. "The incidents do not fall randomly throughout the decade, but occur in clusters" (1981, p. 7). The idea is that one event inspires

another one. Presumably, terrorists knew of these takeovers, most of them successful, from media reports since these incidents took place in a host of different countries on different continents. By late 1979, when the Iran Hostage Crisis began, the "students" who took over the U.S. embassy in Teheran and the Iranian leaders who backed them must have known (via news accounts) about the prominent news coverage such incidents received. After all, of the embassy takeovers during the 1970s, more than half occurred in the last two years of the decade.

Or take as a more recent example the cluster of gruesome beheadings of American, British, Japanese, and South Korean hostages by ruthless terrorists in Iraq and Saudi Arabia starting in the spring of 2004 with the killing of Nicolas Berg, a Philadelphia businessman. Emotionally wrenching videotapes that depicted the hostages begging for their lives were posted on the Internet by the killers and were subsequently reported on by traditional news organizations' in shocking detail. Consider, for example, the following description of an American civilian's decapitation by his terrorist kidnappers as published in a leading U.S. newspaper:

As the insurgent speaks, the gray-bearded man identified as Mr. Armstrong appears to be sobbing, a white blindfold wrapped around his eyes. He is wearing an orange jumpsuit. The masked man then pulls a knife, grabs his head and begins slicing through the neck. The killer places the head atop the body before the video cuts to a shot of him holding up the head and a third, more grainy shot showed the body from a different angle (MacFarquhar, 2004p. 1).

It is likely that the global wave of shock and outrage ignited by Berg's beheading spread the decapitation of hostages as terrorist method in the Middle East. And there were a number of cases in which terrorists beheaded their victims or threatened to do so outside the Middle East. In

Haiti, for example, the bodies of three headless policemen were found; they were victims of terrorists who explained their action as "Operation Baghdad"—a label that had no meaning in Haiti's civil strife, except for the cruel method of murder in Iraq. And then there was the beheading of a Buddhist official in a village in Thailand, which was described as an act of revenge for violence against Muslim rioters. After the shooting of Dutch filmmaker Theo van Gogh (his killer tried to cut his throat as well), self-proclaimed *Jihadis* in the Netherlands threatened to decapitate other critics of Muslim extremists. All of these perpetrators had recognized the shock-value and media attractiveness of this particularly gruesome terrorist tactic from afar.

As one terrorism expert concluded in this context, there "is no doubt that besides direct contacts between terrorist groups and/or individual terrorists, indirect observations of successful terrorist methods and strategies rely on *traditional news* reports and, more recently, *new media* outlets—especially Internet sites" (Sedgwick, 2007, p. 102). Examining the diffusion of suicide terrorism, Mia Bloom explains:

We can discern the direct (patron-client) and indirect (through observation) influences of suicide terror. In some instances, insurgent factions have been physically trained by other organizations and taught how to best use horrifying tactics to devastating effect, who subsequently import the tactic far and wide. . . . On other occasions, factions observe the successful operations of groups from afar—because of the publicity and media attention engendered by spectacular bombings, and then tailored the techniques to suit local circumstances (Bloom, 2005, p. 122).

While suicide terrorism spread inside and outside the Middle East well before 9/11, it became an even more popular weapon after the strikes in New York and Washington, D.C. Examining possible reasons for the post-9/11 wave of suicide terrorism, Paul Marsden and Sharon Attia argued that the media cannot cause "suicide bombings any more than sex (as opposed to HIV) can cause AIDS," but they also suggested that media might be "a vector of transmission that can precipitate its spread" (2005, p. 153). Considering the publicity success of 9/11 from the perspective of al-Qaeda and the organization's supporters and sympathizers, I pointed to the likelihood of spectacular homicide-suicide attacks becoming a most attractive model for future acts of terrorism in one form or the other (Nacos, 2003). While nobody has repeated the flying-of-commercial-airliners-into-buildings scenario so far, there have been many spectacular homicide-suicide attacks since in different countries and continents.[2]

Thus, in sum, besides personal contacts and cooperation between various groups, mass media reports are the most likely sources of information about the efficacy of terror methods and thus important factors in the diffusion of terrorist tactics. Interestingly, based on their analysis of terrorist incidents in the 1960s and 1970s around the globe, Midlarsky, Crenshaw, and Yoshida (1980) concluded that some terrorist methods of attacks (e.g., hijackings, kidnappings, bombings) were more contagious than others (e.g., assassinations, raids). These scholars recognized, too, that publicity provided by the news media was a factor in terrorists' decision to imitate terrorist methods they deemed effective. As they put it, "Visible and unusual violence is in essence newsworthy and attracts international publicity necessary for cross-regional and cross-cultural spread" (Midlarsky, Crenshaw, & Yoshida, 1980, p. 279).

THE SPECIAL CASES OF SUICIDE MISSIONS AND FEMALE TERRORISTS

On August 19, 2003, a Jerusalem a city bus packed with families returning from Judaism's holiest site, the Western Wall, was ripped to pieces by a powerful explosion. It was an unspeakable scene of carnage; 20 people, among them six children, were killed. More than 100 were injured. There were traumatized survivors and witnesses as well as disheartened rescuers. Shortly after the blast and well before the dead and critically injured men, women, and children were identified, a cell of the Palestinian Hamas group released a written press statement claiming responsibility for the attack and a pre-taped video of the "martyr" explaining his deed. The videotape showed 29 year-old Raed Abdul Hamid Misk holding a rifle in one hand and a Qur'an in the other. The father of two young children with a pregnant wife, and the imam of a Hebron mosque, justified his attack on innocents partially in Arabic and partially in English. His wife did not seem surprised when she said, "All his life he was saying, *Oh God, I wish to be a martyr*."[3]

By making the videotape available to the media nearly simultaneously with the explosion, the terrorists calculated correctly that the news media would pay a great deal of attention to Misk. He did not fit the profile of Palestinian suicide bombers—not in terms of his profession, age, or family status. This assured him and his act special media attention around the world when details about his victims were not yet available. During the following days, the media's interest in this unlikely terrorist remained high. Five days after the attack, for example, *The New York Times* illustrated a general story on suicide attacks with a huge color photograph of Misk. Taken three days before he killed himself in order to kill others, the photograph showed the smiling father with his three year-old son and two year-old daughter in his arms. Here was a compelling image that made people wonder what conditions could drive such a man to become a human bomb. This was precisely the effect that terrorists hope for. In this particular case, the news added up to an utterly successful publicity campaign that could not have been better orchestrated by the best experts on Madison Avenue.

No wonder that terrorist organizations with different grievances and in different parts of the world have suicide missions high on their list of tactics that guarantee special media attention.

From the perspective of terrorists, suicide terrorism has a number of advantages compared to other terrorist tactics. According to Bruce Hoffman, "Suicide bombings are inexpensive and effective. They are less complicated and compromising than other kinds of terrorist operations. They guarantee media coverage. The suicide terrorist is the ultimate smart bomb" (2003, June 1, p. 40). The efficacy of the suicide tactic is best understood by terrorists themselves. After interviewing 250 of the most militant Palestinians in the 1990s, Nasra Hassan wrote:

A Palestinian security official pointed out that, apart from a willing young man, all that is needed is such items as nails, gunpowder, a battery, a light switch, and a short cable, mercury (readily obtainable from thermometers), acetone, and the cost of tailoring a belt wide enough to hold six or eight pockets of explosives. The most expensive item is transportation to a distant Israeli town. The total cost of a typical [suicide] operation is about a hundred dollars (Hassan, 2001, November 19, p. 39).

Furthermore, the planners of suicide missions do not have to make escape plans or fear the arrest of their operatives and the revelation of organizational secrets. More importantly, organizations that embrace suicide attacks as their tactic of choice appreciate that this terrorist method is more likely to succeed than most other means.

Military commanders of Hamas and Islamic Jihad remarked that the human bomb was one [of] the surest ways of hitting a target. A senior Hamas leader said, "The main thing is to guarantee that a large number of the enemy will be affected. With an explosive belt or bag, the bomber has control over vision, location, and timing (Hassan, 2001, November 1, p. 39).

Suicide attacks are especially horrifying to target societies—for a number of reasons. First of all, as one expert concluded, this tactic is "reliably deadly" and "on average kills four times as many people as other terrorist acts" (Hoffman, 2003, June 1, p. 40). Secondly, much publicized suicide attacks have lasting effects on the psyche of the target society because no one knows when, where, and how the next suicide attack will occur.

Because of their operational and psychological effectiveness, modern-day suicide attacks spread from Lebanon to an increasing number of other venues, among them Sri Lanka, Turkey, Chechnya, Argentina, and, of course, Israel. Religiously motivated terrorists are not the only ones who have embraced this tactic in the last three decades. To be sure, many of the suicide operations conducted by groups in the Middle East were and are carried out by Muslim extremists. However, secular groups have adopted the same tactic. In Lebanon, only about half of all suicide attacks recorded since the early 1980s were carried out by members of Hezbollah and Amal, both Shi'ite groups; several secular organizations were responsible for the rest. Similarly, although Hamas and the Palestinian Islamic Jihad, both religious Muslim groups, embraced suicide attacks as their most effective weapon against Israelis, the more secular Al-Aksa Martyrs Brigade followed suit beginning in late 2001 (Dolnik, 2003).

The Lebanese Hezbollah that created the mythos of the explosives-laden martyr in the Arab world and beyond—mostly because of the TV images that were broadcast after such attacks. The result was what Christoph Reuter calls an extremely successful "martyr-marketing" (2004, p. 128). This marketing assures that there is never a shortage of individuals willing to die for a cause that they learn to perceive as far more important than their own lives. Hassan (2001, November 19) describes the post-incident glorification efforts after suicide attacks by Palestinian militants, explaining that suicide operations, for example, are not complete with the explosion and the many deaths. Evidence via audiocassette or video of the martyr is distributed to the media and local organizations as a record of success and a tool of encouragement to young men. In this, the act becomes the subject of various public activities and materials (e.g., sermons in mosques, posters, videos, and demonstrations) to celebrate the deed and subsequently inspire other aspiring martyrs. In short, not only newspapers, radio, and television but all kinds of community-based communications spread the word of and praise suicide missions, thereby encouraging predisposed groups and individuals to embrace the same tactics.

Whether they commit suicide terrorism or utilize other terrorist tactics, women involved in terrorist attacks or plots are sure to receive more media attention and are framed differently than their male colleagues. This and the fact that security forces tend to be less suspicious of females than males encourages women to volunteer for terrorist missions and groups to recruit females into their ranks. A recent media content analysis comparing newspaper coverage of one American woman (Colleen LaRose, widely known as "JihadJane") and two American men (Daniel Patrick Boyd and Farooque Ahmed) arrested for terrorism-related offenses affirmed the female-male news divide. To begin with, JihadJane received 8.2 times more coverage than Boyd and 5.5 times more than Ahmed. This imbalance was particularly noteworthy with respect to Ahmed since at the time of this research he had "already been indicted, tried, and sentenced while La Rose was still awaiting sentencing" (Conway & McInerneym, 2012, p. 11). Just as important, the research findings confirmed "the continued existence of [female] media frames, highlighted in the literature, that treat females associated with terrorism in a dramatically different manner to their male counterparts" (Ibid, p. 18). Although women have founded and/or led terrorist groups throughout the history of terrorism, the bottom line is that they are still seen as unlikely terrorists. As one terrorism expert noted:

The media fetishizes [sic] female terrorists. This contributes to the belief that there is something really unique, something just not right about the women who kill. We make assumptions about what these women think, why they do what they do, and what ultimately motivates them (Bloom, 2011, pp. 33-34).

All of this is not lost on terrorists. They are well aware that female terrorists, whether they are killed in suicide missions or survive other forms of attacks, receive far more news coverage than their male counterparts.

INSPIRATIONAL CONTAGION

The adoption of effective terrorist tactics does not cause terrorism, since those tactics are imitated or adapted by organizations that already exist and have embraced terrorism or, as one expert in the field explains:

A particular terrorist technique is only of interest to a group that has already made the decision to adopt a terrorist strategy; a technique cannot on its own cause a resort to terrorism. Similarly, a radical group will normally enter into direct contact with an established terrorist group only once the decision to adopt a terrorist strategy has already been made (Sedgwick, 2007, p. 102).

Inspirational contagion is more alarming for the targets of terrorism because it is the stuff that makes terrorists and leads to the formation of new organizations and cells or the radicalization of lone wolves. The above mentioned recollection of one of the Red Army Faction's founders, Horst Mahler, about the crucial role of televised terrorism news in formulating his group's ideology and thus the RAF's raison d'etre could not have been a surprise for Midlarsky, Crenshaw, and Yoshida whose data analysis revealed the spread of terror-

ist thought from the third world and particularly from Latin-American and Palestinian terrorist leaders and groups, to Western Europe in the early 1970s. Noting that radicals in Germany and elsewhere in Western Europe received this sort of inspirational information from the mass media, the three scholars figured that "physical contacts [for example, between RAF and Palestinian groups] followed rather than preceded the decision to adopt terrorism" (1980, p. 282).

Writing more than a quarter century later and considering David Rapoport's (2004) categorization of four global waves of terrorism, Mark Sedgwick suggests,

"Contagion" is possible at two levels, and can happen in two ways. On one level, a group might copy a particular terrorist technique, and on another level a group might copy a general terrorist strategy. Either of these might happen directly or indirectly. All these forms of contagion take place. The primary form, however, is the adoption of a general terrorist strategy without direct contact. All other forms of contagion are secondary to this (Sedgwick, 2007, p. 102).

The most recent, most lethal, and geographically most diffused inspirational virus originated with Afghan mujahideen fighting Soviet occupiers in the 1980s and, most important, with the establishment of al-Qaeda and its rapidly expanding terrorism network. It is hardly surprising that contagion effects tend to be far stronger among those individuals and groups that share the cultural and religious background of organizations and leaders with inspirational ideologies. Whereas kinship and friendship brought the members of the al-Qaeda Central organization together (Sageman, 2004), the mighty "Afghan wave" that reached literally all continents in the post-9/11 years is now mostly driven by inspirational contagion (Sedgwick, 2007). As Marc Sageman noted:

The Islamist terror networks of the twenty-first century are becoming more fluid, independent, and unpredictable entities than their more structured forebears, who carried out the atrocities of 9/11. The present threat has evolved from a structured group of al Qaeda masterminds, controlling vast resources and issuing commands, to a multitude of informal local groups trying to emulate their predecessors by conceiving and executing operations from the bottom up. These "homegrown" wannabes form a scattered global network, a leaderless jihad (Sageman, 2008, p. vii).

In the first decade of the new millennium the Internet has become the agent of virtual inspirational contagion spread by a multitude of extremist Websites with chat rooms and message boards that condition and inspire especially young men and, increasingly, women within the Muslim world and in the diaspora to form or join autonomous groups or cells and plot terrorist strikes (Nacos, 2010; Sageman, 2008; Weimann, 2006).

But other kinds of ideologies of hate and terror are also disseminated via old and new media and communication technologies. And, no doubt, the inspirational virus is particularly potent when diffused through media forms that are not subject to checks by the traditional media gatekeepers. It is for this reason that inspirational contagion spreads faster and further via books, CDs, and, of course, the Internet.

Timothy McVeigh was inspired by the extremist anti-government and white supremacy doctrines of the militia movement, neo-Nazi groups, and Christian Identity cells, which were synthesized by William Pierce, the founder of the neo-Nazi National Alliance. Using the pseudonym Andrew McDonald, Pierce published the novel *The Turner Diaries* that describes an all out race war—starting with the bombing of FBI headquarters in Washington. McVeigh and Pierce did not have any contact. However, *The Turner Diaries* was the book that inspired McVeigh's extremist worldview and, at the same time, served him as a blueprint for the

actual bombing plot. His accomplice Terry Nichols was inspired by another novel, *Hunter*, authored by Pierce under the McDonald name that was just as racist and violent as *The Turner Diaries*.

Or take the extremist fringe in the anti-abortion movement that uses Websites to spread its hateful agenda in the name of God, displays gruesome pictures of bloody fetuses described as "butchered" children, publicizes the names and locations of abortion providers, celebrates the murderers of abortion providers as inspirational heroes and role models, and cites from the Bible to spread the word that God is on the side of those who serve as soldiers in the "Baby Liberation Army." After Dr. George Tiller, a physician who provided legal abortions in Wichita, Kansas, was shot in May 2009 during Sunday morning service in his church by Scott Roeder, it was revealed that the killer had been a frequent visitor to several of the most notorious anti-abortion sites. On one occasion, he had posted a message on a fake Tiller.com Web site that labeled Dr. Tiller "the concentration camp Mengele of our day" who "needs to be stopped before he and those who protect him bring judgment upon our nation" (The Washington Post, 2009). It is likely that he took this comparison from the Army of God's Web site or similar Internet pages that vilified Tiller by comparing him to Dr. Josef Mengele, a physician in the Auschwitz concentration camp. Not surprisingly, The Army of God praised Roeder's killing of "Tiller the Killer" on its Web site and demanded that Roeder must be found not guilty since he "faced a terrible evil" (Bray, 2009, August 7).

CONCLUSION

To what extent the written and spoken word and visual images encourage people who hold extremist ideologies, to initially adopt attractive terrorist tactics or become terrorists is difficult to assess. The authorities in several European democracies seem convinced that mass media contagion is a real threat. Thus, the Austrian government forced two Websites to remove an on-line "Minaret Game" that called for players to shoot at minarets and thereby prevent calls for prayer at a time of growing anti-Muslim sentiments and deeds. The same game had been posted earlier on an extremist Swiss Web site. In neighboring Germany, the authorities took a board game out of circulation that had been designed and sold to sympathizers by the National Socialist Underground, a terrorist cell responsible for the killing of at least eight Turkish immigrants and German of Greek descent. The fields of designation on the Monopoly-like "Progromly" board were pictures of concentration camps, Hitler portraits, and images of Nazi emblems. In France, as the Interior Ministry declared in 2008, Internet sites with terrorism related content believed to glorify and encourage violence can be blocked. And Germany adopted a law that criminalized the distribution of material that encourages terrorism and teaches terrorist methods regardless of the intent of the material's distributers.

Some counterterrorism experts have no doubt that terrorist propaganda can and does result in copy-cat actions. When this issue became part of the mass-mediated discourse during the trial of the Norwegian terrorist Anders Behring Breivik, Col. Zbigniew Muszynski, the head of Poland's Counterterrorism Center, noted that "security experts believe there have already been violent acts inspired by Breivik, including an Italian extremist's killing of two African immigrants in Florence late last year." Muszynski recognized a risk that some people without knowledge of extremist ideas being exposed to terrorist propaganda, becoming interested, and moving on to commit violence themselves (Gera, 2012).

All told, then, when it comes to international and domestic terrorism, various kinds of media figure to one extent or the other into tactical and/or inspirational contagion. The Internet has moved center-stage in this respect—especially during the last decade. And while counterterrorism experts become increasingly aware of the role of contagion, they have not found effective antidotes to the mass-mediated virus of political violence whether on the Internet or elsewhere in the global media landscape. As Robert Gates in a candid speech before he retired as U.S. Secretary of Defense:

Public relations was invented in the United States, yet we are miserable at communicating to the rest of the world what we are about as a society and a culture, about freedom and democracy, about our policies and our goals. It is just plain embarrassing that al-Qaeda is better at communicating its message on the Internet than America. As one foreign diplomat asked a couple of years ago, "How has one man in a cave managed to out-communicate the world's greatest communication society?" Speed, agility, and cultural relevance are not terms that come readily to mind when discussing U.S. strategic communications (Gates, 2007).

As this chapter suggests, the far greater problem is, however, that besides al-Qaeda and like-minded groups and individuals there are many, many other secular, religious, and pseudo-religious terrorists whose violence attracts news coverage and who self-communicate their incendiary and contagious material.

REFERENCES

Berkowitz, L., & Macaulay, J. (1971). The contagion of criminal violence. *Sociometry, 34*(2), 238–260. doi:10.2307/2786414

Bloom, M. (2005). *Dying to kill: The allure of suicide terror*. New York: Columbia University Press.

Bloom, M. (2011). *Bombshell: The many faces of women terrorists*. London: Hurst.

Bray, M. (2009, August 7). Scott, Scout, and Boo Radley. *The Army of God*. Retrieved August 14, 2009, from http://www.armyofgod.com/Mike-BrayScottScoutandBooRadley.html

Coleman, L. (2004). *The copycat effect: How the media and popular culture trigger mayhem in tomorrow's headlines*. New York: Paraview.

Coleman, L. (2007, April 17). *The copycat effect.* Retrieved from blogspot.com

Conway, M., & McInerneym, L. (2012). What's love got to do with it? Framing JihadJane in the US press. *Media. War & Conflict, 5*(1), 6–21. doi:10.1177/1750635211434373

Dolnik, A. (2003). Die and let die: Exploring links between suicide terrorism and terrorist use of chemical, biological, radiological, and nuclear weapons. *Studies in Conflict and Terrorism, 26*(1), 17–35. doi:10.1080/10576100390145143

Gates, R. (2007, November 26). *Landon lecture.* Paper presented at Kansas State University. Manhattan, KS. Retrieved September 1, 2008, from http://www.defense.gov/speeches/speech.aspx?speechid=1199

Gera, V. (2012, April 25). Breivik's publicity at trial just what he wanted. *Kansas City Star*. Retrieved May 2, 2012, from http://www.kansascity.com/2012/04/25/3575041/breiviks-publicity-at-trial-just.html

Gunter, B. (2008). Media violence: Is there a case for causality? *The American Behavioral Scientist, 51*(8), 1061–1122. doi:10.1177/0002764207312007

Hassan, N. (2001, November 19). An arsenal of believers: Talking to the human bombs. *The New Yorker*. Retrieved July 3, 2013, from http://www.newyorker.com/archive/2001/11/19/011119fa_FACT1

Hoffman, B. (2003, June 1). The logic of suicide terrorism. *The Atlantic*. Retrieved July 3, 2013, from http://www.theatlantic.com/magazine/archive/2003/06/the-logic-of-suicide-terrorism/302739/

Jenkins, B. M. (1981). *The psychological implications of media-covered terrorism (No. RAND-P-6627)*. Santa Monica, CA: The Rand Corporation.

MacFarquhar, N. (2004, June 19). Acting on threat, Saudi group kills captive American. *The New York Times*, p. 1.

Marsden, P., & Attia, S. (2005). A deadly contagion? *The Psychologist, 18*(3), 152–155.

Midlarsky, M. I., Crenshaw, M., & Yoshida, F. (1980). Why violence spreads: The contagion of international terrorism. *International Studies Quarterly, 24*(2), 262–298. doi:10.2307/2600202

Nacos, B. L. (2003). The calculus behind 9-11: A model for future terrorism? *Studies in Conflict and Terrorism, 26*(1), 1–16. doi:10.1080/10576100390145134

Nacos, B. L. (2010). *Terrorism and counterterrorism: Understanding threats and responses in the post-9/11 world*. New York: Longman Pearson.

Picard, R. G. (1986). *News coverage as the contagion of terrorism: Dangerous charges backed by dubious science*. Paper presented at the Annual Meeting of the Association for Education in Journalism and Mass Communication. Norman, OK.

Picard, R. G. (1991). News coverage as the contagion of terrorism: Dangerous charges backed by dubious science. In *Media coverage of terrorism: Methods of diffusion* (pp. 49–62). Newbury Park, CA: Sage Publications.

Post, W. (2009, June 2). *The suspect at a glance*. Retrieved August 20, 2009, from http://www.washingtonpost.com/wp-dyn/content/article/2009/06/01/AR2009060103675_pf.html

Rapoport, D. C. (2004). The four waves of modern terrorism. In A. Cronin, & J. Ludes (Eds.), *Attacking terrorism: Elements of a grand strategy* (pp. 46–73). Washington, DC: Georgetown University Press.

Reuter, C. (2004). *My life is a weapon: A modern history of suicide bombing*. Princeton, NJ: Princeton University Press.

Sageman, M. (2004). *Understanding terror networks*. Philadelphia, PA: University of Pennsylvania Press.

Sageman, M. (2008). *Leaderless Jihad*. Philadelphia, PA: University of Pennsylvania Press.

Schlesinger, P., Murdock, G., & Elliott, P. (1984). *Televising terrorism: Political violence in popular culture*. New York: Charles Scribner's Sons.

Schmid, A. P., & de Graaf, J. (1980). *Insurgent terrorism and the western news media: An exploratory analysis with a Dutch case study*. Leiden, The Netherlands: Center for the Study of Social Conflicts, Dutch State University.

Schmid, A. P., & de Graaf, J. (1982). *Violence and communication: Insurgent terrorism and the Western news media*. London: Sage.

Sedgwick, M. (2007). Inspiration and the origins of global waves of terrorism. *Studies in Conflict and Terrorism*, *30*(2), 97–112. doi:10.1080/10576100601101042

Weimann, G. (2006). *Terror on the internet: The new arena, the new challenges*. Washington, DC: United States Institute of Peace.

Weimann, G., & Winn, C. (1994). *The theater of terror: Mass media and international terrorism*. New York: Longman.

KEY TERMS AND DEFINITIONS

Contagion Theories: Seek to explain networks as conduits for infectious attitudes and behaviors.

Jihad: A vigorous or emotional crusade for an idea or principle my some Muslims.

Media Content Analysis: A methodological investigation into media texts, images, videos, etc.

Suicide Terrorism: An act of terrorism in which the perpetrators kill themselves for the purpose of killing others.

Terrorism Motivations: The reasons, ideologies, principles, or desired outcomes that impel acts of terrorism.

Terrorist Attack: An aggressive move on an adversary orchestrated by terrorists.

Terrorist Strategy: The skillful planning and use of a method created and carried out by terrorists to achieve specific outcomes.

ENDNOTES

1. The account of Breivik's revelations about his attention to and imitation of terrorist tactics used by al-Qaeda and other groups was taken from a multitude of news reports inside and outside the United States.

2. The idea of imitating the 9/11 attacks has been discussed among terrorists. Thus, the Colombian FARC wanted to fly a plane into the presidential palace during President Alvaro Uribe's inauguration but was unable to find a pilot willing to dye for the cause—even though the organization offered to give the suicide pilot's family a two million dollar reward.

3. These quotes were published in many reports both in the print and broadcast media.

Chapter 9
Media–Related Strategies and "War on Terrorism"

Randal Marlin
Carleton University, Canada

ABSTRACT

Terrorist events are breaking news for the media whose ethical responsibility can be debatable. Tactics of terrorism vary from kidnapping, hostage-taking, hijackings, and others up to mass destruction, including the use of nuclear weapons. Media responses and coverage strategies of such tactics also vary, with some reluctant to provide terrorists with the "oxygen of publicity." Some striking similarities have appeared recently between the build-up to the war on Iraq begun by U.S. President George W. Bush's administration in 2002, culminating with the start of war in 2003, and the 2012 push by current U.S. President Barack Obama for action to prevent Iran from acquiring a nuclear weapon. In the earlier case, the presumption was established in the public mind, without adequate evidence, that Iraq possessed or was about to possess weapons of mass destruction, and had the will to use them against the United States. In the latter case, the background presumption is that Iran is actively seeking to produce a nuclear weapon, with Israel as a potential target. This claim also lacks solid evidence at the time of writing, but has come to be accepted in some media as an uncontroversial fact. This chapter looks at aspects of how different English and French Canadian newspapers, as examples, covered the push for war on Iraq. It includes reflections on the use of language in reporting on the war itself. The central concern is with the media role in fear-mongering and propaganda for war.

INTRODUCTION

Terrorist events are breaking news for the media whose ethical responsibility can become ambiguous, divided between the need to inform the public and the unwillingness to provide the "oxygen of publicity" so necessary for terrorism's success. Tactics of terrorism vary from kidnapping, hostage taking, hijackings, and others up to mass destruction, including the use of nuclear weapons. Media responses and coverage strategies of such tactics also vary, and can include endorsement of a "War on Terrorism" in the case of major threats, including nuclear or other weapons of mass destruction. In the wake of a terrorist attack public opinion is likely to be angry against the perpetrators and

DOI: 10.4018/978-1-4666-5776-2.ch009

fearful of further attack. Extremist attacks bring about extremist responses and normally reasonable people who see themselves as terrorism targets tend to prefer their safety to upholding due process and civil liberties. Governments in this situation tend to yield to such extremism and in some cases welcome and harness it, because it allows them to expand their powers. In this situation the media have a hard time resisting such extension of powers because they may alienate readers and be blamed for being "soft on terrorism" if they are seen as restraining government by demanding due process and defending civil liberties in a time of emergency. It is easier to be critical of government when the emergency is past.

This chapter does not focus on the immediate media responses to acts of terrorism, but the media responses to government fear-mongering, war-mongering, and expansion of power in the wake of a terrorist attack, specifically 9/11. In these media responses, some striking similarities have appeared between the build-up to the war on Iraq begun by U.S. President George W. Bush's administration in 2002, culminating with the start of war in 2003, and the 2012 push by current U.S. President Barack Obama for action to prevent Iran from acquiring a nuclear weapon. In the earlier case, the presumption was established in the public mind, without adequate evidence, that Iraq possessed or was about to possess weapons of mass destruction, and had the will to use them against the United States. In the latter case, the background presumption is that Iran is actively seeking to produce a nuclear weapon, with Israel a potential target. This claim also lacks solid evidence at the time of writing, but has come to be accepted in some media as an uncontroversial fact. It is often a cause for alarm how easily mainstream media cooperate with government and private think tank efforts to affect public opinion in ways that promote war.

There appears to be a pattern of behavior wherein media are uncritical of government allegations leading to war. After the war is launched,

the media become more self-critical and work to regain credibility. However, when the government embarks on a similar program of persuasion in a new war, the pattern is repeated (Altheide & Grimes, 2005). This chapter examines how the Canadian media reported on the build-up to the war against Iraq launched by U.S. President George W. Bush in March 19, 2003.

Many Americans reacted with surprise and dismay when Canada failed to join the so-called Coalition of the Willing—countries bent on ousting Saddam Hussein's regime and thereby forcing Iraq to comply with UN requirements relating to weapons of mass destruction. A brief understanding of Canadian political history reveals that a large segment of the French-speaking population has long resisted calls to arms in defense of what they see as imperial interests. Without UN backing, a U.S.-led coalition might seem indistinguishable from imperial designs on Middle East oil. Had Prime Minister Chrétien made the leap he would have handed a vote-getting issue to the flagging "indépendantiste" parties, founded to seek Quebec independence, the Parti Québécois, and the Bloc Québécois. A poll conducted by Ipsos-Reid in late March 2003, revealed that about 83% of Quebec residents were glad Canada stayed out of the war, whereas only 52% of respondents felt that way outside the mainly French-speaking province of Quebec (McCarthy, 2003). The French media of Quebec reflected this strong anti-war stance.

Canadian media coverage of the war build-up is fascinating not just for the English/French divide, but also for the role played by what at the time was the most powerful media conglomerate in English Canada: CanWest Global Communications Corporation. The owner of this conglomerate (no longer in existence in the same form, having been split up and parts sold off) was the Asper family, headed at the time by Israel "Izzy" Asper, a long-time supporter of the then ruling Liberal Party of Canada, and of Zionist causes (he died in October, 2003). The Aspers built up a television network and in 2000 acquired the cross-Canada

Southam chain of newspapers. This chain had earlier cultivated, according to its former owners, a policy of independence for each newspaper in the chain. This changed markedly under the Aspers, who made it clear from the start that control was to be centralized and member newspapers would have to make space for at least some centrally-written editorials for the whole chain. Once policy on a given issue was laid down by central office in Winnipeg newspapers would not be free to disagree editorially, though columns, letters and news were said not to be bound in this way. An outcry resulted from this policy, and two publishers had their employment terminated under circumstances widely acknowledged to stem from differences relating to centralized control.

The Aspers' CanWest Global was not the only media conglomerate in Canada. *The Globe and Mail* with a readership larger than its cross-Canada competitor, *The National Post*, was at the time owned by Bell Globemedia which also owned a major cross-Canada television network, CTV, and was part of a huge conglomerate with telephone and Internet interests. A chain of tabloid newspapers, the *Sun* chain, was also part of Rogers Cable that also owns the widely circulating magazine *Maclean's* (Sun newspapers are now under Québecor ownership.) On the whole, Canadian newspapers presented a wide range of opinions and information concerning the build-up to the Iraq war. The editor of *The Globe and Mail*, Edward Greenspon, who had been recently appointed, allowed some very strong anti-war opinion pieces in that newspaper. In the case of the Aspers the pro-Israel policy of the owners made their newspapers especially interesting objects of study during the war build-up period.

Starting from the most anti-war newspapers, those most skeptical about justification for war, and moving to the most pro-war and least skeptical, these major newspapers can be aligned as follows: First is Montreal independent French newspaper, *Le Devoir*. Then the wider-circulating *La Presse* with the owning Demarais family linked through

marriage to Prime Minister Chrétien. Among English language newspapers the widely circulating *Toronto Star* would come next, followed by *The Globe and Mail*. I would put in last place the Asper-owned *National Post*. As a regular reader of the *Ottawa Citizen*, another paper in the Asper chain, I would put it close to the *National Post*. It has published strongly anti-war letters, but I would never have expected to see an article by Robert Fisk appear there, for example, in contrast to practice under the previous ownership.

Newspapers compete for the largest circulations and it is common for every publisher to assure readers that the highest level of journalistic integrity, objectivity, and professionalism is maintained in their news columns. Those who would accuse a major media outlet of bias will need to provide justification. A general survey of *The National Post* and *Ottawa Citizen* reveals a pro-war bias. In order to examine this idea further, this study chose to look carefully at the coverage given by five different prominent daily newspapers on what was arguably the most important presentation of evidence made by the U.S. administration in its attempt to justify going to war. This was the elaborate display that U.S. Secretary of State Colin Powell presented to the UN Security Council February 5, 2003. The *National Post* showed a clear bias in favor of accepting Powell's evidence and of going to war against Iraq. This is far from conclusive proof of bias more generally, but it will at least count as a solid beginning.

In evaluating coverage, one needs to look not only at what gets published, but also what is left out accidentally or by design. Gilbert Keith Chesterton once wrote,

Tennyson put it very feebly and inadequately when he said that the blackest of lies is the lie that is half a truth. The blackest of lies is the lie that is entirely a truth. Once give me the right to pick out anything and I shall not need to invent anything (Chesterton, 1987, p. 420).

In other words, how a newspaper selects the material is an important factor in determining bias or fairness in reporting. Analysis will require looking at quantity as well as quality and the different ways stories and pictures can have impact on the reader through positioning, type size, order of presentation, and the like.

THREE EXAMPLES OF BIAS

My first example relates to the handling of the death of Abu Nidal, the notorious terrorist who had come to live in Iraq. He was killed and it was widely believed that this was done under orders from Saddam Hussein. An obvious motivation for such killing would have been to provide evidence to the world that Iraq was not interested in harboring or supporting terrorists. It had become clear to many analysts that the U.S. was looking for reasons to justify invasion of Iraq, and by eliminating a notorious resident terrorist Hussein would be would be removing one such reason. However the spin on the story placed by the *Sunday Telegraph*, and reprinted in the *Ottawa Citizen* was that Abu Nidal was killed for not training terrorists. The lead paragraph in the *Ottawa Citizen* August 25, 2002, read: "Abu Nidal, the Palestinian terrorist, was killed on the orders of the [sic] Saddam Hussein after refusing to train al-Qaeda fighters in Iraq, the *Sunday Telegraph* has discovered." By painting Saddam Hussein as a current and militant supporter of al-Qaeda's brand of terrorism, the story supported the Bush administration's line that Hussein was actively supporting worldwide terrorism and was a direct threat to the United States.

The stakes were so high that one would have expected closer scrutiny of the *Sunday Telegraph's* stated source for the story: "Iraqi opposition groups." Certain opposition groups would have a strong self-interest in spreading such a story regardless of its veracity. Yet by using the word "discovered" the *Ottawa Citizen* implicitly en-

dorsed the *Sunday Telegraph* account. To preserve a skeptical stance they should have written, "claims to have discovered" instead.

The story referred to a "U.S. official who has studied the reports" who said, "there is no doubt that Abu Nidal was murdered on Saddam's orders." However, who was this official, what were his credentials, and more importantly, what was his view on the claim made by "Iraqi opposition groups"? If there had been any solid basis for the story, we ought to have heard more about Abu Nidal's relationship with Saddam Hussein in the following months, but the story dropped out of sight after having fixed in many minds the idea that he was bent on training world terrorists despite the more obvious alternative explanation that he was doing his best, albeit ruthlessly, to refute any such terrorist connection.

Thus, it is argued that an uncritical, heavily charged story was foisted on the readership. That the story originated from the British *Sunday Telegraph* does not alter the *Ottawa Citizen's* responsibility. Other instances are available where that newspaper has shown itself to be unreliable (Thomas, 1999). Conrad Black's Hollinger owned the *Sunday Telegraph* and the *Jerusalem Post,* the strongly right-wing views of which should have led to treating their accounts with appropriate circumspection.

As a second example of bias I submit the attack on Prime Minister Chrétien following a television interview on September 11, 2001, in which he suggested that western arrogance toward poor countries might have something to do with terrorist responses. There was a vigorous denunciation of his stance in CanWest Global's most influential paper, *The National Post*. The ensuing columns and editorial in that newspaper were not surprising, nor especially sinister, since in that connection sources were upfront. More insidious was the prominence given to a column reprinted from the *Wall Street Journal,* leaving out an important biographical fact relating to the credibility of the author, Marie-Josée Kravis (formerly Drouin, a newspaper columnist under that name) as a commentator. The column, headed "Canada's Chretien: The 'Schroeder' of the Americas" began with a tendentious question: "Why is Jean Chretien so intent on finding a justification for terrorism?" The question is tendentious, because his reported remarks relate, I believe, to causes of terrorism as distinct from a justification for it. The reference to German Chancellor Gerhard Schroeder came at a time when he was under attack for remarks by his Justice Minister Herta Daeubler-Gmelin, allegedly comparing Bush to Hitler. What she was reported to have said was that Bush's movements against Iraq were a common ploy to divert attention from domestic problems, a technique used "even" by Hitler. She later claimed that she had made no comparison between Bush and Hitler. Schroeder was under attack for not rebuking his minister, and the comparison with Chrétien may well have been calculated to transfer some of the tarnish onto Chrétien. What Kravis wrote was: "Unlike the furor caused by Chancellor Gerhard Schroeder and his justice minister, the remarks of the Canadian PM fell on deaf Yankee ears. Has Canada become so irrelevant in world politics?" This kind of rhetoric evokes some unseemly comparisons in the reader's mind, not excluding a tinge of anti-Semitism.

The column went on to contrast Chrétien with the late former prime minister, Pierre Trudeau, praising the latter for his tough stand in 1970 against the terrorist Front de Libération du Québec (FLQ) when he proclaimed the War Measures Act. She writes: "Mr. Chretien could not resist an opportunity to vent his frustrations about the U.S., and his alleged concern for the poor provided the perfect foil for his anti-Americanism" and "Canada will not be taken seriously as long as its leaders tell Americans that on 9/11 they and the West reaped what they sowed."

Readers of the *Wall Street Journal* will no doubt have been impressed by the credentials cited at the end of the article: "Ms. Kravis is a senior fellow at the Hudson Institute. She was born and raised in Canada." However, she misrepresents Trudeau if she claims that he would have differed from Chrétien on the point at issue. I can recall Mr. Trudeau addressing very forcefully to a large crowd gathered in December 1967, in what was the old railway station in Ottawa, saying that the Third World poor had a just claim to a fair share of the world's riches, and if we did not respond to the demands of justice, they would be right in taking that share from us by force. In Trudeau's case, unlike Chrétien's, there was indeed reference to justification, though not specifically to terrorism, however that might be defined. Also to be borne in mind is that Trudeau took action when in power to rectify some of the injustices that had fueled or might fuel the separatist movement, by enforcing bilingualism in the federal government, investing huge sums in Quebec with government buildings on the Quebec side, allowing the Parti Québécois to take power democratically in Quebec in 1976, setting up a commission which rebuked the RCMP for unlawful and undemocratic measures taken against the Parti Québécois, patriating the constitution and instituting a Charter of Rights and Freedoms, and suchlike.

Both the *National Post* and the *Ottawa Citizen* featured Kravis's article as a news story and as an opinion piece. The headline on a page 2 *National Post* story read "Chrétien soft on terrorism, Wall St. Journal readers told." Ottawa Bureau Chief Robert Fife began the story with "Jean Chrétien was taken to task in the influential *Wall Street Journal* yesterday for 'having a misplaced pity for terrorists' and ignoring Canada's history of confronting terrorism." The story was given more prominence by an accompanying picture of an old Ottawa newspaper headline proclaiming the War Measures Act.

The *Ottawa Citizen* carried the story as the second most prominent on its front page, headlined "PM savaged in Wall Street Journal article." The sub-head stated, "PMO denounces 'distorted' claims of anti-Americanism." The lead paragraph, by Juliet O'Neill, read "Prime Minister Jean Chrétien was portrayed in the influential *Wall Street Journal* yesterday as an anti-American with 'a misplaced pity for terrorists', an irrelevant leader seeking to embellish a meager legacy by pretending he cares for the poor." The article provides some additional revealing facts about Kravis, namely that she "holds directorships at Ford, Seagram and Hollinger, among other corporations, and is married to American financier Henry Kravis. He ranks 351st on *Forbes* magazine's annual list of the world's wealthiest people, with his worth estimated at $1.3 billion." It should be noted that O'Neill's story devotes several paragraphs to responses to the article from the Prime Minister's Office, starting as early as the third paragraph. This certainly mitigates any claim of bias against the *Ottawa Citizen*, showing fairness to the other side by seeking and publishing its response.

However, neither story reveals the additional credibility-affecting fact about Mrs. Kravis's biography that, as reported in the *Washington Times,* she was one of two chairmen of a black-tie gala dinner raising an estimated $30-million for the Republican National Committee on May 14, 2002. She delivered the toast to President George W. Bush who attended the gathering. In other words, she can be seen as a member of the Bush party faithful, not some independent academic voice. And the public should have been informed about this.

While incidental to the main concern of this chapter, it is worth noting that Chrétien's response to this attack was that of a consummate politician. His government announced a few days later that it endorsed military action against Iraq if Saddam Hussein failed to comply with tougher UN resolutions on weapons inspections, and Canada could provide military support. This elicited a banner inch-high headline in *The Globe and Mail*: "Canada backs U.S. on Iraq." The lesson in public relations seems to be the following for a power-holder: if you are under attack with ambiguous but tarnishing rhetoric, then ambiguously appear to act in a way that contradicts what you are under attack for.

My third example relates to attacks by members of the Asper family and their publications on the Canadian Broadcasting Corporation (CBC). Many viewers, myself among them, felt that the CBC did an admirable job of seeking out news and viewpoints from both sides of contentious issues, in particular where Israel-Palestine relations are concerned. By contrast, Israel Asper claimed that the CBC had a pro-Palestinian bias. Because the CBC is publicly financed, the way it is perceived among the public is very important to its survival. With their broadcasting and newspaper empire the Aspers had a great deal of power to influence public perception. Of course, any attack on the CBC is also an attack on a competitor, since Global television competes with the CBC for viewers and advertisers. So on two counts their attacks on the CBC come under suspicion of special interest motivation.

Israel Asper denounced CBC coverage in widely reported public statements, but once again that is not itself of much significance, since an intelligent reader will recognize his perspective and judge his claims accordingly. It is different, though, when someone not so easily identified as someone with an axe to grind mounts the podium for the same purpose. In a column published in the *Ottawa Citizen* December 21, 2002, Norman Spector, a former Canadian ambassador to Israel and a former publisher of the *Jerusalem Post*, wrote to criticize the CBC for not using the word "terrorist" to describe the actions of Hamas and other groups who kill themselves and murder Israeli citizens. He saw an inconsistency in the CBC's using the "T" word in relation to 9/11 and the bombing of a Bali nightclub in 2002, while not using it in relation to murderous acts against Israelis.

Spector's concern was a legitimate one, and Tony Burman, editor in chief of *CBC News, Current Affairs* and *CBC Newsworld* conceded in a letter to the *Ottawa Citizen* on January 2,

2003, that the examples cited were lapses in the CBC's policy of only using the word "terrorist" in cases where use of the word is attributed to others. Anyone who has read Noam Chomsky on terrorism understands the problem. Why should suicide bombers killing innocent Israelis merit the term while Israeli bombings of innocent Palestinians should not? The argument about different intentions regarding selection of targets can bear some, but hardly sufficient weight in practical moral assessments of relative wrongs. So the CBC decided, as a matter of policy, not to use the word with its own authority. It is understandable that such a policy would be difficult to sustain, given the frequency with which the word is used in ordinary discourse, and Burman claimed the lapses were not repeated.

So far, this is all fair debate. However, Spector chose not only to raise a legitimate issue but also to introduce a foul linkage that might be acceptable in private discourse, but when made publicly and repeatedly expressed, as it was, becomes a smear. He claimed that the CBC's coverage of the Mideast affected the mind-set of native leader David Ahenakew, widely denounced by most Canadians for having recently praised Adolf Hitler for the Holocaust. Spector made this claim in his original column, and also in a column printed in reply to Tony Burman on the same day as the latter's letter. Spector's reply took up more than half a page in the more prestigious op-ed page, whereas Berman's letter was a mere ten column-inches.

This kind of linkage is so damning against CBC that one would expect a self-proclaimed (as he was in the first article) friend of CBC to hastily add a lot of appropriate disclaimers in relation to the linkage, so as to discourage a knee-jerk Ahenakew-CBC association. On the contrary, the slur was repeated in his reply and in a later column headed "CBC must stop misleading viewers on Middle East," where he ended with the menacing comment that if Burman "continues to neither change the coverage nor defend it, the time will have come to appoint a new general to clean up an operation

that is stimulating the views of David Ahenakew and his ilk." The slur on the CBC was repeated in news stories as well, such as the report in the *Ottawa Citizen* by Andrew Duffy on January 16, 2003, about a canceled debate between Spector and Burman. A paragraph reminded readers of Spector's allegation that "the CBC's Mideast coverage was creating distorted views of the world, such as those held by native leader David Ahenakew, who praised Adolf Hitler and the Holocaust in a recent speech." Repetition on this scale of such a tendentious claim, without suitable disclaimers, amounts in my view to propaganda.

The attack on the CBC did not appear out of nowhere. The timing was such as to give the appearance of punishing the CBC for exposing an apparently unfounded report claiming that a Hezbollah leader had called for terrorism worldwide. This report, published in the *Washington Times* under the by-line of Paul Martin (not the Canadian Liberal Party leader-in-waiting) did not check out, as the CBC diligently reported, but it was sufficient to get Canada to change its mind about Hezbollah and to include it among terrorist organizations as defined by Bill C-36, the anti-terrorist Act.

What struck me as particularly unfair in Spector's charge of bias was the fact that CBC radio regularly sought out the opinions of both Spector and Robert Fisk on Mideast issues. The two were, and are, well-matched in terms of knowledge and debating skills and I would always find them instructive. By contrast, nowhere in the *Ottawa Citizen* under the Asper ownership have I seen any column by Robert Fisk, even though he is recognized for his superb reporting from that area. He just does not share the pro-Israel stance of Spector.

The above three examples are not conclusive as to bias, any more than Norman Spector's findings of inconsistencies in CBC reporting in certain instances were conclusive. In both cases there are suggestions of bias that need responses.

The question of owner influence is a very difficult one to establish. The influence usually operates at the level of who is appointed to make decisions. Then there is the matter of self-censorship of journalists who may go farther in trying to please the owner than even the owner would wish. Testimony of former Nieman Fellows to the U.S. Commission on Freedom of the Press in 1947, is still revealing on this point:

The significance of owner control doesn't lie in the number of times the own interferes, but when. In nine instances out of ten there is an illusion of freedom, but when the issue is really vital to the owner, then he comes down hard (Chafee, 1947, p. 520, emphasis in original).

In what follows we look at a case where at least some owners were indeed vitally concerned with an issue, namely, that of going to war with Iraq. Thus, we compare the reporting in the different newspapers on this issue to look for bias.

REPORTING ON UN SECURITY COUNCIL FEBRUARY 5, 2003

The date when the interests of pro-war enthusiasts were most in play came on February 5, 2003, when Secretary of State Colin Powell attempted to convince the UN and the world that war against Iraq was necessary and justifiable. The picture presented to the Security Council was that Saddam Hussein had a relationship with al-Qaeda, was ready to use biological and chemical weapons of mass destruction, and was well on the way to having a nuclear bomb and delivery capability to threaten the world, including the United States. By July 12, 2003 even the White House officially doubted Saddam had had nuclear capabilities, alleged six months earlier in President Bush's State of the Union Address in 2003, and in claims repeated by Powell (Sanger & Risen, 2003). A strongly pro-Israel owner with hardliner political

views might be expected to want to discourage skepticism about the U.S. claims allegedly justifying war. If one believes in media influence, one would likewise expect to see a strong antipathy toward skepticism to be reflected not just in the opinion pages, but also in the news reporting. The question then is: did the coverage of the *National Post* show such a tendency?

In what follows I compare the coverage by five of the most influential newspapers in Canada of the crucial presentation February 5, 2003. We are looking, then, at the February 6 issue in each case. Three of these newspapers are English, two French. Canada lacks a genuine left wing daily newspaper of wide distribution, but a few columnists in middle to right wing papers present a somewhat muted representation of left wing viewpoints. I would align the newspapers from pro-war to anti-war as follows: *The National Post, The Globe and Mail, The Toronto Star, La Presse*, and *Le Devoir*. The reader is invited to verify my ranking from the account I give below. My order of presentation will move from *The National Post* to *Le Devoir* for sharpness of contrast, and then to *La Presse*, followed by the *Globe* and the *Star*.

On February 5, 2003, Colin Powell sought not only to influence the UN Security Council, but also the general public to accept his justification for a "coalition of the willing" to wage war in Iraq. The visuals that went along with the presentation gave an aura of authenticity—pictures identified as storage places for chemical munitions, the vial of powder held up by Powell, representing anthrax, freshly graded earth near what was presented as a chemical complex, and so on. To a critical mind, the visuals were far from proof of anything. A chemical bunker looked not much different from an athletic complex, and anyone can hold up a vial of powder.

Looking first at the *National Post* coverage, the impression on the reader is overwhelming that Colin Powell's submission is, in the view of that newspaper, all the proof needed to justify going to war. The banner, inch-high headline screamed in all-capital letters "FACTS ARE 'IRREFUT-ABLE': POWELL." An overline spelled out three different forms of evidence with "United Nations told of Iraq's hidden papers, nuclear designs and connections to Al-Qaeda." A sub-heading reported "Britain convinced, Canada finds evidence 'disturbing', France wants more inspections." A column on the left-hand side, by Mark Steyn, began with two sub-heads of different size. The first, and larger one stated "We're on the road to Baghdad," while the smaller one said "And the United Nations is on the road to oblivion." In all of this, there is little if any skepticism. Even France is not presented as disbelieving, only as wanting more inspections. A boxed insert, "Electronic Intercepts," on the right hand side reproduces talk between Iraqi military officers.

It is assumed the intercepts are authentic, and that they reveal a desire among the Iraqi military to make sure all incriminating materials were properly evacuated before the visit of a UN inspector, and that no references to nerve agents would be found in documents.

A small picture of Powell's hand with the vial was reproduced again on page A15 alongside three large (8x5-inch) photographs of what purported to be "Chemical Weapons Leaving Al-Musayyib," "Bulldozed and Freshly Graded Earth" at the "Al-Musayyib Chemical Complex," and finally "Mobile Production Facilities for Biological Agents." The top two pictures, identified as taken in May and July 2002, respectively, reveal to a critical viewer nothing that is not a matter of interpretation. If you start by believing that they are trucks ready to load up on chemicals, the pictures assist that belief strongly. If you do not start with that presupposition, there is nothing that would indicate they were specially designed for moving chemicals. All the pictures show is four or five very long trucks.

The third picture does present three long trucks that look very incriminating, two of them with

suspicious cylinders joined by piping, one truck also having a large rectangular box. The third truck had only four rectangular boxes, identified as spray dryers and a filling machine. But attentive inspection shows that the picture is not an actual photograph, but a model. The three photographs are weak in the way of logically compelling proof, but the combination of the three photographs has a powerful effect on the imagination.

The quantity of material favoring a given position or outlook can be an indicator of a newspaper's slant, but care is needed to interpret this indicator properly. It would be possible to offset pages of turgid, carelessly written material with a few short paragraphs of well-researched, pertinent, acerbic commentary—provided the proper signals are given so that the reader does not miss it. In the case of the *National Post's* analytical articles, there was no strong countervailing force. Essentially they conveyed that it would be reasonable to accept the evidence Powell presented, even though it was not conclusive. So an article by Peter Goodspeed was headlined "Powell Seeks to Shift Burden of Proof to Iraq," and began "While there was plenty of smoke, there was no smoking gun." He made the point that intelligence information is "by its nature full of uncertainty," in effect excusing Powell for not having anything better to offer.

A separate article, by Jan Cienski, tended to bolster Powell's credibility by painting him as one who had been one of the doves in George W. Bush's cabinet. The story, headlined "A reluctant warrior makes the case for war," argued that as a result of his previous opposition Powell was "the most convincing salesman for the Bush administration's case for action against Iraq." On page A17 some reaction to Powell's case is provided. A story by Michael Friscolanti acknowledges that world leaders opposed to a U.S.-led war in Iraq were "unswayed," but what is stressed in the headline is the impact on some senior democrats: "'Compelling' case made for war: senior democrats." At the top of the page are pictures of two Democrats with quotations from them in eye grabbing type.

Senator Dianne Feinstein, a California Democrat, says, "I think he laid the most comprehensive and compelling case that may have been made. I no longer think that inspections are going to work."

On another page there is an impressive diagram of an international terrorist network stemming from al-Zarqawi. Portrayed are eight faces connected with names and lines. One is identified as a detained al-Qaeda operative. The impact is powerful and bolstered by the adjacent headline: "Iraq a haven for al-Qaeda, Powell says." The claim made by Colin Powell is a very strong one: "Iraq has been working secretly with Osama bin Laden's terrorist network since the mid-nineties, and provided chemical and biological weapons training to al-Qaeda members, Colin Powell . . . charged yesterday." The story goes on to report that Powell accused Saddam Hussein of "training al-Qaeda terrorists and harboring an Iraq-based cell responsible for bomb and poison plots in Europe."

On the Comment page, David Warren in a lengthy article makes his own view of Powell's case very clear: 'Mr. Powell showed irrefutable evidence . . . [and] demonstrated beyond reasonable doubt that Iraq is in flagrant breach of each of the three requirements of Resolution 1441." By the time one reaches the editorial page of the *National Post*, one hardly needs to read the headline above the editorial: "Powell makes the case." The uncritical willingness to accept Powell's accusations has already been a part of the way the news, pictures and comment were all presented.

Let us now look at the sharp contrast to the *National Post* provided by *Le Devoir*, which made doubt about the evidence the central point of attention, instead of the evidence itself. Its banner, front-page headline read: "Doubt persists in the National Security Council" (Cornellier & Lévesque, 2003). There is a picture of a Colin Powell, with a serious, somewhat grim and almost menacing look, as he makes a point with an extended forefinger. The caption straightforwardly reports that for 90 minutes, Powell aligned facts and arguments to show Iraq was hiding materials

from UN inspectors and that al-Qaeda had several agents in Baghdad. A column on the top left-hand side, headed "Prosecutor Powell," begins: "The American war preparations involve a political script in the face of which one does not need to be a skeptic to feel manipulated."

On page five, *Le Devoir* publishes an Agence France-Presse report, which scrupulously distances itself from giving any credence of its own to what Mr. Powell said, putting into quotation marks key words and attributing to him every statement that might be open to doubt. The photograph of the al-Zarqawi chart is reproduced alongside the article, and the caption states: "Above: projection of a slide showing links between certain terrorist cells active in Europe and the Middle-East." Here the word "show" carries an element of ambiguity as to whether the showing is veridical or not, and one could argue that a thoroughly skeptical reporting attitude would have avoided such ambiguity. However, while it might have seemed pedantic to say "purported to show," the three-column headline over story and picture shows no such ambiguity: "Colin Powell tries to establish a 'sinister' link between Baghdad and al-Qaeda. There is no indication here that his attempt to establish this link was successful." Likewise, the sub-head reported "Twenty-odd members of the terrorist network operated in the Iraqi capital according to him."

Turning to the editorial page, there is no doubt about where *Le Devoir* stands on the matter of accepting Colin Powell's word. The cartoon shows Mr. Powell pointing to a picture of an empty desert of sun and sand hills, with "Iraq" written underneath. He says "Nothing! That's the proof that it is well hidden." The editorial, by Serge Truffaut, is headed "Deficiency of proof," and a summary of the editorial states: "The account that Secretary of State Colin Powell presented to the Security Council contained no proof that could authorize those in Washington who are predisposed toward a war against Iraq. Mr. Powell's story was more a politicized version of the Blix report than a speech demonstrating that Iraq had provoked a *casus belli*."

Historically, the French-Canadian population has been fiercely divided on the merits of going to war with either the British who were their conquerors, or the French of France, some of whom thought of Canada as so many acres of snow—"quelques arpents de neige" in Voltaire's words. In recent decades France has rediscovered French-Canada and has encouraged links with Quebec. All the more reason, then, why Prime Minister Jean Chrétien should have tergiversated on the matter of Canadian support for the U.S. war against Iraq. Canada has to keep good relations with the United States, so to give a flat "no" to help was inadvisable. On the other hand, Chrétien would not want to alienate the voters in his Shawinigan riding, who would likely follow the historically conditioned anti-war sentiment. They would also not share the anti-French stereotypes so easily fostered and exploited in the United States, and would tend to feel more of an affinity with the position of French President Jacques Chirac.

The much wider-circulating *La Presse*, owned by the powerful conglomerate called Power Corporation, with family connections to Prime Minister Chrétien, tended to emphasize the skillfulness with which Colin Powell presented his case. The main front-page headline stated, "Powell shows his hand." The sub-head read "Supported by photos and sound tracks, the Secretary of State incriminates Iraq." The story led off with the nature of Powell's accusations against Iraq, without introducing a skeptical stance. An adjacent photograph showed Powell holding up the vial of white silicone-based substance. In this picture he looks mild-mannered, not threatening, and has an appearance of scientific detachment, even curiosity.

The tone of objective presentation is carried into the inside pages, beginning with page three, with pictures of trucks, UN inspectors, Abou Moussab al-Zarkaoui (so-spelled), and aluminum tubes. Five different accusations are laid out with separate headings, under the main headline "What Powell contends against Saddam." On the right-hand side the transcript of the taped conversations (translated into French) between Iraqi military officers is published. At the bottom of the page, a column by Richard Hétu stresses the high reputation of Colin Powell worldwide. It takes note of a *New York Times* report that certain experts in the CIA and the FBI had doubts about links between al-Qaeda and Iraq, but it does not endorse those doubts. The column headline "Powell plays on his reputation" and the column as a whole appear to treat the matter as a standoff between Powell and the doubters—if anything, giving the edge to Powell in the matter.

On the top of page four a diagram showed countries that were for and those that were against military intervention after Powell's speech. A column by Daniel LeMay, headed "Eagle in spite of himself" focused on the drama and nervous energy involved in Powell's presentation, as well as the hope that moderates had placed in him. The message was that Powell had himself become convinced by the evidence. In the absence of calling Powell's credentials into question, the column gives a favorable presentation of Powell and his case, including reference to the concession Powell made to possibly extending the UN inspections beyond February 14.

On the same page a skeptical note is sounded by Isabelle Hachey, *La Presse's* London correspondent who writes that in spite of what Prime Minister Tony Blair has been saying, his government's information services are of the opinion that Saddam Hussein's regime has cultivated "no link to al-Qaeda." By contrast, the Washington correspondent, Martin Vallières, reports a very favorable reception to Powell's speech in both houses of Congress, and among both Democrats and Republicans.

The *La Presse* correspondent in Paris refers to Powell's "proofs" always in quotation marks, but focuses not on his credibility so much as the awkward position France finds itself in "France is boxed in between a rally and the 'historical crisis' with the U.S."

On page 6, *La Presse* carries a story on the Canadian government's reaction to Powell's presentation and tends to give it a large measure of credence. The headline states "Canada's tone hardens" The story is about Canadian support for the idea that Saddam Hussein has not lived up to his international obligations regarding disarmament. Canadian Minister of Foreign Affairs Bill Graham is quoted as saying that he found the presentation "troubling and convincing." An accompanying story, continued from page one, acknowledged that there was no "smoking gun" type of evidence in Powell's presentation.

When we arrive at the editorial and commentary pages, a definite discordant note is sounded, in contrast to the neutral or positive material earlier in the paper. Mario Roy, writing the editorial, repeats favorable comments about Powell's presentation, but introduces an element of caution concerning Powell's credentials: "one should bear in mind, however, that he is bound by a duty of solidarity with the White House." The editorial concludes that in spite of Powell's at times brilliant presentation, war is not the solution to the present crisis. The accompanying cartoon shows "Uncle Powell" boring his audience with slides, saying "Oops! I've got it the wrong way around."

The strongest notes of dissension from Colin Powell's claims are presented on the Forum page opposite the editorial page, under the inch-high headline, "Convaincu?" ("Convinced?"). Jocelyn Coulon, director of the Montréal campus of the Pearson Center for the Maintenance of Peace states in no uncertain terms: "Basically, Colin Powell did not have irrefutable proof of Iraqi violations." A photograph shows Powell holding the vial that, according to the caption "could contain anthrax." Curiously, the caption does not explain that the material in the vials is not in fact anthrax but a kind of white sand. A second columnist, Rémi Landry, focuses on what Powell's speech signifies regarding Washington's intentions. He goes along with

the idea that Saddam Hussein has been fooling the world about his armaments and torturing his people, but questions whether he is an imminent threat to international security. War is a catastrophe that can be legitimately embarked on only in case of defense, he writes. A third columnist, Clifford Lincoln, Liberal member of the Quebec legislature from Lac St-Louis, distinguishes Powell's situation from that of Adlai Stevenson in October 23, 1962 "Nothing like October 23, 1962." Stevenson had irrefutable proof of Soviet missiles in Cuba. By contrast, Powell presented no such proof. Secondly, Stevenson's evidence was for the sake of peace, Powell's for going to war. The evidence to support the idea that war, with its devastating consequences, was necessary to world security just was not there. Let the inspectors continue their work, he wrote. "In the meantime, let us make peace and not war."

Turning again to the English media, Canada's national newspaper of record, *The Globe and Mail*, asserted on the whole a measure of independence from the influence sought by Colin Powell, but the skepticism was not pursued quite as aggressively as we have seen in the French-language newspapers. Lengthy excerpts of Colin Powell's transcript were reprinted on the Comment page, just before the editorial page, under a banner heading "We must not shrink from our duty." With some 52 column inches of text and a 3x8" cartoon of a somewhat menacing Powell with index finger pointed upward the overall impact was one of the paper giving credence to Powell's claims.

A column by Wesley Wark and the newspaper's editorial reinforced this impact.

However, the front page of *The Globe and Mail* played a very different, more skeptical tune, with a powerful, two-line, four-column wide and about inch-high heading: "Powell's dossier on Iraq fails to sway key players." A line over the heading stated, "Dramatic UN presentation sets the stage for a showdown over the need for war." After leading off by straightforwardly reporting Colin Powell's belief that "Iraq is now in further material breach of its obligations," and that "this conclusion is irrefutable and undeniable," reporter Paul Koring switched to focus on the disbelief in the Security Council, writing in the fourth paragraph that "from first reactions, his performance swayed none of the key players at the UN, with only Canada among America's reluctant allies seeming to dance closer to the Bush administration's position. Canada's Foreign Affairs Minister Bill Graham, who had previously taken a stance opposed to war without UN approval, was quoted as saying "Secretary Powell made an absolutely convincing presentation showing that Saddam Hussein is trying to play hide-and-seek with the arms inspectors. . . . It amounts to a transfer of the burden of proof from the United States to Saddam Hussein."

What is interesting about this quotation from Mr. Graham is the way in which it encompasses in its endorsement of Powell's speech aspects of Saddam Hussein's behavior that would only doubtfully be a justification for going to war. He did not, in other words, say he believed that Saddam Hussein had weapons of mass destruction that he could use to damage the U.S., nor did he say that Powell had convinced him that the Iraqi leader was linked in any significant way with al-Qaeda. His expressed agreement was about Saddam Hussein's lack of co-operation with UN inspectors, and the justification for putting more pressure on him to co-operate. The story noted that French Foreign Minister Dominique de Villepin likewise allowed that after Mr. Powell's speech "we must choose to strengthen decisively the means of inspection," if that were the only alternative to war.

Alongside the Koring report was approximately a 6x8 inch photograph of a somewhat menacing Powell, showing his teeth and about to tap the table with the third finger of his right hand. Underneath was an excerpt from intercepted radio conversations between a commander in Iraq's Second Republican Guard Corps and another officer. A list of six elements in Powell's indictment was published alongside the photograph:

"1. Thwarting the UN; 2. Biological Weapons; 3. Chemical weapons; 4. Nuclear weapons; 5. Terrorist connections; 6. Human rights."

Paul Koring had a separate, fully accepting article assessing Colin Powell's presentation on page two, "Powell keeps his best intelligence on Iraq for allies, expert says." The upshot was that while Powell persuaded many people who found his evidence compelling, there was other evidence that could not be revealed because it would tip off the Iraqis to sources and methods used by U.S. intelligence gathering services that they might not know about. Koring's source of information was given as Charles Pena, director of defense policy studies at the Washington-based Cato Institute. James Woolsey, a former director of the CIA, was also quoted as saying that "the only people who don't believe that Iraq has at least chemical and bacteriological weapons would be either people who work for Saddam or human versions of ostriches; there are no other possibilities."

In a final paragraph, Koring shows his assumption that much of what Powell presented is true. Having concluded in the penultimate paragraph that it was evident "the Iraqi regime has been sloppy in at least some of its attempts to hide and deceive," he concludes with: "Moving weapons in daylight, building a new, large and obvious rocket-testing facility, and talking openly on radios about 'nerve weapons' are all indicative of gross failures of elemental rules of military secrecy." The tone of this comment stifles skepticism as to whether the allegations about the existence of the rocket-testing facility or the intercepted talk were actually true.

A story on the bottom of page one covered the drama of the presentation, with the headline "Soldier turned statesman captivates UN." *The Globe and Mail* reporter Miro Cernetig wrote that Powell's voice, "usually controlled and measured, took on a nervous quaver when he gingerly waved a glass vial of white powder and warned about an Iraqi anthrax attack." Yet Cernetig thought that Powell had "pulled off one of the most memorable performances at the United States yesterday." As the story moves to the break page on A10, some doubts about the conclusiveness of the evidence are allowed to surface. The heading on the break is "Powell lacked 'gotcha' moment."

Cernetig makes the comparison with Adlai Stevenson's "smoking gun" presentation to the Security Council of spy-plane photos of Soviet missiles in Cuban territory. Powell's case was not that strong and he faced a "harder and more nuanced sell," in Cernetig's words.

Cernetig usefully calls attention to the fact that Powell's handlers assured the UN press corps that there was no real anthrax in the vial he held up. That the handlers would have felt it necessary to make such an assurance, as Cernetig saw things, indicates it was not made clear in the presentation that the vial contained only a harmless powder! If the news reporters were unsure, what would be the reaction of the average television viewer, directly seeing the vial held up?

The first challenge to the Powell account appears on page nine underneath a four-column, five and a half inch high picture of Kurds in northern Iraq watching Powell's performance on television. The story, by Associated Press reporter Charles Hanley in Baghdad, is headed "Powell's case just 'stunts', and 'special effects'." These opinions are attributed to presidential adviser Lieutenant-General Amer al-Saadi, who suggested the tapes were fabricated, that defector testimony was unreliable and that the satellite photographs "proved nothing."

To the left of the Kurds photograph at the top of the same page, a story with a two-column, three-line headline, "Liberal caucus ordered to cool anti-U.S. talk," attributes to Foreign Affairs Minister Bill Graham the view that Powell's presentation was "strong evidence of Iraqi deception and defiance," and that the onus now shifted to President Saddam Hussein to prove his regime was actively co-operating with inspectors. On the whole this story tended to encourage a favorable reaction to Powell's claims.

More likely to influence readers than the obviously committed Iraqi source were two highly skeptical reactions to Colin Powell's presentation appearing on page 11. These tended to offset somewhat Paul Koring's uncritical presentation. The first, at the top of the page, with a two-column, four-line headline of about half-inch type, consisted of a round-up of expert opinion, summed up in "Terrorism experts doubt bin Laden, Baghdad link." The sub-head stated: "Despite Powell's talk of a 'sinister nexus' few concrete facts offered, observers say, adding it was least compelling argument." Occupying four columns to the right, and about 6 inches deep was the chart Powell presented of Al-Zarqawi with possible links.

Underneath the photograph is a story headed "Bin-Laden-Iraq link suddenly emerges," which seems to be accepting of Powell's claims. The final paragraphs in the story make room for skepticism, however. "If Mr. Zarqawi is so important, it is curious that he does not appear on the FBI's list of 22 most-wanted terrorists, terrorism expert Peter Bergen recently wrote in Britain's *Guardian* newspaper." The story reported Bergen as saying that U.S. intelligence sources thought Mr. Zarqawi was "not a significant al-Qaeda player."

Turning over to page 12, the reader is presented a selection of Powell's photographs and the drawing of trucks outfitted for bacteriological warfare. At the left bottom third of the page the break headline on Paul Koring's story tends to favor Powell: "Burden of proof shifts to Hussein, Graham says," but the right part of the page reflects European skepticism: "U.S. presentation does little to sway leaders or public," reports Alan Freeman from London.

Between the above-mentioned two stories is a significant listing of poll results on page A12. The poll results are of 8,000 people in 14 countries, conducted between November 11 and December 14, 2002, by Ipsos-Reid. The question was: "Do you think your country's leaders should be more or less supportive of American government policies?" Canada came out with 37% favoring more supportive, 48% less supportive, 10% same as now, and 5% do not know. The significance of this poll is that it can be expected to reinforce skeptical attitudes to Powell's presentation.

We can contrast the Ipsos-Reid poll with the Gallup poll reported in the Can-West Global newspaper, the *Ottawa Citizen* on September 9, 2002. The timing of this poll is significant, coming just before the speeches remembering the events of September 11 a year earlier. The front-page one-column headline proclaimed: "Canadians back Bush on Iraq, poll says." The story says "A Gallup poll shows Canadians supporting an invasion to topple the regime of Iraqi dictator Saddam Hussein by a 52 to 43 per cent margin, the highest level of support among the four U.S. allies polled," the other allies being Britain, Spain and Italy. Unfortunately this story does not supply the reader with the exact question asked of respondents, though the reporter, Mike Blanchfield, wrote that the Gallup poll "suggests the majority of Canadians wouldn't mind if [Prime Minister Chrétien] starts to see things the way Mr. Bush does."

Comparatively muted is the reference towards the end of Blanchfield's study, to another poll conducted by Montreal's Leger Marketing, which "found 54 per cent of Canadians were dissatisfied with Mr. Bush's arguments for attacking Iraq, compared with only 22 per cent who thought they were adequate."

Returning to *The Globe and Mail* coverage, counteracting the two page 11 skeptical accounts was a very favorable commentary on page A15, headed "Powell makes his case: The evidence is in, and it's damning," by Wesley Wark, identified as a specialist in security and intelligence issues at the Munk Centre for International Studies at the University of Toronto. There are a few qualifying paragraphs at the end of his article, but the main thrust is reflected in the headline. He gives strong support to Powell's view of things. First, he expresses awe at the intelligence capability of the United States: Satellites overhead, successful eavesdropping on Republican Guard and other Iraqi communication circuits, as well as evidence from defectors and friendly intelligence agencies.

Wark makes the comparison with the Cuban missile crisis, not to draw attention to the absence of a smoking gun as Clifford Lincoln did for *La Presse*, but on the contrary to suggest the evidence was even greater. He wrote: "What's different this time around is the breadth of evidence offered—not just U-2 spy plane photos but a little of everything in the U.S. intelligence dossier, part of what one Bush administration official calls a 'Mount Everest' of information." He mentions uncritically Colin Powell's reference to "Iraq's development of unmanned aerial vehicles" which might in Powell's words "even be deployed directly against the United States" to deliver chemical and biological weapons.

On the alleged nuclear threat from Iraq, Wark notes that Powell did not say that Iraq had the bomb, only that "Saddam Hussein's regime was intent on getting there." The alleged connection with al-Qaeda Wark calls the "most controversial element of the U.S. dossier." But instead of challenging Powell's contention, he states that although the evidence is not "hard enough to conclude that Iraq and al-Qaeda have truly allied" it is enough to "lend credence' to the idea that a "nexus" exists between the two and chemical and biological weapons. Powell's word "nexus," though in quotation marks, is allowed to pass without critical scrutiny.

The Globe and Mail editorial, "Powell's strong case and the coming risk," gave solid, but measured support of Powell's case while expressing concern about the risks that his path to war would involve. Even though many people would be glad to get rid of Saddam Hussein, bringing democratic reform would take five years and 75,000 U.S. troops, according to U.S. government documents, the editorial said, adding: "Many Iraqi citizens will consider the troops a blessing, but many others will consider them occupiers or infidels." It concluded that George W. Bush "must be more open with the American people and with other countries such as Canada, about all that is envisaged. This is a huge step, and it cannot be taken lightly." Although the editorial thought it unlikely that France, China and Russia would wield their vetoes to deny Washington the imprimatur of the UN, as we now know France was later to do just that.

Turning now to the *Toronto Star* we find a more subdued front-page treatment of Powell's presentation. Two photographs taking up four columns by five inches mid-page depict what purport to be a chemical munitions bunker and a sanitized bunker, under a three-quarter inch headline, "Saddam's 'web of lies'." Immediately above the pictures is written "Sanitization of Ammunition Depot at Taji." The lead paragraph in the story by William Walker, of the *Star's* Washington bureau, is puzzling: "U.S. Secretary of State Colin Powell laid out Iraqi President Saddam Hussein's 'web of lies' for the UN Security Council yesterday but it failed to ensnare nations skeptical of the Americans march to war with Iraq." Taken literally, the paragraph seems to be telling us that Hussein's supposed web of lies did not succeed in persuading nations to be skeptical of the Americans' march to war. In other words, if there were skeptical nations, it was not because of Saddam's lies. But how could Walker be sure of what was influencing these skeptical nations? That kind of speculative lead seems hardly suited to a story that, after all, had solid news content. More to the point was the fact that Powell's evidence failed to impress many of the UN delegates at the Security Council meeting.

When we shift to the continuation of Walker's story halfway down page A10, the focus of the break-page headline is British solidarity with the U.S. It reads "'Saddam gambling we'll lose our nerve', Britain maintains." The tenor of the report is one of neutrality, straightforwardly presenting a summary of Powell's evidence, along with comments about the months-long wait for solid

proof. Powell produced no "smoking gun," but he did give a "shopping list" of violations of UN Resolution 1441, in Walker's account.

Interestingly, under "The Case for War" at the top of page A10, there appears a half-inch high, five-column headline over a story giving negative reaction to Powell: "Iraq rips Powell's 'special effects'." The story by Charles Hanley of Associated Press has been described above in connection with the *Globe's* coverage. My own impression is that by placing the story at the top of the page the *Star* gives it more of an appearance of credibility than did the *Globe*. In between the two stories is a picture of Colin Powell holding up the simulated anthrax vial, his fact with a menacing expression, a row of lower teeth visible.

On the top of page two, columnist Joey Slinger writes under "Viewpoint" that Powell was superficially persuasive, in a way that matters for public policy in need of popular support, and that now Ottawa would join the British in supporting the U.S. Having said that, he questions whether democracy is being advanced with a war on Iraq, given the ease with which civil liberties were being dismantled piece by piece.

Three of Powell's visual displays are reproduced in color on page A11, taking up three columns from the top to four inches from the bottom of the page. The captions each include attribution to the U.S. or to Powell. An "Analysis" article to the left of the pictures reports on the cool reaction of France, Russian and China to Powell's presentation, thus keeping the matter of skepticism in the forefront. The headline reads: "Key states not ready to follow U.S. into war." A selection of quotations from senators, representatives, foreign ministers.

On the basis of five other items in the *Star* I would claim that its presentation was noticeably more anti-war than the *Globe's*. Three of them are on page A12. The first is a three-column by seven inches picture of chief UN weapons inspector Hans Blix, shown beside UN Secretary-General Kofi Annan. The expression is of a very unperturbed, smiling, and genial man with the kind of face that has trust written all over it. The picture is placed over an interview with a former Iraqi atomic scientist, the headline of which reads "U.S. argument 'threadbare', ex-Iraqi atomic scientist says." The scientist, Imad Khadduri, left Iraq in 1998 having been involved until Iraq's nuclear effort prior to 1991, and says that the effort came to an end in 1991.

The third item is a story at the top right hand side of the page by Associated Press's Kim Gamel. The headline, "'Irrefutable' evidence sways few at council," carries the skeptical quotation marks over the term "irrefutable," and goes on to mention some of the disbelieving reactions before referring to those who were convinced, including Britain, Spain and the Netherlands.

The fourth item is not a reaction to Powell's speech as such, but to the impression created of a controlling atmosphere in the UN with the covering over of "Guernica" the famous anti-war painting by Picasso. The headline, over a stark AP photo file picture of the tapestry, reads: "Anti-war art doesn't fly at UN" Some official may have thought that the theme of the painting, depicting the horrors of the German bombing of that Basque town in 1937, would be inappropriate at a time when the U.S. State Department was trying to persuade the UN that war with Iraq was necessary. The space in front of the painting is commonly used for interviews and thus the backdrop would likely get included in television broadcasts. It formed a backdrop to Hans Blix's interim report January 27, and would have communicated a vivid anti-war message, as Peter Goddard writes. Goddard points out, however, that UN spokespersons claimed that the cover was to accommodate the needs of the media and not to censor ideas. People would in any case have been able to see only one-tenth of the tapestry, spokesperson Stephane Dujarric told the *Star*.

The editorial page of the *Star* tends to be middling in the range of opinion so far encountered. A cartoon by Patrick Corrigan at the top of the page

shows a heavily armed Colin Powell with a calm, matter of fact but almost bemused expression, presenting his case for war to the Security Council. Written beside him are the words "Material Reach," with the significance presumably that the United States has the military power to enforce its decisions. That is non-committal on the question of whether he is right, but the expression suggests at least that Powell is in control and not malign.

A column underneath the cartoon, "Let the UN seal Saddam's fate," argues that Saddam Hussein's enfeebled regime is no immediate threat to the U.S. and that it would be right for Canada to hold out for UN authorization before going to war. Foreign affairs columnist Gordon Barthos makes the point that although there was no "smoking gun" in Powell's presentation, unlike Adlai Stevenson's in the Cuban missile crisis, it was nevertheless a "forceful indictment." There would be cover for Prime Minister Chrétien to support Bush, but Barthos argues that it would be wrong for Chrétien to take this step.

The editorial, placed below another on medicare and titled *Saddam's web of lies*, endorses Foreign Affairs Minister Bill Graham's view of Powell's presentation as a "disturbing and persuasive" catalogue of suspicious-looking behavior. It says the UN does not have to accept Powell's "less than-persuasive" claim about the connection between Saddam Hussein and al-Qaeda terrorists, but Iraq should be made to comply with Resolution 1441. All peaceful options should be sought first, but war might still be necessary. If so, "another Security Council resolution should be obtained before launching a war."

CONCLUSION

In this chapter, differences in coverage by five different newspapers are reviewed. I think that there is sufficient evidence here to give some substance to a charge of bias against CanWest Global's *National Post* in particular. However, this kind of charge has to be presented tentatively, since more research is required to give appropriate weight to counter-examples, which can no doubt be produced. A further point to bear in mind is that media may depart from good journalistic practice for reasons other than ideological motivation. Fear-mongering, titillation, and gossip may be engaged in with the aim of improving circulation figures. Simplifications and "dumbing down" to reach a wider audience might mistakenly be taken to reflect a desire to promote some cause. It may be difficult to separate the two. However, in the specific case studied there can be no doubt that the coverage of that paper was strongly in support of war, and of Powell's case presented to the UN. There is also evidence to support a

marked difference in French language newspaper coverage, with a robust streak of independence from the conventional wisdom of "mainstream media." Pointing out biases may be thought to be useful to guard readers against being misled by their newspaper sources in future, but for reasons outlined by Altheide and Grimes this may be too much to expect. At least their study and hopefully this one too will increase the likelihood of readers becoming aware of established patterns of deception and eventually overcoming them. For this much depends on creating awareness before the next emergency (real or contrived) because at that time people simply are not so receptive to calls for reason and restraint.

REFERENCES

Altheide, D. L., & Grimes, J. N. (2005). War programming: The propaganda project and the Iraq War. *The Sociological Quarterly*, *46*(4), 617–643. doi:10.1111/j.1533-8525.2005.00029.x

Chafee, Z. (1947). *Government and mass communications: A report*. Chicago, IL: University of Chicago Press.

Chesterton, G. K. (1987). *The collected works of G. K. Chesterton: The illustrated London news, 1908-1910*. San Francisco: Ignatius Press.

Cornellier, M., & Lévesque, C. (2003, February 6). Le doute persiste au counseil de sécurité. *Le Devoir*. Retrieved July 22, 2012, from http://www.ledevoir.com/non-classe/19870/le-doute-persiste-au-conseil-de-securite

McCarthy, S. (2003, March 29). Support for Chrétien's war policy sags. *The Globe and Mail*. Retrieved July 3, 2013, from http://www.theglobeandmail.com/news/national/support-for-chretiens-war-policy-sags/article1159474/

Sanger, D. E., & Risen, J. (2003, July 12). After the war: Intelligence, C.I.A. chief takes blame in assertion on Iraqi uranium. *The New York Times*. Retrieved July 3, 2013, from http://www.nytimes.com/2003/07/12/world/after-the-war-intelligence-cia-chief-takes-blame-in-assertion-on-iraqi-uranium.html?pagewanted=all&src=pm

Thomas, G. (1999). Where there's smoke. In G. Thomas (Ed.), *Words in common: Essays on language, culture, and society* (pp. 279–283). Don Mills, Canada: Addison-Wesley Longman.

KEY TERMS AND DEFINITIONS

English-Canadian News: News created by and directed towards the English population in Canada.

Fear-Mongering: The harassment of fear.

French-Canadian News: News created by and directed towards the French population in Canada.

Implications of Language Use: The impact of words and rhetoric on audiences.

International Relations: The relationships shared among different countries around the world.

Media Ethics: The ethical principles, values, practices, and theories that guide the conceptualization and application of the role of media in society.

Propaganda: Information, ideas, or rumors deliberately disseminated to help or harm a person, group, nation, movement, institution, etc.

Section 5
Terrorism Functioning & Media Employing

Chapter 10
Functioning of Terrorism

Dana Janbek
Lasell College, USA

ABSTRACT

This chapter explores the ways in which terrorist groups operate in today's world. The chapter focuses on the operation of terrorism and the different elements that play a role in this operation, including terrorist groups' missions and their significance in recruitment, what they hope to achieve, their cause, their organizational structure and leadership, the recruitment of terrorists online and offline, including the framing of messages to specific audiences, the reasons why people join their movements, the involvement of women in these operations, and the relationships among organizations. This chapter presents a solid overview of these topics while borrowing examples from a range of organizations to illustrate the different elements of terrorist operations. It highlights specific examples of historically significant events from various parts of the world that mark changes in overall terrorist operations. These include the migration from a centralized operation structure to a decentralized structure in organizations such as al-Qaeda, where its sub-organizations are ideologically aligned but loosely connected. To understand terrorism today, the chapter looks at how terrorist groups have operated historically and examines current developments and trends that will influence the future of terrorist operations.

INTRODUCTION

How do terrorist organizations function? This chapter will take a closer look behind the scenes to explore how organizations labeled as terrorist are managed by their members and leadership. Within the context of how these organizations function, the chapter will touch upon the role of communication in terrorism, the goals and motives of the organizations, the recruitment of future members, the tactics used, and the funding that sustains these organizations.

What is a terrorist organization? Since an international definition of terrorism has proven very difficult to achieve, individual nation states have developed their own lists of foreign terrorist organizations, based on current or perceived threats to their national security. These lists are updated on a regular basis as organizations shift their goals, strengthen in power, or cease to exist. At the time of writing this chapter, the U.S. list was last updated in January of 2012.

The lists of foreign terrorist organizations compiled by different nations are far from identical.

DOI: 10.4018/978-1-4666-5776-2.ch010

There is usually, however, some overlap between these lists, as there are many cases where a number of countries agree on designating a specific organization as "terrorist." A comparison of the United States' list of Foreign Terrorist Organizations (FTOs) (U.S. Department of State: Bureau of Counterterrorism, 2012) with the Proscribed Terror Groups or Organisations list of the United Kingdom (Home Office: Counterterrorism, 2013) reveals some interesting findings. The United States has 50 organizations designated on this list, compared to 58 on the United Kingdom's. Of the U.S.'s 50 organizations, 29 (58%) appear on UK's list. The biggest notable difference between these two lists is U.K.'s designation of 14 northern Irish groups as terrorist groups while the U.S.'s list only includes one, the Continuity Irish Republican Army (CIRA). The United States has some interest and connection to these organizations, as a small portion of Irish Americans residing in the United States has supported the northern Irish cause of expelling the British from Ireland. The influence of these Irish Americans, however, has been minimal to the overall mission of CIRA and its sister organizations.

The perceived threat of extremist organizations varies between nations based on the individual experiences of the nation, geographical proximity to the organization, and the ideological threat that organization poses to the nation. An organization like al-Qaeda, although headquartered thousands of miles away in Afghanistan, has targeted the United States on its land as well as its representatives and allies abroad. Thus, geographical proximity in the case of this organization is irrelevant, while ideological threat maintains significance.

Communication is at the heart of all terrorist acts, and a critical element in organizational function. Consequently, impairments in communication severely hinder organizations from achieving their goals. Communication happens both internally within the organization and externally with outside audiences. Internally, the organization needs to communicate with its members in order to convey relevant information, update them on its latest achievements, and motivate them. Face to face communication continues to be the most secure and reliable type of communication that terrorist organizations rely on, especially for radicalization. However, over the past 10 to 15 years, there has been a trend towards increased reliance on the Internet and other mass media tools by the organizations. Externally, the organization needs to communicate with future recruits, donors, and most importantly the media. The media provide the organization with the opportunity to achieve its goal of publicizing its terrorist activity and terrorizing the enemy and its allies.

It is important to note that much of the communication of these organizations is in fact strategic communication. It is systematic, deliberate, and addresses targeted audiences at carefully chosen times. In his study of the communication strategies of Jihadist organizations, Bockstette (2008) explained that as part of their short-term goals, they rely on persuasive techniques to heighten an Islamic identity by positioning the Muslim world against the "West." This is targeted communication that addresses a specific audience. It is taking place during a time where the "West" has been increasing its efforts in understanding the Muslim world. This technique allows the group to unite against the enemy. He concluded in his analysis that the organizations were strategic in their use of communication as they "defined communication objectives, developed communication tactics and established needed strategies and many Jihadist documents demonstrate that the Jihadists do analyze their communication and media operations in order to enhance its overall effect on mission" (Bockstette, 2008, p. 20).

In the context of the functioning of terrorism, this chapter will briefly touch upon some of the ways by which the Internet had aided terrorist organizations in moving their goals forward.

MOTIVES, MISSION, AND RECRUITMENT

Some terrorism is primarily motivated by religious beliefs, but an argument can be made that in today's world, religion has been politicized. Thus, most scholars of terrorism studies would agree that terrorism is ultimately politically motivated. The destruction of property and the violent killing of civilians is an extreme form of political participation, and is precisely what terrorism is. Motivated by politics, organizations exhibit violence towards people, entities, and states they deem the enemy.

All the organizations listed by the United States as Foreign Terrorist Organizations are motivated by political and religious goals. These organizations usually target the current regime of the country where the terrorist organization operates, or they target present foreign forces if the country or region is currently occupied or at war. The mission of such organizations is to overthrow the current system and replace it with a political system of their own. For example, the main goal of the Islamic Movement of Uzbekistan is to overthrow the current government and establish an Islamic-style state under "sharia" law. Such groups carry out operations targeting locals, government officials, and tourists. While the operations may seem haphazard, the main point of these attacks is to destabilize the government and force it to give up its power to the group.

While some groups are primarily established to resist current legitimate political systems, others are formed because of the presence of a foreign occupation. In Iraq after the U.S. invasion in 2003, resistance groups were formed, partially to fill the void that was left as the previous Iraqi government was collapsing. In some cases, the political goals of the organization are intertwined with religious goals. Such is the case of al-Qaeda, whose primary goal is to rid the lands where they operate of foreign presence and to replace the current political system with "sharia," an Islamic-style system.

Many of the organizations labeled today as terrorist organizations were born as a reaction to the political situation in the region in which they operate. As an example, Al-Aqsa Martyrs Brigade was formed in 2000 during the second Palestinian uprising. Its goal is to rid the West Bank of Israeli forces and settlers and to establish a Palestinian state. Similarly, Hezbollah, a Lebanese-based Shia-group established in 1982, was formed as a reaction to the Israeli invasion of Lebanon. In Northern Ireland, the Continuity Irish Republican Army was formed in 1994 to expel British forces from the region.

So why do people join these movements? Our answers to this question is derived from communication sent by these groups, as well as interviews with current and reformed members. Interviews with members give great insight into the world in which they operate and the host of reasons that motivate them to join such extremist groups. It is important to note, however, that in most cases, each individual is motivated to commit acts of violence by a variety of different factors. Simplistic explanations that blame their actions on only one reason do not accurately capture the complexity of how an individual can develop the motivation to take the lives of others, and in some cases their own, through suicide attacks. Most of the reasons are built on the theory that terrorism is fundamentally a political act.

Most terrorism grows from a sense of perceived injustices. People believe that their religion, ethnicity, or nationality is under attack and is being threatened. They either resist their own government or are in conflict with foreign occupying forces. In civil conflicts, groups may be seeking independence from the nation-state. Such examples include Chechen rebel groups in Russia and the Basque Fatherland and Liberty (ETA) in Spain. The purpose of both of these groups is to separate from the motherland and seek independence. Interestingly, the ETA declared it was ceasing armed activities in 2011 after 52 years of resisting the Spanish and French governments.

Motivated by a sense of nationalism, people may join these organizations to fight for independence. In addition to seeking independence, groups may have a more ambitious political agenda, where they seek to impose their way of life on other people. This approach is different from simply seeking independence where a group wants to maintain its traditions and autonomy. The most prominent example of such groups is al-Qaeda, as they wish to impose their value system on other states. The group mainly increased its power and strength by convincing its members that Islam was under attack by the "West," and that it is the duty of Muslims to spread their religion, even by force.

Some people join terrorist groups because of personal motivations such as seeking revenge for a loved one. Chechnya's "Black Widows," a terrorist group formed by women allegedly seeking revenge for husbands killed by Russian forces, is a prime example of this motivation (British Broadcasting Corporation, 2003). The Black Widows made headlines in 2002 when a group of them held hundreds hostage in a theatre in Moscow, Russia. While the women died three days later during a rescue operation by the Russian government, the incident put a spotlight on the group and their motivations, and the history of turbulent conflict between Chechnya and Russia. Over 100 hostages died during this hostage crisis (Jacinto, 2002). The attack accomplished a number of goals: property damage, a significant casualty count, local and international media attention, and spreading fear and terror among Russians. Chechnya has been seeking independence from Russia. In recent history, these efforts were renewed since the collapse of the Soviet Union in 1991. The past 21 years have witnessed tense relations between Russia and Chechnya highlighted by two wars and a number of terrorist attacks.

Face-to-face communication, when available, continues to be heavily relied on for recruiting future members to join extremist organizations. This is the oldest yet most effective way to change public opinion about a cause, and then convince people to change their behavior by joining a movement. Radicalization is a lengthy process and takes place over several steps. Today, the Internet could play a critical role throughout that process. An individual interested in a cause in which terrorist groups are involved now has the opportunity to seek initial information online. Websites offer information about the cause and ideas on how the person can contribute to the mission of the organization. More importantly, these Websites provide a means through which interested individuals can interact with and be recruited by organization members. This interactivity is key to the radicalization process, as it provides members repeated opportunities to promote and reinforce their organizational narrative. In itself, the availability of static information on terrorist Websites, while significant, does not pose a great threat. Instead, it is the resulting opportunity for a potential recruit to interact with established members of that organization that is critically important.

In 2009, five Virginia men had allegedly traveled to Pakistan to join the Taliban (Witte, Markon, & Hussain, 2009). This trip was organized through an online recruiter for the organization. The initial contact between the recruiter and the Virginia men was made via YouTube by the recruiter. Coded emails were then exchanged and the trip was thus arranged. The men were charged by Pakistan in 2010 on terrorism charges. The government accused them of plotting to kill U.S. soldiers in Afghanistan and eventually target the United States. The men maintained that their visit was a humanitarian one with the intention of helping Muslims displaced by the war in Afghanistan (Markon, Brulliard, & Rizwan, 2010, March 18). What is significant about this case is that the men resided in the United States and through the Internet, specifically YouTube, they were convinced by an online recruiter to participate in a cause in a foreign country.

Online recruitment is growing and is posing a greater threat, especially for "homegrown" terrorism where sympathizers that live thousands of miles away now have the opportunity to join movements from all over the globe. Writing about the use of the Internet by extremist groups in Southeast Asia, scholars confirm that:

[T]he Internet has contributed to radicalisation, will probably grow in regional significance, and might become the dominant factor in radicalisation in the region. And it's not just passive Websites that are important in this context: social networking sites of all kinds, such as blogs and forums, are evolving rapidly (Bergin et al., 2009, p. 1).

So where are these organizations located? Organizations designated by the U.S. government as FTOs are located in a number of regions: The Middle East and North Africa (Afghanistan, Algeria, Egypt, Iran, Iraq, Israel, Lebanon, Libya, Morocco, the Occupied Territories, Pakistan, Somalia, Syria, Turkey, and Yemen), South America (Columbia and Peru), Central Asia (Uzbekistan), East Asia (Japan), South and Southeast Asia (Bangladesh, Philippines, Sri Lanka, India, Indonesia), and Europe (Greece, Ireland, Spain). A number of these organizations launch attacks outside of their main location. Organizations vary in the scope of their focus. Most of al-Qaeda operations in Iraq are somewhat contained within that region. However, its mother organization has influence and reach that extends far beyond a specific location.

The main organization, al-Qaeda, which was originally established in 1988 to fight the Soviet Union in Afghanistan, has evolved its mission over the years. In 1998, it issued a statement telling Muslims it was their duty to kill U.S. citizens and their allies everywhere. This statement is quite broad and can strategically be used to include anyone they target. Wars against organizations like al-Qaeda are harder to fight because such conflict goes beyond a battle against a specific organization—it is more of an ideological fight:

"The war of ideas" is the most complex and difficult for counterterrorism governments to comprehend, and it will be a long-term fight waged over years and decades. Al Qaeda has masterfully conducted an ideological campaign and set the agenda with regards to the role of Islam versus secular ideas throughout the Islamic world. Unfortunately, the United States, and the West overall, have yet to contest this battle space, allowing al Qaeda's narrative to become the dominant, and in many cases the sole, narrative (Howard, Sawyer, & Bajema, 2009, p. 635, emphasis in original).

One relatively new trend in terrorism, which adds further complexity to fighting the war of ideas, is the migration of organizations from a centralized operation structure to a decentralized structure. The main organization and its sub-organizations are ideologically aligned but loosely connected. For example, the decentralized leadership of all the organizations that operate under the name of al-Qaeda is considered a strength. In decentralized structures, decisions are made quickly, there is less hierarchy, and efforts to undermine the enemy are multiplied. The decentralization also forces mid-level members to assume leadership. These new leaders will seek to build connections with like-minded non-members and increase their power through these newly formed alliances.

However, the flip side of such decentralization is the lack of control over the operations of affiliate organizations. When Osama bin Laden was killed on May 1st, 2011, the U.S. team that raided his house in Abbottabad, Pakistan, gathered intelligence from the complex as part of their mission. One of the important findings from the seized documents was how bin Laden viewed the use of his brand, al-Qaeda, by other Jihadi groups. The original goals of al-Qaeda identified the United States and its allies as the enemy. The documents revealed that bin Laden was apparently distraught over the killing of Muslims by other Muslims working for organizations operating under the banner of al-Qaeda. He felt that these groups had essentially hijacked his brand name of al-Qaeda, and proceeded to launch missions that were, in some cases, not closely aligned with the organization's goals. He was displeased with a number of organizations including al-Qaeda in the Arabian Peninsula and issued communication to ask them to redirect their efforts and focus on the United States. As for the Arab Spring, bin Laden seemed excited about the events unraveling across the Arab world because people were revolting against their leaders; the same leaders bin Laden accused of being U.S. allies.

TACTICS, TARGETS, FUNDING, AND MORE

A number of different terrorist groups use similar tactics to help them achieve their goals. The most notorious of these tactics are suicide attacks. The bombs are attached to a person or persons recruited by the terrorist group. This person then walks into a crowded area, such as a shopping mall, where he/she proceeds to detonate the bomb. The purpose of most organizations operating under the banner of Islam is to spread Islam and have it dominate the world through a resurrection of a Caliphate. In the case of these organizations, recruits who engage in a suicide attack are promised a place in heaven as they are told that their actions are helping the mission fulfill its duty towards God. These recruits perceive their work as heroic and noble, since it contributes to the success of a mission that they believe is divinely inspired. In some cases, the families of the recruits are compensated financially for losing their loved one. Donald Rumsfeld, then Secretary of Defense, stated in 2002 that Iraq's late Saddam Hussein compensated the families of suicide bombers in Palestine $25,000 (Kozaryn, 2002). Such attacks are usually very successful for the organization perpetrating the attack as they result in a significant casualty count. Even if the attacks result in few or no deaths, they still achieve their purpose of terrorizing the people in

that area. The timing of the attacks is unpredictable, which makes them that much more effective and harder to control by counterterrorism experts. When women perpetrate such suicide attacks, the shock of these acts are multiplied. In Israel, Al-Aqsa Martyrs Brigade claimed responsibility for the first female suicide attack in 2002. The story of Wafa Idris, the suicide bomber, made international headlines and restarted a public debate about the motivations and rationale behind young people, especially women, committing such violent acts in the name of a cause. The role of women in terrorism will be discussed in greater depth later in this chapter.

Operations are sometimes planned so that multiple suicide attacks take place on the same day, within a few minutes or hours of each other. The chaos created by the suicide attacks is thus multiplied, as is the casualty count and, more importantly, the effect on the spirit of the people witnessing the attacks. Instead of having to deal with one attack only, the country's resources are distributed and dispersed to respond to the multiple incidents.

In 2005, the capital of Jordan, Amman, was victim to one of those synchronized attacks that were masterminded by the late Jordanian al-Qaeda leader Abu Musab Al-Zarqawi. Three nearly simultaneous suicide bombing attacks took place at three hotels, killing over 50 and injuring over 100. As tourists usually stay at hotels, they are considered symbols of "foreign" targets. The attacks, however, resulted in the death of mostly Jordanians, most of who were celebrating a wedding party at the Radisson SAS hotel. The organization claiming responsibility for the attack was allegedly seeking revenge against Jordanians, because the Jordanian government supported the United States and other Western nations. The suicide bombers attacked civilians in an attempt to destabilize the government. Symbolism, like communication, is at the heart of terrorist operations. By killing civilians, the organization is sending a message to protest the government's actions. The attacks targeted "Western" hotels and those who visit the hotels may be considered legitimate targets because they "support" Western interests. The main purpose behind terrorism is to attack interests of the perceived enemy and its allies, and defeat them in physical and psychological terms. Hence, tourist attractions, places of worship, and government symbols such as embassies and military bases are usual targets since they symbolize, to the terrorist group, enemy interests.

Other tactics used include assassinations. These assassinations usually target high profile individuals connected to the perceived enemy. Assassinations are symbolic because they send a clear message to the enemy that the organization is serious about its cause and will resort to violent methods in the attempt to achieve that cause. They are usually not systematic. They target high profile individuals such as ambassadors, ministers, and heads of organizations, all in an effort to destabilize the enemy.

Kidnappings and hostage taking are also methods that organizations rely on to spread terror and gain control of a region (Walt, 2010). In areas in Colombia and Mexico, such methods are used on a regular basis and have the clear effect of terrorizing the people, who live in constant fear of being kidnapped and possibly killed. These kidnappings are used as a bargaining chip for the organization to achieve monetary or political gains. The monetary gains can help in the funding of that organization so it can continue to survive and grow. Governments have the obligation to rescue their citizens, but by doing so, they unintentionally aid the terrorist organization. It is estimated that European governments were paying an average of seven million dollars per citizen in captivity by al-Qaeda. Such sums of money are enough to finance the equipment needed by the organization for weapons and vehicles.

Whatever method is used, the rationale behind all these attacks is to destabilize the government of the enemy, create fear among the people directly affected, utilize the media to spread a message of fear among those indirectly affected, raise awareness about the mission, and raise money to maintain the organization. Ultimately, the goal is to coerce the enemy to surrender to the organization. There is an inherent logic among terrorist groups that terrorism may lead to concrete results, and thus all the aforementioned tactics are used to achieve the overarching goal of the group.

A discussion about the funding of terrorist organizations is needed to gain a better understanding of their finances. The Financial Action Task Force (FATF), an inter-governmental policy making body, divides the financial needs of terrorist organizations into two main categories: operational needs and general requirements. Terrorist organizations need funding for a variety of reasons including funding to "promote a militant ideology, pay operatives and their families, arrange for travel, train new members, forge documents, pay bribes, acquire weapons, and stage attacks" (Financial Action Task Force, 2008, p. 7). As with legitimate organizations, funding is needed for marketing purposes to promote the mission of the organization. Funding is also needed for executing operations that support that mission, although this may be a relatively small expenditure. For example, it is estimated that the operational cost for the infamous al-Qaeda operation against the USS Cole in Yemen in 2000 cost only $10,000. The American ship was attacked by a small boat carrying explosives during a refueling stop in Aden Harbor, resulting in the death of 17 sailors. The monetary cost of this operation was relatively low in comparison to the amount of damage it inflicted on its enemy. However, while the cost of individual attacks is minimal, funding is also needed to create and maintain an environment where the organization can survive and grow. For large organizations, the cost of attacks is a fraction of the dollar amount needed to maintain a terrorist organization. In its 9/11 Commission Report, The National Commission on Terrorist Attacks Upon the United States wrote that "the CIA now estimates that it cost al-Qaeda about $30 million per year to sustain its activities before 9/11 and that this money was raised almost entirely through donations" (2004, p. 169).

So where does all this money come from? The sources vary greatly from one organization to another. Private individuals, specifically persons with means and with a keen interest in the organization, help provide funding. Organizations can also be self-financed, where members contribute to maintaining the organization.

Funding could at times come from the business sector. In the case of al-Qaeda, "American intelligence maintains that bin Laden himself, through a Web of shell companies and associates, owns a network of shops in the Middle East" (Napoleoni, 2003, p. 158). Profits from honey, for example, were used to help fund the organization. Similarly, in the 1970s, the IRA also relied on business to fund its operations. It controlled revenue from the transportation sector (taxis).

In some cases charity groups are used to funnel money into the organization. Funds have been raised through organizations posing as legitimate nonprofits raising money for a charitable cause (Bell, 2008). In 2007, the U.S. Department of the Treasury designated Tamils Rehabilitation Organization as an organization that is acting as a front group for the Liberation Tigers of Tamil Eelam (LTTE), a Foreign Terrorist Organization. LTTE is a Tamil secessionist group that has been fighting Sri Lankan forces since 1976.

In its 2011 annual report, the Office of Foreign Assets Control identified a number of charities inside the United States that they said supported or were controlled by international terrorist groups or individuals. These include the Benevolence International Foundation, the Islamic American Relief Agency, the Al Haramain Islamic, and KindHearts for Charitable Humanitarian Development. Every year, millions of dollars in assets are frozen because of organizations' ties to terrorism. Since 9/11, the U.S. government has significantly increased its efforts to monitor such assets. Such

efforts by the government have often received resistance from the nonprofit sector. Some, including the American Civil Liberties Union, argue that "freezing a charity's assets undermines critical humanitarian aid and the government's own anti-terrorism efforts" (2009, p. 1).

Terrorist organizations also use extortion and the threat of violence to raise the needed funds. The Human Rights Watch found that between 2005 and 2006, "the LTTE launched a massive fundraising drive in Canada and parts of Europe, pressuring individuals and business owners in the Tamil Diaspora to give money for the 'final war'" (2006, p. 2). The Diaspora members were asked to provide specific dollar amounts. While some members of the Diaspora were willing contributors, others who resisted were faced with threats to their lives and their families. The Human Rights Watch interviewed members of the Diaspora affected by this extortion. Stories revealed that representatives of the LTTE, or what is presumed to be front organizations for the LTTE, usually visited the members, in some cases more than once, to ask for contributions. Based on few factors such as the income of the household and the length of time members of the Diaspora had been living abroad, the representatives told the individual or the family how much they owed.

Lastly, terrorist groups also get involved in large-scale organized criminal activities to raise money. In the early 1980s, The Revolutionary Armed Forces of Colombia (FARC), the Colombian rebel group, made a decision to get involved in the coca cultivation business, which proved to be an economically lucrative decision thanks in part to increased U.S. demand for drugs (Cook, 2011). This expansion in revenue assisted the organization in expanding geographically, and in increasing its power. Criminal activity by guerillas in Colombia, including drug trafficking, kidnappings, and extortions, was estimated in 2002 to generate $500 million annually, most of which went to FARC.

According to reports in 2009, British security analysts said that terrorist groups are increasing their reliance on the Internet to help in their fundraising efforts. Gambling sites were one source of income to launder money to their organizations. Raising money online is one of the many ways in which extremist groups are relying on the Internet to advance their cause.

THE ROLE OF WOMEN

The ongoing evolution of terrorist organizations is particularly evident in their changing approach to the recruitment and involvement of women. In the past, women have traditionally played more domestic roles in terrorist organizations, where they acted as supporters for the males in their families. Typically, rhetoric addressed to these women encourages them to support their husbands and sons in their quest to join terrorist organizations, and to help in the recruitment efforts. Women were traditionally less involved in combat roles. Of the almost 3000 suicide attacks tracked by The Chicago Project on Security and Terrorism that took place over a 30-year period between 1981 and 2011, less than 6% were perpetrated by women. A content analysis of organizational Websites reveals that there is disagreement on what types of roles are "appropriate" for women. While there is no consensus on whether women should be permitted to join the battlefield, most organizations would agree that women should play, at the least, a supportive and supplementary role.

More recently, however, an increased number of women have begun to play nontraditional roles involving direct combat, including being the perpetrators of a suicide attack. The Black Widows of Chechnya are an example of such a direct level of involvement. As another example, in 2012, reports surfaced that the Lashkar-e Taiba, a Pakistani/Kashmiri militant group, was establishing and training a group of 21 females in Kashmir to carry out attacks in India (PTI, 2012).

This move was seen by the Indian government as a way for the organization to expand beyond its usual reliance on men.

Lindsey O'Rourke, who has studied this phenomenon through interviews with female suicide attackers, concluded that there is no one profile of female terrorists and that "the main motives and circumstances that drive female suicide attackers are quite similar to those that drive men" (2008, p. 5). O'Rourke discovered that the women represent a wide array of religious and ideological backgrounds, as well as varied personal experiences. A very small percentage was actually coerced to commit these attacks by men. Almost all (95%) of these attacks happened in the context of resisting occupying forces. Secular organizations employing the tactic of suicide attacks were the first to use women, and subsequently inspired religious organizations to do the same.

There are many good strategic reasons to use women in suicide attacks. They typically arouse less suspicion than men do, including at security checkpoints. For terrorist organizations in particular, the biggest advantage of involving women in combative roles is the increased newsworthiness of the attack in the eyes of the media. Terrorism by nature is a newsworthy topic, and terrorist attacks are covered by the media on a regular basis. However, when women are involved in the attacks, the newsworthiness of the event multiplies. Their use in suicide attacks is a much less common phenomenon, thus making it more shocking.

These women provide a challenge for journalists covering their stories. Writing on U.S. media coverage of female suicide bombers, Barbara Friedman (2008) asserts that "women who take up arms or otherwise participate in armed conflict merit news coverage because their actions seem unusual and controversial, two qualities that govern decisions about what is news" (2008, 843). Friedman concludes that five motivational explanations were used by U.S. media to explain these acts: strategic desirability, the influence of men, revenge, desperation, and liberation. Liberation, the least cited motive, referred to the idea that women involved in combative roles had achieved liberation from traditional societal expectations and had become somewhat equal to their male counterparts by participating in the attacks.

The increasing importance of women is clearly illustrated by the efforts of terrorist organizations to specifically target them for recruitment. One of the important developments that took place in 2011 was the launch of a magazine for women by al-Qaeda titled *Al-Shamikha: A Woman Jihadi Islamic Magazine*. The magazine became available and was distributed widely on terrorist Internet forums. The Internet, which became a mass medium in the 1990s and is now available to more than 30% of the world's population, has been used over the past 10 to 15 years to promote al-Qaeda's mission, as well as other terrorist organizations. There are many good reasons for terrorist organizations to use the Internet for marketing purposes: the Internet is relatively censorship-free, authors enjoy some level of anonymity, and the production and distribution of materials online is very cheap in comparison to other printed promotional materials. Similar to legitimate organizations, terrorist organizations rely on all media formats to spread their messages.

Following is a detailed description of this magazine, which provides the readers with an insight into the ideologies and values that govern the organization. The first issue of the magazine, which was 31 pages long, had a purple-pinkish cover with an image of a rifle. Even for non-Arabic speakers, it is clear that the magazine is targeting women with its color choices. The round logo of the magazine is an image of a veiled woman figure, wearing a hijab and a niqab, and posing next to the Quran. The main story in this first issue was an interview with the wife of a mujahed. Included in the issue are additional stories about Jihad and marriage to a mujahed. Interestingly, there was also a generic story about owning a home, which was an added insert to the magazine. The editors and main contacts for the magazine

are both males. The welcome message, which started on the second page, began by reminding the reader that the Islamic nation or "umma" is under attack and is going through a difficult time period, with enemies from the East and the West targeting Muslims. The author then proceeded to acknowledge the importance of women by writing "women represent not only half of society, they represent all of society since they gave birth to the other half." The author proceeded to write that enemies have concealed women's real role in society because they fear what women will do if they reached the battlefield. The author uses this opportunity to re-affirm that women have a very significant role during times of war and that they ought to be aware of their role. Although the author originally implied that women have a role in the battlefield itself, the author proceeded to write that their main role is raising generations of mujahideen. The author ended this welcome letter by reminding Muslim women of how they need to follow God's orders in terms of their appearance and behavior to be real Muslims. The gender of the author is not clear. Since the editor is a male, it can be assumed that this is the welcome letter from the editor. However, throughout the piece, the author uses the feminine version of "we" in the letter.

The magazine is filled with stories about the cruelties of the enemy, the glory of Jihad, and the alleged duties of Islam to engage in Jihadi actions. The stories are emotionally charged, present one side of the story, and are far removed from balanced journalism. In the interview with the wife of a mujahed, the interviewee shared her earlier desires to marry a mujahed as she did not want to continue living a "fake life." She said that similar to her outlook on life, her husband was also searching for a wife who would understand his ways and agree to spend their income on Jihadi activities instead of personal possessions. While it was painful to say goodbye to her husband the day of his departure to participate in an attack, the wife hid her pain and said she did not want to stand as an obstacle between him and Jihad. The interviewee goes on to assure women that their most important role in Jihad is to incite and support their spouses to join the movement. However, women can also join the battlefield if necessary.

The remainder of the magazine sends the same consistent message, which encourages women to promote Jihad and recognize the role they can play in the movement. The articles have a consistently highly conservative tone and are filled with reminders to its female audiences of how to act appropriately in public according to Islamic teachings. One example of this tone is a full-page article titled *The Etiquette of Walking* dedicated to educating Muslim women on how to walk in a way that draws the least attention to themselves. This magazine is an example of how organizations, like al-Qaeda, tailor their messages to specific audiences in their battle to win these women over and have them subscribe to their mission. It is clearly targeting a more culturally and religiously conservative segment of the population whose members would be receptive to such strict codes guiding behavior in public. The content of this magazine serves as a solid reminder of how politics and religion are so closely intertwined for some of these organizations. Thus, to better understand their political cry, one has to be familiar with their interpretation of religion and their perception of what it requires of them.

CONCLUSION

This chapter introduced some of the key elements in the functioning of terrorism. The chapter started by looking at the Foreign Terrorist Organization list as defined by the U.S. Department of State to provide a context for the discussion about what is terrorism. The role that communication plays in the functioning of terrorism was examined briefly as communication is at the heart of terrorism. The text then examined what motivates terrorist organizations to be formed, what their overall mission is, and what goals they hope to accomplish. Recruitment is essential to the functioning of terrorism and thus a look at the radicalization process was necessary. For the organization to survive and expand, a healthy stream of new members is important. The chapter looked at new trends in terrorism including the move from a centralized structure with a well-defined goal and leadership to a decentralized structure for organizations like al-Qaeda. The ramifications of such decentralization are many and essential to understanding how terrorism, as an ideology, can be addressed. The use of the Internet to accomplish tasks such as recruitment was also briefly discussed. This is another significant trend that impacts the way counter-terrorism experts go about their work of curbing terrorism. The tactics used by organizations to terrorize were examined including suicide attacks and extortions. Crucial to that discussion was the use of symbolism in terrorism to draw attention to the mission and cause of organizations. All organizations rely on funds to stay active so a look at the funding was essential. A discussion of the role women play in the functioning of terrorism ensued. The topics covered in this chapter represent some of the most essential elements of terrorism that can help the reader begin to understand how terrorism works.

REFERENCES

American Civil Liberties Union (ACLU). (2009, February 27). *Designating non-profits as terrorist organizations without due process undermines security and humanitarian aid, say groups.* Retrieved July 3, 2013, from http://www.aclu.org/national-security/designating-non-profits-terrorist-organizations-without-due-process-undermines-sec

Bell, J. L. (2008). Terrorist abuse of non-profits and charities: A proactive approach to preventing terrorist financing. *The Kansas Journal of Law & Public Policy, 17*(3), 450–476.

Bergin, A., Osman, S. B., Ungerer, C., & Yasin, N. A. M. (2009, March). *Special report: Countering internet radicalization in Southeast Asia.* S. Rajaratnam School of International Studies and Australian Strategic Policy Institute. Retrieved July 3, 2013, from http://www.cleanitproject.eu/wp-content/uploads/2012/07/2009-Internet-radicalisation-Sout-East-Asia.pdf

Bockstette, C. (2008, December). *Jihadist terrorist use of strategic communication management techniques.* The George C. Marshall European Center for Security Studies. Retrieved July 3, 2013, from http://oai.dtic.mil/oai/oai?verb=getRecord&metadataPrefix=html&identifier=ADA512956

British Broadcasting Corporation. (2003, September 4). *Inside the mind of a black widow.* Retrieved July 3, 2013, from http://news.bbc.co.uk/2/hi/3081126.stm

Chicago Project on Security and Terrorism (CPOST). (2011). Retrieved July 3, 2013, from http://cpost.uchicago.edu/index.php

Cook, T. R. (2011). The financial arm of the FARC: A threat finance perspective. *Journal of Strategic Security, 4*(1), 19–36. doi:10.5038/1944-0472.4.1.2

Financial Action Task Force. (2008, February 29). *Terrorist funding.* Retrieved February 29, 2008, from http://www.fatf-gafi.org/dataoecd/28/43/40285899.pdf

Friedman, B. (2008). Unlikely warriors: How four U.S. news sources explained female suicide bombers. *Journalism & Mass Communication Quarterly, 85*(4), 841–859. doi:10.1177/107769900808500408

Home Office. Counterterrorism. (2013, July 19). *Proscribed terror groups or organizations.* Retrieved August 7, 2011, from https://www.gov.uk/government/publications/proscribed-terror-groups-or-organisations--2

Howard, R., Sawyer, R., & Bajema, N. (2009). *Terrorism and counterterrorism: Understanding the new security environment.* New York: The McGraw Hills Company.

Human Rights Watch. (2006, March 15). *Funding the final war: LTTE intimidation and extortion in the Tamil Diaspora.* Retrieved August 22, 2013, from http://www.hrw.org/reports/2006/03/14/funding-final-war-0

Jacinto, L. (2002, October 29). Chechen black widows bring new fears. *ABC News.* Retrieved July 3, 2012, from http://abcnews.go.com/international/comments?type=story&id=79819#.UdSebhaSBUQ

Kozaryn, L. (2002, April 2). *Rumsfeld: Suicide bombing is terrorism.* U.S. Department of Defense-American Forces Press Service. Retrieved July 3, 2013, from http://www.defense.gov/news/newsarticle.aspx?id=44197

Markon, J., Brulliard, K., & Rizwan, M. (2010, March 18). Pakistan charges 5 Northern Virginia men in alleged terrorism plot. *The Washington Post.* Retrieved July 3, 2013, from http://www.washingtonpost.com/wp-dyn/content/article/2010/03/17/AR2010031700430.html

Napoleoni, L. (2003). *Modern Jihad: Tracing the dollars behind the terror networks*. Sterling, VA: Pluto Press.

National Commission on Terrorist Attacks upon the United States. (2004). *The 9/11 commission report*. Retrieved July 3, 2013, from http://www.9-11commission.gov/report/911Report.pdf

O'Rourke, L. (2008, August 2). Behind the woman behind the bomb. *The New York Times*. Retrieved July 3, 2013, from http://www.nytimes.com/2008/08/02/opinion/02orourke.html?_r=2&pagewanted=all

PTI. (2012, January 3). Lashkar raising 21 female terrorists against India: Army. *The Times of India*. Retrieved July 3, 2013, from http://articles.timesofindia.indiatimes.com/2012-01-03/india/30583991_1_training-camps-terrorists-pok

U.S. Department of State. Bureau of Counterterrorism. (2012, January 27). *Foreign terrorist organizations*. Retrieved July 3, 2013, from http://www.state.gov/j/ct/rls/other/des/123085.htm

U.S. Department of the Treasury. (2007, November 15). *Treasury targets charity covertly supporting violence in Sri Lanka*. Retrieved July 3, 2013, from http://www.treasury.gov/press-center/press-releases/Pages/hp683.aspx

U.S. Department of Treasury. Office of Foreign Assets Control. (2011). *Terrorists assets report*. Retrieved July 3, 2013, from http://www.treasury.gov/resource-center/sanctions/Programs/Documents/tar2011.pdf

Walt, V. (2010, October 12). Terrorist hostage situations: Rescue or ransom? *Time Magazine*. Retrieved July 3, 2013, from http://www.time.com/time/world/article/0,8599,2024420,00.html

Witte, G., Markon, J., & Hussain, S. (2009, December 13). Pakistani authorities hunt for alleged mastermind in plot to send N. Virginia men to Afghanistan to fight U.S. troops. *The Washington Post*. Retrieved May 23, 2012, from http://www.washingtonpost.com/wp-dyn/content/article/2009/12/12/AR2009121201598.html

KEY TERMS AND DEFINITIONS

Communication and Terrorism: The link and interconnectedness of the dissemination of messages for the purposes of communicating terrorism.

Terrorism Organization Funding: The ways in which terrorist organizations obtain resources to sustain their causes.

Terrorist Movements: Events and developments instigated by terrorist activity.

Terrorist Organizational Structure: The way in which a terrorist group or community is hierarchically organized.

Terrorist Recruitment: The process of obtaining members for a terrorist group/organization.

Terrorist Targets: People, places, organizations, and events that terrorists focus on to harm.

Women and Terrorism: The role played by women in and against terrorist activity.

Chapter 11
Employing of Media during Terrorism

Muhammad Ayish
American University of Sharjah, UAE

ABSTRACT

Communication has proven to be an integral component of the terrorism phenomenon. To unravel the opportunities and challenges embedded in employing the media during terrorism, this chapter draws on research findings and practical experiences around the world to identify prime actors associated with this issue and to describe their objectives, tactics, and channels of communication. It is argued here that media constitute a vital resource in the war on terror with both terrorist organizations and states harnessing communication to advance their causes in the public sphere. In this context, four categories of media users have been identified: media institutions, terrorist organizations, governments, and citizen groups. The chapter discusses enduring issues associated with each actor's use of media and calls for evolving new conceptual frameworks for understanding media use during terrorism. It concludes by arguing that while we seem to have a huge pool of research findings and practical experiences related to using the media during terrorism, we seem to have a critical shortage in how we conceptually account for the different variables that define the use of media in terrorism situations.

INTRODUCTION

It is virtually impossible to understand terrorism apart from the way it is communicated to national and international publics.[1] For many scholars and policymakers, while the battle against terrorism is waged in city alleys and rough terrains, it is also fought in the media sphere. Many believe that if it is through media that terrorists make their most stunning impact, it is also through media that they could be defeated. Brigitte L. Nacos argues that

"without massive news coverage, the terrorist act would resemble the proverbial tree falling in the forest: if no one learned of an incident, it would be as if it had not occurred" (2000, p. 174). In an emerging transnational communication environment marked by satellite television and the World Wide Web, the media sphere does not only offer ample opportunities for the global war against terrorism, but it also presents states and societies with serious challenges in that regard. The new media landscape has a greater reach; thrives on

DOI: 10.4018/978-1-4666-5776-2.ch011

multimedia features and draws on interactive information that could be effectively harnessed to discredit terrorists' propaganda. On the other hand, dramatic media transitions have also enabled terrorist organizations to capitalize on new communication channels to promote their orientations and bolster their field plans.

To unravel the opportunities and challenges embedded in employing the media during terrorism, this chapter draws on research findings and practical experiences around the world to identify prime actors associated with this issue and to describe their objectives, tactics, and channels of communication. It is argued here that media constitute a vital resource in the war on terror with both terrorist organizations and states harnessing communication to advance their causes in the public sphere. In this context, four categories of media users have been identified: media institutions, terrorist organizations, governments, and citizen groups. The chapter discusses enduring issues associated with each actor's use of media and calls for evolving new conceptual frameworks for understanding media use during terrorism. It concludes by arguing that while we seem to have a huge pool of research findings and practical experiences relating to the use of media during terrorism, we seem to have a critical shortage in how we conceptually account for the different variables that define the use of media in terrorism situations.

EMPLOYING MEDIA DURING TERRORISM: DEFINING THE PARAMETERS

The emerging media sphere in its real and virtual expressions is a vast communication landscape buzzing with wide-ranging formats, messages, and users. Ever since the introduction of digital technologies in the late 1980s, the communication market has experienced its most dramatic transitions at national and global levels. Fueled by a convergence of media, telecommunications and computer industries, the communication landscape has come to define not our media exposure patterns and habits, but the form and substance of the content we consume. Conventional media institutions remain important forces bearing on our daily communication experiences; but the emerging online media as enabled by the World Wide Web and convergence trends seem to have the most enduring impact on us as individuals and groups. New media have superior interactivity, more convenient accessibility, greater reach, and wider multimedia features than their conventional counterparts. In significant ways, new media, including social media, have not only been empowering for private individuals and groups long marginalized by media institutions, but they have also come to re-define our view of mass communication as a unidirectional process of information.

In this context of shifting media boundaries, it is important at this point to define the parameters of employing media as used in this chapter. Superficially, employing media suggests media channels being harnessed by certain actors to achieve specific effects on target audiences. In a democratic media system where institutions of mass communication pride themselves on being independent, this notion of media being used by other actors suggests some form of manipulation that renders media's editorial autonomy and professional integrity rather irrelevant. To avoid doing injustice to democratic media institutions, employing the media in this chapter is described only in the context of actors using media resources under their disposal according to their established standards. This suggests that journalists working for media institutions apply their professional values and conventions in their reporting of terrorism without falling under other actors' manipulation. Governments use their state-owned and operated media channels to promote their views and ideologies, but there are no formally-defined mechanisms through which governments force their views on media work. Likewise, terrorists harness their own media resources, but when they make headlines in established channels, they do not do that through mutually-agreed formal terms of understanding with media institutions. This also applies to citizen groups who operate their own media and make news in the press primarily because their initiatives are perceived as newsworthy.

COMMUNICATING TERRORISM BY MEDIA INSTITUTIONS: THE SYMBIOSIS DEBATE

In democratic systems where media institutions are functioning as independent channels of communication driven by constitutionally-provided rights of free expression, terrorism is reported according to professionally-recognized news gatekeeping criteria. In significant ways, terrorism-related events carry the full features of competitive news stories (scoops) long sought by journalists: they are dramatic, sensational, have immense consequences, leave critical impact, and far more important, bear on state national security interests. But this congruence of professional journalistic values and conventions, on the one hand, and key features of terrorism-related acts, on the other hand, has generated heated debates on the notion of a media-terrorism symbiosis (Soriano, 2008). Claims of media-terrorism symbiotic relationships have provoked critical reactions from media institutions that feel rather uneasy about them allegedly offering terrorist-favored platforms in the media sphere. Critics of media coverage of terrorism have gone far enough to charge media institutions of caving into terrorists' manipulation tactics in return for some news scoops that would hopefully enhance their exposure profiles.

The dilemma facing media as they cover terrorism has been clearly expressed by a UN counter-terrorism strategy report (United Nations, 2007). On the one hand, showing graphic details of crime scenes, beheadings, and injured victims creates powerful images, exposes emerging threats, and supports freedom of speech. "Each of these can also help build a case against terrorism." On the other hand, these media images can be exploited. For example, by traumatizing victims' families, sensationalizing violence, and repeatedly showing graphic images of destruction, the media can actually advertise the terrorists' cause; reinforce perceptions of the terrorists' "success," and exaggerate the importance and magnitude of the acts, ultimately creating exactly the climate of fear and insecurity that the terrorists are trying to create (United Nations, 2007).

In many ways, most of the critical views of the media-terrorism symbiosis have been inspired by politicians' claims of media providing publicity to terrorists. The traditional metaphor by former British Prime Minister Margaret Thatcher about media publicity as the oxygen for terrorists has long defined arguments on this issue (Muller, Spaaij, & Ruitenberg, 2004). However, all in all, critical views of the media-terrorism symbiosis have been largely benign. Walsh (2010) points out that both terrorists and the media benefit from high levels of public attention to terrorism. Terrorists gain from media attention that communicates their goals and grievances to a wider public while media garner larger audiences and hence, greater profits. Jenkins famously remarks that "terrorism is theater" and that terrorist attacks "are carefully choreographed to attract the attention of the electronic media and international press" (1974, p. 4).

French sociologist Michel Wieviorka (1993) dismisses claims of the terrorism-media symbiosis by identifying four distinct relationships between media and terrorism. The first is described as one of pure indifference, when "terrorists neither seek to frighten a given population group nor to realize a propaganda coup through their acts" (Wieviorka, 1993, p. 43). The "second is that of 'relative indifference', whereby perpetrators of violence remain apathetic about making the headlines because they already have their own channels of communication to discuss and explain their positions." Wieviorka's third relational mode, the media-oriented strategy, covers terrorist efforts to provoke the media into action, and "a calculated manipulation of what they know of media operations" (Ibid, p. 44). The fourth model, termed a total break, is more accurately described as coercion of the media into carrying terrorists' propaganda.

EMPLOYING THE MEDIA BY TERRORISTS: OBJECTIVES, TACTICS AND CHANNELS

Research findings in the past few decades have demonstrated that as much as terrorists are keen on inflicting the heaviest possible human and material damage on their targets, they are also bent on getting their messages resonating among the largest populations. The objectives associated with terrorists' use of media have ranged from ideological indoctrination to political and sectarian mobilization to blackmailing to recruitment to psychological manipulation. Terrorists-sponsored media channels have been found to contain extensive materials that promote their ideological stands and discredit those of their adversaries. They have also been found to contain information that incites populations against governments by invoking political and sectarian backgrounds against which states are framed as corrupt or even blasphemous. In certain cases, terrorists use media channels to apply pressures on governments and communities to submit to their demands. In May 2012, al-Qaeda terrorists in Yemen showed a taped speech by the abducted Saudi Vice Consul in which he appealed to his government to release imprisoned al-Qaeda sympathizers in the Kingdom in return for his freedom (al-Quds al-Arabi, 2012, p. 4). The use of media as tools of recruitment and fundraising has also been noted in numerous cases around the world. Extremists use chat rooms, dedicated servers and Websites, and social networking tools as propaganda machines, as a means of recruitment and organization, for training grounds, and for significant fund-raising through cybercrime (Soriano, 2008). The psychological impact sought by terrorists has been most clear in their endeavors to frighten populations through their stunning mass-mediated acts.

In order to achieve their objectives, terrorist organizations have been found to follow some tactics that ensure their fullest possible employing of media. Perl (1977) notes that any publicity induced by a terrorist act alerts the world about a problem that cannot be ignored and needs to be addressed. He remarks that an unedited interview with one of its leading terrorist figures would be a treasured prize, citing the May 1997 CNN interview with the deceased al-Qaeda leader Osama bin Laden. This media interest seems to have made terrorist groups rather sensitive about the timing of news stories and audience dynamics, prompting them to structure their actions accordingly (Weimann & Winn, 1994). Poland (1988) offers exciting examples of how such media orientations have played into the hands of terrorist groups in cases like the 1974 kidnapping of Patricia Hearst by members of the Symbionese Liberation Army; the 1977 Baader-Meinhof gang suicide in Stammheim prison; the 1977 kidnapping of the Italian Prime Minister, Aldo Moro, by the Red Brigades; the 1983 Armenian Revolutionary Army attack against the Turkish ambassador in Lisbon; and the 1984 bombing of the Grand Hotel in Brighton by the Provisional Irish Republican Army.

But despite extensive discussions of the media-terrorism symbiosis, we still have limited evidence of how terrorist groups handle their relations with media institutions. A policy paper on terrorism and media (COT Institute for Safety, Security and Crisis Management, 2008) identifies three levels of terrorist participation in the media sphere. The first is when terrorists merely carry out an attack and wait to see how media report on it. They could influence the report by choosing location, time, and target, but they have no role in writing the contents of the news. The second level is exemplified by terrorists sending in their messages straight to the media outlets. In this case, they could decide on message content and how it is would be framed. Examples of this practice have been evident in the numerous tapes produced by al-Qaeda and delivered to satellite television channels like al-Jazeera for broadcast to a global audience as a newsworthy development. According to this report, terrorists would gain most influence if they could reach the third level: full control of media outlets. They can create the message and broadcast it exactly the way they want.

One established fact, however, is that terrorist groups' media thinking is too subtle and systematic to be underestimated. Hoffman (2006) argues that terrorists plan their operations in a manner that will shock, impress and intimidate, ensuring that their acts are sufficiently daring and violent to capture attention of media and in turn of the public and government as well. He cites the tactic used by the Red Brigades in choosing Wednesdays and Saturdays as "their preferred communication days" so that their activities would make it into the more robust Thursday and Sunday newspapers. Another example relates to the airing of interviews with Chechen leader Shamil Basayev by several television channels around the world, including those in the U.S., Sweden, and the United Kingdom. On American ABC's *Nightline* show, Basayev claimed responsibility for the terrorist attacks on a theatre in Moscow and a school in Beslan. While the interview seemed to have created a precious media opportunity for Basayev, it in significant ways conferred on him a good deal of credibility fitting only for world leaders (Nacos, 2007).

The repetition of al-Qaeda leaders' platform themes and use of "message projection opportunities" demonstrate a great understanding of human nature, marketing strategy, global media, and world politics (Ciovacco, 2009). The use of the media is so important for al-Qaeda that many within the organization have said that bin Laden is "obsessed" with the international media, "a publicity hound," and that he has "caught the disease of screens, flashes, fans, and applause"

(Gerges, 2005, pp. 194-197). This observation was most conspicuously reflected in the U.S. revelation of what came to be known as the Abbotabad Documents in May 2012, one year after Osama bin Laden was killed by special U.S. forces in 2011 in Pakistan. The 17 documents offer striking details about bin Laden's tactics and methods relating to how communication channels could be harnessed for indoctrination, mobilization, and recruitment. He was reported to show attention to the meticulous details of propaganda and media usage; for instance, he made it clear that he desired his visual statements to be shared with Middle Eastern media outlets, and subsequently translated and shared with Americans (Lahoud et al., 2012). Additionally, Lahound and colleagues (2012) demonstrate that bin Laden's speech, meant to be broadcast on the 10th anniversary of the 9/11 attacks, was envisioned to have a deep impact on worldwide audiences.

The documents suggested al-Qaeda's keenness on building an extensive network of media collaborators around the world, and the list surprisingly included some of the best journalistic figures:

As for the second method, which I suggest, it is close to what the Shaykh mentioned of communicating with 'Abd-al-Bari Atwan and Robert Fisk. I suggest that we send the material-or materials-to a group of writers and professional or independent journalists, who have shown interest in al-Qaeda issues, from different countries. In Britain, the two journalists Atwan and Fisk, and probably others, in America Brian Russ, Simon Hirsh and Jerry Van Dyke and others, in Canada Eric Margolis and Gwynne Dyer. In Europe, the Norwegian journalist who spent some time with the students in Kroner and released a film that was condemned in the West because he shows that the students are humans that have families and children and that they laugh and eat as the rest of the people. In Pakistan, Hamid Mir and Salim Safi, the owner of the program (Jerga) at Geo channel, also Rahimullah Yusuf Zia and Jamal Ismail, and at Al

Jazeera . . . (Put their names here if they exist). In Egypt, Dr. Muhammad 'Abbas and others, in Jordan Dr. Karam Hijazi, in Yemen 'Abd-al-Ilah Haydar Sha'i -if he is released by the government and is still concerned with al-Qa'ida issues, and so on (Lahoud et al., 2012, p. 14).

The documents show how keen al-Qaeda was on using extensive networking tactics to get the best media catch. For instance, they demonstrate that bin Laden had carefully planned a list of journalists who would be contacted with information regarding their tactics. Communication with these selected journalists would outline arguments and incentive as to why they should disseminate such information, creating a networking opportunity for al-Qaeda and media practitioners alike (Lahoud et al., 2012).

It is difficult to single out a specific form of communication that is of special preference for terrorist organizations to spread their messages. However, more or less, it has been found that audio-visual forms of media are receiving the highest attention in light of their most enduring impact. According to Lumbaca and Gray (2011), the audiovisual projects are either posted on terrorist organizations' Websites or sent directly to news agencies. Audio-visual materials often glorify their achievements and advance their goals. Kimmage and Rodolfo (2007) point out that such items generally range from short video clips of attacks on their targets to recorded addresses by leaders to longer films relevant to the terrorist groups' causes. Most video clips posted on Websites are generally short, seeking to identify the group responsible for the message and, conveying an ideological or religious message to target audiences (Ibid).

Around the world, audio-visual materials produced and posted or circulated by terrorist organizations normally carry nationalistic or religious chanting or singing in the background with or without music. Those musical components are meant to serve as supportive ideological contexts

to verbal or visual messages appearing on video. This feature has been typical of most al-Qaeda tapes posted online where religious prayers are said on video scenes of its operatives in full military gear or in field actions. In other cases like those in Iraq, audio-visual materials showing hostages in captivity were used to blackmail governments into submitting to certain demands. Kimmage and Rodolfo (2007) note that both right-wing and leftist groups' use the influence of music not only to capture their audiences' attention, but also to influence their attitudes on social and political issues and even to incite violence. Examples include the song "Your Worst Nightmare," by the white supremacist band *Bound for Glory*, which labels African-Americans as "niggers" and "parasites" as part of its hate campaign against blacks in America. As suggested by the Website *lyricstimes.com*, the song gives a vigilante-like overtone with verses stating, "I'm the man, I'm taking the stand, to rid the world of you is my plan." In some Jihadist Websites, songs glorify insurgents, demonize adversaries, and preach an inevitable victory of good over evil.

However, despite the powerful appeal of audio-visual media for terrorist organizations, printed publications have also received adequate attention. Various groups published weekly and monthly publications or even occasional leaflets to distribute to target audiences. Lumbaca and Gray (2007) note that text-based materials are either distributed in hard form or posted online to communicate with literate audiences. They cite the example of the *Aryan Nation* posting violent literature and publications to their Website with some documents including *Metzgar's War* newspaper and "Essay of a Klansman," by Louis Beam. In the Middle East, *Sawt al-Jihad* (Voice of the Jihad), was noted in 2003 as al-Qaeda's "premiere" online magazine that focused on the Arabian Peninsula's Jihad and mujahidin. The publication focused on al-Qaeda endeavors in Saudi Arabia and aspects of the terrorist movements in Iraq (Kimmage & Rodolfo, 2007). Printed materials have also come to include books authored by leaders of terrorist organizations in which they detailed their ideological visions and goals. One of those books was entitled: *Announcement to the People of the Birth of the Islamic State* authored by Uthman bin Abd al-Rahman al-Tamimi and posted online for users' downloading (Kimmage & Rodolfo, 2007).

While audio-visual and printed materials are highly appreciated by terrorist organizations of all ideological colorations, it is the emerging online media sphere that has been viewed as the ideal resource for mobilization, indoctrination, and recruitment. The Internet seems to be more instrumental than conventional media in enabling terrorists to capture attention and awareness by serving as a virtual worldwide press agency. Cyberspace has been a popular media platform featuring movie clips of bloody beheadings intended to raise awareness, fear, and helplessness among the audience (Weimann, 2004). Lumbaca and Gray (2007) note that virtually all terrorist groups host Websites that share a variety of key characteristics. They have attractive design, colorful and buzzing with "eye-popping" graphics and host a variety of content to capture the individual user's attention. Those Websites publicize the terrorist group's history, mission, ideologies, and their overall goal in defeating its adversaries. Some of them have gone as far as setting up donation sites in hopes of collecting funds from individual and state sympathizers (Hoffman, 2006). The Anti-Defamation League League (2013) notes that the Knights of the Ku Klux Klan (KKK) created the first white supremacist Website, *Stormfront* to spread the Klan's conventional message of hatred towards African-Americans, Jews, and immigrants. However, Hoffman (2006) suggests that the first terrorist organization to use the Internet was actually the Mexican EZLN insurgents, better known as the Zapatistas.

The Internet's ubiquity, convenience of access, interactivity, and multi-media features have turned the Web into a multi-functional platform for ter-

rorist activities (Awan, 2007; Weimann, 2004). Terrorists' use of the Web has come to embrace cyber-terrorism, coordination of attack plans, communication with cells, or propaganda and information (Lumbaca & Gray, 2011). In addition, online media are having a multiplier effect with regular media often reporting on or even copying Internet content (Awan 2007; Weimann 2004). The rising centrality of the Internet in terrorism communication has been eloquently expressed by Michel Moutot of l'Agence France-Presse (AFP), asserting that terrorists no longer require traditional media platforms to disseminate their messages. That is, the "official" media have been replaced by online tools—as they are considerably easier to use and increasingly efficient and effective (Moutot, 2010).

GOVERNMENT USE OF MEDIA TO COMBAT TERRORISM

If terrorists view media channels as vital resources for mobilization, indoctrination, psychological defeat, and recruitment, governments also see communication as important tools for protecting the public order and safeguarding society against the evils of terrorism. During the past decades, governments around the world, especially in the post-9/11 era, have evolved strategies that draw on media as a pivotal element of the counter-terrorism drive. The role of communication in those strategies underscored states' convictions that since an important part of the fight against terrorism is waged in the public sphere, this war would only be won in the media battlefield. But as the experiences of the past few decades suggest, the media sphere has never been a friendly turf for governments seeking a swift victory over terrorism in all fronts. Governments' preference for a controlled flow of information during terrorism seems to run counter to media tendencies to go public and strive for scoops in competitive news markets. But in general, both media and governments have common interests in not seeing media falling victim to terrorists' manipulation tactics (Perl, 1997).

As part of their anti-terrorism drives, governments often cite national security as the key driver of their efforts to keep information under control during terrorism. It is widely believed that any media leaks could potentially jeopardize governments' plans to pre-empt terrorists' attacks and to discredit their propaganda. But from the media side, government controls are often seen as encroachments on their constitutionally-provided freedom of expression and of the press. Graber (2003) notes that the typical freedom-national security trade-off dilemma is starkest when the clashing values are threatened by terrorism or war. Graber identifies three approaches to the dilemma of reconciling the conflicting aspects of press freedom and survival security: the "formal censorship" approach involving legislation that sets forth what may or may not be published; the "opposite free press" approach leaving journalists free to decide what is or is not safe to publish under the circumstances; and the informal censorship scheme as an ingenious combination of both.

Media reporting on terrorism is used extensively by governments to enhance, explain, or propagate their official counter-terrorism efforts (Wilkinson, 2006). An example was the sustained drive by the Bush administration to link Iraq to terrorism and 9/11 before the Anglo-American invasion of that country in March 2003. Domke and colleagues (2006) note that in the United States, the anti-terrorism legislation evolved by the Bush administration just after 9/11 contained an important media component. The "Office of Strategic Influence" was established after 9/11 to provide propaganda to the foreign press in the public relations war linked to the "Global War on Terrorism." In fact, all major U.S. departments have had significant media programs established as part of the counter-terrorism strategy. One approach that has gained popularity over the years has been public diplomacy. Sieb (2011) argues

that the role of public diplomacy in the global war in terror goes beyond branding or image building functions:

[P]ublic diplomacy has larger roles, including as a valuable counterterrorism tool. Envision terrorism as a pyramid. At the tip are Osama bin Laden, Ayman al-Zawahiri, and a relatively small number of others who will never turn aside from the path of violence and must be dealt with accordingly. But as we move toward the base of the pyramid, the numbers grow larger and the commitment to violence lessens. Here are the people—many of them young—who can still be reached. They are certainly being reached by Al Qaeda and other terrorist groups (Sieb, 2011, p. 8).

There are several ways in which governments in democratic societies may react to media handling of terrorism in the public sphere Wilkinson (2006). The first is the policy of laissez-faire, which assumes that no specific steps should be taken concerning media coverage of terrorism at all, regardless of the situation or circumstances. Wilkinson (2006) suggests that this approach is likely to trigger more attacks, which could endanger people's lives.

The dangers of this approach are fairly obvious: sophisticated and media-wise terrorist organizations will exploit the enormous power of the media to enhance their ability to create a climate of fear and disruption, to amplify their propaganda of the deed to publicize their cause or to force concessions of ransoms out of the government or out of companies or wealthy individuals (Wilkinson, 2006, p. 155).

The second policy option is a form of media censorship of statutory regulation. Despite the fact that freedom of speech and political debate is at the very core of the concept of a democratic society, restrictions on the freedom of press and expression might appear as a necessary measure in the fight against terrorism. If the media refuse to cover acts of terrorism, ultimately terrorists will disappear, supporters of regulation measures argue. The third policy option most favored by media organizations is labeled as "voluntary self-restraint." It described media evolution of self-regulations on how to act and work in situations of crisis caused by terrorist acts, without these guidelines being imposed by a government. According to Graber (2003), those measures come partly in response to the fear that government-imposed regulations might otherwise be forced upon them. An editorial in the *Baltimore Sun* on October 15, 2001 about the War on Terrorism stated that "editors, not government, must be the arbiters of what's fit to air or print" and that for a free society "no other alternative is acceptable" (Graber, 2003, p. 41).

The direct censorship approach has been evident in numerous cases. Shortly after 9/11, U.S. Deputy Secretary of State Richard Armitage contacted the board of the Voice of America, to demand scratching a scheduled interview with Taliban leader Mullah Omar. According to a State Department official, the "Voice of America is not the Voice of Mullah Omar and not the Voice of the Taliban." Initially, the board of Voice of America gave in and blocked the broadcast of the interview, but eventually, after heavy protests of the editors, the program was aired some days later (Koppel & Labott, 2001). In another example, Condoleezza Rice and other officials from the U.S. Administration asked major American television stations, just after 9/11, to stop airing bin Laden messages, because they may incite violence against Americans, or even contain secret messages for sleeper cells. The television channels agreed in what was described as "a silky form of censorship" (BBC, 2001). In the UK, the BBC board cancelled a documentary in 1985, after political pressure by Thatcher's government, because it contained an interview with an IRA leader. In fact, also before this, the British government had on several occasions threatened to sue the BBC under the so-called "Prevention of Terrorism Act."

A widely-accepted argument, however, is that government censoring of terrorist activity is not so effective in significantly reducing or even stopping terrorism. Gerrits noted on the United Kingdom that Thatcher's media policy regarding the IRA in the 1980s might have "indeed deprived the terrorists of an important instrument, but they will not be able to destroy thereby the political fanaticism that forms the basis of (armed) resistance" (1992, p. 60). Gerrits quotes Sinn Féin leader Gerry Adams, saying that "censorship alone will certainly not paralyze the movement" (1992, p. 60). Another argument against censorship of terrorism is that if the media do not report on the subject, rumors may be detrimental to state interests. To alleviate the potential effects of media leaks and rumors, Perl (1997) suggests a number of options, none without costs and risks for enhancing the effectiveness of government media-oriented responses to terrorism. These include, p. 1) financing joint media/government training exercises; 2) establishing a government terrorism information response center; 3) promoting use of media pools; 4) promoting voluntary press coverage guidelines; and 5) monitoring terrorism against the media.

According to Biernatzki (2002), government tendencies to control the flow of information about terror events and issues would most likely have adverse effects on balanced and accurate coverage of those events. Information shortages in terror crisis situations are more likely to lead to confusion and rumors with far-reaching implications for the state and society. Governments are typically reserved when it comes to releasing information on ongoing terrorism management situations, claiming that information leaks might be used by terrorists to coordinate further attacks or escape potential entrapments. In numerous cases, governments have blamed unauthorized media leaks for critical security failure that had serious human consequences.

But the gravest challenge before governments as communicators and as sources of information on terrorism lies in cyberspace where it is highly difficult to circumvent the huge deluge of information flows from terrorist organizations or their sympathizers. Seib notes that in Britain, the Research, Information, and Communication Unit (RICU), follows a two-part strategy: "channeling [anti-al-Qaeda] messages through volunteers in Internet forums" and providing the BBC and other media organizations around the world with propaganda designed to "taint the al-Qaeda brand" (2011, p. 10). In May 2012, the U.S. State Departments Strategic Communication Center was reported to be tracking and hacking terrorist Websites by altering their content in a manner detrimental to their mission and ideology (Sky News Arabia, 2012, May 25).

CITIZEN-MEDIA INITIATIVES AGAINST TERRORISM

The use of media to combat terrorism has not been an exclusive government concern, but has come to embrace other sectors of society as well. New views of the war on terrorism as a collective responsibility of society and the state have stimulated widespread interest in community engagement in this battle through the media sphere. The rise of social and other Web-based media has given an enduring momentum to such community engagement with the launch of online Websites and the extensive participation in social media activities on the part of private citizens. Examples include: initiatives adopted by the New South Wales Government (2011) to help protect and resilience within the community in relation to counterterrorism, the Michigan Regional Community Policing Community Counter Terrorism Initiative, and the Las Vegas Police social media initiative to prevent terrorism (StGeorgeUtah. com, 2011). In all community initiatives, media, especially social outlets, have been effectively harnessed to raise public awareness of terrorism in terms of its causes, functions, goals and tactics. Some of those initiatives have training components

seeking to provide individuals with basic skills in handling media coverage of terrorism and in responding to it in their communities in coordination with law-enforcement authorities. In the conventional media sphere, communities around the world have made successful headways with news, features and opinion contents run by daily newspapers on issues relating to the fight against terrorism. This feature has been most conspicuous in countries victimized by terrorist attacks across the United States and Western Europe. In countries where media institutions are owned and operated by governments, communities have also had good access opportunities to the press and airwaves as is the case in Saudi Arabia (Al-Karni, 2005).

CONCLUSION

Communication has proven to be an integral component of the terrorism phenomenon. Media in their institutional and social forms have provided ammunition for both protagonists (governments) and antagonists (terrorist organizations) in the war against terror. While conventional media have been generally resilient to terrorist propaganda, the congruence of media professional values and orientations with the sensational and dramatic features of terror have enabled terrorists to make some headway in the institutional public sphere. This situation has only accentuated the challenges facing governments as they seek to control information flows within their counter-terrorism strategies. For governments, as much as media are indispensible for building up national and global public opinion to combat terrorism, their invocation of freedom of the press rights and their claimed symbiosis with terrorism would only complicate the government drive to defeat terror.

This chapter has identified four employers of media during terrorism: media institutions, terrorist organizations, governments and communities. Each of the four actors has approached employing the media with unique perspectives relevant to its political, professional, social and ideological positions. Each has also followed different tactics to secure a place in the public sphere in order to promote its ideologies and views. The engagement of the four actors in the process of employing the media has given rise to a plethora of issues this chapter has sought to discuss. One of them is the notion of media symbiosis, which claims that both media and terrorists glean mutual benefits from terrorism coverage. Another issue relates to the notion of media information controls as impinging on press freedom to report terrorism news in an independent fashion. A third issue raised by this chapter pertains to how communities could join hands to bolster counter-terrorism drives through education and social awareness programs.

But the most outstanding issue defining employing the media during terrorism relates to the rise of the Internet as a tool of communication in the war against terrorism. It has been argued throughout the chapter that as much as the Web offers good opportunities for governments and communities to win the fight against terror, it also presents society and the state with serious challenges as defined by increasing terrorists' use of online communication to promote their ideas and tactics.

Except for a few conceptual attempts, employing the media during terrorism has been largely addressed on the basis of practical experiences around the world with little theoretical analysis involved. Conceptual frameworks to understand how media are employed during terrorism like the one by Ali Al-Karni (2005) as based on the Saudi experience offer promising prospects for a more systematic understanding of this phenomenon. A more comprehensive model that accounts for media users' objectives, intentions and tactics as well as for media values and conventions would certainly generate useful perspectives. This chapter has identified four prime actors in the process of employing the media: media organizations, terrorists, governments, and communities. It has been argued that despite media claims of independence and governments' elaborate counter-terrorism strategies, the current national and global media environment remains rather vulnerable to terrorist mobilization, indoctrination, and recruitment. An understanding of the dynamics of employing the media as defined by actors' visions, goals, and tactics would certainly be useful not only in fostering the drive against terror, but also in enhancing our understanding of how terrorism is communicated.

REFERENCES

Al-Karni, A. (2005). *A media-terrorism model: The Saudi experience*. Paper presented at the Annual Convention of the International Association for Media and Communication Research. Taipei, Taiwan.

al-Quds al-Arabi. (2012, May 27). *Saudi diplomat appeals to king for his release*, p. 4.

Anti-Defamation League. (2013). *Extremism in America: Don black/stormfront*. Retrieved August 30, 2013, from http://archive.adl.org/learn/ext_us/Don-Black/default.asp?xpicked=2&item=DBlack

Awan, A. (2007). Virtual jihadist media: Function, legitimacy, and radicalizing efficacy. *European Journal of Cultural Studies, 10*(3), 389–408.

Biernatzki, W. E. (2002). Terrorism and mass media. *Communication Research Trends: Center for the Study of Communication and Culture, 21*(1), 3–24.

British Broadcasting Corporation (BBC). (2001, October 11). *US TV limits bin Laden coverage*. Retrieved July 3, 2013, from http://news.bbc.co.uk/2/hi/americas/1593275.stm

Ciovacco, C. J. (2009). The contours of al Qaeda's media strategy. *Studies in Conflict and Terrorism, 32*(10), 853–875.

COT Institute for Safety. Security and Crisis Management. (2008, July 23). *Transnational terrorism and the rule of law: Terrorism and the media*. Retrieved July 3, 2013, from http://www.transnationalterrorism.eu/tekst/publications/WP4%20Del%206.pdf

Domke, D., Graham, E. S., Coe, K., Lockett, S., & Coopman, T. (2006). Going public as political strategy: The Bush administration, an echoing press, and passage of the Patriot Act. *Political Communication, 23*(3), 291–312.

Gerges, F. A. (2005). *The far enemy: Why Jihad went global*. Cambridge, UK: Cambridge University Press.

Gerrits, R. P. J. M. (1992). Terrorists' perspectives: Memoirs. In D. L. Paletz, & A. P. Schmid (Eds.), *Terrorism and the media* (pp. 29–61). London: Sage.

Graber, D. A. (2003). Terrorism, censorship and the 1st amendment: In search of policy guidelines. In P. Norris, M. Kern, & M. Just (Eds.), *Framing terrorism: The news media, the government and the public* (pp. 27–42). New York: Routledge.

Hoffman, B. (2006). *Inside terrorism*. New York: Columbia University Press.

Jenkins, B. M. (1974). International terrorism: A new kind of warfare. The Rand Corporation, 1-16.

Kimmage, D., & Ridolfo, K. (2007). Iraqi insurgent media: The war of ideas and images. *Radio Free Europe/Radio Liberty*. Retrieved July 5, 2013, from http://realaudio.rferl.org/online/OLPDF-files/insurgent.pdf

Koh, H. H. (2002). Preserving American values: The challenge at home and abroad. In *The age of terror: America and the world after September 11* (pp. 143–169). New York: Basic Books.

Koppel, A., & Labott, E. (2001, September 25). VOA asked not to air Taliban leader interview. CNN.com/U.S. Retrieved July 3, 2013, from http://articles.cnn.com/2001-09-24/us/gen.voa.taliban_1_taliban-leader-mullah-mohammad-omar-voa-broadcasts?_s=PM:US

Lahoud, N., Caudill, S., Collins, L., Koehler-Derrick, G., Rassler, D., & al-`Ubaydi, M. (2012). Letters from Abbottabad: Bin Laden sidelined? *Combating Terrorism Centre at Westpoint*. Retrieved July 3, 2013, from http://www.ctc.usma.edu/wp-content/uploads/2012/05/CTC_LtrsFromAbottabad_WEB_v2.pdf

Lumbaca, S., & Gray, D. H. (2011). The media as an enabler for acts of terrorism. *Global Security Studies, 2*(1), 45–54.

Michigan Regional Community Policing Community Counter Terrorism Initiative. (n.d.). Retrieved July 22, 2013, from http://www1.cj.msu.edu/anti_terror/

Moutot, M. (2010, October 9). Al-Qaeda views west terror alert fears as victory: Experts. *Agence France-Presse.* Retrieved July 5, 2013, from http://www.google.com/hostednews/afp/article/ALeqM5iyx1sKrYJT_vrKaMRnR-SMgX9Qrw?docId=CNG.9069423c15ce0426af7f79fa1a9b81e0.a81

Muller, E. R., Spaaij, R. F. J., & Ruitenberg, A. G. W. (2004). *Trends in terrorisme. Alphen aan de Rijn.* Kluwer.

Nacos, B. L. (2000). Accomplice or witness? The media's role in terrorism is the media terrorism's oxygen? A critical examination of how terrorists rely on and use various media. *Current History (New York, N.Y.), 99*(636), 174–178.

Nacos, B. L. (2007). *Mass-mediated terrorism: The central role of the media in terrorism and counterterrorism.* Lanham, MD: Rowman & Littlefield Publishers, Inc.

New South Whales Government. (2011). *Countering terrorism: Community initiatives.* Retrieved July 22, 2013, from http://www.secure.nsw.gov.au/For-individuals-and-community-groups/Community-initiatives.aspx

Perl, R. F. (1997, October 22). Terrorism, the media and the government: Perspectives, trends and options for policy makers. *CRS Issue Brief.* Retrieved July 3, 2013, from http://www.fas.org/irp/crs/crs-terror.htm

Poland, J. M. (1988). *Understanding terrorism: Groups, strategies, and responses.* Englewood Cliffs, NJ: Prentice Hall.

Seib, P. (2011). *Public diplomacy, new media and counterterrorism. USC Center on Public Diplomacy at the Annenberg School.* Los Angeles, CA: Figueroa Press.

Sky News Arabia. (2012, May 25). *Washington chases al-Qaeda in cyberspace.* Retrieved July 3, 2013, from http://www.skynewsarabia.com/Web/article/22803

Soriano, M. R. T. (2008). Terrorism and the mass media after al Qaeda: A change of course? *Athena Intelligence Journal, 3*(2), 1–20.

StGeorgeUtah.com. (2011, May 11). *Las Vegas metro police uses social media to prevent terrorism.* Retrieved July 22, 2013, from http://www.stgeorgeutah.com/news/archive/2011/05/11/las-vegas-metro-police-uses-social-media-to-prevent-terrorism/

United Nations. (2007). *Implementation of the UN counterterrorism strategy.* Paper presented at the 42nd Conference of the United Nations of the Next Decade. St. Michaels, MD.

Walsh, J. I. (2010). Media attention to terrorist attacks: Causes and consequences. *Institute for Home Security Solutions.* Retrieved July 3, 2013, from http://www.jamesigoewalsh.com/ihss.pdf

Weimann, G. (2004). *How modern terrorism uses the internet.* Washington, DC: United States Institute of Peace.

Weimann, G., & Winn, C. (1994). *The theatre of terror: Mass media and international terrorism.* New York: Longman.

Wieviorka, M. (1993). *The making of terrorism.* Chicago: The University of Chicago Press.

Wilkinson, P. (2006). *Terrorism versus democracy: The liberal state response.* London: Routledge.

KEY TERMS AND DEFINITIONS

Citizen Groups: Organized communities made up of people in a given country or nation.

Journalism: The occupation of news reporting.

Media in Terrorism Situations: The role of the media during times of terrorism.

Media Institutions: Mass communication organizations in the business of media.

Media Objectives: The main goals of the media.

Media-Terrorism Symbiosis: The interconnectedness and codependency demonstrated by terrorists and media professionals.

War on Terror: A term applied to an international military campaign initiated by the United States that started after 9/11.

ENDNOTES

[1.] This chapter uses the UN General Assembly definition of terrorism as "criminal acts intended or calculated to provoke a state of terror in the general public, a group of persons or particular persons for political purposes . . . whatever the considerations of a political, philosophical, ideological, racial, ethnic, religious or other nature that may be invoked to justify them" (Koh, 2002, p. 148).

Section 6
New Terrorism & New Media

Chapter 12
New Terrorism and Media

Mahmoud Eid
University of Ottawa, Canada

ABSTRACT

New terrorism has been recently considered a new type of terrorism. The terrorism characteristics that have instigated the introduction of the term stem from the modern evolutions in most aspects of terrorism, such as its organizational structure, financing, recruitment, training, motivations, tactics, reach, targets, and lethality. This chapter reviews discussions surrounding new terrorism, explains its key characteristics and features, and demonstrates the dual role of the media and information technologies. Distinctions from conventional terrorism recognize it as loose, decentralized cell-based networks, using high-intensity weapons, religiously and vaguely motivated, using asymmetrical methods for maximum casualties, and highly skillful in using new media and information technologies. Moreover, the most critical features focus on how the functioning of new terrorism adapts new media technologies, which in turn, contribute to all of its aspects. However, it is concluded that regardless of the label—new or old—attention should be focused on the act and the actors, whether the ways they function utilize the conventional or adapt with the most recent technologies, media, and weapons, and most crucially, recognizing how fast and efficient terrorists are in utilizing the most advanced media and information technologies.

INTRODUCTION

It is debated that terrorism in our modern era may have a "new-look." Terrorism, it is claimed, has entered a new phase, which is referred to as the "new terrorism." At present, terrorism demonstrates new characteristics that have instigated the exploration and the adaptation of the new term (e.g., Adkins, 2013; Burnett & Whyte, 2005; Copeland, 2001; Duyvesteyn, 2004; Grover, 2002; Gurr & Cole, 2005; Field, 2009; Hoffmann, 1999; Kurtulus, 2011; Laqueur, 2000; Lesser et al., 1999;

Martin, 2006; Mockaitis, 2007; Murphy, 2009; Neumann, 2009; Otenyo, 2004; Sandole, 2004; Simon, 2003; Spalek, 2010; Spencer, 2006, 2011; Zimmermann, 2004). The question of whether or not contemporary terrorism should be titled "new terrorism" is contested among many scholars. The idea of the new terrorism has prompted increased concern, scholarly debates, and governmental interventions (Spencer, 2011). Although this shift in nomenclature continues to be debated, it is said to be due to an evolution in this form of violence.

DOI: 10.4018/978-1-4666-5776-2.ch012

Debates involve discussions on how terrorism today has new actors, targets, motivations, weapons, and organizational structures (to name a few), warranting the need for further research and analysis (e.g., Copeland, 2001; Otenyo, 2004). This chapter reviews the discussions around the emergence of new terrorism, explaining the key characteristics and features that have been attributed to terrorism labeling it new in most of its aspects and the ways it functions. It focuses on the dual role of the media and information technologies being both highly used by modern terrorists in almost all aspects and weapons of terrorism and influential in shaping the ways modern terrorists function.

WHAT IN NEW TERRORISM IS "NEW"

A few characteristics and features have been most common in terrorism in recent decades; hence, some tend to label it as "new." Terrorism is argued now to be new in structure, financing, recruitment, training, motivations, tactics, reach, targets, and lethality.

New terrorism is decentralized (Adkins, 2013). New terrorists are less-cohesive organizational entities (Hoffman, 1999). Traditionally, terrorists have relied on state support and sponsorship (Jenkins, 2006; Spencer, 2006). Recently, the financing of terrorism most commonly comes from illegal sources such as credit card fraud, video piracy, drug trafficking, legal business investments, and donations from wealthy charities and individuals (Spencer, 2006). New terrorism is no longer limited to traditional organizations that are exercised by conflicts within specific nations; instead the battleground for new terrorist groups is global (Mythen, 2013). Targets of the new terrorism are also more global in reach (Burnett &Whyte, 2005; Lesser, 1999) and tend to be indiscriminate (Duyvesteyn, 2004). New terrorism is more dangerous and more difficult to

counter than conventional terrorism in that it has a new network structure, facilitated by information technologies, amateur personnel, willingness to cause mass casualties perhaps by using chemical, biological, nuclear, or radiological weapons, and most importantly is no longer in need of state-sponsorship (Tucker, 2001).

Gus Martin (2006) summarizes the most distinguishing characteristics of new terrorism as follow:

- Loose, cell-based networks with minimal lines of command and control
- Desired acquisition of high-intensity weapons and weapons of mass destruction [WMD]
- Politically vague, religious, or mystical motivations
- "Asymmetrical" methods that maximize casualties
- Skillful use of the Internet and manipulation of the media (Martin, 2006, p. 10)

Key characteristics in the weapons and tactics of new terrorism are "the threat of [WMD], indiscriminate targeting, and intentionally high casualty rates"; for instance, the attacks of 9/11 in the United States; March 11, 2004, in Spain; July 7, 2005, in Great Britain; and July 23, 2005, in Saudi Arabia resulted in high rates of victims (Martin, 2006, p. 34). As well, the targets of new terrorism are now different and shifting away from particular states and toward specific ideologies; the new terrorism has a global reach and is considered lethal (Burnett &Whyte, 2005). New terrorists are characterized as "highly funded, technologically articulate groups capable of inflicting devastating damage to a wide range of targets" (Gordon & Ford, 2003, p. 9).

The 9/11 attacks sparked increased attention to terrorism and its functioning in the new millennium. This continues to captivate scholars, politicians, and policymakers who agree that terrorism has changed and entered a new reign of lethality and violence (Spalek, 2010). New terrorism is thought to be much more lethal than terrorism in the past (e.g., Burnett &Whyte, 2005; Duyvesteyn, 2004; Spencer, 2006). The new figures of terrorist incidents and casualties indicate an increase in the number of victims rather than in the number of incidents. For example, while in the 1990s the total number of terrorist incidents worldwide demonstrated a decline, the percentage of terrorist incidents with fatalities has increased (Hoffman, 1999). New terrorism strives to inflict mass-casualties; they are more apocalyptic in their methods and perspectives (Morgan, 2004). Attacks tend to be high-profile that cause tremendous suffering and inflict long-term societal and political consequences (Strandberg, 2013). While old terrorism methods often targeted clearly defined political demands, the new terrorism targets the general destruction of society (Spencer, 2006). New terrorism is "is closely linked to [WMD]" (Field, 2009, p. 200). New terrorists are thought to have an increased willingness to inflict mass violence and bloodshed by using chemical, biological, nuclear, or radiological weapons (e.g., Hirschmann, 2000; Tucker, 2001). While traditional terrorists acted within specific political boundaries and demonstrated little interest in WMD, modern terrorists seem to be more interested in using these lethal weapons; as a result, terrorists are able to achieve highly catastrophic outcomes due to the usage of extremely dangerous weapons that can inflict mass casualties (Field, 2009).

WHEN NEW TERRORISM IS "NEW"

To explore how terrorism has evolved, it is necessary to reflect on the past; however, the existence of terrorism is long and complex (Hawks, 2013). From a historical perspective, "terrorism has been seen as a tactical phenomenon which fluctuates according to geography and culture" (Gearson,

2002, p. 10). When looking to understand whether or not the current state of terrorism warrants a new label (new terrorism), it is important to understand the implications of this shift in labeling. To suggest that an entity has changed implies that a solidified representation of its previous state is understood—this allows for a comparison, granting the process of distinction. However, being that definitions of terrorism remain variable, it is challenging to claim a clear movement from one term to another.

Some distinctions between conventional terrorism and new terrorism have focused on the time in history and the specific actors involved. For example, some proponents of the new terrorism have articulated a precise distinction that traditional terrorist organizations and groups are those of the past during the 1960s, 1970s, and 1980s such as the Red Army Faction, the Red Brigades, the Provisional Irish Republican Army, and the Basque ETA, while new terrorist organizations and groups are those of the 1990s and on, such as al-Qaeda and Aum Shinrikyo (Field, 2009).

While the events of 9/11 can be considered indicative of a new wave of terrorism, the new terrorism began to emerge long before 9/11 (Burnett & Whyte, 2005). Despite the fact that some trace the transformation of terrorism into new terrorism to the beginning of the 1970s (e.g., Rich, 2013), it is commonly stated that this new form of terrorism emerged in the 1990s (e.g., Adkins, 2013; Field, 2009; Hirschmann, 2000; Spencer, 2006): "'new terrorism' refers to a qualitative change in the nature of terrorism, which has allegedly taken place during the 1990s" (Kurtulus, 2011, p. 477). However, Banu Baybars Hawks (2013) explains that modern terrorism "dates back to the mid-19th century. Just as the Jacobins of the French Revolution held a 'Reign of Terror' in 1794, communists and fascists shared a tendency to use terrorism. After World War II, terrorism became known on an international scale, but it can be argued that terrorism today knows no international boundaries. This new terrorism is less centralized, less structured, and less organized, but far more dangerous than the terrorism of the past" (Hawks, 2013, p. 278).

The evolution of terrorism into a more lethal and pervasive form of violence and conflict did not simply happen overnight; the public came to know this shift through the vernacular presented to them through political leaders such as Tony Blair and George W. Bush (Field, 2009), "serving as a rationale for broader geopolitical and strategic international objectives" (Mythen, 2013, p. 386). "Bush warned of 'the growing threat of terror on a catastrophic scale – terror armed with biological, chemical, or nuclear weapons' . . . In much the same way, Blair drew attention to 'the risk of this new global terrorism and its interaction with states or organisations or individuals proliferating WMD'" (Field, 2009, p. 196).

Similar statements have been issued by other senior politicians around the world, many of whom reference the idea of the new terrorism and its potential for lethal outcomes. The general theme of these assertions tends to agree that terrorism has in fact entered a "new" realm, necessitating "an equally 'new' counter-terrorism response" (Field, 2009, p. 195).

HOW NEW TERRORISM IS "NEW"

Despite the controversy surrounding the exact point in which the new terrorism emerged, terrorism has been expanded and enriched (Hirschmann, 2000). Scholars, government analysts, and politicians (to name a few) have articulated "a 'new' concept, which involves different actors, motivations, aims, tactics and actions, compared to the 'old' concept of terrorism used in the mid twentieth century" (Spencer, 2006, p. 4). To distinguish new terrorism from conventional or traditional terrorism, Gus Martin (2006) explains that the latter is typically characterized by the following:

- Clearly identifiable organizations or movements
- Use of conventional weapons, usually small arms and explosives
- Explicit grievances championing specific classes or ethno-national groups
- Relatively "surgical" selection of targets (Martin, 2006, p. 10)

Perhaps one of the most prominent shifts observed in terrorism trends are the changes seen in the ways in which terrorist organizations are structured. Terrorism today demonstrates a different type of organizational structure than that seen in the past among terrorist groups (Jenkins, 2006). Terrorists are now "able and willing to develop network forms of organization for the same reason that businesses are" (Tucker, 2001, p. 1).

While traditional terrorist organizations were characterized by vertical and hierarchical organizational structures, the new terrorist organizations consist of horizontal networks (Kurtulus, 2011). The emerging new terrorism environment is characterized by a horizontal organizational structure in the way terrorist plan, function, and implement their attacks; that is, independent terrorist cells operate autonomously without reporting to a hierarchical (i.e., vertical) command structure (Martin, 2006). These new groups are more resilient than the traditional structure, for if one or more are destroyed, others can carry on, as they are isolated (Tucker, 2001). This is because the terrorist cells within the network are autonomous and do not rely on one defined leader; instead, they are linked by communication to share ideas about their common purpose (e.g., Burnett &Whyte, 2005; Hirschmann, 2000; Spencer, 2006).

This decentralized structure, which is much different from the old controlling hierarchical structure seen by terrorists, is facilitated through communication and information technologies (e.g., Hoffman, 1999; Tucker, 2001). In today's world, technology "is putting into the hands of deviant individuals and groups destructive powers that were once reserved primarily to governments;" it has made "modern societies more vulnerable to large-scale attack" (Nye, 2005, p. 229).

New terrorism is characterized by "asymmetrical tactics, cell-based networks, indiscriminate attacks against 'soft' targets, and the threatened use of high-yield weapons technologies" (Martin, 2006, p. 212). New terrorism has a global reach and the organizations involved are less organized, less structured, and less centralized, but have lethal potential (Hawks, 2013). These new organizations are also a lot more flexible, enjoy tactical independence, and demonstrate a shift away from formally organized, state-sponsored groups (e.g., Spencer, 2006; Zanini & Edwards, 2001).

Despite the fact that asymmetrical warfare[1] was once an old practice throughout the long history of terrorism, it has become recently a central feature in our present era of new terrorism. Nowadays, terrorists can "acquire and wield new high-yield arsenals, strike at unanticipated targets, cause mass casualties, and apply unique and idiosyncratic tactics;" creating a dilemma for both victims and counterterrorism policymakers, as they "can win the initiative and redefine the international security environment" due to the fact that "the traditional protections and deterrent policies used by societies and the global community can be surmounted by dedicated terrorists" (Martin, 2006, p. 270).

Terrorists at present demonstrate a more network-centric mode of organization (e.g., Adkins, 2013; Lesser, 1999; Rich, 2013; Tucker, 2001). New terrorism has become more focused on the transnational dimension, as terrorist cells are growingly "linked to each other across several countries" (Martin, 2006, p. 276). That is, terrorism networks work on a global scale and operate in loosely organized networks (e.g., Cetina, 2005; Duyvesteyn, 2004).

WHY NEW TERRORISM IS "NEW"

New terrorism is a growing threat that "adds a unique dimension to the emerging terrorist environment of the 21st century" because it is "different in character, aiming not at clearly defined political demands but at the destruction of society and the elimination of large sections of the population" (Martin, 2006, p. 40). In looking into the ways new terrorism functions, debates arise around perceptions and motivations that cause extremist behaviors and new acts of terrorism. Terrorism as a "phenomenon in transition," witnesses that new "types of actors have emerged, new means are being deployed, new controversial issues within or between societies make for new motives for extremist behaviour" (Hirschmann, 2000, p. 309). Religiously motivated fundamentalism is considered an important part of the new terrorism (e.g., Duyvesteyn, 2004; Norris, Kern, & Just, 2003). In fact, religiously motivated terrorism can result in mass causalities (Simon, 2003).

A great deal of discussions about new terrorism relates to religion as a central feature, and that new terrorists have religion-related motivations (e.g., Hoffman, 1999; Martin, 2006; Mythen, 2013). A religiously-motivated wave of terrorism, "which started in the 1990's," is "based on religious ideals to justify terrorist activities" (Adkins, 2013, p. 2). Whereas "'old terrorism' was primarily secular in its orientation and inspiration, terrorism linked to religious fanaticism is on the increase" (Spencer, 2006, p. 9). Drawing connections between religion and terrorism has become increasingly popular in recent years. Although religiously motivated terrorism does exist in contemporary times, some faith groups are more frequently associated with terrorist activity than others. Despite this, terrorist acts continue to be committed in the name of various different faith groups.

New terrorism is commonly portrayed as a form of violence that "rejects all other ways and promotes an uncompromising view of the world in accordance with the belief of the religion" (Spencer, 2006, p. 9). Fanaticism rather than political interests is more often the motivation behind the new terrorism (Morgan, 2004). While the controversy surrounding Osama bin Laden's al-Qaeda has seen recent popularization due to 9/11 (Eid, 2008), radicalism among this faith group is not the only form of religiously motivated terrorism (Morgan, 2004). However, it should be noted that terrorism "is not linked to any particular religion or nationality" (Kingshott, 2003, p. 17).[2] While the media are often quick to point fingers at specific faith groups, religiously motivated terrorism can come from any faith group. This feature of the religiously motivated characterizes modern terrorism "since its inception in the activities of Russian anarchists" and it is also found "in many modern terrorist organizations in our century which have had important religious dimensions, i.e., the IRA, EOKA (Cyprus), the FLN (Algeria), and the Irgun (Israel)" (Rapoport, 1984, p. 659).

WHERE IN NEW TERRORISM ARE THE MEDIA

The advancement in traditional media and the emergence of new media have had huge impact on terrorism, contributing to the new phase of terrorism. New terrorism does not only rely on traditional media, as is the case with conventional terrorism, but also on new media. New terrorism often interacts with the media to spread fear through illustrations of their attacks and threats; in fact, the news media can be seen, in some instances, as a co-conspirator when reporting on terrorist events (Walter, 2012). The age of new terrorism demonstrates that terrorists try to gain maximum media publicity and are increasingly dependent on new media and information technologies (Anderson, 2003).

This new trend in using the media is attributed to the shift in how the new media industries work and operate. Today, the media can be considered omnipresent in our society; constantly producing news and contents. As well, the media environment today is highly competitive; they are not only racing against professional competitors, but also social networking sites, such as Twitter and Facebook, which are able to provide audiences with real-time facts similar to journalistic entities. Thus, the media can be attracted by sensational activity, such as terrorist events, making them pivotal participants in the dissemination of information regarding terrorist information.

Due to the global networking and the decentralized nature of new terrorists, they leverage new media and information technologies such as the Internet, mobile phones, and software as well as specialized Websites devoted to various activities such as propaganda, recruitment, training, fundraising, communication, and targeting (Adkins, 2013). Terrorism is now facilitated by new communication and information technologies such as the Internet (e.g., Cetina, 2005; Jenkins, 2006; Tucker, 2001). Technologies allow terrorists to disseminate their propaganda to the world with great ease (Adkins, 2013). The Internet is described as one of the most influential technological inventions of our time (Matusitz & Minei, 2009). It "enables the new terrorists to communicate covertly and to bridge [geographical] distances more easily" (Spencer, 2006, p. 11).

While traditional terrorism relied on members to be present at a specific geographical location to join together to work and learn, today organizations are able to facilitate distance-training practices due to technological developments such as the Internet (Adkins, 2013). In overcoming geographical constraints that have limited communications in the past, new terrorists are able to exchange and connect globally in a timely manner. This has impacted various functions within terrorist activities, such as recruitment and training. Recruiting and training new members for terrorist networks remain consistent practices; terrorists want to find those interested in participating in their cause and train them. New terrorists are commonly amateurs and predominantly receive training and logistical support from information on the Internet (Spencer, 2006).

However, the ways in which members are recruited and trained have changed due to technology. Terrorist organizations no longer rely on traditional means of communication (e.g., word of mouth, face-to-face networking) to attract potential members. Instead, the Internet can be used as a highly efficient means through which terrorists groups can lure in recruits through Websites and online forums; Websites, for example, can easily be designed to reach out and recruit specific audiences (Adkins, 2013). In this, terrorists are able to share information about their cause and attract new members (Anderson, 2003). Moreover, upon recruiting new members, terrorists can train them through online materials, such as videos, forums, and conference calls (Spencer, 2006). Websites are often created to provide members of terrorist organizations with information on how they create weapons or facilitate attacks (Conway, 2006). "Training new recruits no longer requires entering a [foreign] country and attending a terrorist boot camp. By leveraging technology terrorist groups are able to train recruits much like many distance learning classes offered by universities and professional training companies. Many websites offer information and videos on physical training, bomb making, and kidnapping" (Adkins, 2013, p. 3).

In this, terrorist organizations are able to grow and flourish with much greater ease than seen in the past, due to the Internet and its omnipresent role in our society. The Internet is considered a key component in this change; as terrorists increase their use of the Internet, they can increase their reach to potential recruits on a global scale (Conway, 2006). The diffusion of recruitment via the Internet is very much related to the change in terrorist organizational structures, as it provides a highly interactive communication platform for people to learn, participate, and exchange.

Thus, it is important to note how the Internet and communication technologies impact the structure of terrorist organizations. Traditionally, terrorist organizations have abided by a hierarchical structure, in which power is isolated to few powerful individuals; in this, all members are reliant on their orders and abilities to propel the group forward (Tucker, 2001). This structure can be problematic in that it is heavily reliant on the survival of the leaders, and upon their demise, the remaining members can be destabilized. This is not the case for terrorists today. "Organizations can [now] flatten out their pyramids of authority and control and approach a network form, a group of more or less autonomous, dispersed entities, linked by advanced communications and perhaps nothing more than a common purpose. Motivating or compelling the move from hierarchy to network are the advantages that an organization acquires as it transforms itself. It becomes more flexible, adaptive and resilient because each of its units senses and reacts on its own in loose coordination with the others. This multiplies the opportunities for the organization to learn, making it more flexible and adaptive. The organization becomes more resilient because if one or even several of its constituent entities are destroyed, the others carry on. A network, unlike a hierarchy, cannot be destroyed by decapitation" (Tucker, 2001, p. 1).

Thus, being that new terrorist organizations have a decentralized structure, they rely on communication and information technologies to keep them connected (Spencer, 2006). Communication powers afforded by information technologies impact how terrorists function today, allowing them access to increasingly destructive weapons and technologies (Burnett & Whyte, 2005). However, the advantages of new technologies to terrorists do not lie "with the equipment of attack, which is often pre-modem (recall the knives the 9/11 terrorists used on the planes), but with the use of equipment of communication and mediation that enable global coordination" (Cetina, 2005, p. 221). Although in the past terrorist groups have been reliant on traditional news media to report their acts, terrorists now can create their own media platforms with global reach. For instance, nowadays terrorist groups can spread messages via text, images, and video on the Internet that they have created in alignment with their own goals and ideologies: they "can easily portray themselves as victims seeking a peaceful resolution who were forced into acts of violence as a last resort" (Adkins, 2013, p. 2). Additionally, today's terrorists are able to leverage coverage by the media, which can spread their messages around the globe, through massive extraordinary damages and casualties.

Despite the fact that the Internet, "relying on widely separated but interconnected computer systems, was originally designed as a military solution to the threat of communication disruption due to nuclear attack" (Briggs, 2004, p. 453), individuals, groups, or states can now use cyberspace, computers, and information technology, especially the Internet (Conway, 2002; 2006), to threaten, terrorize, and cause harm to both governments and civilians (Eid, 2010). Cyber-terrorism "became very important" in the era of new terrorism (Hirschmann, 2000, p. 309). It is a very attractive option for modern terrorists.[3] However, although the Internet allows terrorists to deploy new social mobilization strategies, the use of the Internet can also result in new vulnerabilities, as it "acts as a leveller: each new advantage for the terrorists is accompanied by a new opportunity to weaken such groups" (Soriano, 2012, p. 274). While terrorist groups are most certainly making considerable use of the Internet, they have yet to launch a major cyber-terrorism attack; albeit, it is likely that new technologies can be limited only to facilitate attacks (Anderson, 2003).

CONCLUSION

A considerable debate has arisen around what has been characterized as "new terrorism." The evolution in this form of violence has contributed to this debate. In addition, discussions looked into how terrorism today can be considered new in most of its aspects, such as: structure, financing, recruitment, training, motivations, tactics, reach, targets, and lethality. Specifically, distinctions have been made to recognize new terrorism as loose, decentralized cell-based networks, using high-intensity weapons such as WMD, religiously and vaguely motivated, using asymmetrical methods for maximum casualties, and highly skillful in using new media and information technologies. Additionally, some distinctions between the new and the old have focused on the time in history and the specific actors involved. A great deal of the discussions has been on how the functioning of new terrorism adapts new media technologies, which in return, contribute to its structure, financing, recruiting, and all other aspects.

However, I would argue here that terrorism is terrorism and terrorists are terrorists, regardless of the label—new or old. Throughout the above discussions, we can acknowledge the fact that terrorism in our modern era is characterized in different ways than those of the past. Despite this, these differences have been seen in most aspects of terrorism. The role of the media, being crucial, has been amplified given the new media and information technologies that facilitate and enhance the functioning of terrorism more and more. But the need to label terrorism as new does not take the sense of inevitability or originality. A key rationale is that some discussions focus on the time in history and the actors involved. The exact point in history to distinguish the emergence of new terrorism is not even agreed-upon by scholars who discuss new terrorism. The same applies to the actors and the specific terrorist groups and organizations, as some of them did not even exist in the near history in order to compare how they had advanced from being old to new.

The current dilemma of labeling terrorism as new or old can be also faced in the future. A decade or two from now, we can probably live a more advanced type of terrorism compared with what we debate to call new terrorism today. In fact, the difference between old and new terrorism is considered artificial and in some ways dangerous because this belief can be employed to justify new rushed and restrictive countermeasures implemented by the government without being democratically debated and publicly discussed (Spencer, 2006).

Therefore, it is suggested here that regardless of the label, our attention should be more focused on the act itself as terrorism and the actors themselves as terrorists, whether the ways they function still utilize the conventional or adapt with the most recent technologies, media, and weapons. However, looking into the functioning of terrorism from an era, decade, year, and even a moment to another should be critically focused on how fast and efficient terrorists are in utilizing, if not even creating, the most advanced media and information technologies.

REFERENCES

Adkins, G. (2013). Red teaming the red team: Utilizing cyber espionage to combat terrorism. *Journal of Strategy Security, 6*(5), 1–9.

Anderson, A. (2003). Risk, terrorism, and the internet. *Knowledge, Technology & Policy, 16*(2), 24–33.

Briggs, W. (2004). North America. In A. S. de Beer, & J. C. Merrill (Eds.), *Global journalism: Topical issues and media systems* (pp. 430–464). Boston: Pearson Education, Inc.

Burnett, J., & Whyte, D. (2005). Embedded expertise and the new terrorism. *Journal for Crime. Conflict and the Media, 1*(4), 1–18.

Cetina, K. K. (2005). Complex global microstructures: The new terrorist societies. *Theory, Culture & Society, 22*(5), 213–234.

Conway, M. (2002). Reality bytes: Cyberterrorism and terrorist 'use' of the internet. *First Monday, 7*(11), 1–17.

Conway, M. (2006). Terrorism and the internet: New media – New threat? *Parliamentary Affairs, 59*(2), 283–298.

Copeland, T. (2001). Is the new terrorism really new? An analysis of the new paradigm for terrorism. *The Journal of Conflict Studies, 21*(2), 91–105.

Duyvesteyn, I. (2004). How new is the new terrorism? *Studies in Conflict and Terrorism, 27*(5), 439–454.

Eid, M. (2008). The two faces of Osama bin Laden: Mass media representations as a force for evil and Arabic hero. In S. J. Drucker, & G. Gumpert (Eds.), *Heroes in a global world* (pp. 151–183). New Jersey: Hampton Press.

Eid, M. (2010). Cyber-terrorism and ethical journalism: A need for rationalism. *International Journal of Technoethics, 1*(4), 1–19.

Field, A. (2009). The new terrorism: Revolution or evolution. *Political Studies Review, 7*(2), 195–207.

Gearson, J. (2002). The nature of modern terrorism. *The Political Quarterly, 73*(1), 7–24.

Gordon, S., & Ford, R. (2003). Cyberterrorism? *Symantec Security Response*. Retrieved October 6, 2013, from http://www.symantec.com/avcenter/reference/cyberterrorism.pdf

Grover, R. (2002). The new state of nature and the new terrorism. *Public Affairs Quarterly, 16*(2), 125–141.

Gurr, N., & Cole, B. (2005). *The new face of terrorism: Threats from weapons of mass destruction*. New York: I. B. Tauris.

Hawks, B. B. (2013). Will peace flourish in the end? The history suffering: Terrorism in Turkey. *Mediterranean Journal of Social Sciences, 4*(10), 278–282.

Hirschmann, K. (2000). The changing face of terrorism. *Internationale Politik und Gesellschaft, 3*, 299–310.

Hoffmann, B. (1999). Terrorism trends and prospects. In I. O. Lesser, B. Hoffman, J. Arquilla, D. Ronfeldt, & M. Zanini (Eds.), *Countering the new terrorism* (pp. 7–38). Santa Monica, CA: RAND Corporation.

Jenkins, B. M. (2006). The new age of terrorism. In D. Kamien (Ed.), Section 2 – Terrorism beyond Al-Qaeda (pp. 117-130). Santa Monica, CA: RAND Corporation.

Kingshott, B. (2003). Terrorism: The new religious war. *Criminal Justice Studies, 16*(1), 15–27.

Kurtulus, E. N. (2011). The new terrorism and its critics. *Studies in Conflict and Terrorism, 34*(6), 476–500.

Laqueur, W. (2000). *The new terrorism: Fanaticism and the arms of mass destruction*. New York: Oxford University Press.

Lesser, I. O. (1999). Countering the new terrorism: Implications for strategy. In I. O. Lesser, B. Hoffman, J. Arquilla, D. Ronfeldt, & M. Zanini (Eds.), *Countering the new terrorism* (pp. 85–144). Santa Monica, CA: RAND Corporation.

Lesser, I. O., Hoffman, B., Arquilla, J., Ronfeldt, D., & Zanini, M. (Eds.). (1999). *Countering the new terrorism*. Santa Monica, CA: RAND Corporation.

Martin, G. (2006). *Understanding terrorism: Challenges, perspectives, and issues*. Thousand Oaks, CA: Sage Publications, Inc.

Matusitz, J., & Minei, E. (2009). Cyberterrorism: Its effects on health-related infrastructures. *Journal of Digital Forensic Practice*, *2*(4), 161–171.

Mockaitis, T. R. (2007). *The new terrorism: Myths and reality*. Westport, CT: Praeger.

Morgan, M. J. (2004). The origins of the new terrorism. *Parameters*, *34*(1), 29–43.

Murphy, J. F. (2009). Challenges of the new terrorism. In D. Armstrong (Ed.), *Routledge handbook of international law* (pp. 281–293). New York: Routeldge.

Mythen, G. (2013). Why should we have to prove we're alright? Counter-terrorism, risk and partial securities. *Sociology*, *47*(2), 383–398.

Neumann, P. (2009). *Old & new terrorism*. Cambridge, UK: Polity Press.

Norris, P., Kern, M., & Just, M. (2003). Introduction: Framing terrorism. In P. Norris, K. Montague, & M. Just (Eds.), *Framing terrorism: The news media, the government and the public* (pp. 3–26). New York: Routledge.

Nye, J. S. (2005). *Understanding international conflicts: An introduction to theory and history*. New York: Pearson Education, Inc.

Otenyo, E. E. (2004). New terrorism: Toward and explanation of cases in Kenya. *African Security Review*, *13*(3), 75–85.

Rapoport, D. C. (1984). Fear and trembling: Terrorism in three religious traditions. *The American Political Science Review*, *78*(3), 658–677.

Rich, P. B. (2013). Understanding terror, terrorism and their representations in media and culture. *Studies in Conflict and Terrorism*, *36*(3), 255–277.

Sandole, D. J. D. (2004). The new terrorism: Causes, conditions and conflict resolution. *Wiener Blätter zur Friedensforschung*, 43-56.

Simon, S. (2003). The new terrorism: Securing the nation against a messianic foe. *The Brookings Review*, *21*(1), 18–24.

Soriano, M. R. T. (2012). The vulnerabilities of online terrorism. *Studies in Conflict and Terrorism*, *35*(4), 263–277.

Spalek, B. (2010). Community policing, trust, and Muslim communities in relation to new terrorism. *Politics & Policy*, *38*(4), 789–815.

Spencer, A. (2006). Questioning the concept of new terrorism. *Peace Conflict & Development*, *8*, 1–33.

Spencer, A. (2011). Comment and debate: Sic[k] of the 'new terrorism' debate? A response to our critics. *Critical Studies on Terrorism*, *4*(3), 459–467.

Strandberg, V. (2013). Rail bound traffic—A prime target for contemporary terrorist attacks? *Journal of Transportation Security*, *6*(3), 271–286.

Tucker, D. (2001). What's new about the new terrorism and how dangerous is it? *Terrorism and Political Violence*, *13*(3), 1–14.

Walter, P. F. (2012). Cyberkill: Melancholia, globalization and media terrorism in American psycho and glamorama. *Arizona Quarterly*, *68*(4), 131–154.

Weimann, G. (2005). Cyberterrorism: The sum of all fears? *Studies in Conflict and Terrorism, 28*(2), 129–149.

Zanini, M., & Edwards, S. J. A. (2001). The networking of terror in the information age. In J. Arquilla, & D. Ronfeldt (Eds.), *Networks and netwars: The future of terror, crime, and militancy* (pp. 29–60). Santa Monica, CA: RAND Corporation.

Zimmermann, D. (2004). Terrorism transformed: The new terrorism, impact scalability, and the dynamic of reciprocal threat perception. *Connections: The Quarterly Journal, 3*(1), 19–40.

KEY TERMS AND DEFINITIONS

Asymmetrical Warfare: Unconventional, unexpected, and nearly unpredictable acts of political violence.

Lethality: Causing great harm or destruction.

New Terrorism: The modern terrorist environment in which the functioning state of terrorism is characterized by utilization of new structure of networking, acquisition of high-intensity weapons, use of asymmetrical methods for massive casualties, and clever use of new media and information technologies.

Terrorism Financing: The ways in which acts of terrorism are funded.

Terrorism Recruitment: The process in which potential members are located to join a terrorist cause, group, or organization.

Terrorism Structure: A complex system of horizontal and/or vertical hierarchy that defines and assigns duties and responsibilities of all members and leaders of one or more terrorist groups or organizations.

Terrorism Training: The process in which terrorists learn about and practice activities that are part of the preparation, planning, facilitation, and/or implementation of acts of terrorism.

ENDNOTES

1. Asymmetrical warfare is a term that refers to "unconventional, unexpected, and nearly unpredictable acts of political violence" (Martin, 2006, p. 270).

2. For example, "although the largest number of suicide terrorist attacks has been carried out by the Liberation Tigers of Tamil Eelam, in Sri Lanka," other groups that embrace suicide attacks include the Kurdistan Workers Party in Turkey, Hezbollah in Lebanon, Hamas and the al-Aqsa Martyrs Brigade in Palestine, and al-Qaeda in East Africa (Kingshott, 2003, p. 17).

3. Cyber-terrorism is a very attractive option for modern terrorists because: 1) it is cheaper than traditional terrorist methods and all what the terrorist needs is a personal computer and an online connection; 2) it is more anonymous than traditional terrorist methods as terrorists use online nicknames or log on to a Website as an unidentified guest user, making it very hard for security agencies and police forces to track down the terrorists' real identity; 3) the variety and number of targets are enormous as the cyber-terrorist can target the computers and computer networks of governments, individuals, public utilities, private airlines, and so on; 4) it can be conducted remotely, a feature that is especially appealing to terrorists because it requires less physical training, psychological investment, risk of mortality, and travel than conventional forms of terrorism; and 5) it has the potential to directly affect a larger number of people than traditional terrorist tactics, thereby generating greater media coverage, which is ultimately a major goal for terrorists (Weimann, 2005).

Chapter 13
New Media and Terrorism

Pauline Hope Cheong
Arizona State University, USA

ABSTRACT

Beyond the widespread coverage of terrorism-related stories on international news outlets, we are witnessing the swift spread of alternative interpretations of these stories online. These alternative narratives typically involve digital transmediation or the remix, remediation, and viral dissemination of textual, audio, and video material on multiple new and social media platforms. This chapter discusses the role of new(er) media in facilitating the transmediated spread of extremist narratives, rumors, and political parody. Drawing from recent case studies based upon multi-modal analyses of digital texts on social media networks, including blogs, vlogs, Twitter, and Jihadist sites associated with acts of terror in Asia, Middle East, and North America, the chapter illustrates how digital transmediation significantly works oftentimes to construct counter narratives to government counter insurgency operations and mainstream media presentations. In discussing these examples, the chapter demonstrates how the new media points to varied narratives and reifies notions of national security, global politics, terrorism, and the media's role in framing the "War on Terrorism." Moreover, a critical examination of remix texts and digital mashups of popular artifacts inform a Web 2.0 understanding of how the creative communication practices of online prosumers (hybrid consumers and producers) contest dominant interests in the online ideological battlefield for hearts and minds.

INTRODUCTION

The relationship between new media and terrorism is profound. It is traditionally charged with the utopic possibilities of new communication technologies to empower and fuel "netwar," yet imbricated with the social and cultural conditions of glocalized contexts and novel user applications. On one hand, control over media content in times of terrorism and conflict historically represents strategic influence over insurgents and contested populations. On the other, the rise of the Internet, including burgeoning patterns of user generated content, raise significant debates about the evolving nature of mediated terrorism in general and propaganda and terrorism related rumors specifically. Participatory digital and social media use allows for increased exposure and interactivity

DOI: 10.4018/978-1-4666-5776-2.ch013

between micro and macro level agencies as non-state actors enter the telecommunications arena and interact online (Payne, 2009; Winn & Zakem, 2009) This participation represents therefore an opportunity for lay persons to consume, construct, and share stories about terrorist events, which should lead us to reconsider the multifaceted nature of mediated terrorism.

Beyond the widespread coverage of terrorism related stories on mainstream and international news outlets, we are witnessing the swift spread of alternative interpretations of these stories online. These alternative narratives typically involve digital transmediation or the remix (Lessig, 2008), remediation (Bolter & Grusin, 2000), and viral dissemination of textual, audio, and video material on multiple and convergent new and social media platforms (Burgess, 2008; Deuze, 2007; Jenkins, 2006). This chapter examines the role of new(er) media in facilitating the transmediated spread of extremist narratives, rumors, and political parody. It illustrates how digital transmediation significantly work to construct counter narratives to government counter insurgency operations and mainstream media presentations. This chapter discusses how new media produsage, which involves lay consumption, creation, and remix practices of digital content (Bruns, 2008), facilitates the discursive and transmediated construction of terrorism-related rumor texts.

New media studies on developing a critical examination of remix texts and digital mashups of popular artifacts help inform a Web 2.0 understanding of how the creative communication practices of online prosumers (hybrid consumers and producers) contest dominant interests in the online ideological battlefield for hearts and minds. Social and political implications of this discussion on new media and strategic influence pertain not only to the viability of digital backchannel communication in a terrorist crisis, but also inform the study of online radicalization.

UNDERSTANDING THE DIGITAL TRANSMEDIATION OF TERRORISM: (RE)PRESENTATIONS IN CONVERGENT NEW AND SOCIAL MEDIA

As the meaning of "truth" is often a key feature of hegemonic struggles, one cardinal dimension in the relationship between new media and terrorism concerns the processes whereby individual and cultural "truth perspectives" may distort veracity, reinforce stigma, and amplify negative stories and images associated with insurgency and counter insurgency operators. In light of the fluorescence of web-enabled technologies, it is important to examine rumors (Sunstein, 2009), particularly how the digital rumor mill functions. That is, in this context, how rumors are created and spread online, by publics linked to the informational war related to terrorism. In many ways, rumors are integrally woven into the fabric of the alleged global war on terror. They reveal information about the narrative landscape, including the expression of social anxieties and the "mentality of the group in which it circulates" (Ellis & Haar, 2004, p. 36). They also help fill knowledge gaps in the wake of a situation of uncertainty and ambiguity (DiFonzo & Prashant, 2007), including the mayhem after a terrorist event.

More importantly, as argued in *Narrative Landmines: Rumors, Islamist extremism, and the struggle for strategic influence* (Bernardi et al., 2012), rumors in war zones can be very dangerous, as they are relatively low-cost and low-tech devices that circulate among lay populations, to instill fear and raise suspicion during times of social conflict, political upheavals, and information uncertainty. As rumors fit into and extend narrative systems and ideologies—and interact with factors particularly in the context of terrorism and counter-terrorism—they can counter elaborate pertinent government initiatives (e.g., outreach programs, strategic communication, etc.). Consequently, the collateral damage caused by rumors, which can be heightened by the virality of content, including rumors on digital platforms—makes it increasingly hard to control (Kibby, 2005) and counter with traditional forms of communication.

In this way, digital media platforms afford new prospects for the democratization of knowledge and the reproduction of alternative sources and voices in the coverage of terrorism-related events. This can highlight various aspects of reality and falsehood beyond traditional, official, or mainstream media coverage. Understanding these changes in the communication landscape is important for strategic communication praxis since the informational access afforded by newer digital and social media presents both opportunities and challenges to dominant states' interests, legitimacy, and support. For example, direct battlefield or ground reports can disseminate via various mediated platforms, such as YouTube (Betz, 2008). The potential of new media to support digital storytelling (Hertzberg & Lundby, 2008) allows the plurality of lay and extremist voices to construct texts to express their anxieties. Additionally, it also allows strategic actors to taint others and manage negative taints, which can drive or mitigate further wedges between constituent populations and between populations and their governing authorities.

Furthermore, in light of burgeoning user-generated content, the notion of media audience/s is in flux, as the same people who read and consume online information and resources increasingly also report and produce it (Livingstone, 1999). In this sense, traditional mass communication distinctions between producer and consumer actions become blurred and indistinct. This gives rise to what influential communication theorist Manuel Castells (2009) calls a form of emerging "communication power" in the relational and hybridized dynamics operant in "the age of mass personal communication." As new media supports digital storytelling among the lay public

(Lessig, 2008), social media may facilitate new and multidirectional ways of interaction. These include collaborative knowledge creation and sharing involving cyber vigilantism and collective intelligence, which may be directed toward spotlighting deviant individuals and public authorities, thereby making them accountable for their actions (Cheong & Gong, 2010). Notably, in the wake of 9/11, Frank (2004) observed how the terrorist attacks inspired vernacular prosumption and manipulation of mediated artifacts including the mass diffusion of photoshopped texts expressing fantasies of humiliation targeted at Osama bin Laden or Afghanistan, and bewilderment of the fate of perished victims. Consequently, the creation of stories and rumors in the contemporary theater of terror now includes new blended groups of producers and consumers, prosumers or "produsers" (Bruns, 2008). This increases the potential agency of everyday non-state actors in communicating facts and falsehoods about extremism and extremist related affairs.

Under wartime fears and social anxieties, creation of rumor texts can help some online participants protest against mainstream media representations. Moreover, as in the case studies discussed below, the use of digital media to perform taint management in the form of satire may be popular during times of insecurity and war, as people attempt to question power behind the shield of parody (Boler, 2008). Additionally, people respond to alternative reports that critique mainstream media and attempt to hold hegemonic regulators accountable (Downing, 2001). The use of humor—such as ridicule and satire—can help reframe and (re)present extremist narratives to erode their authority and weaken the appeal of extremists' messages among contested populations (Goodall et al., 2012). Political humor has historically been used as forms of resistance and control (Benton, 1988) and their contemporary online incarnations can disrupt official storylines and digitally unite protestors globally. In this way, mediated texts highlight the potential of lay responses to counter taken-for-granted truths and navigate tactically a space for themselves amidst national security strategies and the structures of power (de Certeau, 1984).

In the following sections of this chapter, three case study exemplars will be discussed to illustrate the various dimensions and implications of digital transmediation related to terrorism and the struggle for strategic influence. The first example is offered in longer detail as it is based on an unpublished paper in an international conference on new media and terrorism (Cheong & Clow, 2010). The second and third examples are derived from recently published articles (Bernardi et al., 2012; Cheong & Lundry, 2012; Lundry & Cheong, 2011) and provide summarized evidence that showcase the uses of transmediation, rumors, and humor.

MEDIATED TAINT RUMORS: THE CASE OF THE "UNDERWEAR BOMBER"

This section discusses the mediated corpora associated with the "underwear bomber," following the intense and dramatic terrorist attack on December 25, 2009 by 23 year-old Umar Farouk Abdulmutallab. Abdulmutallab tried to detonate an explosive device on board a Northwest airline passenger flight bound for Detroit, Michigan. This case is a fertile context to study the proliferation of online rumors given various ambiguous and suspicions dimensions of the event. In this, information gaps in public perceptions were created, including Abdulmutallab's on board the plane without a passport, the alleged videotaping of the fudged event, and the failure of government officials to revoke Abdulmutallab's visa and place him on the terrorist watch or "no-fly" list. Specifically, the examination below illustrates ways in which online media taint the agents related to terrorism via computer-mediated communication, where the social identities of terrorists and counter insurgency operators' social identities are discursively

performed and contested. Based on an analysis of multiple YouTube, blog, and tweets associated with the underwear bomber, this section illustrates how online interactants intertextually frame the terrorist attack in security branding and national identity discourse. This concomitantly taints state agencies and counter insurgency officials in efforts to resist propaganda and prompts others to combat taints on their national identity to reduce stigma (Cheong & Clow, 2010).

Rumors can serve noetic functions by "tainting" agents associated with the "dirty work" of terrorism. Hughes (1962) first conceptualized "dirty work" as tasks and occupations that were regarded as odious, degrading, or morally insulting. He later observed that society delegates dirty work to groups who act as agents on society's behalf. In this, society then stigmatizes those groups, in effect rejecting the work it has mandated (1962). Dirty work is identified by physical, social, and moral taints (Hughes, cited in Ashforth et al., 2007). Despite past scholarship on this topic, Kreiner, Ashforth, and Sluss (2006) have recommended for more research to examine the broader landscape of stigmatized work. Though little is known about how rumor texts can taint individuals who take on the ground work for terror operations to succeed and agents who act in organizations that counter extremist violence.

It is contended that taint rumors can be applied to the domain of terrorism. This is because stories regarding their dangerous conflicts circulate with reference to suicide bombers who perform the dirty kinetic work of destroying bodies and engaging in bloody sacrifice (Kydd & Walter, 2006). Furthermore, on the other hand, entertainment and mass media representations portray the fight against terrorism as a fearful battle against crime while also justifying the illegal actions of state actors and their criminal conduct to aggressively combat terrorism (Altheide, 2006). At the same time, non-state actors and lay publics are able to exploit the rumor mill and actively propagate satirical or hostile stories about terrorists and counterterrorism state agents. As such, examining taints on multiple levels is important in the sense that it informs shifts in public perceptions of terrorist and state agents, which may potentially undermine strategic communication, diplomatic outreach, and information operations.

In these ways, the spread of taint rumors can have a number of implications for national security, as nations seek to downplay ambient fear, crime, and terror threats in attempts to market a strong "security brand" and reputation worldwide (Coaffee & van Ham, 2008). Specifically, rumors can taint the U.S. brand, which is posited to radiate cultural superiority, political power, and military dominance. Richard Haass, former U.S. State Department's director for policy and planning has argued that his country should assume "the role of international sheriff, one who forges coalitions by posses of states and others for specific tasks" (Haass, cited in van Ham, 2008, p. 243). Consequently, texts that taint the moral basis of U.S. sheriffhood denigrate the state and undermine its authority and credibility to intervene in the global war on terror.

In this case, our analysis involved the archival of 1094 blogs, tweets, YouTube videos, and Jihadist websites. All retrieved texts were published between December 26, 2009 and April, 8, 2010. We examined the top 300 listed blogs, using the keywords "Umar Farouk Abdulmutallab," and the top 300 listed blogs, using the keywords "Underwear Bomber," 73 tweets using the keywords "Umar Farouk Abdulmutallab," and 204 tweets using the keywords "Underwear Bomber," the top 100 viewed videos using the keywords "Umar Farouk Abdulmutallab" and the top 100 viewed videos using the keywords "Underwear Bomber" as well as 17 Jihadist Websites by using the keywords: "Umar Farouk Abdulmutallab or Underwear Bomber," found using the Open Source Center's website (opensource.gov), until the point of data saturation where themes were no longer repeated.

In brief, our analyses showed that there was much discussion on three main themes:

1. Governmental taint and rumors associated with the U.S. government's involvement in staging a fake terrorist attack and fears that the government would use this incident as an excuse to increase surveillance technology expenditure;
2. Taints on the terrorist Umar Farouk Abdulmutallab as an evil and morally lax agent; and
3. Taints associated with the Nigeria national identity.

First, our analyses uncovered taints and rumors associated with the United States "Government." The latter also served in many occasions as a metonym to signify the contiguous operations of the state including its legislature, law enforcement, homeland security, and transportation security administrators. For instance, there were numerous blog postings discussing the incompetence of the U.S. Government's response to the Underwear Bomber. For example, in a blog by Jason Seher entitled "McConnell Attacks Holder on Underwear Bomber, Justice and Security Conflict Grows" (which was the fourth most popular "Underwear Bomber" blog listed by Google), Seher discussed Senate Republican Minority Leader Mitch McConnell's criticisms of President Barack Obama's decision to try Abdulmutallab in a Civil Court (and not a military court). Seher goes on to quote McConnell, who said, in regard to protecting Abdulmutallab's civil rights, "No one denies that a balance must be struck between civil liberties and protecting the homeland . . . but . . . our priorities should be clear: keeping Americans safe should always win out." McConnell believed that Abdulmutallab should have been tried in a military court, so more interrogation could have occurred. McConnell was essentially morally tainting the Government's response to interrogating Abdulmutallab. He suggested that civil rights were taking precedence over the safety of American citizens. In other words, the Government and its legal agencies were being morally reprehensible for choosing a terrorist's civil rights over the safety of its citizens. Additional moral taint of the Government was found in a YouTube video posted by Alex Jones titled "Webster Tarply on Alex Jones Tv 1/6: Underwear Bomber 'Establishment Controlled Patsy!'" In the video (which was viewed over 28,000 times), Jones discussed how Abdulmutallab was a type of "brainwashed" individual being used by the Government to attack Yemen and institute more surveillance of American citizens, suggesting that the Government had dubious and ulterior motives.

In association with federal authorities, our analyses also uncovered taint tumors associated with increased surveillance screening in airports. Many online rumors proposed that the incident was staged so that Government authorities could garner public support for more expenditure on security, whilst furthering their attempts to place more controls on the public. In particular, the online interactants voiced concerns about the potential use and abuses of body scanners (i.e., machines that show a person naked, in order to uncover weapons). For example, in a blog by JackBlood (the 88th most popular "Underwear Bomber" blog listed by Google), titled "Underwear Bomber provides excuse for Kiddie Porn and Massive DNA Destruction!," the author suggested that the Underwear Bomber was being used as a justification to see children naked and harm individuals' health. He then reposted an article by J. Speer-Williams, titled "Crotch Bomber Kicks Off Massive DNA Destruction." That article explained how body-scanners harm DNA, and ends with "it's beginning to appear obvious that some power has far more interest in damaging our DNAs, than keeping us safe while flying." In other words, several blog postings morally tainted the Government officials implementing new airport screening technologies by spreading rumors that

the new screening procedures are used to destroy human DNA.

Second, our analyses revealed moral and social taints cast on terrorists. For example, in a blog by exschoolnerd (which was the 65th most popular "Underwear Bomber" blog listed by Google) titled, "Dear Abdul Umar Farouk 'underwear bomber' Mutallab," the author penned a heartfelt open-letter to the Underwear Bomber. In the blog, the author expressed that she pities Abdulmutallab, because he was just a "horny bastard" who wanted to martyr himself in order to receive "40 virgins" in heaven. She then wrote that she believes that he is not going to heaven, but hell, specifically, that in hell he will see "Hitler on Mondays to Wednesdays . . . idi amin [sic] Wednesdays to Fridays . . . Saturdays and Sundays the devil will take over." By suggesting that Abdulmutallab will go to hell for his actions, she morally taints him, as his actions are deemed worthy of eternal damnation. By doing so, she is also tainting all terrorists, as she suggests that martyring oneself by killing others is worthy of damnation. In another example, the social taint of terrorists (in particular Abdulmutallab) was evident in a tweet by modeknit, who writes "Just heard on @SMS-Show in ref [sic] to underwear bomber: 'What is this, open mike night at the jihad?'" This tweet, and many other online media articles, suggests that Abdulmutallab was a failed terrorist. By associating Abdulmutallab with an "open mike night" (i.e., a night at a comedy club were amateurs are given a chance to perform), modeknit (who has 2551 followers) tainted the Underwear Bomber by calling him an amateur; someone that is not a professional terrorist. This tweet, combined with numerous online texts which refer to the attack as a "failed attack," paints Abdulmutallab as a failure, and by implication terrorism is ridiculed as failed enterprise.

Third, our analyses uncovered taint associated with the national culture of Nigerians. Abdulmutallab's nationality, Nigerian, was widely reported in the media around the time of his failed bombing attack. As a result, Nigerians, as a whole, were socially tainted in the media and the public, with rumors of their corrupt and degenerate identities by drawing references to the infamous "419" advance fee fraud which have led some to label Nigeria as a "financial terrorist" nation on account of the volume of financial crimes that have emanated from the country (Adomi & Igun, 2008). For example, one retweeted message that exemplified this was "John Stewart on why we didn't take the underwear bomber's banker father seriously. 'I also ignore messages from Nigerian bankers.' LOL." By referencing John Stewart's off-color remark about the morality of Nigerians (i.e., past Nigerian banker scams), this disparagement humor suggested that the U.S. government did not take Abdulmutallab's father's warning seriously because Nigerians are cast as crooks and not to be trusted.

Taken together, this case study contributes to a broadened understanding of the social and political implications of prosumption associated with online rumors and texts that taint agents associated with the contemporary global war on terror. Our analyses illustrate how narratives across different media highlight how Abdulmutallab's actions were appropriated and made meaningful in particular ways by different stakeholders for their political ends, to frame the event in ways that both reinforce and complicate our current understandings of the "underwear bomber" in particular, and terrorism in general.

TRANSMEDIATION AND PROSUMPTION: THE CASE OF MAS SELAMAT AND (RE)PRESENTATIONS OF TERRORIST MAN-HUNTING

The second case presented here examines the evolutionary processes and artifacts of prosumption associated with one of the most important yet understudied aspects of the war on terror—finding

and apprehending "persons of national interest" (Marks, Meer, & Nilson, 2007). Drawing upon a study of the man-hunting crisis involving key terrorist leader Mas Selamat bin Kastari (MSK) in Southeast Asia, this section discusses the forms of radical communication behaviors following the outbreak of official news of his escape from a maximum security detention center in Singapore, in order to illustrate how prosumption functions as middle ground resistance (Scott, 1985) because civilians can rarely engage in effective open rebellion without reprisal but can retaliate in prosaic and constant struggles to their minimum disadvantage. Here, it is observed that middle ground resistance enacted by online participants as tactical communication helped them respond and structure a critique of dominant national security ideology (Cheong & Lundry, 2012).

MSK, a prominent leader of the Southeast Asia terrorist group Jemaah Islamiyah with connections to al-Qaeda, broke out of a maximum security detention center and avoided capture despite being hobbled by a leg broken in a previous escape attempt on February 27th, 2008. The official version of events held that MSK slipped out of a window in a toilet stall after asking the guard for permission to change his clothes before a meeting with his family. Yet the escape of such a high profile detainee quickly inspired a tremendous number of rumors, much of it posted on multiple blogs and circulated on social media sites. The emergent rumor family (Bernardi et al., 2012) included speculation that the escape was a cover up as he was murdered, that he was allowed to escape so that he could be followed, that he was still in captivity and this was a civil defense test, that Arab supporters of JI and al-Qaeda paid bribes for his release, and that he used "black magic" (*ilmu tinggi*) to escape.

The spread of these rumors appeared to be undertaken by prosumers with the intent to challenge the official version of events. This represented an implicit critique of the security lapse itself that allowed the escape and the credibility of the government. For example, several bloggers commented that the escape was an "inside job" in collusion with the security forces. Many called for the registration of the Home Affairs Minister and others sarcastically volunteered to quit their jobs in lieu of the Minister's million dollar paycheck and look for MSK themselves. These rumors function as middle ground resistance tactics to taint and character assassinate leaders in power using exaggerated facts to defame the state public authorities.

Another common form of digital transmediation and online resistance observed in the MSK case was parody. In this, for instance, the official "wanted" poster with MSK's headshot was repeatedly doctored and reconstituted, resulting in graphic memes like the "terrorist spotter" poster. The official mug shots of MSK were manipulated to present farcical images of him as a pirate, as Michael Jackson, as a woman, or as a man with an afro, mustache, and sunglasses. Other presumption practices involved recombinant and derivative content from television and movie posters, which exploited the humor linked to a fugitive escape. For example, the most popular parody was based on the American Fox Television series "Prison Break," where a blogger created an advertisement for the television show with MSK's face superimposed over the lead character's and another blogger changed the title of the online graphic poster to "Toilet Break." Other bloggers created similar remixed artifacts using popular film posters, which featured fugitives as righteous but persecuted protagonists, such as "the Limping Man," "V for Vendetta," "the Transformers," "Catch Me If you Can," "Crouching Tiger, Hidden Dragon," and "Escape from Alcatraz." In addition, numerous YouTube videos were created by citizen prosumers, which portrayed the terrorist in various disguises and escape scenarios, and circulated widely.

Third, the modification of games by online prosumers facilitated online resistance through "infotaining play." For example, one blogger posted a game based on the popular "Where's Waldo?" puzzle where participants have to search for Waldo amidst a montage of other faces. This picture game was retitled "Where's MSK?" and incorporated images of the spoof wanted posters showing various disguises. The classic arcade game Pac Man was also recreated to cast online participants into the character of MSK as he is maneuvered around a maze of rewards and obstacles to avoid capture. In this modified game, online interactants earn points by successfully avoiding authority figures and on the second level, every visit their character makes to the bathroom (a reference to the official version of the escape narrative) gains them more time to react to their potential captors.

Here, our analyses of this case show how online political parodies represent a form of middle ground resistance as they remixed text, audio, video, digital games, and the graphic arts to allow prosumers to vent and express their concerns through humor (Boskin, 1997; Tryon, 2008). This case also illustrates how digital remixes can become memes, which cultural dissemination generates virus-like imitations and reproductions that do not have to be exact in order to reinforce beliefs and spur thought contagion in society (Blackmore, 1999). Here, multiple examples of transmediation illustrate the unfolding of media viral codes (Rushkoff, 1996). This can influence a society's agenda or cultivate resistance to state propaganda—particularly among online participants who tend to connect to ideologically similar websites to reinforce their political beliefs (Sunstein, 2009).

POST MORTEM RUMORS AND GENDERED TRANSMEDIATION: THE CASE OF NOORDIN MOHAMMAD TOP

The third case exemplar focuses on the developments following the demise of Southeast Asia's most wanted terrorist, Noordin Mohammad Top (Noordin) in September 2009. This case illustrates how post mortem rumors associated with Noordin tainted him as a perverse, sexual deviant. Based on his forensic examination, Indonesian police announced that he was gay or bisexual. Although the science on which the claim that his funnel shaped anus is caused by sodomy is questionable, the story was nonetheless picked up and reported uncritically by mainstream Indonesian media, online, in print, and via broadcast channels. The announcement led to the creation and propagation of a family of rumors associated with him and digital transmediation of related narratives, allowing for ridicule of the terrorist and delegitimization of his authority (Bernardi et al., 2012).

Our analyses highlight how rumors supported the dominant status quo. For Noordin's gendered construction appeared to be particularly damning and impactful in a heteronormative cultural environment fraught with the conflation of Islamic religious values and national identity (Lundry & Cheong, 2011). In this sense, post-mortem rumors of Noordin functioned to emasculate the terrorist, a figure who is oftentimes portrayed as a hypermasculine hero or martyr. As an accused sodomite, Noordin's status was diminished as feminized and weak. His external image as a degenerate and immoral person became inconsistent with his authority as a leader of an Islamist terrorist organization, which subsequently discredits him as a *munafiq* (hypocrite).

The transmediation of the Noordin Top story began through repostings of the original news stories, often with commentary. Markedly, according to Yahoo, the term "Noordin M. Top" was the most searched term in Indonesia for 2009 (Althaf, 2009). The day after the announcement the al-Yaasin website posted sections of the news articles about the rumor, but added to its content unattributed comments allegedly by psychologists speculating on Noordin's psychological condition. His heterosexual relations with women were de-

scribed as "torture," and his alleged homosexuality was blamed on his "psychopathic" condition.

A slew of other online commentaries turned to parody and crude jokes, many of which were disseminated in the form of striking graphic memes. Many blog postings feminized official images of Noordin Top (from, for example, his wanted posters), by adding a jilbab or feminine physical traits (e.g., long feminine hair, lipstick, flushed cheeks, etc.). Others recycled images of Noordin styled him after American musical pop icons who are similarly rumored to be homosexual and/or have experienced sexual abuse including Michael Jackson and Axl Rose. Online interactants also appropriated video-sharing websites such as Youtube.com by rebroadcasting mainstream stories and editing shots, for example, inserting Noordin's face transposed into women's bodies, which reflected the rumors of his sodomy.

This case illustrates how the spread of rumors regarding Noordin seem to have achieved a chilling effect on his legacy and appeal. Noordin's image was not ascribed with the appearance of green birds that are commonly believed to hold the souls of Muslim martyrs. Recent Internet scholarship on mediated death and social media highlight how fans mourn for their heroes and idols collectively, which further inflames their passion and resurrects the fame of deceased celebrities (Sanderson & Cheong, 2010). In Noordin's case, online discourse appeared not to have any such vivifying effects. Rather, rumor propagation appeared to gain traction on multiple digital media sites to discredit Noordin as a martyred terrorist leader. This is because cultural taboos and moral anxieties surrounding homosexuality were evoked to portray him as a mentally ill and transgressive sinner. Many Muslims and Indonesians view homosexuals as deviant "others" whose sexual identities and practices are inconsistent with the teachings of Islam (Boellstorff, 2005). Additionally, past assertions by Islamists in Indonesia have stressed the need to protect Muslim women from degenerate and immoral influences of the West. Therefore, in many ways, the accusation worked to silence Noordin's followers, and invited ridicule. Notably, a significant portion of online content appeared to taint his legacy and weaken his potential posthumous influence among contested populations and would-be extremists.

CONCLUSION: OXYGENATING TERRORISM VIA NEW MEDIA CONNECTIONS

If publicity is the oxygen of terrorism, as Margaret Thatcher once declared, then it may be said that digital transmediation provides the combustible fuel for terrorism related narratives to circulate virally in contemporary multi-media convergence culture. In the contemporary information environment, rumor mash-ups and remixes amplify its reach and potential influence. This chapter provides an overview of the relationships between new media and terrorism. Given rising interest in Web 2.0 and 3.0 technologies, the focus here is on the recent phenomenon of remix, remediation, and viral dissemination of textual, audio, and video terrorism related material on multiple networks and convergent digital platforms, to facilitate the transmediated spread of extremist narratives, rumors, and political parody. Three case studies were offered as potent evidence of the uses of taints, jocularity, and disparagement humor to cast extremist protagonists as deviants and figures of derision, as well as to generate collective sense-making and promote solidarity among different factions in contested populations after terrorist events.

As creative new and social web practices facilitate plural and (re)presentations and (re)constructions of epistemic authority (Cheong, Poon, & Huang, 2011; Meikle, 2008), what is significant is the competing co-presence of alternative and hegemonic content on the polymorphous Internet (Christensen, 2008). In this, military propaganda, incumbent media, and critical footage can coexist, in striking dissonance, on the same digital platforms (Ibid). Changing social media conditions are now such that strategic communication related to terrorism is not primarily just a struggle between nation-states managing their media and influence, but also implicate non-state actors' communication and resistance. This can in turn disrupt or subvert state ideology and attendant national security branding practices. The multi-dimensional nature of prosumption behaviors should thus prompt further research in the changing nature of strategic communication as well as popular culture (re)presentations and memetic engagements in everyday discourse to shape perceptions and credibility of key strategic actors in the ideational struggles for hearts and minds.

As this chapter has endeavored to point out, attention needs to be paid to the communicative dimensions in contemporary insurgencies and counterinsurgencies involving the creation and circulation of mediated stories and rumors. A critical socio-cultural understanding of the influence of communication technologies is significant because digital and social media interactions often leave lasting traces and imprints in the public sphere, with profound local and global ramifications.

REFERENCES

Adomi, E. E., & Igun, S. E. (2008). Combating cyber crime in Nigeria. *The Electronic Library*, *26*(5), 716–725.

Althaf. (2009, December 12). *Noordin M top rajai Yahoo selama 2009*. Retrieved July 3, 2013, from http://www.arrahmah.com/index.php/news/read/6243/noordin-m-top-

Altheide, D. L. (2006). The mass media, crime and terrorism. *Journal of International Criminal Justice*, *4*(5), 982–997.

Ashforth, B. E., Kreiner, G. E., Clark, M. A., & Fugate, M. (2007). Normalizing dirty work: Managerial tactics for countering occupational taint. *Academy of Management Review*, *50*(1), 149–174.

Benton, G. (1988). The origins of the political joke. In C. Powell, & G. E. C. Paton (Eds.), *Humor in society: Resistance and control* (pp. 33–55). London: The MacMillan Press.

Bernardi, D., Cheong, P. H., Lundry, C., & Ruston, S. (2012). *Narrative landmines: Rumors, Islamist extremism, and the struggle for strategic influence*. New Brunswick, NJ: Rutgers University Press.

Betz, D. (2008). The virtual dimension of contemporary insurgency and counter-insurgency. *Small Wars & Insurgencies*, *19*(4), 510–540.

Blackmore, S. (1999). *The meme machine*. Oxford, UK: Oxford University Press.

Boellstorff, T. (2005). *The gay archipelago: Sexuality and nation in Indonesia*. Princeton, NJ: Princeton University Press.

Boler, M. (2008). The shape of publics: New media and global capitalism. In M. Boler (Ed.), *Digital media and democracy: Tactics in hard times* (pp. 1–51). Cambridge, MA: MIT Press.

Bolter, J. D., & Grusin, R. (2000). *Remediation: Understanding new media*. Cambridge, MA: MIT Press.

Boskin, J. (1997). *Rebellious laughter: People's humor in American culture*. Syracuse, NY: Syracuse University Press.

Bruns, A. (2008). *Blogs, Wikipedia, Second Life, and beyond: From production to produsage*. New York: Peter Lang.

Burgess, J. (2008). All your chocolate rain belong to us? Viral video, YouTube and the dynamics of participatory culture. In *Video vortex reader: Responses to YouTube* (pp. 101–109). Amsterdam: Institute of Network Cultures.

Castells, M. (2009). *Communication power*. Oxford, UK: Oxford University Press.

Cheong, P. H., & Clow, C. (2010). *Understanding the digital transmediation of terrorism: (Re) presentation of the 'underwear bomber' in new and social media*. Paper presented at Terrorism and New Media: Building a Research Network Conference. Dublin, Ireland.

Cheong, P. H., & Gong, J. (2010). Cyber vigilantism, transmedia collective intelligence, and civic participation. *Chinese Journal of Communication*, *3*(4), 471–487.

Cheong, P. H., & Lundry, C. (2012). Prosumption, transmediation and resistance: Terrorism and man-hunting in Southeast Asia. *The American Behavioral Scientist*, *56*(4), 488–510.

Cheong, P. H., Poon, J. H., & Huang, S. H. (2011). Religious communication and epistemic authority of leaders in wired faith organizations. *The Journal of Communication*, *61*(5), 938–958.

Christensen, C. (2008). Uploading dissonance: YouTube and the US occupation of Iraq. *Media. War & Conflict*, *1*(2), 155–175.

Coaffee, J., & van Ham, P. (2008). Security branding: The role of security in marketing the city, region and state. *Place Branding and Public Diplomacy, 4*(3), 191–195.

de Certeau, M. (1984). *The practice of everyday life*. Berkeley, CA: University of California Press.

Deuze, M. (2007). Convergence culture in the creative industries. *International Journal of Cultural Studies, 10*(2), 243–263.

DiFonzo, N., & Prashant, B. (2007). *Rumor psychology*. Washington, DC: American Psychological Association.

Downing, J. (2001). *Radical media: Rebellious communication and social movements*. Thousand Oaks, CA: Sage Publications.

Ellis, S., & Haar, G. T. (2004). *Worlds of power: Religious thought and political practice in Africa*. New York: Oxford University Press.

Frank, R. (2004). When the going gets tough, the tough go photoshopping: September 11 and the newslore of vengeance and victimization. *New Media &. Society, 6*(5), 633–658.

Goodall, H. L., Cheong, P. H., Fleischer, K., & Corman, S. (2012). Rhetorical charms: The promise and pitfalls of humor and ridicule as strategies to counter extremist narratives. *Perspectives on Terrorism, 6*(1), 70–79.

Hertzberg, B. K., & Lundby, K. (2008). Mediatized lives: Autobiography and assumed authenticity in digital storytelling. In K. Lundby (Ed.), *Digital storytelling, mediatized stories: Self-representations in new media* (pp. 105–122). New York: Peter Lang.

Hughes, E. C. (1962). Good people and dirty work. *Social Problems, 10*(1), 3–11.

Jenkins, H. (2006). *Convergence culture: Where old and new media collide*. New York: New York University Press.

Kibby, M. D. (2005). Email forwardables: Folklore in the age of the internet. *New Media &. Society, 7*(6), 770–790.

Kreiner, G. E., Ashforth, B. E., & Sluss, D. M. (2006). Identity dynamics in occupational dirty work: Integrating social identity and system justification perspectives. *Organization Science, 17*(5), 619–636.

Kydd, A. H., & Walter, B. F. (2006). The strategies of terrorism. *International Security, 31*(1), 49–79.

Lessig, L. (2008). *Remix: Making art and commerce thrive in the hybrid economy*. New York: Penguin Press.

Livingstone, S. (1999). New media, new audiences? *New Media & Society, 1*(1), 59–66. doi:10.1177/1461444899001001010

Lundry, C., & Cheong, P. H. (2011). Rumors and strategic communication: The gendered construction and transmediation of a terrorist life story. In T. Kuhn (Ed.), *Matters of communication political, cultural and technological challenges to communication* (pp. 145–166). New York: Hampton Press.

Marks, S. M., Meer, T. M., & Nilson, M. T. (2007). Manhunting: A process to find persons of national interest. In J. J. F. Forest (Ed.), *Countering terrorism and insurgency in the 21st century* (pp. 208–234). Westport, CT: Praeger Security International.

Meikle, G. (2008). Whacking Bush: Tactical media as play. In M. Boler (Ed.), *Digital media and democracy: Tactics in hard times* (pp. 367–382). Cambridge, MA: MIT Press.

Payne, K. (2009). Winning the battle of ideas: Propaganda, ideology, and terror. *Studies in Conflict and Terrorism, 32*(2), 109–128. doi:10.1080/10576100802627738

Rushkoff, D. (1996). *Media virus: Hidden agendas in popular culture*. New York: Ballantine.

Sanderson, J., & Cheong, P. H. (2010). Tweeting prayers and communicating grief over Michael Jackson online. *Bulletin of Science, Technology & Society*, *30*(5), 328–340.

Scott, J. (1985). *Weapons of the weak: Everyday forms of peasant resistance*. New Haven, CT: Yale University Press.

Sunstein, C. R. (2009). *On rumors: How falsehoods spread, why we believe them, what can be done*. New York: Farrar, Straus and Giroux.

Tryon, C. (2008). Pop politics: Online parody videos, intertextuality, and political participation. *Popular Communication*, *6*(4), 209–213. doi:10.1080/15405700802418537

van Ham, P. (2008). Place branding within a security paradigm. *Place Branding and Public Diplomacy*, *4*(3), 240–251. doi:10.1057/pb.2008.14

Winn, A. K., & Zakem, V. L. (2009). Jihad.com 2.0: The new social media and the changing dynamics of mass persuasion. In J. J. F. Forest (Ed.), *Influence warfare: How terrorists and governments fight to shape perceptions in a war of ideas* (pp. 27–48). New York: Praeger.

KEY TERMS AND DEFINITIONS

Communication Power: The influence and ability of communication.

Digital Transmediation: The remix, remediation, and viral dissemination of textual, audio, and video material on multiple and convergent new and social media platforms.

Globalization: A worldwide process of integration and interaction of various aspects of different cultures through economic and cultural activities facilitated by telecommunications and new media.

Memes: A cultural item in the form of an image, video, or phrase that is spread via the Internet and often altered in a creative or humorous manner.

Prosumers: A hybrid term of producers and consumers.

Rumor: A gossip or hearsay.

Social Media: Online means of communication used by large groups of people to share information and develop social and professional contacts.

Section 7
Terrorism & Media
over a Decade

Chapter 14
From "Cyberterrorism" to "Online Radicalism"

Maura Conway
Dublin City University, Ireland

ABSTRACT

This chapter explores the changes that have taken place in the role and functioning of the Internet in terrorism and counter-terrorism in the past decade. It traces the shift in focus from a preoccupation with the threat of so-called "cyberterrorism" in the period pre- and immediately post-9/11 to the contemporary emphasis on the role of the Internet in processes of violent radicalization. The cyberterrorism threat is explained as over-hyped herein, and the contemporary focus, by researchers and policymakers, on the potential of the Internet as a vehicle for violent radicalization viewed as more appropriate albeit not without its difficulties. This change in emphasis is at least partially predicated, it is argued, on the significant changes that occurred in the nature and functioning of the Internet in the last decade: the advent of Web 2.0, with its emphasis on social networking, user generated content, and digital video is treated as particularly salient in this regard. Description and analysis of both "negative" and "positive" Internet-based Counter Violent Extremism (CVE) and online counterterrorism measures and their evolutions are also supplied.

INTRODUCTION

This chapter explores the changes that have taken place in the role and functioning of the Internet in terrorism and counter-terrorism in the more than a decade since 9/11. Although immediately post-9/11 fears about the threat posed by cyberterrorism rose sharply, in the years since the focus has shifted to terrorists' everyday uses of the Internet for information gathering, information provision, radicalization, recruitment, financing, and a host of other purposes. Particular emphasis is now placed on the dissemination of violent political extremist and terrorism-related content and its impacts, which are felt to include the facilitation of both violent radicalization and attack preparation (Bermingham et al., 2009; Conway & McInerney, 2008; Ganor, von Knop, & Duarte, 2007; Stevens & Neumann, 2009). The changes wrought by the events of 9/11 and their aftermath in this area are therefore considerable, with my 2002 observation that "Terrorist 'use' of the Internet has been largely ignored . . . in favor of the more headline-grabbing 'cyberterrorism'"

DOI: 10.4018/978-1-4666-5776-2.ch014

(Conway, 2002, p. 3) having been largely reversed since albeit the cyberterrorism threat continues to fascinate and divide.

This chapter is composed of three main sections. The first section is concerned with cyberterrorism, and contains three arguments on the basis of which it is believed that cyberterrorism is unlikely in the near future. Section two is therefore concerned with the contemporary violent online Jihadi milieu and the changes that have taken place within it in recent years. The current focus on the Internet as a potential vehicle for some individuals' violent radicalization rather than for cyberterrorism purposes are the correct focus; albeit an area in which there are many controversies, some of which are outlined in this section. The chapter's third section briefly describes and discusses Internet-based Counter Violent Extremism (CVE) and present-day online counterterrorism measures.

ON CYBERTERRORISM

Dorothy Denning's (2006) definitions of cyberterrorism are probably the most well known and respected. Her most recent attempt at definition refers to cyberterrorism as composing

...highly damaging computer-based attacks or threats of attack by non-state actors against information systems when conducted to intimidate or coerce governments or societies in pursuit of goals that are political or social. It is the convergence of terrorism with cyberspace, where cyberspace becomes the means of conducting the terrorist act. Rather than committing acts of violence against persons or physical property, the cyberterrorist commits acts of destruction or disruption against digital property (Denning, 2006, p. 124).

Analyses of cyberterrorism can usefully be divided into two broad categories on the basis of where the producers stand on the definition issue: those who agree broadly with Denning versus those who wish to incorporate not just "use," but a host of other activities into the definition (Macdonald et al., 2013). The literature can also be divided on the basis of where the authors stand on the magnitude of the cyberterrorism threat. Dunn-Cavelty (2007) uses the term "Hypers" to describe those who believe a cyberterrorist attack is not just likely, but imminent,[1] and the term "De-Hypers" to describe those who believe such an attack is unlikely. Most journalists, excepting dedicated technology journalists, are hypers as are sizeable numbers of academics. In a recent survey, carried out by the University of Swansea's Cyberterrorism Project, for example, 58% of researchers surveyed view cyberterrorism as a significant threat whilst, in response to a separate question, 49% evinced the view that cyberterrorism has already taken place (Macdonald et al., 2013). Despite the presence of large numbers of terrorist organizations and their supporters online, it is this author's position that no act of cyberterrorism has ever yet occurred and the threat is over-hyped. I am thus emphatically a de-hyper; below, I lay out the three major reasons why.

Three Arguments against Cyberterrorism[4]

The three most compelling arguments against cyberterrorism are:

1. The argument from Technological Complexity;
2. The argument regarding 9/11 and the Image Factor; and
3. The argument regarding 9/11 and the Accident Issue.

The first argument is treated in the academic literature; the second and third arguments are not perspectives to which either journalists, scholars, or policy makers appear to have devoted a lot of thought or given adequate consideration, but ought to.

In a March 2010 speech, FBI Director Robert Mueller observed that "Terrorists have shown a 'clear interest' in pursuing hacking skills" and "They will either train their own recruits or hire outsiders, with an eye toward combining physical attacks with cyber attacks" (Nakashima, 2010, p. 1). That may very well be true, but the argument from Technological Complexity underlines that "wanting" to engage in some activity is quite different from having the ability to do the same. With regard to "training their own recruits," violent Jihadis' IT knowledge is not superior. In research carried out in 2007, for example, it was found that of a random sampling of 404 members of violent Islamist groups, 196 (48.5%) had a higher education, with information about subject areas available for 178 individuals. Of these 178, some 8 (4.5%) had trained in computing, which means that out of the entire sample, less than 2% of the Jihadis came from a computing background (Gambetta & Hertog, 2007), and not even these few could be assumed to have mastery of the complex systems necessary to carry out a successful cyberterrorist attack. Further, what are often viewed as relatively unsophisticated real-world attacks undertaken by highly educated individuals are routinely unsuccessful. One only has to consider the failed car bomb attacks planned and carried out by medical doctors in central London and at Glasgow airport in June 2007. The FBI Director also refers to hiring outsiders, as have others (Clapper, 2013). Hiring outside hackers would be very operationally risky, forcing the terrorists to operate outside their trusted social networks—leaving them ripe for infiltration. Even if they successfully got in contact with "real" hackers, they would be in no position to gauge their competency accurately; they would simply have to put their trust in them. This would, again, be very risky (Conway, 2012).

So on the basis of technical knowhow alone cyberterrorist attack is not imminent, but this is not the only factor one must take into account.

The second argument against cyberterrorism is related to what might be termed terrorism's "image factor." The events of 9/11 underscore that for a truly spectacular terrorist event moving images are crucial. The attacks on the World Trade Center were a defining piece of performance violence; look back on any media roundup of the decade and mention of 9/11 was not just prominent, but images were always provided. The problem with respect to cyberterrorism is that many of the attack scenarios put forward, from shutting down the electric power grid to contaminating a major water supply, fail on this account: they are unlikely to have easily captured, spectacular (i.e., live, moving) images associated with them, something audiences have been primed for by the 9/11 attacks. The only cyberterrorism scenario that would fall into this category is interfering with air traffic control systems to crash planes, but have we not seen that planes can much more easily be employed in spectacular "real-world" terrorism? Additionally, are not all those infrastructures just mentioned much easier and more spectacular to simply blow-up?

The third argument against cyberterrorism is with regard to accident. Strikingly, it is perhaps the most compelling anti-cyberterrorism argument available, yet it is very rarely mentioned perhaps because of the narrow concern in this realm with technologies rather than terrorists/terrorism. This argument was well illustrated by Howard Schmidt, former White House Cybersecurity Coordinator, when he remarked to the U.S. Senate Committee on the Judiciary in 2004, regarding Nimda and Code Red, that "we to this day don't know the source of that. It could have very easily been a terrorist" (Committee on the Judiciary, 2004, p. 28). This observation betrays a fundamental misunderstanding of the nature and purposes of terrorism, particularly its attention getting and communicative functions. A terrorist attack with the potential to be hidden, portrayed as an accident, or otherwise remain unknown is unlikely to be viewed positively by terrorists. In fact, one of the most important aspects of 9/11 from the perpetrators' viewpoint was surely the fact that while the first plane to crash into the World Trade Center could have been accidental, the appearance of the second plane confirmed the incident as a terrorist attack in real time (as did subsequent events in Washington DC and Pennsylvania). Moreover, the crash of the first plane ensured a large audience for the second plane as it hit the second tower. Alternatively, consider the massive electric failure that took place in the north-eastern United States in August 2003: if it was a terrorist attack—and I am not suggesting that it was—but *if it was*, it would have been a spectacular failure.

Given the high cost—not just in terms of money, but also time, commitment, and effort— and the high possibility of failure on the basis of manpower issues, timing, and complexity of a potential cyberterrorist attack, the costs appear to this author to still very largely outweigh the potential publicity benefits. The publicity aspect is a crucial component of terrorism and so the possibility that an attack may be apprehended or portrayed as an accident, which would be highly likely with regard to cyberterrorism, is detrimental. Add the lack of spectacular moving images and it is my belief that cyberterrorism, regardless of what you may read in newspapers, see on television, or obtain via other media sources (Conway, 2008), is not an immediate threat. To be clear, the point is not that cyberterrorism cannot happen or will not happen, but that it has not happened yet and, I am arguing, is unlikely to occur in the near future. My focus in this chapter therefore now shifts to the increasing spread of violent political extremist content online post-9/11 and the potential relationship between this and "real world" terrorism via processes of so-called "online radicalization."

CHANGING INTERNET, CHANGING EMPHASIS: FROM "CYBERTERRORISM" TO "VIOLENT ONLINE RADICALIZATION"

Immediately post-9/11 it was common to refer to "terrorist use of the Net" and "terrorist Websites" as traditional Websites were the most common online communication vehicles at that time, and "terrorist Websites" were those established and run by known terrorist groups. Hezbollah's suite of Websites was established by and continues to be run by the Lebanese Shi'a organization, the Tamil Tigers' Websites were initiated and run by the Tamil organization, the Revolutionary Armed Forces of Colombia site was established and continues to be maintained by that organization, etc. (Conway, 2005a, 2005b). Leaving aside the long-standing and contentious issue of the definition of "terrorism," there are two major reasons why the concept of "violent online political extremism" is preferred in what follows.

First, "cyberterrorism," as discussed above, is the only type of terrorism that is directly linked with cyberspace; all other terrorism is only indirectly linked to the Internet, generally via assertions that perpetrators are being violently radicalized either wholly or partially via their online content consumption and interactions. Second, as discussed below, many contemporary producers and/or distributors of violent online political content have no direct contacts with any individual terrorists or terrorist groups. They are, instead, users who generate content—thence "user-generated content," a hallmark of Web 2.0—in support of particular violent extremist ideologies (e.g., violent Jihadism) and may thus, in the first instance at least, be characterized as "fans." The argument, of which more below, is that some of these fans become violently radicalized as a result of their online activity and that a minority of these take their activities offline and engage in terrorism in the "real world." This matter is complicated however by increasing numbers of online "fans," whom have engaged in no physical acts of terrorism, being prosecuted for terrorism, which is taken-up in section three.

The vast majority of research into violent online political extremism produced to date has focused on the new media practices of violent Jihadis and their supporters (Brachman & Levine, 2011; Conway, 2007; Ducol, 2012; Kimmage, 2008Kimmage & Ridolfo, 2007; Meleagrou-Hitchens, 2011; Seib & Janbek, 2011; Zelin 2013). This is unsurprising given that Jihadis have significantly grown their online presence since 9/11. Increasing numbers of individuals and groups that advocate violent Jihad are known to be using the Internet extensively, both as a tool for spreading their message and, in some instances, attack planning and preparation. Hussain Osman, one of the July 21, 2005 London bombers, claimed to have been influenced by watching Internet video footage of the Iraq conflict and reading about Jihad online, while Arid Uka, the 21-year-old Kosovar who shot dead two U.S. airmen at Frankfurt Airport in March 2010, told a German court he had been radicalized by Jihadist propaganda videos he watched online.[5] Other attacks in which the Internet has played a prominent role are the 2009 Fort Hood shootings, the 2008 Mumbai attacks, and the 2004 Madrid bombings, and in various terrorist plots, including amongst the Netherlands' Hofstad Group, Younis Tsouli (i.e., "Irhabi007") and the Balkan plotters, and Colleen La Rose (i.e., "Jihad Jane") and others plotting to murder the Swedish cartoonist, Lars Vilks.

Jihadis are not alone amongst violent political extremists in recognizing the power of the Net however. According to the European Police Office (2013), in their *EU Terrorism Situation and Trend Report 2013*, the vast majority of EU-wide terrorist attacks in 2012 were carried out by traditional separatist terrorists and not violent Jihadis as some

might expect. Many of these "old" terrorist groups retain a significant online presence, but very little academic research has been conducted on this to date. While the heyday of the Provisional IRA pre-dated the Internet, for example, dissident Irish Republicans (e.g., Real IRA, Continuity IRA, etc.) have an online presence (Bowman-Grieve & Conway, 2012). Other "old" political groups that are in a renewal phase are the many variants of the European extreme right, which have a long history of Internet use, dating to the earliest days of the public Internet (Anti-Defamation League, 1985), and an even longer history of violence and threats of violence against non-whites, religious minorities, ethnic minorities, sexual minorities, and others. The politics of Norway's Anders Behring Breivik, the right-wing extremist responsible for the bomb and gun attacks in Oslo in July 2011 that resulted in 77 fatalities, appears to have been at least partially influenced by his online content consumption and interactions (Archer, 2011).[6]

In short, the amount of online content promoting violent politics is increasing all the time and is not limited to purveyors of any one political ideology. An important point to note here, however, is that not all—or even many—of those who consume violent political extremist material, or indeed produce and/or distribute the same, take their activities offline and engage in "real world" terrorism. The research that addresses links between the Internet and terrorism is largely focused on violent Jihadis' online strategies and their potential offline effects, however, thence the focus upon these in the following sections.

Sketching the Contours of the Contemporary Violent Online Jihadi Milieu

Osama bin Laden's cadres had used the Internet for communication and propaganda purposes prior to 9/11, but their use of the Internet increased exponentially thereafter (Conway, 2002; Seib & Janbek, 2011). This had two interrelated causes:

1) the loss of al-Qaeda's Afghan base and the consequent dispersal of its leaders and fighters; and 2) the rapid development of the Internet itself, the global spread of Internet cafes, and the proliferation of Internet-capable computers and other gadgets, such as mobile telephones (Scheuer, 2004). Until the emergence of Web 2.0, with its emphasis on the integration of user-generated content, social networking, and digital video, bin Laden and "al-Qaeda Central" maintained some level of control over the al-Qaeda's online narrative. It was, however, Abu Musab al-Zarqawi and al-Qaeda in Iraq (AQI), who instigated a separate online strategy in the interregnum between the sunset of the early Web and the full ascent of Web 2.0, that ushered in the beginning of violent Jihad's transformation from a movement with a significant Internet component to a genuine violent online radical community or "milieu." This was cemented over time as the "Jihadisphere" came to encompass a wide cross-section of producers and consumers, from al-Qaeda Central to the media arms of various al-Qaeda franchise organizations, to the globally dispersed array of fans or "jihobbyists" (Brachmann, 2009, p. 19) with no formal links to any violent Jihadist organization, all contributing to the everyday making and remaking of the violent Jihadi narrative via the Internet.

In May 2004, al-Zarqawi pushed the Internet's force-multiplying effect to the maximum by having himself filmed personally cutting off the head of American hostage Nicholas Berg, and posting the footage online.[7] The purpose of this beheading was precisely to videotape it. The images gripped the imaginations of AQI's allies and enemies alike. While making himself a hero to Jihadis worldwide, al-Zarqawi risked nothing in the endeavor (Bergen et al., 2005). It was only after these online exploits that al-Zarqawi was actually endorsed by Osama bin Laden as "Emir" (i.e., leader) of al-Qaeda in Iraq. Government officials' and policymakers' fears of the potential for the Internet to act as a vehicle for violent radicalization spring from the alleged effects of extreme political violence like al-Zarqawi's, combined with the advantages of the cyber world (e.g., potentially vast audience, geographical reach, and multimedia capabilities). However, al-Zarqawi was a terrorist who migrated some of his activity to the Internet, rather than himself emerging out of an online radical milieu. It was the legions of fans inspired by al-Zarqawi's online activity that took up the banner of violent Jihad online, thus generating more of the same, in a spiral effect that eventually coalesced into the contemporary violent Jihadi online milieu.

The exploitation of the Internet by al-Zarqawi was not the only catalyst for heightened concern regarding violent online radicalization. The emergence of the violent Jihadi online milieu was also influenced by changes in the Internet landscape, in terms of both access and technologies that were gaining pace at around the same time al-Zarqawi's publicity strategy came to the world's attention. First, large numbers of people gained cheap and easy access to the Internet. Today, always-on mobile Internet access is speedily becoming the norm, especially among youth who increasingly go online using mobile telephones and other mobile devices. Second, online social networking, an integral part of Web 2.0, took off in the mid-2000s. Consider that Facebook was established in 2004 and is now thought to have a billion regular users,[8] while YouTube, which only came into existence in 2005, currently has 72 hours of video uploaded to it every minute.[9] It was these changes that caused Time magazine to name "You" as their 2006 "Person of the Year" (Grossman, 2006), but also introduced the idea that "You" might through online activity become violently radicalized and potentially be drawn into "real world" terrorism.

No figure immediately emerged from within the ranks of al-Qaeda-affiliated groups to fill the cyber-gap left by al-Zarqawi's death in June 2006. However, such a figure was no longer integral to the buoyancy of violent online Jihadism as official and semi-official Websites and forums are no longer the only important Jihadi cyber spaces

(Seib & Janbek, 2011). Increasing amounts of violent Jihadi online content is available in English, French (Ducol, 2012), German, Spanish, and Dutch, signifying both the rise of violent Jihadism in the West and growing efforts by violent Jihadist voices to reach Western (Muslim) populations online (e.g., European Police Office, 2011). Changes in the nature of the Internet have encouraged increasing numbers of supporters of violent Jihad to post and re-post articles and analyses, exchange information, voice opinions, and debate ideas on blogs, Websites, and social networking pages that they themselves have established. The proliferation of fan sites act as free publicity for the violent Jihadi cause. Today, new Websites appear—and also disappear—frequently, popular forums have stringent admission policies, and most sites display technical savvy on the part of their producers, including all the latest Internet tools and gadgetry. The financing and management of these sites did not and does not come from al-Qaeda; nonetheless, they act as an invaluable force-multiplier for the group's cyber-based incitement strategy.

Recognizing this benefit, al-Qaeda assured its "Internet brothers" early on that "the media war with the oppressive crusader enemy takes a common effort and can use a lot of ideas. We are prepared to help out with these ideas" (Scheuer, 2004, p. 81). From this came al-Qaeda's official media production arm, largely audio and video, known as as-Sahab or "the Clouds" in 2001. This was augmented by the establishment (and subsequent demise) of a host of similar media production outlets in the past decade including, for example, the Global Islamic Media Front (GIMF) and al-Qaeda in the Arabian Peninsula's al-Malahem Media Foundation. Violent Jihadi online content takes four major forms: basic text, including forum postings, books, poetry, and written statements; magazines that are a combination of text and images (e.g., al-Malahem's much-publicized *Inspire* magazine); audio, such as statements by leaders, sermons by violent Jihadi preachers, and *nashid*

(chants); and video. Genres of video include political statements" by al-Qaeda leaders and Western "spokesmen"; attack footage; "pre-martyrdom" videos, such as that made of 7/7 bomber Mohammed Siddique Khan; instructional videos, of both theological and military-operational sorts; memorial videos commemorating persons and/or events; music videos; and beheadings. With the advent of easy digital video composition and fast download, huge amounts of violent Jihad-supporting video began to be produced, distributed, and consumed.

This violent Jihadi content increasingly migrates to global platforms such as Archive.org, Dailymotion, Facebook, Flickr, Instagram, and YouTube, which has the effect of making the content much easier to locate for anyone, regardless of Arabic or other local language skills or level of Internet literacy. Consider too that these global portals are known and attractive to young people in particular, and that multi-media content, especially moving images, is thought to be more convincing than text in terms of its ability to influence. Couple this with the Internet's crowd-sourcing properties, and the violent Jihadi online milieu is born. Masses of violent Jihadi texts that were originally produced in Arabic have now been translated into a multitude of other languages. Large amounts of violent Jihadi video have subtitles, again in multiple languages, added by fans. All of this modified material is then (re-) uploaded for consumption online, or easy copying and dissemination via links embedded in emails and Tweets, instant messages, SMS/text messages (to name a few), but also through VHS tapes, CDs, DVDs, and mobile phones. The importance of the latter is reflected in the increasing availability of Jihadi video specifically formatted for sharing via mobile telephones.

The Role of the Internet in Processes of Violent Radicalization?

Clearly, the effort put into the production and circulation of "images signifying Muslim suffering, Western hypocrisy, Jihadist heroism and so on was intended to create effects; to legitimise violence and recruit and mobilise supporters" (Awan, Hoskins, & O'Loughlin, 2011, p. 128), facilitated by what some analysts term the "new media ecology." However, how effective has this strategy been? Arguments both in favor and against a prominent role for the Internet in processes of violent radicalization have been forwarded by scholars, the outlines of which are sketched in the following paragraphs.

Arguments against a prominent role for the Internet in violent radicalization processes take two main forms. One position holds that claiming violent extremist online content radicalizes individuals into committing violence makes no sense given that other consumers of the same content do not commit violent attacks. Alternatively, it may be argued that while such content can buttress an already sympathetic individual's resolve to engage in violence, it is not generally the originating cause of such a commitment (Githens-Mazer, 2010). The second position suggests that most, though not all, contemporary violent online extremists are dilettantes, in the sense that they restrict themselves to using the Internet to support and encourage violent extremism, but pose no "real world" threat. Put another way, there is the possibility that the "venting" or "purging" that political extremists engage in online satisfies their desire to act. Their Internet activity, rather than becoming an avenue for violent radicalization and leading to potential offline action such as, in the most extreme instances, large-scale terrorist attacks, instead becomes for many a mechanism to dissipate the desire for violent action (Awan, Hoskins, & O'Loughlin, 2011; Ramsay 2009).

The alternative view, of course, is that the violent extremist cyber-world is a progressively more important staging post for "real world" violence. Security personnel and policymakers appear increasingly swayed by this argument, as it relates to violent Jihadists in particular. Europol

has, for example, described the Internet as "a crucial facilitating factor for both terrorists and extremists" (European Police Office, 2011, p. 11). The British government also underscored that:

Al Qa'ida and some Al Qa'ida affiliates have increasingly encouraged acts of terrorism by individuals or small groups independent of the Al Qa'ida chain of command and without reference to, or guidance and instruction from, the leadership. The Internet has enabled this type of terrorism by providing material which encourages and guides radicalisation and instructions on how to plan and conduct operations (UK Home Office, 2011, p. 25).

Manfred Munck, head of the Hamburg branch of Germany's domestic intelligence service, has made similar comments: "The tradition of terrorism is more or less a tradition of groups. But now we see that the group is not always necessary and that the Internet functions as a kind of virtual group" (Maclean, 2011).

Such concerns have been stoked by a rash of both successful and thwarted terrorist attacks in which the Internet played a role, including the failed July 21, 2005 London bomb attacks, the shooting deaths of two U.S. airmen at Frankfurt Airport in March 2010, the failed bombing in New York's Times Square in May 2010, and the so-called "Irhabi007" and "JihadJane" cases. These cases and others have involved Internet users who run the gamut, from prominent figures in the "Jihadisphere" who spent large portions of their lives networking, and producing and/or consuming Jihadi online content, to youths who entered the violent Jihadi online milieu, consumed its products—largely or entirely in isolation from other denizens of the milieu—and acted on the basis of what they absorbed. An example of the former type was Abu Dujana al-Khurasani, a well-known administrator of the al-Hesbah Jihadi forum, who launched a suicide attack at U.S. Forward Operating Base Chapman in Afghanistan in December 2009, killing seven CIA operatives and a member of Jordan's General Intelligence Directorate.[10] He was described by his wife as "constantly reading and writing. He was crazy about online forums" (Awan, Hoskins, & O'Loughlin, 2011, p. 63). British Muslim student Roshonara Choudhry is an example of the other type. She was jailed for life in November 2010 for attempting to murder a British M. P. Ms. Choudhry claimed she was radicalized over the course of just a few weeks after navigating from YouTube to a stream of videos featuring extremist preacher Anwar al-Awlaki (Dodd, 2010).

For many, including policymakers and security practitioners, these cases and others like them illustrate the violent radicalizing properties of radical online milieus. For others however, they raise more questions than answers. Up until recently, al-Awlaki's sermons were widely available on mainstream Islamic Websites. At the time that it came to the attention of U.S. authorities in 2008, for example, his popular lecture "Constants on the Path of Jihad" was available on Ummah.com, a mainstream site that, according to U.S. authorities, was receiving approximately 48,300 visits per month from the United States alone (Meleagrou-Hitchens, 2011). Some of these visitors must surely have viewed "Constants," but presumably never acted on al-Awlaki's advice to carry out attacks within the United States and abroad. Are direct contacts with violent extremists therefore more important than simply consuming violent extremist content? Can this factor explain the attacks carried out by Hasan and Shahzad? If so, what explains Roshonara Choudhry and the influence of al-Awlaki's video sermons on her decision to assassinate a member of the British parliament?

While such questions cannot yet be adequately answered, outright denials of a role for the Internet in the process of violent radicalization, such as the following quote from Jason Burke, seem to be premature:

Twitter will never be a substitute for grassroots activism. In much of the Islamic world, social media is only for super-connected local elites or supporters in far-off countries. Neither are much use on the ground, where it counts. Social media can bring in donations or some foreign recruits. It can aid communication with some logistics and facilitate propaganda operations, but it is not much use in a firefight with Saudi, Iraqi or Pakistani security forces. Twitter won't help al-Shabaab retake Mogadishu or the Taliban reach Kabul in any meaningful way (Burke, 2011, p. 1).

Burke (2011) thus seems to dismiss out of hand all those preparatory steps—donations, foreign recruits, logistics, propaganda—and the potential role of violent online radical milieus in facilitating these that together culminate in "firefights." Burke also draws attention to issues of access; in large parts of the Muslim world, he says, online social networking is restricted to elites and is thus not "much use on the ground, where it counts" (Ibid, p. 1). It is certainly true that home-based Internet penetration rates are low in, for example, the Middle East as compared to the West, but Internet cafes are widely popular and the region is seeing soaring rates of mobile phone usage.

While widespread fast, always-on Internet is doubtless preferable in terms of instituting a durable Web-based political violence strategy, it is not crucial. The Internet, and Web 2.0 in particular, facilitates small contributions—whether of money, content, or other types of virtual labor—by large numbers of people, along with large contributions by small numbers of people, that together can constitute a significant whole. Nor is it necessary for all those engaged in any activist project, violent or non-violent, to be themselves Internet users. Internet-based content can circulate not only online, but can also be disseminated via photocopying, audio tapes, VHS and CDs, text-messaging, and plain old word-of-mouth, depending on its nature. It is also worth remembering that the violent Jihadi online milieu is a component of the wider Jihadi milieu, with ideas and content from each penetrating the other in multiple ways.

INTERNET-BASED COUNTER VIOLENT EXTREMISM (CVE) AND ONLINE COUNTERTERRORISM

The open nature of the online radicalization question has not stopped governments around the world from introducing legislation to tackle the assumed problem. The successful use of the Internet for violent radicalization and other violent extremist purposes is based on the assumption that both users and audiences have access to the messages communicated via the Internet. States therefore believe they can constrain the effectiveness of these cyber-based strategies by limiting user and audience access to Internet technologies, either by actively censoring Internet content or by controlling the Internet infrastructure, or by some combination of the two. There has been a concerted effort to crack down on violent online political extremism globally since 9/11; some commentators view this as a legitimate response to the threat of terrorism, while others see things quite differently. The latter have concerns about the emergence of a "surveillance society" where privacy safeguards are routinely breached in the name of national security and individuals' rights to freedom of speech increasingly narrowed (Fuchs et al., 2011; Lyon, 2003). Described and analyzed below are a selection of both "negative" and "positive" Internet-based Counter Violent Extremism (CVE) and online counterterrorism measures.

Negative Measures

"Negative" Internet-based Counter Violent Extremism (CVE) and online counterterrorism measures are those aimed at the removal of violent political extremist content from the Internet, including legislation outlawing certain types

of content and voluntary codes that advocate similarly. Content control measures instituted by the U.S. and EU since 9/11 are discussed in the following paragraphs.

The First Amendment to the U.S. Constitution guarantees broad freedom of expression, even the right to publish hate-oriented and similar materials. Achieving a workable balance between content control and freedom of expression has therefore proven a considerable challenge and much of the U.S. debate about terrorist use of the Internet and subsequently violent online political extremism more generally has been concerned with finding this balance. First Amendment protections were certainly one of the reasons why many terrorist groups' sites were at one time or another hosted in the United States (Conway, 2007). A commitment to First Amendment rights is also the reason put forward by major U.S. ISPs, such as Facebook, Twitter, and YouTube, for their decisions to decline to censor some content that European states and others find objectionable. In January 2013, Twitter cancelled the account of Somalia's violent Jihadists' al-Shabab following the group tweeting photographs of the body of a French commando whom they had killed followed by explicit threats to execute Kenyan hostages they held. Twitter has described itself as "the free speech wing of the free speech party" (Halliday, 2012) and has in the past refused requests from government officials, activist organizations, and concerned individuals to cancel the accounts of, amongst others, Lebanese Hezbollah, the Afghan Taliban, and Syria's violent Jihadi faction Jabhat al-Nusra. Their decision regarding al-Shabab's account highlighted the lack of transparency surrounding how Twitter takes decisions on which accounts of a violent extremist nature to cancel and which may remain accessible, as Twitter have no detailed and publicly available guidelines on the matter.[11] It also serves to underline the potential difficulties associated with private companies regulating political speech. In the event, al-Shabab reestablished their Twitter account, under a slightly different name, almost immediately and Twitter were once again embroiled in controversy when the group live Tweeted their attack on the Westgate shopping mall in Nairobi, Kenya in September 2013 (Berger, 2013).

U.S. lawmakers have been amongst those exhorting Twitter to cancel accounts they view as "terrorist" (Farmer, 2011; Gettleman, 2011) whilst similar pressures were previously brought to bear upon YouTube (Date, 2008). This dismays many First Amendment advocates concerned about the continuing dilution of many Americans' commitment to free speech principles. Their concerns appear to be borne out by a jury decision in a Boston trial in December 2011, which resulted in the April 2012 sentencing of Tarek Mehanna, a U.S.-born Muslim, to more than 17 years in prison on the basis of his providing "material support" for terrorism via the Internet. The troubling aspect of Mehanna's conviction, from a freedom of speech perspective, is that it was based largely on things he *said* (and wrote and translated) rather than things he *did*. In 2004, Mehanna traveled with a friend to Yemen in search, the prosecution alleged, of a Jihadi training camp; their search was not successful and Mehanna returned to the United States. Mehanna's conviction was not on the basis of his failed attempt at searching out violent Jihadis however, but his online advocacy of violent Jihadism from his Massachusetts home, including translating into English, and then posting online, videos and other documents originally produced by, amongst others, al-Qaeda in the Arabian Peninsula that encouraged violence against American military forces. It is worth noting that the activities described are those engaged in by large numbers of online "fans" of violent Jihadism as described earlier in this chapter.

In the 2010 Supreme Court decision *Holder v. Humanitarian Law Project*, Chief Justice John G. Roberts Jr. declared that for speech to qualify as material support for terrorism, it had to be "expert advice or assistance" delivered "in coordination with or under the control of" a designated foreign terrorist organization (Holder v. Humanitarian Law Project, 2010, pp. 18-20); "independent advocacy" of a terror group's ideology, aims or methods is not a crime, he said (Ibid, p. 18). Justice Roberts underlined that "under the material-support statute, plaintiffs may *say* anything they wish on any topic" (Ibid, p. 20, *emphasis added*) and pointed out that "Congress has not sought to suppress *ideas or opinions* in the form of 'pure political speech'" (Ibid, p. 21, *emphasis added*). There was no question in the Mehanna case that the defendant coordinated with al-Qaeda or any other terrorist organization; the basis of the prosecution was his, admittedly virulently anti-American, political opinions. What the Mehanna conviction suggests is that it is now possible for individuals to be convicted of terrorism offences in the United States on the basis of online speech acts alone and illustrates how engagement in violent online political extremism can, in fact, be prosecuted as terrorism. At the time of Mehnna's conviction, this was flagged as a significant departure from previous jurisprudence in this area and a threat to freedom of speech by activists (e.g., American Civil Liberties Unions, Brennan Center for Justice), journalists (Greenwald, 2012), and others (March, 2012). Mehanna's case is under appeal at time of writing.

The above decision would have been—and indeed similar decisions have been—unremarkable in most European countries where limits on speech are wide-ranging. In April 2008, for example, all 27 member states of the European Union took a unanimous decision on the criminal definition of incitement of terrorism via the Internet (EUR-Lex, 2007, November 6). The decision was an amendment to the Council Framework Decision on Combating Terrorism (2002)[12] and makes "public provocation to commit a terrorist offence . . . punishable behaviour, also when committed through the Internet."[13] In terms of other initiatives undertaken by the EU in the context of content control, recently the EU Commission funded a project titled CleanIT,[14] led by the Dutch

Ministry of Justice's National Counterterrorism Coordinator, to initiate "a structured public-private dialogue between government representatives, academics, Internet industry, Internet users and non-governmental organizations in the European Union" on "Reducing terrorist use of the Internet" (CleanIT, 2013)[15]. CleanIT's final product was a report that lays down a set of nine "conditions for any action taken to reduce the terrorist use of the Internet" and a further 12 "best practices that could reduce terrorist use of the Internet in the EU" (CleanIT, 2013, p. 7). Overall, the final document appears to be positioned as a voluntary code of practice for ISPs and others having control over online content, including potentially violent extremist or terrorist content. CleanIT has faced heavy criticism by participants (e.g., EuroISPA)[16], Members of the European Parliament (MEPs)[17], activists (e.g., Anonymous[18], European Digital Rights, Statewatch) and in media (Farivar, 2012. 2013), both during the dialogue process and on publication of the final report. Criticisms voiced included the subjective nature of what constitutes terrorist online content and concerns about law enforcement activity being transferred to private enterprises (i.e. ISPs).

Finally, in terms of "negative" measures, a much more sweeping content control approach is to simply knock whole violent extremist forums offline using cyber attack methods. Today there are between two and five so-called "top tier" Jihadi forums operating (Zelin, 2013, p. 2). Forums are considered "top tier" that receive new and authentic content for distribution from al-Qaeda's as-Sahab media production outlet and other important producers. These forums are thus the subject of fairly routine attacks that can result in their being offline for days, weeks, or even months. On dates between late March and early April 2012, for example, a majority of the "top tier" Jihadi forums were unavailable for periods ranging from 3 to 16 days (Ibid, p. 9). It is not known what or who was responsible for these outages, but many assume they were the work of one or more states'

intelligence agencies. Such wholesale take-down strategies have been criticised by some; however, they argue that violent extremist online forums and other violent extremist cyberspaces can serve as a provider of open source intelligence for states' intelligence agencies. In fact, this is often forwarded as a reason—oftentimes the major reason—for non-interference on the part of state agencies in the workings of, in particular, violent Jihadi online forums (Lasker, 2005; McCants, 2011; Zelin, 2013). The spread of violent Jihadi content across multiple platforms and in multiple formats can thus be viewed either positively or negatively as it means that it is increasingly difficult to counter, especially because portals such as YouTube and Twitter generally cannot be shut down in the same targeted and sweeping way as dedicated violent extremist forums.

Positive Measures

"Positive" Internet-based Counter Violent Extremism (CVE) and online counterterrorism measures are those that employ online outreach rather than content controls to stem violent radicalization and potentially ultimately terrorism. Most contemporary such campaigns focus upon employment of the Internet, and social media in particular, for spreading positive messages for CVE purposes. These messages tend to target young people believed to be vulnerable to violent online political extremist rhetoric and to be undertaken by non-governmental organizations and concerned individuals, including young people themselves; although some such campaigns have also been undertaken by state agencies.

In 2010, Philip Seib described a visit to the headquarters of the U.S. military's Central Command (CENTCOM)—which oversees U.S. military activity in the Middle East and Central Asia—in Florida, where he observed young civilian employees engaging with users on violent extremist and other online forums:

This Digital Engagement Team's members, who are fluent in Arabic, Farsi, and Urdu, comb through online postings in their respective languages looking for incendiary or inaccurate commentary about U.S. military operations or related activity. When these messages are found, the team prepares "engagements" that challenge the writer's logic or facts. A recent example: a Farsi-speaking member of the team found a commentary defending the suicide bombing in Baghdad that killed more than 40 Iraqi Army recruits. This engagement specialist responded by challenging the premise that such murderous attacks, which kill mostly Muslims, can be justified.

Crucially, members of the CENTCOM teams identify themselves as working for U.S. Central Command in their interactions and this sometimes leads to their being denied further access to forums, according to Seib (2010). CENTCOM has recently been subject to criticism however as a contract has been awarded by it to a California company to develop an automated intervention process through the use of so-called "sock puppets," the name given to fake online personae, multiples of which could be controlled by a single individual. Such "astroturfing" by the U.S. government is likely not just to reverberate negatively globally, but is also likely to run afoul of U.S. laws prohibiting the U.S. government from propagandizing American citizens, despite CENTCOM insisting that no automated English-language interventions will take place (Fielding & Cobain, 2013).

An altogether different approach to "positive" Internet-based CVE has been adopted by the European Union. In 2012, it established a Radicalisation Awareness Network (RAN) (2013) under Directorate General Home Affairs to hinder people from participating in terrorist activities of violent extremist nature or to persuade them to separate themselves from such ideas and methods in the first place. The RAN is composed of eight working groups—composed of CVE researchers, activists, and practitioners (to name a few)—one of which,

RAN@,[19] is tasked with "develop[ing] frontline partnerships around the collation, creation, and dissemination of counter-[violent extremist] and alternative-narratives through the Internet and social media"[20]. Other RAN working groups have also discussed using the Internet to reach out to publics; RAN Voices of Victims of Terrorism (RAN VVT) has, for example, expressed a desire to have the voices of terrorism victims amplified via the Internet and social media for the purposes of CVE (RAN VVT, 2012).

In the same way as ordinary Internet users have contributed to the formation of the online Jihadi milieu, so too have ordinary users from around the globe spoken out against violent Jihadism online. Many of these users have sought to point to what many view as the overly partial or even incorrect interpretation of Jihad forwarded by violent Jihadis and to highlight alternatives. These alternative interpretations have taken many different forms, ranging from online video and other online responses denouncing violent extremism by scholars[21] and imams to wide-ranging multimedia campaigns such as "My Jihad"[22], from ordinary individuals uploading videos to YouTube to more general macro-level positive messaging about Islam targeted at children and youth such as Naif al-Mutawa's comic and animated series, "The 99"[23].

CONCLUDING REMARKS

Terrorism is generally conceived of as physical acts of violence intended to produce fear, and conjures up images of exploding bombs and mutilated bodies. The cyberterrorist threat as portrayed in the mass-media builds upon this aspect of terrorism by seeking to convince the public that cyberterrorism will ultimately result in mass casualties; I have sought to challenge that narrative in this chapter by putting forward three arguments for why cyberterrorism is unlikely in the near future. My arguments from technological complexity, regarding 9/11 and the importance of the image factor, and regarding 9/11 and the accident issue are basically a consideration of the costs and benefits of engaging in cyberterrorism from a terrorism/terrorist's perspective and not from the perspective of unlimited technological capacity as is common.

Immediately post-9/11 the question on many people's lips was "Is cyberterrorism next?" These fears dissipated quite significantly in the decade after as the focus shifted to the actual Internet presences of violent political extremists and terrorists. I focused in this chapter on describing and analyzing the evolution of the violent Jihadi online milieu and the way in which it's development was influenced by the emergence of Web 2.0, particularly the latter's emphasis on social networking, user generated content, and digital video production and distribution. The increased involvement of "fans" of violent Jihadism in spreading its message via global platforms has increased policymakers' and others' concerns as to the effects of this content on its consumers, particularly the likelihood of some of these individuals being drawn into "real world" terrorism, either wholly or partially, on the basis of their exposure to violent online political extremist content and online interactions based on this.

Researchers are divided on the importance of the Internet's role in processes of violent radicalization as briefly outlined herein. There are equal levels of uncertainty surrounding the usefulness of the Internet, and social media in particular, for CVE purposes. This has not stopped governments, ISPs, activist groups, and concerned individuals from getting involved in online CVE and/or Internet-based counterterrorism activity. This activity can be broadly categorized into two sorts: "negative" measures that are generally reliant on removing content identified as violently political

extremist or terrorism-related from the Internet and "positive" measures that focus on using the Internet as a vector for spreading counter violent extremist narratives.

Where to from here?: research into violent online Jihadism mushroomed after 9/11, but from almost nothing prior to that time, and with the effect of pushing research into other areas of violent online political extremism off the agenda. This whole area of research is thus still in its infancy and is therefore largely fragmentary, small scale, and lacking in empirical rigor, with many issues yet to be explored at all. The fast pace of online change is a factor here too. The basic assumption, shared both by actors that espouse violent extremism and policymakers, is that the Internet, and especially Web 2.0, are both making it easier for young people to find and consume violent political content and thus potentially to themselves become ensnared in violent politics, online and in "the real world," but may also be used in order to "fight back" against violent extremism. The problem is that there is a dearth of empirical research exploring the role of the Internet in processes of violent radicalization or CVE. There is an *assumption* that the Internet plays a part in some individuals' radicalization on the basis of self-reporting, anecdotal evidence, etc., but no large-scale, empirically-grounded, social scientific studies showing this to actually be the case or measuring the extent of the Internet's role in such processes. This omission is important even if one believes that there is sufficient anecdotal evidence available to us at this stage to "prove" the Internet's role in contemporary violent radicalization processes. Why? Because successful policy responses can only be crafted on the basis of sound long-term comparative interdisciplinary research and analysis, employing both qualitative and quantitative methods, that identify the factors involved in violent online radicalization.

REFERENCES

Anti-Defamation League. (1985). *Computerized networks of hate*. New York: ADL.

Archer, T. (2011, July 25). Breivik's swamp: Was the Oslo killer radicalized by what he read online? *Foreign Policy*. Retrieved July 3, 2013, from http://www.foreignpolicy.com/articles/2011/07/25/breivik_s_swamp

Awan, A., Hoskins, A., & O'Loughlin, B. (2011). *Radicalisation and media: Connectivity and terrorism in the new media ecology*. London: Routledge.

Bergen, P., Schuster, H., Nasr, O., & Eedle, P. (2005). Al Qaeda's media strategy. In K. J. Greenberg (Ed.), *Al Qaeda now: Understanding today's terrorists* (pp. 112–134). Cambridge, UK: Cambridge University Press. doi:10.1017/CBO9780511510489.009

Berger, J. M. (2013, October 1). Twitter's week of reckoning. *Foreign Policy*. Retrieved October 30, 2013, from http://www.foreignpolicy.com/articles/2013/10/01/twitters_week_of_reckoning

Bermingham, A., McInerney, L., O'Hare, N., & Conway, M. (2009). Combining social network analysis and sentiment analysis to explore the potential for online radicalisation. In *Proceedings of ASONAM 2009: Advances in Social Networks Analysis and Mining* (pp. 231-236). IEEE Computer Society.

Bowman-Grieve, L., & Conway, M. (2012). Exploring the form and function of dissident Irish republican online discourses. *Media. War & Conflict*, *5*(1), 71–85. doi:10.1177/1750635211434371

Brachman, J. M. (2009). *Global Jihadism: Theory and practice*. London: Routledge.

Brachman, J. M., & Levine, A. N. (2011). You too can be Awlaki! *The Fletcher Forum of World Affairs*, *35*(1), 25–46.

British Broadcasting Corporation (BBC). (2004, May 13). *Zarqawi beheaded US man in Iraq*. Retrieved July 3, 2013, from http://news.bbc.co.uk/2/hi/middle_east/3712421.stm

British Broadcasting Corporation (BBC). (2011, August 31). *Kosovan admits shooting US airmen at Frankfurt airport*. Retrieved November 4, 2013, from http://www.bbc.co.uk/news/world-europe-14727975

Burke, J. (2011, December 16). Al-Shabab's tweets won't boost its cause. *The Guardian (UK)*. Retrieved July 3, 2013, from http://www.guardian.co.uk/commentisfree/2011/dec/16/al-shabab-tweets-terrorism-twitter

Clapper, J. R. (2013, March 12). Statement for the record: Worldwide threat assessment of the US intelligence community. *Senate Select Committee on Intelligence*. Retrieved August 7, 2013, from http://www.gwu.edu/~nsarchiv/NSAEBB/NSAEBB424/docs/Cyber-090.pdf

Clean, I. T. (2013). *Reducing terrorist use of the internet*. The Hague: Dutch National Coordinator for Counterterrorism. Retrieved July 3, 2013, from https://www.counterextremism.org/resources/details/id/307/reducing-terrorist-use-of-the-Internet

Committee on the Judiciary. (2004, February 4). *Virtual threat, real terror: Cyberterrorism in the 21ˢᵗ century*. Retrieved July 3, 2013, from http://www.gpo.gov/fdsys/pkg/CHRG-108shrg94639/pdf/CHRG-108shrg94639.pdf

Conway, M. (2002). Reality bytes: Cyberterrorism and terrorist use of the internet. *First Monday*, *7*(11). doi:10.5210/fm.v7i11.1001

Conway, M. (2005a). Cybercortical warfare: Hizbollah's internet strategy. In S. Oates, D. Owen, & R. K. Gibson (Eds.), *The internet and politics: Citizens, voters and activists* (pp. 100–117). London: Routledge.

Conway, M. (2005b). Terrorist web sites: Their contents, functioning and effectiveness. In P. Seib (Ed.), *Media and conflict in the twenty-first century* (pp. 185–215). London: Palgrave.

Conway, M. (2007). Terrorist use of the internet and the challenges of governing cyberspace. In M. D. Cavelty, V. Mauer, & S. F. Krishna-Hensel (Eds.), *Power and security in the information age: Investigating the role of the state in cyberspace* (pp. 95–128). London: Ashgate.

Conway, M. (2008). Media, fear and the hyper-real: The construction of cyberterrorism as the ultimate threat to critical infrastructures. In M. D. Cavelty, & K. S. Kristensen (Eds.), *Securing the homeland: Critical infrastructure, risk, and (in)security*. London: Routledge.

Conway, M. (2011). Against cyberterrorism. *Communications of the ACM*, *54*(2), 26–28. doi:10.1145/1897816.1897829

Conway, M. (2012). What is cyberterrorism and how real is the threat? In P. C. Reich, & E. Gelbstein (Eds.), *Law, technology, and policy: Cyberterrorism, information warfare, and internet immobilization*. Hershey, PA: IGI Global.

Conway, M., & McInerney, L. (2008). *Jihadi video and auto-radicalisation: Evidence from an exploratory YouTube study*. Paper presented at the First European Conference on Intelligence and Security Informatics. Esbjerg, Denmark.

Council of Europe. (2007). *Cyberterrorism: The use of the Internet for terrorist purposes*. Strasbourg, France: Author.

Date, J. (2008, May 19). Lieberman: YouTube not doing enough to remove terrorist content. *ABC News*. Retrieved July 3, 2013, from http://abcnews.go.com/TheLaw/LawPolitics/comments?type=story&id=4889745

Denning, D. (2006). A view of cyberterrorism five years later. In K. E. Himma (Ed.), *Internet security: Hacking, counterhacking, and society* (pp. 123–140). Sudbury, MA: Jones and Bartlett Publishers.

Dodd, V. (2010, November 3). Roshonara Choudhry: Police interview extracts. *The Guardian (UK)*. Retrieved July 3, 2013, from http://www.guardian.co.uk/uk/2010/nov/03/roshonara-choudhry-police-interview

Ducol, B. (2012). Uncovering the French-speaking Jihadisphere: An exploratory analysis. *Media. War & Conflict*, *5*(3), 51–70. doi:10.1177/1750635211434366

Dunn-Cavelty, M. (2007). Cyber-terror—Looming threat or phantom menace? The framing of the US cyber-threat debate. *Journal of Information Technology & Politics*, *4*(1), 19–36. doi:10.1300/J516v04n01_03

EUR-Lex. (2007, November 6). *Proposal for a council framework decision amending framework decision 2002/475/JHA on combating terrorism*. Retrieved July 22, 2013, from http://eur-lex.europa.eu/smartapi/cgi/sga_doc?smartapi!celexplus!prod!DocNumber&lg=en&type_doc=COMfinal&an_doc=2007&nu_doc=650

European Police Office. (2011). *Europol TE-SAT 2011: EU terrorism situation and trend report*. Retrieved July 3, 2013, from https://www.europol.europa.eu/sites/default/files/publications/te-sat2011.pdf

European Police Office. (2013). *Europol TE-SAT 2013: EU terrorism situation and trend report*. Retrieved October 30, 2013, from https://www.europol.europa.eu/sites/default/files/publications/europol_te-sat2013_lr_0.pdf

Facebook. (2013). *Key facts*. Retrieved March 13, 2013, from http://newsroom.fb.com/Key-Facts

Farivar, C. (2012, August 9). Europe's quixotic plan to clean the internet of terrorists. *Ars Technica*. Retrieved July 3, 2013, from http://arstechnica.com/tech-policy/2012/08/europes-quixotic-plan-to-clean-the-Internet-of-terrorists/

Farivar, C. (2013, January 30). EU plan to voluntarily remove terrorist content finally concludes. *Ars Technica*. Retrieved July 3, 2013, from http://arstechnica.com/tech-policy/2013/01/eu-plan-to-voluntarily-remove-terrorist-content-finally-concludes/

Farmer, B. (2011, December 25). Congress calls on Twitter to block Taliban. *The Telegraph (UK)*. Retrieved July 3, 2013, from http://www.telegraph.co.uk/technology/twitter/8972884/Congress-calls-on-Twitter-to-block-Taliban.html

Fielding, N., & Cobain, I. (2013, March 17). Revealed: US spy operation that manipulates social media. *The Guardian (UK)*. Retrieved July 3, 2013, from http://www.guardian.co.uk/technology/2011/mar/17/us-spy-operation-social-networks

Fuchs, C., Boersma, K., Albrechtslund, A., & Sandoval, M. (Eds.). (2011). *Internet and surveillance: The challenges of web 2.0 and social media*. New York: Routledge.

Gambetta, D., & Hertog, S. (2007). *Engineers of Jihad*. University of Oxford. Retrieved July 3, 2013, from http://www.nuff.ox.ac.uk/users/gambetta/engineers%20of%20jihad.pdf

Ganor, B., von Knop, K., & Duarte, C. A. M. (Eds.). (2007). *Hypermedia seduction for terrorist recruiting*. Amsterdam: IOS Press.

Gettleman, J. (2011, December 19). U.S. considers combating Somali militants' Twitter use. *The New York Times*. Retrieved July 3, 2013, from http://www.nytimes.com/2011/12/20/world/africa/us-considers-combating-shabab-militants-twitter-use.html?_r=0

Githens-Mazer, J. (2010, November 4). Radicalisation via YouTube? It's not so simple. *The Guardian (UK)*. Retrieved July 3, 2013, from http://www.guardian.co.uk/commentisfree/2010/nov/04/youtube-radicalisation-roshonara-choudhry

Greenwald, G. (2012, April 13). The real criminals in the Tarek Mehanna case. *Salon*. Retrieved July 3, 2013, from http://www.salon.com/2012/04/13/the_real_criminals_in_the_tarek_mehanna_case/

Grossman, L. (2006, December 25). You—Yes, you—Are TIME's person of the year. *Time Magazine*. Retrieved July 3, 2013, from http://www.time.com/time/magazine/article/0,9171,1570810,00.html

Halliday, J. (2012, March 22). Twitter's Tony Wang: We are the free speech wing of the free speech party. *The Guardian (UK)*. Retrieved July 3, 2013, from http://www.guardian.co.uk/media/2012/mar/22/twitter-tony-wang-free-speech

Holder v. Humanitarian Law Project. (2010). *US Supreme Court 561*. Retrieved July 3, 2013, from http://www.supremecourt.gov/opinions/09pdf/08-1498.pdf

Kimmage, D. (2008, April 14). *The Al-Qaeda media nexus: The virtual network behind the global message*. Washington, DC: Radio Free Europe. Retrieved April 14, 2008, from http://docs.rferl.org/en-US/AQ_Media_Nexus.pdf

Kimmage, D., & Ridolfo, K. (2007, July 13). *Iraqi insurgent media: The war of images and ideas*. Washington, DC: Radio Free Europe/Radio Liberty. Retrieved July 13, 2007, from at http://realaudio.rferl.org/online/OLPDFfiles/insurgent.pdf

Lasker, J. (2005, February 25). Watchdogs sniff out terror sites. *Wired News*. Retrieved July 3, 2013, from http://www.wired.com/politics/security/news/2005/02/66708?currentPage=all

Lyon, D. (2003). *Surveillance after September 11*. Cambridge, MA: Polity.

Macdonald, S., Jarvis, L., Chen, T., & Lavis, S. (2013). *Cyberterrorism: A survey of researchers.* Retrieved July 3, 2013, from http://www.cyberterrorism-project.org/wp-content/uploads/2013/03/Cyberterrorism-Report-2013.pdf

Maclean, W. (2011, September 5). Analysis—Islamist videos, populists stir German worries. *Reuters (UK).* Retrieved July 3, 2013, from http://uk.reuters.com/article/2011/09/05/uk-germany-security-idUKTRE7842HS20110905

March, A. F. (2012, April 21). A dangerous mind? *The New York Times.* Retrieved July 3, 2013, from http://www.nytimes.com/2012/04/22/opinion/sunday/a-dangerous-mind.html?pagewanted=all

McCants, W. (2011, December 6). *Subcommittee hearing: Jihadist use of social media: How to prevent terrorism and preserve innovation.* Retrieved July 3, 2013, from http://homeland.house.gov/hearing/subcommittee-hearing-jihadist-use-social-media-how-prevent-terrorism-and-preserve-innovation

Meleagrou-Hitchens, A. (2011). *As American as apple pie: How Anwar al-Awlaki became the face of western Jihad.* Kings College London: International Centre for the Study of Radicalisation and Political Violence. Retrieved July 3, 2013, from http://icsr.info/2011/09/as-american-as-apple-pie-how-anwar-al-awlaki-became-the-face-of-western-jihad/

Nakashima, E. (2010, March 4). FBI director warns of rapidly expanding cyberterrorism threat. *Washington Post.* Retrieved July 3, 2013, http://www.washingtonpost.com/wp-dyn/content/article/2010/03/04/AR2010030405066.html

Neville, R. (2004, May 29). Who killed Nick Berg? *The Sydney Morning Herald.* Retrieved July 3, 2013, from http://www.smh.com.au/articles/2004/05/28/1085641717320.html

Radicalisation Awareness Network (RAN). (2013). *What we do.* Retrieved July 22, 2013, from http://ec.europa.eu/dgs/home-affairs/what-we-do/networks/radicalisation_awareness_network/index_en.htm

Radicalisation Awareness Network (RAN) Voices of Victims of Terrorism. (VVT). (2012). Proposed policy recommendations for the high level conference from the RAN voices of victims of terrorism working group. *European Commission, DG Home Affairs.* Retrieved July 3, 2013, http://ec.europa.eu/dgs/home-affairs/what-we-do/networks/radicalisation_awareness_network/ran-high-level-conference/docs/proposed_policy_recommendations_ran_vvt_en.pdf

Ramsay, G. (2009). Relocating the virtual war. *Defence Against Terrorism Review, 2*(1), 31–50.

Scheuer, M. (2004). *Imperial hubris: Why the west is losing the war on terror.* Washington, DC: Brasseys.

Seib, P. (2010, August 26). CENTCOM's digital diplomacy. *Huffington Post.* Retrieved July 3, 2013, from http://www.huffingtonpost.com/philip-seib/centcoms-digital-diplomac_b_696448.html

Seib, P., & Janbek, D. M. (2011). *Global terrorism and new media: The post-al Qaeda generation.* London: Routledge.

Stevens, T., & Neumann, P. (2009). *Countering online radicalisation: A strategy for action.* London: ICSR.

Terrorism & Homeland Security. (2004, February 4). *Virtual threat, real terror: Cyberterrorism in the 21st century.* Retrieved February 4, 2004, from http://www.gpo.gov/fdsys/pkg/CHRG-108shrg94639/pdf/CHRG-108shrg94639.pdf

UK Home Office. (2011). *Contest: The United Kingdom's strategy for countering terrorism.* Westminster, UK: Home Office.

Ungerleider, N. (2011, July 25). Examining Oslo terrorist Breivik's internet trail. *Fast Company*. Retrieved July 3, 2013, from http://www.fast-company.com/1768974/examining-oslo-terrorist-breiviks-Internet-trail

Verton, D. (2003). *Black ice: The invisible threat of cyberterrorism*. New York: McGraw-Hill/Osborne.

YouTube. (2013). *Statistics*. Retrieved March 22, 2013, from http://www.youtube.com/yt/press/statistics.html

Zelin, A. (2013). *The state of global Jihad online: A qualitative, quantitative, and cross-lingual analysis*. New America Foundation. Retrieved July 3, 2013, from http://www.newamerica.net/sites/newamerica.net/files/policydocs/Zelin_Global%20Jihad%20Online_NAF.pdf

KEY TERMS AND DEFINITIONS

Cyberterrorism: The convergence of terrorism with cyberspace, where cyberspace becomes the means of conducting the terrorist attack.

Online Radicalization: A process whereby individuals, through their online interactions and exposure to various types of extremist Internet content, come to view violence as a legitimate method of solving social and political conflicts.

Surveillance Society: A term used to describe the emergence of technological tools used by large governing bodies to watch and observe citizens.

Violent Extremism: Violent acts motivated by ideologies considered to be far outside the mainstream attitudes of a society.

ENDNOTES

1. See for example Verton (2003).
2. "The Cyberterrorism Project" Website is at http://www.cyberterrorism-project.org/.
3. Based on 118 responses from academics and other researchers working in 24 countries across six continents. The high percentage of respondents that view cyberterrorism as a significant threat and believe that it has already occurred may be partially explained by the fact that 69% of respondents believe states can engage in cyberterrorism. (Macdonald et al., 2013).
4. The arguments contained in this section were rehearsed in an opinion piece I contributed to *Communications of the ACM* in 2011 (Conway, 2011).
5. One of the videos purported to show U.S. military personnel raping an Iraqi Muslim girl, but was instead a scene from Brian De Palma's 2007 anti-war film, *Redacted* (BBC, 2011, August 31).
6. Breivik also carefully prepared an Internet-based media strategy to accompany his attacks (Ungerleider, 2011, July 25).
7. It is stated on the record by al-Zarqawi that he was Berg's killer. The CIA also identified al-Zarqawi as the likely executioner (BBC, 2004, May 13). However, others have raised doubts as to the authenticity of the beheading video and the likely perpetrator of the beheading (Neville, 2004, May 29).
8. Of these, some 680 million use Facebook mobile products (Facebook, 2013).
9. Further, over 4 billion hours of video are viewed on YouTube each month, one quarter of all YouTube views now come from mobile devices, and 70% of YouTube traffic comes from outside the United States (YouTube, 2013).
10. It has since come to light that the al-Hesbah online discussion forum was actually run by the CIA (Awan, Hoskins & O'Loughlin, 2011).
11. All content removal requests directed at Twitter are however posted on the Chilling Effects Website at http://www.chillingeffects.org.

12. Accessible online at http://www.legislation-line.org/legislation.php?tid=46&lid=5679.

13. As per an EU press release on the amendment http://europa.eu/rapid/pressReleasesAction.do?reference=MEMO/08/255&format=HTML&aged=0&language=EN&guiLanguage=en.

14. The project Website is at http://cleanitproject.eu/.

15. By way of full disclosure, the author was an observer at the final working CleanIT meeting in Vienna on November 5-6, 2012 and contributed to a panel discussion at the projects wrap-up event in Brussels on January 30, 2013.

16. In a statement posted on their Website, the European Internet Service Providers Association (EuroISPA), expressed concern that the Internet industry would be forced to implement ill-designed solutions to a potentially ill-defined problem on the basis of the project outcomes. See http://www.euroispa.org/news/76-reaction-on-cleanit-project.

17. See http://cleanitproject.eu/clean-it-in-european-parliament/ for details of the questions asked by MEPs in the European Parliament in respect of Clean IT and Farivar (2013).

18. See Anonymous' almost three-minute video denunciation of CleanIT at http://www.youtube.com/watch?v=tpE04GZ66KQ.

19. By way of full disclosure, the author is involved with RAN@ and the RAN network more generally.

20. See the RAN@ Webpage at http://ec.europa.eu/dgs/home-affairs/what-we-do/networks/radicalisation_awareness_network/about-ran/ran-at/index_en.htm.

21. In March 2010, for example, Sufi Shakyh Dr. Muhammad Tahir-ul-Qadri issued a 600-page "fatwa" (i.e., religious ruling) in English and Urdu condemning terrorism, which has an accompanying Website at http://www.fatwaonterrorism.com.

22. See "My Jihad" Website at http://myjihad.org/.

23. *The 99's* accompanying Website is at http://www.the99.org/.

Chapter 15
From "Angry Arab" to "Arab Spring"

Samuel P. Winch
Penn State – Harrisburg, USA

ABSTRACT

The 2011 "Arab Spring" revolutions seemed to turn over a new leaf in Western news depictions of the Middle East, shifting from "angry Arab terrorist" visual stereotypes to stereotypes of youthful Internet-savvy-grassroots protesters demanding reasonable democratic reforms. This chapter examines the photographic reportage of the Associated Press wire service photojournalists during the Arab Spring and the decade that preceded it to determine if a measurable shift in coverage did occur. Just as media depictions of the student protesters involved in the 1979 Islamic revolution in Iran shifted the media stereotype of Arab and Persian from Hollywood's vision of oil sheikhs, belly-dancing harem girls, and camel-riding Bedouins to young and angry religious fanatics, the largely secular democratic reforms of the Arab Spring subtly altered media conceptions of the "angry Arab." This chapter examines media depictions of the visible elements of Middle East unrest—from Libya to Pakistan—in the ten-year period from 2002 through the revolutions in Egypt, Tunisia, and Libya in 2011. An examination of news photographs during the period shows subtle shifts in the imagery.

INTRODUCTION

On December 17, 2010, Muhammed Bouazizi, a street vendor selling produce in the small town of Sidi Bouzid in Tunisia, fed up and humiliated by the injustices he had endured from local authorities, went to the street in front of the governor's office and lit himself on fire. Less than a month later, on January 14, 2011, Zine el-Abidene Ben Ali, the President of Tunisia since 1987, left the country on a flight to escape the hordes of protesters inspired by Bouazizi, who had become a revered martyr for democracy. Days later, protests for democracy engulfed Egypt and continued for several weeks until Hosni Mubarak relinquished power after 30 years in 2011.

Thus began the Arab uprising of 2011, or Arab Spring, which eventually included democratic revolutions and protests in Libya, Bahrain, Yemen, Jordan, and Syria. News articles about these

DOI: 10.4018/978-1-4666-5776-2.ch015

revolutions emphasized the role of social media, and the crucial role of young, tech-savvy activists.

In the book, *Tweets from Tahrir*, Idle and Nunns (2011) collected many of the messages the Egyptian pro-democracy protesters in Cairo sent out to the world during their confrontations in Tahrir Square with the government security forces and pro-government factions. "The most compelling coverage was on Twitter, coming directly from the people in the square. The tweets were instant, and so emotional and exciting that anyone following them felt an intense personal connection to what was happening in Tahrir" (Idle & Nunns, 2011, p. 13). Many of the tweeters acted like citizen journalists:

The importance of citizen journalists cannot be overestimated in a country like Egypt with a state controlled media. One of the features of the uprising was the gradual undermining of state TV and newspapers, to the extent that journalists began to resign as the public saw the ludicrous coverage for what it was (Idle & Nunns, 2011, p. 20).

In a previous era, the idea of idealistic young activists in the Middle East might provoke memories of the Iranian revolution of 1979, and thoughts of the American embassy hostages—unpleasant memories for Americans. However, the stories and pictures this time around, particularly from Tunisia and Egypt, seemed especially inspiring for a change. This time around, "The battle cry across the Islamic world . . . is selmiyya, selmiyya or 'peaceful, peaceful'" (Wright, 2011, p. 253).

This chapter[1] provides an examination of the news pictures of the Arab Spring of 2011 and of pictures from the decade prior, to look for visible changes in the way protesters from the Middle East, Pakistan, and Afghanistan have been framed by the photographers of the Associated Press, an international newswire service.

CONCEPTUALIZING THE OTHER

Edward Said (1978) argued that the West has maintained power and domination over the Orient through the telling and retelling of a Eurocentric history of the region. "Orientalism is the general group of ideas . . . shot through with doctrines of European superiority, various kinds of racism, imperialism, and the like, dogmatic views of 'the Oriental' as a kind of ideal and unchanging abstraction" (Said, 1978, p. 8). Western news media depictions of Middle Eastern—and specifically Arab subjects—tend to repeat similar stereotypes and myths. "Islamophobia posits 'Islam' as a conception of the world that is incompatible with modernity, with civilization, and, more important, with Euro-Americanness" (Semati, 2010, p. 267).

Shaheen (2009) says Hollywood continues to replicate the ancient Orientalist stereotypes of Arabs as villains since the beginning of the movie business. Action movies from Hollywood depict "Arabs as backward, as savages (in the eternal struggle with our forces of civilization), and as incompetent" (Semati, 2010, p. 261). Vultee asserts that Edward Said's concept of Orientalism emphasizes the idea that "the East is incapable of representing itself and must be represented by experts" (2009, pp. 624-625).

The 1979 Iranian revolution provided "another caricature of Muslims, mobs of chanting fanatics, was added to the list of negative images that shape the discourse of Islam" (Semati, 2010, p. 259). It also motivated a shift in the framing of Islam in the American press that grew beyond traditional Orientalist depictions of Muslims—from belly dancers and the desert savage to the image of the religious fanatic (Ibrahim, 2011). This is attributed to the ongoing distortions found in western coverage of Islam; specifically, that "Jihad" is commonly translated as "holy war." However, Jihad is not a holy war—it is a conflict involving challenges with the forces of evil. This misinterpretation of Jihad has taken on many violent associations, depicting Islam as a dangerous and confrontational faith group (Ibid). In this, "Arabs are depicted as carriers of primitivism—threatening to upset our cozy modern world with their strange habits and desires" (Greider cited in Shaheen, 2009, p. 12).

Ibrahim analyzed American television news coverage of Muslims in the aftermath of 9/11. While American television news coverage of domestic Muslim-Americans following 9/11 tended to depict "Islam as a religion of peace" (Ibrahim, 2010, p. 123) the news coverage of foreign Muslims focused on angry and irrational America-haters.

Video of aggressive demonstrators accompanied almost every package filed from Islamabad, Peshawar and Quetta, on the Afghan border during the first two weeks after the attacks [of 9/11]. The visuals of these protests were mainly of bearded men shouting in the streets . . . Articulate, intellectual Pakistanis are not news according to how news is shaped and defined by international news agencies. The association of Islam with people who are visibly infuriated is another news convention that objectifies Muslims as "the bad guys" (Ibrahim, 2010, pp. 119-120).

Visual images permeate contemporary media. Pictures affect us on an emotional, almost visceral level, overriding our rational modes of thinking, making us believe things that would otherwise require logical reasoning (Lester, 1995). In a study on the psychological effects of 9/11 media coverage, Huddy and colleagues (2003) found that Americans who watched more visual images of the 9/11 attacks reported more fear and anxiety, while those who read more newspapers did not—visual images had a more powerful effect on emotion. Many researchers are now acknowledging the rhetorical and persuasive power of visual images in communication (Blair, 1996; Foss, 1994).

Blair states that visual messages are most influential "not directly from any arguments they proffer, but from the underlying and hidden identifications and feelings they evoke" (1996, p. 34). Repeated viewing of visual images of a person or a group of persons in certain roles or situations will unconsciously affect the viewer—they begin to identify the subject a certain way, and to develop predictable feelings for that subject or group.

Analyses of images should consider both the internal and external narratives, as described by Banks (2001). The internal narrative is the story the image communicates directly, while the external narrative refers to the social context that produced the image.

Visual images produce and represent an ideological reality that is "bound up with the interests of the social institutions" (Kress & van Leeuwen, 1996, p. 45) in the culture in which they are produced as well as the ones in which they are read or viewed (Ibid). Burton (2002) says visual representations of people in certain stereotypes, repeated and reinforced, typically include the distinguishing features of hair, clothes, age, gender, and social relationships.

The visual images make the storytelling easier, according to Roeh (1981):

If the rhetoric of storytelling includes elements that link the concrete with the general, the rhetoric of the image does so even more. Key pictures (especially the same often-used stills) that symbolize and signal certain topics in the news need little elaboration. Specific news stories change but the stills are there to stay. They serve further to connect new stories with old truths, stock images, repeated stories, and societal conventions (Roeh, 1981, p. 81).

Visual messages can tend to oversimplify complex situations and ideas, unless they are accompanied by verbal information. Blair (1996) says visual arguments rarely tell more than one side of an issue. Roeh, for example, found that television news documentaries on the Israeli-Palestinian conflicts in the 1970s "were continuously packaged to fit simplistic, conventional forms and inherited patterns of storytelling" (1981, p. 87).

Szasz (1994) points out the importance of visual communication in the political context:

[P]olitical communication and production of meaning is increasingly accomplished through images, not words, through visual rather than verbal representation.

[W]e need to find a way of thinking about opinion formation that recognizes the distinctiveness of a process that relies more on image than the word, a process that is more figural than discursive, a process that creates 'meanings' in which the cognitive content is underarticulated and is dominated by visual components (Szasz, 1994, p. 57).

Galtung and Ruge (1965) examined news coverage of crises in foreign countries. The stories that received more coverage tended to be current events that were large enough to pass a newsworthiness threshold, and bad news received more coverage than good news. Predictable events like revolution, war and famine received more coverage as well. Africa gets very little news coverage, except in very special circumstances, and then it resembles a feeding frenzy, or a pack of jackals teaming up to attack the prey. When disaster strikes—an earthquake, coup or something extraordinary, the jackals flock to the scene. The net effect is that news coverage of Africa and the non-Western world is limited to extraordinarily bad events. The tendency of news media to emphasize disaster and bad news, and the whole concept of orientalism, would lead us to expect the coverage of Middle Eastern protest rallies matches the expectations of the photojournalists. We could expect that their pictures would tend to reinforce the expectation that things look bad—they would seek out the worst possible, or most sensational images they could find during a news event.

On the other hand, as Wright (2011) has noted, the Middle East has transformed in the period 2007 to 2011 into what she calls a "counter-Jihad." Public support for terrorism and violence in general in the region are much lower than in the decade prior, with all but a very few having renounced al-Qaeda and its violent solutions to problems. Khaled al-Maeena, the Saudi editor of *Arab News* states that "[T]here's now a younger generation who are sick and tired of violence, and they don't want to be labeled terrorist and carry that collective guilt. They get very upset when they hear the term 'Muslim terrorists'" (Wright, 2011, p. 187). The Moroccan singer Youssra Oukaf, known as *Soultana*, told Wright, "We hate extremists. We look away from militants with their beards and robes. They don't attract the young anymore" (Ibid, p. 120). Ghada Shahbender, an Egyptian poet and activist who was out on the streets during Egypt's uprising explained to Wright that al-Qaeda is just as insignificant to the Islamic world as the Ku Klux Klan is to the Americans. While they exist, Shahbender asserted that al-Qaeda is considered violent and unacceptable to the majority of Muslims. In light of this dramatic increase in the unpopularity of al-Qaeda and extremism, we should expect to see a change in news coverage of protests in the Middle East in the years before and including the Arab Spring uprisings of 2011.

Simon Cottle described the television coverage coming from foreign correspondents in Tahrir Square during the Egyptian uprising in January and February 2011:

Foreign correspondents in Tahrir Square not only helped to focus world attention on these momentous events but also helped grant them a human face. Mass uprising on the streets of Egypt now appeared less distanced, less humanly remote. Visceral scenes and emotional testimonies elicited on the street brought home to watching millions something of the protestors' everyday despair and democratic aspirations as well as their extraordinary courage in confronting, by non-violent means, repressive state violence (Cottle, 2011, p. 648).

Cambie quotes from a *60 Minutes* interview of Wael Gonim, an Egyptian blogger:

Our revolution is like Wikipedia, OK? Everyone is contributing content, [but] you don't know the names of the people contributing content. This is exactly what happened. Revolution 2.0 in Egypt was exactly the same. Everyone contributing small pieces, bits and pieces. We drew this whole picture of a revolution (Cambie, 2012, p. 31).

Thus, the accounts of what happened during the Arab Spring seem to argue that this time was different, the people were different, and the news coverage showed the differences, showed how reasonable they were, how youthful, secular and intelligent they were in their quest for democratic reforms. This study was an effort to see whether and how news pictures of Middle Eastern protesters changed over the decade containing the Arab Spring.

Todd Gitlin's 1980 book, *The Whole World is Watching* examines news media coverage of the 1960s student anti-Vietnam War protest movement in the United States. He shows how the news media generally ignored the movement at first, then began treating it as a fringe group and political oddity. Later coverage tended to focus on the most extreme and fiery rhetoric. Gitlin described media framing as the "persistent patterns" (Gitlin, 1980, p. 7) in which journalists organize stories, both verbally and visually. He found news tended to trivialize the importance, size, and effectiveness of the protest movement, while emphasizing internal conflict within the movement, and tending to portray the movement as "extremists" while relying on quotations and analysis from officials opposed to the protesters. He says news conventions lean toward defining news as events, without examining the underlying condition that led to the event, and often personalize the story to focus the frame on specific details that create a myopic frame of reference for the description. This is exemplified, for instance, when a demonstration (which is meant to be a statement about the world) is depicted as a potential or actual disruption of the peace and proper social order. This type of news media framing suggests that violent extremism is rampant and that political disarray is imminent.

Antonio Gramsci introduced the concept of media hegemony—how ruling classes make sure the dominant values propagated through media and schools reflect the interests of the elite, and the masses are taught to adopt those elite interests as their own, rather than values that might reflect their own working-class interests determined through rational self-interest (Gitlin, 1980). In terms of media coverage of protest movements, we could expect ruling class interests to include maintaining the status quo, and therefore, efforts to marginalize dissent and dissenters, attempts to make them seem deviant and strange. Likewise, American Middle East foreign policy has long been criticized for the tendency to support corrupt autocratic dictators friendly to elite capitalists (particularly oil companies). At the same time, patriotic Americans and political leaders admire the democratic, representative form of government and are supportive of (and inspired by) transitions to democracy in authoritarian countries. In other words, a huge contradiction in American foreign policy is that while the government ostensibly supports emerging democracies, it is also supportive of regimes friendly to capitalism and business. If Gramsci is correct, we should see these dueling purposes and interests reflected in Western media coverage of democracy protest movements in the Middle East: in oil producing countries, news media would tend to be less supportive of democratic revolution, while in non-oil producing countries, news media would tend to produce news coverage more supportive of democratic revolution.

To test these expectations, pictures of Muslim protesters in the Middle East (and Afghanistan and Pakistan) in the ten-year period January 2002 to

December 2011 were examined. It was expected that the pictures of Muslim protesters during the Arab Spring of 2011 would be more sympathetic to the plight of the protesters, and would tend to show Middle Eastern Muslim protesters in a more positive light, moving away from terrorist stereotypes toward more reasonable depictions.

The rhetoric in the photograph captions has been also examined in order to find examples of Western news conventions and ideological assumptions, themes, or frames used to make sense of the events being portrayed. Stuart Hall, writing about news photographs, says,

It is difficult to pin down precisely how and where the themes which convert a photo into an ideological sign arise. . . . The ideological concepts embodied in photos and texts in a newspaper... do not produce new knowledge about the world. They produce recognitions of the world as we have already learned to appropriate it. . . . The dominant ideology always appears, precisely, diffused in and through the particular. Ideology is therefore both the specific interpretation which any photo or text specifies, and the general ambiance within which ideological discourse itself is carried on (Hall, 1973, pp. 239-240).

Dominant ideology is diffused into the subtle decisions and choices made by photojournalists, such as the choices of main subjects—who to focus on, who to leave out of the picture, as well as the depiction of subjects—trying to catch them when they look good, or look strange and angry. Photographers employ conventions and experience to compose their photographs—they must decide whether to zoom-in on one person to convey a closeness and intimacy, or to zoom-out and show the size of the whole group. The late war photojournalist Robert Capa is famous for saying, "If your pictures aren't good enough, you're not close enough" (Magnum Photos, 2012).

CAPTURING THE ARAB SPRING

To understand the implications of images of the Arab Spring in 2011, a content analysis of news photographs and a rhetorical analysis of their captions was conducted. This included the examination of a random sample of 132 pictures from the Associated Press's online archive of news photographs (http://apimages.ap.org). Search terms were "(Islam or Muslim) and protester," including only pictures from Islamic majority countries in the greater Middle East region, including Afghanistan, Bahrain, Egypt, Iran, Iraq, Israel/ Palestine (including Gaza, and the West Bank), Jordan, Lebanon, Libya, Morocco, Pakistan, Saudi Arabia, Syria, Tunisia, and Yemen, for the ten years from January 2002 through December 2011. Pictures were selected from a population of about 700 images (an exact population number was hard to determine, since the search engine did not allow exclusion of non-Middle Eastern countries such as Indonesia and The Philippines, so the exclusion was conducted manually, from a total population of over 5500 images). Pictures that did not include protesters were excluded. Pictures and captions were examined for several features including: date, location, group organizing the protest, actions shown in the pictures, cause of the protest, facial expression of protester (angry, shouting, calm or smiling), threatening messages (either on signs, or quoted in the caption), bearded men, and the degree of closeness (from extreme close-up, to distant overview shot). Two people coded the quantitative data material: the author and a research assistant, a former journalist. Inter-coder reliability tests of the quantitative data showed an agreement of 87.1%.

When coding for real or implied threats, coders read the captions for information about the messages and chants being made by the protesters. If the protesters were chanting "Death to America" (or death to any other country), or if they burned or hanged anyone in effigy, this was coded as threatening. In addition, the presence of weaponry, both real and toy weapons, and pictures of weaponry were considered threatening. Weapons carried by police or security forces were not included, as this study was specifically interested in tracking indications of threats being made by protesters. Additionally, the coders did code for the wearing of beards, because many of the news stories about the young democracy organizers in Egypt emphasized the youthful, modern, secular nature of the movement. The author was curious to see if the pictures of the Arab Spring protesters reflected this, when compared to protesters earlier in the decade. While beard-wearing may be a purely personal choice, the prevailing belief among young people in the Middle East today seems to be that beards are a reliable indication of fundamental Islamic beliefs (Wright, 2011).

Finally, the framing of the pictures was examined—were they zoomed-in close on one subject, or zoomed-out to show a large group? The dominance of the subject within the frame can reflect dimensions of social power, dominance, and familiarity. For example, close-up images of people in photographs can seem more intimate, engaging, and dominant while far away subjects are less engaging, less intimate, more distant, and less imposing (Berger, 1998). However, it is also important to note that Messaris (1994) asserts that motion picture directors move in close to a subject to increase tension.

In addition to the content analysis, the rhetoric in the captions of the photographs was examined, to see whether news expectations or Western assumptions are reflected in the words used to describe the protesters and their causes.

DECONSTRUCTING IMAGES

There were no huge shifts in photojournalistic coverage of Middle East Muslim protesters over the decade. Some subtle shifts were noticeable,

such as the reduction in the use of threats by protesters. For example, a September 21, 2001 picture by B. K. Bangash of protests in Karachi against the impending American attack on Afghanistan focused on a young man holding a picture of a masked man holding a shoulder-fired surface to air missile, with the words (in Arabic) translated as "America, we are coming." A week later, on September 29, 2001, a photograph by Shakeel Adil showed a masked protester in Karachi holding a life size toy gun and a poster of Osama bin Laden. Pictures from the last quarter of the decade examined showed less use of threatening images and tools. From 2002 to 2004, 31% of the images implied a threat, however, in the period from 2009 to 2011, only 9.5% of the images showed a threat being made.

In addition, facial expressions of protesters showed subtle, but statistically insignificant changes during the decade. In particular, it seemed that fewer pictures showed protesters shouting, it became slightly more common to see them calmly and peacefully pressing their causes. For instance, from 2002 to 2004, 54.2% of the images showed people shouting, but between 2009 and 2011, only 28.6% of the images showed people shouting.

While the organizers of the January 25 democracy movement in Egypt saw themselves as young, Westernized, tech-savvy and secular (Wright, 2011), the people being photographed at protests are often not the leaders (Gitlin, 1980). Photographers tend to look for the most extreme (picturesque) examples as subjects, the people shouting the loudest, or the ones with the most visible passion for their cause. "Following the attacks [of 9/11], television news broadcast these 'photogenic' violent images of 'Muslims', often visually represented by Osama bin Laden, Al Qaeda training videos, footage of random men with assault rifles and angry Muslim demonstrators" (Ibrahim, 2010, p. 122).

Further, the number of protesters wearing beards did not vary much during the time period of the study; instead, it seems that beards can be considered a cultural indicator. The prevalence of bearded protesters in Egypt in the images was 19%, while 30.8% in Lebanon and 59.6% in Pakistan were bearded. We can conclude that a large percentage of the protesters in Pakistan wear beards, while few of the Egyptian protesters do.

The subject distance did change over the time period. While the results are not quite statistically significant, there did seem to be a subtle shift toward more overview-type pictures, possibly influenced by efforts to visually convey the immense sizes of the crowds in Tahrir Square. The findings demonstrate that over time, pictures were shot from greater distances. For instance, between 2002 and 2004, 35.7% of the pictures were wide overview-type shots, while between 2009 and 2011, these wider, overview-type shots increased to 60.5% of the pictures. This tendency to move back for wide shots, using a smaller proportion of close-ups could have various effects: for instance, it could mean the wider pictures seem less imposing and less threatening. Or, on the other hand, having fewer close-ups could mean less intimacy, a more distant connection between viewer and subject. Another explanation of the greater percentage of overview and distant group shots is that because the pro-democracy rallies were peaceful ("*selmiyya, selmiyya*"), there was less reason for photojournalists to chase after dramatic close-up shots of conflict and violence. Also, of course, the rallies were huge, particularly in Cairo, and that may have been the news peg—photographers may have been asked to try to show the immensity of the crowds.

IMAGES OF THE 2011 ARAB SPRING: LESSONS LEARNED

Gitlin says, "Editors take arrests as a sign that something significant has taken place" (1980, p. 42). In fact, he quotes from Clifton Daniel, a former editor of *The New York Times* who admitted that one large protest was not assigned news

coverage because "there was not expected to be violence," so it was not considered newsworthy. Gitlin concludes that for protesters, "it took tear gas and bloodied heads to make headlines" (1980, p. 182).

Peaceful protesters are not as exciting to watch, and undoubtedly seem less newsworthy to photojournalists. "As we know, news reports by their very nature cover extraordinary events" (Shaheen, 2009, p. 35). Ordinary, peaceful events are just not newsworthy. Gitlin (1980) noted the tendency to focus on extremists, and this was the case in the pictures of Middle Eastern protesters. An example of showing the protesters as deviant extremists was a September 6, 2010 close-up picture by Musadeq Sadeq of an Afghani protester in Kabul shown shouting with his mouth wide open revealing that he only had three stubs for teeth. Other photographs also seemed to have a mocking, condescending tone, as when the grammatical mistakes in posters and banners written in English seemed to be highlighted. For example, a protest in Lahore in August 2007 showed banners reading "Dath [sic] to Tancredo of America" (additional banners repeated the same misspelling in regard to Bush and Obama). A picture by Anjum Naveed from a May 27, 2005 rally in Islamabad highlighted a protest sign saying "President Bush!! Seek apology from Muslims for desecration of Holy Quran."

To convey extremism, photographers often highlighted subjects making threats. For example, a December 28, 2008 picture from Beirut showed protesters carrying replica rockets. Other protest pictures, such as a picture from Cairo in April 1, 2003 showed protesters dressed as suicide bombers with fake dynamite strapped to their bodies. An April 15, 2011 picture from Jordan showed a protester talking to the crowd with a microphone while holding up a sword.

Sometimes captions seemed written to minimize the significance of the group doing the protest. For example, a November 27, 2007 photograph from Hebron in the Gaza Strip showed a protester being beaten by policemen. The caption described the protesting group, "The Liberation Army, a tiny Islamic group."

Other times, captions seemed to distract from the main protest group by mentioning other, competing groups. For example, the caption from a February 6, 2011 picture from Cairo that showed "representatives of protesters of 25th January movement" meeting with the newly named Vice President Omar Suleiman. The caption continued, "Egypt's largest opposition group, the Muslim Brotherhood, said it would begin talks Sunday with the government to try to end the country's political crisis," drawing attention away from the January 25 group being pictured.

As Robert Karl Manoff noted, "[s]tories also reflect the identities of the people reporters talk to, the places they go, the things they believe, the routines that guide how they work, and the conventions that govern what they write" (1986, pp. 197-198). It works the same way for photojournalists. However, we should not forget the events pictured in the photographs we examined were moments in the decade of 2002 to 2011 when bad things happened to provoke protests. The time period July 1, 2004 through December 31, 2006 contained the highest percentage of angry expressions on protesters' faces. On September 30, 2005 the Danish newspaper *Jyllands-Posten* published 12 editorial cartoons, mostly depicting the Prophet Muhammed. This provoked violent protests for the next several months throughout the Islamic world, resulting in about 100 deaths.

Also, the April 30, 2005 issue of the U.S. weekly newsmagazine *Newsweek* contained a story about the deliberate desecration of a copy of the Quran—flushing it in a toilet—by guards or interrogators at the Guantanamo Bay prison. This also resulted in waves of protest around the Islamic world in mid-2005.

The second largest percentage of angry expressions took place during the last quarter of the decade examined, July 1, 2009 through December 2011. In July 2010, Pastor Terry Jones of a small

Christian church in Gainesville, Florida announced that he would burn 200 copies of the Quran in a September 2010 ceremony to mark the anniversary of the 9/11 attacks. Political and religious leaders throughout the United States and the world hastened to dissuade Jones from his plans, which were eventually scrapped. In September 2010 Jones pledged never to burn a Quran, but Jones did burn a single copy of the Quran during a service held in his church sanctuary on March 30, 2011. Muslim protesters around the world protested Jones's actions in both 2010 and 2011. The initial threat resulted in protests in which over 20 people were killed, and the second action led to an attack on the United Nations Assistance Mission in Mazar-i-Sharif in Afghanistan, resulting in over 30 deaths, including seven foreign U.N. workers.

Many of the most violent protests included in the decade examined in this study came from Palestinian clashes with Israeli security forces in late 2009 concerning access to the Temple Mount, or Haram Ash-Sharif, an ancient holy site in the Old City of Jerusalem. Other violent clashes took place in mid- to late-2011 in Bahrain, where the Shiite majority pressed for representation in the government dominated by the Sunni minority.

One of the limitations of doing a content analysis of archived wire service photographs is that there is no indication of whether the pictures were actually published in newspapers and magazines. Maybe they were seen outside the United States? As Kellner (2004) noted, Western news coverage of the American wars in Afghanistan and Iraq tended to avoid showing pictures of the civilian casualties—pictures that were seen in news coverage shown in every other country in the world. On the other hand, showing radical deviant protesters helps to confirm the worst stereotypes favored by the status quo hegemonic culture. Another limitation of the study is that coverage was spotty—while the AP evidently had several photojournalists stationed in Pakistan, providing a steady stream of pictures of protests there, the coverage of other countries, such as Libya and Tunisia, was scant, if not nonexistent.

A general limitation of quantitative content analyses is that subtle details are rounded off, reduced to categories, eliminating nuance and delicacy. A particular weakness of this study was the relatively small sample of pictures that were analyzed. The Arab Spring revolutions in Tunisia and Egypt happened very quickly in late-December 2010 through early February 2011, so the random sampling employed in this study did not capture a large sample of the images from these short moments in history. In fact, the sample did not include any pictures from Tunisia or Libya, countries that were evidently not regularly receiving news photography coverage from the Associated Press.

While the Arab Spring protests may not have demolished the visual stereotypes of angry Arabs and Middle Eastern Muslim terrorists, it may have opened the door for alternative depictions for Middle Eastern protesters, and especially, more nuanced and sympathetic coverage for pro-democracy movements in Middle Eastern countries.

CONCLUSION

The practice of looking, the capturing of an image, and the process through which visual ideas are shared can have a profound impact on how we understand others and ourselves. Learning through photographs, for example, persists as a pivotal tradition among humans. That is, people often create understandings and associations through observation. However, the deconstruction of the connotation, denotations, and global implications of images is challenging due to the subjective nature of the image. While the risk of subjectivity plagues all who fall (intentionally or unintentionally) in front of the camera lens, Western images of the Middle East are undoubtedly an interesting case.

The "Arab Spring" revolutions certainly demonstrated a subtle shift in how Western images depicted the Middle East. Traditional visual stereotypes moved from the "angry Arab terrorist" to youthful Internet-savvy-grassroots protesters demanding reasonable democratic reforms. Through the examination of the photojournalism of the Associated Press wire in the decade following 9/11, it was possible to dissect the magnitude of such changes.

The main findings of this study were that news photographs of protesters in the Middle East, Pakistan, and Afghanistan tended to fall into the same typifications as photographs from earlier protest movements, but the coverage evolved over the decade. News photographers facing time sensitive deadlines undoubtedly look for the most extreme example—the most dramatic photographs, which come from conflict, anger, violence, and fanaticism. The emphasis on drama leads to pictures of people who look like the stereotypical "Muslim terrorist." When the Arab Spring protests came along and followed a non-violent script, the protesters were less threatening, less angry, and they gathered in huge crowds, so the photographers moved back and showed the mass of humanity pleading for democracy.

The evolution of images traced in this chapter is considered a useful case study, which could be beneficial in guiding the investigation of other instances of photojournalism in conflict. Due to the heightened media activity during conflict, it is important to understand how the images captured during these events depict the realities of others. In a world that is becoming increasing interactive due to technological innovations, images can be shared with great ease. It is suggested that while this study undoubtedly demonstrates interesting findings, further research on the depictions of more current conflict in the Middle East would also yield interesting results.

REFERENCES

Banks, M. (2001). *Visual methods in social research*. Thousand Oaks, CA: Sage.

Berger, A. A. (1998). *Seeing is believing*. Mountain View, CA: Mayfield.

Blair, J. A. (1996). The possibility and actuality of visual arguments. *Argumentation and Advocacy*, *33*(1), 23–39.

Burton, G. (2002). *More than meets the eye: An introduction to media studies*. London: Edward Arnold.

Cambie, S. (2012). Lessons from the front line: The Arab Spring demonstrated the power of people—and social media. *Communication World*, *29*(1), 28–32.

Cottle, S. (2011). Media and the Arab uprisings of 2011: Research notes. *Journalism*, *12*(5), 647–659. doi:10.1177/1464884911410017

Foss, S. (1994). A rhetorical schema for the evaluation of visual imagery. *Communication Studies*, *45*(3-4), 213–224. doi:10.1080/10510979409368425

Gallup Brain. (2012). Retrieved May 28, 2012, from http://institution.gallup.com

Galtung, J., & Ruge, M. H. (1965). The structure of foreign news: The presentation of the Congo, Cuba and Cyprus crises in four Norwegian newspapers. *Journal of Peace Research*, *2*(1), 64–91. doi:10.1177/002234336500200104

Gitlin, T. (1980). *The whole world is watching: Mass media in the making & unmaking of the new left*. Berkeley, CA: University of California Press.

Hall, S. (1973). The determinations of news photographs. In S. Cohen, & J. Young (Eds.), *The manufacture of news: Social problems, deviance and the mass media* (pp. 226–246). London: Constable.

Huddy, L., Feldman, S., Lahav, G., & Taber, C. (2003). Fear and terrorism: Psychological reactions to 9/11. In P. Norris, M. Kern, & M. Just (Eds.), *Framing terrorism: The news media, the government and the public* (pp. 255–278). New York: Routledge.

Ibrahim, D. (2010). The framing of Islam on network news following the September 11th attacks. *The International Communication Gazette*, *72*(1), 111–125. doi:10.1177/1748048509350342

Idle, N., & Nunns, A. (Eds.). (2011). *Tweets from Tahrir*. New York: OR Books.

Kellner, D. (2004). 9/11, spectacles of terror, and media manipulation: A critique of Jihadist and Bush media politics. *Critical Discourse Studies*, *1*(1), 41–64. doi:10.1080/1740590041 0001674515

Kress, G., & van Leeuwen, T. (1996). *Reading images: The grammar of visual design*. New York: Routledge.

Lester, P. M. (1995). *Visual communication: Images with messages*. Belmont, CA: Wadsworth.

Magnum Photos. (2012). *Robert Capa*. Retrieved June 7, 2012, from http://www.magnumphotos. com/C.aspx?VP=XSpecific_MAG.PhotographerDetail_VPage&11=0&pid=2K7O3R14YQ NW&nm=Robert%20Capa

Manoff, R. K. (1986). Writing the news (by telling the story). In R. K. Manoff, & M. Schudson (Eds.), *Reading the news* (pp. 197–229). New York: Pantheon Books.

Messaris, P. (1994). *Visual literacy: Image, mind & reality*. Boulder, CO: Westview Press.

Roeh, I. (1981). Israel in Lebanon: Language and images of storytelling. In W. C. Adams (Ed.), *Television coverage of the Middle East* (pp. 76–88). Norwood, NJ: Ablex Publishing.

Said, E. W. (1978). *Orientalism*. New York: Pantheon Books.

Semati, M. (2010). Islamophobia, culture and race in the age of empire. *Cultural Studies*, *24*(2), 256–275. doi:10.1080/09502380903541696

Shaheen, J. G. (2009). *Reel bad Arabs: How Hollywood vilifies a people*. Northampton, MA: Olive Branch Press.

Szasz, A. (1994). *EcoPopulism: Toxic waste and the movement for environmental justice*. Minneapolis, MN: University of Minnesota Press.

Vultee, F. (2009). Jump back Jack, Mohammed's here: Fox News and the construction of Islamic peril. *Journalism Studies*, *10*(5), 623–638. doi:10.1080/14616700902797333

Wright, R. (2011). *Rock the casbah: Rage and rebellion across the Islamic world*. New York: Simon & Schuster.

KEY TERMS AND DEFINITIONS

Arab Spring of 2011: A term for the revolutionary wave of demonstrations and protests (both non-violent and violent), riots, and civil wars in the Arab world that began on December 18, 2010.

Arabs in the Media: The depiction and representation of Arab peoples in the media.

Citizen Journalism: Public citizens playing an active role in the process of collecting, reporting, analyzing, and disseminating news and information.

Content Analysis: A method in the social sciences for studying the content of various forms of text, images, video, etc.

Middle East: A region that roughly encompasses a majority of Western Asia (excluding the Caucasus) and Egypt.

Orientalism: A term used by scholars for the imitation or depiction of aspects of Middle Eastern and East Asian cultures.

Photojournalism: A particular form of journalism that creates images to tell a story.

ENDNOTES

[1.] The author wishes to thank James Buehner for research assistance and Salam Wahib for insightful advice.

Section 8
Rationality & Responsibility

Chapter 16
Questioning Terrorism/ Counterterrorism Rationality

Joseba Zulaika
University of Nevada, USA

William A. Douglass
University of Nevada, USA

ABSTRACT

In a post-9/11 world, terrorism has become a central focus around the globe, impacting national and international politics. Therefore, understanding the functioning of terrorism and counterterrorism rationality is necessary for furthering this area of study. In this chapter, the authors' key focus in advocating the deconstruction of terrorism is upon the discourse itself: its premises, beliefs, fears, definitions, rhetorical devices, imaginary constructions of the enemy, the inability to distinguish ritual bluff from actual combat, the logic of taboo, the injunction not to humanize the terrorist other, and moral self-righteousness. It is argued that by undermining its claims to apocalyptic powers and fears, terrorism would lose credibility as an effective rhetorical ploy and bellicose weapon for insurgents and governments alike. Thus, this chapter seeks to answer: Are Americans more secure after Afghanistan and Iraq; are Israelis safer behind the wall? Or are we simply doing exactly what is required to foment "terrorism" and make it ever more menacing?

INTRODUCTION

Since 9/11, terrorism has become the very *thing* of international and national politics. Those of us who have long been skeptical about the merits of terrorism discourse and critical of its political manipulations (by perpetrators and governments alike) are now confronted with its omnipresence as the last word regarding international relations and public policy. It seems that any politically and

morally responsible analysis of the contemporary world must start with assuming the centrality of terrorism as the quintessential phenomenon of our times. How can we maintain skepticism towards the ongoing "war on terror," while at the same time taking seriously the worldwide escalation of insurgent and suicidal violence?

Our key focus in advocating the deconstruction of terrorism is upon the discourse itself: its premises, beliefs, fears, definitions, rhetorical devices,

DOI: 10.4018/978-1-4666-5776-2.ch016

imaginary constructions of the enemy, the inability to distinguish ritual bluff from actual combat, the logic of taboo, the injunction not to humanize the terrorist other, and moral self-righteousness. We argued that, by undermining its claims to apocalyptic powers and fears, terrorism would lose credibility as an effective rhetorical ploy and bellicose weapon for insurgents and governments alike (Zulaika & Douglass, 1996). Have the post-9/11 events proven us wrong? Is the enshrinement of terrorism as indisputable worldwide obsession and threat, as well as the "War on Terror" as the single-minded task of American global policy, the unavoidable offshoots of 9/11? Or has the apotheosis of counterterrorism discourse impoverished us analytically and morally, and made us politically more vulnerable while ironically furthering the violence? In practical terms: are Americans more secure after Afghanistan and Iraq; are Israelis safer behind the wall? Or are we simply doing exactly what is required to foment "terrorism" and make it ever more menacing?

Terrorism goes to the heart of "the paradox of sovereignty" which, in Agamben's formulation, "consists in the fact that the sovereign is, at the same time, outside and inside the juridical order" (1998, p. 15). Guantánamo and Abu Ghraib are instances of the sovereign power's capacity to be simultaneously inside and outside of the law. What best typifies the structure of the paradox is that exception becomes the norm. The exception reveals starkly whom has the sovereign power to decide and impose the legal boundaries; when the rules are applicable and when suspended. The omniscient and omnipotent sovereign power decides, for example, what constitutes legitimate torture and terrorist threat, arrogating to *itself* the right to employ the former when interrogating individuals suspected of terrorism (and even their "supporters") and to launch preemptive strikes against sovereign states that *it* classifies as terrorist.

What is at stake regarding the capacity to establish a state of exception is the very possibility of state authority. Recourse to "exception" seeks to exercise control over an exteriority, which then gets included and thereby co-opted by exclusion. Counterterrorism discourse illustrates well this "taking of the outside" through the logic of exception. Empire must control the powers that oppose both its sovereign and indirect rule; hence the implied independence of terrorist exceptionality is intolerable. It is no longer enough (or even possible) to leave terrorists alone. Thus, paradoxically, terrorist outcasts are excluded from the "civilized" world, while simultaneously coming under the purview of imperial control because of the tabooed character of their exceptionality.

THE PATRIOT ACT

Despite the seemingly routine and standard quality of counterterrorism reports, they feed upon and reproduce a veritable "state of exception." The Patriot Act illustrates this best. By the mid-1990s, under Clinton, Reagan's counterterrorism sideshow of the 1980s was a major theme within American politics. However, with the Bush administration, it became the *sine qua non* for defining and then interpreting the everyday life of Americans. If, between 1989 and 1992, it could be argued that the boundaries between the real and the fictional were not clear in American counterterrorism discourse (zero fatalities in the United States, 34 Americans killed abroad and 1,443 published books on terrorism over four years) (Zulaika & Douglass, 1996, p. 31), after the first attack on the Twin Towers and Oklahoma City terror became an important functional reality of American politics that could be deployed in the middle of a crisis such as the Lewinski affair. However, all of that pales compared with President Bush's post-9/11 world in which the war on terror appeared to have become the key, if not sole, purpose of American politics with epoch-making legislative consequences affecting national security at home and international cooperation abroad. The tragic events of 9/11 transformed a president whose election had been the most questionable in American history into the nation's most popular leader ever. If, previously, terrorism had been naturalized into a sort of chaotic principle always ready to strike and create havoc, with Bush it has become the prime *raison d'état*, the common enemy against which civilized (not just American) society must now marshal all of its resources in an unending "war." Welcome to the promised land of terrorism, the one that we predicted in our book "Terror and Taboo" as the possible worst-case scenario.

It is the land of Abu Ghraib, Guantánamo and the Patriot Act. It is the realm in which government after government invokes counterterrorism as the irresistible rationale for abrogating the civil liberties of the citizenry. Only counterterrorism discourse could legitimate the practical suspension of *habeas corpus* in the United States. In its initial Antiterrorism Law, the Clinton administration advocated an anti-*habeas corpus* provision—"the worst cave-in" according to an editorial in *The New York Times* on June 9, 1995. The new powers were sought for the FBI after both the left and the right denounced the Oklahoma City bombing. Even Louis Freeh, the director of the agency, told the Senate that he did not need the relaxation of investigative constraints being proposed by the White House.

Soon after 9/11 the U.S. Congress enacted the Patriot Act virtually overnight. The bill was introduced on October 5 and passed the Senate on October 11 after the briefest of debates. A slightly different one was introduced in the House the next day and approved that afternoon, thus ensuring that not a single member of Congress had read the monumental bill for which he or she had voted. Defenders of civil liberties criticize the Patriot Act for removing most limitations and judicial controls on governmental abuse, for violating core constitutional principles, for fundamentally altering the power of the FBI and the role of the CIA, and for reserving its harshest measures for immigrants. Consider the following summary:

The PATRIOT Act: (1) imposes guilt by association on immigrants, extending the reach of that philosophy beyond the 1996 Act; (2) authorizes executive detention on mere suspicion that an immigrant has at some point engaged in a violent crime or provided humanitarian aid to a proscribed organization; (3) authorized the government to deny entry to aliens for pure speech, resurrecting yet another long-interred relic of the McCarthy era; (4) expands the government's authority to conduct criminal searches and wiretaps without first showing probable cause that the subject is engaged in criminal activity; (5) authorizes secret searches in cases having nothing to do with terrorism; (6) gives the Central Intelligence Agency access to the awesome power of criminal grand juries; and (7) reduces judicial oversight of intrusive information-gathering powers and expands the scope of FBI access to a wide range of records, essentially sanctioning fishing expeditions (Dempsey & Cole, 2002, pp. 152-153).

The Patriot Act has provided the government an extraordinary expansion of surveillance authority that goes beyond the investigation of terrorism and which applies to any federal criminal investigation. The emergency situation after 9/11 facilitated fundamental changes in law enforcement procedures. It eliminated barriers between law enforcement and intelligence gathering. It gave the CIA the benefit of grand jury powers with none of the criminal justice system's protections against their abuse. It granted the FBI unlimited access to specific categories of information, including surveillance of library, bank, hospital, and university records. In short, it radically transformed the realities of both government authority and accountability.

One of the key premises of the Patriot Act is guilt by association. Ethnic profiling has thus been implemented once again with a rationale that is reminiscent of the one used to intern 110,000 persons of Japanese ancestry during World War II. The U.S. government has detained more than 1200 persons, almost all Arabs and Muslims, in connection with its investigation of the 9/11 attacks. Only one of them has been indicted for involvement in a crime. The hearings are held in secret and the names of the detainees are not disclosed.

Such guilt by association is the natural consequence of a counterterrorism culture in which deeply ingrained notions of sin and taboo gain respectability. Anthropologists employ the concepts of ritual pollution and taboo to study the antinomies of norm and anomaly, pattern and chaos, normalcy and pathology. In such foundational dynamics of form and formlessness, civilization and barbarism, a key component has to do with lawfulness and lawlessness. When we wrote "Terror and Taboo" it was impossible to resist the anthropological impulse to draw conceptual and cultural equivalences between the logic of taboo and that of counterterrorism discourse. This is even more so today—politically, militarily, and legally. It seems reasonable, then, to pose the questions of whether counterterrorism is successful in meeting its own objectives.

COUNTERTERRORISM IN THE SERVICE OF TERRORISM

The recent war in Iraq has brought to the fore a question we examined at length in our book, namely, the role of counterterrorism in promoting terrorism. There are many obvious instances with which to argue that counterterrorism policies have fostered more terrorism. The Carter and Reagan administrations provided several examples whereby the slippery/phantasmagoric qualities of their "terrorist" nemesis came to haunt them. Gary Sick, who was the U.S. Department of State expert in charge of Iranian affairs during the hostage crisis, wrote an insider account of the Carter White House's counterterrorism campaign in which reacting to imagined threats played a major part. Whatever policy mistakes were made, the tendency was always to blame them on "intel-

ligence failures" (Sick, 1985, p. 42). However, there was something else far harder to correct regarding that administration's myopia, Sick tells us: "[it] was not so much a failure of sources or observation of data as a structural inadequacy of the system itself to make a conceptual leap from chessboard to hurricane" (1985, p. 42). He complains how, during the Iran crisis, the journalist Robert Moss, who lacked hard evidence and had no qualifications as a specialist on that country, still exerted enormous influence upon top U.S. policymakers when he wrote a piece stating what many in the administration feared, namely, that the Soviets must have been orchestrating the events of the Iranian hostage crisis. Sick (1985) shows how this had a disastrous effect within U.S. policy.

President Reagan´s Iran-Contra fiasco was a classic case of the dangers of a policy based on simplistic premises of good versus evil, while ignoring international legality. First, terrorism was prioritized as almost the only foreign policy issue in the international arena. Then there was the public labeling of whole countries as terrorist, imposing pariah status upon them—a taboo that nevertheless had to be broken when business with the untouchable enemy was in order.

The stage was set for tragic instances of international lawlessness under the guise of counterterrorism, such as the kidnapping and killing of four Iranians—three diplomats and a journalist—after their car bearing diplomatic plates and accompanied by a police escort was stopped by the Israeli-backed Christian militia in Lebanon in 1982. The local governments and the United States ignored the fate of the Iranians, and the incident marked the genesis of dramatic hostage taking in Lebanon that led to the kidnapping of approximately 130 foreigners from 18 nations. Officials in Washington and international diplomats later recognized "that the Iranian abduction established a new context for political violence against the various forces in Lebanon that was later to be widely reenacted" (Jenkins & Wright, 1991, p. 145). It was the sum effect of all these elements in orbit around the Evil of Terrorism that led to the Iran-Contra debacle, a clear example of how the counterterrorist becomes the intimate ally of the terrorist.

Similarly, what is intriguing about the 1993 World Trade Center plotters is that those arrested had been under close police surveillance since 1989, when the FBI photographed them taking target practice on Long Island during four successive weekends. Their reputed leader, Sheik Omar Abdul Rahman, was but another instance of yesterday's friend turned into today's arch-terrorist enemy. That he had been recruited earlier by the CIA to rally support for Islamic anti-Soviet guerrillas in Afghanistan is no secret. The CIA campaigned to set up several "Jihad" offices across the United States. The most important was called Alkifah (Arabic for "the struggle") and was established in Brooklyn where the sheik had settled after coming repeatedly to the United States with visas provided by the CIA. In examining the evidence, Robert Friedman concludes that the CIA's involvement with the first attack on the World Trade Center was "far greater" than was known to the general public and that "the CIA has inadvertently managed to do something that America's enemies have been unable to: give terrorism a foothold in the United States" (Friedman, 1995, pp. 46-47).

The Washington Metro bombing plot, the New York subway plot, the plot to blow up the Sears Tower, the one to bomb a Portland Christmas tree light display, and dozens more across the nation were organized and led by the FBI. Trevor Aaronson's article on "The Informants" concludes:

Informants report to their handlers on people who have, say, made statements sympathizing with terrorists. Those names are then cross- referenced with existing intelligence data, such as immigration and criminal records. FBI agents may then assign an undercover operative to approach the target by posing as a radical. Sometimes the operative will propose a plot, provide explosives, even lead the target in a fake oath to Al Qaeda.

Once enough incriminating information has been gathered, there's an arrest—and a press conference announcing another foiled plot (Aaronson, 2011, September/October, p. 32).

Having examined the prosecutions of 508 defendants in terrorism-related cases, he found that all the high-profile terrorism plots of the last decade, with the exception of three,[1] were FBI stings. The FBI now spends the major portion of its budget ($3.3 billion) on counterterrorism, rather than on organized crime ($2.2 billion). It has 15,000 spies, many of them with the task of infiltrating Muslim communities, paid as much as $100,000 in some cases. As one defense lawyer put, "They're creating crimes to solve crimes so they can claim a victory in the war on terror" (cited in Aaronson, 2011, p. 33). Attorney Eric Holder argued in a speech that sting operations have "proven to be an essential law enforcement tool in uncovering and preventing potential terror attacks" (cited in Ibid, p. 33). But what this view fails to take into account is the extent to which the sting operation is actually creating terrorism. There is no better example of this than the case of the blind sheik, which several analysts consider to be a crucial event leading to 9/11.

John Miller and Michael Stone's (2002) book *The Cell: Inside the 9/11 Plot, And Why the FBI and CIA Failed to Stop It* documents the extent to which the counterterrorists themselves were infiltrated by the FBI and the future terrorists worked at times with agents while leading up to the 1993 assault on the World Trade Center. A key figure was a shadowy informer named Emad Salem, who would later become the main witness against the sheik. According to Miller and Stone, once he infiltrated Abdel-Rahman's group, "Salem was offering to restart the paramilitary training that had lapsed in the year since Nosair's [Alkifah's former leader's] arrest" (2002, p. 72). True to his calling, Salem was soon securing for his fellow plotters "a warehouse in which to build bombs" (Miller & Stone, 2002, p. 74). In other words, although nothing was going on in Abdel-Rahman's circles, it was the FBI agent who advocated engaging in illegal paramilitary activities, including renting a warehouse in which to make bombs. Another undercover agent named "Wilson" had been given on "loan" (and later recalled) for the training operation of Abdel-Rahman's close circle.

Not surprisingly, the FBI was concerned that "the Bureau was training potential terrorists, holy warriors who may not be breaking the law now, but who might one day turn the skills they were acquiring against the U.S" (Miller & Stone, 2002, p. 88). They were aware of "the heat the Bureau would take if it turned out it had assisted a future terrorist," but still, "the subjects were going to get training whether or not the FBI provided it" and "if you weren't willing to get close to the action, to get your hands dirty now and then, how would you ever know what he's plotting to do?" (Ibid, p. 87). In other words, since they were going to be terrorists someday anyway, let us be complicit in order to find out how far they are willing to go!

Later, in April of 1993, two months after 9/11, Salem went to the FBI with the troubling information that Abdel-Rahman's circle was planning a simultaneous bombing of the Lincoln and Holland tunnels, the United Nations, and the New York offices of the FBI. Once again, since the plotters needed a safe house in which to build the bombs, "Salem offered to find one," and then the co-conspirator "accepted the offer" (Miller & Stone, 2002, p. 114).

So who took the initiative? Was it the counter-terrorist informant who "offered" to find a place to build bombs or the terrorist who "accepted?" There was something else that Salem's handlers wanted from him: Abdel-Rahman's blessing on tape for the plotters' murderous intentions. Despite Salem's insistent questioning, the sheik was unresponsive. Soon the FBI's SWAT team would act to foil the "second terrorist plot" in the safe house set up by the agency's own informant Salem. Counterterrorism had triumphed.

After the trial for the plot to bomb New York's landmark buildings, in 1995 Sheik Abdel-Rahman was confined for life to a New York prison on conspiracy charges. Salem was the main witness against him. The American government rewarded him with $1.5 million for his testimony. On March 19, 1995, *The New York Times* reported that Salem "began his testimony by admitting that he had lied to just about everybody he ever met," that he was "always ready with another believe-it-or-not exploit," and that his testimony sounded "like sheer fantasy." An editorial by the same newspaper on October 3, 1995, gave a sense of the type of evidence used to indict the sheik, for it "only required [the government] to prove *the intention* to wage a terror campaign" and in which "only the sketchiest connections [were] established between Sheik Omar Abdel-Rahman and the alleged mastermind of that crime, Ramzi Ahmed Yousef. However, the American public was understandably relieved. The Islamic plotters had been finally caught red-handed. They had been given their lesson—end of the story.

In the event, things would not be that final. If the trial was a sham, even for *The New York Times,* one can imagine how the travesty must have appeared to the Muslims who respected their spiritual leader and who were never allowed to hear his version. In particular, one imagines the enormity of the injustice in the eyes of someone who had been particularly close to the sheik and whose living expenses, while in the United States, had been paid by the American government: Osama bin Laden (Miller & Stone, 2002). He was known at the time as a fund-raiser for the Afghan war. Like Sheik Abdel-Rahman, he had worked with the CIA in Reagan's crusade against the Soviets. Now his friend and spiritual leader was in jail for life, humiliated as scum of the earth, after enduring a mock trial in the alleged land of freedom and human rights. Soon, by January of 1996, President Clinton would sign off on a CIA finding establishing that bin Laden was a threat to national security. A new terrorist enemy had been served. Once again, the former ally was going to transmogrify into the arch-terrorist nemesis.

After the Soviets' defeat in Afghanistan, in 1990 bin Laden had returned home to Saudi Arabia as a war hero and initially gone back to work for his family's construction company. Iraq's invasion of Kuwait mobilized him again. He offered to recruit a Muslim army to drive the Iraqis out of Kuwait. The Saudis turned instead to an American-led coalition force, a decision that then became a critical divide for bin Laden.

After the Iraqis were driven from Kuwait, he declared *Jihad* or holy war against the then communist regime in South Yemen. None of this sat well with the Saudis who placed him under virtual house arrest and soon expelled him "by convincing bin Laden that the U.S. forces stationed in Saudi Arabia had been tasked by the CIA to kill him" (Miller & Stone, 2002, p. 159). By the summer of 1992 he had moved to Sudan with an army of 300 al-Qaeda recruits. To this point they had not committed a single terrorist act.

Osama bin Laden was outraged that U.S. troops had not pulled out of Saudi Arabia as promised, thereby prolonging a western presence—tantamount to the Soviet one in Afghanistan—but this time in Islam's holy land and bin Laden's homeland. Nevertheless, in mid-1993, he opposed a plan to bomb the U.S. embassy in Riyadh because it would endanger civilians. He was not a "terrorist" yet; but by then he was convinced that America was "a snake" in need of beheading (Miller & Stone, 2002, p. 162). It was in 1994 that Sheik Abdel-Rahman had been tried and condemned to life in prison; it was also the year in which bin Laden's assets were frozen and the Saudis tried to assassinate him.

"Real" al-Qaeda terror would begin in August of 1998 with the simultaneous embassy bombings in Kenya and Tanzania, which killed 221 people and injured some 4,500. Earlier that year bin Laden

had told the journalist John Miller that American outrage over the attacks on American civilians revealed a blatant double standard and that there was no longer any difference between military and civilian targets (Miller & Stone, 2002). By then America was treating al-Qaeda as a global terror network.

Meanwhile, had Sheik Abdel-Rahman been forgotten by his followers? His son Saif Rahman was recruiting al-Qaeda members in Afghanistan. A defector told the journalist John Miller in 1999 about a specific bin Laden plan:

The target was a commercial airliner. The objective was to hijack a plane that was carrying a U.S. senator or ambassador and then try and use the dignitary as the bargaining chip to demand the release of the blind sheik from American prison (Miller & Stone, 2002, p. 282).

This was consistent with a report by the CIA that was provided to President Bush a month before 9/11 and which "said that bin Laden's organization had plans to hijack a plane and use the hostages to spring Sheik Omar Abdel-Rahman from U.S. federal prison" (Miller & Stone, 2002, p. 297). No, he had not been forgotten, but only a bold action might free him.

Commandeering planes had become the occasional tactic of terrorist groups. It possessed special efficacy in that it struck fear in the heart of every air traveler while providing hostages. It could possibly be used to obtain the bargaining chip for the freeing of Sheik Abdel-Rahman. Or was it already too late to engage the enemy in an exchange of prisoners? The sheik would certainly understand that there were more important objectives than securing his personal freedom. Perhaps what the enemy needed most was a lesson, an apocryphal performance. September 11 was in the making.

LAW, PREEMPTION AND STATES OF EXCEPTION

The final result of such states of exception has been described by Agamben as one in which "it is impossible to distinguish transgression of the law from the execution of the law, such that what violates a rule and what conforms to it coincide without any reminder" (1988, p. 57). Guantánamo becomes both the ultimate bastion of civilization against terrorism, and also the ultimate repudiation of domestic and international law. What, viewed from the traditional perspectives of civil rights advocates is the most flagrant abuse of the rule of law, is now being tolerated as the law of the land and treated by public opinion and the mainstream media as completely "normal." The anomaly can only be explained in terms of counterterrorism discourse's fundamental premises. The unthinkable, without being thought through, has become normalized because of the premises, fears and self-fulfilling prophecies of a new culture of counterterrorism that is radically subversive of what any proponent of western values and liberal democracy might believe to be the rule of law.

From the perspective of cultural analysis one question that concerns us is the extent to which we attribute such "exceptionality" to semantic definitions and self-serving political expediency. Throughout its recent history counterterrorism played into such a dynamic. Thus, Reagan's 1986 military raid on Libya, for example, was an action later censured by a General Assembly resolution at the United Nations. The *Achille Lauro* affair further undermined American international credibility regarding terrorism when the heinous killing of a paraplegic Jew prompted American overreaction in a way that was unjustified under international law. Antonio Cassesse (1989) devoted a book to the complex legal implications of this affair, including the American interception of an Egyptian airliner and its forced landing in Italy. He concluded that, "The United States preferred violence to law, leaving behind an unfortunate legacy that

has polluted international law and aggravated political and diplomatic relations between states" (Cassesse, 1989, p. 80). The American rationale was an allegory: the terrorists were "a kind of modern incarnation of the pirates of former times" (Ibid, p. 127). Italian Prime Minister Craxi and Egyptian President Mubarak, who spoke of being "stabbed in the back," denounced the American action as an "act of piracy . . . without precedent in any international code or law" (Ibid, p. 129), accusing the Americans of violating their territorial integrity and national sovereignty.

The critical point, and one that can be illustrated with a myriad of examples from Ireland, Great Britain, Germany, Russia, Spain, Israel, Chechnya, Argentina, India, and other states, regards the seemingly irresistible temptation of constituted authority to abrogate its own legal due processes: accusing the Other of terrorist lawlessness allows one to dispense with one's own rule of law.

Counterterrorism discourse is premised upon the dismissal of any notion of legal limits in reacting to terrorism. It begins by portraying terrorism as unique and exceptional; that is, it takes for granted that terrorist violence is unlike any other kind; that it constitutes its own immoral category, that it has no political legitimacy whatsoever and borders on madness; that its means follow no set rules and forms; that its logic is one of irrational chance; that the only civilized reaction to the aberrant phenomenon must be one of utter taboo.

Such premises recall ancient notions regarding barbarians as less than human and therefore outside the realm of law. In our liberal democracies the tension between civilization and barbarism is now configured by terrorism, and its main expression has to do with issues of legality. Not surprisingly, under the guise of fighting terrorism, the United States rejected agreements such as the 1977 Geneva Protocol I, which "provides one clear set of internationally-agreed criteria by which one can assess, and criticize, acts of terrorism" (Roberts, 1989, p. 65). The U.S. view that the Protocol would give recognition and protection to terrorist groups was strongly rejected by other countries (Gasser, 1987). Not surprisingly, some critical legal scholars have had no qualms about describing American counter-terrorism policy as "itself both terroristic and illegal" (Falk, 1988, p. 147).

In short, once the premises of counterterrorism discourse are assimilated and unchallenged, the temptation to use terrorism against terrorism becomes almost irresistible. Counterterrorism's shoot-to-kill policy, its abrogation of due process, its ready resort to torture are all instances that, in the words of Adam Roberts, "point to a central truth—that there are few areas of state activity in which the temptation to abandon important ethical norms is so strong and so pervasive" (1989, p. 62). Prominent counterterrorism specialists in fact have suggested co-opting terrorist strategies as "indirect forms of warfare."

Similarly, counterterrorism policy was criticized in other countries, such as post-Franco Spain. Its otherwise remarkable constitution of 1978 has been faulted by Antonio Vercher for its "substantial amendments . . . in terrorist cases" regarding the rules for detention and trial which are "very much like the antiterrorist decrees and laws that had been inherited from the Franco years" (1992, p. 283). Vercher documents notorious cases of victims tortured to death in democratic Spain, for "judicial control of prolonged detention in terrorist cases is far from effective" (1992, p. 229). It was in Spain that the González government was highly implicated in the GAL scandal. It regarded the creation of a shadowy death squad that crossed the border to kill 27 Spanish Basques exiled in southern France. The subsequent trials were a factor in the electoral defeat of the González government and nearly resulted in an indictment of the president himself (Woodward, 2001).

The perilous doctrine of pre-emption, espoused by the administration of president George W. Bush, would be unthinkable in a nuclear world if not for the rationale provided by counterterrorism. Actually, it is not as innovative as it might seem, since the American military raids on Libya under

the Reagan administration certainly qualify, as would Clinton's missile attacks on Somalia and Afghanistan after the African embassy bombings. Yet Bush extended the doctrine from being an isolated "retaliatory act or warning" to justify a conventional war of invasion and occupation of whole countries. Never mind that an entire war is premised upon faulty intelligence buttressed by counterterrorism's rhetorical ploys, such as that of equating Saddam Hussein with Hitler. There is nothing like counterterrorism to rekindle the age-old mutual dependence between demonizing the enemy while claiming exemption from legal accountability for oneself. Such logic was captured perfectly by the Israeli writer Amos Oz when he replied to Begin's statement that destroying Arafat's headquarters in Beirut made him feel as if he had sent the Israeli defense forces to Berlin to eliminate Hitler in his bunker: "Hitler is already dead, my dear Prime Minister . . . Again and again, Mr. Begin, you reveal to the public eye a strange urge to resuscitate Hitler in order to kill him every day anew in the guise of terrorists" (cited in Margalit, 1994, p. 10).

There is a long list of politicians devoured by the terrorist monster they helped create. From Presidents Carter to Reagan to George Bush father and son, from Giscard d'Estaing to Chirac, from Oliver North to William Casey, from Felipe González to José María Aznar terrorism has come back to haunt them. Both Tony Blair and George W. Bush struggled to survive the consequences of their policies. The politics of counterterrorism deceives nobody more than its proponents.

COUNTERTERRORISM AS SELF-FULFILLING PROPHECY

Counterterrorist thinking bears a peculiar relation to temporality, as threats are largely based on the inevitability of waiting. Actual historical temporality becomes subservient to the feared future. If there are no terrorism attacks, the counterterrorist can claim success in preventing them; but if an attack does occur, then the counterterrorist can claim that "I told you so." At this point terrorism foretold becomes prophecy fulfilled. Such imperviousness to error in actual historical time points to a time warp at the very heart of counterterrorist mythology. The result of this passive temporality regarding events we can do nothing to prevent creates a fateful mind-set in which "terrorism" is seemingly closer to nature than society and politics. At that point there is scarcely any point in looking into the intellectual premises or subjective motivations that guide terrorist actions. The great political victory of the suicide bombers is that they imposed on American politics their own temporality of unending waiting and a culture grounded in the oracular knowledge of secret intelligence. Our response has been declaration of the interminable War on Terror. They waved their cape and we blindly charged!

The self-fulfilling prophecy is, in the beginning, a false definition of the situation evoking a new behavior which makes the original false conception come true. This specious validity of the self-fulfilling prophecy perpetuates a reign of error. For the prophet will cite the actual course of events as proof that he was right from the very beginning . . . Such are the perversities of social logic (Merton, 1968, p. 477).

There was no al-Qaeda in Iraq before the invasion—but there certainly was after it. Anti-American radical Islamists could never afford to have antiaircraft missiles—until the CIA provided Stinger missiles to Afghan rebels battling the Soviets in the middle 1980s. Similarly, over 40 countries are currently developing drone technology to be used as military robots, with the likelihood that in a not so distant future they might fall into the hands of terrorists. Such self-fulfilling prophecy of counterterrorist drones being used by terrorists themselves, we are told, "is not far away" (Caryl, 2011, p. 58).

A central dimension of terrorism, and one that is crucial to understanding its self-fulfilling capacity has to do with threats and the perceptions and reactions they provoke. A threat plays with the future, and we can never know whether its issuer is serious, or just playing with our minds. He might even change his. The Unabomber brought the traffic in California airports to a halt by simply sending a letter to a newspaper with the threat of bringing down an airliner, while mailing another to a different newspaper admitting that the threat was a "prank."

The actual reality of the threat might be nothing but play—a *zero* that can yet have deadly serious consequences. Counterterrorism is a prime example of what Merton labeled "the Thomas theorem:" "If men define situations as real, they are real in their consequences" (1968, p. 475). Once the situation is defined as one of inevitable terrorism and endless waiting, what *could* happen weighs as much as what actually *does*. Once a threat, whose full intent and probability are ultimately unknowable, is taken seriously, that new reality requires that we must react. In a very real sense, then, our option not to overreact becomes severely limited. In this fashion, "terrorism" is a prime catalyst for confusing various semantic levels of linguistic, ritual and military actions.

Anthropologists have examined phenomena such as divination, which manipulates the axis of time in a cultural context of magic and witchcraft. They have compared pre-modern mystical notions of causation and temporality to our own modern rational ones. The central premise of counterterrorism thinking is the oft-repeated formula that "it is not if, but when." The hypotheticals are premised with a conditional "if"—"if A, then B." The premise that characterizes basic counterterrorist knowledge about the next impending attack is that it will happen. In a mind-set that parallels Azande witchcraft, the counterterrorist axiom of "not if" rules out mere hypotheses (Winch, 1977). The revelations are thus "unfulfilled hypotheticals" that will become real over time. Counterterrorist projections are the equivalent of oracular certainties—the horror will happen no matter what. This leads in pragmatic terms to the fatalistic attitude of disregarding actual knowledge and avoiding responsibility for actual decisions—what does it really matter what we decide and do since it is going to happen anyway and is out of our hands? What matters, therefore, is that we sort of *divine* what the course of events will be.

The practical aspect of this temporality of waiting, whereby the certainty of the impending evil is beyond the hypothetical ("not if"), is that we need to act preemptively now against future disasters. The rationale behind nuclear deterrence was that developing armaments now, ready to strike at the push of a button, guaranteed that they would not be used in the future. Many commentators saw in such logic the quintessence of technological madness. But that was not enough. Since future nuclear attacks by terrorists are only a matter of time, we must wage war now preemptively—even in a nuclear fashion—thus breaking with the historic assumption that nuclear arsenals were for deterrence rather than actual deployment. Thus the formula of "not if, but when" becomes a self-fulfilling prophecy. The counterterrorist thinking makes it an imperative that the war must start now—against Saddam Hussein, against al-Qaeda, against Iran, against all potential terrorists.

What happens to the axis of time in the expectations of robotic technology? Robots will have to react in such speed, we are told, that in the decision cycle, reduced from minutes to microseconds, "As the loop gets shorter and shorter, there won't be any time in it for humans" (cited in Singer, 2009, p. 64). It is no longer the "perversion of temporality" in the waiting for terror, but the very elimination of human time—the perfect fantasy whereby humans are left out of a war in which, not only they will not die, but, by reducing time to the category of fiction, they will not have to make the tough decisions and live with the burden of their consequences.

The fact that robotic technologies created to combat terrorism now reinforce self-generating qualities to a frightening degree can be illustrated with the best-known case of terrorism before 9/11: the Pan Am flight 103 devastated over Lockerbie, Scotland, in December 1988, killing the 270 passengers aboard. What the public largely ignored was that this event was preceded in July of that year by the downing of an Iranian airliner with 290 people on board in the Persian Gulf by the U.S.S. *Vincennes*. That was the result of the cruiser being equipped with an Aegis radar system that registered the civilian plane as "Assumed Enemy." The Iranian jet was on a consistent course and broadcasting a civilian radar and radio signal, but the automated Aegis had been designed for dealing with Soviet aircraft and thus the airliner appeared on its computer screen to be an Iranian F-14 fighter. Hard data were telling the crew that it was not a military aircraft, but the computer insisted that it was. What mere mortal could challenge the perfect robotic knowledge of Aegis? And because the *Vincennes* was a Robo-cruiser, the crew could fire the missile without seeking further permission from higher authority. In short, "the computer was trusted even more than any human captain's independent judgment on whether to shoot or not" (Singer, 2009, p. 125). Five months after the tragedy provoked by the *Vincennes* Pan Am 103 was downed and prominent experts saw it as a case of revenge or "blood feuding." It was all a classical case of counterterrorism's spiraling capacity to elicit ever more violence.

DRONES AS THE LATEST SELF-FULFILLING PROPHECY

The latest in counterterrorism, "the only game in town" according to Defense Secretary Leon Panetta, is the killing with drones of hundreds or thousands of Pakistanis, Afghans, and other nationals. It is almost impossible to determine their precise numbers and just how many were civilians—and that is just fine for the overseers of the State of Exception. Maintaining secrecy and the fog of war are very much part of their modus operandi. The drone attacks remain "covert" operations whose very existence must remain secret.

Nevertheless, according to the Conflict Monitoring Center, a private organization that collects Pakistani and foreign news reports, by April of 2012, at least 2717 people been killed in that country by drones, including 175 children. Its Webpage estimates that, of the 609 killed in 2011, only four were al-Qaeda leaders. Of the close to 3,000 people killed, the CIA knows the names of 125 and considers 35 of them as "high value targets" (Ahmad, 2011, June 13). Even a "counterterrorist guru" such as David Kilcullen, author of the book *The Accidental Guerrilla*, took seriously the estimate that until 2009 the ratio of civilians killed for each militant was 50 to one—that is, 98 percent of drone casualties were civilian (Kilcullen & Exum, 2009). This is not a view shared by President Obama, which was expressed in *The New York Times* on February 6, 2012, stating, "actually, drones have not caused a huge number of civilian casualties. For the most part they have been very precise precision strikes against Al Qaeda and their affiliates."

So somewhere in the Nevada desert to the north of Las Vegas a young man, scarcely more than a kid, sits before a computer screen that is but an extension of the virtual reality of the game-playing of his youth—and presses a button that eliminates a target half a world away. He gets in his car and maybe stops to pick up a pizza on his way home to eat while watching the Dodgers' game. Such is the guise of the modern warrior, the avenger in the service of civilization. He probably does not read *Harper's Magazine* so he is oblivious to the wrenching testimony given to the British human rights organization Reprieve by four members of the families of certain Pakistani villagers killed in Datta Khel in the region of North Waziristan

in a drone attack on March 17, 2011. The victims were attending a *jirga* or meeting of tribal elders. One witness stated,

The men who died in this strike were our leaders; the ones we turned to for all forms of support. We always knew that drone strikes were wrong, that they encroached on Pakistan's sovereign territory. We knew that innocent civilians had been killed. However, we did not realize how callous and cruel it could be. The community is now plagued with fear. The tribal elders are afraid to gather together in jirgas, as had been our custom for more than a century. The mothers and wives plead with the men not to congregate together. They do not want to lose anymore of their husbands, sons, brothers, and nephews. People in the same family now sleep apart because they do not want their togetherness to be viewed suspiciously through the eye of the drone. They do not want to become the next target (Harper's Magazine, 2012, p. 18).

What are the practical results of the drone campaign? The number of terrorist attacks in Pakistan has risen sharply and in response to a wave of anti-Americanism. Pakistanis "overwhelmingly believe that most of those who die in the [drone] attacks are civilians" (Caryl, 2011, September 29, p. 56). One concrete instance of such linkage was provided by the testimony of Faisal Shahzad, the Pakistani-American known for his failed bombing attempt in Times Square in May 2010. He declared at his trial that, "I'm avenging the attack" for the "drones [that] kill women, children. . .everybody. . .I am part of the answer" (cited in Hari, 2010). Add to this the stark fact that the C.I.A. drone strikes set a precedent for the nearly 50 other nations, including Pakistan and Iran, which already possess the same unmanned technology.

Counterterrorists know all of this. Yet why is it that these very drones, that help increase terrorist insurgency "exponentially," are still "the only game in town?" In short, counterterrorism knows that its tactics clearly elicit self-fulfilling feedback, and yet there seems to be no other logical response to terrorists. Such a dilemma—if we do nothing, terrorism will flourish; if we do something it will increase even more—shows dramatically the current impasse of counterterrorist knowledge and practice.

CONCLUSION

And what are the costs? The Cold War over, during the last decade the U.S. Defense budget almost doubled. A new enemy, apparently more dangerous than the Soviet Union, has surfaced: the Terrorist. According to the Dana Priest and William Arkin book *Top Secret America*, the vast new security bureaucracy created after 9/11 encompasses some 1,200 government organizations and 1,900 private companies working at over 17,000 locations across the country. In the Washington D.C. area alone, it occupies the equivalent of nearly three Pentagons or 22 U.S. Capitol buildings. Americans with top-secret clearances now number over 850,000; there are more than 250,000 private contractors working on top-secret programs (i.e., counterterrorism). The Pentagon Defense Intelligence agency grew from 7,500 people in 2002 to 16,500 in 2010. By that latter year The Department of Homeland Security had a workforce of no fewer than 230,000.

There is more fear of al-Qaeda as a threat than the Soviet superpower of the Cold War. One estimate by the economist Stiglitz places the total bill of the War on Terror at between $3 and $4 trillion. It is "asymmetric warfare" in which "the United States has so far spent $1.4 million *per dollar of AQ* [al-Qaeda] *investment in the attacks* on the response" (Kilcullen, 2009, p. 274, *emphasis in original*). Stated differently, for years the United States has expended more money *per hour* in Iraq than the entire total of al-Qaeda's financial resources (Singer, 2009).

However, the financial costs are but one (admittedly dire) aspect of our disastrous counterterrorism campaign. There is the state of exception imposed on American politics, evidence of which is there for anyone to see: Guantánamo, indefinite detention, rendition, torture, extra-judicial killings by drones. We have a domestic intelligence network that collects information about tens of thousands of U.S. citizens, involving an apparatus of close to 4,000 federal, state and local organizations. These are staples of the daily news of current politics, officially sanctioned and normalized and broadly accepted by the general public. And yet these are borderline realities at the intersection of law and politics; in the past clearly illegal and deemed anathema, now official policy. The State of Exception means that law-breaking can be approved by the highest officials and go unpunished. Another upshot is that regular crimes are now frequently suspected by law enforcement and intelligence agencies to be possibly linked to terrorism.

To what greater success could al-Qaeda have aspired than to be considered by the United States, and its vast security forces, as a bigger threat than the Soviet superpower at the height of the Cold War? What greater wounds could it have inflicted on its nemesis than to force upon America and its allies a War on Terror that drains national treasuries of trillions of dollars while eroding the very principles of privacy and freedom that underpin any democratic society?

In 1996, we concluded our "Terror and Taboo" book with the following assessment:

In this book we have argued that the American quest for "terrorism" has had a lot to do with a Beckettian theater of the absurd as well as with the political manipulations of collective fantasies of nuclearism and savagery. It doesn't take an uncommon sagacity to perceive that the journalistic and academic fashionings of the "thing" itself are flawed and self deceptive. But, even if we have concentrated on showing how the discursive basis of the culture of terrorism, there is a point in which the thing itself (whether the created category is "race" or "ethnicity" or "taboo"), no matter how reified or distorted or banal, becomes a structural reality and a historical force. It appears that "terrorism" is fast becoming a dominant medium through which American society and domestic politics need to be interpreted. We may laugh at an American public overwhelmingly obsessed with terrorism during the 1980s—a time when little terrorism actually transpired. Yet the rhetorical forces and foreign policy interests that prompted it in the first place are not becoming a thing of the past. Terrorism is now becoming a functional reality of American politics, an autonomous prime mover of enormous consequences affecting na-tional policy and legislation. This is no longer mere phantasmagoria but rather an irreducible dimension of a political ideology that profoundly affects the material reality of American society. Terrorism has been "naturalized" into a constant risk that is omnipresent out there, a sort of chaotic principle always ready to strike and create havoc, and against which society must now marshal all its resources in an unending struggle. Now that it has become a prime raison d'etat, its perpetuation seems guaranteed (Zulaika & Douglass, 1996, p. 238).

Those words were written before 9/11, before the Afghan and Iraq wars, and before the expenditure of the trillions of dollars on the War on Terror that has arguably contributed mightily to the world's current economic crisis!

REFERENCES

Aaronson, T. (2011, September/October). The informants. *Mother Jones*. Retrieved July 3, 2013, from http://www.motherjones.com/politics/2011/08/fbi-terrorist-informants

Agamben, G. (1998). *Homo sacer: Sovereign power and bare life*. Stanford, CA: Stanford University Press.

Ahmad, M. I. (2011, June 13). The magical realism of body counts. *al-Jazeera*. Retrieved July 3, 2013, from http://www.aljazeera.com/indepth/opinion/2011/06/2011613931606455.html

Caryl, C. (2011, September 29). Predators and robots at war. *The New York Review of Books*. Retrieved July 3, 2013, from http://www.nybooks.com/articles/archives/2011/sep/29/predators-and-robots-war/?pagination=false

Cassesse, A. (1989). *Terror, politics, and the law: The Achille Lauro affair*. Princeton, NJ: Princeton University Books.

Dempsey, J. X., & Cole, D. (2002). *Terrorism and the constitution: Sacrificing civil liberties in the name of national security*. New York: New Press.

Falk, R. (1988). *Revolutionaries and functionaries*. New York: E. P. Dutton.

Friedman, R. (1995, March 27). The CIA's Jihad. *JewishComment.com*. Retrieved July 3, 2013, from http://www.jewishcomment.com/cgibin/news.cgi?id=11&command=shownews&newsid=294

Gasser, H.-P. (1987). An appeal for ratification by the United States. *The American Journal of International Law*, *81*(4), 912–925. doi:10.2307/2203418

Hari, J. (2010, October 15). Obama's escalating robot war in Pakistan is making a terror attack more likely. *The Huffington Post*. Retrieved July 3, 2013, from http://www.huffingtonpost.com/johann-hari/obamas-escalating-robot-w_b_763578.html

Harper's Magazine. (2012, June). *Eye of the drone*. Retrieved August 7, 2013, from http://archive.harpers.org/2012/06/pdf/HarpersMagazine-2012-06-0083923.pdf?AWSAccessKeyId=AKIAJXATU3VRJAAA66RA&Expires=1376411645&Signature=mfYaEt%2BLhHMwwOm%2FGSJXkNdnMdo%3D

Jenkins, B., & Wright, R. (1991). Why hostage taking is so popular with terrorists. In B. Schechterman & M. W. Slann (Eds.), Violence and terrorism, (pp. 97-128). Guilford, CT: Dushkin Publishing Group.

Kilcullen, D. (2009). *The accidental guerrilla: Fighting small wars in the midst of a big one*. Oxford, UK: Oxford University Press.

Kilcullen, D., & Exum, A. M. (2009, May 16). Death from above, outrage from below. *The New York Times*. Retrieved July 3, 2013, from http://www.nytimes.com/2009/05/17/opinion/17exum.html?pagewanted=all&_r=0

Margalit, A. (1994, February 17). The uses of the Holocaust. *The New York Review of Books*. Retrieved July 3, 2013, from http://www.nybooks.com/articles/archives/1994/feb/17/the-uses-of-the-holocaust/?pagination=false

Merton, R. K. (1968). *Social theory and social structure*. New York: Free Press.

Miller, J., & Stone, M. (2002). *The cell: Inside the 9/11 plot and why the FBI and CIA failed to stop it*. New York: Hyperion. doi:10.3410/f

Priest, D., & Arkin, W. M. (2011). *Top secret America: The rise of the new American security state*. New York: Back Bay Books.

Roberts, A. (1989). Ethics, terrorism, and counter terrorism. *Terrorism and Political Violence*, *1*(1), 48–69. doi:10.1080/09546558908427013

Sick, G. (1985). *All fall down: America's tragic encounter with Iran*. New York: Random House.

Singer, P. W. (2009). *Wired for war: The robotics revolution and conflict in the 21ˢᵗ century*. New York: Penguin Books.

Vercher, A. (1992). *Terrorism in Europe: An international comparative legal analysis*. Oxford, UK: Oxford University Press.

Winch, P. (1977). Understanding a primitive society. In B. R. Wilson (Ed.), *Rationality* (pp. 78–111). Oxford, UK: Basil Blackwell.

Woodward, P. (2001). *Dirty war, clean hands: ETA, the GAL and Spanish democracy*. Cork, Ireland: Cork University Press.

Zulaika, J., & Douglass, W. A. (1996). *Terror and taboo: The follies, fables and faces of terrorism*. New York: Routledge.

KEY TERMS AND DEFINITIONS

Globalization: A worldwide process of integration and interaction of various aspects of different cultures through economic and cultural activities facilitated by telecommunications and new media.

Osama bin Laden: The founder of al-Qaeda, a Sunni militant organization that claimed responsibility for the attacks on the United States on September 11, 2001.

Power Relations: The ways in which various groups of differing power relate to one another.

State Authority: Power exercised by the state.

State Defense: Protection of a nation facilitated by the state.

The Patriot Act: A ten-letter acronym (USA PATRIOT) that stands for **U**niting and **S**trengthening **A**merica by **P**roviding **A**ppropriate **T**ools **R**equired to **I**ntercept and **O**bstruct **T**errorism Act of 2001.

War on Terror: A term applied to an international military campaign initiated by the United States that started after 9/11.

ENDNOTES

[1.] The three exceptions were Najibulla Zazi who attempted to bomb the New York City subway in September 2009, Hesham Mohamed Hadayet, who fired a gun at the Los Angeles airport's El-Al ticket counter, and Times Square failed bomber Faisal Shahzad.

Chapter 17
Questioning Media Responsibility during Terrorism

Mahmoud Eid
University of Ottawa, Canada

ABSTRACT

The media's dual role during times of terrorism can be as useful as the most effective security and political counterterrorism measures and can be as harmful as exacerbating terrorist events to the worst humanitarian disasters. Media decision-making processes, therefore, are integral to achieving more desired outcomes. This chapter questions the effectiveness of media performance during times of terrorism through the examination of their decision-making processes in terms of rationality and responsibility. The numerous media decisions that are usually made under severe stress during times of terrorism require adherence to both ethical standards and rational thinking. Strategic and goal-directed decision-making that is based on rational choice approach and game theory can help enhance the quality of media decisions. Ethical and socially responsible media performance is fundamental for effective communication. Interweaved, responsible and rational media decision-making are integral to the effectiveness of media decision-making during times of terrorism towards achieving more desired outcomes.

INTRODUCTION

In any terrorist attack, the media may cover what happens, the actors involved, whether anything could have been done to prevent the event, and the people or institutions held accountable, to the extent that "[p]olitical leaders, government officials and first responders would find themselves under siege by the media" (Bergin & Khosa, 2007, p. 1). Media reactions to terrorist acts are not less influential than political counterterrorism measures in de-escalating threats to public safety.

However, the media's role during the terrorist events can be considered a double-edged sword through which the terrorist event may be contained or exacerbated into more violence and destruction. In fact, "[w]hat the news media do cover may well contribute to the problem of political violence rather than to its decrease" (Held, 1997, p. 195). The media can either help overcome the state of uncertainty, misunderstanding, and miscalculation that prevail in a terrorist event or provoke violence. For example, while "[c]lear, rapid and accurate information provided by the media can

DOI: 10.4018/978-1-4666-5776-2.ch017

save lives by contributing to sensible responses in telling people what to do and what not to do," inaccurate coverage could "have the reverse effect" (Bergin & Khosa, 2007, p. 3).

Several theorists have investigated decision-making performances under conditions of stress or uncertainty (e.g., Eid & Fyfe, 2009; Eilon, 1979; Nicholson, 1997; Snyder & Diesing, 1977; Williams, 1976). However, there are significant gaps in research on effective decision-making regarding counterterrorism (e.g., George, 2003; Lebow, 1987) and its impact on the public (Lee & Lemyre, 2009). The research on terrorism tends to study immediate issues: "a great deal about the manifest symptoms of terrorism without ever really delving directly into the roots of the problem" (Silke, 2004, p. 210). This problem is amplified with the global reach a terrorist can achieve when the roots and motivations of terrorism include international goals. Terrorism becomes transnational when "an incident in one country involves perpetrators, victims, targets, institutions, governments, or citizens of another country" (Enders & Sandler, 2004, p. 121) and when "terrorist groups either want to achieve international goals, such as fighting 'American imperialism' all over the world, or are groups that see a greater chance of attaining their national goals by moving beyond their own frontiers" (Frey, 2004, p. 6). Therefore, terrorist threats require effective responses. This can be achieved through effective decision-making that is both ethical and rational (Eid, 2008a). This chapter questions the effectiveness of media performance during times of terrorism through the examination of their decision-making processes in terms of rationality and responsibility.

MEDIA AND COUNTERTERRORISM DECISION-MAKING

Communication, in general, is a decision-making process (Eid, 2008a). In any conflict situation, including terrorist attacks, communication can help define the structure of a conflict so that adversaries can perceive accurately the relative values of the interests at stake when making a decision: "Communication helps to establish the 'rules' of the game in a confrontation, so that the adversaries share common assumptions about the kinds of actions that are legitimate and those that are tacitly, if not formally, prohibited . . . Communication may minimize the likelihood of miscalculation" (Williams, 1976, p. 182).

The media, in particular, play fundamental role in the decision-making process by communicating messages and information about/to the involved actors (terrorists, policymakers, and publics). The media decision-making during terrorist events occurs under conditions of high tension and severe stress, which may negatively affect the functioning of the media and consequently their decisions. Therefore, it is important to look into these decisions and search for ways to enhance the decision-making process.

Journalistic decisions, for example, by writers, presenters, editors, and producers shape news-writing and determine the nature of the final product. Personnel are faced with various choices at various junctures of news production and make numerous decisions in this process (e.g., Dennis & Ismach, 1981; Zinsser, 1998). These decisions are often made under the constraints of time and space, and also economic and political considerations (Zelizer & Allan, 2011), and they vary with circumstances (Wittebols, 1991).

Primarily, knowing what the decision is helps to introduce the process of decision-making as a whole. A decision is "a choice of action—of what to do or not do" (Baron, 2000, p. 6). While many scholars have defined the term "decision," the clearest definition in relation to the process of decision-making is Ofstad's. "To say that a person has made a decision may mean (1) that he has started a series of behavioral reactions in favor of something, or it may mean (2) that he has made up his mind to do a certain action, which he has no doubt that he ought to do. But perhaps the most common use of the term is this: 'to make a decision' means (3) to make a judgment regarding what one ought to do in a certain situation after having deliberated on some alternative courses of action" (Ofstad, cited in Eilon, 1979, pp. 135-136).

The fundamental elements of Ofstad's definition demonstrate that the decision-maker has several options from which to choose and that choice includes a comparison between those options and the evaluation of their outcomes. This explanation provides a sense of the process (including resolution and selection criteria) that the decision-maker goes through to reach a decision.

The media coverage of terrorist events involves a series of decision-making processes. Analysis of some media guidelines[1] for covering acts of terrorism reveal major principles and cautions as most frequently stated; all of them require intensive decision-making (Eid, 2008a). The media guidelines suggest that during a terrorist event, news personnel should do the following:

- Assign experienced staff members to the story.
- Approach the story with care and restraint.
- Report demands of the terrorist(s) after paraphrasing them, instead of presenting them directly.
- Cover the event in a thoughtful and conscientious manner.
- Maintain communication with authorities to seek guidance.
- Consult officials before making publishing decisions.
- Consider recommendations carefully and obey instructions by authorities.
- Avoid interfering in the duties of authorities.
- Do nothing to jeopardize lives.
- Avoid sensationalizing beyond the innate sensation of the story itself.
- Avoid providing a platform for the terrorist propaganda.

- Avoid using inflammatory catchwords or phrases, or reporting rumors. (Eid, 2008a, pp. 23-24)

To take the above important guidelines and cautions into consideration in the process of news-writing about acts of terrorism, it is inevitable to go through a series of decision-making processes. As Dennis and Ismach (1981) argue, news-writing involves decision-making as writers have to make decisions as they produce content. News-writing involves making compromises between one mode of expression and another and deciding which facts go into a story and which ones do not. Dennis and Ismach claim that "the writer, like it or not, becomes a ruthless decision maker, sometimes discarding the very items that seemed essential only a few hours before and choosing the form and style that will most effectively present the information in the space allowed" (1981, p. 109). In writing a news story, a writer goes generally through seven certain stages, each of which is full of decisions that must be made: choosing a subject, planning, news gathering, prewriting, writing, rewriting and polishing, and getting feedback. Decisions, either simple or complex; either made by the writer, news sources, or editors, help shape news-writing and determine what the final product of the reportorial process will look like. "There are *choices* [i.e., decisions] to be made. Think about it: The reporter has more information than she [or he] can use in the story; she [or he] must discard part of it. Some aspects of the remaining information will seem more important and more compelling than others, and thus deserve more emphasis. There are decisions [also] to be made about organizing the story—deciding what sequence the information should follow. And there are questions about rhetoric—the art of writing the story—such as deciding between and among particular words, phrases and sentences. Matters of style must be decided: Should the story be written in terse, spare language, should it be described in more detail? Should information from the meeting take the form of paraphrases or quotations? What combination of words and images will make the most compelling lead or first paragraph?" (Dennis & Ismach, 1981, p. 107).

RATIONAL DECISION-MAKING

It is significant to highlight William Zinsser's (1998) emphasis on thinking before writing. Emphasizing writing decisions as an important part of the writing process, Zinsser demonstrates the many decisions a writer, in general, should make: "This has been a book about decisions—the countless successive decisions that go into every act of writing. Some of the decisions are big ('What should I write about?') and some are as small as the smallest word. But all of them are important . . . big decisions: [such as] matters of shape, structure, compression, focus and intention . . . little decisions [such as]: the hundreds of choices that go into organizing a long article. . . . The hardest decision about any article is how to begin it. The lead must grab the reader with a provocative idea and continue with each paragraph to hold him or her in a tight grip, gradually adding information . . . No less important than decisions about structure are decisions about individual words. . . . [Also a] crucial decision about a piece of writing is where to end it . . . [In sum,] . . . [decide] what you want to do. Then decide to do it. Then do it" (Zinsser, 1998, pp. 265, 266, 270, 283, 285).

As human beings make decisions every day, which may often be difficult or complex, there is an essential need for assistance in the decision-making process, especially in cases of conflicts. Conflict decisions "should be made on the basis of tested knowledge rather than of intuitive guesses" (Nicholson, 1970, p. 162). Indeed, decision theory provides this assistance for the real-life decision-making process. Wayne Lee (1971) clarifies the meaning of *rationality* used in decision theory that a rational person is one who, when confronted with a decision situation, makes the choice (deci-

sion) that is best for him/her. This best decision is called a *rational* or *optimal* decision.

A major approach to the study of conflicts, including terrorist events, in relation to decision-making is the *rational choice approach*. It shares the common assumption that decision-makers are *rational*. Rational choice theory (e.g., Caplan, 2006; Lupia, Mccubbins & Popkin, 2000; Snyder & Diesing, 1977) "can help clarify and discipline the study of terrorism" (Anderton & Carter, 2005, p. 275). Rational decision-making under conflict, where the actions of other calculating actors affect the outcome, is different from decision-making where the outcome depends on some inanimate feature of the situation, such as the weather. In conflict, decision-making involves *strategic decision making* where what actor A does affects actor B, whose actions similarly affect actor A (Nicholson, 1997).

The terms "mass-mediated terrorism" (Nacos, 2007) and "theater of terror" (Weimann & Winn, 1994) highlight the media's central, but dual role during terrorism—the media are "instruments of terrorism," "agents in the spread of terroristic acts," and "tools for manipulation by both terrorists and their adversaries" (Schmid & Jongman, 2008, p. 111). Traditional and new media have been playing key roles in times of terrorism: they "are not simply external actors passively bringing the news of terrorist incidents to global audiences but are increasingly seen as active agents in the actual conceptualization of terrorist events" (Freedman & Thussu, 2012, p. 10). On the other hand, "terrorists themselves also feel 'used' by the media which pick up their action, but offer no guarantee of transmitting their message" (Schmid, 1989, p. 559). Terrorism is neither crazed, random, nor capricious; rather, terrorist attacks are strategic, premeditated, and carefully planned (e.g., Fromkin, 1975; Hoffman, 2006; Whittaker, 2007); therefore, terrorists are described as rational in beliefs and behavior (e.g., Taillon, 2002; Whittaker, 2004).

Rationality means the efficient pursuit of consistent goals (Nicholson, 1996). Terrorists' media-related goals (including publicity, favorable understanding of their cause, legitimacy and identity, and destabilizing the enemy) conflict with those of policymakers (such as publicity, criminality of act, and denying terrorists a platform (e.g., Abrahms, 2012; Combs, 2013). The media's own goals (including getting a scoop, dramatic presentation of news, protection of rights, and personal security) also conflict with goals of terrorists and even of policymakers—hence, the media are a double-edged sword in a conflict that requires careful decision-making in the interests of public safety.

This leads directly to the search for useful tools to help media decision-makers achieve their goals successfully. In light of the sophisticated process of news-writing, the stress under which media decision-makers work, and the speed of events that require *rational* decisions, it is very essential for media decision-makers to have helpful tools, specifically mathematics, and still more specifically game theory, in times of terrorism, that could help them understand what must be done to achieve their sought goals.[2]

There is a great deal of work by major scholars and philosophers who have connected mathematics to knowledge and social sciences in general and communication in particular. Michel Foucault, when discussing two fields of sciences—*a priori* sciences and *a posteriori* sciences—explains that the field of *a priori* sciences is "pure formal sciences, deductive sciences based on logic and mathematics" (1994, p. 246). To illustrate communication as a social science, Stephen Littlejohn explains that communication "involves understanding how people behave in creating, exchanging, and interpreting messages. Consequently, communication inquiry combines both scientific and humanistic methods" (2002, p. 11).

Martin Shubik (1954) argues that without mathematics, researchers analyzing a social phenomenon or problem, which involves multiple factors, could not carry out the analysis without facing substantial difficulty since verbal discussion of the phenomenon would become so complex as to be almost unmanageable. But once the problem is mathematically formulated, little trouble is encountered in re-computing for the adjusted conditions. The analysis of social problems involving multiple factors has to rely on mathematics (Foucault, 1994) because their verbal complexity is unmanageable (Shubik, 1954).

The use of game theory—which is a branch of pure mathematics—in the social sciences is mainly to provide researchers with a tool for examining and formalizing the concepts of information and communication (Shubik, 1954). To study and understand social situations, we need game theory to explain how individuals' decisions are interrelated and how those decisions result in outcomes (Morrow, 1994). Game theory helps understand social situations that involve interactions of individuals, as it explains how their decisions are interrelated and how they result in outcomes; it can be a source of methods that apply to various interactive situations (e.g., Flanagan, 1998; Heap & Varoufakis, 1995; Morrow, 1994; Shubik, 1954).

While there are many important uses for game theory, the most important are the applications to severe stress situations (i.e., conflicts, crises, disasters, and acts of terrorism).[3] The use of game theory as a method in conflict analysis has opened new ways of moving towards effective resolutions. With application on one tactic of terrorism (cyber-terrorism), for instance, the tactics of "the battle between computer security experts and cyberterrorists can be explained through game theory" (Matusitz, 2009, p. 273). Fundamentally, game theory is prescriptive: it recommends a rational[4] course of action and then describes the consequences of such conduct, telling us what would happen if the recommended behavior rules were followed (Nicholson, 1970).

Game theory rests on some basic assumptions[5] regarding the way the interests of different individuals may be related to each other, which can be analyzed mathematically: 1) games always involve two or more players, each with an opportunity to choose between alternatives; 2) each available alternative is fully known to each player; 3) all possible outcomes that might occur to any player may be expressed in terms of numerical measures of utility; and 4) each player will make those choices that will provide the maximum expected utility (Schellenberg, 1996).

Rational behavior, a basic assumption in game theory, can mean many things in our everyday language including reasonable, thoughtful, wise, just, or sane behavior or action. However, for game theory scholars, rational behavior has a more focused and centered meaning than the broad or common meanings of the term rationality. Rational behavior in game theory means "choosing the best means to gain a predetermined set of ends. . . . [It] is goal directed; actors are trying to create more desired outcomes rather than less desired outcomes" (Morrow, 1994, p. 17). Decisions are made "to achieve goals, and they are based on beliefs about what actions will achieve the goals" (Baron, 2000, p. 6). Beliefs, in game theory, play a very important role in finding solutions for actors. Reasonable beliefs have to be consistent with the way the game is played (Aliprantis & Chakrabarti, 2000). The focus in game theory is on how individuals' attempts to achieve their goals are constrained by one another's actions and the structure of the game (Morrow, 1994). So, *rational* behavior is *goal-directed* towards more desired outcomes rather than less desired outcomes.

Communication plays a central role in game theory in order for players to reach desired outcomes. No cooperation can be formed between two players if there is no communication, leading to negative outcomes for both players, as in the Prisoners' Dilemma Game. However, if they can communicate and engage in cooperative behavior, the outcome would be quite different, as in the Communication Game (Eid, 2008a), where a modified prisoners' dilemma game illustrates how Canada and the Arab World, during the 2003 War on Iraq, communicated through the media and diplomacy to play a more effective role during the crisis than that which had been imposed on them due to their relations to the main adversaries (United States and Iraq, respectively).

RESPONSIBLE DECISION-MAKING

Ethics and responsibility (e.g., Day, 2006; Leslie, 2000) are fundamental to the effective performance of the media: "communication cannot be effective without being ethical and socially responsible" (Wright, 1996, p. 521). Ethical journalism, for example, requires adherence to basic principles that include truth telling, accuracy, fairness, balance, verification, and maintaining context (e.g., Eid, 2008a; Elliott, 2003; Gordon, 1999; Harris & Spark, 1997; Hindman, 1997; Kittross, 1999; Kovach & Rosenstiel, 2001).

Given the important role of the media in society, their ethical performance is vital—particularly in times of terrorism. Journalism, as in most other professions, has codes of ethics to guide personnel. They attempt to instill a moral balance in the interests of the media, the public, and policymakers (Gordon, 1999), and require careful decision-making (Eid, 2008a). Responsibility is "the core theme and larger umbrella of most . . . codes of ethics under which fall most other principles and values of journalistic conduct;" specifically, responsibility towards the public "exceeds any other responsibility, particularly towards employers and authorities" (Eid, 2008a, p. 130).

There are numerous responsibilities of the media when covering political violence in general and terrorism in particular. These responsibilities include, among many others, the dilemmas of labeling actors (whether to be called freedom fighters, retaliators, or terrorists) and choosing whether to cover or not (following officials' requests to avoid specific situations that favor terrorists' goals).

However, it is often difficult to find journalists who adhere to their institutional codes when facing severe stress situations. Critics have found the media's ethical performance sorely lacking (Held, 1997). After 9/11 the media "fell short on all three of the fundamental obligations that are stated in the 'Statement of Principles' of the American Society of Newspaper Editors," as they did not "inform the public fully about the most important events, developments, issues, and problems concerning counterterrorism;" "provide a forum for real debate;" or "scrutinize the selling of fear and the so-called war on terrorism" (Nacos, Bloch-Elkon, & Shapiro, 2011, p. 197). The safety of some members of the public who share ethnicity or a religion with terrorist groups is even jeopardized by stereotypical media portrayals (e.g., Bramadat & Seljak, 2005; Bullock & Jafri, 2000; Byng, 2010; Cañas, 2008; Dakroury, 2008; Eid, 2008b; Eid & Khan, 2011; Haque, 2010; Henry, 2010; Khan, 2000; Ruby, 2006; Steuter & Wills, 2009). Also, photojournalism sometimes lacks responsible conduct when covering terrorism: "newsmagazine photographs primarily serve established narrative themes within official discourse: that published photographs most often offer prompts for prevailing government versions of events and rarely contribute independent, new or unique visual information" (Griffin, 2004, p. 381).

Informing the public is the media's fundamental role; however, the issue here is not whether the media should cover terrorist events, but rather what kind of coverage should be devoted to terrorist events (Nacos, 2012). Political violence "is newsworthy and should not be ignored, though it should be covered truthfully rather than as a drama that can be exploited to increase ratings" (Held, 1997, p. 193).

Responsibility as an overriding ethical principle also requires that some of those ethical principles be rationally considered according to the rules of the game relevant to the terrorist event. A central characteristic of ethics is that "it is rational" (Markel, 2001, p. 31). This is a clear link between ethics and rationality. In the mathematical Truth Game, media decision-makers are motivated to tell the truth (i.e., following a major journalistic ethical principle) based on the calculation that rational thinking leads to achieving their desired goals and helps them practice their responsible role in society (Eid, 2008a).

CONCLUSION

It is in the public interest that journalistic choices are guided by ethics and rationality. The media's role during acts of terrorism involves a high level of responsibility. Media policies have to be "planned ahead, if those policies could hope to have effect" (Shpiro, 2002, p. 77). Choices in the ways messages are delivered and plans for audience reception are integral to a sound media strategy (e.g., Goodall, Trethewey, & Corman, 2008; Wilkinson, 1997).

Apart from being a strategy of violence (e.g., Bassiouni, 1981; Fromkin, 1975), terrorism is also "a form of communication that interacts with other forms of social and political communication, whether by nonstate actors or state actors" (Crelinsten, 2002, p. 77). Terrorist acts are designed to communicate political messages (e.g., Crenshaw, 1981; Hoffman, 2006; Rohner & Frey, 2007). Communication in these circumstances needs to be strategic and purposeful; it can be directive, intentional, and controlled, based on goals, plans, and understanding (Kellermann, 2009). Strategy[6] entails the development of plans of action with intentions to achieve specific outcomes (Zack, 1999). It is a continuous process, which requires consecutive decisions to ensure that the techniques and alternative courses of action are appropriately conceptualized for desired outcomes (Pettigrew, 1977).

Communication strategy is a logical response by individuals, groups, or organizations to unfamiliar circumstances (Moore, 2010). It entails three phases: preparation, mobilization, and implementation (Mei, Lee, & Al-Hawamdeh, 2004). Strategic communication is effective when situated in alignment with the communicator's overall goals to enhance his/her strategic positions (e.g., Argenti, Howell, & Beck, 2005; Brown, 2003; Gudykunst, 2005; Hallahan et al., 2007; Kumar, 1997; Najafbagy, 2008; Ray, 1999). Effective decision-making entails a maximization of logic and rationality (e.g., Adair, 2009; Eisenhardt & Zbaracki, 1992; Elbanna & Child, 2007). There-fore, it is important to ensure that "the practice of communication by individuals and institutions is instrumental and goal directed" (Mody & Lee, 2002, p. 381).

Media decision-making during times of ter-rorism can be effective by being both rational and responsible. The interweavement of ethics and rational thinking in the media decision-making process is inevitable to achieve more desired outcomes that are goal-directed. Challenges exist for media decision-makers to adhere to the ethical standards and guidelines. Sophisticated rational decisions are even more difficult to achieve. How-ever, each is fundamental to the effectiveness of the decision-making, especially during times of severe stress situations such as terrorism. Moreover, in the media coverage of terrorism, adherence to ethical principles and making rational decisions are not exclusive to one another; instead, they feed each other towards more desired outcomes.

REFERENCES

Abrahms, M. (2012). The political effectiveness of terrorism revisited. *Comparative Political Studies*, *45*(3), 366–393. doi:10.1177/0010414011433104

Adair, J. (2009). *Effective decision making: The essential guide to thinking for management success*. London, UK: Pan Books.

Alexander, Y., & Latter, R. (Eds.). (1990). Terrorism and the media: Dilemmas for government, journalists and the public. Washington, DC: Brassey's (US), Inc.

Aliprantis, C. D., & Chakrabarti, S. K. (2000). *Games and decision making*. New York: Oxford University Press.

Anderton, C. H., & Carter, J. R. (2005). On rational choice theory and the study of terrorism. *Defence and Peace Economics*, *16*(4), 275–282. doi:10.1080/1024269052000344864

Argenti, P. A., Howell, R. A., & Beck, K. A. (2005). The strategic communication imperative. *MIT Sloan Management Review*, *46*(3), 82–89.

Baron, J. (2000). *Thinking and deciding*. Cambridge, UK: Cambridge University Press.

Bassiouni, M. C. (1981). Terrorism, law enforcement, and the mass media: Perspectives, problems, proposals. *The Journal of Criminal Law & Criminology*, *72*(1), 1–51. doi:10.2307/1142904

Bergin, A., & Khosa, R. (2007). The Australian media and terrorism. *ASPI: Australian Strategic Policy Institute*, *11*, 1–8.

Bramadat, P., & Seljak, D. (Eds.). (2005). *Religion and ethnicity in Canada*. Toronto: Longman.

Brown, R. (2003). Spinning the war: Political communications, information operations and public diplomacy in the war on terrorism. In D. K. Thussu, & D. Freedman (Eds.), *War and the media: Reporting conflict 24/7* (pp. 87–100). London, UK: Sage. doi:10.4135/9781446215579.n7

Bullock, K. H., & Jafri, G. J. (2000). Media (mis) representations: Muslim women in the Canadian nation. *Canadian Woman Studies*, *20*(2), 35–40.

Byng, M. D. (2010). Symbolically Muslim: Media, hijab, and the West. *Critical Sociology*, *36*(1), 109–129. doi:10.1177/0896920509347143

Cañas, S. (2008). The little mosque on the prairie: Examining (multi)cultural spaces of nation and religion. *Cultural Dynamics*, *20*(3), 195–211. doi:10.1177/0921374008096309

Caplan, B. (2006). Terrorism: The relevance of the rational choice model. *Public Choice*, *128*(1-2), 91–107. doi:10.1007/s11127-006-9046-8

Combs, C. C. (2013). *Terrorism in the twenty-first century*. Boston: Pearson.

Crelinsten, R. D. (2002). Analysing terrorism and counter-terrorism: A communication model. *Terrorism and Political Violence*, *14*(2), 77–122. doi:10.1080/714005618

Crenshaw, M. (1981). The causes of terrorism. *Comparative Politics*, *13*(4), 379–399. doi:10.2307/421717

Dakroury, A. (2008). CBC's Little Mosque on the Prairie: Just a 'little masquerade'? *Media Development*, *55*(3), 42–46.

Day, L. A. (2006). *Ethics in media communications: Cases and controversies*. Belmont, CA: Thomson Wadsworth.

Dennis, E. E., & Ismach, A. H. (1981). *Reporting processes and practices: Newswriting for today's readers*. Belmont, CA: Wadsworth Publishing Company.

Eid, M. (2008a). *Interweavement: International media ethics and rational decision-making*. Boston, MA: Pearson.

Eid, M. (2008b). The two faces of Osama bin Laden: Mass media representations as a force for evil and Arabic hero. In S. J. Drucker, & G. Gumpert (Eds.), *Heroes in a global world* (pp. 151–183). Hampton Press.

Eid, M., & Fyfe, T. (2009). Globalisation and crisis communication: Competencies for decision-making in the government of Canada. *The Journal of International Communication, 15*(2), 7–27. doi:10.1080/13216597.2009.9674748

Eid, M., & Khan, S. (2011). A new-look for Muslim women in the Canadian media: CBC's little mosque on the prairie. *Middle East Journal of Culture and Communication, 4*(2), 184–202. doi:10.1163/187398611X571355

Eilon, S. (1979). *Management control*. Oxford, UK: Pergamon Press.

Eisenhardt, K. M., & Zbaracki, M. J. (1992). Strategic decision making. *Strategic Management Journal, 13*(S2), 17–37. doi:10.1002/smj.4250130904

Elbanna, S., & Child, J. (2007). Influences on strategic decision effectiveness: Development and test of an integrative model. *Strategic Management Journal, 28*(4), 431–453. doi:10.1002/smj.597

Elliott, D. (2003). Balance and context: Maintaining media ethics. *Phi Kappa Phi Forum, 83*(2), 16-21.

Enders, W., & Sandler, T. (2004). What do we know about the substitution effect in transnational terrorism? In A. Silke (Ed.), *Research on terrorism: Trends, achievements and failures* (pp. 119–137). London: Frank Cass. doi:10.4324/9780203500972.ch7

Flanagan, T. (1998). *Game theory and Canadian politics*. Toronto: University of Toronto Press.

Foucault, M. (1994). *The order of things: An archaeology of the human sciences*. New York: Vintage Books.

Freedman, D., & Thussu, D. K. (2012). Introduction: Dynamics of media and terrorism. In D. Freedman, & D. K. Thussu (Eds.), *Media & terrorism: Global perspectives* (pp. 1–20). London: Sage. doi:10.4135/9781446288429.n1

Frey, B. S. (2004). *Dealing with terrorism – Stick or carrot?* Cheltenham, UK: Edward Elgar. doi:10.4337/9781845421465

Fromkin, D. (1975). The strategy of terrorism. *Foreign Affairs, 53*(4), 683–698. doi:10.2307/20039540

George, A. L. (2003). Analysis and judgment in policymaking. In S. A. Renshon, & D. W. Larson (Eds.), *Good judgment in foreign policy: Theory and application* (pp. 259–268). Lanham, MD: Rowman & Littlefield Publishers, Inc.

Goodall, H. L., Trethewey, A., & Corman, S. R. (2008). Strategery: Missed opportunities and the consequences of obsolete strategic communication theory. In S. R. Corman, A. Trethewey, & H. L. Goodall (Eds.), *Weapons of mass persuasion: Strategic communication to combat violent extremism* (pp. 3–26). New York: Peter Lang.

Gordon, A. D. (1999). Truth precludes any need for further ethical concerns in journalism and public relations. In A. D. Gordon, & J. M. Kittross (Eds.), *Controversies in media ethics* (pp. 73–80). New York: Longman.

Griffin, M. (2004). Picturing America's 'war on terrorism' in Afghanistan and Iraq: Photographic motifs as news frames. *Journalism, 5*(4), 381–402. doi:10.1177/1464884904044201

Gudykunst, W. B. (Ed.). (2005). *Theorizing about intercultural communication*. Thousand Oaks, CA: Sage.

Hallahan, K., Holtzhausen, D., van Ruler, B., Verčič, D., & Sriramesh, K. (2007). Defining strategic communication. *International Journal of Strategic Communication, 1*(1), 3–35. doi:10.1080/15531180701285244

Haque, E. (2010). Homegrown, Muslim and other: Tolerance, secularism and the limits of multiculturalism. *Social Identities*, *16*(1), 79–101. doi:10.1080/13504630903465902

Harris, G., & Spark, D. (1997). *Practical newspaper reporting*. Oxford, UK: Focal Press.

Heap, S. P. H., & Varoufakis, Y. (1995). *Game theory: A critical introduction*. New York: Routledge. doi:10.4324/9780203199275

Held, V. (1997). The media and political violence. *The Journal of Ethics*, *1*(2), 187–202. doi:10.1023/A:1009797007570

Henry, L. (2010). Minorities in Canadian media: Islam and the case of Aqsa Parvez. *The Laurier M.A. Journal of Religion and Culture*, *2*, 39–56.

Hindman, E. B. (1997). *Rights vs. responsibilities: The Supreme Court and the media*. Westport, CT: Greenwood Press.

Hoffman, B. (2006). *Inside terrorism*. New York: Columbia University Press.

Kellermann, K. (2009). Communication: Inherently strategic and primarily automatic. *Communication Monographs*, *59*(3), 288–300. doi:10.1080/03637759209376270

Khan, S. (2000). *Muslim women: Crafting a North American identity*. Gainesville, FL: University Press of Florida.

Kittross, J. M. (1999). The social value of journalism and public relations requires high-quality practices reflecting ethical considerations that go beyond truth and objectivity to accuracy and fairness. In A. D. Gordon, & J. M. Kittross (Eds.), *Controversies in media ethics* (pp. 80–89). New York: Longman.

Kovach, B., & Rosenstiel, T. (2001). *The elements of journalism: What newspeople should know and the public should expect*. New York: Crown Publishers.

Kumar, N. (1997). *Communication and management*. New Delhi: Gyan Publishing House.

Lebow, R. N. (1987). Is crisis management always possible? *Political Science Quarterly*, *102*(2), 181–192. doi:10.2307/2151348

Lee, J. E. C., & Lemyre, L. (2009). A social-cognitive perspective of terrorism risk perception and individual response in Canada. *Risk Analysis*, *29*(9), 1265–1280. doi:10.1111/j.1539-6924.2009.01264.x PMID:19650811

Lee, W. (1971). *Decision theory and human behavior*. New York: John Wiley & Sons, Inc.

Leslie, L. Z. (2000). *Mass communication ethics: Decision making in postmodern culture*. Boston: Houghton Mifflin Company.

Littlejohn, S. W. (2002). *Theories of human communication*. Wadsworth, Thomson Learning.

Lupia, A., Mccubbins, M. D., & Popkin, S. L. (2000). Beyond rationality: Reason and the study of politics. In A. Lupia, M. D. Mccubbins, & S. L. Popkin (Eds.), *Elements of reason: Cognition, choice, and the bounds of rationality* (pp. 1–20). Cambridge, UK: Cambridge University Press. doi:10.1017/CBO9780511805813.001

Markel, M. (2001). *Ethics in technical communication: A critique and synthesis*. Westport, CT: Ablex Publishing.

Matusitz, J. (2009). A postmodern theory of cyberterrorism: Game theory. *Information Security Journal: A Global Perspective*, *18*(6), 273-281.

Mei, Y. M., Lee, S. T., & Al-Hawamdeh, S. (2004). Formulating a communication strategy for effective knowledge sharing. *Journal of Information Science*, *30*(1), 12–22. doi:10.1177/0165551504041674

Mody, B., & Lee, A. (2002). Differing traditions of research on international media influence. In W. B. Gudykunst, & B. Mody (Eds.), *Handbook of international and intercultural communication* (pp. 381–398). Thousand Oaks, CA: Sage Publications.

Moore, S. (2010). The origins of strategic communication: Precedents and parallels in ancient states. *Atlantic Journal of Communication, 18*(5), 227–240. doi:10.1080/15456870.2010.521469

Morrow, J. D. (1994). *Game theory for political scientists*. Princeton, NJ: Princeton University Press.

Nacos, B. L. (2007). *Mass-mediated terrorism: The central role of the media in terrorism and counterterrorism*. Lanham, MD: Rowman & Littlefield Publishers.

Nacos, B. L. (2012). *Terrorism and counterterrorism*. Boston: Longman.

Nacos, B. L., Bloch-Elkon, Y., & Shapiro, R. Y. (2011). *Selling fear: Counterterrorism, the media, and public opinion*. Chicago: The University of Chicago Press. doi:10.7208/chicago/9780226567204.001.0001

Najafbagy, R. (2008). Problems of effective cross-cultural communication and conflict resolution. *Palestine – Israel Journal of Politics. Economics, and Culture, 15*(16), 146–150.

Nicholson, M. (1970). *Conflict analysis*. London: The English Universities Press Limited.

Nicholson, M. (1996). *Causes and consequences in international relations: A conceptual study*. London: Pinter.

Nicholson, M. (1997). *Rationality and the analysis of international conflict*. Cambridge, UK: Cambridge University Press.

Pettigrew, A. M. (1977). Strategy formulation as a political process. *International Studies of Management and Organization, 7*(2), 78–87.

Ray, S. J. (1999). *Strategic communication in crisis management: Lessons from the airline industry*. Westport, CT: Quorum Books.

Rohner, D., & Frey, B. S. (2007). Blood and ink! The common-interest-game between terrorists and the media. *Public Choice, 133*, 129–145. doi:10.1007/s11127-007-9182-9

Ruby, T. F. (2006). Listening to the voices of hijab. *Women's Studies International Forum, 29*(1), 54–66. doi:10.1016/j.wsif.2005.10.006

Schellenberg, J. A. (1996). *Conflict resolution: Theory, research, and practice*. Albany, NY: State University of New York Press.

Schmid, A. P. (1989). Terrorism and the media: The ethics of publicity. *Terrorism and Political Violence, 1*(4), 539–565. doi:10.1080/09546558908427042

Schmid, A. P., & Jongman, A. J. (2008). *Political terrorism: A new guide to actors, authors, concepts, data bases, theories, & literature*. London: Transaction Publishers.

Shpiro, S. (2002). Conflict media strategies and the politics of counter-terrorism. *Politics, 22*(2), 76–85. doi:10.1111/1467-9256.00162

Shubik, M. (1954). Introduction to the nature of game theory. In M. Shubik (Ed.), *Readings in game theory and political behavior* (pp. 1–11). New York: Doubleday & Company, Inc.

Silke, A. (2004). The road less travelled: Recent trends in terrorism research. In A. Silke (Ed.), *Research on terrorism: Trends, achievements and failures* (pp. 186–213). London: Frank Cass. doi:10.4324/9780203500972.ch10

Snyder, G. H., & Diesing, P. (1977). *Conflict among nations: Bargaining, decision making, and system structure in international crises.* Princeton, NJ: Princeton University Press.

Steuter, E., & Wills, D. (2009). Discourses and dehumanization: Enemy construction and the Canadian media complicity in the framing of the war on terror. Global Media Journal – Canadian Ed., 2(2), 7-24.

Taillon, P. de B. (2002). *Hijacking and hostages: Government responses to terrorism.* Westport, CT: Praeger.

Weimann, G., & Winn, C. (1994). *The theater of terror: Mass media and international terrorism.* New York: Longman.

Whittaker, D. J. (2004). *Terrorists and terrorism in the contemporary world.* Westport, CT: Praeger.

Whittaker, D. J. (2007). *Terrorism: Understanding the global threat.* Harlow, UK: Longman.

Wilkinson, P. (1997). The media and terrorism: A reassessment. *Terrorism and Political Violence,* 9(2), 51–64. doi:10.1080/09546559708427402

Williams, P. (1976). *Crisis management: Confrontation and diplomacy in the nuclear age.* London: Martin Robertson & Co. Ltd.

Wittebols, J. H. (1991). The politics and coverage of terrorism: From media images to public consciousness. *Communication Theory, 1*(3), 253–266. doi:10.1111/j.1468-2885.1991.tb00018.x

Wright, D. K. (1996). Communication ethics. In M. B. Salwen, & D. W. Stacks (Eds.), *An integrated approach to communication theory and research* (pp. 519–535). Hoboken, NJ: Lawrence Erlbaum Associates, Publishers.

Zack, M. H. (Ed.). (1999). *Knowledge and strategy.* Woburn, MA: Butterworth-Heinemann.

Zelizer, B., & Allan, S. (Eds.). (2011). *Journalism after September 11.* London: Routledge.

Zinsser, W. (1998). *On writing well: The classic guide to writing nonfiction.* New York: HarperPerennial, A Division of HarperCollins Publishers.

KEY TERMS AND DEFINITIONS

Codes of Ethics: Adopted by organizations to assist members in understanding the difference between right and wrong conducts.

Communication: There are numerous definitions of communication. The emphasized definition in this chapter is that communication is a decision-making process.

Counterterrorism: Strategies and measures employed to stop or prevent terrorism.

Decision-Making: A cognitive process through which one makes a decision.

Rationality: The quality or state of being reasonable; usually based on facts or reason rather than emotions or feelings.

Responsibility: The state of being accountable for something within one's power, control, or management.

Strategy: A plan, method, or series of maneuvers to achieve specific outcomes.

ENDNOTES

[1.] The analyzed media guidelines for covering terrorism are those of CBS News Standards, *The Courier-Journal* and *The Louisville Times*, *The Sun-Times* and *Daily News* Standards for Coverage of Terrorism, and the United Press International (Alexander & Latter, 1990).

[2.] The sought goals could be those of the media organization, the national media system, or the government if they are identical to those of the media.

[3.] To explain some of the basic concepts of game theory, Michael Nicholson (1970)

considers a simple form, which still preserves the characteristics of a game, one of a class or type called zero-sum games, by which is meant that whatever one player wins, the other loses, so that the total benefit of the two players is always zero. As for non-zero sum games, two very simple games of this type have played an essential role in the analysis of conflicts—Prisoners' Dilemma and Chicken games. Another classification for game theory, in addition to zero-sum (pure conflict) or non-zero-sum (cooperation) is based on the number of persons, groups, or nations involved: two-person games and multi- or *n*-person games.

4. Game theory belongs to a family of methodologies variously known as rational choice, public choice, social choice, and collective choice (Flanagan, 1998).

5. There are three key assumptions: 1) agents are instrumentally rational; 2) they have common knowledge of this rationality; and 3) they know the rules of the game (Heap & Varoufakis, 1995).

6. Strategies are the choices that the players can make within the rules of the game; a strategy is a complete set of choices from beginning to end of the game, while a solution is the set of payoffs arising from the strategies that rational players would choose under the rules of the game (Flanagan, 1998).

Related References

To continue our tradition of advancing media and communications research, we have compiled a list of recommended IGI Global readings. These references will provide additional information and guidance to further enrich your knowledge and assist you with your own research and future publications.

Aas, B. G. (2012). What's real? Presence, personality and identity in the real and online virtual world. In N. Zagalo, L. Morgado, & A. Boa-Ventura (Eds.), *Virtual worlds and metaverse platforms: New communication and identity paradigms* (pp. 88–99). Hershey, PA: Information Science Reference.

Aceti, V., & Luppicini, R. (2013). Exploring the effect of mhealth technologies on communication and information sharing in a pediatric critical care unit: A case study. In J. Tan (Ed.), *Healthcare information technology innovation and sustainability: Frontiers and adoption* (pp. 88–108). Hershey, PA: Medical Information Science Reference. doi:10.4018/978-1-4666-2797-0.ch006

Acilar, A. (2013). Factors affecting mobile phone use among undergraduate students in Turkey: An exploratory analysis. In I. Lee (Ed.), *Strategy, adoption, and competitive advantage of mobile services in the global economy* (pp. 234–246). Hershey, PA: Information Science Reference.

Adams, A. (2013). Situated e-learning: Empowerment and barriers to identity changes. In S. Warburton, & S. Hatzipanagos (Eds.), *Digital identity and social media* (pp. 159–175). Hershey, PA: Information Science Reference.

Adeoye, B. F. (2013). Culturally different learning styles in online learning environments: A case of Nigerian university students. In L. Tomei (Ed.), *Learning tools and teaching approaches through ICT advancements* (pp. 228–240). Hershey, PA: Information Science Reference.

Agarwal, N., & Mahata, D. (2013). Grouping the similar among the disconnected bloggers. In G. Xu, & L. Li (Eds.), *Social media mining and social network analysis: Emerging research* (pp. 54–71). Hershey, PA: Information Science Reference.

Aiken, M., Wang, J., Gu, L., & Paolillo, J. (2013). An exploratory study of how technology supports communication in multilingual groups. In N. Kock (Ed.), *Interdisciplinary applications of electronic collaboration approaches and technologies* (pp. 17–29). Hershey, PA: Information Science Reference.

Aikins, S. K., & Chary, M. (2013). Online participation and digital divide: An empirical evaluation of U.S. midwestern municipalities. In I. Association (Ed.), *Digital literacy: Concepts, methodologies, tools, and applications* (pp. 63–85). Hershey, PA: Information Science Reference.

Al Disi, Z. A., & Albadri, F. (2013). Arab youth and the internet: Educational perspective. In F. Albadri (Ed.), *Information systems applications in the Arab education sector* (pp. 163–178). Hershey, PA: Information Science Reference.

Al Omoush, K. S., Alqirem, R. M., & Shaqrah, A. A. (2013). The driving internal beliefs of household internet adoption among Jordanians and the role of cultural values. In A. Zolait (Ed.), *Technology diffusion and adoption: global complexity, global innovation* (pp. 130–151). Hershey, PA: Information Science Reference. doi:10.4018/978-1-4666-2791-8.ch009

Al-Dossary, S., Al-Dulaijan, N., Al-Mansour, S., Al-Zahrani, S., Al-Fridan, M., & Househ, M. (2013). Organ donation and transplantation: Processes, registries, consent, and restrictions in Saudi Arabia. In M. Cruz-Cunha, I. Miranda, & P. Gonçalves (Eds.), *Handbook of research on ICTs for human-centered healthcare and social care services* (pp. 511–528). Hershey, PA: Medical Information Science Reference. doi:10.4018/978-1-4666-3986-7.ch027

Al-Khaffaf, M. M., & Abdellatif, H. J. (2013). The effect of information and communication technology on customer relationship management: Jordan public shareholding companies. In R. Eid (Ed.), *Managing customer trust, satisfaction, and loyalty through information communication technologies* (pp. 342–350). Hershey, PA: Business Science Reference.

Al-Nuaim, H. A. (2012). Evaluation of Arab municipal websites. In I. Management Association (Ed.), *Wireless technologies: Concepts, methodologies, tools and applications* (pp. 1170-1185). Hershey, PA: Information Science Reference. doi: doi:10.4018/978-1-61350-101-6.ch505

Al-Nuaim, H. A. (2013). Developing user profiles for interactive online products in practice. In M. Garcia-Ruiz (Ed.), *Cases on usability engineering: Design and development of digital products* (pp. 57–79). Hershey, PA: Information Science Reference. doi:10.4018/978-1-4666-4046-7.ch003

Al-Shqairat, Z. I., & Altarawneh, I. I. (2013). The role of partnership in e-government readiness: The knowledge stations (KSs) initiative in Jordan. In A. Mesquita (Ed.), *User perception and influencing factors of technology in everyday life* (pp. 192–210). Hershey, PA: Information Science Reference.

AlBalawi, M. S. (2013). Web-based instructions: An assessment of preparedness of conventional universities in Saudi Arabia. In M. Khosrow-Pour (Ed.), *Cases on assessment and evaluation in education* (pp. 417–451). Hershey, PA: Information Science Reference.

Alejos, A. V., Cuiñas, I., Expósito, I., & Sánchez, M. G. (2013). From the farm to fork: Information security accomplishment in a RFID based tracking chain for food sector. In P. Lopez, J. Hernandez-Castro, & T. Li (Eds.), *Security and trends in wireless identification and sensing platform tags: Advancements in RFID* (pp. 237–270). Hershey, PA: Information Science Reference.

Alkazemi, M. F., Bowe, B. J., & Blom, R. (2013). Facilitating the Egyptian uprising: A case study of Facebook and Egypt's April 6th youth movement. In N. Azab (Ed.), *Cases on web 2.0 in developing countries: Studies on implementation, application, and use* (pp. 256–282). Hershey, PA: Information Science Reference.

Almutairi, M. S. (2012). M-government: Challenges and key success factors – Saudi Arabia case study. In I. Management Association (Ed.), *Wireless technologies: Concepts, methodologies, tools and applications* (pp. 1698-1717). Hershey, PA: Information Science Reference. doi: doi:10.4018/978-1-61350-101-6.ch611

Alyagout, F., & Siti-Nabiha, A. K. (2013). Public sector transformation: Privatization in Saudi Arabia. In N. Pomazalová (Ed.), *Public sector transformation processes and internet public procurement: Decision support systems* (pp. 17–31). Hershey, PA: Engineering Science Reference.

Amirante, A., Castaldi, T., Miniero, L., & Romano, S. P. (2013). Protocol interactions among user agents, application servers, and media servers: Standardization efforts and open issues. In D. Kanellopoulos (Ed.), *Intelligent multimedia technologies for networking applications: Techniques and tools* (pp. 48–63). Hershey, PA: Information Science Reference.

Andres, H. P. (2013). Shared mental model development during technology-mediated collaboration. In N. Kock (Ed.), *Interdisciplinary applications of electronic collaboration approaches and technologies* (pp. 125–142). Hershey, PA: Information Science Reference.

Andrus, C. H., & Gaynor, M. (2013). Good IT requires good communication. In S. Sarnikar, D. Bennett, & M. Gaynor (Eds.), *Cases on healthcare information technology for patient care management* (pp. 122–125). Hershey, PA: Medical Information Science Reference.

Annafari, M. T., & Bohlin, E. (2013). Why is the diffusion of mobile service not an evolutionary process? In I. Lee (Ed.), *Mobile services industries, technologies, and applications in the global economy* (pp. 25–38). Hershey, PA: Information Science Reference.

Anupama, S. (2013). Gender evaluation of rural e-governance in India: A case study of E-Gram Suraj (e-rural good governance) scheme1. In I. Association (Ed.), *Digital literacy: Concepts, methodologies, tools, and applications* (pp. 1059–1074). Hershey, PA: Information Science Reference.

Ariely, G. (2013). Boundaries of socio-technical systems and IT for knowledge development in military environments. In J. Abdelnour-Nocera (Ed.), *Knowledge and technological development effects on organizational and social structures* (pp. 224–238). Hershey, PA: Information Science Reference.

Arsenio, A. M. (2013). Intelligent approaches for adaptation and distribution of personalized multimedia content. In D. Kanellopoulos (Ed.), *Intelligent multimedia technologies for networking applications: Techniques and tools* (pp. 197–224). Hershey, PA: Information Science Reference.

Artail, H., & Tarhini, T. (2013). Runtime discovery and access of web services in mobile environments. In I. Lee (Ed.), *Mobile services industries, technologies, and applications in the global economy* (pp. 193–213). Hershey, PA: Information Science Reference.

Asino, T. I., Wilder, H., & Ferris, S. P. (2013). Innovative use of ICT in Namibia for nationhood: Special emphasis on the Namibian newspaper. In H. Rahman (Ed.), *Cases on progressions and challenges in ICT utilization for citizen-centric governance* (pp. 205–216). Hershey, PA: Information Science Reference.

Atici, B., & Bati, U. (2013). Identity of virtual supporters: Constructing identity of Turkish football fans on digital media. In S. Warburton, & S. Hatzipanagos (Eds.), *Digital identity and social media* (pp. 256–274). Hershey, PA: Information Science Reference.

Azab, N., & Khalifa, N. (2013). Web 2.0 and opportunities for entrepreneurs: How Egyptian entrepreneurs perceive and exploit web 2.0 technologies. In N. Azab (Ed.), *Cases on web 2.0 in developing countries: Studies on implementation, application, and use* (pp. 1–32). Hershey, PA: Information Science Reference.

Bainbridge, W. S. (2013). Ancestor veneration avatars. In R. Luppicini (Ed.), *Handbook of research on technoself: Identity in a technological society* (pp. 308–321). Hershey, PA: Information Science Reference.

Baporikar, N. (2013). Critical review of academic entrepreneurship in India. In A. Szopa, W. Karwowski, & P. Ordóñez de Pablos (Eds.), *Academic entrepreneurship and technological innovation: A business management perspective* (pp. 29–52). Hershey, PA: Information Science Reference.

Barroca, L., & Gimenes, I. M. (2013). Computing postgraduate programmes in the UK and Brazil: Learning from experience in distance education with web 2.0 support. In N. Azab (Ed.), *Cases on web 2.0 in developing countries: Studies on implementation, application, and use* (pp. 147–171). Hershey, PA: Information Science Reference.

Barton, S. M. (2013). Facilitating learning by going online: Modernising Islamic teaching and learning in Indonesia. In E. McKay (Ed.), *ePedagogy in online learning: New developments in web mediated human computer interaction* (pp. 74–92). Hershey, PA: Information Science Reference. doi:10.4018/978-1-4666-3649-1.ch005

Barzilai-Nahon, K., Gomez, R., & Ambikar, R. (2013). Conceptualizing a contextual measurement for digital divide/s: Using an integrated narrative. In I. Association (Ed.), *Digital literacy: Concepts, methodologies, tools, and applications* (pp. 279–293). Hershey, PA: Information Science Reference.

Bénel, A., & Lacour, P. (2012). Towards a participative platform for cultural texts translators. In C. El Morr, & P. Maret (Eds.), *Virtual community building and the information society: Current and future directions* (pp. 153–162). Hershey, PA: Information Science Reference.

Bentley, C. M. (2013). Designing and implementing online collaboration tools in West Africa. In N. Azab (Ed.), *Cases on web 2.0 in developing countries: Studies on implementation, application, and use* (pp. 33–60). Hershey, PA: Information Science Reference.

Berg, M. (2012). Checking in at the urban playground: Digital geographies and electronic flâneurs. In F. Comunello (Ed.), *Networked sociability and individualism: Technology for personal and professional relationships* (pp. 169–194). Hershey, PA: Information Science Reference.

Bers, M. U., & Ettinger, A. B. (2013). Programming robots in kindergarten to express identity: An ethnographic analysis. In I. Management Association (Ed.), *Industrial engineering: Concepts, methodologies, tools, and applications* (pp. 1952-1968). Hershey, PA: Engineering Science Reference. doi: doi:10.4018/978-1-4666-1945-6.ch105

Binsaleh, M., & Hassan, S. (2013). Systems development methodology for mobile commerce applications. In I. Khalil, & E. Weippl (Eds.), *Contemporary challenges and solutions for mobile and multimedia technologies* (pp. 146–162). Hershey, PA: Information Science Reference.

Bishop, J. (2013). Cooperative e-learning in the multilingual and multicultural school: The role of "classroom 2.0" for increasing participation in education. In P. Pumilia-Gnarini, E. Favaron, E. Pacetti, J. Bishop, & L. Guerra (Eds.), *Handbook of research on didactic strategies and technologies for education: Incorporating advancements* (pp. 137–150). Hershey, PA: Information Science Reference.

Bishop, J. (2013). Increasing capital revenue in social networking communities: Building social and economic relationships through avatars and characters. In J. Bishop (Ed.), *Examining the concepts, issues, and implications of internet trolling* (pp. 44–61). Hershey, PA: Information Science Reference. doi:10.4018/978-1-4666-2803-8.ch005

Bishop, J. (2013). Lessons from the emotive project for increasing take-up of big society and responsible capitalism initiatives. In P. Pumilia-Gnarini, E. Favaron, E. Pacetti, J. Bishop, & L. Guerra (Eds.), *Handbook of research on didactic strategies and technologies for education: Incorporating advancements* (pp. 208–217). Hershey, PA: Information Science Reference.

Blau, I. (2013). E-collaboration within, between, and without institutions: Towards better functioning of online groups through networks. In N. Kock (Ed.), *Interdisciplinary applications of electronic collaboration approaches and technologies* (pp. 188–203). Hershey, PA: Information Science Reference.

Boskic, N., & Hu, S. (2013). Blended learning: The road to inclusive and global education. In E. Jean Francois (Ed.), *Transcultural blended learning and teaching in postsecondary education* (pp. 283–301). Hershey, PA: Information Science Reference.

Botero, A., Karhu, K., & Vihavainen, S. (2012). Exploring the ecosystems and principles of community innovation. In A. Lugmayr, H. Franssila, P. Näränen, O. Sotamaa, J. Vanhala, & Z. Yu (Eds.), *Media in the ubiquitous era: Ambient, social and gaming media* (pp. 216–234). Hershey, PA: Information Science Reference.

Bowe, B. J., Blom, R., & Freedman, E. (2013). Negotiating boundaries between control and dissent: Free speech, business, and repressitarian governments. In J. Lannon, & E. Halpin (Eds.), *Human rights and information communication technologies: Trends and consequences of use* (pp. 36–55). Hershey, PA: Information Science Reference.

Brandão, J., Ferreira, T., & Carvalho, V. (2012). An overview on the use of serious games in the military industry and health. In M. Cruz-Cunha (Ed.), *Handbook of research on serious games as educational, business and research tools* (pp. 182–201). Hershey, PA: Information Science Reference. doi:10.4018/978-1-4666-0149-9.ch009

Brost, L. F., & McGinnis, C. (2012). The status of blogging in the republic of Ireland: A case study. In T. Dumova, & R. Fiordo (Eds.), *Blogging in the global society: Cultural, political and geographical aspects* (pp. 128–147). Hershey, PA: Information Science Reference.

Burns, J., Blanchard, M., & Metcalf, A. (2013). Bridging the digital divide in Australia: The potential implications for the mental health of young people experiencing marginalisation. In I. Association (Ed.), *Digital literacy: Concepts, methodologies, tools, and applications* (pp. 772–793). Hershey, PA: Information Science Reference.

Cagliero, L., & Fiori, A. (2013). News document summarization driven by user-generated content. In G. Xu, & L. Li (Eds.), *Social media mining and social network analysis: Emerging research* (pp. 105–126). Hershey, PA: Information Science Reference.

Camillo, A., & Di Pietro, L. (2013). Managerial communication in the global cross-cultural context. In B. Christiansen, E. Turkina, & N. Williams (Eds.), *Cultural and technological influences on global business* (pp. 397–419). Hershey, PA: Business Science Reference. doi:10.4018/978-1-4666-3966-9.ch021

Canazza, S., De Poli, G., Rodà, A., & Vidolin, A. (2013). Expressiveness in music performance: Analysis, models, mapping, encoding. In J. Steyn (Ed.), *Structuring music through markup language: Designs and architectures* (pp. 156–186). Hershey, PA: Information Science Reference.

Carrasco, J. G., Ovide, E., & Puyal, M. B. (2013). Closing and opening of cultures. In F. García-Peñalvo (Ed.), *Multiculturalism in technology-based education: Case studies on ICT-supported approaches* (pp. 125–142). Hershey, PA: Information Science Reference.

Carreras, I., Zanardi, A., Salvadori, E., & Miorandi, D. (2013). A distributed monitoring framework for opportunistic communication systems: An experimental approach. In V. De Florio (Ed.), *Innovations and approaches for resilient and adaptive systems* (pp. 220–236). Hershey, PA: Information Science Reference.

Carter, M., Grover, V., & Thatcher, J. B. (2013). Mobile devices and the self: developing the concept of mobile phone identity. In I. Lee (Ed.), *Strategy, adoption, and competitive advantage of mobile services in the global economy* (pp. 150–164). Hershey, PA: Information Science Reference.

Caruso, F., Giuffrida, G., Reforgiato, D., & Zarba, C. (2013). Recommendation systems for mobile devices. In I. Lee (Ed.), *Mobile services industries, technologies, and applications in the global economy* (pp. 221–242). Hershey, PA: Information Science Reference.

Casamassima, L. (2013). eTwinning project: A virtual orchestra. In P. Pumilia-Gnarini, E. Favaron, E. Pacetti, J. Bishop, & L. Guerra (Eds.) Handbook of research on didactic strategies and technologies for education: Incorporating advancements (pp. 703-709). Hershey, PA: Information Science Reference. doi: doi:10.4018/978-1-4666-2122-0.ch061

Caschera, M. C., D'Ulizia, A., Ferri, F., & Grifoni, P. (2012). Multiculturality and multimodal languages. In G. Ghinea, F. Andres, & S. Gulliver (Eds.), *Multiple sensorial media advances and applications: New developments in MulSeMedia* (pp. 99–114). Hershey, PA: Information Science Reference.

Catagnus, R. M., & Hantula, D. A. (2013). The virtual individual education plan (IEP) team: Using online collaboration to develop a behavior intervention plan. In N. Kock (Ed.), *Interdisciplinary applications of electronic collaboration approaches and technologies* (pp. 30–45). Hershey, PA: Information Science Reference.

Ch'ng, E. (2013). The mirror between two worlds: 3D surface computing for objects and environments. In D. Harrison (Ed.), *Digital media and technologies for virtual artistic spaces* (pp. 166–185). Hershey, PA: Information Science Reference. doi:10.4018/978-1-4666-2961-5.ch013

Chand, A. (2013). Reducing digital divide: The case of the 'people first network' (PFNet) in the Solomon Islands. In I. Association (Ed.), *Digital literacy: Concepts, methodologies, tools, and applications* (pp. 1571–1605). Hershey, PA: Information Science Reference.

Chatterjee, S. (2013). Ethical behaviour in technology-mediated communication. In J. Bishop (Ed.), *Examining the concepts, issues, and implications of internet trolling* (pp. 1–9). Hershey, PA: Information Science Reference. doi:10.4018/978-1-4666-2803-8.ch001

Chen, C., Chao, H., Wu, T., Fan, C., Chen, J., Chen, Y., & Hsu, J. (2013). IoT-IMS communication platform for future internet. In V. De Florio (Ed.), *Innovations and approaches for resilient and adaptive systems* (pp. 68–86). Hershey, PA: Information Science Reference.

Chen, J., & Hu, X. (2013). Smartphone market in China: Challenges, opportunities, and promises. In I. Lee (Ed.), *Mobile services industries, technologies, and applications in the global economy* (pp. 120–132). Hershey, PA: Information Science Reference.

Chen, Y., Lee, B., & Kirk, R. M. (2013). Internet use among older adults: Constraints and opportunities. In R. Zheng, R. Hill, & M. Gardner (Eds.), *Engaging older adults with modern technology: Internet use and information access needs* (pp. 124–141). Hershey, PA: Information Science Reference.

Cheong, P. H., & Martin, J. N. (2013). Cultural implications of e-learning access (and divides): Teaching an intercultural communication course online. In A. Edmundson (Ed.), *Cases on cultural implications and considerations in online learning* (pp. 82–100). Hershey, PA: Information Science Reference.

Chhanabhai, P., & Holt, A. (2013). The changing world of ICT and health: Crossing the digital divide. In I. Association (Ed.), *Digital literacy: Concepts, methodologies, tools, and applications* (pp. 794–811). Hershey, PA: Information Science Reference.

Chuling, W., Hua, C. M., & Chee, C. J. (2012). Investigating the demise of radio and television broadcasting. In R. Sharma, M. Tan, & F. Pereira (Eds.), *Understanding the interactive digital media marketplace: Frameworks, platforms, communities and issues* (pp. 392–405). Hershey, PA: Information Science Reference.

Ciaramitaro, B. L. (2012). Introduction to mobile technologies. In B. Ciaramitaro (Ed.), *Mobile technology consumption: Opportunities and challenges* (pp. 1–15). Hershey, PA: Information Science Reference.

Cicconetti, C., Mambrini, R., & Rossi, A. (2013). A survey of wireless backhauling solutions for ITS. In R. Daher, & A. Vinel (Eds.), *Roadside networks for vehicular communications: Architectures, applications, and test fields* (pp. 57–70). Hershey, PA: Information Science Reference.

Ciptasari, R. W., & Sakurai, K. (2013). Multimedia copyright protection scheme based on the direct feature-based method. In K. Kondo (Ed.), *Multimedia information hiding technologies and methodologies for controlling data* (pp. 412–439). Hershey, PA: Information Science Reference.

Code, J. (2013). Agency and identity in social media. In S. Warburton, & S. Hatzipanagos (Eds.), *Digital identity and social media* (pp. 37–57). Hershey, PA: Information Science Reference.

Comunello, F. (2013). From the digital divide to multiple divides: Technology, society, and new media skills. In I. Association (Ed.), *Digital literacy: Concepts, methodologies, tools, and applications* (pp. 1622–1639). Hershey, PA: Information Science Reference.

Consonni, A. (2013). About the use of the DMs in CLIL classes. In F. García-Peñalvo (Ed.), *Multiculturalism in technology-based education: Case studies on ICT-supported approaches* (pp. 9–27). Hershey, PA: Information Science Reference.

Constant, J. (2012). Digital approaches to visualization of geometric problems in wooden sangaku tablets. In A. Ursyn (Ed.), *Biologically-inspired computing for the arts: Scientific data through graphics* (pp. 240–253). Hershey, PA: Information Science Reference. doi:10.4018/978-1-4666-0942-6.ch013

Cossiavelou, V., Bantimaroudis, P., Kavakli, E., & Illia, L. (2013). The media gatekeeping model updated by R and I in ICTs: The case of wireless communications in media coverage of the olympic games. In M. Bartolacci, & S. Powell (Eds.), *Advancements and innovations in wireless communications and network technologies* (pp. 262–288). Hershey, PA: Information Science Reference.

Cropf, R. A., Benmamoun, M., & Kalliny, M. (2013). The role of web 2.0 in the Arab Spring. In N. Azab (Ed.), *Cases on web 2.0 in developing countries: Studies on implementation, application, and use* (pp. 76–108). Hershey, PA: Information Science Reference.

Cucinotta, A., Minnolo, A. L., & Puliafito, A. (2013). Design and implementation of an event-based RFID middleware. In N. Karmakar (Ed.), *Advanced RFID systems, security, and applications* (pp. 110–131). Hershey, PA: Information Science Reference.

D'Andrea, A., Ferri, F., & Grifoni, P. (2013). Assessing e-health in Africa: Web 2.0 applications. In N. Azab (Ed.), *Cases on web 2.0 in developing countries: Studies on implementation, application, and use* (pp. 442–467). Hershey, PA: Information Science Reference.

de Guinea, A. O. (2013). The level paradox of e-collaboration: Dangers and solutions. In N. Kock (Ed.), *Interdisciplinary applications of electronic collaboration approaches and technologies* (pp. 166–187). Hershey, PA: Information Science Reference.

Dhar-Bhattacharjee, S., & Takruri-Rizk, H. (2012). An Indo-British comparison. In C. Romm Livermore (Ed.), *Gender and social computing: Interactions, differences and relationships* (pp. 50–71). Hershey, PA: Information Science Publishing.

Díaz-Foncea, M., & Marcuello, C. (2013). ANOBIUM, SL: The use of the ICT as niche of employment and as tool for developing the social market. In T. Torres-Coronas, & M. Vidal-Blasco (Eds.), *Social e-enterprise: Value creation through ICT* (pp. 221–242). Hershey, PA: Information Science Reference.

Díaz-González, M., Froufe, N. Q., Brena, A. G., & Pumarola, F. (2013). Uses and implementation of social media at university: The case of schools of communication in Spain. In B. Pătruţ, M. Pătruţ, & C. Cmeciu (Eds.), *Social media and the new academic environment: Pedagogical challenges* (pp. 204–222). Hershey, PA: Information Science Reference. doi:10.4018/978-1-4666-2851-9.ch010

Ditsa, G., Alwahaishi, S., Al-Kobaisi, S., & Snášel, V. (2013). A comparative study of the effects of culture on the deployment of information technology. In A. Zolait (Ed.), *Technology diffusion and adoption: Global complexity, global innovation* (pp. 77–90). Hershey, PA: Information Science Reference. doi:10.4018/978-1-4666-2791-8.ch006

Donaldson, O., & Duggan, E. W. (2013). Assessing mobile value-added preference structures: The case of a developing country. In I. Lee (Ed.), *Strategy, adoption, and competitive advantage of mobile services in the global economy* (pp. 349–370). Hershey, PA: Information Science Reference.

Douai, A. (2013). "In YouTube we trust": Video exchange and Arab human rights. In J. Lannon, & E. Halpin (Eds.), *Human rights and information communication technologies: Trends and consequences of use* (pp. 57–71). Hershey, PA: Information Science Reference.

Dromzée, C., Laborie, S., & Roose, P. (2013). A semantic generic profile for multimedia document adaptation. In D. Kanellopoulos (Ed.), *Intelligent multimedia technologies for networking applications: Techniques and tools* (pp. 225–246). Hershey, PA: Information Science Reference.

Drucker, S., & Gumpert, G. (2012). The urban communication infrastructure: Global connection and local detachment. In I. Management Association (Ed.), *Wireless technologies: Concepts, methodologies, tools and applications* (pp. 1150–1169). Hershey, PA: Information Science Reference. doi: doi:10.4018/978-1-61350-101-6.ch504

Drula, G. (2013). Media and communication research facing social media. In M. Pătruţ, & B. Pătruţ (Eds.), *Social media in higher education: Teaching in web 2.0* (pp. 371–392). Hershey, PA: Information Science Reference. doi:10.4018/978-1-4666-2970-7.ch019

Dueck, J., & Rempel, M. (2013). Human rights and technology: Lessons from Alice in Wonderland. In J. Lannon, & E. Halpin (Eds.), *Human rights and information communication technologies: Trends and consequences of use* (pp. 1–20). Hershey, PA: Information Science Reference.

Dumova, T. (2012). Social interaction technologies and the future of blogging. In T. Dumova, & R. Fiordo (Eds.), *Blogging in the global society: Cultural, political and geographical aspects* (pp. 249–274). Hershey, PA: Information Science Reference.

Dunn, H. S. (2013). Information literacy and the digital divide: Challenging e-exclusion in the global south. In I. Association (Ed.), *Digital literacy: Concepts, methodologies, tools, and applications* (pp. 20–38). Hershey, PA: Information Science Reference.

Eid, M. (2012). Cyber-terrorism and ethical journalism: A need for rationalism. In R. Lupiccini (Ed.), *Ethical impact of technological advancements and applications in society* (pp. 263–283). Hershey, PA: Information Science Reference.

Elias, N. (2013). Immigrants' internet use and identity from an intergenerational perspective: Immigrant senior citizens and youngsters from the former Soviet Union in Israel. In R. Luppicini (Ed.), *Handbook of research on technoself: Identity in a technological society* (pp. 293–307). Hershey, PA: Information Science Reference.

Elizabeth, L. S., Ismail, N., & Tun, M. S. (2012). The future of the printed book. In R. Sharma, M. Tan, & F. Pereira (Eds.), *Understanding the interactive digital media marketplace: Frameworks, platforms, communities and issues* (pp. 416–429). Hershey, PA: Information Science Reference.

Erne, R. (2012). Knowledge worker performance in a cross-industrial perspective. In S. Brüggemann, & C. d'Amato (Eds.), *Collaboration and the semantic web: Social networks, knowledge networks, and knowledge resources* (pp. 297–321). Hershey, PA: Information Science Reference. doi:10.4018/978-1-4666-0894-8.ch015

Ertl, B., Helling, K., & Kikis-Papadakis, K. (2012). The impact of gender in ICT usage, education and career: Comparisons between Greece and Germany. In C. Romm Livermore (Ed.), *Gender and social computing: Interactions, differences and relationships* (pp. 98–119). Hershey, PA: Information Science Publishing.

Estapé-Dubreuil, G., & Torreguitart-Mirada, C. (2013). ICT adoption in the small and medium-size social enterprises in Spain: Opportunity or priority? In T. Torres-Coronas, & M. Vidal-Blasco (Eds.), *Social e-enterprise: Value creation through ICT* (pp. 200–220). Hershey, PA: Information Science Reference.

Eze, U. C., & Poong, Y. S. (2013). Consumers' intention to use mobile commerce and the moderating roles of gender and income. In I. Lee (Ed.), *Strategy, adoption, and competitive advantage of mobile services in the global economy* (pp. 127–148). Hershey, PA: Information Science Reference.

Farrell, R., Danis, C., Erickson, T., Ellis, J., Christensen, J., Bailey, M., & Kellogg, W. A. (2012). A picture and a thousand words: Visual scaffolding for mobile communication in developing regions. In W. Hu (Ed.), *Emergent trends in personal, mobile, and handheld computing technologies* (pp. 341–354). Hershey, PA: Information Science Reference. doi:10.4018/978-1-4666-0921-1.ch020

Fidler, C. S., Kanaan, R. K., & Rogerson, S. (2013). Barriers to e-government implementation in Jordan: The role of wasta. In A. Mesquita (Ed.), *User perception and influencing factors of technology in everyday life* (pp. 179–191). Hershey, PA: Information Science Reference.

Filho, J. R. (2013). ICT and human rights in Brazil: From military to digital dictatorship. In J. Lannon, & E. Halpin (Eds.), *Human rights and information communication technologies: Trends and consequences of use* (pp. 86–99). Hershey, PA: Information Science Reference.

Fiordo, R. (2012). Analyzing blogs: A hermeneutic perspective. In T. Dumova, & R. Fiordo (Eds.), *Blogging in the global society: Cultural, political and geographical aspects* (pp. 231–248). Hershey, PA: Information Science Reference.

Fischer, G., & Herrmann, T. (2013). Socio-technical systems: A meta-design perspective. In J. Abdelnour-Nocera (Ed.), *Knowledge and technological development effects on organizational and social structures* (pp. 1–36). Hershey, PA: Information Science Reference.

Fleury, M., & Al-Jobouri, L. (2013). Techniques and tools for adaptive video streaming. In D. Kanellopoulos (Ed.), *Intelligent multimedia technologies for networking applications: Techniques and tools* (pp. 65–101). Hershey, PA: Information Science Reference.

Freeman, I., & Freeman, A. (2013). Capacity building for different abilities using ICT. In T. Torres-Coronas, & M. Vidal-Blasco (Eds.), *Social e-enterprise: Value creation through ICT* (pp. 67–82). Hershey, PA: Information Science Reference. doi:10.4018/978-1-4666-4422-9.ch014

Gallon, R. (2013). Communication, culture, and technology: Learning strategies for the unteachable. In R. Lansiquot (Ed.), *Cases on interdisciplinary research trends in science, technology, engineering, and mathematics: Studies on urban classrooms* (pp. 91–106). Hershey, PA: Information Science Reference.

García, M., Lloret, J., Bellver, I., & Tomás, J. (2013). Intelligent IPTV distribution for smart phones. In D. Kanellopoulos (Ed.), *Intelligent multimedia technologies for networking applications: Techniques and tools* (pp. 318–347). Hershey, PA: Information Science Reference.

García-Plaza, A. P., Zubiaga, A., Fresno, V., & Martínez, R. (2013). Tag cloud reorganization: Finding groups of related tags on delicious. In G. Xu, & L. Li (Eds.), *Social media mining and social network analysis: Emerging research* (pp. 140–155). Hershey, PA: Information Science Reference.

Gerpott, T. J. (2013). Attribute perceptions as factors explaining mobile internet acceptance of cellular customers in Germany: An empirical study comparing actual and potential adopters with distinct categories of access appliances. In I. Lee (Ed.), *Strategy, adoption, and competitive advantage of mobile services in the global economy* (pp. 19–48). Hershey, PA: Information Science Reference.

Giambona, G. J., & Birchall, D. W. (2012). Collaborative e-learning and ICT tools to develop SME managers: An Italian case. In I. Management Association (Ed.), Wireless technologies: Concepts, methodologies, tools and applications (pp. 1606-1617). Hershey, PA: Information Science Reference. doi: doi:10.4018/978-1-61350-101-6.ch605

Giannakos, M. N., Pateli, A. G., & Pappas, I. O. (2013). Identifying the direct effect of experience and the moderating effect of satisfaction in the Greek online market. In A. Scupola (Ed.), *Mobile opportunities and applications for e-service innovations* (pp. 77–97). Hershey, PA: Information Science Reference.

Giorda, M., & Guerrisi, M. (2013). Educating to democracy and social participation through a "history of religion" course. In P. Pumilia-Gnarini, E. Favaron, E. Pacetti, J. Bishop, & L. Guerra (Eds.), *Handbook of research on didactic strategies and technologies for education: Incorporating advancements* (pp. 152–161). Hershey, PA: Information Science Reference.

Goggins, S., Schmidt, M., Guajardo, J., & Moore, J. L. (2013). 3D virtual worlds: Assessing the experience and informing design. In B. Medlin (Ed.), *Integrations of technology utilization and social dynamics in organizations* (pp. 194–213). Hershey, PA: Information Science Reference.

Gold, N. (2012). Rebels, heretics, and exiles: Blogging among estranged and questioning American Hasidim. In T. Dumova, & R. Fiordo (Eds.), *Blogging in the global society: Cultural, political and geographical aspects* (pp. 108–127). Hershey, PA: Information Science Reference.

Görgü, L., Wan, J., O'Hare, G. M., & O'Grady, M. J. (2013). Enabling mobile service provision with sensor networks. In I. Lee (Ed.), *Mobile services industries, technologies, and applications in the global economy* (pp. 175–192). Hershey, PA: Information Science Reference.

Gregory, S. J. (2013). Evolution of mobile services: An analysis. In I. Lee (Ed.), *Mobile services industries, technologies, and applications in the global economy* (pp. 104–119). Hershey, PA: Information Science Reference.

Grieve, G. P., & Heston, K. (2012). Finding liquid salvation: Using the Cardean ethnographic method to document second life residents and religious cloud communities. In N. Zagalo, L. Morgado, & A. Boa-Ventura (Eds.), *Virtual worlds and metaverse platforms: New communication and identity paradigms* (pp. 288–305). Hershey, PA: Information Science Reference.

Guha, S., Thakur, B., Konar, T. S., & Chakrabarty, S. (2013). Web enabled design collaboration in India. In N. Kock (Ed.), *Interdisciplinary applications of electronic collaboration approaches and technologies* (pp. 96–111). Hershey, PA: Information Science Reference.

Gulati, G. J., Yates, D. J., & Tawileh, A. (2013). Explaining the global digital divide: The impact of public policy initiatives on e-government capacity and reach worldwide. In I. Association (Ed.), *Digital literacy: Concepts, methodologies, tools, and applications* (pp. 39–62). Hershey, PA: Information Science Reference.

Gupta, J. (2013). Digital library initiatives in India. In T. Ashraf, & P. Gulati (Eds.), *Design, development, and management of resources for digital library services* (pp. 80–93). Hershey, PA: Information Science Reference.

Gururajan, R., Hafeez-Baig, A., Danaher, P. A., & De George-Walker, L. (2012). Student perceptions and uses of wireless handheld devices: Implications for implementing blended and mobile learning in an Australian university. In I. Management Association (Ed.), Wireless technologies: Concepts, methodologies, tools and applications (pp. 1323-1338). Hershey, PA: Information Science Reference. doi: doi:10.4018/978-1-61350-101-6.ch512

Gwilt, I. (2013). Data-objects: Sharing the attributes and properties of digital and material culture to creatively interpret complex information. In D. Harrison (Ed.), *Digital media and technologies for virtual artistic spaces* (pp. 14–26). Hershey, PA: Information Science Reference. doi:10.4018/978-1-4666-2961-5.ch002

Hackley, D. C., & Leidman, M. B. (2013). Integrating learning management systems in K-12 supplemental religious education. In A. Ritzhaupt, & S. Kumar (Eds.), *Cases on educational technology implementation for facilitating learning* (pp. 1–22). Hershey, PA: Information Science Reference. doi:10.4018/978-1-4666-3676-7.ch001

Hale, J. R., & Fields, D. (2013). A cross-cultural measure of servant leadership behaviors. In M. Bocarnea, R. Reynolds, & J. Baker (Eds.), *Online instruments, data collection, and electronic measurements: Organizational advancements* (pp. 152–163). Hershey, PA: Information Science Reference.

Hanewald, R. (2012). Using mobile technologies as research tools: Pragmatics, possibilities and problems. In I. Management Association (Ed.), Wireless technologies: Concepts, methodologies, tools and applications (pp. 130-150). Hershey, PA: Information Science Reference. doi: doi:10.4018/978-1-61350-101-6.ch108

Hanewald, R. (2013). Professional development with and for emerging technologies: A case study with Asian languages and cultural studies teachers in Australia. In J. Keengwe (Ed.), *Pedagogical applications and social effects of mobile technology integration* (pp. 175–192). Hershey, PA: Information Science Reference. doi:10.4018/978-1-4666-2985-1.ch010

Hayhoe, S. (2012). Non-visual programming, perceptual culture and mulsemedia: Case studies of five blind computer programmers. In G. Ghinea, F. Andres, & S. Gulliver (Eds.), *Multiple sensorial media advances and applications: New developments in MulSeMedia* (pp. 80–98). Hershey, PA: Information Science Reference.

Henschke, J. A. (2013). Nation building through andragogy and lifelong learning: On the cutting edge educationally, economically, and governmentally. In V. Wang (Ed.), *Handbook of research on technologies for improving the 21st century workforce: Tools for lifelong learning* (pp. 480–506). Hershey, PA: Information Science Publishing.

Hermida, J. M., Meliá, S., Montoyo, A., & Gómez, J. (2013). Developing rich internet applications as social sites on the semantic web: A model-driven approach. In D. Chiu (Ed.), *Mobile and web innovations in systems and service-oriented engineering* (pp. 134–155). Hershey, PA: Information Science Reference.

Hernández-García, Á., Agudo-Peregrina, Á. F., & Iglesias-Pradas, S. (2013). Adoption of mobile video-call service: An exploratory study. In I. Lee (Ed.), *Strategy, adoption, and competitive advantage of mobile services in the global economy* (pp. 49–72). Hershey, PA: Information Science Reference.

Hesapci-Sanaktekin, O., & Somer, I. (2013). Mobile communication: A study on smart phone and mobile application use. In I. Lee (Ed.), *Strategy, adoption, and competitive advantage of mobile services in the global economy* (pp. 217–233). Hershey, PA: Information Science Reference.

Hill, S. R., Troshani, I., & Freeman, S. (2013). An eclectic perspective on the internationalization of Australian mobile services SMEs. In I. Lee (Ed.), *Mobile services industries, technologies, and applications in the global economy* (pp. 55–73). Hershey, PA: Information Science Reference.

Ho, V. (2013). The need for identity construction in computer-mediated professional communication: A Community of practice perspective. In R. Luppicini (Ed.), *Handbook of research on technoself: Identity in a technological society* (pp. 502–530). Hershey, PA: Information Science Reference.

Hudson, H. E. (2013). Challenges facing municipal wireless: Case studies from San Francisco and Silicon Valley. In A. Abdelaal (Ed.), *Social and economic effects of community wireless networks and infrastructures* (pp. 12–26). Hershey, PA: Information Science Reference. doi:10.4018/978-1-4666-2997-4.ch002

Humphreys, S. (2012). Unravelling intellectual property in a specialist social networking site. In A. Lugmayr, H. Franssila, P. Näränen, O. Sotamaa, J. Vanhala, & Z. Yu (Eds.), *Media in the ubiquitous era: Ambient, social and gaming media* (pp. 248–266). Hershey, PA: Information Science Reference. doi:10.4018/978-1-4666-2136-7.ch016

Iglesias, A., Ruiz-Mezcua, B., López, J. F., & Figueroa, D. C. (2013). New communication technologies for inclusive education in and outside the classroom. In D. Griol Barres, Z. Callejas Carrión, & R. Delgado (Eds.), *Technologies for inclusive education: Beyond traditional integration approaches* (pp. 271–284). Hershey, PA: Information Science Reference. doi:10.4018/978-1-4666-4422-9.ch088

Igun, S. E. (2013). Gender and national information and communication technology (ICT) policies in Africa. In B. Maumbe, & J. Okello (Eds.), *Technology, sustainability, and rural development in Africa* (pp. 284–297). Hershey, PA: Information Science Reference. doi:10.4018/978-1-4666-3607-1.ch018

Ikolo, V. E. (2013). Gender digital divide and national ICT policies in Africa. In I. Association (Ed.), *Digital literacy: Concepts, methodologies, tools, and applications* (pp. 812–832). Hershey, PA: Information Science Reference.

Imran, A., & Gregor, S. (2013). A process model for successful e-government adoption in the least developed countries: A case of Bangladesh. In I. Association (Ed.), *Digital literacy: Concepts, methodologies, tools, and applications* (pp. 213–241). Hershey, PA: Information Science Reference.

Ionescu, A. (2013). ICTs and gender-based rights. In J. Lannon, & E. Halpin (Eds.), *Human rights and information communication technologies: Trends and consequences of use* (pp. 214–234). Hershey, PA: Information Science Reference.

Iyamu, T. (2013). The impact of organisational politics on the implementation of IT strategy: South African case in context. In J. Abdelnour-Nocera (Ed.), *Knowledge and technological development effects on organizational and social structures* (pp. 167–193). Hershey, PA: Information Science Reference.

Jadhav, V. G. (2013). Integration of digital reference service for scholarly communication in digital libraries. In T. Ashraf, & P. Gulati (Eds.), *Design, development, and management of resources for digital library services* (pp. 13–20). Hershey, PA: Information Science Reference.

Jäkälä, M., & Berki, E. (2013). Communities, communication, and online identities. In S. Warburton, & S. Hatzipanagos (Eds.), *Digital identity and social media* (pp. 1–13). Hershey, PA: Information Science Reference.

Janneck, M., & Staar, H. (2013). Playing virtual power games: Micro-political processes in inter-organizational networks. In B. Medlin (Ed.), *Integrations of technology utilization and social dynamics in organizations* (pp. 171–192). Hershey, PA: Information Science Reference.

Januska, I. M. (2013). Communication as a key factor in cooperation success and virtual enterprise paradigm support. In P. Renna (Ed.), *Production and manufacturing system management: Coordination approaches and multi-site planning* (pp. 145–161). Hershey, PA: Engineering Science Reference.

Jayasingh, S., & Eze, U. C. (2013). Consumers' adoption of mobile coupons in Malaysia. In I. Lee (Ed.), *Strategy, adoption, and competitive advantage of mobile services in the global economy* (pp. 90–111). Hershey, PA: Information Science Reference.

Jean Francois, E. (2013). Transculturality. In E. Jean Francois (Ed.), *Transcultural blended learning and teaching in postsecondary education* (pp. 1–14). Hershey, PA: Information Science Reference.

Jensen, S. S. (2012). User-driven content creation in second life a source of innovation? Three case studies of business and public service. In N. Zagalo, L. Morgado, & A. Boa-Ventura (Eds.), *Virtual worlds and metaverse platforms: New communication and identity paradigms* (pp. 1–15). Hershey, PA: Information Science Reference.

Johnston, W. J., Komulainen, H., Ristola, A., & Ulkuniemi, P. (2013). Mobile advertising in small retailer firms: How to make the most of it. In I. Lee (Ed.), *Strategy, adoption, and competitive advantage of mobile services in the global economy* (pp. 283–298). Hershey, PA: Information Science Reference.

Kadas, G., & Chatzimisios, P. (2013). The role of roadside assistance in vehicular communication networks: Security, quality of service, and routing issues. In R. Daher, & A. Vinel (Eds.), *Roadside networks for vehicular communications: Architectures, applications, and test fields* (pp. 1–37). Hershey, PA: Information Science Reference.

Kale, S. H., & Spence, M. T. (2012). A trination analysis of social exchange relationships in e-dating. In C. Romm Livermore (Ed.), *Gender and social computing: Interactions, differences and relationships* (pp. 257–271). Hershey, PA: Information Science Publishing.

Kamoun, F. (2013). Mobile NFC services: Adoption factors and a typology of business models. In I. Lee (Ed.), *Mobile services industries, technologies, and applications in the global economy* (pp. 254–272). Hershey, PA: Information Science Reference.

Kaneda, K., & Iwamura, K. (2013). New proposals for data hiding in paper media. In K. Kondo (Ed.), *Multimedia information hiding technologies and methodologies for controlling data* (pp. 258–285). Hershey, PA: Information Science Reference.

Kastell, K. (2013). Seamless communication to mobile devices in vehicular wireless networks. In O. Strobel (Ed.), *Communication in transportation systems* (pp. 324–342). Hershey, PA: Information Science Reference. doi:10.4018/978-1-4666-2976-9.ch012

Kaye, B. K., & Johnson, T. J. (2012). Net gain? Selective exposure and selective avoidance of social network sites. In F. Comunello (Ed.), *Networked sociability and individualism: Technology for personal and professional relationships* (pp. 218–237). Hershey, PA: Information Science Reference.

Kaye, B. K., Johnson, T. J., & Muhlberger, P. (2012). Blogs as a source of democratic deliberation. In T. Dumova, & R. Fiordo (Eds.), *Blogging in the global society: Cultural, political and geographical aspects* (pp. 1–18). Hershey, PA: Information Science Reference.

Kefi, H., Mlaiki, A., & Peterson, R. L. (2013). IT offshoring: Trust views from client and vendor perspectives. In J. Wang (Ed.), *Perspectives and techniques for improving information technology project management* (pp. 113–130). Hershey, PA: Information Science Reference.

Khan, N. A., & Batoo, M. F. (2013). Stone inscriptions of Srinagar: A digital panorama. In T. Ashraf, & P. Gulati (Eds.), *Design, development, and management of resources for digital library services* (pp. 58–79). Hershey, PA: Information Science Reference.

Kim, P. (2012). "Stay out of the way! My kid is video blogging through a phone!": A lesson learned from math tutoring social media for children in underserved communities. In I. Management Association (Ed.), *Wireless technologies: Concepts, methodologies, tools and applications* (pp. 1415-1428). Hershey, PA: Information Science Reference. doi: doi:10.4018/978-1-61350-101-6.ch517

Kisubi, A. T. (2013). A critical perspective on the challenges for blended learning and teaching in Africa's higher education. In E. Jean Francois (Ed.), *Transcultural blended learning and teaching in postsecondary education* (pp. 145–168). Hershey, PA: Information Science Reference.

Koole, M., & Parchoma, G. (2013). The web of identity: A model of digital identity formation in networked learning environments. In S. Warburton, & S. Hatzipanagos (Eds.), *Digital identity and social media* (pp. 14–28). Hershey, PA: Information Science Reference.

Kordaki, M., Gorghiu, G., Bîzoi, M., & Glava, A. (2012). Collaboration within multinational learning communities: The case of the virtual community collaborative space for sciences education European project. In A. Juan, T. Daradoumis, M. Roca, S. Grasman, & J. Faulin (Eds.), *Collaborative and distributed e-research: Innovations in technologies, strategies and applications* (pp. 206–226). Hershey, PA: Information Science Reference. doi:10.4018/978-1-4666-0125-3.ch010

Kovács, J., Bokor, L., Kanizsai, Z., & Imre, S. (2013). Review of advanced mobility solutions for multimedia networking in IPv6. In D. Kanellopoulos (Ed.), *Intelligent multimedia technologies for networking applications: Techniques and tools* (pp. 25–47). Hershey, PA: Information Science Reference.

Kreps, D. (2013). Performing the discourse of sexuality online. In S. Warburton, & S. Hatzipanagos (Eds.), *Digital identity and social media* (pp. 118–132). Hershey, PA: Information Science Reference.

Ktoridou, D., Kaufmann, H., & Liassides, C. (2012). Factors affecting WiFi use intention: The context of Cyprus. In I. Management Association (Ed.), *Wireless technologies: Concepts, methodologies, tools and applications* (pp. 1760-1781). Hershey, PA: Information Science Reference. doi: doi:10.4018/978-1-61350-101-6.ch703

Kumar, N., Nero Alves, L., & Aguiar, R. L. (2013). Employing traffic lights as road side units for road safety information broadcast. In R. Daher, & A. Vinel (Eds.), *Roadside networks for vehicular communications: Architectures, applications, and test fields* (pp. 118–135). Hershey, PA: Information Science Reference.

Kvasny, L., & Hales, K. D. (2013). The evolving discourse of the digital divide: The internet, black identity, and the evolving discourse of the digital divide. In I. Association (Ed.), *Digital literacy: Concepts, methodologies, tools, and applications* (pp. 1350–1366). Hershey, PA: Information Science Reference.

L'Abate, L. (2013). Of paradigms, theories, and models: A conceptual hierarchical structure for communication science and technoself. In R. Luppicini (Ed.), *Handbook of research on technoself: Identity in a technological society* (pp. 84–104). Hershey, PA: Information Science Reference.

Laghos, A. (2013). Multimedia social networks and e-learning. In D. Kanellopoulos (Ed.), *Intelligent multimedia technologies for networking applications: Techniques and tools* (pp. 365–379). Hershey, PA: Information Science Reference.

Lappas, G. (2012). Social multimedia mining: Trends and opportunities in areas of social and communication studies. In I. Ting, T. Hong, & L. Wang (Eds.), *Social network mining, analysis, and research trends: Techniques and applications* (pp. 1–16). Hershey, PA: Information Science Reference.

Lawrence, J. E. (2013). Barriers hindering ecommerce adoption: A case study of Kurdistan region of Iraq. In A. Zolait (Ed.), *Technology diffusion and adoption: Global complexity, global innovation* (pp. 152–165). Hershey, PA: Information Science Reference. doi:10.4018/978-1-4666-2791-8.ch010

Lawrence, K. F. (2013). Identity and the online media fan community. In S. Warburton, & S. Hatzipanagos (Eds.), *Digital identity and social media* (pp. 233–255). Hershey, PA: Information Science Reference.

Lee, M. J., Dalgarno, B., Gregory, S., Carlson, L., & Tynan, B. (2013). How are Australian and New Zealand higher educators using 3D immersive virtual worlds in their teaching? In B. Tynan, J. Willems, & R. James (Eds.), *Outlooks and opportunities in blended and distance learning* (pp. 169–188). Hershey, PA: Information Science Reference.

Lee, S., Alfano, C., & Carpenter, R. G. (2013). Invention in two parts: Multimodal communication and space design in the writing center. In R. Carpenter (Ed.), *Cases on higher education spaces: Innovation, collaboration, and technology* (pp. 41–63). Hershey, PA: Information Science Reference.

Leichsenring, C., Tünnermann, R., & Hermann, T. (2013). Feelabuzz: Direct tactile communication with mobile phones. In J. Lumsden (Ed.), *Developments in technologies for human-centric mobile computing and applications* (pp. 145–154). Hershey, PA: Information Science Reference.

Lemos, A., & Marques, F. P. (2013). A critical analysis of the limitations and effects of the Brazilian national broadband plan. In A. Abdelaal (Ed.), *Social and economic effects of community wireless networks and infrastructures* (pp. 255–274). Hershey, PA: Information Science Reference. doi:10.4018/978-1-4666-2997-4.ch014

Leung, C. K., Medina, I. J., & Tanbeer, S. K. (2013). Analyzing social networks to mine important friends. In G. Xu, & L. Li (Eds.), *Social media mining and social network analysis: Emerging research* (pp. 90–104). Hershey, PA: Information Science Reference.

Li, B. (2012). Toward an infrastructural approach to understanding participation in virtual communities. In H. Li (Ed.), *Virtual community participation and motivation: Cross-disciplinary theories* (pp. 103–123). Hershey, PA: Information Science Reference. doi:10.4018/978-1-4666-0312-7.ch007

Li, L., Xiao, H., & Xu, G. (2013). Recommending related microblogs. In G. Xu, & L. Li (Eds.), *Social media mining and social network analysis: Emerging research* (pp. 202–210). Hershey, PA: Information Science Reference.

Liddell, T. (2013). Historical evolution of adult education in America: The impact of institutions, change, and acculturation. In V. Wang (Ed.), *Handbook of research on technologies for improving the 21st century workforce: Tools for lifelong learning* (pp. 257–271). Hershey, PA: Information Science Publishing.

Liljander, V., Gummerus, J., Pihlström, M., & Kiehelä, H. (2013). Mobile services as resources for consumer integration of value in a multi-channel environment. In I. Lee (Ed.), *Strategy, adoption, and competitive advantage of mobile services in the global economy* (pp. 259–282). Hershey, PA: Information Science Reference.

Litaay, T., Prananingrum, D. H., & Krisanto, Y. A. (2013). Indonesian legal perspectives on biotechnology and intellectual property rights. In I. Association (Ed.), *Digital rights management: Concepts, methodologies, tools, and applications* (pp. 834–845). Hershey, PA: Information Science Reference.

Little, G. (2013). Collection development for theological education. In S. Holder (Ed.), *Library collection development for professional programs: Trends and best practices* (pp. 112–127). Hershey, PA: Information Science Reference.

Losh, S. C. (2013). American digital divides: Generation, education, gender, and ethnicity in American digital divides. In I. Association (Ed.), *Digital literacy: Concepts, methodologies, tools, and applications* (pp. 932–958). Hershey, PA: Information Science Reference.

Lovari, A., & Parisi, L. (2012). Public administrations and citizens 2.0: Exploring digital public communication strategies and civic interaction within Italian municipality pages on Facebook. In F. Comunello (Ed.), *Networked sociability and individualism: Technology for personal and professional relationships* (pp. 238–263). Hershey, PA: Information Science Reference.

Maamar, Z., Faci, N., Mostéfaoui, S. K., & Akhter, F. (2013). Towards a framework for weaving social networks into mobile commerce. In D. Chiu (Ed.), *Mobile and web innovations in systems and service-oriented engineering* (pp. 333–347). Hershey, PA: Information Science Reference.

Maia, I. F., & Valente, J. A. (2013). Digital identity built on a cooperative relationship. In S. Warburton, & S. Hatzipanagos (Eds.), *Digital identity and social media* (pp. 58–73). Hershey, PA: Information Science Reference.

Maity, M. (2013). Consumer information search and decision-making on m-commerce: The role of product type. In I. Lee (Ed.), *Strategy, adoption, and competitive advantage of mobile services in the global economy* (pp. 73–89). Hershey, PA: Information Science Reference.

Malinen, S., Virjo, T., & Kujala, S. (2012). Supporting local connections with online communities. In A. Lugmayr, H. Franssila, P. Näränen, O. Sotamaa, J. Vanhala, & Z. Yu (Eds.), *Media in the ubiquitous era: Ambient, social and gaming media* (pp. 235–250). Hershey, PA: Information Science Reference.

Mantoro, T., Milišic, A., & Ayu, M. (2013). Online authentication using smart card technology in mobile phone infrastructure. In I. Khalil, & E. Weippl (Eds.), *Contemporary challenges and solutions for mobile and multimedia technologies* (pp. 127–144). Hershey, PA: Information Science Reference.

Marcato, E., & Scala, E. (2013). Moodle: A platform for a school. In P. Pumilia-Gnarini, E. Favaron, E. Pacetti, J. Bishop, & L. Guerra (Eds.), *Handbook of research on didactic strategies and technologies for education: Incorporating advancements* (pp. 107–116). Hershey, PA: Information Science Reference.

Markaki, O. I., Charalabidis, Y., & Askounis, D. (2013). Measuring interoperability readiness in south eastern Europe and the Mediterranean: The interoperability observatory. In A. Scupola (Ed.), *Mobile opportunities and applications for e-service innovations* (pp. 210–230). Hershey, PA: Information Science Reference.

Martin, J. D., & El-Toukhy, S. (2012). Blogging for sovereignty: An analysis of Palestinian blogs. In T. Dumova, & R. Fiordo (Eds.), *Blogging in the global society: Cultural, political and geographical aspects* (pp. 148–160). Hershey, PA: Information Science Reference.

Matei, S. A., & Bruno, R. J. (2012). Individualist motivators and community functional constraints in social media: The case of Wikis and Wikipedia. In F. Comunello (Ed.), *Networked sociability and individualism: Technology for personal and professional relationships* (pp. 1–23). Hershey, PA: Information Science Reference.

Matsuoka, H. (2013). Acoustic OFDM technology and system. In K. Kondo (Ed.), *Multimedia information hiding technologies and methodologies for controlling data* (pp. 90–103). Hershey, PA: Information Science Reference.

McCarthy, J. (2013). Online networking: Integrating international students into first year university through the strategic use of participatory media. In F. García-Peñalvo (Ed.), *Multiculturalism in technology-based education: Case studies on ICT-supported approaches* (pp. 189–210). Hershey, PA: Information Science Reference.

McDonald, A., & Helmer, S. (2013). A comparative case study of Indonesian and UK organisational culture differences in IS project management. In A. Mesquita (Ed.), *User perception and influencing factors of technology in everyday life* (pp. 46–55). Hershey, PA: Information Science Reference.

McDonough, C. (2013). Mobile broadband: Substituting for fixed broadband or providing value-added. In I. Lee (Ed.), *Mobile services industries, technologies, and applications in the global economy* (pp. 74–86). Hershey, PA: Information Science Reference.

McKeown, A. (2013). Virtual communitas, "digital place-making," and the process of "becoming". In D. Harrison (Ed.), *Digital media and technologies for virtual artistic spaces* (pp. 218–236). Hershey, PA: Information Science Reference. doi:10.4018/978-1-4666-2961-5.ch016

Medeni, T. D., Medeni, I. T., & Balci, A. (2013). Proposing a knowledge amphora model for transition towards mobile government. In A. Scupola (Ed.), *Mobile opportunities and applications for e-service innovations* (pp. 170–192). Hershey, PA: Information Science Reference.

Melo, A., Bezerra, P., Abelém, A. J., Neto, A., & Cerqueira, E. (2013). PriorityQoE: A tool for improving the QoE in video streaming. In D. Kanellopoulos (Ed.), *Intelligent multimedia technologies for networking applications: Techniques and tools* (pp. 270–290). Hershey, PA: Information Science Reference.

Mendoza-González, R., Rodríguez, F. Á., & Arteaga, J. M. (2013). A usability study of mobile text based social applications: Towards a reliable strategy for design evaluation. In M. Garcia-Ruiz (Ed.), *Cases on usability engineering: Design and development of digital products* (pp. 195–219). Hershey, PA: Information Science Reference. doi:10.4018/978-1-4666-4046-7.ch009

Metzger, M. J., Wilson, C., Pure, R. A., & Zhao, B. Y. (2012). Invisible interactions: What latent social interaction can tell us about social relationships in social network sites. In F. Comunello (Ed.), *Networked sociability and individualism: Technology for personal and professional relationships* (pp. 79–102). Hershey, PA: Information Science Reference.

Millo, G., & Carmeci, G. (2013). Insurance in Italy: A spatial perspective. In G. Borruso, S. Bertazzon, A. Favretto, B. Murgante, & C. Torre (Eds.), *Geographic information analysis for sustainable development and economic planning: New technologies* (pp. 158–178). Hershey, PA: Information Science Reference.

Mingqing, X., Wenjing, X., & Junming, Z. (2012). The future of television. In R. Sharma, M. Tan, & F. Pereira (Eds.), *Understanding the interactive digital media marketplace: Frameworks, platforms, communities and issues* (pp. 406–415). Hershey, PA: Information Science Reference.

Miscione, G. (2013). Telemedicine and development: Situating information technologies in the Amazon. In J. Abdelnour-Nocera (Ed.), *Knowledge and technological development effects on organizational and social structures* (pp. 132–145). Hershey, PA: Information Science Reference.

Modegi, T. (2013). Spatial and temporal position information delivery to mobile terminals using audio watermarking techniques. In K. Kondo (Ed.), *Multimedia information hiding technologies and methodologies for controlling data* (pp. 182–207). Hershey, PA: Information Science Reference.

Montes, J. A., Gutiérrez, A. C., Fernández, E. M., & Romeo, A. (2012). Reality mining, location based services and e-business opportunities: The case of city analytics. In I. Management Association (Ed.), Wireless technologies: Concepts, methodologies, tools and applications (pp. 1520-1532). Hershey, PA: Information Science Reference. doi: doi:10.4018/978-1-61350-101-6.ch601

Moreno, A. (2012). The social construction of new cultural models through information and communication technologies. In M. Safar, & K. Mahdi (Eds.), *Social networking and community behavior modeling: Qualitative and quantitative measures* (pp. 68–84). Hershey, PA: Information Science Reference.

Morris, J. Z., & Thomas, K. D. (2013). Implementing BioSand filters in rural Honduras: A case study of his hands mission international in Copán, Honduras. In H. Muga, & K. Thomas (Eds.), *Cases on the diffusion and adoption of sustainable development practices* (pp. 468–496). Hershey, PA: Information Science Reference.

Mura, G. (2012). The MultiPlasticity of new media. In G. Ghinea, F. Andres, & S. Gulliver (Eds.), *Multiple sensorial media advances and applications: New developments in MulSeMedia* (pp. 258–271). Hershey, PA: Information Science Reference.

Murray, C. (2012). Imagine mobile learning in your pocket. In I. Management Association (Ed.), *Wireless technologies: Concepts, methodologies, tools and applications* (pp. 2060-2088). Hershey, PA: Information Science Reference. doi: doi:10.4018/978-1-61350-101-6.ch807

Mutohar, A., & Hughes, J. E. (2013). Toward web 2.0 integration in Indonesian education: Challenges and planning strategies. In N. Azab (Ed.), *Cases on web 2.0 in developing countries: Studies on implementation, application, and use* (pp. 198–221). Hershey, PA: Information Science Reference.

Nandi, B., & Subramaniam, G. (2012). Evolution in broadband technology and future of wireless broadband. In I. Management Association (Ed.), *Wireless technologies: Concepts, methodologies, tools and applications* (pp. 1928-1957). Hershey, PA: Information Science Reference. doi: doi:10.4018/978-1-61350-101-6.ch801

Naser, A., Jaber, I., Jaber, R., & Saeed, K. (2013). Information systems in UAE education sector: Security, cultural, and ethical issues. In F. Albadri (Ed.), *Information systems applications in the Arab education sector* (pp. 148–162). Hershey, PA: Information Science Reference.

Nemoianu, I., & Pesquet-Popescu, B. (2013). Network coding for multimedia communications. In D. Kanellopoulos (Ed.), *Intelligent multimedia technologies for networking applications: Techniques and tools* (pp. 1–24). Hershey, PA: Information Science Reference.

Nezlek, G., & DeHondt, G. (2013). Gender wage differentials in information systems: 1991 – 2008 a quantitative analysis. In B. Medlin (Ed.), *Integrations of technology utilization and social dynamics in organizations* (pp. 31–47). Hershey, PA: Information Science Reference.

Nishimura, A., & Kondo, K. (2013). Information hiding for audio signals. In K. Kondo (Ed.), *Multimedia information hiding technologies and methodologies for controlling data* (pp. 1–18). Hershey, PA: Information Science Reference.

Norder, J. W., & Carroll, J. W. (2013). Applied geospatial perspectives on the rock art of the lake of the woods region of Ontario, Canada. In D. Albert, & G. Dobbs (Eds.), *Emerging methods and multidisciplinary applications in geospatial research* (pp. 77–93). Hershey, PA: Information Science Reference.

O'Brien, M. A., & Rogers, W. A. (2013). Design for aging: Enhancing everyday technology use. In R. Zheng, R. Hill, & M. Gardner (Eds.), *Engaging older adults with modern technology: Internet use and information access needs* (pp. 105–123). Hershey, PA: Information Science Reference.

O'Hanlon, S. (2013). Health information technology and human rights. In J. Lannon, & E. Halpin (Eds.), *Human rights and information communication technologies: Trends and consequences of use* (pp. 235–246). Hershey, PA: Information Science Reference.

Odella, F. (2012). Social networks and communities: From traditional society to the virtual sphere. In M. Safar, & K. Mahdi (Eds.), *Social networking and community behavior modeling: Qualitative and quantitative measures* (pp. 1–25). Hershey, PA: Information Science Reference.

Okazaki, S., Romero, J., & Campo, S. (2012). Capturing market mavens among advergamers: A case of mobile-based social networking site in Japan. In I. Ting, T. Hong, & L. Wang (Eds.), *Social network mining, analysis, and research trends: Techniques and applications* (pp. 291–305). Hershey, PA: Information Science Reference.

Omojola, O. (2012). Exploring the impact of Google Igbo in South East Nigeria. In R. Lekoko, & L. Semali (Eds.), *Cases on developing countries and ICT integration: Rural community development* (pp. 62–73). Hershey, PA: Information Science Reference.

Ovide, E. (2013). Intercultural education with indigenous peoples and the potential of digital technologies to make it happen. In F. García-Peñalvo (Ed.), *Multiculturalism in technology-based education: Case studies on ICT-supported approaches* (pp. 59–78). Hershey, PA: Information Science Reference.

Owusu-Ansah, A. (2013). Exploring Hofstede's cultural dimension using Hollins' structured dialogue to attain a conduit for effective intercultural experiences. In E. Jean Francois (Ed.), *Transcultural blended learning and teaching in postsecondary education* (pp. 52–74). Hershey, PA: Information Science Reference.

Özdemir, E. (2012). Gender and e-marketing: The role of gender differences in online purchasing behaviors. In C. Romm Livermore (Ed.), *Gender and social computing: Interactions, differences and relationships* (pp. 72–86). Hershey, PA: Information Science Publishing. doi:10.4018/978-1-4666-1598-4.ch044

Palmer, M. H., & Hanney, J. (2012). Geographic information networks in American Indian governments and communities. In S. Dasgupta (Ed.), *Technical, social, and legal issues in virtual communities: Emerging environments: Emerging environments* (pp. 52–62). Hershey, PA: Information Science Reference. doi:10.4018/978-1-4666-1553-3.ch004

Pande, R. (2013). Gender gaps and information and communication technology: A case study of India. In I. Association (Ed.), *Digital literacy: Concepts, methodologies, tools, and applications* (pp. 1425–1439). Hershey, PA: Information Science Reference.

Park, J., Chung, T., & Hur, W. (2013). The role of consumer innovativeness and trust for adopting internet phone services. In A. Scupola (Ed.), *Mobile opportunities and applications for e-service innovations* (pp. 22–36). Hershey, PA: Information Science Reference.

Parke, A., & Griffiths, M. (2013). Poker gambling virtual communities: The use of computer-mediated communication to develop cognitive poker gambling skills. In R. Zheng (Ed.), *Evolving psychological and educational perspectives on cyber behavior* (pp. 190–204). Hershey, PA: Information Science Reference.

Paschou, M., Sakkopoulos, E., Tsakalidis, A., Tzimas, G., & Viennas, E. (2013). An XML-based customizable model for multimedia applications for museums and exhibitions. In D. Kanellopoulos (Ed.), *Intelligent multimedia technologies for networking applications: Techniques and tools* (pp. 348–363). Hershey, PA: Information Science Reference.

Pauwels, L. (2013). Images, self-images, and idealized identities in the digital networked world: Reconfigurations of family photography in a web-based mode. In S. Warburton, & S. Hatzipanagos (Eds.), *Digital identity and social media* (pp. 133–147). Hershey, PA: Information Science Reference.

Peachey, A., & Withnail, G. (2013). A sociocultural perspective on negotiating digital identities in a community of learners. In S. Warburton, & S. Hatzipanagos (Eds.), *Digital identity and social media* (pp. 210–224). Hershey, PA: Information Science Reference.

Peixoto, E., Martins, E., Anjo, A. B., & Silva, A. (2012). Geo@NET in the context of the platform of assisted learning from Aveiro University, Portugal. In M. Cruz-Cunha (Ed.), *Handbook of research on serious games as educational, business and research tools* (pp. 648–667). Hershey, PA: Information Science Reference. doi:10.4018/978-1-4666-0149-9.ch033

Pillay, N. (2013). The use of web 2.0 technologies by students from developed and developing countries: A New Zealand case study. In N. Azab (Ed.), *Cases on web 2.0 in developing countries: Studies on implementation, application, and use* (pp. 411–441). Hershey, PA: Information Science Reference.

Pimenta, M. S., Miletto, E. M., Keller, D., Flores, L. V., & Testa, G. G. (2013). Technological support for online communities focusing on music creation: Adopting collaboration, flexibility, and multiculturality from Brazilian creativity styles. In N. Azab (Ed.), *Cases on web 2.0 in developing countries: Studies on implementation, application, and use* (pp. 283–312). Hershey, PA: Information Science Reference.

Pina, P. (2013). Between scylla and charybdis: The balance between copyright, digital rights management and freedom of expression. In I. Association (Ed.), *Digital rights management: Concepts, methodologies, tools, and applications* (pp. 1355–1367). Hershey, PA: Information Science Reference.

Pitsillides, S., Waller, M., & Fairfax, D. (2013). Digital death: What role does digital information play in the way we are (re)membered? In S. Warburton, & S. Hatzipanagos (Eds.), *Digital identity and social media* (pp. 75–90). Hershey, PA: Information Science Reference.

Polacek, P., & Huang, C. (2013). QoS scheduling with opportunistic spectrum access for multimedia. In M. Ku, & J. Lin (Eds.), *Cognitive radio and interference management: Technology and strategy* (pp. 162–178). Hershey, PA: Information Science Reference.

Potts, L. (2013). Balancing McLuhan with Williams: A sociotechnical view of technological determinism. In J. Abdelnour-Nocera (Ed.), *Knowledge and technological development effects on organizational and social structures* (pp. 109–114). Hershey, PA: Information Science Reference.

Prescott, J., & Bogg, J. (2013). Stereotype, attitudes, and identity: Gendered expectations and behaviors. In *Gendered occupational differences in science, engineering, and technology careers* (pp. 112–135). Hershey, PA: Information Science Reference.

Preussler, A., & Kerres, M. (2013). Managing social reputation in Twitter. In S. Warburton, & S. Hatzipanagos (Eds.), *Digital identity and social media* (pp. 91–103). Hershey, PA: Information Science Reference.

Prieger, J. E., & Church, T. V. (2013). Deployment of mobile broadband service in the United States. In I. Lee (Ed.), *Mobile services industries, technologies, and applications in the global economy* (pp. 1–24). Hershey, PA: Information Science Reference.

Puumalainen, K., Frank, L., Sundqvist, S., & Tuppura, A. (2012). The critical mass of wireless communications: Differences between developing and developed economies. In I. Management Association (Ed.), *Wireless technologies: Concepts, methodologies, tools and applications* (pp. 1719-1736). Hershey, PA: Information Science Reference. doi: doi:10.4018/978-1-61350-101-6.ch701

Rabino, S., Rafiee, D., Onufrey, S., & Moskowitz, H. (2013). Retention and customer share building: Formulating a communication strategy for a sports club. In H. Kaufmann, & M. Panni (Eds.), *Customer-centric marketing strategies: Tools for building organizational performance* (pp. 511–529). Hershey, PA: Business Science Reference.

Rahman, H., & Kumar, S. (2012). Mobile computing: An emerging issue in the digitized world. In A. Kumar, & H. Rahman (Eds.), *Mobile computing techniques in emerging markets: Systems, applications and services* (pp. 1–22). Hershey, PA: Information Science Reference. doi:10.4018/978-1-4666-0080-5.ch001

Ratten, V. (2013). Adoption of mobile reading devices in the book industry. In I. Lee (Ed.), *Strategy, adoption, and competitive advantage of mobile services in the global economy* (pp. 203–216). Hershey, PA: Information Science Reference.

Ratten, V. (2013). Mobile banking in the youth market: Implications from an entrepreneurial and learning perspective. In I. Lee (Ed.), *Strategy, adoption, and competitive advantage of mobile services in the global economy* (pp. 112–126). Hershey, PA: Information Science Reference.

Ratten, V. (2013). Social e-enterprise through technological innovations and mobile social networks. In T. Torres-Coronas, & M. Vidal-Blasco (Eds.), *Social e-enterprise: Value creation through ICT* (pp. 96–109). Hershey, PA: Information Science Reference.

Rego, P. A., Moreira, P. M., & Reis, L. P. (2012). New forms of interaction in serious games for rehabilitation. In M. Cruz-Cunha (Ed.), *Handbook of research on serious games as educational, business and research tools* (pp. 1188–1211). Hershey, PA: Information Science Reference. doi:10.4018/978-1-4666-0149-9.ch062

Reinhard, C. D. (2012). Virtual worlds and reception studies: Comparing engagings. In N. Zagalo, L. Morgado, & A. Boa-Ventura (Eds.), *Virtual worlds and metaverse platforms: New communication and identity paradigms* (pp. 117–136). Hershey, PA: Information Science Reference.

Rieser, M. (2013). Mobility, liminality, and digital materiality. In D. Harrison (Ed.), *Digital media and technologies for virtual artistic spaces* (pp. 27–45). Hershey, PA: Information Science Reference. doi:10.4018/978-1-4666-2961-5.ch003

Rodrigues, R. G., Pinheiro, P. G., & Barbosa, J. (2012). Online playability: The social dimension to the virtual world. In M. Cruz-Cunha (Ed.), *Handbook of research on serious games as educational, business and research tools* (pp. 391–421). Hershey, PA: Information Science Reference. doi:10.4018/978-1-4666-0149-9.ch021

Romm-Livermore, C., Somers, T. M., Setzekorn, K., & King, A. L. (2012). How e-daters behave online: Theory and empirical observations. In C. Romm Livermore (Ed.), *Gender and social computing: Interactions, differences and relationships* (pp. 236–256). Hershey, PA: Information Science Publishing.

Rosaci, D., & Sarnè, G. M. (2012). An agent-based approach to adapt multimedia web content in ubiquitous environment. In S. Bagchi (Ed.), *Ubiquitous multimedia and mobile agents: Models and implementations* (pp. 60–84). Hershey, PA: Information Science Reference.

Rosas, O. V., & Dhen, G. (2012). One self to rule them all: A critical discourse analysis of French-speaking players' identity construction in World of Warcraft. In N. Zagalo, L. Morgado, & A. Boa-Ventura (Eds.), *Virtual worlds and metaverse platforms: New communication and identity paradigms* (pp. 337–366). Hershey, PA: Information Science Reference.

Rouibah, K., & Abbas, H. A. (2012). Effect of personal innovativeness, attachment motivation and social norms on the acceptance of camera mobile phones: An empirical study in an Arab country. In W. Hu (Ed.), *Emergent trends in personal, mobile, and handheld computing technologies* (pp. 302–323). Hershey, PA: Information Science Reference. doi:10.4018/978-1-4666-0921-1.ch018

Ruiz-Mafé, C., Sanz-Blas, S., & Martí-Parreño, J. (2013). Web 2.0 goes mobile: Motivations and barriers of mobile social networks use in Spain. In N. Azab (Ed.), *Cases on web 2.0 in developing countries: Studies on implementation, application, and use* (pp. 109–146). Hershey, PA: Information Science Reference.

Rybas, S. (2012). Community embodied: Validating the subjective performance of an online class. In H. Li (Ed.), *Virtual community participation and motivation: Cross-disciplinary theories* (pp. 124–141). Hershey, PA: Information Science Reference. doi:10.4018/978-1-4666-0312-7.ch008

Sabelkin, M., & Gagnon, F. (2013). Data transmission oriented on the object, communication media, application, and state of communication systems. In M. Bartolacci, & S. Powell (Eds.), *Advancements and innovations in wireless communications and network technologies* (pp. 117–132). Hershey, PA: Information Science Reference.

Sajeva, S. (2013). Towards a conceptual knowledge management system based on systems thinking and sociotechnical thinking. In J. Abdelnour-Nocera (Ed.), *Knowledge and technological development effects on organizational and social structures* (pp. 115–130). Hershey, PA: Information Science Reference.

Salo, M., Olsson, T., Makkonen, M., & Frank, L. (2013). User perspective on the adoption of mobile augmented reality based applications. In I. Lee (Ed.), *Strategy, adoption, and competitive advantage of mobile services in the global economy* (pp. 165–188). Hershey, PA: Information Science Reference.

Samanta, S. K., Woods, J., & Ghanbari, M. (2013). Automatic language translation: An enhancement to the mobile messaging services. In A. Mesquita (Ed.), *User perception and influencing factors of technology in everyday life* (pp. 57–75). Hershey, PA: Information Science Reference.

Santo, A. E., Rijo, R., Monteiro, J., Henriques, I., Matos, A., & Rito, C. et al. (2012). Games improving disorders of attention deficit and hyperactivity. In M. Cruz-Cunha (Ed.), *Handbook of research on serious games as educational, business and research tools* (pp. 1160–1174). Hershey, PA: Information Science Reference. doi:10.4018/978-1-4666-0149-9.ch060

Sarker, S., Campbell, D. E., Ondrus, J., & Valacich, J. S. (2012). Mapping the need for mobile collaboration technologies: A fit perspective. In N. Kock (Ed.), *Advancing collaborative knowledge environments: New trends in e-collaboration* (pp. 211–233). Hershey, PA: Information Science Reference.

Sasajima, M., Kitamura, Y., & Mizoguchi, R. (2013). Method for modeling user semantics and its application to service navigation on the web. In G. Xu, & L. Li (Eds.), *Social media mining and social network analysis: Emerging research* (pp. 127–139). Hershey, PA: Information Science Reference.

Scheel, C., & Pineda, L. (2013). Building industrial clusters in Latin America: Paddling upstream. In J. Abdelnour-Nocera (Ed.), *Knowledge and technological development effects on organizational and social structures* (pp. 146–166). Hershey, PA: Information Science Reference.

Sell, A., Walden, P., & Carlsson, C. (2013). Segmentation matters: An exploratory study of mobile service users. In D. Chiu (Ed.), *Mobile and web innovations in systems and service-oriented engineering* (pp. 301–317). Hershey, PA: Information Science Reference.

Sermon, P., & Gould, C. (2013). Site-specific performance, narrative, and social presence in multi-user virtual environments and the urban landscape. In D. Harrison (Ed.), *Digital media and technologies for virtual artistic spaces* (pp. 46–58). Hershey, PA: Information Science Reference. doi:10.4018/978-1-4666-2961-5.ch004

Servaes, J. (2012). The role of information communication technologies within the field of communication for social change. In I. Management Association (Ed.), Wireless technologies: Concepts, methodologies, tools and applications (pp. 1117-1135). Hershey, PA: Information Science Reference. doi: doi:10.4018/978-1-61350-101-6.ch502

Seth, N., & Patnayakuni, R. (2012). Online matrimonial sites and the transformation of arranged marriage in India. In C. Romm Livermore (Ed.), *Gender and social computing: Interactions, differences and relationships* (pp. 272–295). Hershey, PA: Information Science Publishing.

Shaffer, G. (2013). Lessons learned from grassroots wireless networks in Europe. In A. Abdelaal (Ed.), *Social and economic effects of community wireless networks and infrastructures* (pp. 236–254). Hershey, PA: Information Science Reference. doi:10.4018/978-1-4666-2997-4.ch013

Shen, J., & Eder, L. B. (2013). An examination of factors associated with user acceptance of social shopping websites. In A. Mesquita (Ed.), *User perception and influencing factors of technology in everyday life* (pp. 28–45). Hershey, PA: Information Science Reference.

Shen, K. N. (2012). Identification vs. self-verification in virtual communities (VC): Theoretical gaps and design implications. In C. El Morr, & P. Maret (Eds.), *Virtual community building and the information society: Current and future directions* (pp. 208–236). Hershey, PA: Information Science Reference.

Shi, Y., & Liu, Z. (2013). Cultural models and variations. In I. Management Association (Ed.), Industrial engineering: Concepts, methodologies, tools, and applications (pp. 1560-1573). Hershey, PA: Engineering Science Reference. doi: doi:10.4018/978-1-4666-1945-6.ch083

Shiferaw, A., Sehai, E., Hoekstra, D., & Getachew, A. (2013). Enhanced knowledge management: Knowledge centers for extension communication and agriculture development in Ethiopia. In B. Maumbe, & C. Patrikakis (Eds.), *E-agriculture and rural development: Global innovations and future prospects* (pp. 103–116). Hershey, PA: Information Science Reference.

Simão de Vasconcellos, M., & Soares de Araújo, I. (2013). Massively multiplayer online role playing games for health communication in Brazil. In K. Bredl, & W. Bösche (Eds.), *Serious games and virtual worlds in education, professional development, and healthcare* (pp. 294–312). Hershey, PA: Information Science Reference. doi:10.4018/978-1-4666-3673-6.ch018

Simour, L. (2012). Networking identities: Geographies of interaction and computer mediated communication1. In S. Dasgupta (Ed.), *Technical, social, and legal issues in virtual communities: Emerging environments: Emerging environments* (pp. 235–246). Hershey, PA: Information Science Reference. doi:10.4018/978-1-4666-1553-3.ch016

Singh, G. R. (2013). Cyborg in the village: Culturally embedded resistances to blended teaching and learning. In E. Jean Francois (Ed.), *Transcultural blended learning and teaching in postsecondary education* (pp. 75–90). Hershey, PA: Information Science Reference.

Singh, M., & Iding, M. K. (2013). Does credibility count?: Singaporean students' evaluation of social studies web sites. In R. Zheng (Ed.), *Evolving psychological and educational perspectives on cyber behavior* (pp. 230–245). Hershey, PA: Information Science Reference.

Singh, S. (2013). Information and communication technology and its potential to transform Indian agriculture. In B. Maumbe, & C. Patrikakis (Eds.), *E-agriculture and rural development: Global innovations and future prospects* (pp. 140–168). Hershey, PA: Information Science Reference.

Siqueira, S. R., Rocha, E. C., & Nery, M. S. (2012). Brazilian occupational therapy perspective about digital games as an inclusive resource to disabled people in schools. In M. Cruz-Cunha (Ed.), *Handbook of research on serious games as educational, business and research tools* (pp. 730–749). Hershey, PA: Information Science Reference. doi:10.4018/978-1-4666-0149-9.ch037

Siti-Nabiha, A., & Salleh, D. (2013). Public sector transformation in Malaysia: Improving local governance and accountability. In N. Pomazalová (Ed.), *Public sector transformation processes and internet public procurement: Decision support systems* (pp. 276–290). Hershey, PA: Engineering Science Reference.

Siwar, C., & Abdulai, A. (2013). Sustainable development and the digital divide among OIC countries: Towards a collaborative digital approach. In I. Association (Ed.), *Digital literacy: Concepts, methodologies, tools, and applications* (pp. 242–261). Hershey, PA: Information Science Reference.

Smith, P. A. (2013). Strengthening and enriching audit practice: The socio-technical relevance of "decision leaders". In J. Abdelnour-Nocera (Ed.), *Knowledge and technological development effects on organizational and social structures* (pp. 97–108). Hershey, PA: Information Science Reference.

Smith, P. A., & Cockburn, T. (2013). Generational demographics. In *Dynamic leadership models for global business: Enhancing digitally connected environments* (pp. 230–256). Hershey, PA: Business Science Reference. doi:10.4018/978-1-4666-2836-6.ch009

Smith, P. A., & Cockburn, T. (2013). Leadership, global business, and digitally connected environments. In *Dynamic leadership models for global business: Enhancing digitally connected environments* (pp. 257–296). Hershey, PA: Business Science Reference. doi:10.4018/978-1-4666-2836-6.ch010

Sohrabi, B., Gholipour, A., & Amiri, B. (2013). The influence of information technology on organizational behavior: Study of identity challenges in virtual teams. In N. Kock (Ed.), *Interdisciplinary applications of electronic collaboration approaches and technologies* (pp. 79–95). Hershey, PA: Information Science Reference.

Soitu, L., & Paulet-Crainiceanu, L. (2013). Student-faculty communication on Facebook: Prospective learning enhancement and boundaries. In B. Pătruţ, M. Pătruţ, & C. Cmeciu (Eds.), *Social media and the new academic environment: Pedagogical challenges* (pp. 40–67). Hershey, PA: Information Science Reference. doi:10.4018/978-1-4666-2851-9.ch003

Solvoll, T. (2013). Mobile communication in hospitals: What is the problem? In C. Rückemann (Ed.), *Integrated information and computing systems for natural, spatial, and social sciences* (pp. 287–301). Hershey, PA: Information Science Reference.

Somboonviwat, K. (2013). Topic modeling for web community discovery. In G. Xu, & L. Li (Eds.), *Social media mining and social network analysis: Emerging research* (pp. 72–89). Hershey, PA: Information Science Reference.

Speaker, R. B., Levitt, G., & Grubaugh, S. (2013). Professional development in a virtual world. In J. Keengwe, & L. Kyei-Blankson (Eds.), *Virtual mentoring for teachers: Online professional development practices* (pp. 122–148). Hershey, PA: Information Science Reference.

Stevenson, G., & Van Belle, J. (2013). Using social media technology to improve collaboration: A case study of micro-blogging adoption in a South African financial services company. In N. Azab (Ed.), *Cases on web 2.0 in developing countries: Studies on implementation, application, and use* (pp. 313–341). Hershey, PA: Information Science Reference.

Strang, K. D. (2013). Balanced assessment of flexible e-learning vs. face-to-face campus delivery courses at an Australian university. In M. Khosrow-Pour (Ed.), *Cases on assessment and evaluation in education* (pp. 304–339). Hershey, PA: Information Science Reference.

Strömberg-Jakka, M. (2013). Social assistance via the internet: The case of Finland in the European context. In J. Lannon, & E. Halpin (Eds.), *Human rights and information communication technologies: Trends and consequences of use* (pp. 177–195). Hershey, PA: Information Science Reference.

Sultanow, E., Weber, E., & Cox, S. (2013). A semantic e-collaboration approach to enable awareness in globally distributed organizations. In N. Kock (Ed.), *Interdisciplinary applications of electronic collaboration approaches and technologies* (pp. 1–16). Hershey, PA: Information Science Reference.

Sun, H., Gui, N., & Blondia, C. (2013). A generic adaptation framework for mobile communication. In V. De Florio (Ed.), *Innovations and approaches for resilient and adaptive systems* (pp. 196–207). Hershey, PA: Information Science Reference.

Surgevil, O., & Özbilgin, M. F. (2012). Women in information communication technologies. In C. Romm Livermore (Ed.), *Gender and social computing: Interactions, differences and relationships* (pp. 87–97). Hershey, PA: Information Science Publishing.

Sylaiou, S., White, M., & Liarokapis, F. (2013). Digital heritage systems: The ARCO evaluation. In M. Garcia-Ruiz (Ed.), *Cases on usability engineering: Design and development of digital products* (pp. 321–354). Hershey, PA: Information Science Reference. doi:10.4018/978-1-4666-4046-7.ch014

Sylvester, O. A. (2013). Impact of information and communication technology on livestock production: The experience of rural farmers in Nigeria. In B. Maumbe, & C. Patrikakis (Eds.), *E-agriculture and rural development: Global innovations and future prospects* (pp. 68–75). Hershey, PA: Information Science Reference.

Taha, K., & Elmasri, R. (2012). Social search and personalization through demographic filtering. In I. Ting, T. Hong, & L. Wang (Eds.), *Social network mining, analysis, and research trends: Techniques and applications* (pp. 183–203). Hershey, PA: Information Science Reference.

Tai, Z. (2012). Fame, fantasy, fanfare and fun: The blossoming of the Chinese culture of blogmongering. In T. Dumova, & R. Fiordo (Eds.), *Blogging in the global society: Cultural, political and geographical aspects* (pp. 37–54). Hershey, PA: Information Science Reference.

Taifi, N., & Gharbi, K. (2013). Technology integration in strategic management: The case of a micro-financing institutions network. In T. Torres-Coronas, & M. Vidal-Blasco (Eds.), *Social e-enterprise: Value creation through ICT* (pp. 263–279). Hershey, PA: Information Science Reference.

Talib, S., Clarke, N. L., & Furnell, S. M. (2013). Establishing a personalized information security culture. In I. Khalil, & E. Weippl (Eds.), *Contemporary challenges and solutions for mobile and multimedia technologies* (pp. 53–69). Hershey, PA: Information Science Reference.

Tamura, H., Sugasaka, T., & Ueda, K. (2012). Lovely place to buy!: Enhancing grocery shopping experiences with a human-centric approach. In A. Lugmayr, H. Franssila, P. Näränen, O. Sotamaa, J. Vanhala, & Z. Yu (Eds.), *Media in the ubiquitous era: Ambient, social and gaming media* (pp. 53–65). Hershey, PA: Information Science Reference.

Tawileh, W., Bukvova, H., & Schoop, E. (2013). Virtual collaborative learning: Opportunities and challenges of web 2.0-based e-learning arrangements for developing countries. In N. Azab (Ed.), *Cases on web 2.0 in developing countries: Studies on implementation, application, and use* (pp. 380–410). Hershey, PA: Information Science Reference.

Teixeira, P. M., Félix, M. J., & Tavares, P. (2012). Playing with design: The universality of design in game development. In M. Cruz-Cunha (Ed.), *Handbook of research on serious games as educational, business and research tools* (pp. 217–231). Hershey, PA: Information Science Reference. doi:10.4018/978-1-4666-0149-9.ch011

Teusner, P. E. (2012). Networked individualism, constructions of community and religious identity: The case of emerging church bloggers in Australia. In F. Comunello (Ed.), *Networked sociability and individualism: Technology for personal and professional relationships* (pp. 264–288). Hershey, PA: Information Science Reference.

Tezcan, M. (2013). Social e-entrepreneurship, employment, and e-learning. In T. Torres-Coronas, & M. Vidal-Blasco (Eds.), *Social e-enterprise: Value creation through ICT* (pp. 133–147). Hershey, PA: Information Science Reference.

Thatcher, B. (2012). Approaching intercultural rhetoric and professional communication. In *Intercultural rhetoric and professional communication: Technological advances and organizational behavior* (pp. 1–38). Hershey, PA: Information Science Reference.

Thatcher, B. (2012). Borders and etics as units of analysis for intercultural rhetoric and professional communication. In *Intercultural rhetoric and professional communication: Technological advances and organizational behavior* (pp. 39–74). Hershey, PA: Information Science Reference.

Thatcher, B. (2012). Core competencies in intercultural teaching and research. In *Intercultural rhetoric and professional communication: Technological advances and organizational behavior* (pp. 318–342). Hershey, PA: Information Science Reference.

Thatcher, B. (2012). Distance education and e-learning across cultures. In *Intercultural rhetoric and professional communication: Technological advances and organizational behavior* (pp. 186–215). Hershey, PA: Information Science Reference.

Thatcher, B. (2012). Information and communication technologies and intercultural professional communication. In *Intercultural rhetoric and professional communication: Technological advances and organizational behavior* (pp. 97–123). Hershey, PA: Information Science Reference.

Thatcher, B. (2012). Intercultural rhetorical dimensions of health literacy and medicine. In *Intercultural rhetoric and professional communication: Technological advances and organizational behavior* (pp. 247–282). Hershey, PA: Information Science Reference.

Thatcher, B. (2012). Legal traditions, the universal declaration of human rights, and intercultural professional communication. In *Intercultural rhetoric and professional communication: Technological advances and organizational behavior* (pp. 216–246). Hershey, PA: Information Science Reference.

Thatcher, B. (2012). Organizational theory and communication across cultures. In *Intercultural rhetoric and professional communication: Technological advances and organizational behavior* (pp. 159–185). Hershey, PA: Information Science Reference.

Thatcher, B. (2012). Teaching intercultural rhetoric and professional communication. In *Intercultural rhetoric and professional communication: Technological advances and organizational behavior* (pp. 343–378). Hershey, PA: Information Science Reference.

Thatcher, B. (2012). Website designs as an indicator of globalization. In *Intercultural rhetoric and professional communication: Technological advances and organizational behavior* (pp. 124–158). Hershey, PA: Information Science Reference.

Thatcher, B. (2012). Writing instructions and how-to-do manuals across cultures. In *Intercultural rhetoric and professional communication: Technological advances and organizational behavior* (pp. 283–317). Hershey, PA: Information Science Reference.

Thirumal, P., & Tartakov, G. M. (2013). India's Dalits search for a democratic opening in the digital divide. In I. Association (Ed.), *Digital literacy: Concepts, methodologies, tools, and applications* (pp. 852–871). Hershey, PA: Information Science Reference.

Thomas, G. E. (2013). Facilitating learning with adult students in the transcultural classroom. In E. Jean Francois (Ed.), *Transcultural blended learning and teaching in postsecondary education* (pp. 193–215). Hershey, PA: Information Science Reference.

Tripathi, S. N., & Siddiqui, M. H. (2013). Designing effective mobile advertising with specific reference to developing markets. In I. Lee (Ed.), *Strategy, adoption, and competitive advantage of mobile services in the global economy* (pp. 299–324). Hershey, PA: Information Science Reference.

Truong, Y. (2013). Antecedents of consumer acceptance of mobile television advertising. In A. Mesquita (Ed.), *User perception and influencing factors of technology in everyday life* (pp. 128–141). Hershey, PA: Information Science Reference.

Tsuneizumi, I., Aikebaier, A., Ikeda, M., Enokido, T., & Takizawa, M. (2013). Design and implementation of hybrid time (HT) group communication protocol for homogeneous broadcast groups. In N. Bessis (Ed.), *Development of distributed systems from design to application and maintenance* (pp. 282–293). Hershey, PA: Information Science Reference.

Tzoulia, E. (2013). Legal issues to be considered before setting in force consumer-centric marketing strategies within the European Union. In H. Kaufmann, & M. Panni (Eds.), *Customer-centric marketing strategies: Tools for building organizational performance* (pp. 36–56). Hershey, PA: Business Science Reference.

Underwood, J., & Okubayashi, T. (2013). Comparing the characteristics of text-speak used by English and Japanese students. In R. Zheng (Ed.), *Evolving psychological and educational perspectives on cyber behavior* (pp. 258–271). Hershey, PA: Information Science Reference.

Unoki, M., & Miyauchi, R. (2013). Method of digital-audio watermarking based on cochlear delay characteristics. In K. Kondo (Ed.), *Multimedia information hiding technologies and methodologies for controlling data* (pp. 42–70). Hershey, PA: Information Science Reference.

Usman, L. M. (2013). Adult education and sustainable learning outcome of rural widows of central northern Nigeria. In V. Wang (Ed.), *Technological applications in adult and vocational education advancement* (pp. 215–231). Hershey, PA: Information Science Reference.

Usoro, A., & Khan, I. U. (2013). Trust as an aspect of organisational culture: Its effects on knowledge sharing in virtual communities. In R. Colomo-Palacios (Ed.), *Enhancing the modern organization through information technology professionals: Research, studies, and techniques* (pp. 182–199). Hershey, PA: Business Science Reference.

Utz, S. (2012). Social network site use among Dutch students: Effects of time and platform. In F. Comunello (Ed.), *Networked sociability and individualism: Technology for personal and professional relationships* (pp. 103–125). Hershey, PA: Information Science Reference.

Vasilescu, R., Epure, M., & Florea, N. (2013). Digital literacy for effective communication in the new academic environment: The educational blogs. In B. Pătruţ, M. Pătruţ, & C. Cmeciu (Eds.), *Social media and the new academic environment: Pedagogical challenges* (pp. 368–390). Hershey, PA: Information Science Reference. doi:10.4018/978-1-4666-2851-9.ch018

Vladimirschi, V. (2013). An exploratory study of cross-cultural engagement in the community of inquiry: Instructor perspectives and challenges. In Z. Akyol, & D. Garrison (Eds.), *Educational communities of inquiry: Theoretical framework, research and practice* (pp. 466–489). Hershey, PA: Information Science Reference.

Vuokko, R. (2012). A practice perspective on transforming mobile work. In I. Management Association (Ed.), *Wireless technologies: Concepts, methodologies, tools and applications* (pp. 1104-1116). Hershey, PA: Information Science Reference. doi: doi:10.4018/978-1-61350-101-6.ch501

Wall, M., & Kirdnark, T. (2012). The blogosphere in the "land of smiles": Citizen media and political conflict in Thailand. In T. Dumova, & R. Fiordo (Eds.), *Blogging in the global society: Cultural, political and geographical aspects* (pp. 19–36). Hershey, PA: Information Science Reference.

Warburton, S. (2013). Space for lurking: A pattern for designing online social spaces. In S. Warburton, & S. Hatzipanagos (Eds.), *Digital identity and social media* (pp. 149–158). Hershey, PA: Information Science Reference.

Warren, S. J., & Lin, L. (2012). Ethical considerations for learning game, simulation, and virtual world design and development. In H. Yang, & S. Yuen (Eds.), *Handbook of research on practices and outcomes in virtual worlds and environments* (pp. 1–18). Hershey, PA: Information Science Publishing.

Wasihun, T. A., & Maumbe, B. (2013). Information and communication technology uses in agriculture: Agribusiness industry opportunities and future challenges. In B. Maumbe, & C. Patrikakis (Eds.), *E-agriculture and rural development: Global innovations and future prospects* (pp. 235–251). Hershey, PA: Information Science Reference.

Webb, L. M., Fields, T. E., Boupha, S., & Stell, M. N. (2012). U.S. political blogs: What aspects of blog design correlate with popularity? In T. Dumova, & R. Fiordo (Eds.), *Blogging in the global society: Cultural, political and geographical aspects* (pp. 179–199). Hershey, PA: Information Science Reference.

Weeks, M. R. (2012). Toward an understanding of online community participation through narrative network analysis. In H. Li (Ed.), *Virtual community participation and motivation: Cross-disciplinary theories* (pp. 90–102). Hershey, PA: Information Science Reference. doi:10.4018/978-1-4666-0312-7.ch006

White, J. R. (2013). Language economy in computer-mediated communication: Learner autonomy in a community of practice. In B. Zou, M. Xing, Y. Wang, M. Sun, & C. Xiang (Eds.), *Computer-assisted foreign language teaching and learning: Technological advances* (pp. 75–90). Hershey, PA: Information Science Reference.

Whitworth, B., & Liu, T. (2013). Politeness as a social computing requirement. In J. Bishop (Ed.), *Examining the concepts, issues, and implications of internet trolling* (pp. 88–104). Hershey, PA: Information Science Reference. doi:10.4018/978-1-4666-2803-8.ch008

Wichowski, D. E., & Kohl, L. E. (2013). Establishing credibility in the information jungle: Blogs, microblogs, and the CRAAP test. In M. Folk, & S. Apostel (Eds.), *Online credibility and digital ethos: Evaluating computer-mediated communication* (pp. 229–251). Hershey, PA: Information Science Reference.

Williams, J. (2013). Social cohesion and free home internet in New Zealand. In A. Abdelaal (Ed.), *Social and economic effects of community wireless networks and infrastructures* (pp. 135–159). Hershey, PA: Information Science Reference. doi:10.4018/978-1-4666-2997-4.ch008

Williams, S., Fleming, S., Lundqvist, K., & Parslow, P. (2013). This is me: Digital identity and reputation on the internet. In S. Warburton, & S. Hatzipanagos (Eds.), *Digital identity and social media* (pp. 104–117). Hershey, PA: Information Science Reference.

Winning, R. (2013). Behind the sonic veil: Considering sound as the mediator of illusory life in variable and screen-based media. In D. Harrison (Ed.), Digital media and technologies for virtual artistic spaces (pp. 117-134). Hershey, PA: Information science reference. doi: doi:10.4018/978-1-4666-2961-5.ch009

Wolfe, A. (2012). Network perspective on structures related to communities. In M. Safar, & K. Mahdi (Eds.), *Social networking and community behavior modeling: Qualitative and quantitative measures* (pp. 26–50). Hershey, PA: Information Science Reference.

Worden, S. (2013). The earth sciences and creative practice: Exploring boundaries between digital and material culture. In D. Harrison (Ed.), *Digital media and technologies for virtual artistic spaces* (pp. 186–204). Hershey, PA: Information Science Reference. doi:10.4018/978-1-4666-2961-5.ch014

Xing, M., Zou, B., & Wang, D. (2013). A wiki platform for language and intercultural communication. In B. Zou, M. Xing, Y. Wang, M. Sun, & C. Xiang (Eds.), *Computer-assisted foreign language teaching and learning: Technological advances* (pp. 1–15). Hershey, PA: Information Science Reference.

Xu, G., Gu, Y., & Yi, X. (2013). On group extraction and fusion for tag-based social recommendation. In G. Xu, & L. Li (Eds.), *Social media mining and social network analysis: Emerging research* (pp. 211–223). Hershey, PA: Information Science Reference. doi:10.4018/978-1-4666-2806-9.ch014

Yakura, E. K., Soe, L., & Guthrie, R. (2012). Women in IT careers: Investigating support for women in the information technology workforce. In C. Romm Livermore (Ed.), *Gender and social computing: Interactions, differences and relationships* (pp. 35–49). Hershey, PA: Information Science Publishing.

Yang, Y., Rahim, A., & Karmakar, N. C. (2013). 5.8 GHz portable wireless monitoring system for sleep apnea diagnosis in wireless body sensor network (WBSN) using active RFID and MIMO technology. In N. Karmakar (Ed.), *Advanced RFID systems, security, and applications* (pp. 264–303). Hershey, PA: Information Science Reference.

Yu, Z., Liang, Y., Yang, Y., & Guo, B. (2013). Supporting social interaction in campus-scale environments by embracing mobile social networking. In G. Xu, & L. Li (Eds.), *Social media mining and social network analysis: Emerging research* (pp. 182–201). Hershey, PA: Information Science Reference.

Zaman, M., Simmers, C. A., & Anandarajan, M. (2013). Using an ethical framework to examine linkages between "going green" in research practices and information and communication technologies. In B. Medlin (Ed.), *Integrations of technology utilization and social dynamics in organizations* (pp. 243–262). Hershey, PA: Information Science Reference.

Zarmpou, T., Saprikis, V., & Vlachopoulou, M. (2013). Examining behavioral intention toward mobile services: An empirical investigation in Greece. In A. Scupola (Ed.), *Mobile opportunities and applications for e-service innovations* (pp. 37–56). Hershey, PA: Information Science Reference.

Zavala Pérez, J. M. (2012). Registry culture and networked sociability: Building individual identity through information records. In F. Comunello (Ed.), *Networked sociability and individualism: Technology for personal and professional relationships* (pp. 41–62). Hershey, PA: Information Science Reference.

Zemliansky, P., & Goroshko, O. (2013). Social media and other web 2.0 technologies as communication channels in a cross-cultural, web-based professional communication project. In B. Pătruţ, M. Pătruţ, & C. Cmeciu (Eds.), *Social media and the new academic environment: Pedagogical challenges* (pp. 256–272). Hershey, PA: Information Science Reference. doi:10.4018/978-1-4666-2851-9.ch013

Zervas, P., & Alexandraki, C. (2013). The realisation of online music services through intelligent computing. In D. Kanellopoulos (Ed.), *Intelligent multimedia technologies for networking applications: Techniques and tools* (pp. 291–317). Hershey, PA: Information Science Reference.

Zhang, J., & Mao, E. (2013). The effects of consumption values on the use of location-based services on smartphones. In I. Lee (Ed.), *Strategy, adoption, and competitive advantage of mobile services in the global economy* (pp. 1–18). Hershey, PA: Information Science Reference.

Zhang, S., Köbler, F., Tremaine, M., & Milewski, A. (2012). Instant messaging in global software teams. In N. Kock (Ed.), *Advancing collaborative knowledge environments: New trends in e-collaboration* (pp. 158–179). Hershey, PA: Information Science Reference.

Zhang, T., Wang, C., Luo, Z., Han, S., & Dong, M. (2013). RFID enabled vehicular network for ubiquitous travel query. In D. Chiu (Ed.), *Mobile and web innovations in systems and service-oriented engineering* (pp. 348–363). Hershey, PA: Information Science Reference.

Zhang, W. (2012). Virtual communities as subaltern public spheres: A theoretical development and an application to the Chinese internet. In H. Li (Ed.), *Virtual community participation and motivation: Cross-disciplinary theories* (pp. 143–159). Hershey, PA: Information Science Reference. doi:10.4018/978-1-4666-0312-7.ch009

Zhang, X., Wang, L., Li, Y., & Liang, W. (2013). Global community extraction in social network analysis. In G. Xu, & L. Li (Eds.), *Social media mining and social network analysis: Emerging research* (pp. 156–171). Hershey, PA: Information Science Reference.

Zhang, X., Wang, L., Li, Y., & Liang, W. (2013). Local community extraction in social network analysis. In G. Xu, & L. Li (Eds.), *Social media mining and social network analysis: Emerging research* (pp. 172–181). Hershey, PA: Information Science Reference.

Zulu, S. F. (2013). Emerging information and communication technology policy framework for Africa. In B. Maumbe, & J. Okello (Eds.), *Technology, sustainability, and rural development in Africa* (pp. 236–256). Hershey, PA: Information Science Reference. doi:10.4018/978-1-4666-3607-1.ch016

Compilation of References

Aaronson, T. (2011, September/October). The informants. *Mother Jones*. Retrieved July 3, 2013, from http://www.motherjones.com/politics/2011/08/fbi-terrorist-informants

Aas, B. G. (2012). What's real? Presence, personality and identity in the real and online virtual world. In N. Zagalo, L. Morgado, & A. Boa-Ventura (Eds.), *Virtual worlds and metaverse platforms: New communication and identity paradigms* (pp. 88–99). Hershey, PA: Information Science Reference.

Abrahamian, E. (2003). The US media, Huntington and September 11. *Third World Quarterly*, 24(3), 529–544. doi:10.1080/0143659032000084456

Abrahms, M. (2012). The political effectiveness of terrorism revisited. *Comparative Political Studies*, 45(3), 366–393. doi:10.1177/0010414011433104

Aceti, V., & Luppicini, R. (2013). Exploring the effect of mhealth technologies on communication and information sharing in a pediatric critical care unit: A case study. In J. Tan (Ed.), *Healthcare information technology innovation and sustainability: Frontiers and adoption* (pp. 88–108). Hershey, PA: Medical Information Science Reference. doi:10.4018/978-1-4666-2797-0.ch006

Acilar, A. (2013). Factors affecting mobile phone use among undergraduate students in Turkey: An exploratory analysis. In I. Lee (Ed.), *Strategy, adoption, and competitive advantage of mobile services in the global economy* (pp. 234–246). Hershey, PA: Information Science Reference.

Adair, J. (2009). *Effective decision making: The essential guide to thinking for management success*. London, UK: Pan Books.

Adams, A. (2013). Situated e-learning: Empowerment and barriers to identity changes. In S. Warburton, & S. Hatzipanagos (Eds.), *Digital identity and social media* (pp. 159–175). Hershey, PA: Information Science Reference.

Adeoye, B. F. (2013). Culturally different learning styles in online learning environments: A case of Nigerian university students. In L. Tomei (Ed.), *Learning tools and teaching approaches through ICT advancements* (pp. 228–240). Hershey, PA: Information Science Reference.

Adkins, G. (2013). Red teaming the red team: Utilizing cyber espionage to combat terrorism. *Journal of Strategy Security*, 6(5), 1–9.

Adomi, E. E., & Igun, S. E. (2008). Combating cyber crime in Nigeria. *The Electronic Library*, 26(5), 716–725.

Agamben, G. (1998). *Homo sacer: Sovereign power and bare life*. Stanford, CA: Stanford University Press.

Agarwal, N., & Mahata, D. (2013). Grouping the similar among the disconnected bloggers. In G. Xu, & L. Li (Eds.), *Social media mining and social network analysis: Emerging research* (pp. 54–71). Hershey, PA: Information Science Reference.

Ahmad, M. I. (2011, June 13). The magical realism of body counts. *al-Jazeera*. Retrieved July 3, 2013, from http://www.aljazeera.com/indepth/opinion/2011/06/2011613931606455.html

Aiken, M., Wang, J., Gu, L., & Paolillo, J. (2013). An exploratory study of how technology supports communication in multilingual groups. In N. Kock (Ed.), *Interdisciplinary applications of electronic collaboration approaches and technologies* (pp. 17–29). Hershey, PA: Information Science Reference.

Aikins, S. K., & Chary, M. (2013). Online participation and digital divide: An empirical evaluation of U.S. midwestern municipalities. In I. Association (Ed.), *Digital literacy: Concepts, methodologies, tools, and applications* (pp. 63–85). Hershey, PA: Information Science Reference.

Akram, S. M., & Karmely, M. (2005). Immigration and constitutional consequences of post-9/11 policies involving Arabs and Muslims in the United States: Is alienage a distinction without a difference? *University of California Davis Law Review, 38*(3), 609–700.

Al Disi, Z. A., & Albadri, F. (2013). Arab youth and the internet: Educational perspective. In F. Albadri (Ed.), *Information systems applications in the Arab education sector* (pp. 163–178). Hershey, PA: Information Science Reference.

Al Omoush, K. S., Alqirem, R. M., & Shaqrah, A. A. (2013). The driving internal beliefs of household internet adoption among Jordanians and the role of cultural values. In A. Zolait (Ed.), *Technology diffusion and adoption: global complexity, global innovation* (pp. 130–151). Hershey, PA: Information Science Reference. doi:10.4018/978-1-4666-2791-8.ch009

AlBalawi, M. S. (2013). Web-based instructions: An assessment of preparedness of conventional universities in Saudi Arabia. In M. Khosrow-Pour (Ed.), *Cases on assessment and evaluation in education* (pp. 417–451). Hershey, PA: Information Science Reference.

Albright, K., Abrams, C. B., & Panofsky, A. L. (2009). After the fall: The changing experiential conditions of post-9/11 New York and their political implications. *The American Behavioral Scientist, 53*(1), 80–98. doi:10.1177/0002764209338787

Al-Dossary, S., Al-Dulaijan, N., Al-Mansour, S., Al-Zahrani, S., Al-Fridan, M., & Househ, M. (2013). Organ donation and transplantation: Processes, registries, consent, and restrictions in Saudi Arabia. In M. Cruz-Cunha, I. Miranda, & P. Gonçalves (Eds.), *Handbook of research on ICTs for human-centered healthcare and social care services* (pp. 511–528). Hershey, PA: Medical Information Science Reference. doi:10.4018/978-1-4666-3986-7.ch027

Alejos, A. V., Cuiñas, I., Expósito, I., & Sánchez, M. G. (2013). From the farm to fork: Information security accomplishment in a RFID based tracking chain for food sector. In P. Lopez, J. Hernandez-Castro, & T. Li (Eds.), *Security and trends in wireless identification and sensing platform tags: Advancements in RFID* (pp. 237–270). Hershey, PA: Information Science Reference.

Alexander, Y., & Latter, R. (Eds.). (1990). Terrorism and the media: Dilemmas for government, journalists and the public. Washington, DC: Brassey's (US), Inc.

Alexander, Y. (2006). Introduction. In Y. Alexander (Ed.), *Counterterrorism strategies: Success and failures of six nations* (pp. 1–8). Washington, DC: Potomac Books.

Alger, D. E. (1989). *The media and politics*. Upper Saddle River, NJ: Prentice Hall.

Aliprantis, C. D., & Chakrabarti, S. K. (2000). *Games and decision making*. New York: Oxford University Press.

Ali, Z., Iqbal, A., Jan, M., & Ahmad, A. (2012). Coverage of Pak-U.S. relations on issue of counter terrorism by U.S. leading news magazines. *Middle-East Journal of Scientific Research, 15*(10), 1464–1471.

Al-Karni, A. (2005). *A media-terrorism model: The Saudi experience*. Paper presented at the Annual Convention of the International Association for Media and Communication Research. Taipei, Taiwan.

Alkazemi, M. F., Bowe, B. J., & Blom, R. (2013). Facilitating the Egyptian uprising: A case study of Facebook and Egypt's April 6th youth movement. In N. Azab (Ed.), *Cases on web 2.0 in developing countries: Studies on implementation, application, and use* (pp. 256–282). Hershey, PA: Information Science Reference.

Al-Khaffaf, M. M., & Abdellatif, H. J. (2013). The effect of information and communication technology on customer relationship management: Jordan public shareholding companies. In R. Eid (Ed.), *Managing customer trust, satisfaction, and loyalty through information communication technologies* (pp. 342–350). Hershey, PA: Business Science Reference.

Allan, S. (2004). The culture of distance: Online reporting of the Iraq war. In S. Allan, & B. Zelizer (Eds.), *Reporting war: Journalism in wartime* (pp. 347–364). London: Routledge.

Almutairi, M. S. (2012). M-government: Challenges and key success factors – Saudi Arabia case study. In I. Management Association (Ed.), Wireless technologies: Concepts, methodologies, tools and applications (pp. 1698-1717). Hershey, PA: Information Science Reference. doi: doi:10.4018/978-1-61350-101-6.ch611

Al-Nuaim, H. A. (2012). Evaluation of Arab municipal websites. In I. Management Association (Ed.), Wireless technologies: Concepts, methodologies, tools and applications (pp. 1170-1185). Hershey, PA: Information Science Reference. doi: doi:10.4018/978-1-61350-101-6.ch505

Al-Nuaim, H. A. (2013). Developing user profiles for interactive online products in practice. In M. Garcia-Ruiz (Ed.), *Cases on usability engineering: Design and development of digital products* (pp. 57–79). Hershey, PA: Information Science Reference. doi:10.4018/978-1-4666-4046-7.ch003

al-Quds al-Arabi. (2012, May 27). *Saudi diplomat appeals to king for his release*, p. 4.

Al-Shqairat, Z. I., & Altarawneh, I. I. (2013). The role of partnership in e-government readiness: The knowledge stations (KSs) initiative in Jordan. In A. Mesquita (Ed.), *User perception and influencing factors of technology in everyday life* (pp. 192–210). Hershey, PA: Information Science Reference.

Alsultany, E. (2012). *Arabs and Muslims in the media: Race and representation after 9/11*. New York: New York University Press.

Alsultany, E. (2013). Arabs and Muslims in the media after 9/11: Representational strategies for a postrace era. *American Quarterly, 65*(1), 161–169. doi:10.1353/aq.2013.0008

Althaf. (2009, December 12). *Noordin M top rajai Yahoo selama 2009*. Retrieved July 3, 2013, from http://www.ar-rahmah.com/index.php/news/read/6243/noordin-m-top-

Altheide, D. L. (1987). Format and symbols in TV coverage of terrorism in the United States and Great Britain. *International Studies Quarterly, 31*(2), 161–176. doi:10.2307/2600451

Altheide, D. L. (2006). The mass media, crime and terrorism. *Journal of International Criminal Justice, 4*(5), 982–997.

Altheide, D. L., & Grimes, J. N. (2005). War programming: The propaganda project and the Iraq War. *The Sociological Quarterly, 46*(4), 617–643. doi:10.1111/j.1533-8525.2005.00029.x

Alyagout, F., & Siti-Nabiha, A. K. (2013). Public sector transformation: Privatization in Saudi Arabia. In N. Pomazalová (Ed.), *Public sector transformation processes and internet public procurement: Decision support systems* (pp. 17–31). Hershey, PA: Engineering Science Reference.

al-Zawahiri, A. (2005). *Letter from Ayman al-Zawahiri to Abu Musab al-Zarqawi*. Council on Foreign Relations. Retrieved May 16, 2012, from http://www.cfr.org/iraq/letter-ayman-al-zawahiri-abu-musab-al-zarqawi/p9862

American Civil Liberties Union (ACLU). (2009, February 27). *Designating non-profits as terrorist organizations without due process undermines security and humanitarian aid, say groups*. Retrieved July 3, 2013, from http://www.aclu.org/national-security/designating-non-profits-terrorist-organizations-without-due-process-undermines-sec

Amirante, A., Castaldi, T., Miniero, L., & Romano, S. P. (2013). Protocol interactions among user agents, application servers, and media servers: Standardization efforts and open issues. In D. Kanellopoulos (Ed.), *Intelligent multimedia technologies for networking applications: Techniques and tools* (pp. 48–63). Hershey, PA: Information Science Reference.

Andersen, R. (2006). *A century of media, a century of war*. New York: Peter Lang Publishers.

Anderson, A. (2003). Risk, terrorism, and the internet. *Knowledge, Technology & Policy, 16*(2), 24–33.

Anderton, C. H., & Carter, J. R. (2005). On rational choice theory and the study of terrorism. *Defence and Peace Economics*, *16*(4), 275–282. doi:10.1080/1024269052000344864

Andres, H. P. (2013). Shared mental model development during technology-mediated collaboration. In N. Kock (Ed.), *Interdisciplinary applications of electronic collaboration approaches and technologies* (pp. 125–142). Hershey, PA: Information Science Reference.

Andrus, C. H., & Gaynor, M. (2013). Good IT requires good communication. In S. Sarnikar, D. Bennett, & M. Gaynor (Eds.), *Cases on healthcare information technology for patient care management* (pp. 122–125). Hershey, PA: Medical Information Science Reference.

Annafari, M. T., & Bohlin, E. (2013). Why is the diffusion of mobile service not an evolutionary process? In I. Lee (Ed.), *Mobile services industries, technologies, and applications in the global economy* (pp. 25–38). Hershey, PA: Information Science Reference.

Anti-Defamation League. (1985). *Computerized networks of hate*. New York: ADL.

Anti-Defamation League. (2013). *Extremism in America: Don black/stormfront*. Retrieved August 30, 2013, from http://archive.adl.org/learn/ext_us/Don-Black/default.asp?xpicked=2&item=DBlack

Anupama, S. (2013). Gender evaluation of rural e-governance in India: A case study of E-Gram Suraj (e-rural good governance) scheme1. In I. Association (Ed.), *Digital literacy: Concepts, methodologies, tools, and applications* (pp. 1059–1074). Hershey, PA: Information Science Reference.

Arce, D. G., & Sandler, T. (2007). Terrorist signaling and the value of intelligence. *British Journal of Political Science*, *37*, 573–586. doi:10.1017/S0007123407000324

Archer, T. (2011, July 25). Breivik's swamp: Was the Oslo killer radicalized by what he read online? *Foreign Policy*. Retrieved July 3, 2013, from http://www.foreignpolicy.com/articles/2011/07/25/breivik_s_swamp

Arena, M., & Arrigo, B. (2004). Identity and the terrorist threat: An interpretive and explanatory model. *International Criminal Justice Review*, *14*, 124–163.

Argenti, P. A., Howell, R. A., & Beck, K. A. (2005). The strategic communication imperative. *MIT Sloan Management Review*, *46*(3), 82–89.

Ariely, G. (2013). Boundaries of socio-technical systems and IT for knowledge development in military environments. In J. Abdelnour-Nocera (Ed.), *Knowledge and technological development effects on organizational and social structures* (pp. 224–238). Hershey, PA: Information Science Reference.

Arquilla, J., & Ronfeldt, D. (1996). *The advent of netwar*. Santa Monica, CA: RAND Corporation.

Arquilla, J., & Ronfeldt, D. (2001). *Networks and netwars: The future of terror, crime, and militancy*. Santa Monica, CA: RAND Corporation.

Arquilla, J., Ronfeldt, D., & Zanini, M. (1999). Networks, netwar, and information-age terrorism. In I. O. Lesser, B. Hoffman, J. Arquilla, D. Ronfeldt, & M. Zanini (Eds.), *Countering the new terrorism* (pp. 39–41). Santa Monica, CA: RAND Corporation.

Arsenio, A. M. (2013). Intelligent approaches for adaptation and distribution of personalized multimedia content. In D. Kanellopoulos (Ed.), *Intelligent multimedia technologies for networking applications: Techniques and tools* (pp. 197–224). Hershey, PA: Information Science Reference.

Artail, H., & Tarhini, T. (2013). Runtime discovery and access of web services in mobile environments. In I. Lee (Ed.), *Mobile services industries, technologies, and applications in the global economy* (pp. 193–213). Hershey, PA: Information Science Reference.

Ashforth, B. E., Kreiner, G. E., Clark, M. A., & Fugate, M. (2007). Normalizing dirty work: Managerial tactics for countering occupational taint. *Academy of Management Review*, *50*(1), 149–174.

Asino, T. I., Wilder, H., & Ferris, S. P. (2013). Innovative use of ICT in Namibia for nationhood: Special emphasis on the Namibian newspaper. In H. Rahman (Ed.), *Cases on progressions and challenges in ICT utilization for citizen-centric governance* (pp. 205–216). Hershey, PA: Information Science Reference.

Aslan, R. (2010). *Beyond fundamentalism: Confronting religious extremism in the age of globalization.* New York: Random House.

Atici, B., & Bati, U. (2013). Identity of virtual supporters: Constructing identity of Turkish football fans on digital media. In S. Warburton, & S. Hatzipanagos (Eds.), *Digital identity and social media* (pp. 256–274). Hershey, PA: Information Science Reference.

Atran, S. (2003). Genesis of suicide terrorism. *Review Social Science, 299,* 1534–1539. PMID:12624256

Atran, S. (2006). The moral logic and growth of suicide terrorism. *The Washington Quarterly, 29*(2), 127–147. doi:10.1162/wash.2006.29.2.127

Atton, C. (2009). Alternative and citizen journalism. In K. Wahl-Jorgensen, & T. Hanitzsch (Eds.), *The handbook of journalism studies* (pp. 265–278). New York: Routledge.

Atton, C., & Hamilton, J. F. (2008). *Alternative journalism.* Los Angeles, CA: Sage.

Aussaresses, P. (2001). *Services spéciaux Algérie 1955-1957.* Paris: Perrin.

Awan, A. (2007). Virtual jihadist media: Function, legitimacy, and radicalizing efficacy. *European Journal of Cultural Studies, 10*(3), 389–408.

Awan, A., Hoskins, A., & O'Loughlin, B. (2011). *Radicalisation and media: Connectivity and terrorism in the new media ecology.* London: Routledge.

Azab, N., & Khalifa, N. (2013). Web 2.0 and opportunities for entrepreneurs: How Egyptian entrepreneurs perceive and exploit web 2.0 technologies. In N. Azab (Ed.), *Cases on web 2.0 in developing countries: Studies on implementation, application, and use* (pp. 1–32). Hershey, PA: Information Science Reference.

Bainbridge, W. S. (2013). Ancestor veneration avatars. In R. Luppicini (Ed.), *Handbook of research on technoself: Identity in a technological society* (pp. 308–321). Hershey, PA: Information Science Reference.

Bamber, D., & Palmer, A. (2003, March 31). UK forces aided Ulster loyalists. *The Age.* Retrieved March 31, 2003, from http://www.theage.com.au/articles/2003/03/30/1048962644995.html?oneclick=true

Bankoff, G. (2003). Region of risk: Western discourses on terrorism and the significance of Islam. *Studies in Conflict and Terrorism, 26*(6), 413–428. doi:10.1080/10576100390242929

Banks, M. (2001). *Visual methods in social research.* Thousand Oaks, CA: Sage.

Baporikar, N. (2013). Critical review of academic entrepreneurship in India. In A. Szopa, W. Karwowski, & P. Ordóñez de Pablos (Eds.), *Academic entrepreneurship and technological innovation: A business management perspective* (pp. 29–52). Hershey, PA: Information Science Reference.

Baratieri, D. (2010). *Memories and silences haunted by fascism: Italian colonialism, MCMXXX-MCMLX.* Bern, Switzerland: Peter Lang.

Barkan, S. E., & Snowden, L. L. (2001). *Collective violence.* Boston: Allyn & Bacon.

Barnett, T. P. M. (2005b, February). *Thomas Barnett draws a new map for peace.* [podcast radio program]. Monterey, CA: TED Talks. Retrieved May 5, 2012, from http://www.ted.com/talks/thomas_barnett_draws_a_new_map_for_peace.html

Barnett, T. P. M. (2005a). *The Pentagon's new map: War and peace in the twenty-first Century.* New York: Putnam's.

Barnhurst, K. G. (1991). Contemporary terrorism in Peru: Sendero luminoso and the media. *The Journal of Communication, 41*(4), 75–89. doi:10.1111/j.1460-2466.1991.tb02332.x

Baron, J. (2000). *Thinking and deciding.* Cambridge, UK: Cambridge University Press.

Barroca, L., & Gimenes, I. M. (2013). Computing post-graduate programmes in the UK and Brazil: Learning from experience in distance education with web 2.0 support. In N. Azab (Ed.), *Cases on web 2.0 in developing countries: Studies on implementation, application, and use* (pp. 147–171). Hershey, PA: Information Science Reference.

Barton, S. M. (2013). Facilitating learning by going online: Modernising Islamic teaching and learning in Indonesia. In E. McKay (Ed.), *ePedagogy in online learning: New developments in web mediated human computer interaction* (pp. 74–92). Hershey, PA: Information Science Reference. doi:10.4018/978-1-4666-3649-1.ch005

Barzilai-Nahon, K., Gomez, R., & Ambikar, R. (2013). Conceptualizing a contextual measurement for digital divide/s: Using an integrated narrative. In I. Association (Ed.), *Digital literacy: Concepts, methodologies, tools, and applications* (pp. 279–293). Hershey, PA: Information Science Reference.

Bassiouni, M. C. (1981). Terrorism, law enforcement, and the mass media: Perspectives, problems, proposals. *The Journal of Criminal Law & Criminology*, *72*(1), 1–51. doi:10.2307/1142904

Beck, E. R. (1986). *Under the bombs: The German home front, 1942-1945*. Lexington, KY: The University Press of Kentucky.

Becker, J. (1982). Communication and peace: The empirical and theoretical relation between two categories in social sciences. *Journal of Peace Research*, *19*(3), 227–240. doi:10.1177/002234338201900302

Beiber, F. (2003). Approaches to political violence and terrorism in former Yugoslavia. *Journal of Southern Europe and the Balkans*, *5*(1), 39–51.

Bell, D. A. (2007). *The first total war: Napoleon's Europe and the birth of war as we know it*. New York: Houghton Mifflin Company.

Bell, J. L. (2008). Terrorist abuse of non-profits and charities: A proactive approach to preventing terrorist financing. *The Kansas Journal of Law & Public Policy*, *17*(3), 450–476.

Bénel, A., & Lacour, P. (2012). Towards a participative platform for cultural texts translators. In C. El Morr, & P. Maret (Eds.), *Virtual community building and the information society: Current and future directions* (pp. 153–162). Hershey, PA: Information Science Reference.

Bennett, S. (1999). Commercial aircraft bomb-proofing technologies: A social science critique. *Risk Management*, *1*(3), 49–61. doi:10.1057/palgrave.rm.8240004

Benramdane, D. (2004, March). Les rouages d'une guerre secrete. *Le Monde Diplomatique*. Retrieved July 3, 2013, from http://www.monde-diplomatique.fr/2004/03/BEN-RAMDANE/11094

Bentley, C. M. (2013). Designing and implementing online collaboration tools in West Africa. In N. Azab (Ed.), *Cases on web 2.0 in developing countries: Studies on implementation, application, and use* (pp. 33–60). Hershey, PA: Information Science Reference.

Benton, G. (1988). The origins of the political joke. In C. Powell, & G. E. C. Paton (Eds.), *Humor in society: Resistance and control* (pp. 33–55). London: The MacMillan Press.

Berezovsky, B. (2005). Putin is terrorist number one. *New Perspectives Quarterly*, *22*(1), 59–61. doi:10.1111/j.1540-5842.2005.00730.x

Bergen, P., Schuster, H., Nasr, O., & Eedle, P. (2005). Al Qaeda's media strategy. In K. J. Greenberg (Ed.), *Al Qaeda now: Understanding today's terrorists* (pp. 112–134). Cambridge, UK: Cambridge University Press. doi:10.1017/CBO9780511510489.009

Berger, J. M. (2013, October 1). Twitter's week of reckoning. *Foreign Policy*. Retrieved October 30, 2013, from http://www.foreignpolicy.com/articles/2013/10/01/twitters_week_of_reckoning

Berger, A. A. (1998). *Seeing is believing*. Mountain View, CA: Mayfield.

Bergesen, A. J., & Lizardo, O. (2004). International terrorism and the world-system. *Sociological Theory*, *22*(1), 38–52. doi:10.1111/j.1467-9558.2004.00203.x

Bergin, A., Osman, S. B., Ungerer, C., & Yasin, N. A. M. (2009, March). *Special report: Countering internet radicalization in Southeast Asia*. S. Rajaratnam School of International Studies and Australian Strategic Policy Institute. Retrieved July 3, 2013, from http://www.clean-itproject.eu/wp-content/uploads/2012/07/2009-Internet-radicalisation-Sout-East-Asia.pdf

Bergin, A., & Khosa, R. (2007). The Australian media and terrorism. *ASPI: Australian Strategic Policy Institute*, *11*, 1–8.

Berg, M. (2012). Checking in at the urban playground: Digital geographies and electronic flâneurs. In F. Comunello (Ed.), *Networked sociability and individualism: Technology for personal and professional relationships* (pp. 169–194). Hershey, PA: Information Science Reference.

Berkowitz, L., & Macaulay, J. (1971). The contagion of criminal violence. *Sociometry*, *34*(2), 238–260. doi:10.2307/2786414

Berman, E. (2009). *Radical, religious, and violent: The new economics of terrorism*. Boston: MIT Press.

Bermingham, A., McInerney, L., O'Hare, N., & Conway, M. (2009). Combining social network analysis and sentiment analysis to explore the potential for online radicalisation. In *Proceedings of ASONAM 2009: Advances in Social Networks Analysis and Mining* (pp. 231-236). IEEE Computer Society.

Bernardi, D., Cheong, P. H., Lundry, C., & Ruston, S. (2012). *Narrative landmines: Rumors, Islamist extremism, and the struggle for strategic influence*. New Brunswick, NJ: Rutgers University Press.

Berner, S. (2003). Cyber-terrorism: Reality or paranoia? *South African Journal of Information Management*, *5*(1), 1–4.

Bers, M. U., & Ettinger, A. B. (2013). Programming robots in kindergarten to express identity: An ethnographic analysis. In I. Management Association (Ed.), *Industrial engineering: Concepts, methodologies, tools, and applications* (pp. 1952-1968). Hershey, PA: Engineering Science Reference. doi: doi:10.4018/978-1-4666-1945-6.ch105

Betz, D. (2008). The virtual dimension of contemporary insurgency and counter-insurgency. *Small Wars & Insurgencies*, *19*(4), 510–540.

Biernatzki, W. E. (2002). Terrorism and mass media. *Communication Research Trends: Center for the Study of Communication and Culture*, *21*(1), 3–24.

Binsaleh, M., & Hassan, S. (2013). Systems development methodology for mobile commerce applications. In I. Khalil, & E. Weippl (Eds.), *Contemporary challenges and solutions for mobile and multimedia technologies* (pp. 146–162). Hershey, PA: Information Science Reference.

Bird, K., & Lifschultz, L. (Eds.). (1998). *Hiroshima's shadow*. Branford, CT: The Pamphleteers Press Inc.

Bishop, J. (2013). Cooperative e-learning in the multilingual and multicultural school: The role of "classroom 2.0" for increasing participation in education. In P. Pumilia-Gnarini, E. Favaron, E. Pacetti, J. Bishop, & L. Guerra (Eds.), *Handbook of research on didactic strategies and technologies for education: Incorporating advancements* (pp. 137–150). Hershey, PA: Information Science Reference.

Bishop, J. (2013). Increasing capital revenue in social networking communities: Building social and economic relationships through avatars and characters. In J. Bishop (Ed.), *Examining the concepts, issues, and implications of internet trolling* (pp. 44–61). Hershey, PA: Information Science Reference. doi:10.4018/978-1-4666-2803-8.ch005

Bishop, J. (2013). Lessons from the emotivate project for increasing take-up of big society and responsible capitalism initiatives. In P. Pumilia-Gnarini, E. Favaron, E. Pacetti, J. Bishop, & L. Guerra (Eds.), *Handbook of research on didactic strategies and technologies for education: Incorporating advancements* (pp. 208–217). Hershey, PA: Information Science Reference.

Black, D. (2004). The geometry of terrorism. *Sociological Theory*, *22*(1), 14–25. doi:10.1111/j.1467-9558.2004.00201.x

Blackmore, S. (1999). *The meme machine*. Oxford, UK: Oxford University Press.

Blair, J. A. (1996). The possibility and actuality of visual arguments. *Argumentation and Advocacy, 33*(1), 23–39.

Blake, C., Sheldon, B., Strzelecki, R., & Williams, P. (2012). *Policing terrorism.* London: Learning Matters.

Blau, I. (2013). E-collaboration within, between, and without institutions: Towards better functioning of online groups through networks. In N. Kock (Ed.), *Interdisciplinary applications of electronic collaboration approaches and technologies* (pp. 188–203). Hershey, PA: Information Science Reference.

Bloom, M. (2005). *Dying to kill: The allure of suicide terror.* New York: Columbia University Press.

Bloom, M. (2011). *Bombshell: The many faces of women terrorists.* London: Hurst.

Blum, A., Asal, V., & Wilkenfeld, J. (2005). Nonstate actors, terrorism, and weapons of mass destruction. *International Studies Review, 7,* 133–170. doi:10.1111/j.1521-9488.2005.479_1.x

Bockstette, C. (2008, December). *Jihadist terrorist use of strategic communication management techniques.* The George C. Marshall European Center for Security Studies. Retrieved July 3, 2013, from http://oai.dtic.mil/oai/oai?verb=getRecord&metadataPrefix=html&identifier=ADA512956

Boellstorff, T. (2005). *The gay archipelago: Sexuality and nation in Indonesia.* Princeton, NJ: Princeton University Press.

Boggs, C. (2002). Militarism and terrorism: The deadly cycle. *Democracy and Nature, 8*(2), 241–259. doi:10.1080/10855660220148598

Boler, M. (2008). The shape of publics: New media and global capitalism. In M. Boler (Ed.), *Digital media and democracy: Tactics in hard times* (pp. 1–51). Cambridge, MA: MIT Press.

Bolter, J. D., & Grusin, R. (2000). *Remediation: Understanding new media.* Cambridge, MA: MIT Press.

Boskic, N., & Hu, S. (2013). Blended learning: The road to inclusive and global education. In E. Jean Francois (Ed.), *Transcultural blended learning and teaching in postsecondary education* (pp. 283–301). Hershey, PA: Information Science Reference.

Boskin, J. (1997). *Rebellious laughter: People's humor in American culture.* Syracuse, NY: Syracuse University Press.

Botero, A., Karhu, K., & Vihavainen, S. (2012). Exploring the ecosystems and principles of community innovation. In A. Lugmayr, H. Franssila, P. Näränen, O. Sotamaa, J. Vanhala, & Z. Yu (Eds.), *Media in the ubiquitous era: Ambient, social and gaming media* (pp. 216–234). Hershey, PA: Information Science Reference.

Bowe, B. J., Blom, R., & Freedman, E. (2013). Negotiating boundaries between control and dissent: Free speech, business, and repressitarian governments. In J. Lannon, & E. Halpin (Eds.), *Human rights and information communication technologies: Trends and consequences of use* (pp. 36–55). Hershey, PA: Information Science Reference.

Bowman-Grieve, L., & Conway, M. (2012). Exploring the form and function of dissident Irish republican online discourses. *Media. War & Conflict, 5*(1), 71–85. doi:10.1177/1750635211434371

Boyle, M. P., Schmierbach, M., Armstrong, C. L., McLeod, D. M., Shah, D. V., & Pan, Z. (2004). Information seeking and emotional reaction to the September 11 terrorist attacks. *Journalism & Mass Communication Quarterly, 81*(1), 155–167. doi:10.1177/107769900408100111

Brachman, J. M. (2009). *Global Jihadism: Theory and practice.* London: Routledge.

Brachman, J. M., & Levine, A. N. (2011). You too can be Awlaki! *The Fletcher Forum of World Affairs, 35*(1), 25–46.

Brackett, D. W. (1996). *Holy terror: Armageddon in Tokyo.* New York: Weatherhill.

Braithwaite, A. (2013). The logic of public fear in terrorism and counter-terrorism. *Journal of Police and Criminal Psychology, 28,* 95–101. doi:10.1007/s11896-013-9126-x

Bramadat, P., & Seljak, D. (Eds.). (2005). *Religion and ethnicity in Canada.* Toronto: Longman.

Brandão, J., Ferreira, T., & Carvalho, V. (2012). An overview on the use of serious games in the military industry and health. In M. Cruz-Cunha (Ed.), *Handbook of research on serious games as educational, business and research tools* (pp. 182–201). Hershey, PA: Information Science Reference. doi:10.4018/978-1-4666-0149-9.ch009

Bray, M. (2009, August 7). Scott, Scout, and Boo Radley. *The Army of God.* Retrieved August 14, 2009, from http://www.armyofgod.com/MikeBrayScottScoutandBooRadley.html

Breckenridge, J. N., & Zimbardo, P. G. (2007). The strategy of terrorism and the psychology of mass-mediated fear. In B. Bongar, L. M. Brown, L. E. Beutler, J. N. Breckenridge, & P. G. Zimbardo (Eds.), *Psychology of terrorism* (pp. 116–133). New York: Oxford University Press.

Breen, G.-M. (2008). Examining existing counter-terrorism tactics and applying social network theory to fight cyberterrorism: An interpersonal communication perspective. *Journal of Applied Security Research, 3*(2), 191–204. doi:10.1080/19361610802135888

Briggs, W. (2004). North America. In A. S. de Beer, & J. C. Merrill (Eds.), *Global journalism: Topical issues and media systems* (pp. 430–464). Boston: Pearson Education, Inc.

British Broadcasting Corporation (BBC). (2001, October 11). *US TV limits bin Laden coverage.* Retrieved July 3, 2013, from http://news.bbc.co.uk/2/hi/americas/1593275.stm

British Broadcasting Corporation (BBC). (2004, May 13). *Zarqawi beheaded US man in Iraq.* Retrieved July 3, 2013, from http://news.bbc.co.uk/2/hi/middle_east/3712421.stm

British Broadcasting Corporation (BBC). (2011, August 31). *Kosovan admits shooting US airmen at Frankfurt airport.* Retrieved November 4, 2013, from http://www.bbc.co.uk/news/world-europe-14727975

British Broadcasting Corporation. (2003, September 4). *Inside the mind of a black widow.* Retrieved July 3, 2013, from http://news.bbc.co.uk/2/hi/3081126.stm

Brost, L. F., & McGinnis, C. (2012). The status of blogging in the republic of Ireland: A case study. In T. Dumova, & R. Fiordo (Eds.), *Blogging in the global society: Cultural, political and geographical aspects* (pp. 128–147). Hershey, PA: Information Science Reference.

Brown, R. (2003). Spinning the war: Political communications, information operations and public diplomacy in the war on terrorism. In D. K. Thussu, & D. Freedman (Eds.), *War and the media: Reporting conflict 24/7* (pp. 87–100). London, UK: Sage. doi:10.4135/9781446215579.n7

Brown, W. J. (1990). The persuasive appeal of mediated terrorism: The case of the TWA flight 847 hijacking. *Western Journal of Speech Communication, 54,* 219–236. doi:10.1080/10570319009374337

Bruce, G. (2013). Definition of terrorism: Social and political effects. *Journal of Military and Veteran's Health, 21*(2), 26–30.

Bruggemann, M., & Schulz-Forberg, H. (2009). Becoming pan-European? Transnational media and the European public sphere. *The International Communication Gazette, 71*(8), 693–712. doi:10.1177/1748048509345064

Bruns, A. (2008). *Blogs, Wikipedia, Second Life, and beyond: From production to produsage.* New York: Peter Lang.

Bullock, K. H., & Jafri, G. J. (2000). Media (mis)representations: Muslim women in the Canadian nation. *Canadian Woman Studies, 20*(2), 35–40.

Burgess, J. (2008). All your chocolate rain belong to us? Viral video, YouTube and the dynamics of participatory culture. In *Video vortex reader: Responses to YouTube* (pp. 101–109). Amsterdam: Institute of Network Cultures.

Burke, J. (2011, December 16). Al-Shabab's tweets won't boost its cause. *The Guardian (UK).* Retrieved July 3, 2013, from http://www.guardian.co.uk/commentisfree/2011/dec/16/al-shabab-tweets-terrorism-twitter

Burleigh, M. (2009). *Blood and rage: A cultural history of terrorism.* New York: Harper.

Burnett, J., & Whyte, D. (2005). Embedded expertise and the new terrorism. *Journal for Crime. Conflict and the Media, 1*(4), 1–18.

Burns, J., Blanchard, M., & Metcalf, A. (2013). Bridging the digital divide in Australia: The potential implications for the mental health of young people experiencing marginalisation. In I. Association (Ed.), *Digital literacy: Concepts, methodologies, tools, and applications* (pp. 772–793). Hershey, PA: Information Science Reference.

Burton, G. (2002). *More than meets the eye: An introduction to media studies.* London: Edward Arnold.

Byng, M. D. (2010). Symbolically Muslim: Media, hijab, and the West. *Critical Sociology, 36*(1), 109–129. doi:10.1177/0896920509347143

Cagliero, L., & Fiori, A. (2013). News document summarization driven by user-generated content. In G. Xu, & L. Li (Eds.), *Social media mining and social network analysis: Emerging research* (pp. 105–126). Hershey, PA: Information Science Reference.

Cambie, S. (2012). Lessons from the front line: The Arab Spring demonstrated the power of people—and social media. *Communication World, 29*(1), 28–32.

Camillo, A., & Di Pietro, L. (2013). Managerial communication in the global cross-cultural context. In B. Christiansen, E. Turkina, & N. Williams (Eds.), *Cultural and technological influences on global business* (pp. 397–419). Hershey, PA: Business Science Reference. doi:10.4018/978-1-4666-3966-9.ch021

Cañas, S. (2008). The little mosque on the prairie: Examining (multi)cultural spaces of nation and religion. *Cultural Dynamics, 20*(3), 195–211. doi:10.1177/0921374008096309

Canazza, S., De Poli, G., Rodà, A., & Vidolin, A. (2013). Expressiveness in music performance: Analysis, models, mapping, encoding. In J. Steyn (Ed.), *Structuring music through markup language: Designs and architectures* (pp. 156–186). Hershey, PA: Information Science Reference.

Caplan, B. (2006). Terrorism: The relevance of the rational choice model. *Public Choice, 128*(1-2), 91–107. doi:10.1007/s11127-006-9046-8

Carrasco, J. G., Ovide, E., & Puyal, M. B. (2013). Closing and opening of cultures. In F. García-Peñalvo (Ed.), *Multiculturalism in technology-based education: Case studies on ICT-supported approaches* (pp. 125–142). Hershey, PA: Information Science Reference.

Carreras, I., Zanardi, A., Salvadori, E., & Miorandi, D. (2013). A distributed monitoring framework for opportunistic communication systems: An experimental approach. In V. De Florio (Ed.), *Innovations and approaches for resilient and adaptive systems* (pp. 220–236). Hershey, PA: Information Science Reference.

Carter, D. L. (2009). *Law enforcement intelligence: A guide for state, local and tribal agencies*. United States Department of Justice. Retrieved July 30, 2010 from, http://www.cops.usdoj.gov/pdf/e09042536.pdf

Carter, M., Grover, V., & Thatcher, J. B. (2013). Mobile devices and the self: developing the concept of mobile phone identity. In I. Lee (Ed.), *Strategy, adoption, and competitive advantage of mobile services in the global economy* (pp. 150–164). Hershey, PA: Information Science Reference.

Caruso, F., Giuffrida, G., Reforgiato, D., & Zarba, C. (2013). Recommendation systems for mobile devices. In I. Lee (Ed.), *Mobile services industries, technologies, and applications in the global economy* (pp. 221–242). Hershey, PA: Information Science Reference.

Caryl, C. (2011, September 29). Predators and robots at war. *The New York Review of Books.* Retrieved July 3, 2013, from http://www.nybooks.com/articles/archives/2011/sep/29/predators-and-robots-war/?pagination=false

Casamassima, L. (2013). eTwinning project: A virtual orchestra. In P. Pumilia-Gnarini, E. Favaron, E. Pacetti, J. Bishop, & L. Guerra (Eds.) Handbook of research on didactic strategies and technologies for education: Incorporating advancements (pp. 703-709). Hershey, PA: Information Science Reference. doi: doi:10.4018/978-1-4666-2122-0.ch061

Caschera, M. C., D'Ulizia, A., Ferri, F., & Grifoni, P. (2012). Multiculturality and multimodal languages. In G. Ghinea, F. Andres, & S. Gulliver (Eds.), *Multiple sensorial media advances and applications: New developments in MulSeMedia* (pp. 99–114). Hershey, PA: Information Science Reference.

Cassesse, A. (1989). *Terror, politics, and the law: The Achille Lauro affair*. Princeton, NJ: Princeton University Books.

Castells, M. (2009). *Communication power*. Oxford, UK: Oxford University Press.

Catagnus, R. M., & Hantula, D. A. (2013). The virtual individual education plan (IEP) team: Using online collaboration to develop a behavior intervention plan. In N. Kock (Ed.), *Interdisciplinary applications of electronic collaboration approaches and technologies* (pp. 30–45). Hershey, PA: Information Science Reference.

Cebrowsky, A. K. (2004). *Netwar*. Paper presented at the Assistant Secretary of Defense Conference on Special Operations. Alexandria, VA.

Cebrowsky, A. K., & Barnett, T. P. M. (2003). The American way of war. In *Proceedings of U.S. Naval Institute*, (pp. 42-43). Retrieved July 30, 2013, from http://thomaspmbarnett.com/globlogization/2010/8/12/blast-from-my-past-the-american-way-of-war-2003.html

Cetina, K. K. (2005). Complex global microstructures: The new terrorist societies. *Theory, Culture & Society*, 22(5), 213–234.

Ch'ng, E. (2013). The mirror between two worlds: 3D surface computing for objects and environments. In D. Harrison (Ed.), *Digital media and technologies for virtual artistic spaces* (pp. 166–185). Hershey, PA: Information Science Reference. doi:10.4018/978-1-4666-2961-5.ch013

Chafee, Z. (1947). *Government and mass communications: A report*. Chicago, IL: University of Chicago Press.

Chakravorti, R. (1994). Terrorism: Past, present and future. *Economic and Political Weekly*, 29(36), 2340–2343.

Chand, A. (2013). Reducing digital divide: The case of the 'people first network' (PFNet) in the Solomon Islands. In I. Association (Ed.), *Digital literacy: Concepts, methodologies, tools, and applications* (pp. 1571–1605). Hershey, PA: Information Science Reference.

Chatterjee, S. (2013). Ethical behaviour in technology-mediated communication. In J. Bishop (Ed.), *Examining the concepts, issues, and implications of internet trolling* (pp. 1–9). Hershey, PA: Information Science Reference. doi:10.4018/978-1-4666-2803-8.ch001

Chen, C., Chao, H., Wu, T., Fan, C., Chen, J., Chen, Y., & Hsu, J. (2013). IoT-IMS communication platform for future internet. In V. De Florio (Ed.), *Innovations and approaches for resilient and adaptive systems* (pp. 68–86). Hershey, PA: Information Science Reference.

Chen, J., & Hu, X. (2013). Smartphone market in China: Challenges, opportunities, and promises. In I. Lee (Ed.), *Mobile services industries, technologies, and applications in the global economy* (pp. 120–132). Hershey, PA: Information Science Reference.

Chen, Y., Lee, B., & Kirk, R. M. (2013). Internet use among older adults: Constraints and opportunities. In R. Zheng, R. Hill, & M. Gardner (Eds.), *Engaging older adults with modern technology: Internet use and information access needs* (pp. 124–141). Hershey, PA: Information Science Reference.

Cheong, P. H., & Clow, C. (2010). *Understanding the digital transmediation of terrorism: (Re)presentation of the 'underwear bomber' in new and social media*. Paper presented at Terrorism and New Media: Building a Research Network Conference. Dublin, Ireland.

Cheong, P. H., & Gong, J. (2010). Cyber vigilantism, transmedia collective intelligence, and civic participation. *Chinese Journal of Communication*, 3(4), 471–487.

Cheong, P. H., & Lundry, C. (2012). Prosumption, transmediation and resistance: Terrorism and man-hunting in Southeast Asia. *The American Behavioral Scientist*, 56(4), 488–510.

Cheong, P. H., & Martin, J. N. (2013). Cultural implications of e-learning access (and divides): Teaching an intercultural communication course online. In A. Edmundson (Ed.), *Cases on cultural implications and considerations in online learning* (pp. 82–100). Hershey, PA: Information Science Reference.

Cheong, P. H., Poon, J. H., & Huang, S. H. (2011). Religious communication and epistemic authority of leaders in wired faith organizations. *The Journal of Communication*, 61(5), 938–958.

Chermak, S. (2003). Marketing fear: Representing terrorism after September 11. *Journal for Crime. Conflict and the Media*, 1(1), 5–22.

Chesterton, G. K. (1987). *The collected works of G. K. Chesterton: The illustrated London news, 1908-1910*. San Francisco: Ignatius Press.

Chhanabhai, P., & Holt, A. (2013). The changing world of ICT and health: Crossing the digital divide. In I. Association (Ed.), *Digital literacy: Concepts, methodologies, tools, and applications* (pp. 794–811). Hershey, PA: Information Science Reference.

Chicago Project on Security and Terrorism (CPOST). (2011). Retrieved July 3, 2013, from http://cpost.uchicago.edu/index.php

Cho, J., Boyle, M. P., Keum, H., Shevy, M. D., McLeod, D. M., Shah, D. V., & Pan, Z. (2003). Media, terrorism, and emotionality: Emotional differences in media content and public reactions to the September 11ᵗʰ terrorist attacks. *Journal of Broadcasting & Electronic Media*, *47*(3), 309–327. doi:10.1207/s15506878jobem4703_1

Chomsky, N., & Herman, E. (1979). *The Washington connection and third world fascism: The political economy of human rights* (Vol. 1). Boston: South End Press.

Christensen, C. (2008). Uploading dissonance: YouTube and the US occupation of Iraq. *Media. War & Conflict*, *1*(2), 155–175.

Chuling, W., Hua, C. M., & Chee, C. J. (2012). Investigating the demise of radio and television broadcasting. In R. Sharma, M. Tan, & F. Pereira (Eds.), *Understanding the interactive digital media marketplace: Frameworks, platforms, communities and issues* (pp. 392–405). Hershey, PA: Information Science Reference.

Ciaramitaro, B. L. (2012). Introduction to mobile technologies. In B. Ciaramitaro (Ed.), *Mobile technology consumption: Opportunities and challenges* (pp. 1–15). Hershey, PA: Information Science Reference.

Cicconetti, C., Mambrini, R., & Rossi, A. (2013). A survey of wireless backhauling solutions for ITS. In R. Daher, & A. Vinel (Eds.), *Roadside networks for vehicular communications: Architectures, applications, and test fields* (pp. 57–70). Hershey, PA: Information Science Reference.

Ciovacco, C. J. (2009). The contours of al Qaeda's media strategy. *Studies in Conflict and Terrorism*, *32*(10), 853–875.

Ciptasari, R. W., & Sakurai, K. (2013). Multimedia copyright protection scheme based on the direct feature-based method. In K. Kondo (Ed.), *Multimedia information hiding technologies and methodologies for controlling data* (pp. 412–439). Hershey, PA: Information Science Reference.

Clapper, J. R. (2013, March 12). Statement for the record: Worldwide threat assessment of the US intelligence community. *Senate Select Committee on Intelligence*. Retrieved August 7, 2013, from http://www.gwu.edu/~nsarchiv/NSAEBB/NSAEBB424/docs/Cyber-090.pdf

Clark, W. (2001). *Waging modern war*. New York: Public Affairs.

Clausewitz, C. (1984). *On war* (M. Howard, & P. Paret, Trans.). Princeton, NJ: Princeton University Press.

Clean, I. T. (2013). *Reducing terrorist use of the internet*. The Hague: Dutch National Coordinator for Counterterrorism. Retrieved July 3, 2013, from https://www.counterextremism.org/resources/details/id/307/reducing-terrorist-use-of-the-Internet

Cluterbuck, R. C. (1975). *Living with terrorism*. London: Faber & Faber.

Clutterbuck, R. (1982). Terrorism and urban violence. *Proceedings of the Academy of Political Science*, *34*(4), 165–175. doi:10.2307/3700978

Coady, C. A. J. (2004). Terrorism and innocence. *The Journal of Ethics*, *8*(1), 37–58. doi:10.1023/B:JOET.0000012251.24102.a5

Coaffee, J., & van Ham, P. (2008). Security branding: The role of security in marketing the city, region and state. *Place Branding and Public Diplomacy*, *4*(3), 191–195.

Code, J. (2013). Agency and identity in social media. In S. Warburton, & S. Hatzipanagos (Eds.), *Digital identity and social media* (pp. 37–57). Hershey, PA: Information Science Reference.

Cohan, J. A. (2006). Necessity, political violence and terrorism. *Stetson Law Review*, *35*(3), 903–981.

Cole, J. (2006, November 10). 655000 dead in Iraq since Bush. *Informed Comment*. Retrieved July 17, 2013, from http://www.juancole.com/2006/10/655000-dead-in-iraq-since-bush.html

Coleman, L. (2007, April 17). *The copycat effect*. Retrieved from blogspot.com

Coleman, L. (2004). *The copycat effect: How the media and popular culture trigger mayhem in tomorrow's headlines*. New York: Paraview.

Collins, S. D. (2004). Dissuading state support of terrorism: Strikes or sanctions? An analysis of dissuasion measures employed against Libya. *Studies in Conflict and Terrorism*, *27*(1), 1–18. doi:10.1080/10576100490262115

Combs, C. C. (2013). *Terrorism in the twenty-first century*. Boston, MA: Pearson.

Committee on the Judiciary. (2004, February 4). *Virtual threat, real terror: Cyberterrorism in the 21ˢᵗ century.* Retrieved July 3, 2013, from http://www.gpo.gov/fdsys/pkg/CHRG-108shrg94639/pdf/CHRG-108shrg94639.pdf

Comunello, F. (2013). From the digital divide to multiple divides: Technology, society, and new media skills. In I. Association (Ed.), *Digital literacy: Concepts, methodologies, tools, and applications* (pp. 1622–1639). Hershey, PA: Information Science Reference.

Consonni, A. (2013). About the use of the DMs in CLIL classes. In F. García-Peñalvo (Ed.), *Multiculturalism in technology-based education: Case studies on ICT-supported approaches* (pp. 9–27). Hershey, PA: Information Science Reference.

Constant, J. (2012). Digital approaches to visualization of geometric problems in wooden sangaku tablets. In A. Ursyn (Ed.), *Biologically-inspired computing for the arts: Scientific data through graphics* (pp. 240–253). Hershey, PA: Information Science Reference. doi:10.4018/978-1-4666-0942-6.ch013

Conway, M., & McInerney, L. (2008). *Jihadi video and auto-radicalisation: Evidence from an exploratory YouTube study.* Paper presented at the First European Conference on Intelligence and Security Informatics. Esbjerg, Denmark.

Conway, M. (2002). Reality bytes: Cyberterrorism and terrorist 'use' of the internet. *First Monday, 7*(11), 1–17.

Conway, M. (2005a). Cybercortical warfare: Hizbollah's internet strategy. In S. Oates, D. Owen, & R. K. Gibson (Eds.), *The internet and politics: Citizens, voters and activists* (pp. 100–117). London: Routledge.

Conway, M. (2005b). Terrorist web sites: Their contents, functioning and effectiveness. In P. Seib (Ed.), *Media and conflict in the twenty-first century* (pp. 185–215). London: Palgrave.

Conway, M. (2006). Terrorism and the internet: New media – New threat? *Parliamentary Affairs, 59*(2), 283–298.

Conway, M. (2007). Terrorist use of the internet and the challenges of governing cyberspace. In M. D. Cavelty, V. Mauer, & S. F. Krishna-Hensel (Eds.), *Power and security in the information age: Investigating the role of the state in cyberspace* (pp. 95–128). London: Ashgate.

Conway, M. (2008). Media, fear and the hyperreal: The construction of cyberterrorism as the ultimate threat to critical infrastructures. In M. D. Cavelty, & K. S. Kristensen (Eds.), *Securing the homeland: Critical infrastructure, risk, and (in)security.* London: Routledge.

Conway, M. (2011). Against cyberterrorism. *Communications of the ACM, 54*(2), 26–28. doi:10.1145/1897816.1897829

Conway, M. (2012). What is cyberterrorism and how real is the threat? In P. C. Reich, & E. Gelbstein (Eds.), *Law, technology, and policy: Cyberterrorism, information warfare, and internet immobilization.* Hershey, PA: IGI Global.

Conway, M., & McInerney, L. (2012). Terrorism in old and new media. *Media. War & Conflict, 5*(1), 3–5. doi:10.1177/1750635211434349

Conway, M., & McInerneym, L. (2012). What's love got to do with it? Framing JihadJane in the US press. *Media. War & Conflict, 5*(1), 6–21. doi:10.1177/1750635211434373

Cook, T. R. (2011). The financial arm of the FARC: A threat finance perspective. *Journal of Strategic Security, 4*(1), 19–36. doi:10.5038/1944-0472.4.1.2

Cooper, H. H. A. (1978). Terrorism: The problem of the problem of definition. *Chitty's Law Journal, 26*(3), 105–108.

Cooper, H. H. A. (2001). Terrorism: The problem of definition revisited. *The American Behavioral Scientist, 44*(6), 881–893. doi:10.1177/00027640121956575

Copeland, T. (2001). Is the new terrorism really new? An analysis of the new paradigm for terrorism. *The Journal of Conflict Studies, 21*(2), 91–105.

Cordesman, A. H. (2002). *Terrorism, asymmetric warfare, and weapons of mass destruction: Defending the U.S. homeland.* Westport, CT: Praeger.

Cornellier, M., & Lévesque, C. (2003, February 6). Le doute persiste au counseil de sécurité. *Le Devoir.* Retrieved July 22, 2012, from http://www.ledevoir.com/non-classe/19870/le-doute-persiste-au-conseil-de-securite

Cossiavelou, V., Bantimaroudis, P., Kavakli, E., & Illia, L. (2013). The media gatekeeping model updated by R and I in ICTs: The case of wireless communications in media coverage of the olympic games. In M. Bartolacci, & S. Powell (Eds.), *Advancements and innovations in wireless communications and network technologies* (pp. 262–288). Hershey, PA: Information Science Reference.

COT Institute for Safety. Security and Crisis Management. (2008, July 23). *Transnational terrorism and the rule of law: Terrorism and the media*. Retrieved July 3, 2013, from http://www.transnationalterrorism.eu/tekst/publications/WP4%20Del%206.pdf

Cottle, S. (2011). Media and the Arab uprisings of 2011: Research notes. *Journalism*, *12*(5), 647–659. doi:10.1177/1464884911410017

Council of Europe. (2007). *Cyberterrorism: The use of the Internet for terrorist purposes*. Strasbourg, France: Author.

Crelinsten, R. D. (1989). Terrorism and the media: Problems, solutions, and counterproblems. *Political Communication and Persuasion*, *6*(4), 311–339. doi:10.1080/10584609.1989.9962881

Crelinsten, R. D. (2002). Analysing terrorism and counterterrorism: A communication model. *Terrorism and Political Violence*, *14*(2), 77–122. doi:10.1080/714005618

Crenshaw Hutchinson, M. (1972). The concept of revolutionary terrorism. *The Journal of Conflict Resolution*, *16*(3), 383–396.

Crenshaw, M. (1981). The causes of terrorism. *Comparative Politics*, *13*(4), 379–399. doi:10.2307/421717

Crenshaw, M. (2000). The psychology of terrorism: An agenda for the 21st century. *Political Psychology*, *21*(2), 405–420. doi:10.1111/0162-895X.00195

Cropf, R. A., Benmamoun, M., & Kalliny, M. (2013). The role of web 2.0 in the Arab Spring. In N. Azab (Ed.), *Cases on web 2.0 in developing countries: Studies on implementation, application, and use* (pp. 76–108). Hershey, PA: Information Science Reference.

Cucinotta, A., Minnolo, A. L., & Puliafito, A. (2013). Design and implementation of an event-based RFID middleware. In N. Karmakar (Ed.), *Advanced RFID systems, security, and applications* (pp. 110–131). Hershey, PA: Information Science Reference.

Curran, J. (2012). Reinterpreting the Internet. In J. Curran, N. Fenton, & D. Freedman (Eds.), *Misunderstanding the internet* (pp. 3–33). London: Routledge.

Curtis, L. (1984). *Ireland: The propaganda war*. London: Pluto Press.

D'Andrea, A., Ferri, F., & Grifoni, P. (2013). Assessing e-health in Africa: Web 2.0 applications. In N. Azab (Ed.), *Cases on web 2.0 in developing countries: Studies on implementation, application, and use* (pp. 442–467). Hershey, PA: Information Science Reference.

Dakroury, A. (2008). CBC's Little Mosque on the Prairie: Just a 'little masquerade'? *Media Development*, *55*(3), 42–46.

Danner, M. (2004). *Torture and truth: America, Abu Ghraib and the war on terror*. New York: NYRB Books.

Date, J. (2008, May 19). Lieberman: YouTube not doing enough to remove terrorist content. *ABC News*. Retrieved July 3, 2013, from http://abcnews.go.com/TheLaw/Law-Politics/comments?type=story&id=4889745

Davis, J. M., Planje, E., Davis, C. J., Page, J., Whitely, M., O'Neil, S., & West, D. (2013). Definitions of war, torture, and terrorism in Great Britain, Northern Ireland, Australia, Canada, and the United States. In K. Malley-Morrison, S. McCarthy, & D. Hines (Eds.), *International handbook of war, torture, and terrorism* (pp. 27–48). New York: Springer.

Day, L. A. (2006). *Ethics in media communications: Cases and controversies*. Belmont, CA: Thomson Wadsworth.

De Bussière, M., Méadel, C., & Ulmann-Mauriat, C. (Eds.). (1999). *Radios et télévision au temps des événements d'Algérie*. Paris: L'Harmattan.

de Certeau, M. (1984). *The practice of everyday life*. Berkeley, CA: University of California Press.

De Goede, M. (2008). Beyond risk: Premediation and post-9/11 security imagination. *Security Dialogue*, *39*(2-3), 155–176. doi:10.1177/0967010608088773

de Guinea, A. O. (2013). The level paradox of e-collaboration: Dangers and solutions. In N. Kock (Ed.), *Interdisciplinary applications of electronic collaboration approaches and technologies* (pp. 166–187). Hershey, PA: Information Science Reference.

Delli Carpini, M. X., & Williams, B. A. (1987). Television and terrorism: Patterns of presentation and occurrences, 1969 to 1980. *The Western Political Quarterly*, *40*(1), 45–64. doi:10.1177/106591298704000105

Dempsey, J. X., & Cole, D. (2002). *Terrorism and the constitution: Sacrificing civil liberties in the name of national security.* New York: New Press.

Denning, D. (2006). A view of cyberterrorism five years later. In K. E. Himma (Ed.), *Internet security: Hacking, counterhacking, and society* (pp. 123–140). Sudbury, MA: Jones and Bartlett Publishers.

Denning, D. E. (2000). Activism, hacktivism, and cyberterrorism: The internet as a tool for influencing foreign policy. *Computer Security Journal*, *16*(3), 15–35.

Dennis, E. E., & Ismach, A. H. (1981). *Reporting processes and practices: Newswriting for today's readers.* Belmont, CA: Wadsworth Publishing Company.

Der Derian, J. (2005). Imaging terror: Logos, pathos and ethos. *Third World Quarterly*, *26*(1), 23–37. doi:10.1080/0143659042000322883

Deuze, M. (2007). Convergence culture in the creative industries. *International Journal of Cultural Studies*, *10*(2), 243–263.

Devine, P. E., & Rafalko, R. J. (1982). On terror. *The Annals of the American Academy of Political and Social Science*, *463*, 39–53. doi:10.1177/0002716282463001004

Dhar-Bhattacharjee, S., & Takruri-Rizk, H. (2012). An Indo-British comparison. In C. Romm Livermore (Ed.), *Gender and social computing: Interactions, differences and relationships* (pp. 50–71). Hershey, PA: Information Science Publishing.

Díaz-Foncea, M., & Marcuello, C. (2013). ANOBIUM, SL: The use of the ICT as niche of employment and as tool for developing the social market. In T. Torres-Coronas, & M. Vidal-Blasco (Eds.), *Social e-enterprise: Value creation through ICT* (pp. 221–242). Hershey, PA: Information Science Reference.

Díaz-González, M., Froufe, N. Q., Brena, A. G., & Pumarola, F. (2013). Uses and implementation of social media at university: The case of schools of communication in Spain. In B. Pătruţ, M. Pătruţ, & C. Cmeciu (Eds.), *Social media and the new academic environment: Pedagogical challenges* (pp. 204–222). Hershey, PA: Information Science Reference. doi:10.4018/978-1-4666-2851-9.ch010

DiFonzo, N., & Prashant, B. (2007). *Rumor psychology.* Washington, DC: American Psychological Association.

Ditsa, G., Alwahaishi, S., Al-Kobaisi, S., & Snášel, V. (2013). A comparative study of the effects of culture on the deployment of information technology. In A. Zolait (Ed.), *Technology diffusion and adoption: Global complexity, global innovation* (pp. 77–90). Hershey, PA: Information Science Reference. doi:10.4018/978-1-4666-2791-8.ch006

Dodd, V. (2010, November 3). Roshonara Choudhry: Police interview extracts. *The Guardian (UK)*. Retrieved July 3, 2013, from http://www.guardian.co.uk/uk/2010/nov/03/roshonara-choudhry-police-interview

Dolnik, A. (2003). Die and let die: Exploring links between suicide terrorism and terrorist use of chemical, biological, radiological, and nuclear weapons. *Studies in Conflict and Terrorism*, *26*(1), 17–35. doi:10.1080/10576100390145143

Domke, D., Graham, E. S., Coe, K., Lockett, S., & Coopman, T. (2006). Going public as political strategy: The Bush administration, an echoing press, and passage of the Patriot Act. *Political Communication*, *23*(3), 291–312.

Donaldson, O., & Duggan, E. W. (2013). Assessing mobile value-added preference structures: The case of a developing country. In I. Lee (Ed.), *Strategy, adoption, and competitive advantage of mobile services in the global economy* (pp. 349–370). Hershey, PA: Information Science Reference.

Douai, A. (2013). "In YouTube we trust": Video exchange and Arab human rights. In J. Lannon, & E. Halpin (Eds.), *Human rights and information communication technologies: Trends and consequences of use* (pp. 57–71). Hershey, PA: Information Science Reference.

Dower, J. W. (2010). *Cultures of war*. New York: W. W. Norton.

Downing, J. (2001). *Radical media: Rebellious communication and social movements*. Thousand Oaks, CA: Sage Publications.

Downing, J. D. H. (2007). The imperiled American: Visual culture, nationality, and U.S. foreign policy. *International Journal of Communication, 1*(1), 318–341.

Downing, J. D. H., & Husband, C. H. (1995). Media flows, ethnicity, racism and xenophobia. *The Electronic Journal of Communication, 5*(2), 91–95.

Drakos, K., & Gofas, A. (2006). The devil you know but are afraid to face: Underreporting bias and its distorting effects on the study of terrorism. *The Journal of Conflict Resolution, 50*(5), 714–735. doi:10.1177/0022002706291051

Dromzée, C., Laborie, S., & Roose, P. (2013). A semantic generic profile for multimedia document adaptation. In D. Kanellopoulos (Ed.), *Intelligent multimedia technologies for networking applications: Techniques and tools* (pp. 225–246). Hershey, PA: Information Science Reference.

Drucker, S., & Gumpert, G. (2012). The urban communication infrastructure: Global connection and local detachment. In I. Management Association (Ed.), *Wireless technologies: Concepts, methodologies, tools and applications* (pp. 1150-1169). Hershey, PA: Information Science Reference. doi: doi:10.4018/978-1-61350-101-6.ch504

Drula, G. (2013). Media and communication research facing social media. In M. Pătruţ, & B. Pătruţ (Eds.), *Social media in higher education: Teaching in web 2.0* (pp. 371–392). Hershey, PA: Information Science Reference. doi:10.4018/978-1-4666-2970-7.ch019

Ducol, B. (2012). Uncovering the French-speaking Jihadisphere: An exploratory analysis. *Media. War & Conflict, 5*(3), 51–70. doi:10.1177/1750635211434366

Dueck, J., & Rempel, M. (2013). Human rights and technology: Lessons from Alice in Wonderland. In J. Lannon, & E. Halpin (Eds.), *Human rights and information communication technologies: Trends and consequences of use* (pp. 1–20). Hershey, PA: Information Science Reference.

Dumova, T. (2012). Social interaction technologies and the future of blogging. In T. Dumova, & R. Fiordo (Eds.), *Blogging in the global society: Cultural, political and geographical aspects* (pp. 249–274). Hershey, PA: Information Science Reference.

Dunn-Cavelty, M. (2007). Cyber-terror—Looming threat or phantom menace? The framing of the US cyber-threat debate. *Journal of Information Technology & Politics, 4*(1), 19–36. doi:10.1300/J516v04n01_03

Dunn, H. S. (2013). Information literacy and the digital divide: Challenging e-exclusion in the global south. In I. Association (Ed.), *Digital literacy: Concepts, methodologies, tools, and applications* (pp. 20–38). Hershey, PA: Information Science Reference.

Duyvesteyn, I. (2004). How new is the new terrorism? *Studies in Conflict and Terrorism, 27*(5), 439–454.

Ehrenfeld, R. (1990). *Narco terrorism*. New York: Basic Books.

Eid, M. (2008a). *Interweavement: International media ethics and rational decision-making*. Boston, MA: Pearson.

Eid, M. (2008b). The two faces of Osama bin Laden: Mass media representations as a force for evil and Arabic hero. In S. J. Drucker, & G. Gumpert (Eds.), *Heroes in a global world* (pp. 151–183). New Jersey: Hampton Press.

Eid, M. (2010). Cyber-terrorism and ethical journalism: A need for rationalism. *International Journal of Technoethics, 1*(4), 1–19. doi:10.4018/jte.2010100101

Eid, M. (2013). The new era of media and terrorism. [Review of the three books *Terrorism in the twenty-first century, Mass-mediated terrorism: The central role of the media in terrorism and counterterrorism,* and *Fueling our fears: Stereotyping, media coverage, and public opinion of Muslim Americans*]. *Studies in Conflict and Terrorism, 36*(7), 609–615. doi:10.1080/1057610X.2013.793638

Eid, M., & Fyfe, T. (2009). Globalisation and crisis communication: Competencies for decision-making in the government of Canada. *The Journal of International Communication, 15*(2), 7–27. doi:10.1080/13216597.2009.9674748

Eid, M., & Khan, S. (2011). A new-look for Muslim women in the Canadian media: CBC's little mosque on the prairie. *Middle East Journal of Culture and Communication, 4*(2), 184–202. doi:10.1163/187398611X571355

Eilon, S. (1979). *Management control.* Oxford, UK: Pergamon Press.

Eisenhardt, K. M., & Zbaracki, M. J. (1992). Strategic decision making. *Strategic Management Journal, 13*(S2), 17–37. doi:10.1002/smj.4250130904

Elbanna, S., & Child, J. (2007). Influences on strategic decision effectiveness: Development and test of an integrative model. *Strategic Management Journal, 28*(4), 431–453. doi:10.1002/smj.597

Elias, N. (2013). Immigrants' internet use and identity from an intergenerational perspective: Immigrant senior citizens and youngsters from the former Soviet Union in Israel. In R. Luppicini (Ed.), *Handbook of research on technoself: Identity in a technological society* (pp. 293–307). Hershey, PA: Information Science Reference.

Elizabeth, L. S., Ismail, N., & Tun, M. S. (2012). The future of the printed book. In R. Sharma, M. Tan, & F. Pereira (Eds.), *Understanding the interactive digital media marketplace: Frameworks, platforms, communities and issues* (pp. 416–429). Hershey, PA: Information Science Reference.

Elliott, D. (2003). Balance and context: Maintaining media ethics. *Phi Kappa Phi Forum, 83*(2), 16-21.

Ellis, S., & Haar, G. T. (2004). *Worlds of power: Religious thought and political practice in Africa.* New York: Oxford University Press.

Elmquist, S. (1990). The scope and limits of cooperation between the media and the authorities. In Y. Alexander & R. Latter (Eds.), Terrorism and the media: Dilemmas for government, journalists and the public (pp. 74-80). Washington, DC: Brassey's (US), Inc.

Enders, W., & Sandler, T. (2004). What do we know about the substitution effect in transnational terrorism? In A. Silke (Ed.), *Research on terrorism: Trends, achievements and failures* (pp. 119–137). London: Frank Cass. doi:10.4324/9780203500972.ch7

Enders, W., & Sandler, T. (2005). Transnational terrorism 1968-2000: Thresholds, persistence, and forecasts. *Southern Economic Journal, 71*(3), 467–482. doi:10.2307/20062054

Erne, R. (2012). Knowledge worker performance in a cross-industrial perspective. In S. Brüggemann, & C. d'Amato (Eds.), *Collaboration and the semantic web: Social networks, knowledge networks, and knowledge resources* (pp. 297–321). Hershey, PA: Information Science Reference. doi:10.4018/978-1-4666-0894-8.ch015

Ertl, B., Helling, K., & Kikis-Papadakis, K. (2012). The impact of gender in ICT usage, education and career: Comparisons between Greece and Germany. In C. Romm Livermore (Ed.), *Gender and social computing: Interactions, differences and relationships* (pp. 98–119). Hershey, PA: Information Science Publishing.

Estapé-Dubreuil, G., & Torreguitart-Mirada, C. (2013). ICT adoption in the small and medium-size social enterprises in Spain: Opportunity or priority? In T. Torres-Coronas, & M. Vidal-Blasco (Eds.), *Social e-enterprise: Value creation through ICT* (pp. 200–220). Hershey, PA: Information Science Reference.

EUR-Lex. (2007, November 6). *Proposal for a council framework decision amending framework decision 2002/475/JHA on combating terrorism.* Retrieved July 22, 2013, from http://eur-lex.europa.eu/smartapi/cgi/sga_doc?smartapi!celexplus!prod!DocNumber&lg=en&type_doc=COMfinal&an_doc=2007&nu_doc=650

European Police Office. (2011). *Europol TE-SAT 2011: EU terrorism situation and trend report.* Retrieved July 3, 2013, from https://www.europol.europa.eu/sites/default/files/publications/te-sat2011.pdf

European Police Office. (2013). *Europol TE-SAT 2013: EU terrorism situation and trend report.* Retrieved October 30, 2013, from https://www.europol.europa.eu/sites/default/files/publications/europol_te-sat2013_lr_0.pdf

Ezeldin, A. (1987). *Terrorism & political violence: An Egyptian perspective.* Chicago, IL: Office of International Criminal Justice, University of Illinois at Chicago.

Eze, U. C., & Poong, Y. S. (2013). Consumers' intention to use mobile commerce and the moderating roles of gender and income. In I. Lee (Ed.), *Strategy, adoption, and competitive advantage of mobile services in the global economy* (pp. 127–148). Hershey, PA: Information Science Reference.

Facebook. (2013). *Key facts*. Retrieved March 13, 2013, from http://newsroom.fb.com/Key-Facts

Falk, R. (1988). *Revolutionaries and functionaries*. New York: E. P. Dutton.

Falk, R. A. (2003). A dual reality: Terrorism against the state and terrorism by the state. In C. W. Kegley (Ed.), *The new global terrorism: Characteristics, causes, controls* (pp. 53–59). Upper Saddle River, NJ: Prentice Hall.

Fallows, J., Bergen, P., Hoffman, B., & Simon, S. (2005). Al Qaeda then and now. In K. J. Greenberg (Ed.), *Al Qaeda now: Understanding today's terrorists* (pp. 3–26). Cambridge, UK: Cambridge University Press. doi:10.1017/CBO9780511510489.004

Farivar, C. (2012, August 9). Europe's quixotic plan to clean the internet of terrorists. *Ars Technica*. Retrieved July 3, 2013, from http://arstechnica.com/tech-policy/2012/08/europes-quixotic-plan-to-clean-the-Internet-of-terrorists/

Farivar, C. (2013, January 30). EU plan to voluntarily remove terrorist content finally concludes. *Ars Technica*. Retrieved July 3, 2013, from http://arstechnica.com/tech-policy/2013/01/eu-plan-to-voluntarily-remove-terrorist-content-finally-concludes/

Farmer, B. (2011, December 25). Congress calls on Twitter to block Taliban. *The Telegraph (UK)*. Retrieved July 3, 2013, from http://www.telegraph.co.uk/technology/twitter/8972884/Congress-calls-on-Twitter-to-block-Taliban.html

Farrell, R., Danis, C., Erickson, T., Ellis, J., Christensen, J., Bailey, M., & Kellogg, W. A. (2012). A picture and a thousand words: Visual scaffolding for mobile communication in developing regions. In W. Hu (Ed.), *Emergent trends in personal, mobile, and handheld computing technologies* (pp. 341–354). Hershey, PA: Information Science Reference. doi:10.4018/978-1-4666-0921-1.ch020

Fidler, C. S., Kanaan, R. K., & Rogerson, S. (2013). Barriers to e-government implementation in Jordan: The role of wasta. In A. Mesquita (Ed.), *User perception and influencing factors of technology in everyday life* (pp. 179–191). Hershey, PA: Information Science Reference.

Field, A. (2009). The new terrorism: Revolution or evolution. *Political Studies Review*, 7(2), 195–207.

Fielding, N., & Cobain, I. (2013, March 17). Revealed: US spy operation that manipulates social media. *The Guardian (UK)*. Retrieved July 3, 2013, from http://www.guardian.co.uk/technology/2011/mar/17/us-spy-operation-social-networks

Filho, J. R. (2013). ICT and human rights in Brazil: From military to digital dictatorship. In J. Lannon, & E. Halpin (Eds.), *Human rights and information communication technologies: Trends and consequences of use* (pp. 86–99). Hershey, PA: Information Science Reference.

Financial Action Task Force. (2008, February 29). *Terrorist funding*. Retrieved February 29, 2008, from http://www.fatf-gafi.org/dataoecd/28/43/40285899.pdf

Finn, J. E. (1990). Media coverage of political terrorism and the first amendment: Reconciling the public's right to know with public order. In Y. Alexander & R. Latter (Eds.), Terrorism and the media: Dilemmas for government, journalists and the public (pp. 47-56). Washington, DC: Brassey's (US), Inc.

Fiordo, R. (2012). Analyzing blogs: A hermeneutic perspective. In T. Dumova, & R. Fiordo (Eds.), *Blogging in the global society: Cultural, political and geographical aspects* (pp. 231–248). Hershey, PA: Information Science Reference.

Fischer, G., & Herrmann, T. (2013). Socio-technical systems: A meta-design perspective. In J. Abdelnour-Nocera (Ed.), *Knowledge and technological development effects on organizational and social structures* (pp. 1–36). Hershey, PA: Information Science Reference.

Flanagan, T. (1998). *Game theory and Canadian politics*. Toronto: University of Toronto Press.

Fletcher, G. P. (2006). The indefinable concept of terrorism. *Journal of International Criminal Justice*, 4(5), 894–911. doi:10.1093/jicj/mql060

Fleury, M., & Al-Jobouri, L. (2013). Techniques and tools for adaptive video streaming. In D. Kanellopoulos (Ed.), *Intelligent multimedia technologies for networking applications: Techniques and tools* (pp. 65–101). Hershey, PA: Information Science Reference.

Fleury-Villatte, B. (2000). *La mémoire télévisuelle de la guerre d'Algérie*. Paris: Institut National de l'Audiovisuel/ L'Harmattan.

Fontaine, R. W. (1988). *Terrorism: The Cuban connection*. New York: Crane Russak.

Fosl, P. S. (2013). Anarchism and authenticity, or why SAMCRO shouldn't fight history. In G. A. Dunn, & J. T. Eberl (Eds.), *Sons of anarchy and philosophy: Brains before bullets* (pp. 201–214). West Sussex, UK: John Wiley & Sons. doi:10.1002/9781118641712.ch18

Foss, S. (1994). A rhetorical schema for the evaluation of visual imagery. *Communication Studies*, *45*(3-4), 213–224. doi:10.1080/10510979409368425

Foucault, M. (1994). *The order of things: An archaeology of the human sciences*. New York: Vintage Books.

Frank, R. (2004). When the going gets tough, the tough go photoshopping: September 11 and the newslore of vengeance and victimization. *New Media &. Society*, *6*(5), 633–658.

Freedman, D., & Thussu, D. K. (2012). Introduction: Dynamics of media and terrorism. In D. Freedman, & D. K. Thussu (Eds.), *Media & terrorism: Global perspectives* (pp. 1–20). London: Sage. doi:10.4135/9781446288429.n1

Freeman, I., & Freeman, A. (2013). Capacity building for different abilities using ICT. In T. Torres-Coronas, & M. Vidal-Blasco (Eds.), *Social e-enterprise: Value creation through ICT* (pp. 67–82). Hershey, PA: Information Science Reference. doi:10.4018/978-1-4666-4422-9.ch014

Frey, B. S. (2004). *Dealing with terrorism – Stick or carrot?* Cheltenham, UK: Edward Elgar. doi:10.4337/9781845421465

Friedman, R. (1995, March 27). The CIA's Jihad. *JewishComment.com*. Retrieved July 3, 2013, from http://www.jewishcomment.com/cgibin/news.cgi?id=11&command=shownews&newsid=294

Friedman, B. (2008). Unlikely warriors: How four U.S. news sources explained female suicide bombers. *Journalism & Mass Communication Quarterly*, *85*(4), 841–859. doi:10.1177/107769900808500408

Frohardt, M., & Temin, J. (2003). Use and abuse of media in vulnerable societies. *United States Institute of Peace*. Retrieved July 30, 2013, from http://www.usip.org/sites/default/files/sr110.pdf

Fromkin, D. (1975). The strategy of terrorism. *Foreign Affairs*, *53*(4), 683–698. doi:10.2307/20039540

Fuchs, C., Boersma, K., Albrechtslund, A., & Sandoval, M. (Eds.). (2011). *Internet and surveillance: The challenges of web 2.0 and social media*. New York: Routledge.

Gallon, R. (2013). Communication, culture, and technology: Learning strategies for the unteachable. In R. Lansiquot (Ed.), *Cases on interdisciplinary research trends in science, technology, engineering, and mathematics: Studies on urban classrooms* (pp. 91–106). Hershey, PA: Information Science Reference.

Gallup Brain. (2012). Retrieved May 28, 2012, from http://institution.gallup.com

Galtung, J. (1990). Cultural violence. *Journal of Peace Research*, *27*(3), 291–305. doi:10.1177/0022343390027003005

Galtung, J., & Ruge, M. (1965). The structure of foreign news: The presentation of the Congo, Cuba and Cyprus crises in four Norwegian newspapers. *Journal of Peace Research*, *2*(1), 64–90. doi:10.1177/002234336500200104

Gambetta, D., & Hertog, S. (2007). *Engineers of Jihad*. University of Oxford. Retrieved July 3, 2013, from http://www.nuff.ox.ac.uk/users/gambetta/engineers%20of%20jihad.pdf

Ganor, B. (2002). Defining terrorism: Is one man's terrorist another man's freedom fighter? *Police Practice and Research*, *3*(4), 287–304. doi:10.1080/1561426022000032060

Ganor, B., von Knop, K., & Duarte, C. A. M. (Eds.). (2007). *Hypermedia seduction for terrorist recruiting*. Amsterdam: IOS Press.

García, M., Lloret, J., Bellver, I., & Tomás, J. (2013). Intelligent IPTV distribution for smart phones. In D. Kanellopoulos (Ed.), *Intelligent multimedia technologies for networking applications: Techniques and tools* (pp. 318–347). Hershey, PA: Information Science Reference.

García, P. (1995). *El drama de la autonomía militar*. Madrid: Alianza Editorial.

García-Plaza, A. P., Zubiaga, A., Fresno, V., & Martínez, R. (2013). Tag cloud reorganization: Finding groups of related tags on delicious. In G. Xu, & L. Li (Eds.), *Social media mining and social network analysis: Emerging research* (pp. 140–155). Hershey, PA: Information Science Reference.

Garrison, A. H. (2004). Defining terrorism: Philosophy of the bomb, propaganda by deed and change through fear and violence. *Criminal Justice Studies*, *17*(3), 259–279. doi:10.1080/1478601042000281105

Gasser, H.-P. (1987). An appeal for ratification by the United States. *The American Journal of International Law*, *81*(4), 912–925. doi:10.2307/2203418

Gates, R. (2007, November 26). *Landon lecture*. Paper presented at Kansas State University. Manhattan, KS. Retrieved September 1, 2008, from http://www.defense.gov/speeches/speech.aspx?speechid=1199

Gearson, J. (2002). The nature of modern terrorism. *The Political Quarterly*, *73*(1), 7–24.

George, A. L. (2003). Analysis and judgment in policy-making. In S. A. Renshon, & D. W. Larson (Eds.), *Good judgment in foreign policy: Theory and application* (pp. 259–268). Lanham, MD: Rowman & Littlefield Publishers, Inc.

Gera, V. (2012, April 25). Breivik's publicity at trial just what he wanted. *Kansas City Star*. Retrieved May 2, 2012, from http://www.kansascity.com/2012/04/25/3575041/breiviks-publicity-at-trial-just.html

Gerbner, G., Gross, L., Morgan, M., & Signorielli, N. (1986). Living with television: The dynamics of the cultivation process. In J. Bryant, & D. Zillman (Eds.), *Perspectives on media effects* (pp. 17–40). Hillsdale, NJ: Lawrence Erlbaum Associates.

Gerges, F. A. (2005). *The far enemy: Why Jihad went global*. Cambridge, UK: Cambridge University Press.

Gerpott, T. J. (2013). Attribute perceptions as factors explaining mobile internet acceptance of cellular customers in Germany: An empirical study comparing actual and potential adopters with distinct categories of access appliances. In I. Lee (Ed.), *Strategy, adoption, and competitive advantage of mobile services in the global economy* (pp. 19–48). Hershey, PA: Information Science Reference.

Gerrits, R. P. J. M. (1992). Terrorists' perspectives: Memoirs. In D. L. Paletz, & A. P. Schmid (Eds.), *Terrorism and the media* (pp. 29–61). London: Sage.

Gettleman, J. (2011, December 19). U.S. considers combating Somali militants' Twitter use. *The New York Times*. Retrieved July 3, 2013, from http://www.nytimes.com/2011/12/20/world/africa/us-considers-combating-shabab-militants-twitter-use.html?_r=0

Giambona, G. J., & Birchall, D. W. (2012). Collaborative e-learning and ICT tools to develop SME managers: An Italian case. In I. Management Association (Ed.), Wireless technologies: Concepts, methodologies, tools and applications (pp. 1606-1617). Hershey, PA: Information Science Reference. doi: doi:10.4018/978-1-61350-101-6.ch605

Giannakos, M. N., Pateli, A. G., & Pappas, I. O. (2013). Identifying the direct effect of experience and the moderating effect of satisfaction in the Greek online market. In A. Scupola (Ed.), *Mobile opportunities and applications for e-service innovations* (pp. 77–97). Hershey, PA: Information Science Reference.

Gibbs, J. P. (1989). Conceptualization of terrorism. *American Sociological Review*, *54*(3), 329–340. doi:10.2307/2095609

Giorda, M., & Guerrisi, M. (2013). Educating to democracy and social participation through a "history of religion" course. In P. Pumilia-Gnarini, E. Favaron, E. Pacetti, J. Bishop, & L. Guerra (Eds.), *Handbook of research on didactic strategies and technologies for education: Incorporating advancements* (pp. 152–161). Hershey, PA: Information Science Reference.

Githens-Mazer, J. (2010, November 4). Radicalisation via YouTube? It's not so simple. *The Guardian (UK)*. Retrieved July 3, 2013, from http://www.guardian.co.uk/commentisfree/2010/nov/04/youtube-radicalisation-roshonara-choudhry

Gitlin, T. (1984). *The whole world is watching: Mass media in the making and unmaking of the new left*. Berkley, CA: University of California Press.

Glancey, J. (2003, April 19). Our last occupation: Gas, chemicals, bombs: Britain has used them all before in Iraq. *The Guardian*. Retrieved July 3, 2013, from http://www.guardian.co.uk/comment/story/0,3604,939608,00.html

Glavin, T. (2011). *Come from the shadows: The long and lonely struggle for peace in Afghanistan*. Vancouver, BC: Douglas & McIntyre.

Goggins, S., Schmidt, M., Guajardo, J., & Moore, J. L. (2013). 3D virtual worlds: Assessing the experience and informing design. In B. Medlin (Ed.), *Integrations of technology utilization and social dynamics in organizations* (pp. 194–213). Hershey, PA: Information Science Reference.

Golden, T. (2004, October 24). After terror: A secret reviewing of military law. *The New York Times*. Retrieved July 17, 2013, from http://www.nytimes.com/2004/10/24/international/worldspecial2/24gitmo.html?_r=0

Golden, T., & Van Natta, D. (2004, October 25). Threats and responses: Tough justice, administration officials split over stalled military tribunals. *The New York Times*. Retrieved July 17, 2013, from http://query.nytimes.com/gst/fullpage.html?res=9D05E4D7163DF936A15753C1A9629C8B63

Golding, P., & Elliott, P. (1979). *Making the news*. London: Longman.

Gold, N. (2012). Rebels, heretics, and exiles: Blogging among estranged and questioning American Hasidim. In T. Dumova, & R. Fiordo (Eds.), *Blogging in the global society: Cultural, political and geographical aspects* (pp. 108–127). Hershey, PA: Information Science Reference.

Goodall, H. L., Cheong, P. H., Fleischer, K., & Corman, S. (2012). Rhetorical charms: The promise and pitfalls of humor and ridicule as strategies to counter extremist narratives. *Perspectives on Terrorism, 6*(1), 70–79.

Goodall, H. L., Trethewey, A., & Corman, S. R. (2008). Strategery: Missed opportunities and the consequences of obsolete strategic communication theory. In S. R. Corman, A. Trethewey, & H. L. Goodall (Eds.), *Weapons of mass persuasion: Strategic communication to combat violent extremism* (pp. 3–26). New York: Peter Lang.

Goody, J. (2002). What is a terrorist? *History and Anthropology, 13*(2), 139–143. doi:10.1080/0275720022000001219

Gordon, S., & Ford, R. (2003). Cyberterrorism? *Symantec Security Response*. Retrieved October 6, 2013, from http://www.symantec.com/avcenter/reference/cyberterrorism.pdf

Gordon, A. D. (1999). Truth precludes any need for further ethical concerns in journalism and public relations. In A. D. Gordon, & J. M. Kittross (Eds.), *Controversies in media ethics* (pp. 73–80). New York: Longman.

Gordon, M. R., & Trainor, B. E. (2006). *Cobra II: The inside story of the invasion and occupation of Iraq*. New York: Pantheon Books.

Görgü, L., Wan, J., O'Hare, G. M., & O'Grady, M. J. (2013). Enabling mobile service provision with sensor networks. In I. Lee (Ed.), *Mobile services industries, technologies, and applications in the global economy* (pp. 175–192). Hershey, PA: Information Science Reference.

Graber, D. A. (2003). Terrorism, censorship and the 1st amendment: In search of policy guidelines. In P. Norris, M. Kern, & M. Just (Eds.), *Framing terrorism: The news media, the government and the public* (pp. 27–42). New York: Routledge.

Grayling, A. C. (2006). *Among the dead cities: Is the targeting of civilians in war ever justified?* London: Bloomsbury Publishing.

Greenwald, G. (2012, April 13). The real criminals in the Tarek Mehanna case. *Salon*. Retrieved July 3, 2013, from http://www.salon.com/2012/04/13/the_real_criminals_in_the_tarek_mehanna_case/

Gregory, S. J. (2013). Evolution of mobile services: An analysis. In I. Lee (Ed.), *Mobile services industries, technologies, and applications in the global economy* (pp. 104–119). Hershey, PA: Information Science Reference.

Grieve, G. P., & Heston, K. (2012). Finding liquid salvation: Using the Cardean ethnographic method to document second life residents and religious cloud communities. In N. Zagalo, L. Morgado, & A. Boa-Ventura (Eds.), *Virtual worlds and metaverse platforms: New communication and identity paradigms* (pp. 288–305). Hershey, PA: Information Science Reference.

Griffin, M. (2004). Picturing America's 'war on terrorism' in Afghanistan and Iraq: Photographic motifs as news frames. *Journalism*, *5*(4), 381–402. doi:10.1177/1464884904044201

Grinyaev, S. (2003). The mass media and terrorism: A Russian view. *European Security*, *12*(2), 85–88. doi:10.1080/09662830412331308086

Grossman, L. (2006, December 25). You—Yes, you—Are TIME's person of the year. *Time Magazine*. Retrieved July 3, 2013, from http://www.time.com/time/magazine/article/0,9171,1570810,00.html

Grover, R. (2002). The new state of nature and the new terrorism. *Public Affairs Quarterly*, *16*(2), 125–141.

Gudykunst, W. B. (Ed.). (2005). *Theorizing about intercultural communication*. Thousand Oaks, CA: Sage.

Guha, S., Thakur, B., Konar, T. S., & Chakrabarty, S. (2013). Web enabled design collaboration in India. In N. Kock (Ed.), *Interdisciplinary applications of electronic collaboration approaches and technologies* (pp. 96–111). Hershey, PA: Information Science Reference.

Gulati, G. J., Yates, D. J., & Tawileh, A. (2013). Explaining the global digital divide: The impact of public policy initiatives on e-government capacity and reach worldwide. In I. Association (Ed.), *Digital literacy: Concepts, methodologies, tools, and applications* (pp. 39–62). Hershey, PA: Information Science Reference.

Gunter, B. (2008). Media violence: Is there a case for causality? *The American Behavioral Scientist*, *51*(8), 1061–1122. doi:10.1177/0002764207312007

Gupta, J. (2013). Digital library initiatives in India. In T. Ashraf, & P. Gulati (Eds.), *Design, development, and management of resources for digital library services* (pp. 80–93). Hershey, PA: Information Science Reference.

Gurr, N., & Cole, B. (2005). *The new face of terrorism: Threats from weapons of mass destruction*. New York: I. B. Tauris.

Gururajan, R., Hafeez-Baig, A., Danaher, P. A., & De George-Walker, L. (2012). Student perceptions and uses of wireless handheld devices: Implications for implementing blended and mobile learning in an Australian university. In I. Management Association (Ed.), Wireless technologies: Concepts, methodologies, tools and applications (pp. 1323-1338). Hershey, PA: Information Science Reference. doi: doi:10.4018/978-1-61350-101-6.ch512

Gwilt, I. (2013). Data-objects: Sharing the attributes and properties of digital and material culture to creatively interpret complex information. In D. Harrison (Ed.), *Digital media and technologies for virtual artistic spaces* (pp. 14–26). Hershey, PA: Information Science Reference. doi:10.4018/978-1-4666-2961-5.ch002

Hackett, R. A. (2006). Is peace journalism possible? Three frameworks for assessing structure and agency in news media. *Conflict and Communication Online*, *5*(2), 1–13.

Hackett, R. A. (2007a). Journalism versus peace? Notes on a problematic relationship. *Global Media Journal*, *2*(1), 47–53.

Hackett, R. A. (2007b). Media terror? *Media Development*, *46*(3), 3–6.

Hackett, R. A. (2010). Journalism for peace and justice: Towards a comparative analysis of media paradigms. *Studies in Social Justice*, *4*(2), 145–164.

Hackett, R. A. (2012). Militarizing Canadian culture: Our government and media not just excusing war, but glorifying it. *The CCPA Monitor*, *18*(8), 39.

Hackett, R. A., & Carroll, W. K. (2006). *Remaking media: The struggle to democratize public communication*. London: Routledge.

Hackett, R. A., & Zhao, Y. (1998). *Sustaining democracy? Journalism and the politics of objectivity*. Toronto: Garamond.

Hackley, D. C., & Leidman, M. B. (2013). Integrating learning management systems in K-12 supplemental religious education. In A. Ritzhaupt, & S. Kumar (Eds.), *Cases on educational technology implementation for facilitating learning* (pp. 1–22). Hershey, PA: Information Science Reference. doi:10.4018/978-1-4666-3676-7.ch001

Hale, J. R., & Fields, D. (2013). A cross-cultural measure of servant leadership behaviors. In M. Bocarnea, R. Reynolds, & J. Baker (Eds.), *Online instruments, data collection, and electronic measurements: Organizational advancements* (pp. 152–163). Hershey, PA: Information Science Reference.

Hallahan, K., Holtzhausen, D., van Ruler, B., Verčič, D., & Sriramesh, K. (2007). Defining strategic communication. *International Journal of Strategic Communication, 1*(1), 3–35. doi:10.1080/15531180701285244

Halliday, J. (2012, March 22). Twitter's Tony Wang: We are the free speech wing of the free speech party. *The Guardian (UK)*. Retrieved July 3, 2013, from http://www.guardian.co.uk/media/2012/mar/22/twitter-tony-wang-free-speech

Hall, S. (1973). The determinations of news photographs. In S. Cohen, & J. Young (Eds.), *The manufacture of news: Social problems, deviance and the mass media* (pp. 226–246). London: Constable.

Hammond, P. (2003). The media war on terrorism. *Journal for Crime. Conflict and the Media, 1*(1), 23–36.

Hanewald, R. (2012). Using mobile technologies as research tools: Pragmatics, possibilities and problems. In I. Management Association (Ed.), *Wireless technologies: Concepts, methodologies, tools and applications* (pp. 130-150). Hershey, PA: Information Science Reference. doi: doi:10.4018/978-1-61350-101-6.ch108

Hanewald, R. (2013). Professional development with and for emerging technologies: A case study with Asian languages and cultural studies teachers in Australia. In J. Keengwe (Ed.), *Pedagogical applications and social effects of mobile technology integration* (pp. 175–192). Hershey, PA: Information Science Reference. doi:10.4018/978-1-4666-2985-1.ch010

Hanitzsch, T. et al. (2012). Worlds of journalism: Journalistic cultures, professional autonomy, and perceived influences across 18 nations. In D. H. Weaver, & L. Willnat (Eds.), *The global journalist: In the 21ˢᵗ century* (pp. 473–494). New York: Routledge.

Haque, E. (2010). Homegrown, Muslim and other: Tolerance, secularism and the limits of multiculturalism. *Social Identities, 16*(1), 79–101. doi:10.1080/13504630903465902

Harcup, T., & O'Neill, D. (2001). What is news? Galtung and Ruge revisited. *Journalism Studies, 2*(2), 261–280. doi:10.1080/14616700118449

Hari, J. (2010, October 15). Obama's escalating robot war in Pakistan is making a terror attack more likely. *The Huffington Post*. Retrieved July 3, 2013, from http://www.huffingtonpost.com/johann-hari/obamas-escalating-robot-w_b_763578.html

Harper's Magazine. (2012, June). *Eye of the drone*. Retrieved August 7, 2013, from http://archive.harpers.org/2012/06/pdf/HarpersMagazine-2012-06-0083923.pdf?AWSAccessKeyId=AKIAJXATU3VRJAAA66RA&Expires=1376411645&Signature=mfYaEt%2BLhHMwwOm%2FGSJXkNdnMdo%3D

Harris, D. (2010, July 1). Deadly Arkansas shootings by Jerry and Joe Kane who shun U.S. law. *ABC News*. Retrieved 3 July, 2013, from http://abcnews.go.com/WN/deadly-arkansas-shooting-sovereign-citizens-jerry-kane-joseph/story?id=11065285

Harris, G., & Spark, D. (1997). *Practical newspaper reporting*. Oxford, UK: Focal Press.

Hartmann, P., & Husband, C. (1974). *Racism and the mass media: A study of the role of the mass media in the formation of white beliefs and attitudes in Britain.* London: Davis-Poynter.

Hassan, N. (2001, November 19). An arsenal of believers: Talking to the human bombs. *The New Yorker*. Retrieved July 3, 2013, from http://www.newyorker.com/archive/2001/11/19/011119fa_FACT1

Hawks, B. B. (2013). Will peace flourish in the end? The history suffering: Terrorism in Turkey. *Mediterranean Journal of Social Sciences, 4*(10), 278–282.

Hayhoe, S. (2012). Non-visual programming, perceptual culture and mulsemedia: Case studies of five blind computer programmers. In G. Ghinea, F. Andres, & S. Gulliver (Eds.), *Multiple sensorial media advances and applications: New developments in MulSeMedia* (pp. 80–98). Hershey, PA: Information Science Reference.

Heap, S. P. H., & Varoufakis, Y. (1995). *Game theory: A critical introduction*. New York: Routledge. doi:10.4324/9780203199275

Heining, A. (2010, February 18). Who is Joe Stack? *The Christian Science Monitor*. Retrieved June 12, 2012, from http://www.csmonitor.com/USA/2010/0218/Who-is-Joe-Stack

Held, V. (1997). The media and political violence. *The Journal of Ethics*, *1*(2), 187–202. doi:10.1023/A:1009797007570

Held, V. (2004). Terrorism and war. *The Journal of Ethics*, *8*(1), 59–75. doi:10.1023/B:JOET.0000012252.68332.ff

Helfstein, S. (2012). Edges of radicalization: Ideas, individuals and networks in violent extremism. *Combating Terrorism Center at West Point: United State Military Academy*. Retrieved February 17, 2012, from http://www.ctc.usma.edu/posts/edges-of-radicalization-ideas-individuals-and-networks-in-violent-extremism

Hennebelle, G., Berrah, M., & Stora, B. (Eds.). (1997). *La guerre d'Algérie à l'écran*. Paris: Éditions Corlet-Télérama.

Henry, L. (2010). Minorities in Canadian media: Islam and the case of Aqsa Parvez. *The Laurier M.A. Journal of Religion and Culture*, *2*, 39–56.

Henschke, J. A. (2013). Nation building through andragogy and lifelong learning: On the cutting edge educationally, economically, and governmentally. In V. Wang (Ed.), *Handbook of research on technologies for improving the 21st century workforce: Tools for lifelong learning* (pp. 480–506). Hershey, PA: Information Science Publishing.

Hensgen, T., Desouza, K. C., Evaristo, J. R., & Kraft, G. D. (2003). Playing the cyber terrorism game towards a semiotic definition. *Human Systems Management*, *22*(2), 51–61.

Herman, E. S., & Chomsky, N. (1988). *Manufacturing consent: The political economy of the mass media*. New York: Pantheon.

Hermida, J. M., Meliá, S., Montoyo, A., & Gómez, J. (2013). Developing rich internet applications as social sites on the semantic web: A model-driven approach. In D. Chiu (Ed.), *Mobile and web innovations in systems and service-oriented engineering* (pp. 134–155). Hershey, PA: Information Science Reference.

Hernández-García, Á., Agudo-Peregrina, Á. F., & Iglesias-Pradas, S. (2013). Adoption of mobile video-call service: An exploratory study. In I. Lee (Ed.), *Strategy, adoption, and competitive advantage of mobile services in the global economy* (pp. 49–72). Hershey, PA: Information Science Reference.

Hertzberg, B. K., & Lundby, K. (2008). Mediatized lives: Autobiography and assumed authenticity in digital storytelling. In K. Lundby (Ed.), *Digital storytelling, mediatized stories: Self-representations in new media* (pp. 105–122). New York: Peter Lang.

Herz, M. (2006). Prime time terror: The case of La Jetee and 12 Monkeys. In A. P. Kavoori, & T. Fraley (Eds.), *Media, terrorism, and theory: A reader* (pp. 53–68). Lanham, MD: Rowman & Littlefield.

Hesapci-Sanaktekin, O., & Somer, I. (2013). Mobile communication: A study on smart phone and mobile application use. In I. Lee (Ed.), *Strategy, adoption, and competitive advantage of mobile services in the global economy* (pp. 217–233). Hershey, PA: Information Science Reference.

Hill, S. R., Troshani, I., & Freeman, S. (2013). An eclectic perspective on the internationalization of Australian mobile services SMEs. In I. Lee (Ed.), *Mobile services industries, technologies, and applications in the global economy* (pp. 55–73). Hershey, PA: Information Science Reference.

Hindman, E. B. (1997). *Rights vs. responsibilities: The Supreme Court and the media*. Westport, CT: Greenwood Press.

Hirschmann, K. (2000). The changing face of terrorism. *Internationale Politik und Gesellschaft*, *3*, 299–310.

Hoffman, B. (2003, June 1). The logic of suicide terrorism. *The Atlantic*. Retrieved July 3, 2013, from http://www.theatlantic.com/magazine/archive/2003/06/the-logic-of-suicide-terrorism/302739/

Hoffman, B. (2002). Rethinking terrorism and counterterrorism since 9/11. *Studies in Conflict and Terrorism, 25*(1), 303–316. doi:10.1080/105761002901223

Hoffman, B. (2006). *Inside terrorism.* New York: Columbia University Press.

Hoffman, B. (2008a). The myth of grass roots terrorism. *Foreign Affairs, 87*(3), 133–138.

Hoffman, B. (2008b). Hoffman replies. *Foreign Affairs, 87*(4), 165–166.

Hoffman, F. G. (2008c). Al Qaeda's demise or evolution? *United States Naval Institute Proceedings, 134*(9), 18–22.

Hoffmann, B. (1999). Terrorism trends and prospects. In I. O. Lesser, B. Hoffman, J. Arquilla, D. Ronfeldt, & M. Zanini (Eds.), *Countering the new terrorism* (pp. 7–38). Santa Monica, CA: RAND Corporation.

Holder v. Humanitarian Law Project. (2010). *US Supreme Court 561.* Retrieved July 3, 2013, from http://www.supremecourt.gov/opinions/09pdf/08-1498.pdf

Hollywood Reporter. (2002, April 16). *24 seeing ratings action.* Author.

Home Office. Counterterrorism. (2013, July 19). *Proscribed terror groups or organizations.* Retrieved August 7, 2011, from https://www.gov.uk/government/publications/proscribed-terror-groups-or-organisations--2

Homer-Dixon, T. (2002). The rise of complex terrorism. *Foreign Affairs, 81*(1), 52–62.

Horgan, J. (2007). *Preventing incitement to terrorism and radicalisation: What role for the media?* Paper presented at the EuroMed Conference. Dublin, Ireland.

Horgan, J. (2005). *The psychology of terrorism.* New York: Routledge. doi:10.4324/9780203496961

Horgan, J. (2009). *Walking away from terrorism.* New York: Routledge.

Ho, V. (2013). The need for identity construction in computer-mediated professional communication: A Community of practice perspective. In R. Luppicini (Ed.), *Handbook of research on technoself: Identity in a technological society* (pp. 502–530). Hershey, PA: Information Science Reference.

Howard, R., Sawyer, R., & Bajema, N. (2009). *Terrorism and counterterrorism: Understanding the new security environment.* New York: The McGraw Hills Company.

Huddy, L., Feldman, S., Lahav, G., & Taber, C. (2003). Fear and terrorism: Psychological reactions to 9/11. In P. Norris, M. Kern, & M. Just (Eds.), *Framing terrorism: The news media, the government and the public* (pp. 255–278). New York: Routledge.

Hudson, H. E. (2013). Challenges facing municipal wireless: Case studies from San Francisco and Silicon Valley. In A. Abdelaal (Ed.), *Social and economic effects of community wireless networks and infrastructures* (pp. 12–26). Hershey, PA: Information Science Reference. doi:10.4018/978-1-4666-2997-4.ch002

Hudson, R. A. (1999). *The sociology and psychology of terrorism: Who becomes a terrorist and why?* Washington, DC: Federal Research Division: Library of Congress. doi:10.1037/e622272007-001

Hughes, E. C. (1962). Good people and dirty work. *Social Problems, 10*(1), 3–11.

Human Rights Watch. (2006, March 15). *Funding the final war: LTTE intimidation and extortion in the Tamil Diaspora.* Retrieved August 22, 2013, from http://www.hrw.org/reports/2006/03/14/funding-final-war-0

Humphreys, S. (2012). Unravelling intellectual property in a specialist social networking site. In A. Lugmayr, H. Franssila, P. Näränen, O. Sotamaa, J. Vanhala, & Z. Yu (Eds.), *Media in the ubiquitous era: Ambient, social and gaming media* (pp. 248–266). Hershey, PA: Information Science Reference. doi:10.4018/978-1-4666-2136-7.ch016

Huntington, S. P. (1996). *The clash of civilizations and the remaking of world order.* New York: Touchstone.

Iadicola, P., & Shupe, A. (1998). *Violence, inequality, and human freedom.* Dix Hills, NY: General Hall.

Ibrahim, D. (2010). The framing of Islam on network news following the September 11th attacks. *The International Communication Gazette, 72*(1), 111–125. doi:10.1177/1748048509350342

Idle, N., & Nunns, A. (Eds.). (2011). *Tweets from Tahrir.* New York: OR Books.

If Americans Knew. (2013, May 15). Retrieved July 17, 2013, from http://www.ifamericansknew.org

Iglesias, A., Ruiz-Mezcua, B., López, J. F., & Figueroa, D. C. (2013). New communication technologies for inclusive education in and outside the classroom. In D. Griol Barres, Z. Callejas Carrión, & R. Delgado (Eds.), *Technologies for inclusive education: Beyond traditional integration approaches* (pp. 271–284). Hershey, PA: Information Science Reference. doi:10.4018/978-1-4666-4422-9.ch088

Ignatieff, M. (2004). *The lesser evil: Political ethics in an age of terror*. Toronto: Penguin Canada. doi:10.3366/edinburgh/9780748618729.001.0001

Igun, S. E. (2013). Gender and national information and communication technology (ICT) policies in Africa. In B. Maumbe, & J. Okello (Eds.), *Technology, sustainability, and rural development in Africa* (pp. 284–297). Hershey, PA: Information Science Reference. doi:10.4018/978-1-4666-3607-1.ch018

Ikolo, V. E. (2013). Gender digital divide and national ICT policies in Africa. In I. Association (Ed.), *Digital literacy: Concepts, methodologies, tools, and applications* (pp. 812–832). Hershey, PA: Information Science Reference.

Imran, A., & Gregor, S. (2013). A process model for successful e-government adoption in the least developed countries: A case of Bangladesh. In I. Association (Ed.), *Digital literacy: Concepts, methodologies, tools, and applications* (pp. 213–241). Hershey, PA: Information Science Reference.

Ionescu, A. (2013). ICTs and gender-based rights. In J. Lannon, & E. Halpin (Eds.), *Human rights and information communication technologies: Trends and consequences of use* (pp. 214–234). Hershey, PA: Information Science Reference.

Ismail, A., & Berkowitz, D. (2009). Terrorism meets press system: The *New York Times* and *China Daily* before and after 9/11. *Global Media Journal, 4*(1), 15-28.

Iyamu, T. (2013). The impact of organisational politics on the implementation of IT strategy: South African case in context. In J. Abdelnour-Nocera (Ed.), *Knowledge and technological development effects on organizational and social structures* (pp. 167–193). Hershey, PA: Information Science Reference.

Jacinto, L. (2002, October 29). Chechen black widows bring new fears. *ABC News*. Retrieved July 3, 2012, from http://abcnews.go.com/international/comments?type=story&id=79819#.UdSebhaSBUQ

Jadhav, V. G. (2013). Integration of digital reference service for scholarly communication in digital libraries. In T. Ashraf, & P. Gulati (Eds.), *Design, development, and management of resources for digital library services* (pp. 13–20). Hershey, PA: Information Science Reference.

Jager, S., & Link, J. (1993). *Die vierte gewalt: Rassismus und die medien*. Duisburg: DISS.

Jaggar, A. M. (2003). Responding to the evil of terrorism. *Hypatia, 18*(1), 175–182. doi:10.1111/j.1527-2001.2003.tb00787.x

Jäkälä, M., & Berki, E. (2013). Communities, communication, and online identities. In S. Warburton, & S. Hatzipanagos (Eds.), *Digital identity and social media* (pp. 1–13). Hershey, PA: Information Science Reference.

Janneck, M., & Staar, H. (2013). Playing virtual power games: Micro-political processes in inter-organizational networks. In B. Medlin (Ed.), *Integrations of technology utilization and social dynamics in organizations* (pp. 171–192). Hershey, PA: Information Science Reference.

Januska, I. M. (2013). Communication as a key factor in cooperation success and virtual enterprise paradigm support. In P. Renna (Ed.), *Production and manufacturing system management: Coordination approaches and multi-site planning* (pp. 145–161). Hershey, PA: Engineering Science Reference.

Jayasingh, S., & Eze, U. C. (2013). Consumers' adoption of mobile coupons in Malaysia. In I. Lee (Ed.), *Strategy, adoption, and competitive advantage of mobile services in the global economy* (pp. 90–111). Hershey, PA: Information Science Reference.

Jean Francois, E. (2013). Transculturality. In E. Jean Francois (Ed.), *Transcultural blended learning and teaching in postsecondary education* (pp. 1–14). Hershey, PA: Information Science Reference.

Jenkins, B. (1984, November). The who, what, when, where, how, and why of terrorism. In *Proceedings of the Detroit Police Department Conference on Urban Terrorism: Planning or Chaos?* Detroit, MI: Detroit Police Department.

Jenkins, B. (2004a). The operational code of the jihadists: A briefing prepared for the Army science board. *RAND Corporation*. Retrieved July 30, 2013, from http://www.au.af.mil/au/awc/awcgate/army/asb_op_code_jihadists.pdf

Jenkins, B. (2004b). Where I draw the line. *The Christian Science Monitor.* Retrieved July 3, 2013, from http://www.csmonitor.com/specials/terrorism/%20lite/expert.html

Jenkins, B. M. (1974). International terrorism: A new kind of warfare. The Rand Corporation, 1-16.

Jenkins, B. M. (2006). The new age of terrorism. In D. Kamien (Ed.), Section 2 – Terrorism beyond Al-Qaeda (pp. 117-130). Santa Monica, CA: RAND Corporation.

Jenkins, B., & Wright, R. (1991). Why hostage taking is so popular with terrorists. In B. Schechterman & M. W. Slann (Eds.), Violence and terrorism, (pp. 97-128). Guilford, CT: Dushkin Publishing Group.

Jenkins, B. (1987). Will terrorists go nuclear? In W. Laqueur, & Y. Alexander (Eds.), *The terrorism reader*. New York: Meridian.

Jenkins, B. (2006). *Unconquerable nation: Knowing our enemy, strengthening ourselves.* Santa Monica, CA: RAND Corporation.

Jenkins, B. M. (1981). *The psychological implications of media-covered terrorism (No. RAND-P-6627)*. Santa Monica, CA: The Rand Corporation.

Jenkins, B. M. (1983). Research in terrorism: Areas of consensus, areas of ignorance. In B. Eichelman, D. A. Soskis, & W. H. Reid (Eds.), *Terrorism: Interdisciplinary perspectives* (pp. 153–177). Washington, DC: American Psychiatric Association.

Jenkins, H. (2006). *Convergence culture: Where old and new media collide.* New York: New York University Press.

Jensen, S. S. (2012). User-driven content creation in second life a source of innovation? Three case studies of business and public service. In N. Zagalo, L. Morgado, & A. Boa-Ventura (Eds.), *Virtual worlds and metaverse platforms: New communication and identity paradigms* (pp. 1–15). Hershey, PA: Information Science Reference.

Johnston, W. J., Komulainen, H., Ristola, A., & Ulkuniemi, P. (2013). Mobile advertising in small retailer firms: How to make the most of it. In I. Lee (Ed.), *Strategy, adoption, and competitive advantage of mobile services in the global economy* (pp. 283–298). Hershey, PA: Information Science Reference.

Jones, J. (2008). *Blood that cries out from the Earth: The psychology of religious terrorism.* New York: Oxford University Press. doi:10.1093/acprof:oso/9780195335972.001.0001

Juergensmeyer, M. (2003). *Terror in the mind of God: The global rise of religious violence.* Berkley, CA: University of California Press.

Juergensmeyer, M. (2009). *Global rebellion: Religious challenges to the secular state from Christian militias to Al Qaeda.* Berkeley, CA: University of California Press.

Kadas, G., & Chatzimisios, P. (2013). The role of roadside assistance in vehicular communication networks: Security, quality of service, and routing issues. In R. Daher, & A. Vinel (Eds.), *Roadside networks for vehicular communications: Architectures, applications, and test fields* (pp. 1–37). Hershey, PA: Information Science Reference.

Kale, S. H., & Spence, M. T. (2012). A trination analysis of social exchange relationships in e-dating. In C. Romm Livermore (Ed.), *Gender and social computing: Interactions, differences and relationships* (pp. 257–271). Hershey, PA: Information Science Publishing.

Kamoun, F. (2013). Mobile NFC services: Adoption factors and a typology of business models. In I. Lee (Ed.), *Mobile services industries, technologies, and applications in the global economy* (pp. 254–272). Hershey, PA: Information Science Reference.

Kaneda, K., & Iwamura, K. (2013). New proposals for data hiding in paper media. In K. Kondo (Ed.), *Multimedia information hiding technologies and methodologies for controlling data* (pp. 258–285). Hershey, PA: Information Science Reference.

Karmasin, M., Melischek, G., Seethaler, J., & Wöhlert, R. (2013). Perspectives on the changing role of the mass media in hostile conflicts. In J. Seethaler, M. Karmasin, G. Melischek, & R. Wöhlert (Eds.), *The role of the mass media in hostile conflicts from World War I to the war on terror* (p. ix-1). Chicago: University of Chicago Press.

Kastell, K. (2013). Seamless communication to mobile devices in vehicular wireless networks. In O. Strobel (Ed.), *Communication in transportation systems* (pp. 324–342). Hershey, PA: Information Science Reference. doi:10.4018/978-1-4666-2976-9.ch012

Katz, S. M. (2004). *Raging within: Ideological terrorism.* Minneapolis, MN: Lerner Publications Company.

Kaye, B. K., & Johnson, T. J. (2012). Net gain? Selective exposure and selective avoidance of social network sites. In F. Comunello (Ed.), *Networked sociability and individualism: Technology for personal and professional relationships* (pp. 218–237). Hershey, PA: Information Science Reference.

Kaye, B. K., Johnson, T. J., & Muhlberger, P. (2012). Blogs as a source of democratic deliberation. In T. Dumova, & R. Fiordo (Eds.), *Blogging in the global society: Cultural, political and geographical aspects* (pp. 1–18). Hershey, PA: Information Science Reference.

Kefi, H., Mlaiki, A., & Peterson, R. L. (2013). IT offshoring: Trust views from client and vendor perspectives. In J. Wang (Ed.), *Perspectives and techniques for improving information technology project management* (pp. 113–130). Hershey, PA: Information Science Reference.

Kellermann, K. (2009). Communication: Inherently strategic and primarily automatic. *Communication Monographs*, *59*(3), 288–300. doi:10.1080/03637759209376270

Kellner, D. (2004). 9/11, spectacles of terror, and media manipulation: A critique of Jihadist and Bush media politics. *Critical Discourse Studies*, *1*(1), 41–64. doi:10.1080/17405900410001674515

Kelly, M. J. (1989). The seizure of the Turkish embassy in Ottawa: Managing terrorism and the media. In U. Rosenthal, M. T. Charles, & P. T. Hart (Eds.), *Coping with crises: The management of disasters, riots and terrorism* (pp. 117–138). Charles C. Thomas Publisher.

Kelly, M. J., & Mitchell, T. H. (1981). Transnational terrorism and the Western elite press. *Political Communication*, *1*(3), 269–296. doi:10.1080/10584609.1981.9962729

Khan, N. A., & Batoo, M. F. (2013). Stone inscriptions of Srinagar: A digital panorama. In T. Ashraf, & P. Gulati (Eds.), *Design, development, and management of resources for digital library services* (pp. 58–79). Hershey, PA: Information Science Reference.

Khan, S. (2000). *Muslim women: Crafting a North American identity.* Gainesville, FL: University Press of Florida.

Kibby, M. D. (2005). Email forwardables: Folklore in the age of the internet. *New Media &. Society*, *7*(6), 770–790.

Kilcullen, D., & Exum, A. M. (2009, May 16). Death from above, outrage from below. *The New York Times.* Retrieved July 3, 2013, from http://www.nytimes.com/2009/05/17/opinion/17exum.html?pagewanted=all&_r=0

Kilcullen, D. (2009). *The accidental guerrilla: Fighting small wars in the midst of a big one.* Oxford, UK: Oxford University Press.

Kim, P. (2012). "Stay out of the way! My kid is video blogging through a phone!": A lesson learned from math tutoring social media for children in underserved communities. In I. Management Association (Ed.), Wireless technologies: Concepts, methodologies, tools and applications (pp. 1415-1428). Hershey, PA: Information Science Reference. doi: doi:10.4018/978-1-61350-101-6.ch517

Kimery, A. L. (2009, August 13). Rejection of Jihadist, war on terrorism terms draws fire, debate. *Homeland Security Today.* Retrieved July 3, 2013, from http://www.hstoday.us/blogs/the-kimery-report/blog/rejection-of-jihadist-war-on-terrorism-terms-draws-fire-debate/7a2ac6715e2f3671f040bfca2cb55f57.html

Kimmage, D. (2008, April 14). *The Al-Qaeda media nexus: The virtual network behind the global message.* Washington, DC: Radio Free Europe. Retrieved April 14, 2008, from http://docs.rferl.org/en-US/AQ_Media_Nexus.pdf

Kimmage, D., & Ridolfo, K. (2007). Iraqi insurgent media: The war of ideas and images. *Radio Free Europe/Radio Liberty.* Retrieved July 5, 2013, from http://realaudio.rferl.org/online/OLPDFfiles/insurgent.pdf

Kimmage, D., & Ridolfo, K. (2007, July 13). *Iraqi insurgent media: The war of images and ideas*. Washington, DC: Radio Free Europe/Radio Liberty. Retrieved July 13, 2007, from at http://realaudio.rferl.org/online/OLPDF-files/insurgent.pdf

Kingshott, B. (2003). Terrorism: The new religious war. *Criminal Justice Studies, 16*(1), 15–27.

Kisubi, A. T. (2013). A critical perspective on the challenges for blended learning and teaching in Africa's higher education. In E. Jean Francois (Ed.), *Transcultural blended learning and teaching in postsecondary education* (pp. 145–168). Hershey, PA: Information Science Reference.

Kittross, J. M. (1999). The social value of journalism and public relations requires high-quality practices reflecting ethical considerations that go beyond truth and objectivity to accuracy and fairness. In A. D. Gordon, & J. M. Kittross (Eds.), *Controversies in media ethics* (pp. 80–89). New York: Longman.

Koh, H. H. (2002). Preserving American values: The challenge at home and abroad. In *The age of terror: America and the world after September 11* (pp. 143–169). New York: Basic Books.

Koole, M., & Parchoma, G. (2013). The web of identity: A model of digital identity formation in networked learning environments. In S. Warburton, & S. Hatzipanagos (Eds.), *Digital identity and social media* (pp. 14–28). Hershey, PA: Information Science Reference.

Koppel, A., & Labott, E. (2001, September 25). VOA asked not to air Taliban leader interview. CNN.com/U.S. Retrieved July 3, 2013, from http://articles.cnn.com/2001-09-24/us/gen.voa.taliban_1_taliban-leader-mullah-mohammad-omar-voa-broadcasts?_s=PM:US

Kordaki, M., Gorghiu, G., Bîzoi, M., & Glava, A. (2012). Collaboration within multinational learning communities: The case of the virtual community collaborative space for sciences education European project. In A. Juan, T. Daradoumis, M. Roca, S. Grasman, & J. Faulin (Eds.), *Collaborative and distributed e-research: Innovations in technologies, strategies and applications* (pp. 206–226). Hershey, PA: Information Science Reference. doi:10.4018/978-1-4666-0125-3.ch010

Kovach, B., & Rosenstiel, T. (2001). *The elements of journalism: What newspeople should know and the public should expect*. New York: Crown Publishers.

Kovács, J., Bokor, L., Kanizsai, Z., & Imre, S. (2013). Review of advanced mobility solutions for multimedia networking in IPv6. In D. Kanellopoulos (Ed.), *Intelligent multimedia technologies for networking applications: Techniques and tools* (pp. 25–47). Hershey, PA: Information Science Reference.

Kozaryn, L. (2002, April 2). *Rumsfeld: Suicide bombing is terrorism*. U.S. Department of Defense-American Forces Press Service. Retrieved July 3, 2013, from http://www.defense.gov/news/newsarticle.aspx?id=44197

Kreiner, G. E., Ashforth, B. E., & Sluss, D. M. (2006). Identity dynamics in occupational dirty work: Integrating social identity and system justification perspectives. *Organization Science, 17*(5), 619–636.

Kreps, D. (2013). Performing the discourse of sexuality online. In S. Warburton, & S. Hatzipanagos (Eds.), *Digital identity and social media* (pp. 118–132). Hershey, PA: Information Science Reference.

Kress, G., & van Leeuwen, T. (1996). *Reading images: The grammar of visual design*. New York: Routledge.

Ktoridou, D., Kaufmann, H., & Liassides, C. (2012). Factors affecting WiFi use intention: The context of Cyprus. In I. Management Association (Ed.), Wireless technologies: Concepts, methodologies, tools and applications (pp. 1760-1781). Hershey, PA: Information Science Reference. doi: doi:10.4018/978-1-61350-101-6.ch703

Kumar, N. (1997). *Communication and management*. New Delhi: Gyan Publishing House.

Kumar, N., Nero Alves, L., & Aguiar, R. L. (2013). Employing traffic lights as road side units for road safety information broadcast. In R. Daher, & A. Vinel (Eds.), *Roadside networks for vehicular communications: Architectures, applications, and test fields* (pp. 118–135). Hershey, PA: Information Science Reference.

Kupperman, R. H., van Opstal, D., & Williamson, D. (1982). Terror, the strategic tool: Response and control. *The Annals of the American Academy of Political and Social Science, 463*, 24–38. doi:10.1177/0002716282463001003

Kurtulus, E. N. (2011). The new terrorism and its critics. *Studies in Conflict and Terrorism, 34*(6), 476–500.

Kushner, H. (1998). *Terrorism in America: A structured approach to understanding the terrorist threat.* Springfield, IL: Charles C Thomas.

Kvasny, L., & Hales, K. D. (2013). The evolving discourse of the digital divide: The internet, black identity, and the evolving discourse of the digital divide. In I. Association (Ed.), *Digital literacy: Concepts, methodologies, tools, and applications* (pp. 1350–1366). Hershey, PA: Information Science Reference.

Kydd, A. H., & Walter, B. F. (2006). The strategies of terrorism. *International Security, 31*(1), 49–79.

L'Abate, L. (2013). Of paradigms, theories, and models: A conceptual hierarchical structure for communication science and technoself. In R. Luppicini (Ed.), *Handbook of research on technoself: Identity in a technological society* (pp. 84–104). Hershey, PA: Information Science Reference.

Laghos, A. (2013). Multimedia social networks and e-learning. In D. Kanellopoulos (Ed.), *Intelligent multimedia technologies for networking applications: Techniques and tools* (pp. 365–379). Hershey, PA: Information Science Reference.

Lahoud, N., Caudill, S., Collins, L., Koehler-Derrick, G., Rassler, D., & al-`Ubaydi, M. (2012). Letters from Abbottabad: Bin Laden sidelined? *Combating Terrorism Centre at Westpoint.* Retrieved July 3, 2013, from http://www.ctc.usma.edu/wp-content/uploads/2012/05/CTC_LtrsFromAbottabad_WEB_v2.pdf

Lappas, G. (2012). Social multimedia mining: Trends and opportunities in areas of social and communication studies. In I. Ting, T. Hong, & L. Wang (Eds.), *Social network mining, analysis, and research trends: Techniques and applications* (pp. 1–16). Hershey, PA: Information Science Reference.

Laqueur, W. (1976). The futility of terrorism. *Harper's Magazine, 252*(1510), 99-105.

Laqueur, W. (1987). *The age of terrorism.* Boston: Little Brown.

Laqueur, W. (2000). *The new terrorism: Fanaticism and the arms of mass destruction.* New York: Oxford University Press.

Lasker, J. (2005, February 25). Watchdogs sniff out terror sites. *Wired News.* Retrieved July 3, 2013, from http://www.wired.com/politics/security/news/2005/02/66708?currentPage=all

Latora, V., & Marchioni, M. (2004). How the science of complex networks can help developing strategies against terrorism. *Chaos, Solitons, and Fractals, 20*(1), 69–75. doi:10.1016/S0960-0779(03)00429-6

Lawrence, J. E. (2013). Barriers hindering ecommerce adoption: A case study of Kurdistan region of Iraq. In A. Zolait (Ed.), *Technology diffusion and adoption: Global complexity, global innovation* (pp. 152–165). Hershey, PA: Information Science Reference. doi:10.4018/978-1-4666-2791-8.ch010

Lawrence, K. F. (2013). Identity and the online media fan community. In S. Warburton, & S. Hatzipanagos`(Eds.), *Digital identity and social media* (pp. 233–255). Hershey, PA: Information Science Reference.

Lebow, R. N. (1987). Is crisis management always possible? *Political Science Quarterly, 102*(2), 181–192. doi:10.2307/2151348

Lee, J. E. C., & Lemyre, L. (2009). A social-cognitive perspective of terrorism risk perception and individual response in Canada. *Risk Analysis, 29*(9), 1265–1280. doi:10.1111/j.1539-6924.2009.01264.x PMID:19650811

Lee, M. J., Dalgarno, B., Gregory, S., Carlson, L., & Tynan, B. (2013). How are Australian and New Zealand higher educators using 3D immersive virtual worlds in their teaching? In B. Tynan, J. Willems, & R. James (Eds.), *Outlooks and opportunities in blended and distance learning* (pp. 169–188). Hershey, PA: Information Science Reference.

Lee, P. (2007). Editorial. *Media Development, 56*(3), 2.

Lee, S., Alfano, C., & Carpenter, R. G. (2013). Invention in two parts: Multimodal communication and space design in the writing center. In R. Carpenter (Ed.), *Cases on higher education spaces: Innovation, collaboration, and technology* (pp. 41–63). Hershey, PA: Information Science Reference.

Lee, W. (1971). *Decision theory and human behavior.* New York: John Wiley & Sons, Inc.

Leichsenring, C., Tünnermann, R., & Hermann, T. (2013). Feelabuzz: Direct tactile communication with mobile phones. In J. Lumsden (Ed.), *Developments in technologies for human-centric mobile computing and applications* (pp. 145–154). Hershey, PA: Information Science Reference.

Leith, S. (2011). *You talkin' to me? Rhetoric from Aristotle to Obama.* London: Profile Books Ltd.

Lemos, A., & Marques, F. P. (2013). A critical analysis of the limitations and effects of the Brazilian national broadband plan. In A. Abdelaal (Ed.), *Social and economic effects of community wireless networks and infrastructures* (pp. 255–274). Hershey, PA: Information Science Reference. doi:10.4018/978-1-4666-2997-4.ch014

Leslie, L. Z. (2000). *Mass communication ethics: Decision making in postmodern culture.* Boston: Houghton Mifflin Company.

Lesser, I. O. (1999). Countering the new terrorism: Implications for strategy. In I. O. Lesser (Ed.), *Countering the new terrorism* (pp. 85–144). Santa Monica, CA: Rand Corporation.

Lesser, I., Arquilla, J., Hoffman, B., Ronfeldt, D. F., & Zanini, M. (1999). *Countering the new terrorism.* Santa Monica, CA: RAND.

Lessig, L. (2008). *Remix: Making art and commerce thrive in the hybrid economy.* New York: Penguin Press.

Lester, P. M. (1995). *Visual communication: Images with messages.* Belmont, CA: Wadsworth.

Leung, C. K., Medina, I. J., & Tanbeer, S. K. (2013). Analyzing social networks to mine important friends. In G. Xu, & L. Li (Eds.), *Social media mining and social network analysis: Emerging research* (pp. 90–104). Hershey, PA: Information Science Reference.

Li, B. (2012). Toward an infrastructural approach to understanding participation in virtual communities. In H. Li (Ed.), *Virtual community participation and motivation: Cross-disciplinary theories* (pp. 103–123). Hershey, PA: Information Science Reference. doi:10.4018/978-1-4666-0312-7.ch007

Liddell, T. (2013). Historical evolution of adult education in America: The impact of institutions, change, and acculturation. In V. Wang (Ed.), *Handbook of research on technologies for improving the 21st century workforce: Tools for lifelong learning* (pp. 257–271). Hershey, PA: Information Science Publishing.

Liebes, T., & Kampf, Z. (2004). The PR of terror: How new-style wars give voice to terrorists. In S. Allan, & B. Zelizer (Eds.), *Reporting war: Journalism in wartime* (pp. 77–95). London: Routledge.

Likar, L. E. (2011). *Eco-warriors, nihilistic terrorists, and the environment.* Santa Barbara, CA: Praeger.

Li, L., Xiao, H., & Xu, G. (2013). Recommending related microblogs. In G. Xu, & L. Li (Eds.), *Social media mining and social network analysis: Emerging research* (pp. 202–210). Hershey, PA: Information Science Reference.

Liljander, V., Gummerus, J., Pihlström, M., & Kiehelä, H. (2013). Mobile services as resources for consumer integration of value in a multi-channel environment. In I. Lee (Ed.), *Strategy, adoption, and competitive advantage of mobile services in the global economy* (pp. 259–282). Hershey, PA: Information Science Reference.

Litaay, T., Prananingrum, D. H., & Krisanto, Y. A. (2013). Indonesian legal perspectives on biotechnology and intellectual property rights. In I. Association (Ed.), *Digital rights management: Concepts, methodologies, tools, and applications* (pp. 834–845). Hershey, PA: Information Science Reference.

Little, G. (2013). Collection development for theological education. In S. Holder (Ed.), *Library collection development for professional programs: Trends and best practices* (pp. 112–127). Hershey, PA: Information Science Reference.

Littlejohn, S. W. (2002). *Theories of human communication.* Wadsworth, Thomson Learning.

Littleton, C. (2002, October 31). 24 return kick-starts Fox just in time for Nov. sweep. *The Hollywood Reporter.* Retrieved July 22, 2013, from http://www.imdb.com/news/ni0187566/

Livingstone, S. (1999). New media, new audiences? *New Media & Society, 1*(1), 59–66. doi:10.1177/1461444899001001010

Lockyer, A. (2003). *The relationship between the media and terrorism*. The Australian National University: Strategic and Defence Studies Centre.

Losh, S. C. (2013). American digital divides: Generation, education, gender, and ethnicity in American digital divides. In I. Association (Ed.), *Digital literacy: Concepts, methodologies, tools, and applications* (pp. 932–958). Hershey, PA: Information Science Reference.

Louw, E. (2005). *The media and political process*. London: Sage.

Louw, P. E. (2003). The war against terrorism. *Gazette: The International Journal for Communication Studies, 65*(3), 211–230. doi:10.1177/0016549203065003001

Lovari, A., & Parisi, L. (2012). Public administrations and citizens 2.0: Exploring digital public communication strategies and civic interaction within Italian municipality pages on Facebook. In F. Comunello (Ed.), *Networked sociability and individualism: Technology for personal and professional relationships* (pp. 238–263). Hershey, PA: Information Science Reference.

Loza, W. (2007). The psychology of extremism and terrorism: A middle-eastern perspective. *Aggression and Violent Behavior, 12*(2), 141–155. doi:10.1016/j.avb.2006.09.001

Lumbaca, S., & Gray, D. H. (2011). The media as an enabler for acts of terrorism. *Global Security Studies, 2*(1), 45–54.

Lundry, C., & Cheong, P. H. (2011). Rumors and strategic communication: The gendered construction and transmediation of a terrorist life story. In T. Kuhn (Ed.), *Matters of communication political, cultural and technological challenges to communication* (pp. 145–166). New York: Hampton Press.

Luostarinen, H. (1999). *Media and collective identities*. Unpublished Manuscript.

Lupia, A., Mccubbins, M. D., & Popkin, S. L. (2000). Beyond rationality: Reason and the study of politics. In A. Lupia, M. D. Mccubbins, & S. L. Popkin (Eds.), *Elements of reason: Cognition, choice, and the bounds of rationality* (pp. 1–20). Cambridge, UK: Cambridge University Press. doi:10.1017/CBO9780511805813.001

Lutz, J., & Lutz, B. (2013). *Global terrorism*. New York: Routledge.

Lynch, J., & McGoldrick, A. (2005). *Peace journalism*. Stroud, UK: Hawthorn Press.

Lyon, D. (2003). *Surveillance after September 11*. Cambridge, MA: Polity.

Maamar, Z., Faci, N., Mostéfaoui, S. K., & Akhter, F. (2013). Towards a framework for weaving social networks into mobile commerce. In D. Chiu (Ed.), *Mobile and web innovations in systems and service-oriented engineering* (pp. 333–347). Hershey, PA: Information Science Reference.

Macdonald, S., Jarvis, L., Chen, T., & Lavis, S. (2013). *Cyberterrorism: A survey of researchers*. Retrieved July 3, 2013, from http://www.cyberterrorism-project.org/wp-content/uploads/2013/03/Cyberterrorism-Report-2013.pdf

MacFarquhar, N. (2004, June 19). Acting on threat, Saudi group kills captive American. *The New York Times*, p. 1.

Maclean, W. (2011, September 5). Analysis—Islamist videos, populists stir German worries. *Reuters (UK)*. Retrieved July 3, 2013, from http://uk.reuters.com/article/2011/09/05/uk-germany-security-idUK-TRE7842HS20110905

Magnum Photos. (2012). *Robert Capa*. Retrieved June 7, 2012, from http://www.magnumphotos.com/C.aspx?VP=XSpecific_MAG.PhotographerDetail_VPage&l1=0&pid=2K7O3R14YQNW&nm=Robert%20Capa

Maia, I. F., & Valente, J. A. (2013). Digital identity built on a cooperative relationship. In S. Warburton, & S. Hatzipanagos (Eds.), *Digital identity and social media* (pp. 58–73). Hershey, PA: Information Science Reference.

Maity, M. (2013). Consumer information search and decision-making on m-commerce: The role of product type. In I. Lee (Ed.), *Strategy, adoption, and competitive advantage of mobile services in the global economy* (pp. 73–89). Hershey, PA: Information Science Reference.

Malinen, S., Virjo, T., & Kujala, S. (2012). Supporting local connections with online communities. In A. Lugmayr, H. Franssila, P. Näränen, O. Sotamaa, J. Vanhala, & Z. Yu (Eds.), *Media in the ubiquitous era: Ambient, social and gaming media* (pp. 235–250). Hershey, PA: Information Science Reference.

Mander, J. (1978). *Four arguments for the elimination of television.* New York: William Morrow.

Manoff, R. K. (1986). Writing the news (by telling the story). In R. K. Manoff, & M. Schudson (Eds.), *Reading the news* (pp. 197–229). New York: Pantheon Books.

Mantoro, T., Milišic, A., & Ayu, M. (2013). Online authentication using smart card technology in mobile phone infrastructure. In I. Khalil, & E. Weippl (Eds.), *Contemporary challenges and solutions for mobile and multimedia technologies* (pp. 127–144). Hershey, PA: Information Science Reference.

Marcato, E., & Scala, E. (2013). Moodle: A platform for a school. In P. Pumilia-Gnarini, E. Favaron, E. Pacetti, J. Bishop, & L. Guerra (Eds.), *Handbook of research on didactic strategies and technologies for education: Incorporating advancements* (pp. 107–116). Hershey, PA: Information Science Reference.

March, A. F. (2012, April 21). A dangerous mind? *The New York Times.* Retrieved July 3, 2013, from http://www.nytimes.com/2012/04/22/opinion/sunday/a-dangerous-mind.html?pagewanted=all

Margalit, A. (1994, February 17). The uses of the Holocaust. *The New York Review of Books.* Retrieved July 3, 2013, from http://www.nybooks.com/articles/archives/1994/feb/17/the-uses-of-the-holocaust/?pagination=false

Markaki, O. I., Charalabidis, Y., & Askounis, D. (2013). Measuring interoperability readiness in south eastern Europe and the Mediterranean: The interoperability observatory. In A. Scupola (Ed.), *Mobile opportunities and applications for e-service innovations* (pp. 210–230). Hershey, PA: Information Science Reference.

Markel, M. (2001). *Ethics in technical communication: A critique and synthesis.* Westport, CT: Ablex Publishing.

Markon, J., Brulliard, K., & Rizwan, M. (2010, March 18). Pakistan charges 5 Northern Virginia men in alleged terrorism plot. *The Washington Post.* Retrieved July 3, 2013, from http://www.washingtonpost.com/wp-dyn/content/article/2010/03/17/AR2010031700430.html

Marks, S. M., Meer, T. M., & Nilson, M. T. (2007). Manhunting: A process to find persons of national interest. In J. J. F. Forest (Ed.), *Countering terrorism and insurgency in the 21ˢᵗ century* (pp. 208–234). Westport, CT: Praeger Security International.

Marsden, P., & Attia, S. (2005). A deadly contagion? *The Psychologist, 18*(3), 152–155.

Marsden, S. V., & Schmid, A. P. (2011). Typologies of terrorism and political violence. In A. P. Schmid (Ed.), *The Routledge handbook of terrorism research* (pp. 158–200). New York: Routledge.

Martinez, J. S. (2008). Process and substance in the war on terror. *Columbia Law Review, 108*(5), 1013–1092.

Martin, G. (2006). *Understanding terrorism: Challenges, perspectives, and issues.* Thousand Oaks, CA: Sage Publications, Inc.

Martin, J. D., & El-Toukhy, S. (2012). Blogging for sovereignty: An analysis of Palestinian blogs. In T. Dumova, & R. Fiordo (Eds.), *Blogging in the global society: Cultural, political and geographical aspects* (pp. 148–160). Hershey, PA: Information Science Reference.

Matei, S. A., & Bruno, R. J. (2012). Individualist motivators and community functional constraints in social media: The case of Wikis and Wikipedia. In F. Comunello (Ed.), *Networked sociability and individualism: Technology for personal and professional relationships* (pp. 1–23). Hershey, PA: Information Science Reference.

Matsuoka, H. (2013). Acoustic OFDM technology and system. In K. Kondo (Ed.), *Multimedia information hiding technologies and methodologies for controlling data* (pp. 90–103). Hershey, PA: Information Science Reference.

Matusitz, J. (2009). A postmodern theory of cyberterrorism: Game theory. *Information Security Journal: A Global Perspective, 18*(6), 273-281.

Matusitz, J. (2005). Cyberterrorism: How can American foreign policy be strengthened in the information age? *American Foreign Policy Interests, 27*(2), 137–147.

Matusitz, J., & Minei, E. (2009). Cyberterrorism: Its effects on health-related infrastructures. *Journal of Digital Forensic Practice, 2*(4), 161–171.

Mayer, J. (2007, February 19). Whatever it takes: The politics of the man behind 24. *The New Yorker.* Retrieved July 3, 2013, from http://www.newyorker.com/reporting/2007/02/19/070219fa_fact_mayer

Mazumdar, R. (2004). Cracks in the urban frame: The visual politics of 9/11. In Sarai reader 04: Crisis/media (pp. 209-216). Delhi, India: Sarai, the Centre for the Study of Developing Societies.

McCants, W. (2011, December 6). *Subcommittee hearing: Jihadist use of social media: How to prevent terrorism and preserve innovation*. Retrieved July 3, 2013, from http://homeland.house.gov/hearing/subcommittee-hearing-jihadist-use-social-media-how-prevent-terrorism-and-preserve-innovation

McCarthy, S. (2003, March 29). Support for Chrétien's war policy sags. *The Globe and Mail*. Retrieved July 3, 2013, from http://www.theglobeandmail.com/news/national/support-for-chretiens-war-policy-sags/article1159474/

McCarthy, J. (2013). Online networking: Integrating international students into first year university through the strategic use of participatory media. In F. García-Peñalvo (Ed.), *Multiculturalism in technology-based education: Case studies on ICT-supported approaches* (pp. 189–210). Hershey, PA: Information Science Reference.

McChesney, R. W. (2004). *The problem of the media: U.S. communication politics in the twenty-first century*. New York: Monthly Review Press.

McCoy, A. W. (2006). *A question of torture: CIA interrogation from the Cold War to the war on terror*. New York: Metropolitan/Owl Books, Henry Holt & Company.

McDonald, A., & Helmer, S. (2013). A comparative case study of Indonesian and UK organisational culture differences in IS project management. In A. Mesquita (Ed.), *User perception and influencing factors of technology in everyday life* (pp. 46–55). Hershey, PA: Information Science Reference.

McDonough, C. (2013). Mobile broadband: Substituting for fixed broadband or providing value-added. In I. Lee (Ed.), *Mobile services industries, technologies, and applications in the global economy* (pp. 74–86). Hershey, PA: Information Science Reference.

McGuffin, J. (1974). *The guinea-pigs*. Harmondsworth, UK: Penguin Books.

McKeown, A. (2013). Virtual communitas, "digital place-making," and the process of "becoming". In D. Harrison (Ed.), *Digital media and technologies for virtual artistic spaces* (pp. 218–236). Hershey, PA: Information Science Reference. doi:10.4018/978-1-4666-2961-5.ch016

McKibben, B. (1999). Living second hand: An environmental view of the mass media. In K. Duncan (Ed.), *Liberating alternatives: The founding convention of the cultural environment movement* (pp. 43–47). Cresskill, NJ: Hampton Press.

McMillian, N. (2004). Beyond representation: Cultural understandings of the September 11 attacks. *Australian and New Zealand Journal of Criminology, 37*(3), 380–400. doi:10.1375/acri.37.3.380

McNair, B. (1998). *The sociology of journalism*. London: Oxford University Press.

McNair, B. (2003). *An introduction to political communication*. London: Routledge.

Medeni, T. D., Medeni, I. T., & Balci, A. (2013). Proposing a knowledge amphora model for transition towards mobile government. In A. Scupola (Ed.), *Mobile opportunities and applications for e-service innovations* (pp. 170–192). Hershey, PA: Information Science Reference.

Meikle, G. (2008). Whacking Bush: Tactical media as play. In M. Boler (Ed.), *Digital media and democracy: Tactics in hard times* (pp. 367–382). Cambridge, MA: MIT Press.

Mei, Y. M., Lee, S. T., & Al-Hawamdeh, S. (2004). Formulating a communication strategy for effective knowledge sharing. *Journal of Information Science, 30*(1), 12–22. doi:10.1177/0165551504041674

Meleagrou-Hitchens, A. (2011). *As American as apple pie: How Anwar al-Awlaki became the face of western Jihad*. Kings College London: International Centre for the Study of Radicalisation and Political Violence. Retrieved July 3, 2013, from http://icsr.info/2011/09/as-american-as-apple-pie-how-anwar-al-awlaki-became-the-face-of-western-jihad/

Melo, A., Bezerra, P., Abelém, A. J., Neto, A., & Cerqueira, E. (2013). PriorityQoE: A tool for improving the QoE in video streaming. In D. Kanellopoulos (Ed.), *Intelligent multimedia technologies for networking applications: Techniques and tools* (pp. 270–290). Hershey, PA: Information Science Reference.

Meltzer, A. (1996). *Anarchism: Arguments for and against.* Edinburgh, UK: AK Press.

Mendoza-González, R., Rodríguez, F. Á., & Arteaga, J. M. (2013). A usability study of mobile text based social applications: Towards a reliable strategy for design evaluation. In M. Garcia-Ruiz (Ed.), *Cases on usability engineering: Design and development of digital products* (pp. 195–219). Hershey, PA: Information Science Reference. doi:10.4018/978-1-4666-4046-7.ch009

Merola, L. M. (2013). Transmitting the threat: Media coverage and the discussion of terrorism and civil liberties since 9/11. *Behavioral Sciences of Terrorism and Political Aggression, 5*(1), 1–19. doi:10.1080/1943447 2.2011.571531

Merton, R. K. (1968). *Social theory and social structure.* New York: Free Press.

Messaris, P. (1994). *Visual literacy: Image, mind & reality.* Boulder, CO: Westview Press.

Metzger, M. J., Wilson, C., Pure, R. A., & Zhao, B. Y. (2012). Invisible interactions: What latent social interaction can tell us about social relationships in social network sites. In F. Comunello (Ed.), *Networked sociability and individualism: Technology for personal and professional relationships* (pp. 79–102). Hershey, PA: Information Science Reference.

Michigan Regional Community Policing Community Counter Terrorism Initiative. (n.d.). Retrieved July 22, 2013, from http://www1.cj.msu.edu/anti_terror/

Midlarsky, M. I., Crenshaw, M., & Yoshida, F. (1980). Why violence spreads: The contagion of international terrorism. *International Studies Quarterly, 24*(2), 262–298. doi:10.2307/2600202

Miller, J., & Stone, M. (2002). *The cell: Inside the 9/11 plot and why the FBI and CIA failed to stop it.* New York: Hyperion. doi:10.3410/f

Millo, G., & Carmeci, G. (2013). Insurance in Italy: A spatial perspective. In G. Borruso, S. Bertazzon, A. Favretto, B. Murgante, & C. Torre (Eds.), *Geographic information analysis for sustainable development and economic planning: New technologies* (pp. 158–178). Hershey, PA: Information Science Reference.

Mingqing, X., Wenjing, X., & Junming, Z. (2012). The future of television. In R. Sharma, M. Tan, & F. Pereira (Eds.), *Understanding the interactive digital media marketplace: Frameworks, platforms, communities and issues* (pp. 406–415). Hershey, PA: Information Science Reference.

Miscione, G. (2013). Telemedicine and development: Situating information technologies in the Amazon. In J. Abdelnour-Nocera (Ed.), *Knowledge and technological development effects on organizational and social structures* (pp. 132–145). Hershey, PA: Information Science Reference.

Mitliaga, V. (2001). Cyber-terrorism: A call for governmental action? In *Proceedings of 16th BILETA Annual Conference.* Retrieved October 9, 2009, from http://www.bileta.ac.uk/01papers/mitliaga.html

Mockaitis, T. R. (2008). *The new terrorism: Myths and reality.* Stanford, CA: Stanford University Press.

Modegi, T. (2013). Spatial and temporal position information delivery to mobile terminals using audio watermarking techniques. In K. Kondo (Ed.), *Multimedia information hiding technologies and methodologies for controlling data* (pp. 182–207). Hershey, PA: Information Science Reference.

Mody, B., & Lee, A. (2002). Differing traditions of research on international media influence. In W. B. Gudykunst, & B. Mody (Eds.), *Handbook of international and intercultural communication* (pp. 381–398). Thousand Oaks, CA: Sage Publications.

Montes, J. A., Gutiérrez, A. C., Fernández, E. M., & Romeo, A. (2012). Reality mining, location based services and e-business opportunities: The case of city analytics. In I. Management Association (Ed.), *Wireless technologies: Concepts, methodologies, tools and applications* (pp. 1520-1532). Hershey, PA: Information Science Reference. doi: doi:10.4018/978-1-61350-101-6.ch601

Moore, S. (2010). The origins of strategic communication: Precedents and parallels in ancient states. *Atlantic Journal of Communication, 18*(5), 227–240. doi:10.1080/15456870.2010.521469

Moreno, A. (2012). The social construction of new cultural models through information and communication technologies. In M. Safar, & K. Mahdi (Eds.), *Social networking and community behavior modeling: Qualitative and quantitative measures* (pp. 68–84). Hershey, PA: Information Science Reference.

Morgan, M. (Ed.). (2002). *Against the mainstream: The selected words of George Gerbner*. New York: Peter Lang.

Morgan, M. J. (2004). The origins of the new terrorism. *Parameters, 34*(1), 29–43.

Morris, J. Z., & Thomas, K. D. (2013). Implementing BioSand filters in rural Honduras: A case study of his hands mission international in Copán, Honduras. In H. Muga, & K. Thomas (Eds.), *Cases on the diffusion and adoption of sustainable development practices* (pp. 468–496). Hershey, PA: Information Science Reference.

Morrow, J. D. (1994). *Game theory for political scientists*. Princeton, NJ: Princeton University Press.

Mothana, I. (2012, June 13). How drone strikes help al Qaeda. *The New York Times*. Retrieved June 13, 2012, from http://www.nytimes.com/2012/06/14/opinion/how-drones-help-al-qaeda.html

Moutot, M. (2010, October 9). Al-Qaeda views west terror alert fears as victory: Experts. *Agence France-Presse*. Retrieved July 5, 2013, from http://www.google.com/hostednews/afp/article/ALeqM5iyx1sKrYJT_vrKaM-RnR-SMgX9Qrw?docId=CNG.9069423c15ce0426af7f79fa1a9b81e0.a81

Muller, E. R., Spaaij, R. F. J., & Ruitenberg, A. G. W. (2004). *Trends in terrorisme. Alphen aan de Rijn*. Kluwer.

Mura, G. (2012). The MultiPlasticity of new media. In G. Ghinea, F. Andres, & S. Gulliver (Eds.), *Multiple sensorial media advances and applications: New developments in MulSeMedia* (pp. 258–271). Hershey, PA: Information Science Reference.

Murphy, J. F. (2009). Challenges of the new terrorism. In D. Armstrong (Ed.), *Routledge handbook of international law* (pp. 281–293). New York: Routeldge.

Murray, C. (2012). Imagine mobile learning in your pocket. In I. Management Association (Ed.), *Wireless technologies: Concepts, methodologies, tools and applications* (pp. 2060-2088). Hershey, PA: Information Science Reference. doi: doi:10.4018/978-1-61350-101-6.ch807

Murray, J. (2005). Policing terrorism: A threat to community policing or just a shift in priorities? *Police Practice and Research, 6*(4), 347–361. doi:10.1080/15614260500293986

Murray, R. (2003). *State violence: Northern Ireland 1969-1997*. Cork, Ireland: Mercier Press.

Mutohar, A., & Hughes, J. E. (2013). Toward web 2.0 integration in Indonesian education: Challenges and planning strategies. In N. Azab (Ed.), *Cases on web 2.0 in developing countries: Studies on implementation, application, and use* (pp. 198–221). Hershey, PA: Information Science Reference.

Mythen, G. (2013). Why should we have to prove we're alright? Counter-terrorism, risk and partial securities. *Sociology, 47*(2), 383–398.

Mythen, G., & Walklate, S. (2006). Communicating the terrorist risk: Harnessing a culture of fear? *Crime, Media, Culture, 2*(2), 123–142. doi:10.1177/1741659006065399

Nacos, B. L. (2000). Accomplice or witness? The media's role in terrorism is the media terrorism's oxygen? A critical examination of how terrorists rely on and use various media. *Current History (New York, N.Y.), 99*(636), 174–178.

Nacos, B. L. (2003). The calculus behind 9-11: A model for future terrorism? *Studies in Conflict and Terrorism, 26*(1), 1–16. doi:10.1080/10576100390145134

Nacos, B. L. (2003a). Terrorism as breaking news: Attack on America. *Political Science Quarterly, 118*(1), 23–52. doi:10.1002/j.1538-165X.2003.tb00385.x

Nacos, B. L. (2005). The portrayal of female terrorists in the media: Similar framing patters in the news coverage of women in politics and in terrorism. *Studies in Conflict and Terrorism, 28*(5), 435–451. doi:10.1080/10576100500180352

Nacos, B. L. (2006). *Terrorism and counterterrorism: Understanding threats and responses in the post-9/11 world*. New York: Longman.

Nacos, B. L. (2007). *Mass-mediated terrorism: The central role of the media in terrorism and counterterrorism.* Lanham, MD: Rowman & Littlefield Publishers, Inc.

Nacos, B. L. (2012). *Terrorism and counterterrorism.* Boston: Longman.

Nacos, B. L., Bloch-Elkon, Y., & Shapiro, R. Y. (2011). *Selling fear: Counterterrorism, the media, and public opinion.* Chicago: The University of Chicago Press. doi:10.7208/chicago/9780226567204.001.0001

Najafbagy, R. (2008). Problems of effective cross-cultural communication and conflict resolution. *Palestine – Israel Journal of Politics. Economics, and Culture, 15*(16), 146–150.

Nakashima, E. (2010, March 4). FBI director warns of rapidly expanding cyberterrorism threat. *Washington Post.* Retrieved July 3, 2013, http://www.washingtonpost.com/wp-dyn/content/article/2010/03/04/AR2010030405066.html

Nandi, B., & Subramaniam, G. (2012). Evolution in broadband technology and future of wireless broadband. In I. Management Association (Ed.), Wireless technologies: Concepts, methodologies, tools and applications (pp. 1928-1957). Hershey, PA: Information Science Reference. doi: doi:10.4018/978-1-61350-101-6.ch801

Napoleoni, L. (2003). *Modern Jihad: Tracing the dollars behind the terror networks.* Sterling, VA: Pluto Press.

Naser, A., Jaber, I., Jaber, R., & Saeed, K. (2013). Information systems in UAE education sector: Security, cultural, and ethical issues. In F. Albadri (Ed.), *Information systems applications in the Arab education sector* (pp. 148–162). Hershey, PA: Information Science Reference.

Nasir, M., Khan, A. A., & Jalil, H. H. (2013). Exploring the relationship between media and terrorism: A panel study of south Asian countries. *Economic Bulletin, 33*(1), 714–720.

National Commission on Terrorist Attacks upon the United States. (2004). *The 9/11 commission report.* Retrieved July 3, 2013, from http://www.9-11commission.gov/report/911Report.pdf

Nemoianu, I., & Pesquet-Popescu, B. (2013). Network coding for multimedia communications. In D. Kanellopoulos (Ed.), *Intelligent multimedia technologies for networking applications: Techniques and tools* (pp. 1–24). Hershey, PA: Information Science Reference.

Neumann, P. (2009). *Old and new terrorism.* Malden, MA: Polity Press.

Neville, R. (2004, May 29). Who killed Nick Berg? *The Sydney Morning Herald.* Retrieved July 3, 2013, from http://www.smh.com.au/articles/2004/05/28/1085641717320.html

New South Whales Government. (2011). *Countering terrorism: Community initiatives.* Retrieved July 22, 2013, from http://www.secure.nsw.gov.au/For-individuals-and-community-groups/Community-initiatives.aspx

Nezlek, G., & DeHondt, G. (2013). Gender wage differentials in information systems: 1991 – 2008 a quantitative analysis. In B. Medlin (Ed.), *Integrations of technology utilization and social dynamics in organizations* (pp. 31–47). Hershey, PA: Information Science Reference.

Nia, M. M. (2010). From old to new terrorism: The changing nature of international security. *Global Studies Journal, 18*, 1–20.

Nicholson, M. (1970). *Conflict analysis.* London: The English Universities Press Limited.

Nicholson, M. (1996). *Causes and consequences in international relations: A conceptual study.* London: Pinter.

Nicholson, M. (1997). *Rationality and the analysis of international conflict.* Cambridge, UK: Cambridge University Press.

Nishimura, A., & Kondo, K. (2013). Information hiding for audio signals. In K. Kondo (Ed.), *Multimedia information hiding technologies and methodologies for controlling data* (pp. 1–18). Hershey, PA: Information Science Reference.

Noelle-Neumann, E. (1973). Return to the concept of the powerful mass media. *Studies in Broadcasting, 9*, 67–112.

Nonneman, G. (2010). Terrorism and political violence in the Middle East and North Africa. In A. Siniver (Ed.), *International terrorism post-9/11: Comparative dynamics and responses* (pp. 12–36). New York: Routledge.

Norder, J. W., & Carroll, J. W. (2013). Applied geospatial perspectives on the rock art of the lake of the woods region of Ontario, Canada. In D. Albert, & G. Dobbs (Eds.), *Emerging methods and multidisciplinary applications in geospatial research* (pp. 77–93). Hershey, PA: Information Science Reference.

Norris, P., Kern, M., & Just, M. (2003). Introduction: Framing terrorism. In P. Norris, K. Montague, & M. Just (Eds.), *Framing terrorism: The news media, the government and the public* (pp. 3–26). New York: Routledge.

Nye, J. S. (2005). *Understanding international conflicts: An introduction to theory and history*. New York: Pearson Education, Inc.

O'Brien, M. A., & Rogers, W. A. (2013). Design for aging: Enhancing everyday technology use. In R. Zheng, R. Hill, & M. Gardner (Eds.), *Engaging older adults with modern technology: Internet use and information access needs* (pp. 105–123). Hershey, PA: Information Science Reference.

O'Connor, T. R. (2006). The criminology of terrorism: History, law, definitions, typologies. *Cults and Terror*. Retrieved June 14, 2012, from http://www.cultsandterror.org/sub-file/TOConnor%20Lecture.htm

O'Hanlon, S. (2013). Health information technology and human rights. In J. Lannon, & E. Halpin (Eds.), *Human rights and information communication technologies: Trends and consequences of use* (pp. 235–246). Hershey, PA: Information Science Reference.

O'Kane, R. H. T. (2012). *Terrorism*. Harlow, UK: Pearson.

O'Rourke, L. (2008, August 2). Behind the woman behind the bomb. *The New York Times*. Retrieved July 3, 2013, from http://www.nytimes.com/2008/08/02/opinion/02orourke.html?_r=2&pagewanted=all

Oberschall, A. (2004). Explaining terrorism: The contribution of collective action theory. *Sociological Theory*, *22*(1), 26–37. doi:10.1111/j.1467-9558.2004.00202.x

Odella, F. (2012). Social networks and communities: From traditional society to the virtual sphere. In M. Safar, & K. Mahdi (Eds.), *Social networking and community behavior modeling: Qualitative and quantitative measures* (pp. 1–25). Hershey, PA: Information Science Reference.

Okazaki, S., Romero, J., & Campo, S. (2012). Capturing market mavens among advergamers: A case of mobile-based social networking site in Japan. In I. Ting, T. Hong, & L. Wang (Eds.), *Social network mining, analysis, and research trends: Techniques and applications* (pp. 291–305). Hershey, PA: Information Science Reference.

Omojola, O. (2012). Exploring the impact of Google Igbo in South East Nigeria. In R. Lekoko, & L. Semali (Eds.), *Cases on developing countries and ICT integration: Rural community development* (pp. 62–73). Hershey, PA: Information Science Reference.

Otenyo, E. E. (2004). New terrorism: Toward and explanation of cases in Kenya. *African Security Review*, *13*(3), 75–85.

Ovide, E. (2013). Intercultural education with indigenous peoples and the potential of digital technologies to make it happen. In F. García-Peñalvo (Ed.), *Multiculturalism in technology-based education: Case studies on ICT-supported approaches* (pp. 59–78). Hershey, PA: Information Science Reference.

Owens, D. D. (2005). Law versus war: Competing approaches to fighting terrorism. *Strategic Studies Institute, US Army War College*. Retrieved November 10, 2011, from http://www.au.af.mil/au/awc/awcgate/ssi/boyne_law_terr.pdf

Owusu-Ansah, A. (2013). Exploring Hofstede's cultural dimension using Hollins' structured dialogue to attain a conduit for effective intercultural experiences. In E. Jean Francois (Ed.), *Transcultural blended learning and teaching in postsecondary education* (pp. 52–74). Hershey, PA: Information Science Reference.

Özdemir, E. (2012). Gender and e-marketing: The role of gender differences in online purchasing behaviors. In C. Romm Livermore (Ed.), *Gender and social computing: Interactions, differences and relationships* (pp. 72–86). Hershey, PA: Information Science Publishing. doi:10.4018/978-1-4666-1598-4.ch044

Palmer, M. H., & Hanney, J. (2012). Geographic information networks in American Indian governments and communities. In S. Dasgupta (Ed.), *Technical, social, and legal issues in virtual communities: Emerging environments: Emerging environments* (pp. 52–62). Hershey, PA: Information Science Reference. doi:10.4018/978-1-4666-1553-3.ch004

Pande, R. (2013). Gender gaps and information and communication technology: A case study of India. In I. Association (Ed.), *Digital literacy: Concepts, methodologies, tools, and applications* (pp. 1425–1439). Hershey, PA: Information Science Reference.

Parachini, J. (2003). Putting WMD terrorism into perspective. *The Washington Quarterly*, *26*(4), 37–50. doi:10.1162/016366003322387091

Parke, A., & Griffiths, M. (2013). Poker gambling virtual communities: The use of computer-mediated communication to develop cognitive poker gambling skills. In R. Zheng (Ed.), *Evolving psychological and educational perspectives on cyber behavior* (pp. 190–204). Hershey, PA: Information Science Reference.

Park, J., Chung, T., & Hur, W. (2013). The role of consumer innovativeness and trust for adopting internet phone services. In A. Scupola (Ed.), *Mobile opportunities and applications for e-service innovations* (pp. 22–36). Hershey, PA: Information Science Reference.

Paschou, M., Sakkopoulos, E., Tsakalidis, A., Tzimas, G., & Viennas, E. (2013). An XML-based customizable model for multimedia applications for museums and exhibitions. In D. Kanellopoulos (Ed.), *Intelligent multimedia technologies for networking applications: Techniques and tools* (pp. 348–363). Hershey, PA: Information Science Reference.

Pauwels, L. (2013). Images, self-images, and idealized identities in the digital networked world: Reconfigurations of family photography in a web-based mode. In S. Warburton, & S. Hatzipanagos (Eds.), *Digital identity and social media* (pp. 133–147). Hershey, PA: Information Science Reference.

Payne, K. (2009). Winning the battle of ideas: Propaganda, ideology, and terror. *Studies in Conflict and Terrorism*, *32*(2), 109–128. doi:10.1080/10576100802627738

Peachey, A., & Withnail, G. (2013). A sociocultural perspective on negotiating digital identities in a community of learners. In S. Warburton, & S. Hatzipanagos (Eds.), *Digital identity and social media* (pp. 210–224). Hershey, PA: Information Science Reference.

Peixoto, E., Martins, E., Anjo, A. B., & Silva, A. (2012). Geo@NET in the context of the platform of assisted learning from Aveiro University, Portugal. In M. Cruz-Cunha (Ed.), *Handbook of research on serious games as educational, business and research tools* (pp. 648–667). Hershey, PA: Information Science Reference. doi:10.4018/978-1-4666-0149-9.ch033

Pellicani, L. (2003). *Revolutionary apocalypse: Ideological roots of terrorism*. Westport, CT: Praeger.

Perl, R. F. (1997, October 22). Terrorism, the media and the government: Perspectives, trends and options for policy makers. *CRS Issue Brief*. Retrieved July 3, 2013, from http://www.fas.org/irp/crs/crs-terror.htm

Perl, R. F. (2001). *Terrorism, the future, and U.S. foreign policy*. Washington, DC: Congressional Research Service, The Library of Congress.

Pettigrew, A. M. (1977). Strategy formulation as a political process. *International Studies of Management and Organization*, *7*(2), 78–87.

Pfeiffer, C. P. (2012). Terrorism and its oxygen: A game-theoretic perspective on terrorism and the media. *Behavioral Sciences of Terrorism and Political Aggression*, *4*(3), 212–228. doi:10.1080/19434472.2011.594629

Picard, R. G. (1986). *News coverage as the contagion of terrorism: Dangerous charges backed by dubious science*. Paper presented at the Annual Meeting of the Association for Education in Journalism and Mass Communication. Norman, OK.

Picard, R. G. (1991). News coverage as the contagion of terrorism: Dangerous charges backed by dubious science. In *Media coverage of terrorism: Methods of diffusion* (pp. 49–62). Newbury Park, CA: Sage Publications.

Pillar, P. (2005). Perceptions of terrorism: Continuity and change. *Strategic Studies Institute, US Army War College*. Retrieved June 25, 2012, from http://www.au.af.mil/au/awc/awcgate/ssi/boyne_law_terr.pdfhttp://www.strategic-studiesinstitute.army.mil/pubs/display.cfm?pubID=613

Pillay, N. (2013). The use of web 2.0 technologies by students from developed and developing countries: A New Zealand case study. In N. Azab (Ed.), *Cases on web 2.0 in developing countries: Studies on implementation, application, and use* (pp. 411–441). Hershey, PA: Information Science Reference.

Pimenta, M. S., Miletto, E. M., Keller, D., Flores, L. V., & Testa, G. G. (2013). Technological support for online communities focusing on music creation: Adopting collaboration, flexibility, and multiculturality from Brazilian creativity styles. In N. Azab (Ed.), *Cases on web 2.0 in developing countries: Studies on implementation, application, and use* (pp. 283–312). Hershey, PA: Information Science Reference.

Pina, P. (2013). Between scylla and charybdis: The balance between copyright, digital rights management and freedom of expression. In I. Association (Ed.), *Digital rights management: Concepts, methodologies, tools, and applications* (pp. 1355–1367). Hershey, PA: Information Science Reference.

Pitsillides, S., Waller, M., & Fairfax, D. (2013). Digital death: What role does digital information play in the way we are (re)membered? In S. Warburton, & S. Hatzipanagos (Eds.), *Digital identity and social media* (pp. 75–90). Hershey, PA: Information Science Reference.

Polacek, P., & Huang, C. (2013). QoS scheduling with opportunistic spectrum access for multimedia. In M. Ku, & J. Lin (Eds.), *Cognitive radio and interference management: Technology and strategy* (pp. 162–178). Hershey, PA: Information Science Reference.

Poland, J. M. (2005). *Understanding terrorism: Groups, strategies, and responses*. Englewood Cliffs, NJ: Pearson Education, Inc.

Post, W. (2009, June 2). *The suspect at a glance*. Retrieved August 20, 2009, from http://www.washingtonpost.com/wp-dyn/content/article/2009/06/01/AR2009060103675_pf.html

Potts, L. (2013). Balancing McLuhan with Williams: A sociotechnical view of technological determinism. In J. Abdelnour-Nocera (Ed.), *Knowledge and technological development effects on organizational and social structures* (pp. 109–114). Hershey, PA: Information Science Reference.

Prescott, J., & Bogg, J. (2013). Stereotype, attitudes, and identity: Gendered expectations and behaviors. In *Gendered occupational differences in science, engineering, and technology careers* (pp. 112–135). Hershey, PA: Information Science Reference.

Preussler, A., & Kerres, M. (2013). Managing social reputation in Twitter. In S. Warburton, & S. Hatzipanagos (Eds.), *Digital identity and social media* (pp. 91–103). Hershey, PA: Information Science Reference.

Prieger, J. E., & Church, T. V. (2013). Deployment of mobile broadband service in the United States. In I. Lee (Ed.), *Mobile services industries, technologies, and applications in the global economy* (pp. 1–24). Hershey, PA: Information Science Reference.

Priest, D., & Arkin, W. M. (2011). *Top secret America: The rise of the new American security state*. New York: Back Bay Books.

Protheroe, A. H. (1990). Terrorism, journalism, and democracy. In Y. Alexander & R. Latter (Eds.), Terrorism and the media: Dilemmas for government, journalists and the public (pp. 64-69). Washington, DC: Brassey's (US), Inc.

PTI. (2012, January 3). Lashkar raising 21 female terrorists against India: Army. *The Times of India*. Retrieved July 3, 2013, from http://articles.timesofindia.indiatimes.com/2012-01-03/india/30583991_1_training-camps-terrorists-pok

Purpura, P. P. (2007). *Terrorism and homeland security: An introduction with applications*. Burlington, MA: Elsevier.

Puumalainen, K., Frank, L., Sundqvist, S., & Tuppura, A. (2012). The critical mass of wireless communications: Differences between developing and developed economies. In I. Management Association (Ed.), Wireless technologies: Concepts, methodologies, tools and applications (pp. 1719-1736). Hershey, PA: Information Science Reference. doi: doi:10.4018/978-1-61350-101-6.ch701

Rabino, S., Rafiee, D., Onufrey, S., & Moskowitz, H. (2013). Retention and customer share building: Formulating a communication strategy for a sports club. In H. Kaufmann, & M. Panni (Eds.), *Customer-centric marketing strategies: Tools for building organizational performance* (pp. 511–529). Hershey, PA: Business Science Reference.

Radicalisation Awareness Network (RAN) Voices of Victims of Terrorism. (VVT). (2012). Proposed policy recommendations for the high level conference from the RAN voices of victims of terrorism working group. *European Commission, DG Home Affairs*. Retrieved July 3, 2013, http://ec.europa.eu/dgs/home-affairs/what-we-do/networks/radicalisation_awareness_network/ran-high-level-conference/docs/proposed_policy_recommendations_ran_vvt_en.pdf

Radicalisation Awareness Network (RAN). (2013). *What we do*. Retrieved July 22, 2013, from http://ec.europa.eu/dgs/home-affairs/what-we-do/networks/radicalisation_awareness_network/index_en.htm

Rahman, H., & Kumar, S. (2012). Mobile computing: An emerging issue in the digitized world. In A. Kumar, & H. Rahman (Eds.), *Mobile computing techniques in emerging markets: Systems, applications and services* (pp. 1–22). Hershey, PA: Information Science Reference. doi:10.4018/978-1-4666-0080-5.ch001

Ramadani, S. (2004, April 9). Iraqis told them to go from day one. *The Guardian*. Retrieved July 3, 2013, from http://www.guardian.co.uk/comment/story/0,1188857,00.html

Ramsay, G. (2009). Relocating the virtual war. *Defence Against Terrorism Review*, 2(1), 31–50.

Rana, P. S. J. B. (2011, July 29). Terrorism by other name. *The Kathmandu Post*. Retrieved July 30, 2013, from http://www.ekantipur.com/the-kathmandu-post/2011/07/28/related_articles/terrorism-by-other-name/224547.html

Rapoport, D. (1988). *Inside terrorist organizations*. New York: Columbia University Press.

Rapoport, D. C. (1984). Fear and trembling: Terrorism in three religious traditions. *The American Political Science Review*, 78(3), 658–677.

Rapoport, D. C. (2004). The four waves of modern terrorism. In A. Cronin, & J. Ludes (Eds.), *Attacking terrorism: Elements of a grand strategy* (pp. 46–73). Washington, DC: Georgetown University Press.

Ratten, V. (2013). Adoption of mobile reading devices in the book industry. In I. Lee (Ed.), *Strategy, adoption, and competitive advantage of mobile services in the global economy* (pp. 203–216). Hershey, PA: Information Science Reference.

Ratten, V. (2013). Mobile banking in the youth market: Implications from an entrepreneurial and learning perspective. In I. Lee (Ed.), *Strategy, adoption, and competitive advantage of mobile services in the global economy* (pp. 112–126). Hershey, PA: Information Science Reference.

Ratten, V. (2013). Social e-enterprise through technological innovations and mobile social networks. In T. Torres-Coronas, & M. Vidal-Blasco (Eds.), *Social e-enterprise: Value creation through ICT* (pp. 96–109). Hershey, PA: Information Science Reference.

Ray, S. J. (1999). *Strategic communication in crisis management: Lessons from the airline industry*. Westport, CT: Quorum Books.

Rego, P. A., Moreira, P. M., & Reis, L. P. (2012). New forms of interaction in serious games for rehabilitation. In M. Cruz-Cunha (Ed.), *Handbook of research on serious games as educational, business and research tools* (pp. 1188–1211). Hershey, PA: Information Science Reference. doi:10.4018/978-1-4666-0149-9.ch062

Reinhard, C. D. (2012). Virtual worlds and reception studies: Comparing engagings. In N. Zagalo, L. Morgado, & A. Boa-Ventura (Eds.), *Virtual worlds and metaverse platforms: New communication and identity paradigms* (pp. 117–136). Hershey, PA: Information Science Reference.

Reuter, C. (2004). *My life is a weapon: A modern history of suicide bombing*. Princeton, NJ: Princeton University Press.

Richardson, L. (2007). *What terrorists want: Understanding the enemy, containing the threat*. New York: Random House.

Richler, N. (2012). What we talk about when we talk about war. Fredericton: Goose Lane Ed.s.

Rich, P. B. (2013). Understanding terror, terrorism and their representations in media and culture. *Studies in Conflict and Terrorism*, 36(3), 255–277.

Ricks, T. E. (2006). *Fiasco: The American military adventure in Iraq*. New York: Penguin.

Rieser, M. (2013). Mobility, liminality, and digital materiality. In D. Harrison (Ed.), *Digital media and technologies for virtual artistic spaces* (pp. 27–45). Hershey, PA: Information Science Reference. doi:10.4018/978-1-4666-2961-5.ch003

Rivoire, J.-B., & Aggoun, L. (2004). *Françalgérie: Crimes et mensonges d'État*. Paris: La Découverte.

Roberts, A. (1989). Ethics, terrorism, and counter terrorism. *Terrorism and Political Violence*, *1*(1), 48–69. doi:10.1080/09546558908427013

Robinson, P. (2000). The policy-media interaction model: Measuring media power during humanitarian crisis. *Journal of Peace Research*, *37*(5), 613–633. doi:10.1177/0022343300037005006

Rodrigues, R. G., Pinheiro, P. G., & Barbosa, J. (2012). Online playability: The social dimension to the virtual world. In M. Cruz-Cunha (Ed.), *Handbook of research on serious games as educational, business and research tools* (pp. 391–421). Hershey, PA: Information Science Reference. doi:10.4018/978-1-4666-0149-9.ch021

Roeh, I. (1981). Israel in Lebanon: Language and images of storytelling. In W. C. Adams (Ed.), *Television coverage of the Middle East* (pp. 76–88). Norwood, NJ: Ablex Publishing.

Rohner, D., & Frey, B. S. (2007). Blood and ink! The common-interest-game between terrorists and the media. *Public Choice*, *133*, 129–145. doi:10.1007/s11127-007-9182-9

Romm-Livermore, C., Somers, T. M., Setzekorn, K., & King, A. L. (2012). How e-daters behave online: Theory and empirical observations. In C. Romm Livermore (Ed.), *Gender and social computing: Interactions, differences and relationships* (pp. 236–256). Hershey, PA: Information Science Publishing.

Rosaci, D., & Sarnè, G. M. (2012). An agent-based approach to adapt multimedia web content in ubiquitous environment. In S. Bagchi (Ed.), *Ubiquitous multimedia and mobile agents: Models and implementations* (pp. 60–84). Hershey, PA: Information Science Reference.

Rosas, O. V., & Dhen, G. (2012). One self to rule them all: A critical discourse analysis of French-speaking players' identity construction in World of Warcraft. In N. Zagalo, L. Morgado, & A. Boa-Ventura (Eds.), *Virtual worlds and metaverse platforms: New communication and identity paradigms* (pp. 337–366). Hershey, PA: Information Science Reference.

Rosie, G. (1987). *The dictionary of international terrorism*. New York: Paragon House.

Ross, J. I. (2007). Deconstructing the terrorism-news media relationship. *Crime, Media, Culture*, *3*(2), 215–225. doi:10.1177/1741659007078555

Rouibah, K., & Abbas, H. A. (2012). Effect of personal innovativeness, attachment motivation and social norms on the acceptance of camera mobile phones: An empirical study in an Arab country. In W. Hu (Ed.), *Emergent trends in personal, mobile, and handheld computing technologies* (pp. 302–323). Hershey, PA: Information Science Reference. doi:10.4018/978-1-4666-0921-1.ch018

Rubenstein, R. E. (1974). *Alchemists of revolution: Terrorism in the modern world*. New York: Basic Books.

Ruby, C. L. (2002). The definition of terrorism. *Analyses of Social Issues and Public Policy (ASAP)*, *2*(1), 9–14. doi:10.1111/j.1530-2415.2002.00021.x

Ruby, T. F. (2006). Listening to the voices of hijab. *Women's Studies International Forum*, *29*(1), 54–66. doi:10.1016/j.wsif.2005.10.006

Ruddock, A. (1996). Unarmed and dangerous: The Gibraltar killings meet the press. In M. Morgan, & S. Leggett (Eds.), *Mainstream(s) and margins: Cultural politics in the 90s* (pp. 143–158). Westport, CT: Greenwood Publishing Group.

Ruiz-Mafé, C., Sanz-Blas, S., & Martí-Parreño, J. (2013). Web 2.0 goes mobile: Motivations and barriers of mobile social networks use in Spain. In N. Azab (Ed.), *Cases on web 2.0 in developing countries: Studies on implementation, application, and use* (pp. 109–146). Hershey, PA: Information Science Reference.

Rushkoff, D. (1996). *Media virus: Hidden agendas in popular culture*. New York: Ballantine.

Rybas, S. (2012). Community embodied: Validating the subjective performance of an online class. In H. Li (Ed.), *Virtual community participation and motivation: Cross-disciplinary theories* (pp. 124–141). Hershey, PA: Information Science Reference. doi:10.4018/978-1-4666-0312-7.ch008

Sabelkin, M., & Gagnon, F. (2013). Data transmission oriented on the object, communication media, application, and state of communication systems. In M. Bartolacci, & S. Powell (Eds.), *Advancements and innovations in wireless communications and network technologies* (pp. 117–132). Hershey, PA: Information Science Reference.

Sadaba, T. (2002). Each to his own... September 11 in Basque media. *Television & New Media*, *3*(2), 219–222. doi:10.1177/152747640200300214

Sageman, M. (2004). *Understanding terror networks*. Philadelphia, PA: University of Pennsylvania.

Sageman, M. (2008). *Leaderless Jihad: Terror networks in the twenty-first century*. Philadelphia, PA: University of Pennsylvania Press.

Said, E. W. (1978). *Orientalism*. New York: Pantheon Books.

Sajeva, S. (2013). Towards a conceptual knowledge management system based on systems thinking and sociotechnical thinking. In J. Abdelnour-Nocera (Ed.), *Knowledge and technological development effects on organizational and social structures* (pp. 115–130). Hershey, PA: Information Science Reference.

Salo, M., Olsson, T., Makkonen, M., & Frank, L. (2013). User perspective on the adoption of mobile augmented reality based applications. In I. Lee (Ed.), *Strategy, adoption, and competitive advantage of mobile services in the global economy* (pp. 165–188). Hershey, PA: Information Science Reference.

Samanta, S. K., Woods, J., & Ghanbari, M. (2013). Automatic language translation: An enhancement to the mobile messaging services. In A. Mesquita (Ed.), *User perception and influencing factors of technology in everyday life* (pp. 57–75). Hershey, PA: Information Science Reference.

Sanderson, J., & Cheong, P. H. (2010). Tweeting prayers and communicating grief over Michael Jackson online. *Bulletin of Science, Technology & Society*, *30*(5), 328–340.

Sandler, T., Tschirhart, J. T., & Cauley, J. (1983). A theoretical analysis of transnational terrorism. *The American Political Science Review*, *77*(1), 36–54. doi:10.2307/1956010

Sandole, D. J. D. (2004). The new terrorism: Causes, conditions and conflict resolution. *Wiener Blätter zur Friedensforschung*, 43-56.

Sanger, D. E., & Risen, J. (2003, July 12). After the war: Intelligence, C.I.A. chief takes blame in assertion on Iraqi uranium. *The New York Times*. Retrieved July 3, 2013, from http://www.nytimes.com/2003/07/12/world/after-the-war-intelligence-cia-chief-takes-blame-in-assertion-on-iraqi-uranium.html?pagewanted=all&src=pm

Santo, A. E., Rijo, R., Monteiro, J., Henriques, I., Matos, A., & Rito, C. et al. (2012). Games improving disorders of attention deficit and hyperactivity. In M. Cruz-Cunha (Ed.), *Handbook of research on serious games as educational, business and research tools* (pp. 1160–1174). Hershey, PA: Information Science Reference. doi:10.4018/978-1-4666-0149-9.ch060

Sarker, S., Campbell, D. E., Ondrus, J., & Valacich, J. S. (2012). Mapping the need for mobile collaboration technologies: A fit perspective. In N. Kock (Ed.), *Advancing collaborative knowledge environments: New trends in e-collaboration* (pp. 211–233). Hershey, PA: Information Science Reference.

Sasajima, M., Kitamura, Y., & Mizoguchi, R. (2013). Method for modeling user semantics and its application to service navigation on the web. In G. Xu, & L. Li (Eds.), *Social media mining and social network analysis: Emerging research* (pp. 127–139). Hershey, PA: Information Science Reference.

Schechter, D. (2003). *Embedded: Weapons of mass deception*. Amherst, NY: Prometheus Books.

Scheel, C., & Pineda, L. (2013). Building industrial clusters in Latin America: Paddling upstream. In J. Abdelnour-Nocera (Ed.), *Knowledge and technological development effects on organizational and social structures* (pp. 146–166). Hershey, PA: Information Science Reference.

Schellenberg, J. A. (1996). *Conflict resolution: Theory, research, and practice*. Albany, NY: State University of New York Press.

Scheuer, M. (2002). *Through our enemies' eyes: Osama bin Laden, radical Islam, and the future of America*. Washington, DC: Potomac Books.

Scheuer, M. (2004). *Imperial hubris: Why the west is losing the war on terror*. Washington, DC: Brasseys.

Schlesinger, P. (1987). *Putting reality together: BBC news*. London: Routledge.

Schlesinger, P. (1991). *Media, state and nation: Political violence and collective identities*. London: Sage Publications.

Schlesinger, P., Murdock, G., & Elliott, P. (1983). *Televising terrorism: Political violence in popular culture*. London: Comedia.

Schmid, A. P. (1989). Terrorism and the media: The ethics of publicity. *Terrorism and Political Violence*, *1*(4), 539–565. doi:10.1080/09546558908427042

Schmid, A. P. (2005). Terrorism as psychological warfare. *Democracy and Security*, *1*, 137–146. doi:10.1080/17419160500322467

Schmid, A. P., & de Graaf, J. (1980). *Insurgent terrorism and the western news media: An exploratory analysis with a Dutch case study*. Leiden, The Netherlands: Center for the Study of Social Conflicts, Dutch State University.

Schmid, A. P., & de Graaf, J. (1982). *Violence as communication: Insurgent terrorism and the Western news media*. London: Sage.

Schmid, A. P., & Jongman, A. J. (2008). *Political terrorism: A new guide to actors, authors, concepts, data bases, theories, & literature*. London: Transaction Publishers.

Schneider, M. (2002, August 15). FX to clock 24 Labor Day marathon. *Daily Variety*. Retrieved July 22, 2013, from http://variety.com/2002/scene/news/fx-net-to-clock-24-marathon-on-sept-1-1117871260/

Schulz, W. F. (1982). News structure and people's awareness of political events. *International Communication Gazette*, *30*(3), 139–153. doi:10.1177/001654928203000301

Schweitzer, Y., & Ferber, S. G. (2005). *Al-Qaeda and the internationalization of suicide terrorism*. Jerusalem, Israel: Jaffee Center for Strategic Studies.

Scott, J. (1985). *Weapons of the weak: Everyday forms of peasant resistance*. New Haven, CT: Yale University Press.

Sederberg, P. C. (1989). *Terrorist myths: Illusion, rhetoric, and reality*. Englewood Cliffs, NJ: Prentice Hall.

Sedgwick, M. (2007). Inspiration and the origins of global waves of terrorism. *Studies in Conflict and Terrorism*, *30*(2), 97–112. doi:10.1080/10576100601101042

Seib, P. (2010, August 26). CENTCOM's digital diplomacy. *Huffington Post*. Retrieved July 3, 2013, from http://www.huffingtonpost.com/philip-seib/centcoms-digital-diplomac_b_696448.html

Seib, P. (2011). *Public diplomacy, new media and counterterrorism. USC Center on Public Diplomacy at the Annenberg School*. Los Angeles, CA: Figueroa Press.

Seib, P. (2012). *Real-time diplomacy: Politics and power in the social media era*. New York: Palgrave MacMillan. doi:10.1057/9781137010902

Seib, P., & Janbek, D. M. (2011). *Global terrorism and new media: The post-al Qaeda generation*. London: Routledge.

Sell, A., Walden, P., & Carlsson, C. (2013). Segmentation matters: An exploratory study of mobile service users. In D. Chiu (Ed.), *Mobile and web innovations in systems and service-oriented engineering* (pp. 301–317). Hershey, PA: Information Science Reference.

Semati, M. (2010). Islamophobia, culture and race in the age of empire. *Cultural Studies*, *24*(2), 256–275. doi:10.1080/09502380903541696

Sermon, P., & Gould, C. (2013). Site-specific performance, narrative, and social presence in multi-user virtual environments and the urban landscape. In D. Harrison (Ed.), *Digital media and technologies for virtual artistic spaces* (pp. 46–58). Hershey, PA: Information Science Reference. doi:10.4018/978-1-4666-2961-5.ch004

Servaes, J. (2012). The role of information communication technologies within the field of communication for social change. In I. Management Association (Ed.), Wireless technologies: Concepts, methodologies, tools and applications (pp. 1117-1135). Hershey, PA: Information Science Reference. doi: doi:10.4018/978-1-61350-101-6.ch502

Seth, N., & Patnayakuni, R. (2012). Online matrimonial sites and the transformation of arranged marriage in India. In C. Romm Livermore (Ed.), *Gender and social computing: Interactions, differences and relationships* (pp. 272–295). Hershey, PA: Information Science Publishing.

Shaffer, G. (2013). Lessons learned from grassroots wireless networks in Europe. In A. Abdelaal (Ed.), *Social and economic effects of community wireless networks and infrastructures* (pp. 236–254). Hershey, PA: Information Science Reference. doi:10.4018/978-1-4666-2997-4.ch013

Shaheen, J. G. (2009). *Reel bad Arabs: How Hollywood vilifies a people.* Northampton, MA: Olive Branch Press.

Sheehan, S. (2003). *Anarchism.* London: Reaktion Books.

Shen, J., & Eder, L. B. (2013). An examination of factors associated with user acceptance of social shopping websites. In A. Mesquita (Ed.), *User perception and influencing factors of technology in everyday life* (pp. 28–45). Hershey, PA: Information Science Reference.

Shen, K. N. (2012). Identification vs. self-verification in virtual communities (VC): Theoretical gaps and design implications. In C. El Morr, & P. Maret (Eds.), *Virtual community building and the information society: Current and future directions* (pp. 208–236). Hershey, PA: Information Science Reference.

Sherry, M. (1987). *The rise of American air power.* New Haven, CT: Yale University Press.

Shi, Y., & Liu, Z. (2013). Cultural models and variations. In I. Management Association (Ed.), Industrial engineering: Concepts, methodologies, tools, and applications (pp. 1560-1573). Hershey, PA: Engineering Science Reference. doi: doi:10.4018/978-1-4666-1945-6.ch083

Shiferaw, A., Sehai, E., Hoekstra, D., & Getachew, A. (2013). Enhanced knowledge management: Knowledge centers for extension communication and agriculture development in Ethiopia. In B. Maumbe, & C. Patrikakis (Eds.), *E-agriculture and rural development: Global innovations and future prospects* (pp. 103–116). Hershey, PA: Information Science Reference.

Shipley, T. (2013). The NHL and the new Canadian militarism. *Canadian Dimension, 47*(2), 32–34.

Shpiro, S. (2002). Conflict media strategies and the politics of counter-terrorism. *Politics, 22*(2), 76–85. doi:10.1111/1467-9256.00162

Shubik, M. (1954). Introduction to the nature of game theory. In M. Shubik (Ed.), *Readings in game theory and political behavior* (pp. 1–11). New York: Doubleday & Company, Inc.

Sick, G. (1985). *All fall down: America's tragic encounter with Iran.* New York: Random House.

Silke, A. (2004). The road less travelled: Recent trends in terrorism research. In A. Silke (Ed.), *Research on terrorism: Trends, achievements and failures* (pp. 186–213). London: Frank Cass. doi:10.4324/9780203500972.ch10

Simão de Vasconcellos, M., & Soares de Araújo, I. (2013). Massively multiplayer online role playing games for health communication in Brazil. In K. Bredl, & W. Bösche (Eds.), *Serious games and virtual worlds in education, professional development, and healthcare* (pp. 294–312). Hershey, PA: Information Science Reference. doi:10.4018/978-1-4666-3673-6.ch018

Simon, S. (2003). The new terrorism: Securing the nation against a messianic foe. *The Brookings Review, 21*(1), 18–24.

Simons, G. (2010). *Mass media and modern warfare: Reporting on the Russian war on terrorism.* Bulington, VT: Ashgate.

Simour, L. (2012). Networking identities: Geographies of interaction and computer mediated communication1. In S. Dasgupta (Ed.), *Technical, social, and legal issues in virtual communities: Emerging environments: Emerging environments* (pp. 235–246). Hershey, PA: Information Science Reference. doi:10.4018/978-1-4666-1553-3.ch016

Singer, P. W. (2009). *Wired for war: The robotics revolution and conflict in the 21st century.* New York: Penguin Books.

Singh, G. R. (2013). Cyborg in the village: Culturally embedded resistances to blended teaching and learning. In E. Jean Francois (Ed.), *Transcultural blended learning and teaching in postsecondary education* (pp. 75–90). Hershey, PA: Information Science Reference.

Singh, M., & Iding, M. K. (2013). Does credibility count?: Singaporean students' evaluation of social studies web sites. In R. Zheng (Ed.), *Evolving psychological and educational perspectives on cyber behavior* (pp. 230–245). Hershey, PA: Information Science Reference.

Singh, S. (2013). Information and communication technology and its potential to transform Indian agriculture. In B. Maumbe, & C. Patrikakis (Eds.), *E-agriculture and rural development: Global innovations and future prospects* (pp. 140–168). Hershey, PA: Information Science Reference.

Siochru, O. S. (2005). Finding a frame: Towards a transnational advocacy campaign to democratize communication. In R. A. Hackett & Y. Zhao (Eds.), Democratizing global media: One world, many struggles (pp. 289-311). Lanham, MD: Rowman & Littlefield.

Siqueira, S. R., Rocha, E. C., & Nery, M. S. (2012). Brazilian occupational therapy perspective about digital games as an inclusive resource to disabled people in schools. In M. Cruz-Cunha (Ed.), *Handbook of research on serious games as educational, business and research tools* (pp. 730–749). Hershey, PA: Information Science Reference. doi:10.4018/978-1-4666-0149-9.ch037

Siti-Nabiha, A., & Salleh, D. (2013). Public sector transformation in Malaysia: Improving local governance and accountability. In N. Pomazalová (Ed.), *Public sector transformation processes and internet public procurement: Decision support systems* (pp. 276–290). Hershey, PA: Engineering Science Reference.

Sivard, R. L. (1991). *World military and social expenditures 1991*. Washington, DC: World Priorities Inc.

Siwar, C., & Abdulai, A. (2013). Sustainable development and the digital divide among OIC countries: Towards a collaborative digital approach. In I. Association (Ed.), *Digital literacy: Concepts, methodologies, tools, and applications* (pp. 242–261). Hershey, PA: Information Science Reference.

Sky News Arabia. (2012, May 25). *Washington chases al-Qaeda in cyberspace*. Retrieved July 3, 2013, from http://www.skynewsarabia.com/Web/article/22803

Smith, P. A. (2013). Strengthening and enriching audit practice: The socio-technical relevance of "decision leaders". In J. Abdelnour-Nocera (Ed.), *Knowledge and technological development effects on organizational and social structures* (pp. 97–108). Hershey, PA: Information Science Reference.

Smith, P. A., & Cockburn, T. (2013). Generational demographics. In *Dynamic leadership models for global business: Enhancing digitally connected environments* (pp. 230–256). Hershey, PA: Business Science Reference. doi:10.4018/978-1-4666-2836-6.ch009

Smith, P. A., & Cockburn, T. (2013). Leadership, global business, and digitally connected environments. In *Dynamic leadership models for global business: Enhancing digitally connected environments* (pp. 257–296). Hershey, PA: Business Science Reference. doi:10.4018/978-1-4666-2836-6.ch010

Snyder, G. H., & Diesing, P. (1977). *Conflict among nations: Bargaining, decision making, and system structure in international crises*. Princeton, NJ: Princeton University Press.

Sohrabi, B., Gholipour, A., & Amiri, B. (2013). The influence of information technology on organizational behavior: Study of identity challenges in virtual teams. In N. Kock (Ed.), *Interdisciplinary applications of electronic collaboration approaches and technologies* (pp. 79–95). Hershey, PA: Information Science Reference.

Soitu, L., & Paulet-Crainiceanu, L. (2013). Student-faculty communication on Facebook: Prospective learning enhancement and boundaries. In B. Pătruţ, M. Pătruţ, & C. Cmeciu (Eds.), *Social media and the new academic environment: Pedagogical challenges* (pp. 40–67). Hershey, PA: Information Science Reference. doi:10.4018/978-1-4666-2851-9.ch003

Solvoll, T. (2013). Mobile communication in hospitals: What is the problem? In C. Rückemann (Ed.), *Integrated information and computing systems for natural, spatial, and social sciences* (pp. 287–301). Hershey, PA: Information Science Reference.

Somboonviwat, K. (2013). Topic modeling for web community discovery. In G. Xu, & L. Li (Eds.), *Social media mining and social network analysis: Emerging research* (pp. 72–89). Hershey, PA: Information Science Reference.

Somerville, I., & Wood, E. (2007). Public relations, politics and the media. In A. Theaker (Ed.), *The public relations handbook* (pp. 32–51). New York: Routledge.

Sontag, S. (2003). *Regarding the pain of others*. New York: Farrar, Straus & Giroux.

Soriano, M. R. T. (2008). Terrorism and the mass media after al Qaeda: A change of course? *Athena Intelligence Journal, 3*(2), 1–20.

Soriano, M. R. T. (2012). The vulnerabilities of online terrorism. *Studies in Conflict and Terrorism, 35*(4), 263–277.

Spalek, B. (2010). Community policing, trust, and Muslim communities in relation to new terrorism. *Politics & Policy, 38*(4), 789–815.

Speaker, R. B., Levitt, G., & Grubaugh, S. (2013). Professional development in a virtual world. In J. Keengwe, & L. Kyei-Blankson (Eds.), *Virtual mentoring for teachers: Online professional development practices* (pp. 122–148). Hershey, PA: Information Science Reference.

Spencer, A. (2006). Questioning the concept of new terrorism. *Peace Conflict & Development, 8,* 1–33.

Spencer, A. (2011). Comment and debate: Sic[k] of the 'new terrorism' debate? A response to our critics. *Critical Studies on Terrorism, 4*(3), 459–467.

Steer, G. L. (2012). *The tree of Gernika: A field study of modern war.* London: Faber & Faber.

Stern, J. (2003). *Terror in the name of God: Why religious militants kill.* New York: Harper Collins.

Stern, J. (2003). *Why religious militants kill: Terror in the name of God.* New York: HarperCollins.

Stetler, B. (2013, May 13). Revival of 24 is more like 12. *The New York Times.* Retrieved August 30, 2013, from http://www.nytimes.com/2013/05/14/business/media/fox-to-bring-back-24-and-jack-bauer.html?_r=0

Steuter, E., & Wills, D. (2009). Discourses and dehumanization: Enemy construction and the Canadian media complicity in the framing of the war on terror. Global Media Journal – Canadian Ed., 2(2), 7-24.

Steuter, E. (1990). Understanding the media/terrorism relationship: An analysis of ideology and the news in Time magazine. *Political Communication and Persuasion, 7*(4), 257–278. doi:10.1080/10584609.1990.9962902

Stevenson, G., & Van Belle, J. (2013). Using social media technology to improve collaboration: A case study of micro-blogging adoption in a South African financial services company. In N. Azab (Ed.), *Cases on web 2.0 in developing countries: Studies on implementation, application, and use* (pp. 313–341). Hershey, PA: Information Science Reference.

Stevenson, J. (2003). How Europe and America defend themselves. *Foreign Affairs, 82*(2), 75–90. doi:10.2307/20033505

Stevens, T., & Neumann, P. (2009). *Countering online radicalisation: A strategy for action.* London: ICSR.

StGeorgeUtah.com. (2011, May 11). *Las Vegas metro police uses social media to prevent terrorism.* Retrieved July 22, 2013, from http://www.stgeorgeutah.com/news/archive/2011/05/11/las-vegas-metro-police-uses-social-media-to-prevent-terrorism/

Stora, B. (2007). Still fighting: The battle of Algiers, censorship and the memory wars. *Interventions, 9*(3), 65–70. doi:10.1080/13698010701618596

Storm, K. J., & Eyerman, J. (2008). *Interagency cooperation: Lessons learned from the London subway bombings.* Office of Justice Programs, United States Department of Justice. Retrieved May 15, 2012, from http://www.ojp.usdoj.gov/nij/journals/261/coordination.htm

Strandberg, V. (2013). Rail bound traffic—A prime target for contemporary terrorist attacks? *Journal of Transportation Security, 6*(3), 271–286.

Strang, K. D. (2013). Balanced assessment of flexible e-learning vs. face-to-face campus delivery courses at an Australian university. In M. Khosrow-Pour (Ed.), *Cases on assessment and evaluation in education* (pp. 304–339). Hershey, PA: Information Science Reference.

Strömberg-Jakka, M. (2013). Social assistance via the internet: The case of Finland in the European context. In J. Lannon, & E. Halpin (Eds.), *Human rights and information communication technologies: Trends and consequences of use* (pp. 177–195). Hershey, PA: Information Science Reference.

Sultanow, E., Weber, E., & Cox, S. (2013). A semantic e-collaboration approach to enable awareness in globally distributed organizations. In N. Kock (Ed.), *Interdisciplinary applications of electronic collaboration approaches and technologies* (pp. 1–16). Hershey, PA: Information Science Reference.

Sun, H., Gui, N., & Blondia, C. (2013). A generic adaptation framework for mobile communication. In V. De Florio (Ed.), *Innovations and approaches for resilient and adaptive systems* (pp. 196–207). Hershey, PA: Information Science Reference.

Sunstein, C. R. (2009). *On rumors: How falsehoods spread, why we believe them, what can be done.* New York: Farrar, Straus and Giroux.

Surette, R., Hansen, K., & Noble, G. (2009). Measuring media oriented terrorism. *Journal of Criminal Justice, 37,* 360–370. doi:10.1016/j.jcrimjus.2009.06.011

Surgevil, O., & Özbilgin, M. F. (2012). Women in information communication technologies. In C. Romm Livermore (Ed.), *Gender and social computing: Interactions, differences and relationships* (pp. 87–97). Hershey, PA: Information Science Publishing.

Suskind, R. (2008). *The way of the world: A story of truth and hope in the age of terrorism.* New York: HarperCollins.

Sutton, M. (1994). *Bear in mind these dead: An index of deaths from the conflict in Ireland (1969-1993).* Belfast, Ireland: Beyond the Pale Publications.

Sylaiou, S., White, M., & Liarokapis, F. (2013). Digital heritage systems: The ARCO evaluation. In M. Garcia-Ruiz (Ed.), *Cases on usability engineering: Design and development of digital products* (pp. 321–354). Hershey, PA: Information Science Reference. doi:10.4018/978-1-4666-4046-7.ch014

Sylvester, O. A. (2013). Impact of information and communication technology on livestock production: The experience of rural farmers in Nigeria. In B. Maumbe, & C. Patrikakis (Eds.), *E-agriculture and rural development: Global innovations and future prospects* (pp. 68–75). Hershey, PA: Information Science Reference.

Symeonidou-Kastanidou, E. (2004). Defining terrorism. *European Journal of Crime Criminal Law and Criminal Justice, 12*(1), 14–35. doi:10.1163/1571817041268883

Szasz, A. (1994). *EcoPopulism: Toxic waste and the movement for environmental justice.* Minneapolis, MN: University of Minnesota Press.

Taha, K., & Elmasri, R. (2012). Social search and personalization through demographic filtering. In I. Ting, T. Hong, & L. Wang (Eds.), *Social network mining, analysis, and research trends: Techniques and applications* (pp. 183–203). Hershey, PA: Information Science Reference.

Taifi, N., & Gharbi, K. (2013). Technology integration in strategic management: The case of a micro-financing institutions network. In T. Torres-Coronas, & M. Vidal-Blasco (Eds.), *Social e-enterprise: Value creation through ICT* (pp. 263–279). Hershey, PA: Information Science Reference.

Taillon, P. de B. (2002). *Hijacking and hostages: Government responses to terrorism.* Westport, CT: Praeger.

Tai, Z. (2012). Fame, fantasy, fanfare and fun: The blossoming of the Chinese culture of blogmongering. In T. Dumova, & R. Fiordo (Eds.), *Blogging in the global society: Cultural, political and geographical aspects* (pp. 37–54). Hershey, PA: Information Science Reference.

Talib, S., Clarke, N. L., & Furnell, S. M. (2013). Establishing a personalized information security culture. In I. Khalil, & E. Weippl (Eds.), *Contemporary challenges and solutions for mobile and multimedia technologies* (pp. 53–69). Hershey, PA: Information Science Reference.

Tamura, H., Sugasaka, T., & Ueda, K. (2012). Lovely place to buy!: Enhancing grocery shopping experiences with a human-centric approach. In A. Lugmayr, H. Franssila, P. Näränen, O. Sotamaa, J. Vanhala, & Z. Yu (Eds.), *Media in the ubiquitous era: Ambient, social and gaming media* (pp. 53–65). Hershey, PA: Information Science Reference.

Tassadit, Y. (2004, February). Révélations sur les camps de la guerre d'Algérie. *Le Monde Diplomatique.* Retrieved July 3, 2013, from http://www.monde-diplomatique.fr/2004/02/TASSADIT/11020

Tawileh, W., Bukvova, H., & Schoop, E. (2013). Virtual collaborative learning: Opportunities and challenges of web 2.0-based e-learning arrangements for developing countries. In N. Azab (Ed.), *Cases on web 2.0 in developing countries: Studies on implementation, application, and use* (pp. 380–410). Hershey, PA: Information Science Reference.

Taylor, P. M. (2009). Public diplomacy and strategic communications. In N. Snow, & P. M. Taylor (Eds.), *Routledge handbook of public diplomacy* (pp. 12–16). London: Routledge.

Tehranian, M. (2002). Peace journalism: Negotiating global media ethics. *Harvard Journal of Press/Politics, 7*(2), 58-83.

Teichman, J. (1989). How to define terrorism. *Philosophy (London, England), 64*(250), 505–517. doi:10.1017/S0031819100044260

Teixeira, P. M., Félix, M. J., & Tavares, P. (2012). Playing with design: The universality of design in game development. In M. Cruz-Cunha (Ed.), *Handbook of research on serious games as educational, business and research tools* (pp. 217–231). Hershey, PA: Information Science Reference. doi:10.4018/978-1-4666-0149-9.ch011

Terrorism & Homeland Security. (2004, February 4). *Virtual threat, real terror: Cyberterrorism in the 21st century*. Retrieved February 4, 2004, from http://www.gpo.gov/fdsys/pkg/CHRG-108shrg94639/pdf/CHRG-108shrg94639.pdf

Terzis, G. (2001). Think local, teach global: National identity and media education. *Media Development, 48*(3), 62–66.

Teusner, P. E. (2012). Networked individualism, constructions of community and religious identity: The case of emerging church bloggers in Australia. In F. Comunello (Ed.), *Networked sociability and individualism: Technology for personal and professional relationships* (pp. 264–288). Hershey, PA: Information Science Reference.

Tezcan, M. (2013). Social e-entrepreneurship, employment, and e-learning. In T. Torres-Coronas, & M. Vidal-Blasco (Eds.), *Social e-enterprise: Value creation through ICT* (pp. 133–147). Hershey, PA: Information Science Reference.

Thackrah, J. R. (2013). *Dictionary of terrorism*. New York: Routledge.

Thatcher, B. (2012). Approaching intercultural rhetoric and professional communication. In *Intercultural rhetoric and professional communication: Technological advances and organizational behavior* (pp. 1–38). Hershey, PA: Information Science Reference.

Thatcher, B. (2012). Borders and etics as units of analysis for intercultural rhetoric and professional communication. In *Intercultural rhetoric and professional communication: Technological advances and organizational behavior* (pp. 39–74). Hershey, PA: Information Science Reference.

Thatcher, B. (2012). Core competencies in intercultural teaching and research. In *Intercultural rhetoric and professional communication: Technological advances and organizational behavior* (pp. 318–342). Hershey, PA: Information Science Reference.

Thatcher, B. (2012). Distance education and e-learning across cultures. In *Intercultural rhetoric and professional communication: Technological advances and organizational behavior* (pp. 186–215). Hershey, PA: Information Science Reference.

Thatcher, B. (2012). Information and communication technologies and intercultural professional communication. In *Intercultural rhetoric and professional communication: Technological advances and organizational behavior* (pp. 97–123). Hershey, PA: Information Science Reference.

Thatcher, B. (2012). Intercultural rhetorical dimensions of health literacy and medicine. In *Intercultural rhetoric and professional communication: Technological advances and organizational behavior* (pp. 247–282). Hershey, PA: Information Science Reference.

Thatcher, B. (2012). Legal traditions, the universal declaration of human rights, and intercultural professional communication. In *Intercultural rhetoric and professional communication: Technological advances and organizational behavior* (pp. 216–246). Hershey, PA: Information Science Reference.

Thatcher, B. (2012). Organizational theory and communication across cultures. In *Intercultural rhetoric and professional communication: Technological advances and organizational behavior* (pp. 159–185). Hershey, PA: Information Science Reference.

Thatcher, B. (2012). Teaching intercultural rhetoric and professional communication. In *Intercultural rhetoric and professional communication: Technological advances and organizational behavior* (pp. 343–378). Hershey, PA: Information Science Reference.

Thatcher, B. (2012). Website designs as an indicator of globalization. In *Intercultural rhetoric and professional communication: Technological advances and organizational behavior* (pp. 124–158). Hershey, PA: Information Science Reference.

Thatcher, B. (2012). Writing instructions and how-to-do manuals across cultures. In *Intercultural rhetoric and professional communication: Technological advances and organizational behavior* (pp. 283–317). Hershey, PA: Information Science Reference.

Thirumal, P., & Tartakov, G. M. (2013). India's Dalits search for a democratic opening in the digital divide. In I. Association (Ed.), *Digital literacy: Concepts, methodologies, tools, and applications* (pp. 852–871). Hershey, PA: Information Science Reference.

Thomas, G. (1999). Where there's smoke. In G. Thomas (Ed.), *Words in common: Essays on language, culture, and society* (pp. 279–283). Don Mills, Canada: Addison-Wesley Longman.

Thomas, G. E. (2013). Facilitating learning with adult students in the transcultural classroom. In E. Jean Francois (Ed.), *Transcultural blended learning and teaching in postsecondary education* (pp. 193–215). Hershey, PA: Information Science Reference.

Thomassen, N. (1992). *Communicative ethics in theory and practice* (J. Irons, Trans.). New York: St. Martin's Press.

Thompson, E. P. (1980). Protest and survive. In E. P. Thompson, & D. Smith (Eds.), *Protest and survive* (pp. 9–61). Harmondsworth, UK: Penguin.

Tilly, C. (2004). Terror, terrorism, terrorists. *Sociological Theory*, *22*(1), 5–13. doi:10.1111/j.1467-9558.2004.00200.x

Trapp, K. N. (2011). *State responsibility for international terrorism*. Oxford, UK: Oxford University Press. doi:10.1093/acprof:oso/9780199592999.001.0001

Tripathi, S. N., & Siddiqui, M. H. (2013). Designing effective mobile advertising with specific reference to developing markets. In I. Lee (Ed.), *Strategy, adoption, and competitive advantage of mobile services in the global economy* (pp. 299–324). Hershey, PA: Information Science Reference.

Truong, Y. (2013). Antecedents of consumer acceptance of mobile television advertising. In A. Mesquita (Ed.), *User perception and influencing factors of technology in everyday life* (pp. 128–141). Hershey, PA: Information Science Reference.

Tryon, C. (2008). Pop politics: Online parody videos, intertextuality, and political participation. *Popular Communication*, *6*(4), 209–213. doi:10.1080/15405700802418537

Tsfati, Y., & Weimann, G. (2002). Terror on the internet. *Studies in Conflict and Terrorism*, *25*(5), 317–332. www.terrorism.com doi:10.1080/10576100290101214

Tsuneizumi, I., Aikebaier, A., Ikeda, M., Enokido, T., & Takizawa, M. (2013). Design and implementation of hybrid time (HT) group communication protocol for homogeneous broadcast groups. In N. Bessis (Ed.), *Development of distributed systems from design to application and maintenance* (pp. 282–293). Hershey, PA: Information Science Reference.

Tucker, D. (2001). What's new about the new terrorism and how dangerous is it? *Terrorism and Political Violence*, *13*(3), 1–14.

Tucker, J. B. (Ed.). (2000). *Toxic terror: Assessing terrorist use of chemical and biological weapons*. Cambridge, MA: MIT Press.

Tzoulia, E. (2013). Legal issues to be considered before setting in force consumer-centric marketing strategies within the European Union. In H. Kaufmann, & M. Panni (Eds.), *Customer-centric marketing strategies: Tools for building organizational performance* (pp. 36–56). Hershey, PA: Business Science Reference.

U.S. Department of State. Bureau of Counterterrorism. (2012, January 27). *Foreign terrorist organizations*. Retrieved July 3, 2013, from http://www.state.gov/j/ct/rls/other/des/123085.htm

U.S. Department of the Treasury. (2007, November 15). *Treasury targets charity covertly supporting violence in Sri Lanka*. Retrieved July 3, 2013, from http://www.treasury.gov/press-center/press-releases/Pages/hp683.aspx

U.S. Department of Treasury. Office of Foreign Assets Control. (2011). *Terrorists assets report*. Retrieved July 3, 2013, from http://www.treasury.gov/resource-center/sanctions/Programs/Documents/tar2011.pdf

UK Home Office. (2011). *Contest: The United Kingdom's strategy for countering terrorism.* Westminster, UK: Home Office.

Underwood, J., & Okubayashi, T. (2013). Comparing the characteristics of text-speak used by English and Japanese students. In R. Zheng (Ed.), *Evolving psychological and educational perspectives on cyber behavior* (pp. 258–271). Hershey, PA: Information Science Reference.

Ungerleider, N. (2011, July 25). Examining Oslo terrorist Breivik's internet trail. *Fast Company.* Retrieved July 3, 2013, from http://www.fastcompany.com/1768974/examining-oslo-terrorist-breiviks-Internet-trail

United Nations. (1999). *International convention for the suppression of the financing of terrorism.* Article 2(b) Adopted by the General Assembly of the United Nations in resolution 54/109 on 9 December 1999. Retrieved January 20, 2014, from http://www.un.org/law/cod/finterr.htm

United Nations. (2007). *Implementation of the UN counterterrorism strategy.* Paper presented at the 42nd Conference of the United Nations of the Next Decade. St. Michaels, MD.

United States Department of State Publication Office of the Coordinator of Counterterrorism. (2009). *Country reports on terrorism.* Retrieved July 30, 2013, from http://www.state.gov/documents/organization/141114.pdf

Unoki, M., & Miyauchi, R. (2013). Method of digital-audio watermarking based on cochlear delay characteristics. In K. Kondo (Ed.), *Multimedia information hiding technologies and methodologies for controlling data* (pp. 42–70). Hershey, PA: Information Science Reference.

Usman, L. M. (2013). Adult education and sustainable learning outcome of rural widows of central northern Nigeria. In V. Wang (Ed.), *Technological applications in adult and vocational education advancement* (pp. 215–231). Hershey, PA: Information Science Reference.

Usoro, A., & Khan, I. U. (2013). Trust as an aspect of organisational culture: Its effects on knowledge sharing in virtual communities. In R. Colomo-Palacios (Ed.), *Enhancing the modern organization through information technology professionals: Research, studies, and techniques* (pp. 182–199). Hershey, PA: Business Science Reference.

Utz, S. (2012). Social network site use among Dutch students: Effects of time and platform. In F. Comunello (Ed.), *Networked sociability and individualism: Technology for personal and professional relationships* (pp. 103–125). Hershey, PA: Information Science Reference.

Valentine, D. (2000). The phoenix program. New York: Authors Guild Backinprint.com.

van Dijk, T. A. (1991). *Racism and the press.* London: Routledge.

van Dijk, T. A. (Ed.). (1997). *Discourse as structure and process.* London: Sage.

van Ginneken, J. (1998). *Understanding global news: A critical introduction.* London: Sage Publications.

van Ham, P. (2008). Place branding within a security paradigm. *Place Branding and Public Diplomacy, 4*(3), 240–251. doi:10.1057/pb.2008.14

Vasilescu, R., Epure, M., & Florea, N. (2013). Digital literacy for effective communication in the new academic environment: The educational blogs. In B. Pătruţ, M. Pătruţ, & C. Cmeciu (Eds.), *Social media and the new academic environment: Pedagogical challenges* (pp. 368–390). Hershey, PA: Information Science Reference. doi:10.4018/978-1-4666-2851-9.ch018

Vercher, A. (1992). *Terrorism in Europe: An international comparative legal analysis.* Oxford, UK: Oxford University Press.

Verton, D. (2003). *Black ice: The invisible threat of cyberterrorism.* New York: McGraw-Hill/Osborne.

Vladimirschi, V. (2013). An exploratory study of cross-cultural engagement in the community of inquiry: Instructor perspectives and challenges. In Z. Akyol, & D. Garrison (Eds.), *Educational communities of inquiry: Theoretical framework, research and practice* (pp. 466–489). Hershey, PA: Information Science Reference.

Vultee, F. (2009). Jump back Jack, Mohammed's here: Fox News and the construction of Islamic peril. *Journalism Studies, 10*(5), 623–638. doi:10.1080/14616700902797333

Vuokko, R. (2012). A practice perspective on transforming mobile work. In I. Management Association (Ed.), *Wireless technologies: Concepts, methodologies, tools and applications* (pp. 1104-1116). Hershey, PA: Information Science Reference. doi: doi:10.4018/978-1-61350-101-6.ch501

Waldron, J. (2004). Terrorism and the uses of terror. *The Journal of Ethics*, *8*(1), 5–35. doi:10.1023/B:JOET.0000012250.78840.80

Wall, M., & Kirdnark, T. (2012). The blogosphere in the "land of smiles": Citizen media and political conflict in Thailand. In T. Dumova, & R. Fiordo (Eds.), *Blogging in the global society: Cultural, political and geographical aspects* (pp. 19–36). Hershey, PA: Information Science Reference.

Walsh, J. I. (2010). Media attention to terrorist attacks: Causes and consequences. *Institute for Home Security Solutions*. Retrieved July 3, 2013, from http://www.jamesigoewalsh.com/ihss.pdf

Walt, V. (2010, October 12). Terrorist hostage situations: Rescue or ransom? *Time Magazine*. Retrieved July 3, 2013, from http://www.time.com/time/world/article/0,8599,2024420,00.html

Walter, P. F. (2012). Cyberkill: Melancholia, globalization and media terrorism in American psycho and glamorama. *Arizona Quarterly*, *68*(4), 131–154.

Warburton, S. (2013). Space for lurking: A pattern for designing online social spaces. In S. Warburton, & S. Hatzipanagos (Eds.), *Digital identity and social media* (pp. 149–158). Hershey, PA: Information Science Reference.

Wardlaw, G. (1982). *Political terrorism: Theory, tactics, and counter-measures*. London: Cambridge University Press.

Warren, S. J., & Lin, L. (2012). Ethical considerations for learning game, simulation, and virtual world design and development. In H. Yang, & S. Yuen (Eds.), *Handbook of research on practices and outcomes in virtual worlds and environments* (pp. 1–18). Hershey, PA: Information Science Publishing.

Wasihun, T. A., & Maumbe, B. (2013). Information and communication technology uses in agriculture: Agribusiness industry opportunities and future challenges. In B. Maumbe, & C. Patrikakis (Eds.), *E-agriculture and rural development: Global innovations and future prospects* (pp. 235–251). Hershey, PA: Information Science Reference.

Webb, L. M., Fields, T. E., Boupha, S., & Stell, M. N. (2012). U.S. political blogs: What aspects of blog design correlate with popularity? In T. Dumova, & R. Fiordo (Eds.), *Blogging in the global society: Cultural, political and geographical aspects* (pp. 179–199). Hershey, PA: Information Science Reference.

Weeks, M. R. (2012). Toward an understanding of online community participation through narrative network analysis. In H. Li (Ed.), *Virtual community participation and motivation: Cross-disciplinary theories* (pp. 90–102). Hershey, PA: Information Science Reference. doi:10.4018/978-1-4666-0312-7.ch006

Weimann, G. (2004). *How modern terrorism uses the internet*. Washington, DC: United States Institute of Peace.

Weimann, G. (2005). Cyberterrorism: The sum of all fears? *Studies in Conflict and Terrorism*, *28*(2), 129–149.

Weimann, G. (2006). *Terror on the internet: The new arena, the new challenges*. Washington, DC: United States Institute of Peace.

Weimann, G., & Winn, C. (1994). *The theatre of terror: Mass media and international terrorism*. New York: Longman.

Westra, L. (2012). *Faces of state terrorism*. Leiden, The Netherlands: Brill. doi:10.1163/9789004225695

White, J. R. (2001). Political eschatology: A theology of antigovernment extremism. *The American Behavioral Scientist*, *44*(6), 937–956. doi:10.1177/00027640121956601

White, J. R. (2006). *Terrorism and homeland security*. Mason, OH: Thomson Wadsworth.

White, J. R. (2013). Language economy in computer-mediated communication: Learner autonomy in a community of practice. In B. Zou, M. Xing, Y. Wang, M. Sun, & C. Xiang (Eds.), *Computer-assisted foreign language teaching and learning: Technological advances* (pp. 75–90). Hershey, PA: Information Science Reference.

Whittaker, D. J. (2004). *Terrorists and terrorism in the contemporary world*. Westport, CT: Praeger.

Whittaker, D. J. (2007). *Terrorism: Understanding the global threat*. Harlow, UK: Longman.

Whitworth, B., & Liu, T. (2013). Politeness as a social computing requirement. In J. Bishop (Ed.), *Examining the concepts, issues, and implications of internet trolling* (pp. 88–104). Hershey, PA: Information Science Reference. doi:10.4018/978-1-4666-2803-8.ch008

Wichowski, D. E., & Kohl, L. E. (2013). Establishing credibility in the information jungle: Blogs, microblogs, and the CRAAP test. In M. Folk, & S. Apostel (Eds.), *Online credibility and digital ethos: Evaluating computer-mediated communication* (pp. 229–251). Hershey, PA: Information Science Reference.

Wieviorka, M. (1993). *The making of terrorism*. Chicago: The University of Chicago Press.

Wilkinson, P. (1974). *Political terrorism*. London: Macmillan.

Wilkinson, P. (1997). The media and terrorism: A reassessment. *Terrorism and Political Violence, 9*(2), 51–64. doi:10.1080/09546559708427402

Wilkinson, P. (2001). Current and future trends in domestic and international terrorism: Implications for democratic government and the international community. *Strategic Review for Southern Africa, 23*(2), 106–123.

Wilkinson, P. (2006). *Terrorism versus democracy: The liberal state response*. London: Routledge.

Williams, J. (2013). Social cohesion and free home internet in New Zealand. In A. Abdelaal (Ed.), *Social and economic effects of community wireless networks and infrastructures* (pp. 135–159). Hershey, PA: Information Science Reference. doi:10.4018/978-1-4666-2997-4.ch008

Williams, P. (1976). *Crisis management: Confrontation and diplomacy in the nuclear age*. London: Martin Robertson & Co. Ltd.

Williams, S., Fleming, S., Lundqvist, K., & Parslow, P. (2013). This is me: Digital identity and reputation on the internet. In S. Warburton, & S. Hatzipanagos (Eds.), *Digital identity and social media* (pp. 104–117). Hershey, PA: Information Science Reference.

Willnat, L., & Martin, J. (2012). Foreign correspondents—An endangered species? In D. H. Weaver, & L. Willnat (Eds.), *The global journalist: In the 21ˢᵗ century* (pp. 495–510). New York: Routledge.

Winch, P. (1977). Understanding a primitive society. In B. R. Wilson (Ed.), *Rationality* (pp. 78–111). Oxford, UK: Basil Blackwell.

Winn, A. K., & Zakem, V. L. (2009). Jihad.com 2.0: The new social media and the changing dynamics of mass persuasion. In J. J. F. Forest (Ed.), *Influence warfare: How terrorists and governments fight to shape perceptions in a war of ideas* (pp. 27–48). New York: Praeger.

Winning, R. (2013). Behind the sonic veil: Considering sound as the mediator of illusory life in variable and screen-based media. In D. Harrison (Ed.), Digital media and technologies for virtual artistic spaces (pp. 117-134). Hershey, PA: Information science reference. doi: doi:10.4018/978-1-4666-2961-5.ch009

Wiseman, P. (2003, December 16). Cluster bombs kill, even after shooting ends. *USA Today*. Retrieved July 3, 2013, from http://www.usatoday.com/news/world/iraq/2003-12-10-cluster-bomb-cover_x.htm

Witte, G., Markon, J., & Hussain, S. (2009, December 13). Pakistani authorities hunt for alleged mastermind in plot to send N. Virginia men to Afghanistan to fight U.S. troops. *The Washington Post*. Retrieved May 23, 2012, from http://www.washingtonpost.com/wp-dyn/content/article/2009/12/12/AR2009121201598.html

Wittebols, J. H. (1991). The politics and coverage of terrorism: From media images to public consciousness. *Communication Theory, 1*(3), 253–266. doi:10.1111/j.1468-2885.1991.tb00018.x

Wittebols, J. H. (1992). Media and the institutional perspective: U.S. & Canadian coverage of terrorism. *Political Communication, 9*(4), 267–278. doi:10.1080/10584609.1992.9962950

Wolfe, A. (2012). Network perspective on structures related to communities. In M. Safar, & K. Mahdi (Eds.), *Social networking and community behavior modeling: Qualitative and quantitative measures* (pp. 26–50). Hershey, PA: Information Science Reference.

Woodward, P. (2001). *Dirty war, clean hands: ETA, the GAL and Spanish democracy*. Cork, Ireland: Cork University Press.

Worden, S. (2013). The earth sciences and creative practice: Exploring boundaries between digital and material culture. In D. Harrison (Ed.), *Digital media and technologies for virtual artistic spaces* (pp. 186–204). Hershey, PA: Information Science Reference. doi:10.4018/978-1-4666-2961-5.ch014

Worlds of Journalism Study. (2013). Retrieved July 30, 2013, from http://www.worldsofjournalism.org/pilot.htm

Wright, D. K. (1996). Communication ethics. In M. B. Salwen, & D. W. Stacks (Eds.), *An integrated approach to communication theory and research* (pp. 519–535). Hoboken, NJ: Lawrence Erlbaum Associates, Publishers.

Wright, R. (2011). *Rock the casbah: Rage and rebellion across the Islamic world*. New York: Simon & Schuster.

Xing, M., Zou, B., & Wang, D. (2013). A wiki platform for language and intercultural communication. In B. Zou, M. Xing, Y. Wang, M. Sun, & C. Xiang (Eds.), *Computer-assisted foreign language teaching and learning: Technological advances* (pp. 1–15). Hershey, PA: Information Science Reference.

Xu, G., Gu, Y., & Yi, X. (2013). On group extraction and fusion for tag-based social recommendation. In G. Xu, & L. Li (Eds.), *Social media mining and social network analysis: Emerging research* (pp. 211–223). Hershey, PA: Information Science Reference. doi:10.4018/978-1-4666-2806-9.ch014

Yakura, E. K., Soe, L., & Guthrie, R. (2012). Women in IT careers: Investigating support for women in the information technology workforce. In C. Romm Livermore (Ed.), *Gender and social computing: Interactions, differences and relationships* (pp. 35–49). Hershey, PA: Information Science Publishing.

Yang, Y., Rahim, A., & Karmakar, N. C. (2013). 5.8 GHz portable wireless monitoring system for sleep apnea diagnosis in wireless body sensor network (WBSN) using active RFID and MIMO technology. In N. Karmakar (Ed.), *Advanced RFID systems, security, and applications* (pp. 264–303). Hershey, PA: Information Science Reference.

You-Li, S. (1993). *China and the origins of the Pacific War, 1931-1941*. New York: St. Martin's Press.

YouTube. (2013). *Statistics*. Retrieved March 22, 2013, from http://www.youtube.com/yt/press/statistics.html

Yu, Z., Liang, Y., Yang, Y., & Guo, B. (2013). Supporting social interaction in campus-scale environments by embracing mobile social networking. In G. Xu, & L. Li (Eds.), *Social media mining and social network analysis: Emerging research* (pp. 182–201). Hershey, PA: Information Science Reference.

Zack, M. H. (Ed.). (1999). *Knowledge and strategy*. Woburn, MA: Butterworth-Heinemann.

Zafirovski, M., & Rodeheaver, D. G. (2013). *Modernity and terrorism: From anti-modernity to global terror*. Leiden, The Netherlands: Brill. doi:10.1163/9789004242883

Zaman, M., Simmers, C. A., & Anandarajan, M. (2013). Using an ethical framework to examine linkages between "going green" in research practices and information and communication technologies. In B. Medlin (Ed.), *Integrations of technology utilization and social dynamics in organizations* (pp. 243–262). Hershey, PA: Information Science Reference.

Zanini, M., & Edwards, S. J. A. (2001). The networking of terror in the information age. In J. Arquilla, & D. Ronfeldt (Eds.), *Networks and netwars: The future of terror, crime, and militancy* (pp. 29–60). Santa Monica, CA: RAND Corporation.

Zarmpou, T., Saprikis, V., & Vlachopoulou, M. (2013). Examining behavioral intention toward mobile services: An empirical investigation in Greece. In A. Scupola (Ed.), *Mobile opportunities and applications for e-service innovations* (pp. 37–56). Hershey, PA: Information Science Reference.

Zavala Pérez, J. M. (2012). Registry culture and networked sociability: Building individual identity through information records. In F. Comunello (Ed.), *Networked sociability and individualism: Technology for personal and professional relationships* (pp. 41–62). Hershey, PA: Information Science Reference.

Zelin, A. (2013). *The state of global Jihad online: A qualitative, quantitative, and cross-lingual analysis.* New America Foundation. Retrieved July 3, 2013, from http://www.newamerica.net/sites/newamerica.net/files/policydocs/Zelin_Global%20Jihad%20Online_NAF.pdf

Zelizer, B., & Allan, S. (Eds.). (2011). *Journalism after September 11.* London: Routledge.

Zemliansky, P., & Goroshko, O. (2013). Social media and other web 2.0 technologies as communication channels in a cross-cultural, web-based professional communication project. In B. Pătruţ, M. Pătruţ, & C. Cmeciu (Eds.), *Social media and the new academic environment: Pedagogical challenges* (pp. 256–272). Hershey, PA: Information Science Reference. doi:10.4018/978-1-4666-2851-9.ch013

Zervas, P., & Alexandraki, C. (2013). The realisation of online music services through intelligent computing. In D. Kanellopoulos (Ed.), *Intelligent multimedia technologies for networking applications: Techniques and tools* (pp. 291–317). Hershey, PA: Information Science Reference.

Zhang, J., & Mao, E. (2013). The effects of consumption values on the use of location-based services on smartphones. In I. Lee (Ed.), *Strategy, adoption, and competitive advantage of mobile services in the global economy* (pp. 1–18). Hershey, PA: Information Science Reference.

Zhang, S., Köbler, F., Tremaine, M., & Milewski, A. (2012). Instant messaging in global software teams. In N. Kock (Ed.), *Advancing collaborative knowledge environments: New trends in e-collaboration* (pp. 158–179). Hershey, PA: Information Science Reference.

Zhang, T., Wang, C., Luo, Z., Han, S., & Dong, M. (2013). RFID enabled vehicular network for ubiquitous travel query. In D. Chiu (Ed.), *Mobile and web innovations in systems and service-oriented engineering* (pp. 348–363). Hershey, PA: Information Science Reference.

Zhang, W. (2012). Virtual communities as subaltern public spheres: A theoretical development and an application to the Chinese internet. In H. Li (Ed.), *Virtual community participation and motivation: Cross-disciplinary theories* (pp. 143–159). Hershey, PA: Information Science Reference. doi:10.4018/978-1-4666-0312-7.ch009

Zhang, X., Wang, L., Li, Y., & Liang, W. (2013). Global community extraction in social network analysis. In G. Xu, & L. Li (Eds.), *Social media mining and social network analysis: Emerging research* (pp. 156–171). Hershey, PA: Information Science Reference.

Zhang, X., Wang, L., Li, Y., & Liang, W. (2013). Local community extraction in social network analysis. In G. Xu, & L. Li (Eds.), *Social media mining and social network analysis: Emerging research* (pp. 172–181). Hershey, PA: Information Science Reference.

Zhao, Y., & Hackett, R. A. (2005). Media globalization, media democratization: Challenges, issues and paradoxes. In R. Hackett, & Y. Zhao (Eds.), *Democratizing global media: One world, many struggles* (pp. 1–36). Lanham, MD: Rowman & Littlefield.

Zimmermann, D. (2004). Terrorism transformed: The new terrorism, impact scalability, and the dynamic of reciprocal threat perception. *Connections: The Quarterly Journal, 3*(1), 19–40.

Zinsser, W. (1998). *On writing well: The classic guide to writing nonfiction.* New York: HarperPerennial, A Division of HarperCollins Publishers.

Zulaika, J., & Douglass, W. A. (1996). *Terror and taboo: The follies, fables and faces of terrorism.* New York: Routledge.

Zulu, S. F. (2013). Emerging information and communication technology policy framework for Africa. In B. Maumbe, & J. Okello (Eds.), *Technology, sustainability, and rural development in Africa* (pp. 236–256). Hershey, PA: Information Science Reference. doi:10.4018/978-1-4666-3607-1.ch016

About the Contributors

Mahmoud Eid is an Associate Professor at the Department of Communication, University of Ottawa, Canada. Dr. Eid is the author of *Interweavement: International Media Ethics and Rational Decision-Making* (2008), co-author of *Mission Invisible: Race, Religion, and News at the Dawn of the 9/11 Era* (2014), editor of *Research Methods in Communication* (2011), and co-editor of *Basics in Communication and Media Studies* (2012) and *The Right to Communicate: Historical Hopes, Global Debates, and Future Premises* (2009). Dr. Eid is the Editor of the *Global Media Journal – Canadian Edition*, serves on the editorial boards of several academic journals and as an organizing committee member for various international conferences, contributed several book chapters and journal articles, and presented numerous papers at global conferences. He has led and collaborated in projects for Public Safety Canada, Citizenship and Immigration Canada, Canadian Broadcasting Corporation, and various other Canadian and international institutions. His research interests focus on international communication and media studies, communication and media ethics and effects, terrorism, crisis management, conflict resolution, Islam, Arab culture, Middle East politics, media representations and ethnic studies, research methods, and the political economy of communication.

* * *

Muhammad Ayish is a Professor and Head of the Mass Communication Department at the American University of Sharjah, United Arab Emirates. During the past 20 years, Dr. Ayish has worked at several universities in Jordan and the United Arab Emirates where he had served as Dean of the College of Communication at the University of Sharjah from 2002-2008. His research interests include Arab World broadcasting, new media technologies, women and media, and political communication. He is the author of *The New Arab Public Sphere* (2008), has published over 50 journal articles and book chapters in both Arabic and English, and has contributed numerous research papers in international conferences of media and communication.

Pauline Hope Cheong is an Associate Professor at the Hugh Downs School of Human Communication, Arizona State University, United States. Her research interests are in the socio-cultural implications of communication technologies, particularly the mediation of leadership and influence. This includes analyzing authority and power, civic participation, and community building, with a multidisciplinary and international perspective. Dr. Cheong's research has been published widely in leading peer-reviewed journals. She is the lead editor of two volumes, *Digital Religion, Social Media and Culture: Perspectives, Practices and Future* (2012) and *New Media and Intercultural Communication: Identity, Community* *and Politics* (2012), and is the co-author of *Narrative Landmines: Rumors, Islamist Extremism, and the Struggle for Strategic Influence* (2012). She has received multiple grants, speaking honors and awards, including outstanding research awards from the International Communication Association and the National Communication Association. She serves on the Editorial boards of *Journal of Communication* and *Western Journal of Communication*.

Maura Conway is a Senior Lecturer in the School of Law and Government at Dublin City University in Dublin, Ireland. Her principal research interests are in the area of terrorism and the Internet, including academic and media discourses on cyberterrorism, the functioning and effectiveness of violent political extremist online content, and violent online radicalization. She has presented upon these issues before the United Nations in New York, the Commission of the European Union in Brussels, the Royal United Services Institute in London, and elsewhere. Her articles have appeared in, amongst others, *Current History*, *First Monday*, *Media, War & Conflict*, and *Parliamentary Affairs*.

William A. Douglass is Coordinator Emeritus of the Center of Basque Studies at The University of Nevada-Reno that he helped found in 1967 and then directed for 33 years. His research interests include ethnic groups and ethnicity maintenance, Basque society, Mediterranean social structure, family history, immigration, and identity. He is the author of *Death in Murelaga: The Social Significance of Funerary Ritual in a Spanish Basque Village* (1969) and *Emigration in a South Italian Hill Town: An Anthropological History* (1984). He co-authored the acclaimed books *Amerikanuak: Basques in the New World* (2005, with Jon Bilbao) and *Terror and Taboo: The Follies, Fables, and Faces of Terrorism* (1996, with Joseba Zulaika).

John D. H. Downing is Professor Emeritus of International Communication at the College of Mass Communication and Media Arts, Southern Illinois University and currently affiliated to the Information & Media Studies Department at Aarhus University, Denmark. He is well known for his research on alternative media and social movements. Dr. Downing is founding Director of the Global Media Research Center and was Vice-President of the International Association for Media and Communication Research (2008-2012). He is a founding Executive Editorial Committee member, *Global Media & Communication* (2005-) and an elected Editor, *Communication, Culture & Critique* (2011-2013), an official journal of the International Communication Association. He is the author of *Internationalizing Media Theory: Transition, Power, Culture* (1996), co-author of *Radical Media: Rebellious Communication and Social Movements* (2001), and Editor-in-Chief of *Sage Encyclopedia of Social Movement Media* (2010).

Robert A. Hackett is a Professor in the Faculty of Communication at Simon Fraser University, Vancouver, Canada. His current research interests include journalism studies, media democratization, media activism, communication rights, news analysis during peace and war, and peace journalism. He is an editor of *Expanding Peace Journalism: Comparative and Critical Approaches* (2011, with Ibrahim Seaga Shaw and Jake Lynch), and co-author of *Remaking Media: The Struggle to Democratize Public Communication* (2006, with William K. Carroll). Dr. Hackett has also conducted numerous media interviews and public talks, written policy briefs, and has helped to found several community-based media action and education initiatives, including NewsWatch Canada (initially a Canadian version of Project Censored) at Simon Fraser University, OpenMedia.ca, and Vancouver's annual Media Democracy Days.

Dana Janbek is Assistant Professor of Public Relations at Lasell College in Newton, Massachusetts, United States. Her research focuses on terrorist use of the Internet as a media outlet and the use of information and communication technologies in the Middle East including within refugee populations. As a doctoral student she served as a research assistant intern at the Middle East Institute in Washington, D.C. Prior to entering academia, she worked for the Embassy of the Hashemite Kingdom of Jordan in Washington, D.C. Earlier in her career, she served as the Director of World Communities of Louisville. Dr. Janbek is the co-author of *Global Terrorism and New Media: The Post Al-Qaeda Generation* (2010, with Philip Seib).

Randal Marlin is Adjunct Professor of Philosophy at Carleton University and at Dominican University College, Ottawa, Canada. He retired in 2001 from full-time teaching after 35 years at Carleton University. Throughout his career, Dr. Marlin's research interests were focused on propaganda. He is a board member of the International Jacques Ellul Society and the Civil Liberties Association, National Capital Region. Dr. Marlin is the author of *Propaganda and the Ethics of Persuasion* (2002), and *The David Levine Affair: Separatist Betrayal or McCarthyism North?* (1998).

Clarence Augustus "Gus" Martin is Associate Vice President for Human Resources Management at California State University, Dominguez Hills, United States. He began his academic career as a member of the faculty of the Graduate School of Public and International Affairs, University of Pittsburgh, where he was an Administration of Justice professor. He is author and editor of several books on the subject of terrorism, including *Understanding Homeland Security* (2014), *Essentials of Terrorism: Concepts and Controversies* (2014), *Understanding Terrorism: Challenges, Perspectives, and Issues* (2013), *The Sage Encyclopedia of Terrorism* (2012), *Terrorism and Homeland Security* (2011), and *The New Era of Terrorism: Selected Readings* (2004). He has served as a panelist for university and community symposia and interviews on the subjects of administration of justice and terrorism.

Brigitte L. Nacos is an Adjunct Professor in political science at Columbia University, New York, United States, where she has taught courses in American politics and government for more than 15 years. Her research concentrates on the links between the media, public opinion, and decision-making and on domestic and international terrorism and counterterrorism. She is the author of various books, such as *Terrorism and the Media* (1996), *Decisionmaking in a Glass House: Mass Media, Public Opinion, and American and European Foreign Policy in the 21ˢᵗ Century* (2000), *Mass Mediated Terrorism: The Central Role of the Media in Terrorism and Counterterrorism* (2002), and *Fueling Our Fears: Stereotyping, Media Coverage, and Public Opinion of Muslim Americans* (2006).

Georgios Terzis is an Associate Professor at Vesalius College, Vrije Universiteit Brussel, and Head of the Media and Global Security Governance unit of the Global Governance Institute, Belgium. He is the founding Chair of the Journalism Studies Section of the European Communication Research and Education Association. His research focuses on media and ethnopolitical conflict, media governance, journalism education, and the development of transnational media. He has been involved in academic work and administrative duties in journalism and communication departments of many universities for more than 15 years. He has also been involved in several international research projects and networks.

He has authored, co-authored, and edited 6 books, 13 book chapters, and 17 refereed and non-refereed journal articles. He is currently an editorial board member of the journals, *Journalism Practice*, *Journal of Applied Journalism and Media Studies*, and *Communication Management Quarterly*.

Jonathan R. White is the Dean of Social Sciences at Grand Valley State University, Grand Rapids, Michigan, United States. He is an expert on the topic of terrorism and Middle Eastern extremism and has served as Director for State and Local Anti-Terrorism Training with the Institute of Intergovernmental Research. As Director, he managed a nation-wide counterterrorist information gathering, analysis, and dissemination program in conjunction with the FBI. He is also a leader in Homeland Security, serving as Executive Director of the Homeland Defense Initiative. Furthermore, Dr. White has worked as an Adjunct Instructor with the State and Local Anti-Terrorism Training (SLATT) Program. He is the author of numerous key books in the field, including *Terrorism and Homeland Security* (2013) and *Defending the Homeland* (2003).

Samuel P. Winch is an Associate Professor of Communications and Humanities and program coordinator for the Master of Arts in Communications at Penn State Harrisburg of Pennsylvania State University, United States. His research interests include media ethics, visual communication, and professionalism in journalism. Dr. Winch has written two books: *Mapping the Cultural Space of Journalism: How Journalists Distinguish News from Entertainment* (1997) and *Handbook for Visual Journalists* (2000). His research has also been published in several scholarly journals, including *Journalism Studies*, *Journal of Mass Media Ethics*, *Visual Communication Quarterly*, and *Journal of Computer Mediated Communication*. In addition to his research, Dr. Winch continues to produce award-winning photography. His photographs have been published in many magazines and books, and exhibited in several juried shows.

Joseba Zulaika is a Professor at the Center for Basque Studies at University of Nevada, Reno, Nevada, United States. His primary research interests include Basque culture and politics, the international discourse of terrorism, diasporic and global cultures, history of anthropological thought, theories of symbolism, ritual, and discourse. He is the author of various books on political violence, such as *Basque Violence: Metaphor and Sacrament* (1988), *Terror and Taboo: The Follies, Fables and Faces of Terrorism* (1996, with William A. Douglass), *Polvo de ETA* (2006), and *Terrorism: The Self-Fulfilling Prophecy* (2009). He has published articles in various journals, such as *Critical Terrorism Studies*, *Etnologia*, and *Comparative Studies in Society and History*.

Index